CHILDREN OF TIME AND SPACE OF ACTION AND IMPULSE

RUDOLF EKSTEIN, Ph. D.

Director, Project: Childhood Psychosis,
Reiss-Davis Child Study Center
Los Angeles, California

With Contributions by

ELAINE CARUTH, Ph.D.
SEYMOUR W. FRIEDMAN, M.D.
ARTHUR MANDELBAUM, M.S.W.
JUDITH WALLERSTEIN, M.S.W.
DOROTHY G. WRIGHT, M.S.

Children
of
Time and Space
of
Action and Impulse

Clinical Studies on the Psychoanalytic
Treatment of Severely Disturbed Children

NEW YORK • JASON ARONSON • LONDON

New Printing 1983

ISBN: 0-87668-733-8

Library of Congress Catalog Number: 76-52312

Manufactured in the United States of America.

To the patients, the students, and collaborators at the Southard School, Topeka, Kansas, and the Reiss-Davis Child Study Center, Los Angeles, California

ACKNOWLEDGMENTS

I am grateful to all the colleagues from whom I have learned. I wish particularly to express my thanks to the patients, the staff, and the students at Southard School and at the Reiss-Davis Child Study Center. I also acknowledge my appreciation to the publishers and editors of journals and books (listed below) who have granted permission to reprint or to quote from previously published material. I want to thank the publisher of this volume and his editor and their respective staffs in preparing it. Expressions of appreciation also go to Sylvia B. Harary, who has done all the editorial work on this manuscript before it went to the publisher, and to Hella Freud Bernays for her copyediting and preparation of the index.

In slightly different form, "The Opening Gambit in Psychotherapeutic Work with a Severely Disturbed Adolescent Girl," "The Space Child's Time Machine," "Cross-sectional Views of the Psychotherapeutic Process with an Adolescent Recovering from a Psychotic Episode," and "Special Training Problems in Psychotherapeutic Work with Psychotic and Borderline Children" originally appeared in *American Journal of Orthopsychiatry*; "A Technical Problem in the Beginning Phase of Psychotherapy with a Borderline Psychotic Boy" in G. Gardner's *Case Studies in Childhood Emotional Disabilities, II*, American Orthopsychiatric Association; "The Nature of the Interpretive Process," in M. Levitt's *Readings in Psychoanalytic Psychology*, Appleton-Century-Crofts; "Vicissitudes of the 'Internal Image' during the Recovery Process," "Choice of Interpretation in the Treatment of Borderline and Psychotic Children," "The Space Child," and "The Working Alliance with the Monster" in *Bulletin of the Menninger Clinic*; "The Meaning of Play in Childhood Psychosis" in L. Jessner and E. Pavenstedt's *Dynamic Psychopathology in Childhood*, Grune & Stratton; "A Psychotherapeutic Session with the Space Child" in *International Record of Medicine*; "Interpretation within the Metaphor: Further Considerations" in *Journal of the Academy of Child Psychiatry*; "The Therapeutic Use of a Quasi-religious Experience" and "The Function of Acting Out, Play Action, and Play Acting in the Psychotherapeutic Process" in *Journal of the American Psychoanalytic Association*; "Pleasure and Reality, Play and Work,

Thought and Action" in *Journal of Humanistic Psychology;* "Observations on the Psychotherapy of Borderline and Psychotic Children," "Observations on the Psychology of Borderline and Psychotic Children," "Counter-transference in the Residential Treatment of Children," and "Puppet Play of a Psychotic Adolescent Girl in the Psychotherapeutic Process" in *Psychoanalytic Study of the Child;* "The Acquisition of Speech in the Autistic Child" in *Reiss-Davis Clinic Bulletin;* and the quoted material in the introduction from "Childhood Schizophrenia and Allied Conditions" in L. Bellak's *Schizophrenia: A Review of the Syndrome,* Logos Press.

RUDOLF EKSTEIN

CONTENTS

PREFACE TO THE SECOND EDITION

This work, first published 15 years ago, describes two decades of clinical investigations conducted by myself and my collaborators at the Menninger Foundation in Topeka, and later at the Reiss-Davis Child Study Center in Los Angeles, then under the directorship of Rocco L. Motto. Many inquiries and requests for the original book have resulted in this updated edition.

I have often suggested that the work in childhood psychosis and related disorders can be separated into two classes, following the guidelines of William McDougall (1926) who spoke of two types of mental disorders: those arising from organic lesions of the nervous system and those that do not suggest such lesions and which should be called *functional disorders*. One is reminded of the two ways of looking at mental phenomena as expressed in the works of Freud and Pavlov. In America a similar dichotomy exists between dynamic psychiatry and behavior modification. Szurek and his collaborators[1] stress environmental causes, while Bender and her collaborators[2] stress biological and organic ones. I have suggested that the different points of view concerning etiology hide preferences as to methods of treatment. Therefore, I suggest that we do not look for the cause of the illness but rather for the cause of the cure.

DIAGNOSTIC AND PHENOMENOLOGICAL ISSUES
Laufer and Gair[3] find a refinement of classification essential in etiological and therapeutic work with this broad group of seriously ill children. However, the refinement of classification does not necessarily guarantee the improvement of etiological and therapeutic studies. Menninger and Mayman warn us about the danger of classification systems.[4] The need for

order is sometimes no more than the denial of existing disorder; classifications, particularly in child psychiatry, have frequently created pseudo-order.

My contributions on single case studies avoid a textbook approach, because my experience suggests that we are not yet in a position to generalize. Each case must be treated as unique. Freud's great teacher, Jean Martin Charcot, wrote that one must look at the phenomena until they seem to tell the story by themselves. He felt that intuitive and empathic understanding would allow us to discover previously unnoticed features.

The nature of the phenomena is more than suddenly discovered hidden truth. Rather, such truth is our subjective way of systematizing these phenomena according to new ways of therapeutic action. We might then slowly discover that different psychotic syndromes are not simply separate entities but are interrelated, perhaps part of a curve, similar to those syndromes described in the epigenetic schemes developed by Freud in 1905 and enlarged upon by Erikson.[5] My colleagues and I have reviewed childhood schizophrenia and allied conditions, and discussed the shift of mood characteristic of the literature in this field from therapeutic nihilism to optimism. We agree with Goldfarb, who speaks of autistic, symbiotic, and schizophrenic conditions as different phases in the universe of childhood schizophrenia, rather than supporting views which place each symptom picture in strictly defined categories, as is possible to some extent in the establishment of diagnostic categories for adults.[7]

Very early forms of childhood psychosis are described by Kanner as infantile autism.[8] Mahler speaks of autistic psychoses and symbiotic syndromes.[9] Milder forms of these difficulties have been referred to as childhood and adolescent borderline conditions (Ekstein[10]; Masterson[11]). Rather than succumb to the temptation of classifying these different syndromes as if they were separate and defineable disease units, we should view them in terms of dominant features. Likewise, differential development should also be viewed in terms of phase dominance.

Bettelheim's book *The Empty Fortress*[12] graphically describes our difficulty in reaching the autistic child classically described by Kanner[13], and in overcoming, in Erikson's terminology,[14] the lack of *sending power* for the infant or the child. I emphasize that the adult caretaker's deficit is small in comparison to the autistic child's lack of *receiving power*.[15] Goldfarb, Bettelheim, and Rohde-Dascher make similar attempts to reassure the often desperate adult caretaker. Goldfarb refers to the *perplexed parent*, who does have sending power vis-a-vis other children in the family, but who feels hopeless when confronted with the autistic child's lack of receiving power.[16] Bettelheim describes the child's attempt to ward off emotional encounters with the surrounding world.[17] The German author Rohde-Dascher speaks of defensive positions rather than an ego deficit or ego defect.[18]

One might say that the autistic infant or growing child learns the art of defense before developing the capacity to encounter the world. This results in an inability to develop the necessary internal world, or its differentiation of functions. The personality of the autistic child seems empty, lacking the capacity to develop functions of self or to maintain a level of pathological identity, a kind of individualism without the world, a self without object. What should have been the developmental state of the infant living merely for the fulfillment of his anaclitic needs, in a private paradise, becomes pathological autism. Mahler and her co-workers suggest that the nonself, the autistic self, precedes the birth of the self.[19] She describes the symbiotic phase, in which a differentiation of self from nonself is not yet established. In her view the autistic and symbiotic position is normal, a part of the growth process that leads to separation between self and non-self and toward genuine individuation.[20, 21]

The autistic and symbiotic conditions of childhood psychoses and related disorders are thus regressions or fixations to earlier phases. The inability to deal with separation and individuation can be seen in borderline conditions as well as in childhood schizophrenia. We see in childhood schizophrenia very impaired reality testing or a break with reality, primitive thought and language systems in which a separation between thought, act and impulse is not yet established. Borderline conditions show fluctuations of normal and abnormal mental states and are nearer to adult conditions.[22]

Frequently we stress the *thought disorder* of the schizophrenic, and in childhood schizophrenia we refer to the child's responses as characteristic of dreamlike rather than reality-oriented thinking. I wrote that the term "thought disorder" might prevent us from discovering the secret order of this type of thinking, and hence serve as a barrier to communication with the schizophrenic child.[23] This way of communicating may have nihilistic consequences. We should not allow our own autistic barriers to stand in the way of entering the child's inner world.

Lorenzer, in trying to analyze language, sees the neurosis or the psychosis as *language destruction* and psychoanalytic therapy as the reconstruction of language.[24] I prefer to think of the patient as an inventor of a new language, by means of which he or she can express his difficulties best, albeit a language that is not understood by the therapist. Rather than reconstruct the language of the patient, the therapist finds its secret rules and grammar and creates a bridge of communication through his own language of interpretation. Interpretation in turn creates a new bridge to communication between therapist and patient. In "From the Language of Play to Play with Language" I pointed out different languages of patients who used verbal communications.[25] Therapists' languages have to be studied as well in order for patient and psychotherapist to communicate rather than utilizing language destruction as a defense. In the latter condition the patient is an empty fortress with pulled-up bridges, refusing conventional communication in order to provide for pathological security, bewildering the therapist who insists on using his own language as the only legitimate one. Freud's *Interpretation of Dreams* shows how the discovery of the rules, the secret grammar of the dreamer's language, allows for the translation of manifest content into latent meanings.[26]

While psychotic conditions of early childhood and latency cannot be easily differentiated or categorized, those of adolescence can be classified according to systems used in the diagnosis of adults, such as hysterical psychosis, schizophrenia, catatonic states, paranoid states, psychotic-like psychopathology, psychotic acting out, and the borderline conditions. For borderline conditions of adolescence, fluctuations between psychotic and normal adjustments frequently are characteristic. Models of the psychic apparatus are useful in observing psychic states that occur with somewhat predictable regularity, particularly differentiated functions capable of adaptation to the tasks and conflicts of life. I have suggested the following:[27]

> *Freudian psychoanalysis, for example, has used the tripartite model, with differentiation among ego, superego, and id functions. They have a special relation to each other and allow for mutual influences, a system of checks and balances, and, guided by the adaptive mechanisms, the synthetic functions of ego organization. Fully developed structures allow enabling operations within the normally expected environment. Such a full personality organization develops out of simpler forms of psychic life. Under the average conditions of mothering and parenting, of social nutriment and appropriate frustrations, the mental life of the infant develops from undifferentiated psychic functioning. This is the source of the organization of the drive systems, the expression of need, the inhibiting and guiding systems that bring about a compromise between id and superego functions and allow for the development of perception, cognition, and reality testing and for the move from conflict solution to task solution. The structure of the mind as a fully developed psychic organization is pictured in the spatial model of Freud[28] both in terms of the basic three functions of the mind and in terms of the*

qualities of these mental functions. The qualities were described in the topographic model through the concepts of the conscious, pre-conscious, and unconscious systems of mind.

This tridimensionality consists of many layers that have to be stripped away to reach the deeper layers that originated earlier. These endless layers—a hierarchy of id, superego, and ego func-tions—have grown out of a steady interchange between the psychic organism and its growth-facilitating environment. Functional dis-orders are usually understood to be caused by the lack of impairment of a facilitating environment. [29]

The use of spatial models leads often to concrete pictures rather than to a functional language. Nevertheless, simplifications concerning the phenomenology of functional childhood psychosis can be enlightening. For example, one topographical model of conscious, preconscious and un-conscious thought is of the layers of an onion. This metaphor allows us, in referring to the many layers of the onion, to characterize what is normal, stable, and predictable. Other concrete images may be used to gain some elementary insight into the childhood psychoses.

In this book I have used the image of the eggshell of a cobra to portray the psyche of the psychotic child. Unlike the ordinary egg, which does not allow us to see through its shell, the cobra egg is thin and translucent; we can see the cobra unhatched, rolled up. The inner structure is confined by the outer organization of the shell; but if the shell breaks from outside or inside pressure, the snake is ready to strike, fully equipped with poisonous fangs. There is no parenting, no early feeding. This picture might well compare with that of the autistic personality, ready to fend for itself at birth, equipped with only those functions of gratification which provide defense against external disaster. If one thinks of an unhatched cobra, it is impossible to imagine it developing systems of communication, such as with a mother cobra. The need for togetherness and fusion, for object rela-tions, is unnecessary. The autistic child is experienced by the caretaker as unreachable, lacking the normal infant's capacity to invite mother's love and respond to love and tenderness. The autistic child, like the fully developed baby cobra ready to strike, does not proceed from appeal to signal functions and finally to symbolic speech. Rather, he engenders feel-ings of anxiety, bewilderment, hopelessness, and isolation. Such a condi-tion excludes empathy, identification, and internalization.

No wonder therapeutic schools based on conditioning and training, rather than on dynamically oriented psychotherapy and education, at-tempt to help the child to move from primitive states of mind to higher states of mental functioning. These schools rely on a stimulus–response model of the psychic apparatus. A positive or a negative stimulus slowly brings about a change of response, which allows the response system itself to adjust to new conditions of stimulation.

Another way to define childhood schizophrenia as a characteristic defensive way of creating distance between self and nonself, self and object, appropriate to the difficulties of the patient. The patient's distance devices thus take on interpersonal meaning. The therapist is portrayed as trying to overcome the distance between himself and the patient. For example, a phobic person might slowly be taught to discover that a seemingly dangerous object can be tolerated. In these terms, mental health can be measured by the distance between the person and his object world. Appropriate distance would allow for object as well as self constancy. Too much distance leads to autistic states, and too little distance results in symbiotic arrangements which do not allow for the development of a self. Thus, in viewing the psychic apparatus in isolation, the interpersonal, object world must also be stressed.[30]

Any one model has only limited value in portraying the different clinical conditions in childhood psychosis. Other models, such as the Moebius strip, provide a better understanding of a particular condition and its treatment techniques.[31] The strip, with its inverted ring, allows us to see that what is on the outside leads to the inside. Thus this model dramatizes that the therapeutic process with schizophrenic patients moves from surface to dream and from dream to surface without warning. In the same way that an ordinary person moves back and forth between the rhythms of being awake and asleep, schizophrenic patients move back and forth between primary and secondary process, autistic and symbiotic states, withdrawal and fusion. Fusion states constantly occur between perception and memory, between past and present. This endless fluctuation indicates the patient's capacity for having reliable defenses against psychotic material.

This model also describes the borderline conditions and their interpersonal aspects. Harry Stack Sullivan viewed psychiatry as a science of interpersonal relations. He referred to the special technical conditions of psychotherapy with borderline cases, but did not include investigation of the intrapsychic aspects. Interpersonal models encourage us to study the the nonfacilitating environment and allow us to develop therapeutic environments that facilitate adaptive processes.[32] When considering intrapsychic processes, however, it might also be helpful to go back to the image of the cobra egg, which illustrates the patient's mental and physical dispositions and defensive and adaptive structure deficits.

THE DIAGNOSTIC PROCESS

Both the psychological and medical literature differentiate between diagnosis and treatment. Traditionally, psychiatric clinics have assigned the tasks of treatment and diagnosis to different teams. Diagnosis may indicate whether treatment is necessary or unnecessary. A review of the literature indicates that few authors share my point of view in referring to the *diagnostic process* rather than simply to diagnosis. It is my belief that diagnosis is a dynamic process, an intervention in itself that marks the beginning of treatment. Friedman suggests that the diagnostic process helps determine to what degree child and parents are capable of entering treatment and of making use of the therapist, the therapeutic milieu, and the social resources available.[33]

This concept of diagnosis as a process has been explored by the staff of the Menninger Clinic Children's Division.[34] The diagnostic process is a team process, involving not only the sick child and his family but also the psychiatric team, usually consisting of a psychiatrist or psychoanalyst, a social worker, a clinical psychologist, and perhaps a neurologist or an internist, as well as teachers and referring physicians. A speech pathologist, researchers, and others may help to assess the total psychological and social situation. Each team member employs the specific skills of his field of expertise and also participates in a process which integrates the observations and experiences of the other team members. This approach not only provides a picture of the child's illness, his mental and emotional functions, and his inner world; it also gives us a picture of family interaction and the social world of the child and the family—of individual as well as group pathology.

This method of diagnosis, although sometimes painful and lengthy, raises various questions. Can the child or adolescent be treated by means of psychotherapy or psychoanalysis? Can this be done in a private office? Will the parents be included in the treatment process, and in what way? Do they need psychotherapy? Do they need casework help, which has a different focus than psychotherapy? Is it possible to treat the child while he continues to live in the family group, or is separation necessary? Does the child need a special school, a residential center, or a hospital? Can one work via a day treatment center, and have the child live with the parents? Not only is there the problem as to what should be prescribed; the team must also carefully assess its own resources as to whether the clinic, the hospital or the residential center and its psychotherapists, teachers, recreational workers, occupational therapists, and nurses have the technical resources necessary for a successful program.

In the Menninger team approach, the employment of standardized procedures and tests must be weighed against the need for flexibility.

When would a standardized test such as the Rorschach Test be appropriate, and would it serve only to produce anxiety and resistance in a
patient?

The diagnostic team must consider the developing transference situation, the feelings and actions of the child and the family involved, and also
the kinds of countertransferences the test procedure stimulate or provoke
in the team. Bettelheim stresses that treatability is a two-way process requiring continual assessment of the treatment facility and its staff. There
may be very poor chances of treatability in one setting, but good conditions for treatment in another.

Both treatability and diagnosis can only be determined after a long process. In spite of a cautious team approach, we are repeatedly confronted
by failures or near failures of treatment. This volume reports failures to
diagnose the strengths of an illness and the weakness of specific healing
factors, especially in the beginning of the treatment process. Understanding the errors in the diagnostic process that others have made can be as
much a learning experience as accounts of successes—and more germane
to the reality of our own experiences.

Elsewhere, I have spoken about changes in the social climate concerning mental health facilities in the United States and most likely in Europe
as well.[35] There are few long-term treatment centers available. Rising
hospital costs, accompanied by diminishing federal and local funds, have
led to the necessity of treating children within the home. The support
system consists of devoted and dedicated parents often overwhelmed by
their difficulties. One task of the diagnostic process is to determine
whether the parents can help to create a facilitating environment. Frequently parents are perceived by clinicians as being the cause of the illness, when instead we should consider whether they can serve as one of
the causes of the cure.

The strength of any psychotherapeutic process depends on the support
system. In conventional psychotherapeutic or psychoanalytic work, the
maintenance of the therapeutic alliance is to some extent assured, despite
difficulties the patient may have with members of his family or in his social
or work life. In the case of psychotic and borderline children and
adolescents, however, the support system is of extraordinary importance.
The diagnostic team and the parents must understand that it is not the illness alone which determines prognosis, but the complexity of the illness
within a constantly changing interpersonal context. Psychotic and borderline children are usually brought to us by desperate parents after many
other attempted treatments have failed. The family and the child, driven
by a sense of panic and hopelessness, start the diagnostic process in the
spirit of a last appeal for help. The team's task is to turn the emergency

appeal of child and parents into trust and hope in a participatory process of healing. Many of the examples in this book demonstrate the diagnostic process necessary for this to occur.

THE PSYCHOTHERAPEUTIC PROCESS

Earlier in this introduction I compared metaphors which permit us to envision the psychic apparatus of very disturbed children whose difficulties do not fit conventional models of the psychotherapeutic process and therefore require some rethinking. Classic analytic treatment allows for the development of a stable therapeutic situation, the development of the transference neurosis, the analysis of transference and resistance, the resolution of conflicts, and the slow dissolution of the transference neurosis which is the repetition of the infantile neurosis. Psychoanalysis and analytic psychotherapy with neurotic children show many analogues, although differences in means of communication should be stressed. Free association in adult psychoanalysis, based primarily on verbal communication, is substituted in child analysis by play. As Erikson suggests, play is the child's royal road to the unconscious.[36]

In therapeutic work with the nonpsychotic child or adolescent, treatment procedures can be developed on the basis of the child's capacity to differentiate between self and object and on the degree of selfobject constancy. The nonpsychotic child can distinguish between play and real action, fantasy and reality, and can thus participate in the therapeutic process and observe therapeutic material. Although this capacity may not always be stable, it can usually be well maintained during the therapeutic experience. The child's socialization is generally stable enough to keep acting out within the socially acceptable limits of the family and school system.

The personality of the child or adolescent who is amenable to conventional psychoanalytic or psychotherapeutic treatment can be compared to a stable, predictable organization which undergoes a slow rate of change during development and maturation. One might use, as indicated earlier, the analogy of the layers of an onion. As one after another layer is removed and studied, a comparatively predictable structure is discovered. It includes systems of communication, developed and developing speech, the capacity for play, a certain degree of available trust, and expressions of love and hate.

This predictable structure breaks down completely in the case of the psychotic or borderline child, in whom no ordinary defense organization or adaptive capacity exists. Behind a thin facade of reality-oriented communication, we find instead primary process, the logic of the dream, psychotic thought disorder. Here the therapist is not dealing with the predictable layers of an onion, but with the thin shell of the cobra egg, behind which can be seen the deadly cobra coiled, ready to strike. The only predictable element is the lack of predictability. The therapist must be ready for endless surprises.

A brief example of unpredictable psychotic transference is the case of Theresa Esperanza, an adolescent girl discussed in this volume. She enters the therapist's office and wants her new dress to be admired. Receiving a compliment, she suddenly asks if she looks like Snow White. The therapist is a little hasty and suggests that Theresa looks much better than Snow White, since she is real and Snow White is merely a fairy tale. But Theresa insists that Snow White is much prettier and starts to describe beautiful Snow White in her coffin, poisoned by the mother, unable to move. Her beauty is so admired by the dwarfs who guard her that instead of burying her, they put her in a glass coffin where she can be seen forever. A handsome prince opens her glass coffin, and Theresa continues the story by saying, ''The prince kisses me on the mouth, and I ride off with him on his white charger to the castle, where I live with him happily ever after.''

Theresa's inability to maintain her identity is apparent here. She fuses with the fantasy character; substitutes the psychotherapist with the representation of the prince; who for her is an inner reality, and escapes from and denies external reality. The psychotherapeutic situation is placed on an entirely different dreamlike level, contact with the patient is lost, and she returns to her private delusional world. Only later might she be able to turn her delusion into an observed fantasy.

In psychotic transferences, past and present are fused, and reality and fantasy are combined with a rapid destruction of the capacity for interpersonal contact. In the material above we see the hidden aspects of negative, hostile symbiosis: fusion with the mother or father, and fragments of the perception of the mother as hostile and devouring. Ordinary communication is destroyed and communion occurs, but lacking the safety of a positive mother-infant relationship. There is only the hostility of mutual devouring, mutual destruction, and mutual incorporation.

The therapist must therefore discover and develop a system of communication which avoids the extremes of either distance or closeness. I have suggested that metaphoric language can serve as the link to the patient's unconscious material and simultaneously offer the patient a safety valve by means of which optimum distance can slowly be created and preserved.

Metaphoric language may occur in the modes of space, time, and distance, and its fluctuations may be expressed in terms of religious and biblical allegories, or by acting out. It may sometimes take the form of science fiction, fairy tales, mythology, poetry, or the technical language of machine building. Language may be one of symbolic realization, as was used by Madame Sechehaye.[37] During certain phases of treatment, forms of communication which make use of metaphor, simile, and allegory merely hint at problems without achieving insight on a higher level of secondary process functioning. Metaphoric language spans communication and communion. It creates a bridge between patient and therapist and satisfies the patient temporarily with primitive mutual understanding. One need only remember that the first understanding between the infant and the maternal figure is one of mutual satisfaction, out of which verbal language develops. First, language consist of appeal and counterappeal, demand and counterdemand; only later does it attain a truly symbolic function.[38] All echolalic language—like the metaphor, that link between echolalia and symbolic representation, between emotional bond and communication—serves as a solid bridge from one state of mind to another.

Elaine, another patient described in this book, after extended contact along the axis of metaphor, frequently in the form of religious and biblical allegories, wondered why she and her therapist continued to talk in such different and strange ways, even though both knew what they really meant. At that moment, therapist and patient were ready to abandon metaphoric communication, which had served as merely a preliminary means of communication. With the patient's use of her newfound capacities, therapy could now be conducted along the more conventional modes of psychotherapeutic dialogue.

Establishing communication and unthreatening, helpful contact with autistic children is a particularly difficult task. Peller speaks of the autistic child's language as uniting as well as separating the child from the mother.[39] In Bowlby's terms, language tries to bring about attachment and also to make separation possible.[40] The autistic child does not trust the possibility of uniting with and remaining attached to the mother, and neither does he accept the risk of separation from her. Such a child does not see language as a bridge to the mother; language is experienced as a terrible exit which leads farther away from her, towards increasing anxiety, panic, and destruction, and resulting in the autistic, nonspeaking position that Mahler has described. The autistic child's negativism is a way of insisting that he does not want to believe in communication, only in communion. Communion without language is seen as a guarantee to maintaining the object, albeit an anaclitic object. The child's positive world is symbiotic; there is no true separation between self and nonself, and the other self, the object, has not yet been discovered.

The autistic monologue has to be slowly developed into a psychotherapeutic dialogue.[41] The psychotherapist's task is to help the child experience language as an opportunity for growing autonomy, achievable without losing the mother. How can the psychotherapist convince the child of an emotional situation that allows for separation leading to individuation rather than to annihilation?

The technical problems involved are extremely difficult because the patient has not yet attained self or object constancy. He frequently has not moved beyond fragmentary mental representations of objects and self. In addition, the synthetic function has not been established. Therefore, we can often observe, as the patient forms object relations and allows himself to get near to the object, that his inner transformation of the object shifts from a positive representation to a negative one. Primitive splitting mechanisms prevail, as in the case described earlier of Theresa Esperanza. In telling her therapist the story of Snow White, Theresa herself becomes Snow White, whose mother attempts to destroy her and who is rescued by a magical kiss from the prince. Although Theresa seeks contact with her therapist, she is suddenly overwhelmed by a fantasy, actually a delusion, that he is a powerful creature who is persecuting and destroying her. She must free herself from him by withdrawing into a shell. Any object constancy that she might have achieved with the therapist is shattered by his premature comment, and she escapes with her prince, a distant, psychotic elaboration of the unavailable parent figure. Contact with the therapist is lost, and she at once removes herself from the real world, which her delusion, like a dream, mirrors. In this situation, fragments of the psychotherapeutic dialogue are transformed into a delusional monologue.

The longing for fusion—for communion—then turns into the fear of fusion, as in the case of Elaine. She wants to unite with Jesus Christ and be like him, but then bitterly accuses herself of the sinful, frivolous thought that she could be Christ. Advanced mechanisms of identification that normally lead to idealization fall apart and reassemble as primitive introjects, that is, incorporative devices leading to terror and panic.

In clinical situations such as these, the metaphor of the Moebius strip becomes useful in clarifying the technical task of the therapist. The therapist travels with the patient along the axis of an inner world that imperceptibly becomes the outer world, and which projects onto the outer world the inner struggle. The child's inability to separate inner and outer reality creates special technical difficulties that are resolved with the therapist's subtle use of metaphor, allegory, simile or allusion, via the child's use of regressed means of communication and communion, or other distance devices.

Thus, only selected cases can be treated in private practice, and psychotherapy alone is not always the treatment of choice. We must develop a total treatment program, taking into account the severity of the psychotic illness or borderline condition, and also the ability of the family to be supportive of treatment. Psychotherapy is only part of the total psychiatric armamentarium, and it should never be thought of as the only method available. However, it must also be stressed that psychotherapy allows much insight into other problem areas. The psychotherapist is like the pilot of a ship who, although assisted by the captain and crew, is the one who actually guides the ship into safe harbor.

Any psychotherapeutic work with psychotic children must take into account the difficulties the therapist faces in addition to those inherent in his personality and training. Psychotherapeutic work usually lasts for many years, and results are unpredictable. The therapist may succeed in some cases and have partial success in others, but the total success will seem insignificant. As part of his professional identity, the therapist must adopt a completely new attitude toward the measurement of achievement. Is the therapist able to work in unpredictable situations, with parents who may themselves have serious difficulties and who may not be very cooperative? Can he work with or against a community that is often critical? And can he face up to illnesses which are heartbreaking, provoking, time consuming, full of emergencies, and often unique, and which constantly demand the use of his intuition and his ability for innovation and experimentation? Is he willing to undertake such difficult work without a clear program of action?

The therapist must continually be aware that psychotic and borderline children provoke powerful countertransference reactions. Winnicott[56] warns of reactions of murderous rage, hate, hopelessness, and fear that may be brought forth in the therapist.[42] The continuing work of therapists, supervisors, and teachers in this area, as well as a growing body of research, will help us develop the necessary clinical skills for the effective treatment of such children.

I believe that understanding and restoration of choice must be the primary technique and goal in treatment, and must not be sacrificed to the expediency of manipulative techniques which aim at control and conformity.[57]

PSYCHOTHERAPEUTIC GROUP PROCESSES

The literature rarely refers to group psychotherapy techniques with children who are diagnosed as psychotic or schizophrenic, or of the borderline type. One notable exception is Speers and Lansing, who believe that group psychotherapy should not be considered the only mode of treatment, although it may be used as the dominant method.[43] They treated severely disturbed young children in small groups of about five, with collateral groups conducted for the parents. In this psychoanalytically oriented study, correlations were made between the material produced by the adults' and children's groups, with a focus on the nature of the mother-child symbiosis and on the mother's relationship to the child in the treatment process. Speers and Lansing found that fathers were less involved in the treatment situation, and the mother's self-image and her image of her child were usually very poor. They attempted to turn neurotic family interactions into positive ones through the group situation. According to the authors, therapeutic results indicated that the children could be brought to a level of socialization that made it possible for them to enter the kindergarten or first grade of a regular elementary school. The treatment techniques used by the therapists in the study focused on variables of biological defect in the child, the pathology of the mother, tenaciousness of the mother-child symbiosis, the psychologically absent father, and the overall interaction of the family. This approach enabled the therapists to alter the network of pathological reactions which enmeshed the family.

Speers and Lansing do not claim their treatment modality produced a cure, but treatment did bring about improvement which allowed the patient to return to more normal group experiences. They suggest that the combination of group and individual therapy may result in more effective therapeutic interaction.

Other authors, such as Mayer and Blum, Fant, and Tuss and Saltzman have made similar suggestions in a symposium on residential treatment utilizing the group situation.[44] All residential treatment, hospitalization, special boarding homes, and day treatment centers rely to a large extent on the use of therapeutic group interaction. These groups usually include nonpsychotic children.

CONCERNING THE USE OF HOSPITALIZATION, MILIEU TREATMENT, AND RESIDENTIAL CENTERS

The history of psychiatry, especially the history of work with severely disturbed patients, reveals a movement from total neglect and restraint towards more human and therapeutic practices. In the past, the attitude of society towards the mentally ill was based on a fear of real or imaginary dangers. Hospitalization was considered a last resort, an expression of helplessness. In *A Home for the Heart,* Bruno Bettelheim describes his struggle to turn hospitals for chronically ill patients into positive, therapeutic environments.[45] Today, in spite of the work of such pioneers as Bettelheim, Szurek and Berlin, Kanner, and Bender, hospitals are too frequently thought of merely as storehouses for unmanageable patients, and in some hospitals, neglect or even overt abuse of patients may occur.

Psychotic children, especially when they are very young, are usually treated as long as possible in the home or occasionally in boarding homes. It is commonly assumed that home is the best place for the child. Hospitalization is used as a temporary measure for acute situations, since it is considered an added trauma, an undesirable intervention to be postponed as long as possible, and is feared by parents and physicians alike. Some acute psychotic and borderline conditions may require temporary therapeutic residential arrangements.

The range of an illness indicates whether outpatient or office treatment alone can be the treatment of choice. Most authors view the hospital as a positive milieu or facilitating environment and discuss methods of arranging the milieu to help restore the patient to a more functional level. Szurek et al. have described 25 years of collaborative treatment at the Langley Porter Children's Service, where a gamut of psychiatric intervention is used, including a psychotherapeutic milieu.[46] Much emphasis is placed on developing a nursing staff that can help with the 24-hour care of the child.

Brunstetter discusses milieu treatment for psychotic children, and he emphasizes the task of grouping children in order to meet the needs of each individual.[47] He believes a milieu program should provide a framework for the child's normal growth with activities and opportunities that support the work of the psychotherapist and psychiatric nurses, and that reduce conflict. He sees the milieu program as a substitute for family living, an addendum to the psychotherapeutic treatment, not merely an emergency measure as is true in many centers today.

Similar technical procedures are described by Goldfarb and his co-workers.[48] They use hospital as well as day treatment programs to bring about the corrective socialization of the child. The milieu becomes an effective therapeutic climate, more important than brief encounters between child and therapist. They suggest that total programs be carried out by a staff which includes educators, and which is trained to know what the necessary corrections are for the defects characteristic of schizophrenic children. This program of corrective socialization is used to stimulate and reinforce the development of adaptive functions that the child lacks as well as to strengthen functions which he already possesses.

Goldfarb and his collaborators believe that child care workers and teachers can carry out programs within the context of institutional life.[49] The program is run in a structured setting, following special time patterns, and employing repetition and regularity of routines. Goldfarb et al. emphasize the imposition of structure from without as a means of encouraging the growth of the child's inner structure. Their program avoids encouraging regression or illusory fulfillment. Immediate appropriate responses to the child as well as highly structured and predictable rewards and limit-setting counteracts the schizophrenic child's fantasy of noncompliance and insistence on timelessness, formlessness, and informational vagueness.

My own point of view combines behavior modification and dynamic psychotherapy. Rather than accept Skinner's *Walden II* and his philosophy expressed in *Beyond Freedom and Dignity,* I recommend a "Walden III" philosophy, which integrates structure and meaning.

Bettelheim, as well as his successors at the Orthogenic School, are working on an integrative model of treatment for psychotic children and adolescents.[50] Their stress is the positive milieu, a total therapeutic environment in which the children and the child care staff live and work together. The therapeutic setting is a residential center with living space, a total *Lebensraum*, physically and psychologically developed. Furniture, sleeping arrangements, availability of staff, and the permanence and continuity of relationships among staff and children are all carefully planned. The staff is intensively involved in the psychotherapeutic community and most of them literally live in this organization. Comparable, although less intensive therapeutic communities exist at the Southard School, the Children's Division of the Menninger Foundation, and also at Bellefaire.

The goal of most of these treatment centers is to bring children to a point where separation from the hospital program is possible. Some of the centers believe in very short hospitalization; those mentioned above allow for longer placements until the children are ready to move back into the community. Usually interim steps are encouraged, such as day treatment centers, special schools, boarding and foster homes, or partial return to the family.

THERAPEUTIC PROCESSES AND CASEWORK PROCESSES WITH PARENTS

As stressed earlier, psychotic conditions and borderline states in childhood and adolescence usually carry a strong component of pathology relating to the child's special tie with the mother or the parent surrogate. Therefore, it is necessary to develop special modes of technical help for the parents. This subject was treated by Bowlby in his contributions concerning attachment, separation and loss.[51] Among the most outstanding contributions are those made by Mahler and her collaborators, Pine and Bergman, concerning symbiosis and the vicissitudes of individuation, especially in infantile psychosis.[52] Their work provides a clinical and theoretical basis for the development of techniques in working with parents. Bowlby stresses interpersonal aspects of parents problems, and interpersonal, Mahler and her colleagues stress intrapsychic features.

Many other authors discuss the impact of mother and child on each other in severe childhood disturbances. Goldfarb discusses two paradigms: the somatically inadequate child's impact on parents and, at the other extreme, the impact of the deviant family on the child which encourages the development of pathological symptoms and defenses. The second paradigm also stresses the issue of parental *perplexity*, the parent's inability to develop sending power when the child has no receiving power. Goldfarb stresses the necessity of working with parents.[53]

In his early contributions, Bettelheim advised removing the child from the pathological environment and placing him in a nonpathological environment, a total treatment milieu.[54] His basic attitude with regard to parents was not to involve them in the treatment program, but "rather, separate them from the child completely in an attempt to bring about a new situation." Bettelheim's view is reflected in earlier psychoanalytic writings, in which the parent was seen as the cause of the child's illness. The therapist, identifying with the child's view of having been traumatized by the parents, shared the child's overt or covert blaming of the parents.

Modern treatment techniques have grown beyond an overidentification with the child's suffering and now include the parents. With very young children it is frequently useful to see the mother and the small child at the same time. The mother can learn to respond appropriately to the child by picking up cues from the therapist, who serves as a temporary auxiliary mother. As the nonpathological link between mother and child, the therapist is able to break the pathological pattern between them.

Helping the mother to separate from the child and to give up the symbiotic arrangement and its pathological consequences for both is the central aim of therapy. Giving up this early tie, which is a kind of bondage, in exchange for normal relations, allowing for separation, growth, and individuation, is a painful and torturous process. In some cases counseling and case work focusing on social planning suffices. In other cases family or individual psychotherapy has to be initiated, or psychotherapy or psychoanalysis with the parents may be necessary. The psychiatric team can serve as a healthy model for the family. Therapy provides a situation in which the parent, who may be puzzled, bewildered, ineffective, or besieged by his own difficulties or marital problems, may become a positive force and help to maintain the treatment situation, despite unbelievably trying conditions.

Work with parents must not merely be focused around the treatment of the child, but must also be concerned with the parents' adequate functioning and happiness. The parents are not just tools to help us, but individuals with their own personal problems. The psychiatrist should try to free the parents from their unbearable burdens, help them to allow for separation if necessary, and help them work through their mourning in having to give up the possible illusion of their child's complete recovery. The parents must learn to accept whatever improvement may be possible, and to cope with further planning, including possible permanent institutionalization. The parents must forsake any delusion of the omnipotentiality of the child and accept the child with all his flaws (such as the clubfoot of Oedipus), some of which may be beyond the possibility of change. The child also must abandon the fantasy that his parents are allpowerful and accept the subsequent disillusionment of seeing them as ordinary mortals.

One of the greatest difficulties for the clinician in this field is discovering and tolerating the fact that work with parents never proceeds smoothly. Parents create emergencies similar to those the child creates, and thus the maintenance of the treatment situation is constantly endangered. Part of the parents' transference paradigm is a fluctuation between the naive expectation that the therapist is an omnipotent miracle worker, and the equally dangerous fantasy that the therapist has nothing to offer, has never helped, and is a destroyer of hopes. Shifting attitudes and violent transferences also occur in the therapeutic team or individual therapist, and with it the fluctuation between despair and hope that is part of the challenge of treating psychotic children.

CONCLUSION

More hospital beds are currently occupied by schizophrenic patients than by patients in any other diagnostic category, psychiatric or medical. Methods of prevention, methods of training personnel for the treatment of schizophrenia and allied conditions, and investments in research do not keep pace with the enormity of this social problem. This is also true of the treatment of children suffering from psychotic and borderline conditions, even though the literature indicates vast improvements.[55] Present-day treatment modalities and facilities are still understaffed and underfinanced, setting an almost impossible task for the helping professions, which humanistic impulses and compassion alone are not enough to meet. Thirty years ago Bettleheim stated this fact in *Love Is Not Enough*. We need opportunities for long term treatment; facilities with continuity; leaders who combine compassion, curiosity, research interests, and the will to help and communities willing to support them.

Many of the pioneers in the field have created powerful centers of activity, but frequently these individuals work in isolation. Their theoretical differences and their different languages, theory, or practice keep them apart, and their students are almost like members of medieval guilds who do not join other guilds and believe only in their own master. The task before us requires integration of effort, a synthesis of the many fragments of knowledge that have accumulated in years past.

Creative people, often ahead of the mainstream of clinical activity, create their own isolation. It is as if they can work only on small islands of activity. Their work must be supplemented by imaginative and thorough research on causes—not only the causes of illness as now studied, but also causes of the cures. We must ensure that the accomplishments of such pioneers will make a significant difference in clinical activity and social influence. We must work to increase the readiness of the helping professions as well as the total community to support new programs. Resources must be provided for such programs, many of which in recent years have become endangered and frequently dissolved. Finally, we must develop clinical research on every level.

What is needed, I feel, and this is documented throughout the work presented in this volume, are many small pilot programs that allow research in childhood psychosis and related disorders to be conducted without strings attached. Small groups should be supported, even when they do not follow the exact rules and regulations of the money-granting foundations or government agencies. These small research groups can overcome theoretical, often merely ideological differences in order to draw knowledge from each other and to make use of the insights and findings of all the clinical and behavioral sciences.

REFERENCES

[1] Szurek, S.A., and Berlin, I.N. Clinical Studies in Childhood Psychoses. Brunner/Mazel, New York: 1973.

[2] Bender, L. Childhood schizophrenia. Nerv. Child, 1:138, 1942; Childhood schizophrenia. Psychiatric Quarterly, 27:663, 1953; Childhood schizophrenia: a review. J. Hillside Hospital, 16:10, 1967.

[3] Laufer, M.W., and Gair, D.S. Childhood Schizophrenia. In The Schizophrenic Syndrome, Bellak, L., and Loeb, L., editors. New York: Grune & Stratton, 1969, p. 378.

[4] Menninger, K., and Mayman, M. The Vital Balance. New York The Viking Press, 1963.

[5] Erikson, E. Childhood and Society, New York: W.W. Norton & Co., 1964.

[6] Ekstein, R., Bryant, K., and Friedman, S. Childhood schizophrenia and allied conditions. In Schizophrenia: A Review of The Syndrome. Bellak, L. (editor). New York: Logos Press, 1958.

[7]Goldfarb, W. Childhood schizophrenia. Int. Psychiatry Clin., 1:821, 1964.

[8]Kanner, L. Autistic disturbances of affective contact. Nerv. Child, 2:217, 1943; Early infantile autism. J. Pediatri., 25:211, 1944.

[9]Mahler, M.S. Autism and symbiosis: Two extreme disturbances of identity. Int. J. Psychoanal., 39:77, 1958; On early infantile psychosis; The Symbiotic and autistic syndromes. J. Am. Acad. Child Psychiatry, 4:554, 1965.

[10]Ekstein, R. The Challenge: Despair and Hope in the Conquest of Inner Space. New York Brunner/Mazel, 1971; Borderline states and ego disturbances. In Treatment of Emotional Disorders in Children and Adolescents. Sholevar, P., Benson, R. and Blinder, B., (editors). New York: Spectrum Publications, 1980, p. 403.

[11]Masterson, J. Treatment of the Borderline Adolescent. New York: John Wiley and Sons, 1975.

[12]Bettelheim, B. The Empty Fortress. New York: Free Press of Glencoe (Macmillan), 1967.

[13]Kanner, L. Autistic disturbances of affective contact. Nerv. Child, 2:217, 1943; Early infantile autism. J. Pediatri., 25:211, 1944.

[14]Erikson, E. Childhood and Society. New York: W.W. Norton, 1964.

[15]Ekstein, R. Children of Time and Space, of Action and Impulse. New York: Appleton-Century-Crofts, 1966.

[16]Goldfarb, W. The mutual impact of mother and child in childhood schizophrenia. Am. J. Orthopsychiatry, 31:738, 1961.

[17]Bettelheim, B. The Empty Fortress.

[18]Rohde-Dascher, C. Das Borderline Syndrom. Verlag Hans Huber, Bern, Stuttgart, Wien, 1979.

[19]Mahler, M.S., Pine, F., and Bergman, A. The Psychological Birth of the Human Infant—Symbiosis and Individuation. New York: Basic Books, 1975.

[20]Mahler, M.S. On early infantile psychosis: The symbiotic and autistic syndromes, 1965.

[21]Mahler, M.S. On Human Symbiosis and The Vicissitudes of Individuation. Vol I: Infantile Psychosis. New York: International Universities Press, 1968.

[22]Ekstein, R., and Wallerstein, J. Observations on the psychology of borderline and psychotic children. In Psychoanalytic Study of the Chld, 9:344, 1954.

[23]Meyer, M.M., and Ekstein, R. The psychotic pursuit of reality. In The Challenge: Despair and Hope in the Conquest of Inner Space, New York: Brunner/Mazel, 1971.

[24]Lorenzer, A. Sprachzerstorung und Rekonstruktion Vorarbeinten Zu Einer Metatheorie der Psychoanalyse. Suhrkamp, 1970.

[25]Ekstein, R. From the language of play to play with language. In Adol. Psychiatry, 4:142-162, 1975.

[26]Freud S. (1900) Interpretation of Dreams (standard edition). London: Hogarth Press, 1953.

[27]Ekstein, R. Functional Psychoses in children: clinical features and treatment. In Comprehensive Textbook of Psychiatry. Freedman, A.M., Kaplan,

H.I., and Sadock, B.J. (editors). Baltimore: Williams and Wilkins, 1975, p. 2189.

[28]Freud, S. (1923). Group Psychology and the Analysis of the Ego (standard edition). London: Hogarth Press, 1955.

[29]Winnicott, D. The Maturational Processes and the Facilitating Environment. London: Hogarth Press, 1965.

[30]Ekstein, R. Children of Time and Space, of Action and Impulse, 1966; Ekstein, R., Friedman, S., and Caruth, E. The psychoanalytic treatment of childhood schizophrenia. In Manual of Child Psychopathology, Wolman, B.B. (editor). New York: McGraw-Hill, 1972.

[31]Caruth, E. The onion and the moebius strip: Rational and irrational models for the secondary and primary process. In The Challenge: Despair and Hope in the Conquest of Inner Space. Ekstein, E. (editor). New York: Brunner/Mazel, 1971, p. 334.

[32]Winnicott, D. The Maturational Processes and the Facilitating Environment, 1965.

[33]Friedman, S. The diagnostic process during the evaluation of an adolescent girl. In Children of Time and Space, of Action and Impulse, Ekstein, R. (editor). New York: Appleton-Century-Crofts, 1966, p. 15.

[34]Staff of the Menninger Clinic Children's Foundation, The Menninger Clinic. Disturbed Children. San Francisco: Jossey-Bass, 1969.

[35]Ekstein, R. The Challenge, 1971.

[36]Erikson, E. Childhood and Society, 1964.

[37]Sechehaye, M.A. The transference in symbolic realization. Int. J. Psychoanal., 37:270, 1956.

[38]Ekstein, R. Functional psychoses in children: clinical features and treatment, 1975.

[39]Peller, L.E. Freud's contribution to language development. Psychoanal. Study of the Child, 21:459, 1966.

[40]Bowlby, J. Attachment and Loss. New York: Basic Books, 1969; Attachment and Loss: Separation, Anxiety, and Anger. Vol. 2, New York: Basic Books, 1973; Attachment and Loss: Loss, Sadness, and Depression. Vol. 3. New York: Basic Books, 1980.

[41]Ekstein, R. and Nelston, T. The birth of the psychotherapeutic dialogue. In Psychiatric Clinics of North America. Philadelphia: W.B. Saunders, 1981.

[42]Winnicott, D. Hate in the countertransference. Int. J. Psychoanal., 20:69, 1949.

[43]Speers, R.W., and Lansing, C. Group Therapy and Childhood Psychosis. Chapel Hill: University of North Carolina Press, 1965.

[44]Tuss, K., and Saltzman, E.S., Special education in residential treatment. In Healing Through Living. Mayer, M.F. and Blum, A., (editors). Springfield: Charles C. Thomas, 1971, p. 127.

[45]Bettelheim, B. A Home for the Heart. New York: Alfred A. Knopf, 1974.

[46]Szurek, S.A., and Berlin, I.N. Clinical Studies in Childhood Psychoses,

1973.

[47]Brunstetter, R.W. Milieu treatment for psychotic children. In Clinical Studies in Childhood Psychoses. New York: Brunner/Mazel, 1973, p. 174.

[48]Goldfarb, W., Mintz, I., and Stroock, C.W. A Time to Heal Corrective Socialization: A Treatment Approach to Childhood Schizophrenia. New York: International Universities Press, 1969.

[49]Goldfarb, W., Mintz, I., and Stroock, C.W. A Time to Heal Corrective Socialization, 1969.

[50]Bettelheim, B. A Home for the Heart, 1974.

[51]Bowlby, J. Attachment and Loss, 1969, 1973, 1980.

[52]Mahler, M.S. On Human Symbiosis, 1968; Mahler, M.S., Pine, F., and Bergman, A. The Psychological Birth of the Human Infant, 1975.

[53]Goldfarb, W. The mutual impact of mother and child in childhood schizophrenia, 1961.

[54]Bettelheim, B. Love Is Not Enough: The Treatment of Emotionally Disturbed Children. New York: Free Press of Glencoe (Macmillan), 1950; Truants from Life: The Rehabilitation of Emotionally Disturbed Children. New York: Free Press of Glencoe (Macmillan), 1955.

[55]Ekstein, R., Bryant, K., and Friedman, S. Childhood Schizophrenia and allied conditions, 1958.

INTRODUCTION

Looking back, then, over the patchwork of my life's labors, I can say that I have made many beginnings and thrown out many suggestions. Something will come of them in the future, though I cannot tell myself whether it will be much or little. I can, however, express a hope that I have opened up a pathway for an important advance in our knowledge.

SIGMUND FREUD

To study the phenomena of disease without books is to sail an uncharted sea. To study books without patients is not to go to sea at all.

SIR WILLIAM OSLER

INTRODUCTION

The work presented in this book, covering about two decades of clinical investigation, received its first stimulus in the late forties. At that time I was the director of psychotherapy at the Southard School, a facility for disturbed children. It offered inpatient and outpatient services; a thorough diagnostic service; a rigorous intake process in terms of suitability for the treatment program; an analytic psychotherapy program; a formal school program, recreational and occupational therapy; a staff of psychiatrists, social workers, psychologists, teachers, recreational workers, house-parents —all of them exposed to continued clinical training as well as the impetus which comes from a research-oriented organization.

It was during the late forties that we first developed a structured program of supervision for all the therapists, a systematic method of recording psychotherapeutic sessions which enabled us to collect comparable and thorough data on our work. The data were then utilized for an expanding clinical, research, and training program, including clinical seminars and supervisory conferences.

We were puzzled by a number of cases which did not seem to yield to the usual analytic techniques despite our theoretical understanding of the patients' productions. This particular group of children could be described as suffering from borderline disorders, different forms of childhood schizophrenia, or severe character disorders. Supervision and seminar work then grew beyond the scope of the regular teaching program. The program then turned to research and a re-evaluation of our theoretical and technical tools.

Investigations of therapeutic techniques require not only a study of the specific difficulties of the child, but must aim toward an understanding of the therapist's special capacities as well. This led us to pay attention to the supervisory process, the study of staff dynamics and of the nature of data collection, individual recording, evaluation of test data and of electric recording devices.

The studies in this volume contain material from all of these areas, including work with very young children and also with adolescents. The chapters actually reflect the work of a number of clinicians who, at first under supervision and later as collaborators of the author, contributed to this field. The earlier investigations were primarily carried on at Southard School, and deal with children who were first placed there and later frequently continued treatment as outpatients. The more recent work was carried out at the Reiss-Davis Child Study Center, an outpatient facility where I function as Director of a Project on Childhood Psychosis.

Thus, my collaborators and my students were able to follow the treatment of inpatient and outpatient children, including both clinic and private-practice patients, each modality posing its unique problems of selection and treatment technique.

In addition to the advantage of drawing from work within different settings, these studies also benefit from the fact that they do not present merely one man's style, elaborated in a fully developed school of thought, but rather reflect a collaborative effort, best characterized perhaps through the philosophy of orthopsychiatry. The author is a psychoanalyst who has also had training as a clinical psychologist and social worker. The other contributors come from the fields of psychoanalysis, social work, clinical psychology, and psychiatry.

In order to evaluate these almost two decades of work against the background of the total social scene, I want to remind the reader of the situation at the beginning of this endeavor. In 1958, the author, together with Friedman and Bryant, reviewed the literature in this field published between 1946 and 1956.[1] These authors felt then that:

The scientific and social significance of work in the field of childhood schizophrenia during the last decade can perhaps be more fully evaluated if seen in historical perspective. An earlier representative survey of this kind, covering the period from 1936 to 1946, was published in 1948 . . . by Bellak who lists a total bibliography of 54 items concerning dementia praecox in childhood. A breakdown of these items reveals that 52 deal with etiology, symptomatology, diagnosis and problems of differential diagnosis; only two are concerned with problems of treatment and these describe the use of metrazol. His review chapter mentions psychotherapy without going into specific details, thus indicating that at that time no technical literature was available concerning psychotherapy with schizophrenic children. A review by Escalona (1948) is extremely cautious concerning psychotherapy with psychotic children. She states: "Adequate therapeutic measures, in cases of childhood psychosis, can be developed—if at all— only if the nature and causes of these conditions can be understood much more fully than they are at present." Her reference list does not include a single item concerning psychoanalytic work with psychotic children.

Thus this decade was primarily oriented toward diagnosis and etiology and is represented by literature that is rather pessimistic in regard to the success of therapeutic measures.

As we review the literature from 1946 to 1956, we find an immense increase in the number of contributions in this area. The new decade is represented by 515 items, approximately ten times as many as were published in the preceding decade. A breakdown of these items reveals that about 325 are concerned primarily with problems of etiology, symptomatology and diagnosis; approximately 90 deal mainly with psychotherapy; about 80 consider residential or hospital treatment, and about 20 are concerned with somatic treatment in the field of childhood schizophrenia and related disorders. This tremendous tenfold increase in contributions to the field of childhood schizophrenia is indeed puzzling and deserves our interest. There is no question that the total field of psychiatry has received enormous impetus since the Second World War. This is reflected in increased research and increased therapeutic optimism concerning mental illness in general, and specifically in apparent progress in the field of child psychiatry.

Approximately 40 per cent—190 items—of the scientific contributions in the field of childhood schizophrenia and related disorders in the last decade are therapeutically oriented; in the preceding decade only 4 per cent —2 items—represented expressed explicit interest in therapy. One might exaggerate and say that therapeutic optimism was a hundred times stronger between 1946 and 1956 than it was in the preceding ten years.

Lest we fall victim to statistical oversimplification, we must guard against a variety of possible errors. As the interest in early and serious childhood disorders has grown, we have developed a tendency to apply our concepts loosely and sometimes vaguely. The diagnostic category of childhood schizophrenia has become a rather broad concept which is used with many shades of meaning by a variety of authors. It is therefore quite possible that the new literature includes cases which were not considered in the studies characteristic of the period before 1946. A good many conditions which are referred to by authors as "atypical," "borderline," "schizoid," "pre-schizophrenic," "autistic," "symbiotic," etc., are reflected in the literature. Unless one wants to introduce an additional definition of childhood schizophrenia, more concise perhaps than those definitions used in our literature, and would then wish to confine oneself to the literature which fits this very new definition, one must incorporate in a survey of this kind a good many "doubtful" items. The Annotated Bibliography of Childhood Schizophrenia, by Goldfarb and Dorsen (1956)[2] which covers the literature up to 1954, is a case in point, since these authors, too, employ the broadest possible definition of childhood schizophrenia.

A review of so vast an area of literature would hardly be of benefit to the reader if it were simply an attempt to abstract various articles. We prefer to discuss developing trends in the field and we will try to see these trends against the background of a number of basic convictions which the authors hold. One of these is the assumption that diagnostic work is directly related to treatment. Many of the differences in diagnostic philosophy, which will be described in detail, can be understood better if seen as based on explicit or implicit decisions concerning treatability and concerning treatment techniques. This also holds true, of course, for studies in etiology, which are often merely indirect statements as to treatment philosophy, including, quite frequently, the pessimistic view that nothing can be offered but custodial care. The question as to what causes a mental condition is directly related to treatment decisions, even though a cloud of quasi-philosophical issues usually does not permit us to see this fact.

The literature on treatment can also be better integrated if it is seen against the background of a rather simple but nevertheless useful idea. This idea stems from a clarification of the concept of "choice of treatment." Any rational method of treatment usually bases its choice of therapy on an understanding of the afflicted personality organization, and the proper choice of treatment is then explained in terms of the patient's illness. The concept of the "choice of treatment" does not, however, immediately reveal the fact that choices depend not only on the nature of the patient's illness but on the tools of treatment which society, or a specific physician, or a specific treatment organization has available in order to make a specific choice. The treatment possibilities in the area of childhood schizophrenia have obviously increased in the last decade. The rich material on residential centers which treat these severely disturbed children is a case in point, as is the literature on psychotherapy, particularly psychoanalytically oriented psychotherapy concerning this specific syndrome.

Choices of treatment depend on the kind of support the community offers the therapist who wishes to treat such children. Psychoanalytic literature contains very little on the treatment of either adult schizophrenics or of schizophrenic children in the era before 1946, since psychotherapy was carried out primarily in private practice, but, on the other hand, subsequent placement in institutions merely meant custodial care for many of these children. Therefore, we find that most of the material before 1946 contains pessimistic notions concerning prognosis. Ideal conditions even then would perhaps have allowed genuine successes in the treatment of such patients, but the limited choices that society provided us with further hampered our efforts. The situation today is far from ideal but the different listings, concerning, for example, residential treatment centers, indicate the progress that has been made. Another limitation in the "choice of treatment" concerns the slow development of training in child psychiatry and child care as well as in psychotherapy with children, particularly borderline and psychotic children. Only during the last decade have training in these fields and opportunities for work with such children under optimum treatment conditions been developed. As a result, a variety of practitioners, whose work is reflected in the literature, have appeared on the scene.

Thus, . . . a variety of centers and sub-groups have developed which are concerned with studies of childhood schizophrenia. The rise in therapeutic optimism is perhaps but a reflection of improved training, of increased social responsibility on the part of the general public, of better social resources which have given us many more "choices of treatment." However, while intensive long-term psychotherapy of a psychotic child under optimum conditions in a residential treatment center with trained personnel is still the exception today in terms of availability to the large group of sufferers, it is at the same time for many cases the "ideal choice of treatment." Our survey then will reflect the problem of choice of treatment, not only in terms of increased knowledge about schizophrenic personality organization in childhood, but also in terms of the availability of tools and trained personnel. A good many of the differences of opinion are not differences in basic principles and therefore might permit us to integrate a variety of trends that seem irreconcilable on the surface.

Beyond the basic assumptions just discussed, we will not offer a partisan view, but rather will try to provide an objective account of developments in this field. Since we, too, have contributed to the literature, we are aware of the immense difficulties entailed and the necessity for study, for cross-fertilization of different views, for combining many different approaches. Partisan points of view have no place here. The field is too young; all of us are still groping in the dark. The more objectively the worker can approach open questions, and study the partial answers to others, the better equipped he will be to contribute toward the solution of the double problem which is implied in the phrase "ideal choice of treatment," namely, on the one hand, the study of the schizophrenic and schizophrenic-like personality organization, and on the other, the development of resources, of techniques and theories in the hands of those who are concerned with the problems of prevention and treatment.

When I first started my investigations, I had little to go by, since the field was undeveloped and the literature was only then beginning to deal with such issues as concerned us. I truly groped in the dark, and what seemed to be enormous insights in 1950 were considered but preliminary notions in 1960.

Psychoanalytic work necessitates slow and painstaking reconstruction. There is no final insight; revision of earlier insights, the sharpening of older concepts, the updating of fragments of theory are the order of the day. I continue to be confronted with that feeling that made Freud speak of the "patchwork of my life's labor" and that in all probability kept him from ever attempting to write a textbook or a definitive technique of psychoanalysis.

I, too, at present, do not want to attempt this, since we want to stress the fact that our opinions are fluid, that we are ready to face new clinical facts and to dispense with methods should they prove to be useless for a specific case.

The reader who searches for the consistency of that final version, the commitment to a fixed therapeutic prescription, a perfect theoretical explanation, will be disappointed. But he who wants to follow us in our successful trials, as well as in our desperate failures, will find stimulation.

I like to think of this book as representing the results of organized effort at clinical research and I seek to share the labors and results of the last two decades with a growing group of clinicians who are interested in this area and who, in turn, have stimulated us immensely. In the aforementioned survey, in which we tried to integrate all relevant work during a period of ten years, an effort which we have maintained throughout the succeeding years, we characterized the historical situation as it points toward the future as:

The markedly widened scope of interest within the decade 1946–1956 in the nature of the psychotic processes constituting childhood schizophrenia has great significance for the development of child psychiatry, when this trend is contrasted with the limited, often nihilistic views about psychosis, and more specifically, of schizophrenia in childhood, of preceding decades. This tendency, paralleling a remarkable interest in both the processes of child and ego development, has been reflected in the search for etiological factors in those fundamental areas involving the basic nature of the organism itself, its hereditary antecedents, constitutional organic structure, biological functions, physico-chemical and psychological dynamics, and the host of environmental influences related to the area of object-and-interpersonal relations. Diagnostically, the major trend of the decade under review has undergone the shift of the pendulum from concern with the clarification and establishment of psychopathologic categories and classifications of childhood schizophrenia as a diagnostic label to an intensively active and investigative understanding of the psychodynamic problems and peculiar modes of mental functioning of the ego of the schizophrenic personality. Similarly, in the area of differential diagnosis, the major contributions have led to increased clarification of the more precise and specific criteria which have aided in the establishment of the identity of childhood schizophrenia as an illness; it has also led to differentiation from related and allied conditions. Of historical interest are the extreme changes which have taken place in our view of childhood schizophrenia. Whereas formerly its existence was denied, it is now regarded as being of such a global, all-encompassing nature, that for purposes of differential diagnosis its possibility must be considered in every serious emotional and mental disturbance of childhood.

The powerful optimism which pervades the literature concerning the treatment of a number of schizophrenic children is as yet not supported by evidence concerning the prognosis for the whole group. Most reports represent enthusiastic pioneer efforts and permit the expectation that another survey ten years from now will report consolidated gains. The years from 1936 to 1946 were characterized by an emphasis on diagnosis and therapeutic pessimism. The phase from 1946 to 1956 has been one of therapeutic experimentation and optimism. One may predict then, or certainly hope, on the basis of accumulated evidence, that the period from 1956 to 1966 will bring further improved treatment techniques which may shift the emphasis from an uncertain prognosis for childhood schizophrenia to one in which there will be increased probability of recovery.

Even as this volume goes to press we are engaged in clinical research which constantly carries us into new fields. In the most recent report on our current interests and activities [3] we stated that:

The research for answers must be preceded by a proper search for questions, which stem from our work with patients during the treatment process, during the careful and continued scanning of our therapeutic activities. These questions are pursued for a while, abandoned later in order to give way to more emergent questions which are always cued by the patients who, in their way, search for answers and thrust the questions of ongoing research upon us.

These patients force upon us new methods concerning the study of our data. The therapist's recording of therapeutic sessions afford but lopsided data. The comparison of these process notes with the actual electric tape record has given us new insights beyond those which arise when we rely on memory only.[4] The therapist's record, influenced by his own style of remembering, dominated by secondary-process goal-oriented thinking, is comparable to the recollection of the manifest dream.

Much of our work elaborates the concept of distance, but most recent considerations lead us to further refinements and to redefinitions, such as are expressed in a simile based upon a topological consideration of distancing devices. We feel that, in the analysis of psychotic organization, the moebius strip for which there is no clearcut inside and outside in the conventional sense, rather than the picture of defensive layers within the personality, will provide us with more suitable models.[5] In our new work we deal, of course, with the issue of parents.[6] We have also started to be concerned with the problem of schooling.[7] Finally, the area of testing is steadily being refined and this is also reflected in some of the ongoing work.[8]

My collaborators and I hope that the professional community will receive this work as substantiating, in part, our prediction of improved treatment techniques and increased probability of recovery for the categories of disorders with which we deal, as well as of expanding our theoretical understanding of the issues involved.

The struggles of our child patients at times seem to be but a microscopic reflection of the global anxieties about survival and of the violent conflicts about human organizational patterns. As mankind looks for new positive heroic and creative effort, we marvel at the scientific achievements in the conquest of what is no longer completely uncharted outer space. Yet our child patients might inspire us to new commitments, in a new dimension of that heroic American quest which conquers the wilderness and expands the frontiers: the uncharted wilderness of psychological inner space.

The time may well come in which current pilot projects, experimental efforts such as are reflected in work with these patients, will not be isolated from the mainstream of social attempts at cure of emotional and mental illness. The time may well come when these efforts will be supported by vast backup teams, which will turn into a social reality what is true today for only a comparatively few research patients. That conquest of inner psychological space may well be the companion effort necessary for technical scientific advance to benefit mankind rather than to threaten its destruction. The insights of psychoanalysis have helped us to make the first tentative steps in that direction. An unfaltering dedication to the task of exploring inner psychological space and its mastery might help us close the gap between the physical sciences and our present knowledge of social and psychological adaptation.

REFERENCES

[1] Ekstein, R., Friedman, S. W., and Bryant, K. Childhood schizophrenia and allied conditions, in Schizophrenia—a Review of the Syndrome, L. Bellak, ed., New York, Logos Press, 1958.

[2] Goldfarb, W., and Dorsen, M. The Annotated Bibliography of Childhood Schizophrenia, New York, Basic Books, 1956.

[3] Ekstein, R. The project on childhood psychosis: an introduction, Reiss-Davis Clin. Bull., 2:57, 1964.

[4] Examples of this are presented in Chapters 3 and 12; also in Caruth, E., and Ekstein, R. Certain phenomenological aspects of the countertransference in the treatment of schizophrenic children, Reiss-Davis Clin. Bull., 2:80, 1964; also in the same authors' To sleep but not to dream: on the use of electrical tape recording in clinical research, Reiss-Davis Clin. Bull., 2:87, 1965.

[5] Ekstein, R., and Meyer, M. M. Distancing devices in childhood schizophrenia and allied conditions: quantitative and qualitative aspects of "distancing" in the psychotherapeutic process, Psycholog. Reports, 9:145, 1961; Ekstein, R., and Caruth, E. The concept of distance revisited, unpublished; and Caruth

E. The onion, the moebius: rational and irrational modes for the primary and secondary process, unpublished.

[6]——— The parent turning into the sibling, Amer. J. Orthopsychiat., 3:519, 1963; Cooper, B. The parallel process as it emerges in casework, Reiss-Davis Clin. Bull., 2:89, 1964; Casework with a psychotic adolescent in the pursuit of reality, unpublished.

[7]——— and Motto, R. L. The borderline child in the school situation, Professional School Psychology, M. B. and G. B. Gottsegen, eds., New York, Grune & Stratton, 1960, p. 249.

[8] Meyer, M. M., and Caruth, E. Inner and outer reality testing on the Rorschach, Reiss-Davis Clin. Bull., 2:100, 1964; same authors, Rorschach indices of ego processes, J. Projective Tech., 2:200, 1965; Meyer, M. M., and Ekstein, R. The psychotic pursuit of reality, unpublished.

PART ONE

THE DIAGNOSTIC PROCESS AND THE BEGINNING OF TREATMENT

Anyone who hopes to learn the noble game of chess from books will soon discover that only the opening and closing moves admit of an exhaustive systematic presentation and that the infinite variety of moves which develop after the opening defy any such description. This gap in instruction can only be filled by a diligent study of games fought out by masters. The rules which can be laid down for the practice of psycho-analytic treatment are subject to similar limitations.

In what follows, I shall endeavor to collect together for the use of practicing analysts some of the rules for the beginning of the treatment. Among them there are some which may seem to be petty details, as, indeed they are. Their justification is that they are simply rules of the game which acquire their importance from their relation to the general plan of the game.

SIGMUND FREUD

1

THE DIAGNOSTIC PROCESS
DURING THE EVALUATION OF AN
ADOLESCENT GIRL*

Until these gaps are filled by more clinical data from the psycho-analytical investigation of single children, it will be necessary not to confine examinations to shortcuts of any kind, helpful as they may be in furnishing additional data, but to adhere to the former, lengthy, laborious and groping methods of individual approach.

ANNA FREUD

Eugen Bleuler, in his classic *Dementia Praecox or the Group of Schizo-phrenias* [1] observed that while in most cases it was relatively simple to diagnose schizophrenia, this was not always so. Bleuler was, of course, referring to the conception of diagnosis as it usually applies in medical parlance and practice, of identifying, classifying, and labeling an illness according to onset, history, course, and observation of the clinical signs and symptoms.

Bleuler's observation reflected the universal capacity of man to recognize in other men those deviations from appropriate thinking and behavior that would make them a potential threat or a real danger to the community. Similarly, throughout the history of medicine, physicians have keenly detected and diagnosed through the sense of sight, hearing, smell, and touch many forms of physical illness that could endanger the well population.

The diagnosis of mental illness, especially in its more blatant forms, has always been the ken of layman and physician alike, although progressing centuries and times had given changing purpose and understanding to the awareness and recognition of mental illness. Recognition and

* Seymour W. Friedman is the author of this chapter.

diagnosis of mental illness, rather than serving as a sign to worship or an alarm to punitive action, now serve as a signal and plea for corrective action. Recognition of the severely disturbed person is quite frequently within the easy diagnostic acumen of the layman as well as of the physician. The thought and behavioral deviations of the severely psychotic and schizophrenic person are usually quickly recognized on sight in a social or public situation as well as in the back wards of a mental institution. Their easy recognition attests to Bleuler's original observation.

With children a diagnosis of schizophrenia may not be so readily made and generally requires the experienced sensitivity of a psychiatrically trained person. One of the unique and central problems of psychiatric diagnosis in childhood lies in the inherent nature of the state of childhood itself. Personality is still maturationally "immature" and in *status nascendi*; rapid, freely shifting psychological and related biological changes are characteristic and normal. In this stage of expected transience and fluctuations, it is not enough to recognize that deviations from the established norm are present, and then to describe and classify them into their proper category. Another facet of diagnosis is now the qualitative evaluation of these deviations, an understanding of their origin and meaning for the functioning of the personality, and an appraisal of the potential capacity of the personality for further growth, maturation, and a more successful adaptation to life.

Bleuler's systematic dynamic classification of schizophrenia, following Kraepelin's brilliant phenomenological contribution, created the scientific model for modern medical psychiatry and enhanced its status with professional medical prestige. Within traditional medical practice, psychiatric diagnosis at first concerned itself with establishing the classification of a disease for which a known treatment could be prescribed and applied. The physician's proclamation of a diagnosis confirmed the patient's personal experience of a disease, informed him of its medical nature, and prescribed a course of action to cure the illness. Dynamic psychiatry extended the concept and purpose of diagnosis to include a thorough evaluation and understanding of the multifaceted aspects of the development of the illness, and to regard it as a psychological process within the interpersonal relationship between patient and physician, as the initial phase of the total treatment process itself.

Child psychiatry arose out of modern psychiatry with its theoretical and methodological emphasis on the dynamic interrelationship of the internal forces of development and maturation with the external environmental pressures. Modern child psychiatry concerned itself with how growth-promoting and growth-retarding forces in the child's life interact and produce a variety of conflicts, and of the specific modes of resolving them. The emphasis shifted from identifying pathological entities to understanding psychological processes which must be evaluated against the total functioning of the child's ego. Assets and strengths are delineated as well as conflicts and deficits. The diagnosis must assess the specific conflicts and anxieties and evaluate the healthy capacities of the ego for adaptation in the light of the normal and/or pathological developmental tasks of the specific child in a specific setting. The diagnostic philosophy assumes that the illness itself represents a regression to earlier conflict areas. It must be understood, therefore, both as a defensive withdrawal maneuver and as a constructive adaptive attempt to rally the child's strengths in the service of restitution and recovery. The child's ego functioning must also be considered against the framework of his inter-relationships with his parents and with society, the representatives of the world of human reality.

In the mutually interacting relationship of the child and those around him each is modified and influenced by the other, so that the child and the parents exert a two-way influence. For example, certain constitutional factors in a child may lower his inherent capacity for effective utilization of positive life stimuli. This may modify and limit his resultant positive life experiences even though their potential was available in the environment. A child's chronic failure to reward the mothering efforts may generate tensions in the mother. The result may be the vicious cycle of the chronically uncomforted child and a frustrated mother trying vainly to make of herself a nurturing mother to the child. On the other hand, the mother, beset by unresolved and unconscious conflicts, could react to the child as a symbol of her own inner turmoil and unrewarding life and displace her hostility and dissatisfactions onto him. In another instance she might never realistically perceive the child as a separate individual with separate needs of his own. Deprived of needed gratifications, the child might fail to receive from the mother the psychological nutriment neces-sary for normal ego development. Thus a normal symbiosis with the potential push for individuation and maturation is never obtained, and the noxious environmental agent in the development of the atypical or psychotic ego is established.

As modern child psychiatry deepened its understanding of the dynamic and process nature of personality development and mental illness, it gradually developed a recognition of the dynamic and process nature of the diagnostic procedure itself. The early goal of psychiatric medical diagnosis, to recognize illness, identify the disease, and to prescribe treat-ment, assumed that illness was only a source of distress to the patient and was, therefore, totally unwelcome and unacceptable to him. The rational desire to eliminate pain was presumed naturally to lead the patient to accept eagerly the physician's authority as to how to rid himself of his distressing affliction. Repeated experience that the patient frequently did not accept and follow the physician's advice called attention to the limitations of the application of the techniques of medical diagnosis to psychiatric illness, evoking a scientific curiosity about this behavior of the mentally ill person. Motives that desperately impelled the individual to seek relief from his pain were in conflict with motives that drove him to struggle against the very help he sought. Resistance phenomena became recognized as a crucial central problem in the psychic life of all human beings. In the mentally ill person one of the basic dilemmas is that hate and aggression are turned against one's self. Such self-destructiveness has important implications for the concept and practice of diagnosis as well as of treatment. Dynamic psychiatry, in penetrating beyond the mere phenomenological description of disturbed and surface behavior and in seeking explanations beyond the rational and observable—in order to comprehend the seemingly irrational—began to apprehend the mysterious paradoxes and contradictions of unconscious motivation.

Mental illness has to be understood not as an intolerable foreign body from which the "afflicted" patient seeks to release himself but rather as an adaptive process of both positive and negative value to the patient's psychic economy. The hated undesirable illness is also needed and serves a function. Therefore the patient unconsciously must oppose those very efforts to cure him which, out of conscious rational desires, he seeks.

This inherent conflict came to be understood as an integral part of the illness itself. Outwardly, the patient consciously and earnestly seeks help while inwardly he must oppose it. It now became clear that one of the tasks of the diagnostic evaluation was to initiate in the patient a recognition of this paradox, or in other words, to initiate the beginning phase of a total process, the next phase of which is a rational course of treatment. Diagnosis constructs the initial framework of a working process, out of which the increased capacity for the widening of alternatives and choices for solutions and effective rational courses of action can emerge. The diagnostic process attempts to introduce the process of psychotherapy, its methods, aims, and purposes, to the child and his parents as they are initiated into the process of facing their problems together with the help of the professional person. Diagnosis and treatment, rather than being separate and different tasks, are to be understood merely as different phases of a total process.

In the diagnostic evaluation of those psychological disturbances in which the child's ego more closely approximates the normal organization dominated by mature, integrated, secondary-process functioning, the process usually develops as an orderly procedure adhering to the rules and structure of a conventional medical diagnostic evaluation. Child and parents, having achieved a higher degree of ego integration and function, can accept rules and structure and can delay action in the service of future goals, including the delay inherent in the nature of the process itself. They can, with relative objectivity, give historical information and enter into discussion for the professional purpose of evaluating their problems and of exploring alternative programs of treatment. The diagnostic process, under these circumstances, is guided and directed more by purposeful design then by chaotic emotional pressures. Maintaining their sense of separate identity, the participants can outwardly make objective use of the procedure, while inwardly they have the power successfully to resist the pressure of the process itself. Thus they retain a critical, observing relationship to this process essentially without sacrificing their own autonomy To some degree, the diagnostic process enables such patients to arrive at a rational decision which they can then execute into effective action for treatment. In other patients, however, with a comparably effective ego organization, the diagnostic process may serve more as an intellectual discussion procedure. Such patients may acknowledge the value of the diagnostic evaluation and find immediate gratification in it, without, however, permitting it to enable them to overcome their inward resistance to accepting the recommendation for treatment emerging from the diagnostic evaluation.

This situation is quite contrary to that in the case of the psychotic child whose parents also are usually so severely disturbed that no rational, orderly procedure can be adhered to in the evaluation. Lacking the capacity for delay, driven by uncontrollable panic that motivated their search for professional help, and deficient in a sense of separate identity and individuation, such child and parents are unable to tolerate the delay, structure, and purpose imposed by the diagnostic evaluation. The psychotic child and his parents, as if immediately driven into a transference psychosis, are unable to maintain separateness among themselves and from the process. They are drawn into a fusion state, with the helping person as the representative of the rescue process, and plunge headlong into the evaluation. They irresistibly reveal their undefended conflicts via their characteristic psychotic mode of relationships. These relationships are now acted out as a living experience in the diagnostic process itself. Outwardly child and parents resent and reject the rules, structure, and procedure of the evaluation, and seem immediately to seize control over its direction. Inwardly they cannot resist the driving impulse to become part of it, any more than they can extricate themselves from the symbiosis inherent in their psychotic mode of living together. This irresistible acting out of their psychotic symbiotic mode of object relationships in the immediate trans-ference psychosis serves as the vehicle for communication of the very conflicts and problems that they consciously intend to conceal. Unable to accept delay in the gratification of their urgent need for help, they struggle against the diagnostic process at the same time that they become deeply involved with its therapeutic purpose. Unable to differentiate the imme-diate diagnostic purpose of the process, they often seize upon it as a source of help and demand that it immediately become the therapeutic agent in itself. Thus, they may attempt to compel the physician to accept their need for immediate, emergency action. This results in impulsive, irra-tional, and ultimately self-defeating action, motivated by forces of the ill-ness rather than by appropriate therapeutic considerations.

In the malignant, schizophrenic, psychotic ego organization, the need for therapeutic intervention is patently manifest and the diagnosis evident. The evaluation serves the purpose of the diagnostic process chiefly in its function to mobilize the capacity of the parent and child to accept and to initiate appropriate treatment on a rational basis. In contrast, in the neurotic organization, the evaluation answers the questions whether an emotional illness is present, what is the relative degree of mobility or rigidity of its organization, and what kind of treatment would be re-quired.

The basic assumption now is that the diagnostic process is a collabora-tive process, utilizing the specialized methods and techniques of the various professional disciplines, each with its unique skill in investigating a specific area of the child's functioning. This has become the basis for the team approach to diagnosis in all child-diagnostic facilities organized around a group structure. In the private practice of child psychiatry where no such group structure prevails, the basic philosophy of this collaborative, inte-grated approach can also be utilized in the diagnostic process. Here, the psychiatrist alone fills the separate specialized functions of the various disciplines as much as his inclination and skill permit.

In the recent past I had occasion to evaluate Rena, a 17 year old girl whose severe psychotic illness gave me the opportunity to observe at close quarters a number of problems encountered in the diagnostic process with such children. My initial telephone contact with Rena's mother, Mrs. R., was a mournful announcement of their desperate need to be rescued from an unbearable dilemma, and furnished me with an ominous foreboding of the complex psychological forces standing in the way of their obtaining help. Sounding depressed and plaintive, the mother's plea for aid both described and presaged the tenor of her endeavors to escape from an ap-parently insoluble predicament. It also predicted the inevitable conflicts within the mother and between the mother and daughter and their way of involving in these conflicts the psychiatrist whom they sought out for a diagnostic consultation.

In the first telephone communication, Mrs. R. spoke of the glowing recommendation given me by the referring physician. She then sank into a mournful account of her daughter's loneliness as her only source of trouble, and of her futile attempts to stimulate her daughter's interest in friends and social activities. With increasing anger she reproached the school authorities who steadily had reduced Rena's academic load rather than enlarging her capacity for increased participation. As she ended her plaintive tirade, she pleaded with me to help her daughter and tried to exact a promise that I would end her own state of misery and restore her daughter to her former sweet self. I gave her an appointment to see her alone before I would arrange to see Rena, and stressed the importance of this appointment with her. She said that she understood and eagerly confirmed the appointment for the following day.

Mrs. R. arrived late for her appointment, appearing with Rena. I met them in the waiting-room. Almost defiantly, she informed me that Rena had a severe irritation in her mouth and would need a prescription from me for medicine. For a split second, she seemed to hang back, looking for my reaction to this contrary response to my request to see her alone. I sensed the message that flashed across her face; she could not bear to come alone, nor to bring herself to inform Rena of the purpose of this visit. I decided to accept her silent communication and turned to Rena.

It took but a moment's glance to determine that Rena was a severely psychotic adolescent girl. Her bizarre appearance was caused by her jet black hair streaming in disarray down her neck and face, the vacant depth of her eyes, and the vapid, flattened mood imprinted on her blotched, irritated face, atop a sturdy-framed body that drooped at the shoulders and seemed to slump and sag at the hips and knees. She called to mind the familiar sight of the severe, chronic hebephrenic patient in the back wards of a mental institution, for whom living had become an intolerable burden to both spirit and body. Rena hung back as if awaiting her cue. She peered intently into my eyes with almost closed, fluttering eyelids, her face falling into a lifeless, chimeric grin. In a high-pitched cackle sounding like a combination of small child and ugly witch, she rapidly intoned, "What do you prescribe?"

Rena's echo of her mother's demand for a prescription did not come as a surprise. A child so obviously severely psychotic could exist only as an extension of another ego that maintained a precarious hold upon her own psychological life. Although aware of her shadow existence, I chose to recognize the remnants of her individual identity, and responded directly to Rena: "This irritation in your mouth must trouble you a great deal. I can see how you would want me to give you a medicine right away. But I would like to talk with you about it first. We'd want to find the very best medicine to give you. Can you come with me so we can talk about it?"

Mrs. R. immediately appeared alarmed and moved forward to come with us, while Rena hung back without any apparent intention to accompany me. I tried to assure them both that the daughter would be all right with me alone. I would see to it that she would get back to Mother safely when we had finished talking together. Mrs. R., recovering from her alarm, asked that the door remain open. Rena, she informed me, was very frightened of strangers and would need to know that her mother was close by. I assured Rena that I could see her with the door open or closed, with or without her mother, and held my hand out to her and encouraged her to come along with me. Again she squinted, peered intently at my face, and then waddled into the office, leaving the door open.

In the next few minutes Rena peered into the corners of the room, behind the desk, over the couch and chairs, seeming to sniff the air as if to explore and sort out the dangers and any familiar sights and scents present in this unfamiliar place. Satisfied momentarily with her safety, Rena turned to me and again silently fixed me with her stare that registered no perceptual recognition of me as a person. I felt her searching scrutiny of my face, looking for clues as to my intentions toward her, just as she had peered and sniffed as if to identify the office surroundings. Squinting through her still almost closed, fluttering eyelids, her fleeting expressions seemed to disclose the conflict between her desperate attempt to make some contact with a representative of external reality and her opposing drive to shut her eyes to the world. At best, she could permit only the faintest images to filter through the curtain drawn against her inner world by her fluttering eyelids.

Suddenly, in her high-pitched cackling voice, there gushed forth a rapid surge of questions: "Are you a medical doctor? What is my diagnosis? Look at my mouth. What do you prescribe? Are you going to prescribe a medicine?" The words tumbled out in a torrent, stumbling over themselves in her seeming haste to rid herself of them and to deluge and capture me. Opening her mouth, she insisted that I examine the irritation. The rapidity of her questions and the onslaught of her words and demands momentarily served their purpose of fending me off. I found myself overwhelmed and groping for an elusive response. Rena had succeeded in diverting my attention and in thwarting my efforts to remain in contact and in communication with her. But she had also succeeded in heightening my inquiring interest. I told her I wished to answer all of her questions but didn't quite know which one to answer first. I confessed that I felt she was trying to find out much more than her questions seemed to ask.

She had asked so many questions so quickly that I also felt that she was running away before she could even get my answers. If she could stop for a moment and listen, I would try to understand what I thought she wanted me to know and perhaps I could give some answers, too. Rena paused and again silently fixed me with her penetrating squint. She seemed to be inviting me to talk and I told her what I thought of her questions.

I said that from the few remarks her mother had made about her before she herself had come to see me, I surmised that for some time now she must have been having some very distressing trouble and must need help at once. I could fully understand that she would need to know if I were a doctor who could help her right away as well as to be assured that I knew what her trouble was about and would be smart enough to prescribe the right medicine for the mouth irritation. I could see that this must be such a terrible situation for her that she was determined to take no chances that I would not help her, even if she had to force me to do something for her right away. I was interested in knowing the best way to help her, but to do that we would first have to understand and know more about her trouble. Could she wait long enough for us to do this together before I prescribed the medicine?

The repetitious, pressing flow of her urgent plea for help was momentarily stopped. Alternately she explored the office and returned to peer into my face with her characteristic grimace, as if she were playing with the choice of seeking to help herself or of listening to me. Repeatedly and abruptly she resorted to the same questioning. It was as if she were determined not to permit me to make my presence or influence felt and to make certain that she would receive merely those answers that she immediately required, to receive no more nor less than the magic medicine that would ease the painful irritation in her mouth. I was to be merely the extension of her self and was to give her her own prescription and her own diagnosis.

As the interview continued, the process increasingly assumed the form of a struggle. Rena persevered her demands for the magic medicine, while I attempted to extract from her the sacrificial effort to relinquish her panic-stricken tenacity to maintain absolute autonomy and control over the manner of her satisfaction. I did not yield to her stubborn demand for absolute autonomy as to how she was to be helped, nor to her infantile omnipotent command immediately to gratify her only as she wished to be gratified. Instead, I sought to explore her capacity for delay, her tolerance for frustration of her gratification, and her reserve of trust that would enable her to yield her sovereignty to the judgment and authority of the helping person. As the hour proceeded, I increasingly appreciated how desperate was her need to be helped immediately, before it was too late and her hope was completely shattered. I could realize how intolerable might be her anxiety that every second of waiting must raise the haunting fear that help would never come. I communicated to her my awareness of her anxiety and expressed my hope that she might still be able to give up her immediate need for a final prescription. I thought she should and would accept and tolerate the painful delay in order for us to explore her trouble so that we could find the best medicine for her.

My attempt to enlist the cooperation and the participation of her remaining ego resources momentarily caught her attention. She seemed engaged in dogged and conflicting efforts to hold onto my words and to struggle against the irresistible impulse to withdraw. At the same time that she was holding onto me, she was also holding me off, as if in seizing me by the hand she could also hold me off at arm's length. Abruptly she would turn away from me to search the office, responded in private whispers to auditory hallucinations and finally in one panic-driven flight retreated to the waiting-room where she sought the protective haven of her mother.

Grasping her mother's arm in alarm, Rena cackled, "Come on, come on, we're going." Mrs. R. threw me a swift look of anger and reproval, grasped Rena's hand, and quickly started for the door. I intervened quickly, speaking directly to Rena. "There's no need to run, Rena. I know how scared you are with me and I know how frightened you must feel that I might separate you from your mother. There's no special way that I plan to help you. I'm only interested in seeing how together we can find the best method to help you and in such a way that you have something to say about it, too. When we finish our talk, you'll still be with your mother and you can go home with her." Rena at first appeared not to listen. She frantically pulled at her mother's arm, demanding to leave now. Mrs. R.'s expression of alarm and urgency became relaxed. She paused in her flight with Rena and turned to me for further cues. I said to Rena, "You see, your mother knows I don't want to keep you here forever or take you away from her. Can you finish your time with me?" Rena screwed up her face and searched my face as if to discover the deceit and treachery she was prepared to find. Then she released her grasp of her mother's hand and slowly and triumphantly waddled back to the office. She sniffed again and appeared to await my next move.

For the moment, Rena seemed to have made an independent, almost defiant move vis-à-vis her mother. She had acceded to my wish that she permit herself, within the remaining functioning of her autonomous ego, to determine her choice to come with me. Mrs. R., resenting her daughter's independent move, and feeling threatened by this apparent defection to the side of another ally, now became the anxious mother faced with the loss of her daughter. As if driven by an irresistible impulse, Mrs. R. bounded into the office, looked at Rena in alarm, and then dropped onto the couch. She assumed the pose of a passive, disinterested observer but listened attentively to the proceedings. She looked at the magazine in her idle hands, and threw furtive glances at me as Rena continued to ply me with her demands to know my diagnosis and to be given the magic medicine. But, unable to contain her mounting irritation, Mrs. R. abruptly erupted into anger, "For God's sake, all Rena wants is a prescription. Why don't you give it to her?" Her own explosiveness apparently had taken her by surprise. Testily she explained that her own physician was out of town and so could not prescribe the medicine for Rena, but that he had assured her she could have the utmost confidence in me. Why did it take so long to do such a simple thing?

Rena, without displaying the slightest trace of an emotional response to her mother's reaction, now asked me if I were a medical doctor. Did I treat physical disease? Did I know about physical disease? I perceived that the tide had turned and that it was now the mother who was threatened by the separation from her daughter and who needed the quasi-delusional alibi that it was only Rena's physical complaint that needed attention. It was only a simple physical irritation to be soothed by the doctor's magic medicine without surgically interrupting the symbiotic relationship between mother and daughter. And it was now Rena who could momentarily relinquish her delusional autism and return to the quest for reality by seeking the reality of my identity. I could see the trap of mother's and daughter's determined efforts to gain an alliance, each at the expense of the other. It was imperative for me to maintain my neutrality and to ally myself only with the immediate purpose of sustaining communication both with Rena herself and with the mother's will to permit the continuance of the diagnostic evaluation. This could be achieved only by maintaining the status quo of the symbiotic relationship and doing nothing to imply its disruption.

Speaking to Rena, I said, "Your mouth irritation has been rough for both of you, Rena. It hurts you; your mother wants to get help for you right away and your own doctor is away. You have to come to me, a stranger, whom you know nothing about. Can't we find out more about it to be sure that we've found the best medicine for it?" Rena turned to me, opened her mouth wide, and pointed inside. She asked me to look at it. I said I was glad that she could let me see this irritation and I would be happy to look at it. I was interested in seeing and knowing all I could about it. There must be so much more about it that I couldn't see just by looking in her mouth. I would need to talk more about it with her and would like her to tell me as much as she could about it, too.

Mrs. R. seemed satisfied. She permitted Rena's examination to proceed and left the office for the waiting room. Rena continued her demand for me to look, to diagnose, and to prescribe the medicine. I held to the position that now that she wanted me to look at it, we were ready to see all we could and to understand as much as we could to help her to feel better. In the meantime I would also want to see her mother alone and I wanted to make an appointment with her. Rena appeared not to hear my request to terminate the interview. She perseverated her demands for me to look and to prescribe and repeatedly opened her mouth and insisted that I look at it. Repeated efforts to reassure her that I was interested in knowing and understanding the trouble she was having and of continuing with her to find a way to help her, and my appreciation of how hard it was for her to wait for the medicine brought only more frantic and determined repetitions of her demand. Her anxiety about leaving me was now as great as it had been earlier about staying, and I conveyed this understanding to her. "Now that you want me to help you, Rena, you don't want to go away without knowing what your trouble is about and without the medicine for it, but I will see you again. Perhaps you would not like me to see your mother before I see you as if that would hurt your chances to get my help, but I hope that in talking with her I'll be able to do more for you. This time with her is just to help you."

Rena seemed unimpressed but made no motion to leave. She was determined to know what I would prescribe. I said, "I don't know at this moment what it will be, but I do know that now that I am prescribing we should understand you and your trouble better in order to prescribe the best medicine for you. Not just any medicine, but one that is right for you and one that you can take. And I prescribe that we stop now and wait until we meet again to talk about it some more." For the first time a faint smile flickered across Rena's face but it quickly disappeared. "What do you prescribe?" she intoned. I answered, "I've already prescribed to you, but you don't like my prescription, Rena. I don't think you can take any prescription I would give you now. You want it but you can't take it and you can't use it. The way you ask for it, you're really telling me that you're going to decide your own treatment. You don't dare to take anything from me as long as you don't know anything about me and whether I can help you. You ask for a prescription in the same way that your mother asks for a prescription, as if you feel you have to imitate her. As soon as I would prescribe something and try to help you in my way, both you and your mother would be afraid that I would be trying to take you away from her, to separate you from each other." Rena turned away, rapidly babbling a number of words that I could barely follow. But from her word salad I could pick out "blue eyes," "white eyes," and "brown eyes." Rena peered into my eyes and then with a resigned shrug waddled into the waiting-room to rejoin her mother.

The delusional myth of physical illness, of a minor mouth irritation, compellingly adhered to by both Rena and her mother, served as the only possible means of enabling Mrs. R. to bring Rena to the diagnostic evaluation. As a denial of Rena's dreaded emotional illness, of which Mrs. R. was all too acutely aware, and as the manifestation of the mother's psychotic acting out, it shielded mother's and daughter's mutually related psychological illness from full observation. It also served as a stage upon which they could re-enact in the diagnostic process their folie à deux, the symbiosis, and the meager remnants of mutual reciprocity characterizing their object- and their interpersonal-relationship.

Within the safe distance of telephonic communication, Mrs. R. was able to assess critically the psychological and emotional nature of Rena's profound illness. As long as she could remain its detached reporter, she could acknowledge its existence and take appropriate action necessary for the wished-for change. Inevitably, however, as she found herself actually engaged in the process of actively seeking help to cure Rena, and thus inevitably started to dissolve the symbiotic relationship, she was faced with the threatening loss of her only available object, and the dissolution of her own ego integrity. This threat she could meet only in a manner parallel to that of her daughter: with psychotic regression to the delusional denial of the mental illness and retreat to the safety of a somatic illness. A minor physical irritation reduced the entire problem to a minor situation, which lessened her guilt and also gave greater assurance that there could be treatment and help for an illness which she was unconsciously convinced could not be cured. A physical phenomenon supported the mother's need and demand for some authoritative action from which she could be disengaged. But most important of all, such a physical phenomenon provided the basis for hope that here was an illness that could be treated with some minor medical prescription and that did not require the radical, catastrophic psychic surgery that the mother fearfully anticipated in the dissolution of the symbiotic relationship with her daughter. Mrs. R., in distorting the true purpose of the consultation, also revealed her fear of Rena's rage and her own inability to provide a strong protective authority figure with whom Rena's crumbling ego could maintain a borrowed integrity.

For Rena, the somatic delusion served a similar purpose of denying the emotional illness that she, too, could not cope with. With attention focused on her mouth rather than on her inner world, she could sustain her autistic remoteness and her control over the diagnostic procedure, thus maintaining the circumscribed structure with which she could cope. Demanding a prescription for the irritation in her mouth, Rena maintained and re-enforced the symbiotic relationship with her mother by echoing her mother's description of the purpose of this procedure and of the relationship with the doctor, thereby guaranteeing that the doctor could not sever her own needed attachment to the mother.

My own efforts in the diagnostic procedure were directed at accepting the delusional somatic symptom as a metaphoric expression of Rena's illness and as the body-language basis for communication between us. I attempted to introduce her to the notion that her verbalized irritation was a metaphoric expression of the deep problems of her whole life, and to assure her that no action would be taken to destroy the status quo which I recognized that she needed in order to survive. Her mother was unable to communicate the reality purpose of the diagnostic evaluation to her. The initial task of the diagnostic process was to introduce the valid purpose and limits of this procedure and to attempt to engage and to recruit the remnants of secondary-process functioning of her ego in utilizing the purpose of this procedure, i.e., of observing and evaluating an appropriate mode of action rather than of plunging into impulsive and emergency action. Rena, in her intolerable anxiety and her incapacity to wait for appropriate treatment, wanted to turn the diagnostic process into a treatment situation. The task of the psychiatrist was to establish its diagnostic limits and purpose, and to give support to Rena's ego that would enable her to utilize the evaluation both as a process separate from treatment and as an integral part of the future treatment.

In the next session, Mrs. R. came to her appointment alone, appearing resentful and doleful. Were it not for her melancholy, peevish mood, she would have given the impression of an energetic, intelligent, executive woman in her late forties, inclined to direct, to dominate, and to command. Slowly and resistively she entered the consultation office at my invitation, took the proffered chair, and looked about her disdainfully, almost haughtily. She then bitterly complained that the waiting-room was so dark, ugly, and small, she hated to sit in it. She took in the office with a slow, sweeping glance and denounced its color scheme, decor, drabness, and lifelessness. She despised and hated darkness. She could not breathe and felt that she was being smothered. Ruefully she wished I would change the oppressive and cheerless color scheme to let the sunlight and cheerfulness come in. For a few minutes she voiced her bitter complaints and then fell silent.

I said I knew how she felt. I could well understand the dark and mournful mood that enclosed her. It must be extremely difficult and depressing to live with so terrible an illness as Rena's. As a constant part of her life, it must be a most oppressive burden that must make her whole world seem dismal, dark, and joyless. It must be like a crushing weight that could indeed suffocate her.

Mrs. R. stared at me quizzically and incredulously. Her chin began to tremble and, yielding to uncontrollable convulsive weeping, she sobbed that it was terribly agonizing to see Rena turning into something she no longer could recognize. What had happened to her beautiful baby? She had lost her. She was more than dead. And as if she had not had enough sorrow and anguish, her own mother had to die, too. It was more than she could bear and she didn't see how she could live through it. On and on she lamented her agonized bewilderment over Rena's awful transformation into a dead stranger to her. And her own mother, who had been her inspiration and source of strength, had also left her. She felt abandoned and lost, and saw no way out of her distress.

After her sobbing slowly subsided, she fell into a depressed silence. Then she looked up at me and asked, "What have I done to my darling Rena? I should have seen how sick she was long ago, but I thought that she was only lonely and shy. I thought that all she needed was to be with friends. I pushed her into social life, I brought friends to our house, I made parties. Maybe I pushed her too hard. Was it the wrong thing to do? How does a mother know when she's doing right or wrong when her daughter seems lonely?" Mrs. R. went on, recalling her attempts to help Rena and her disbelief as her daughter seemed to withdraw and act more strangely despite her own efforts to help. Alternately berating and defending herself, she appeared torn with guilt and overcome by the turbulent mixed emotions she could neither identify nor recognize. As she continued her self-accusation for her cruelty to her daughter, for her negligence in not recognizing that Rena had been ill, she alternately wondered whether the girl was really sick or just lonely. Everyone who had told her that Rena was sick must be wrong. She recanted her confessions and defended her former efforts to help Rena. She really had done the right thing, the way a mother knew what to do. She had tried to tear Rena away from her loneliness and had only the best of intentions toward her.

As her depressive mood deepened, Mrs. R. recounted her experiences with the doctors to whom she had been urged to go when it had become all too evident that Rena was ill. The first time she took Rena to see Dr. B., he had wanted to keep her in the hospital. It was an awful place. The doctors were cold and hateful. Rena was so frightened that she couldn't leave her there with them. She took her home the next day. Then there had been the visit with Dr. L. She hated him on sight and wouldn't dare leave Rena with him. Dr. H. was a kind and sensitive woman. But when she had told Rena that she wanted her to be in a hospital, Rena would not return to see her. Mrs. R. protested that it was ridiculous that

Rena had to be in a hospital. She would be much too frightened there. Home was the best place for her. All she really needed were friends and a good mother's care. Besides, Rena could not live with strange adults. She needed friends her own age, young people to bring cheer and joy into her life.

As if exhausted from the confessional torment, Mrs. R. lapsed into silence and I told her that I could well understand how difficult all this must have been for her. She had been frantically trying to find ways to help Rena and to avert the sickness that she saw coming over her. Now, fearing that she had failed, it was ever so much more difficult for her to have to turn to someone else, when it had been so terribly important for her to see her own effort rewarded by Rena's becoming a happy child. No wonder she could bring her to see me only on condition that Rena had a physical illness that needed medical attention. It must be much too difficult for the mother to remain convinced that Rena was suffering with a serious emotional illness; that was why she kept struggling against accepting it and had to deny that it really existed.

Mrs. R. ruefully agreed that she didn't know what to tell Rena about her coming to see me. The girl had been so afraid of the other doctors that she was certain Rena would never have come had she known I was a psychiatrist. I added, "And it must have been as threatening for you as it was for her, so that you couldn't get yourself to tell her the real reason for coming." Mrs. R. pleaded such confusion and exhaustion, she no longer knew what to think. What could she do? Restoring Rena's health was the only task left in her life but she didn't know how. Now she was ready to do anything that I asked, to tell me anything I wanted to know.

I asked her if she felt up to telling me about Rena's life and what led up to her present illness. Mrs. R. launched into an account of Rena's life from infancy up to the present, that, in the main, seemed coherent and reliable, but was filled with nostalgic reminiscences and longing for the precious past that she was so certain both she and Rena had lost. Her account flowed in relatively undisturbed continuity, interspersed with fits of weeping, protestations of her guilt, agonizing confessions of her cruelty, insensitivity, and failure to understand her child. She had bursts of defensive anger against those who were so certain that Rena was ill and would have to be taken away from her for a chance to recover. Imperiled by the flood of her emotions, she would angrily berate the doctors who had dared to suggest that Rena be taken away from her, and would furiously scold me for wasting precious time with her when it was Rena who needed my time and help. My understanding of her guilt feelings, her painful exposure to her own disturbing conflict over Rena's illness, and to her feelings of herself as a bad and destructive mother, permitted her to continue until we had a relatively coherent account of the history of Rena's illness.

Rena was the only child of a 20-year marriage, that from its very inception seemed to have been instigated and manipulated by Mrs. R., for whom it was the second marriage, while for Mr. R. it was the first. After a series of unsatisfactory romantic relationships and an unhappy short-lived marriage to an older man whose family did not accept her, Mrs. R. met her current husband in a casual business contact. Captivated by his boyish charm and bashful shyness, she determined to win him over into marriage. With calculated maneuvers, she unrestrainedly wooed him until she succeeded.

Mr. R. did not participate in the diagnostic evaluation, ostensibly because of his absence from home on a business trip. Mrs. R. dramatized his absence as having been characteristic of his relationship with her and Rena. Bitterly she portrayed him as having been remote from the family, negligent of his daughter, a complete failure as a lover, husband, and father. Spreading out her hands in a gesture of resigned helplessness, Mrs. R. observed, "Is it any wonder that Rena should have come to this?" I empathized with her feeling of aloneness and with her sorrow at having no one with whom to share the task of creating a family relationship that could have better fulfilled the lives of its members. Mrs. R. nodded her head in a plaintive gesture of martyrdom and continued her bitter diatribe against her husband's passivity and emotional absenteeism which had left her life empty of love. It seemed to her that his life had centered almost completely around his engineering profession, deliberately avoiding all relationships with her and with Rena as he sought out his male friends in preference to them. She pictured him as having no capacity for, nor interest in, an emotional human relationship with a woman or with a child. In her determined efforts to tie him into their family life, and against his rebellious protestations, she literally forced him to participate in social activities that she arranged. Rena often witnessed the frequent quarreling and temper outbursts between the parents and would shrink in terror from them or entreat her parents to love each other.

As Mrs. R. recalled her long years of loneliness she sank deeper into a morass of despair and self-pity, and fell into a mournful account of her mother's recent death, which she experienced as a final crushing assault. I empathized with her grief, with her terrible feelings of loneliness and emptiness. Mrs. R. recovered from her despair and brightly began to relate her admiration for her mother. She glowingly recalled her image as a tower of strength upon whom she had felt dependent all her life, as a source of her own strength and determination. It soon became apparent that her relationship with her own mother had been a profound mixture of adoration, adulation, envy, and secret hatred and resentment. Proudly, as if eagerly drawing renewed life from the image of her mother's greatness, Mrs. R. related her mother's accomplishment as a highly intellectual scholar of literature and the arts; a gifted actress; a resourceful person who could meet adversity with courage and skill. But most of all she retained the image of her mother as a warm, loving mother whose death had left her feeling abandoned, and had plunged her into a state of emotional and physical collapse. In contrast, Mrs. R. recalled only bitter memories of her father who had deserted her mother and her during her early childhood.

Again Mrs. R. fell into a lugubrious silence and I empathized with her deep feelings of loss. Rena's illness was as tragic a loss to her as was her mother's death. She must feel deserted and abandoned by all who were important to her to maintain her feeling of being alive. "That's true," she asserted, "Rena is dead, too, she's no longer my beautiful, wonderful baby—I've lost her. Can I ever get her back again?" Mrs. R. shook her head as if to rid herself of her depressing despair and related how difficult it was to understand how Rena had so completely changed. Rena had been a perfect baby, an angel from the time of her birth. She had never been a problem in any way, only a source of pride and satisfaction. Mrs. R. described Rena's developmental achievements in eating habits, weaning, walking, talking, sleep patterning, personal and early social relationships as a model of ideal maturation and development. Throughout her childhood Rena had impressed adults with her age maturity, meeting every phase of her growth with ease. Mrs. R.'s friends, lamenting the misbehavior of their own children, enviously admired her child as a mother's blessing.

Despite the joyous satisfaction she accorded her, Rena could not continue to fulfill her mother's narcissistic needs. Mrs. R. found herself becoming increasingly discontented with her husband, her marriage, and her life. When Rena was about two and a half years old, Mrs. R. arranged for her mother to live with them to care for Rena, enabling her to escape from the intolerable boredom and conflict of her home life into community welfare activities. With characteristic energy and the need to wrest the utmost gratification from her relationships and her endeavors, she threw herself into her newly created duties with complete abandon. In a short time her skillful and expert executive services were eagerly sought for fund-raising for hospitals and community clinics. Rena was left in the grandmother's exclusive care, and the mother for a number of years had little contact with her.

Rena's easy adjustment in school and her subsequent performance were a source of intense pride and pleasure to Mrs. R. She glowed as she told how the teachers adored Rena and had the highest praise for her performance and talents, predicting a great artistic career for her. Nevertheless, Rena was shy, and remained on the fringe of social relationships and group activities. Mrs. R., as if suddenly made aware of this deficiency in Rena's perfection, mused that she must have overlooked this as a symptom of a deeper problem. She reflected that her long absence from Rena's intimate care could have caused Rena's illness. But, she defended herself, her own mother had cared for her with such fondness and devotion. Rena had not been rejected or deserted. Mrs. R. continued alternately to defend and attack herself. Somehow she must have been derelict in her responsibility to Rena. She had never spoken with her about sex, had never volunteered information, nor had she ever encouraged her to ask questions. She reflected that, perhaps unknown to herself, she must have felt the need to protect her daughter from knowledge of sexual matters out of fear that Rena might succumb to sexual impulses.

At this point I expressed puzzlement over the inconsistency between her image of Rena as a perfectly behaved and proper child, and the mother's implicit fear that mere information about the "forbidden things" in life might tempt Rena to act on such impulses. Could she have felt that Rena could remain perfect only as long as she remained ignorant of the so-called bad things of life and might not have been able to control her behavior had she known that these things existed? This question seemed to startle Mrs. R. She pleaded confusion about what might have been going on inside her mind. Perhaps she hadn't understood Rena as she thought she had. Rena had always seemed only a very proper, well-mannered, beautiful girl with refined, cultural, and artistic tastes and interests. An excellent student, she had also been an avid, voracious reader. She seemed to love learning, and devoured knowledge as if it were a life-giving food. She loved flowers and found pleasure in gardening. Mrs. R. continued to recount how Rena had been like her own mother in so many ways. The grandmother's cultural interests and the high value that she placed on learning and intellectual pursuits had become an ideal with which Rena had identified. And from her grandmother's strength and perfect control of her emotions, Rena had seemed to acquire her apparent control of aggression which she never outwardly displayed in any form, but which presumably emerged in disguised, symptomatic form in her shyness, timidity, and reluctance to enter into social relationships.

Rena was ten years old when her grandmother left their home, at Mrs. R.'s request. Motivated by a variety of feelings—including a growing dissatisfaction with her community activities; a stirring sense of guilt toward Rena who, she felt, would need her maternal guidance as she was entering puberty; and a vague sense of longing for her daughter who she feared would become a stranger to her, as well as a growing envy of her own mother's close relationship to Rena—Mrs. R. decided to return to a full-time role of mother and homemaker. At this time the grandmother discovered that she herself was suffering from a chronic illness, but that she could live alone and care for herself. Mrs. R., feeling guilty over the eviction of her mother and separating her from Rena, sought relief by drawing closer to Rena and freely indulging her in the gratification of her wishes.

Rena's menarche appeared when she was about twelve and a half without noticeable anxiety or problems. Entering junior high school, she timidly began to demonstrate an interest in boys and her desire to become more acceptable to friends. For the first time, her feminine interests became apparent to the parents who were more anxious and concerned than pleased over this social awareness. As if liberated from her restraints, Rena burst out in excessive pursuit of her newly longed-for social relationships. She became overly concerned about her appearance, constantly expressing anxiety over her looks; and began to monopolize the family bathroom, fussing over herself for hours. Her behavior provoked her father into fits of anger that led him to bar her from the toilet for prolonged periods and to refuse to permit her to enjoy her privacy there.

The changes that seemed to mark the onset of her illness began to occur, in the mother's retrospect, during her last year in junior high school when Rena was about fourteen. She began to withdraw from peer contacts, expressing doubt about her worth, and voicing fears that she was disliked and unwanted by girl friends. She refused to accept dates and invitations from boys, and developed a lassitude towards sports and physical activities in which she had previously excelled. She became increasingly confused and obtuse in her thinking, and found it increasingly difficult to concentrate on and to comprehend her studies. She began to fear all adults and pleaded for her mother's help in understanding them.

Upon entering high school, as if starting anew, Rena initially reconstituted herself and made energetic attempts to recapture her normality. She forced herself to enter social relationships with peers of both sexes, becoming more deeply emotionally involved with a boy than she could manage. His pursuit of her and his teasing, as well as her own sexual and hostile feelings towards him frightened her, until she felt driven to beseech her father to protect her from him. Her intense anxiety, manifested by profuse perspiration and complaints of coldness, became apparent to her mother. Mrs. R. became concerned about Rena's emotional distress but, with characteristic denial, she related her daughter's confusion to normal adolescent turmoil. Rena's anxiety state increased to near-panic proportions as she became preoccupied with the incomprehensible nature and behavior of people. They began to appear to her as strange and weird, and she was particularly distressed with their acts of cruelty and their inhumanity. Her fearfulness became overt and inescapable. She could not sleep, and withdrew more completely into herself. In spite of the obvious turn of events, Mrs. R. could not actively entertain the realization that Rena was becoming ill, and continued to regard her disturbance as normal adolescent procedure. To ward off the terrible preconscious insight into Rena's growing illness, Mrs. R. intensified her own defense of denial and rationalization, and thrust Rena more into social and physical activities.

For the next two years Rena managed to maintain a tenuous equilibrium, although at tremendous emotional cost to her heavily strained defensive energies. She managed to contain her mounting tension and anxiety but inwardly experienced a growing dread of impending disaster and dissolution of her personality organization. Her academic work steadily declined as she drove herself furiously to maintain her parity with her schoolmates. She doggedly pursued strenuous physical activities, driven by her mother's encouragement and her own compelling urgency to hold on to her rapidly waning normality and her tenuous contact with the world of reality. She tired easily and her efforts left her exhausted.

By the time she was sixteen, Rena exhibited a very marked and alarming change in her entire behavior pattern and total functioning. Most noticeable for a period of time was the bizarre shifting pattern of her eating habits, periods of fasting alternating with binges of voracious, indiscriminate devouring of any food within reach. She continued to throw herself feverishly into school activities and social relationships that were unbearable to her. Failing in her efforts, she would withdraw in defeat with harsh self-castigation and depreciation. Seeking out her friends and attempting to relate to them, she would begin to babble incoherently and retreat in terror. School officials, observing her futile struggle to maintain her school performance, and observing its demoralizing effects upon her, encouraged her to decrease her academic load. Nonetheless, her school performance continued to deteriorate.

The first dramatic change that pierced Mrs. R.'s denial of Rena's illness occurred at the end of the academic year. For the first time Mrs. R. became overtly alarmed at her daughter's behavior as Rena manifested a complete break with reality, directly implicating her mother in her delusional system. She babbled about the world coming to an end and spoke incoherently and in terrified outbursts about the invasion of the earth by horrible moon creatures intent on attacking and kidnapping her. In this delusion she hallucinated her mother as being one of these terrifying creatures with their evil design upon her life. In stark panic she would run away from her mother. Prevailing on the minute residue of reality-testing functioning in Rena's ego and the remnants of her own image as a loving, protecting figure, Mrs. R., on the common assumption that a vacation restores health, persuaded Rena to accompany her on a long holiday away from home. Although desperately clinging to her faith and trust in her mother, Rena's ambivalent delusional perception of her mother as an invading moon creature led her to behave as if she were in the clutches of death. She repeatedly attempted to escape from her, would run into the street and grasp onto strange girls, beseeching them to rescue her. In spite of the internal turmoil that rocked her very existence, Rena insisted on returning to school for the summer session. As with a dying person's gasping effort to hold onto life, she again plunged into an over-committed, heavy academic program. Finally in a state of complete collapse, she stormed out of the school in utter terror, screaming out that the world was coming to an end.

In futile desperation, Mrs. R. again prevailed upon her to take another holiday trip out of town. Again Rena repeated her terrified struggle to escape from the mother whom she hallucinated as the monstrous moon creature, and whose resemblance to her mother's real image she could now identify only in her babbling of incoherent, fragmented thoughts about "blue eyes," "white skin," "white hair," "red hair." At times she was in actual danger of being killed: she would jump from the moving car in order to escape the delusional danger of her mother's hatred. Taken home again, Rena continued to run away, and a number of times sought refuge at the home of a girl friend. Her parents could not persuade her to return home, and only after threats of police intervention did Rena, rather than face the reality danger of the police, return to her psychotic struggle with the blue-eyed invaders from the moon.

This total collapse and departure from reality—inescapably recognizable—finally forced Mrs. R. to seek professional help for Rena, although she still resisted all-out efforts to obtain treatment for her. Only under the pressure of urgent advice of numerous friends and physicians whom she consulted, and out of a sense of shame and guilt that she was not assuming responsibility for the proper care of Rena's illness—now openly exposed to public view—did Mrs. R. finally consult a psychiatrist who requested that Rena be hospitalized immediately.

Mrs. R. brought Rena to the recommended psychiatric hospital but insisted on remaining with her daughter. Suspicious and intrusive because of intolerable anxiety at being separated from Rena, she inquired into every admission and examination procedure. She demanded in a commanding, provocative manner to be informed of every move that the doctor made and refused to permit any procedure without her consent.

As she related this frantic experience, Mrs. R. imitated the physician's outburst of anger against her when he could no longer contain his heavily taxed impatience: "I can't stand you, and I'm not sick. How can your daughter possibly stand being with you when she is so sick?" The physician's anger, the hostility she felt from the hospital staff, and Rena's panic-stricken demands to leave this strange, frightening place and return home, provided Mrs. R. with the excuse to withdraw her daughter from the hospital the following day.

Clutching at a disappearing straw, attempting to stave off the catastrophic impending separation from her daughter, Mrs. R. hoped for the miracle that, having undergone the frightening experience of a threatened separation from her mother, Rena would recover. But, when on Rena's seventeenth birthday, Mrs. R.'s own mother died, the additional stress to the status quo became overwhelming to Mrs. R. She collapsed into a psychotic grief associated with deep feelings of depersonalization and depression. She experienced her mother's death as a chaotic state of abandonment, and as the loss of her own identity. It was as if she were experiencing her own psychic death, which she could still critically observe, and against which she could still bring to bear some reasoning and reality testing. She conceded that it was impossible for her to cope both with this new emotional upheaval and with Rena's psychotic threat to her own integrity. Once more she yielded to the urgent advice of friends to seek psychiatric treatment for her daughter.

On that occasion, Rena's father accompanied Rena and her mother to the consultation, serving as Rena's support to which she clung during the interview. The mother, however, repeated her previous experience with the psychiatrist. In her deep anxiety over the expected separation from Rena, she defeated the success of this search for help which she saw only as a catastrophic threat to her own integrity. She immediately experienced an enormous hatred for the psychiatrist whom she stigmatized as cold, forbidding, and frightening. She intruded herself into the examination and monopolized the psychiatrist's time by commanding the father to comfort Rena outside the office. She berated the psychiatrist for being inhuman and cold, challenged his competence, and violently disputed his urgent recommendation for immediate hospitalization. She brusquely terminated this second attempt to arrange for Rena's treatment.

Her own intolerable feelings of depersonalization and depression now intensified the compelling urge to seek help for Rena. Shortly thereafter she brought Rena to a woman psychiatrist who agreed to see Rena and her mother, initially on an outpatient basis, with the understanding that this should be solely an exploratory and tentative arrangement until a more definitive treatment could be formulated. Rena seemed to reach out to the psychiatrist and offered no resistance to making the visits alone. Mrs. R. was seen on a similar basis. When the psychiatrist felt that she had sufficient rapport with Rena, she suggested that treatment would be facilitated by her admission to a hospital, but with the continuation of their relationship. At the end of this therapeutic session, Rena tenderly kissed the therapist good-by and avowed that she would not see her again.

Rena kept her word and refused to return to the psychiatrist. Mrs. R., however, continued her therapeutic relationship with her, and at the recommendation of Rena's life-long pediatrician contacted me.

Ending her historical account of Rena's illness, Mrs. R. sat silent, seemingly exhausted by the revival of the terrible past. Her manner was subdued and expectant, and I admiringly commented on Rena's courage, and what superhuman effort Mrs. R., too, had mobilized to help her. But I remarked how terrible their suffering must have been through all this. If only they could have accepted help from someone and had shared this impossible responsibility with others, they might have spared themselves much grief and anguish. But that seemed to be the way with such an illness. On the one hand, it made the victim helpless, while on the other it destroyed all trust and hopefulness to accept the help of others.

Mrs. R. nodded in silent agreement. Then, in mournful tones, she confided that she didn't see any way out and that she was certain that Rena was dead to her, and that her own life had ended, too. "But you came expecting that there could be some way to free you from this trouble," I said. "Do you see any way to help?" she challenged. "Should Rena be in a hospital? Is that what you recommend, too?" I told her that I realized part of her dilemma was the expectation that Rena's recovery would necessitate separation from her. Her dilemma was indeed terrible because she wanted desperately to save both their lives, yet felt that their rescue would involve separation, which meant the loss of both their lives.

Mrs. R. pursued this interpretation and eagerly agreed that she could not live without Rena and that Rena could not live without her. But everyone had told her that Rena had to go to a hospital. What if this were the only way of helping her? Did everyone think she was a bad mother, that the only way to save Rena was to take her away from her? Had she really destroyed Rena's life and must she now pay with her own life to restore Rena's life? Again the threat of separation overwhelmed her and in a frightened voice, she asked, "Do you, too, think Rena should be in a hospital?" I told her that at this point I could not determine what arrangement might be necessary for Rena's treatment. I could see that the whole problem seemed insoluble to her, that perhaps the thing to do now was to see what could be done that she could go along with. If hospitalizing Rena were a necessary part of her treatment, it posed a big problem for us since this was something that she, the mother, could not accept. We would really have to understand much more of Rena's illness, how it involved her parents' life and her whole living situation before I could make a final recommendation for a treatment program. I would like to discuss this with her and her husband at greater length, and to see Rena again. Then we might create a better basis for arriving at an appropriate decision. Mrs. R. became impatient, brusquely demanding, and openly angry. She questioned whether I would have to talk with her any more. Didn't I already see that Rena was sick and needed help immediately? She could not see the point of my seeing her or her husband. It was Rena who needed the help and we were just wasting more precious time.

I agreed that the situation was urgent. Rena did need help at once. But could she wait long enough for us to determine the best form of treatment in order to give Rena a chance for recovery? Mrs. R. saw no point to judicious delay. If I thought I could help Rena, why should I not start at once? I reminded her that I had not promised that I could help Rena nor guaranteed how much could be done for her. But I did understand Mrs. R.'s urgency and her demand to waste no further time. She could not tolerate my waiting approach since that implied that I, too, had doubts that something could be done for Rena. I could also understand her terror that further discussion might convince me that she had been a terrible, destructive mother and that the only solution possible would be to separate her and Rena. Her tremendous fear of this eventuality was such that she must have absolute control of the situation, decide what treatment was necessary, and demand instant action to prevent this dreaded possibility.

The hour had come to an end and I asked Mrs. R. to return for another appointment before I would see Rena again. Mrs. R. doggedly held on, determined not to leave without a definite promise from me to plunge immediately into Rena's treatment. Further interpretation of her anxious urgency provided no relief. However, with the assurance that I would make no decisions or recommendations without our mutual agreement, Mrs. R. reluctantly accepted the time for our next appointment.

Rena's illness presents a classical, self-evident illustration of the phenomenology and psychodynamics of the prehistory, onset, and course of development of an adolescent schizophrenic. The insatiable need for self-esteem of this severely narcissistic mother throve on her daughter's perfection and accomplishments. In her dependence upon her daughter as a source for this emotional gratification, she reversed the usual mother-child roles. Thus, the girl's infantile ego was prematurely forced to assume a maternal role of psychologically nurturing the infantile mother. The father's physical and psychological absenteeism deprived Rena of a father-image needed by the ego as an object in whom she could have invested aggressive and libidinal energy. This could have diluted the cathexis on the mother and decreased the emotional conflict with her which later might have prevented the deep and irreparable split of the maternal introject into separate love-and-hate polarities.

In Rena's history there was a premature psychological loss of the mother as an immediate cathexic object. Before Rena's ego had achieved individuation from the original primary maternal ego, the grandmother replaced the real mother as the object. This substitute mother was lost, however, when Rena was on the threshold of puberty, the real mother having literally evicted the substitute mother. In this act, Mrs. R.'s unconscious ambivalence, envy, and hatred toward her own mother were simultaneously acted out against both her mother and daughter. Having relinquished her own maternal object as the recipient of her hostile feelings, Mrs. R. now displaced the hostility from her mother to her daughter. In an attempt to expiate her guilt over her hostility to Rena and over having forcibly repossessed her from the grandmother, Mrs. R. now indulged Rena with excessive gratification. For this she also exacted a greater levy of perfection for the gratification of her own narcissistic needs from Rena's goodness.

The mother's relationship with her husband unconsciously repeated her own earlier relationship with a father who had deserted her. In her vindictive rage towards her own father, she inculcated into Rena a hated ungiving father-image which further intensified the domination of the destructive matriarchal relationship.

Unable therefore adequately to channel and neutralize a vast reservoir of aggressive and libidinal energy, Rena was unable to achieve in her object relationship with either parent the optimum distance for adequate and permanent identifications. In latency years she managed to control this reservoir of poorly neutralized energy by her shyness and peripheral interpersonal relationships, thereby maintaining the necessary distance from human objects. However, the basic absence of adequate object relationships and the poorly internalized identifications with the primary objects resulted in a deficient ego functioning in the areas of internal controls, choice of defenses, and the permanent integrity of reality testing.

With her ego surviving on a minimum energy reserve that would henceforth be progressively drained, Rena's entry into puberty and adolescence led inevitably to the one course of action left to the ego. She regressed to an infantile stage of longed-for narcissistic gratification and omnipotence as a haven of safety to preserve her own meager narcissistic supplies from the mother's parasitic demands.

This course was dramatically enacted in Rena's conflicted but progressive withdrawal of her energies from reality, despite her desperate efforts to maintain her normal manner of living by her compulsive defenses and despite the tenacious attempts of her ego to maintain its cathexis on the external world. In this struggle were involved all her human relationships, school and social activities, the composite representatives of her entire world, but more especially, her fundamental relationship with her mother, without whom she could no longer carry on her psychological life. With the final loss of her primary maternal object, her internal world collapsed and with it the image of the external world, manifested in her classic delusion of world destruction. The concomitant dissolution of psychic structure, with its resultant release of deneutralized energy as the dominant supply of energy available to the ego for its task of restitution, resulted in the classical schizophrenic psychosis so patently demonstrated in Rena's manifest illness.

Mrs. R. came to her next appointment in high spirits and engaged in friendly small talk until her freely emerging thoughts led to her concern over the question of Rena's hospitalization. For the remainder of the hour she defended her conviction that Rena's cure could only be accomplished at home where she would have Mother's loving care rather than be neglected by a cold, hostile hospital staff. She attacked me for not forcibly assuming the doctor's authority and responsibility to carry out what the patient needed, even to placing Rena in a hospital if that were necessary. And alternately, she lamented that both she and Rena would die if they were to be separated from each other, and castigated herself for her excessive demands upon Rena and her outbursts of impatient hatred toward her that must have driven her into her illness.

Repeatedly she flared into open vituperative anger against me. I was wasting precious time; I must stop this nonsensical procedure of seeing her; I must immediately terminate this evaluation and start treating Rena.

The immediate therapeutic task of this session was to diminish the mother's sense of urgency that impelled her to plunge into action, whether to force me into impulsive quasi-therapeutic action or abruptly to terminate the evaluation and forestall all future therapeutic intervention. Her obsessive conflicts concerned her anger towards me both for threatening her attachment to Rena and for not assuming an authoritarian role; her alternate attacks were against the physicians who had threatened to destroy Rena and herself by separating them, and against herself for having destroyed Rena. They were interpreted as an unconscious maneuver to create a stalemate and to prevent the carrying out of any treatment program that she was certain would require Rena to be removed from home —a fearsome threat to her autonomy and control over Rena's life, and confirmation that she had been a bad mother.

Again, maintaining the structure of the diagnostic evaluation and its assurance of maintaining the status quo for the present, enabled Mrs. R. to continue the process. She accepted an appointment for Rena, despite her plea of confusion and her resigned protest as to its futility.

At the start of our next appointment, Rena accepted my invitation to enter the office with me, leaving her mother in the waiting-room. Her fluttering eyelids again almost closed, she peered intently at my face, searching me out as if to identify me, without a trace of recognition in her vacant expression. I said to Rena that she looked as if she didn't recognize me from our last visit and that she seemed to be trying to make out who I was. Her peering glance relaxed and she looked away. Again she turned to me and began to ply me with questions and demands about the irritation in her mouth. I said I remembered that she had an irritation in her mouth. I was glad she asked me about it again. Peering at me, she asked what I would prescribe for it. I said that we were not ready to prescribe anything for it yet and hoped that she could tell me more about it. In her infantile voice she repeated, "What do you prescribe?" I answered, "I prescribe that you and I talk more about your mouth, how it irritates you, what makes it hurt—all the things you can tell me so we can find the best way to help it." Rena closely surveyed my face and a number of slight expressions flitted quickly across her face and mouth. Her lips curled into an expression of disdain and impatience and she repeated, "What do you prescribe?" She opened her mouth wide and begged me to look in. I said, "I guess you want me to look for myself to see what's wrong. It must be hard for you to tell me anything about it. But that's what you expect a good doctor to do—to be able to see what's wrong and to know instantly how to cure it."

Rena listened intently, sniffed, and continued to fix her intent gaze upon my face. She seemed to invite me to continue to talk. "There must be much more that you want to tell me than that you have an irritation in your mouth, Rena. Your mother has been telling me about the terrible time you have been having and it sounds as if your whole life has been irritated and upset. It must be your whole life that needs my medicine, and this must be your way of telling me this." Rena's lips moved silently, her nose twitched, and she sniffed again. Her vacant stare continued. I went on, "I understand that you're trying to tell me, Rena, that your mouth is the most important part of you, of your body, of yourself, and of your life. Your mother has been telling me of the awful time you've been having, of your terror of being killed. It must be a terrible thing for you to feel that your life is dwindling away, as if something were eating your life away. Maybe your mouth is the only remaining part of you that keeps you in touch with the world and keeps you alive. You eat with it, you talk with it, you taste with it, but it also hurts you. I can see how you would want some medicine that would very quickly take care of your mouth before any more harm comes to it."

A slight, fleeting, almost mechanical smile flickered over her lips. I silently wondered if I had understood her regressed schizophrenic perception of herself as being represented mainly by her mouth—like an infant whose elemental mode of survival and main contact with the outside world and with the supporting mother is its mouth. I asked her if I had understood her correctly. Rena remained silent, relaxed her intent, peering glance, and then waddled about the room. It was as if she were now permitting herself to seek further contact with the surroundings as an extension of myself, or perhaps to seek a safe distance from my attempts to penetrate the autistic barrier protecting her from the prying and dangerous external world.

After a few moments she returned and reiterated her demands for a prescription for her mouth irritation. I said that I wondered if her mouth had gotten irritated by something that she had eaten. Had her mother given her some very bad food that was now causing her so much discomfort and pain? Rena stared into my eyes but did not respond. "Your mother told me how frightened you've been lately of being killed," I said. "She told me how terrified you've been of her, too, and that you've been running away from her. I think you have been telling me that Mother, like your mouth, has made you sick, has caused you so much pain, and is making it so very hard for you to live. That makes for a very difficult dilemma—to need your mother to feed you in order to live and yet to feel that how Mother feeds you makes you sick so that you can't eat and can't use your mouth. No wonder you keep repeating that you want a prescription. You must know that any medicine I prescribe now would not really help you, would not be the right medicine. And you are right, Rena, because what I do now is no prescription for this irritation, since there is no simple answer nor simple medicine for it. It's a problem that needs a lot of help to cure it."

Rena seemed to listen intently to my words, but gave no indication that she understood. She continued to fix me with her perplexed, vacant facial expressions and I had the feeling that she was trying desperately to penetrate a dense fog of confusion, a fog that so enshrouded my image that she could perceive me only dimly. She seemed locked in a paralyzing conflict between accepting and rejecting me, between listening to me and blocking out my words. She seemed to be weighing what I had to say, struggling with the urge to understand my words as a bridge for contact with reality, yet being driven inexorably by the impulse to distrust me, to deny my existence. Like a frightened child in a temper tantrum, she seemed to be holding her hands over her ears to block out the mother's attempts to reach her, stubbornly holding on to her autonomy and refusing to accept anything—except what she wanted—shutting me out with the mechanical reiteration of her question, "What do you prescribe?"

I told her that it didn't seem to matter what I would prescribe. She probably couldn't take anything that I would give her. Rena asked, "Then you won't prescribe anything?" I told her that I had been trying to tell her that I did want to prescribe and that what we were doing now was a prescription—a way of discovering what was troubling her and of our trying to understand it together. But I could see that understanding, and the kind of help people could give each other didn't seem like help to her. Two people talking to each other could not feel like help, perhaps because people no longer seemed to be real to her, and she no longer felt real and alive as a person either. The only things that must seem real and meaningful to her now were things like prescriptions and medicines—things that she could hear, see, touch, taste, and feel. Apparently unaware of the mechanical expression of her compliance, Rena's head nodded almost imperceptibly as if in confirmation of my understanding of her de-animated, dehumanized schizophrenic world. The hour had come to an end and I asked her to come again. Nodding her head, as if satisfied that she had been given a prescription, and as if there were no further use in staying, she waddled into the waiting-room and led her mother out.

Rena started the following appointment by holding onto her mother's hand as she entered the office. Mrs. R. explained that Rena wanted her to be with her today. Rena squinted and peered at me, sniffed and cackled, "Are you a medical doctor? Do you take care of physical sickness?" I said that I was interested in helping her as best I could and asked what she would like me to do for her. After a long, silent look into my eyes she turned away, squirmed, tugged at her skirt, and began to act somewhat giggly. She turned her face upward, her lips moving in a faint whisper, and she appeared to be responding to auditory hallucinations. Mrs. R., sitting on the couch, could no longer contain her silent peripheral position. Testily, she remarked that Rena had been having a vaginal discharge and had been complaining of much irritation in her vagina. She explained that Rena frequently had this trouble during and shortly after her menstrual periods.

Rena's perseverative demand for a prescription for the irritation of her mouth, the psychotic displacement upward of the representation of the forbidden genital area was the elaborate defense against the terror aroused by the delusion of genital castration with its transformation into oral aggression. The irritation in her mouth had perhaps served as a psychotic, somatic, hypochondriacal defense against her anxiety about revealing the dangerous secrets of her fantasies and wishes. It also seemed to express the transference wish of being satisfied by the male therapist—the first "move" in the process from mouth to vaginal sensations.

I turned to Rena and said that she had so many irritations plaguing her. Her mouth and her vagina irritated her and she doubtless had many more things disturbing her. It looked as if we had a lot to talk about because there seemed to be many things that needed to be relieved. Rena stayed close to her mother, continuing to squirm and hallucinate. Mechanically, as if it were a detached part of herself, her body began to gyrate in almost imperceptible, seductive movements. Mrs. R.'s annoyance began to mount and she blurted out, "It's a simple thing for you. Why don't you prescribe something for her irritation? You make such an issue of it." In disgust she quickly withdrew to the waiting-room and glowered over a magazine.

Rena remained with me. Her lips moved more jerkily and quickly as she became more and more excited in response to the hallucinated voices. The scene that had just been enacted seemed to have burst forth suddenly into her psychotic delusional system and I couldn't immediately grasp all of its implications. I tried to intrude into Rena's hallucinated autistic fortress and to recapture some contact with her. "Your mother's anger and your wanting me to know about the irritation in your vagina must have frightened you, Rena," I said, "so that you would have to run away into the world where you have so much power, and to listen to other voices than my own. You guard this world so well that you must find it the only protection you have left. You keep your enemies out— like myself, like your mother, everyone who you believe could destroy you when you're afraid." Rena continued her hallucinated conversation as if she were oblivious of me and my words, as if I did not actually exist.

I continued to try to make myself understood. "I can understand why you wanted your mother with you today when you wanted me to know about the irritation in your vagina. You would need to have your mother at your side to share such a dangerous secret with me. Your mother protects you from me and from your fear that you are not sharing your secret with her. I suppose that you must be afraid that your mother could become very jealous that she would be left out of something private between us, between you and me. You show her that she also may know what you want me to know. I can see how afraid you are of her, as if she could be very dangerous to you."

The façade of obliviousness vanished from Rena's face. For a moment an expression of terror and alarm sprang into her eyes; she had become alive, but only to experience fear. She pierced me with an angry look, and then poured out an animated, but incoherent babbling flood of delusional references to dark people, black skin, white skin, black hair, brown hair, red hair, blond hair, blue eyes, brown eyes. It was done in such rapid-fire chatter that it was impossible for me to find the continuity in her chain of broken thoughts. I was impressed by the immense terror that so completely overwhelmed her that her only refuge was a completely separate, internal world of her own in which she was omnipotent and un-challenged. But it was also a world so terrifying and dangerous, with for-bidden archaic fantasies and wishes and with unleashed uncontrollable aggression, that it, too, would only disintegrate into the broken pieces. This was portrayed in the fragmentary, dissected image of herself as mouth or vagina, brown eyes, dark skin, and dark hair, while her mother became blue eyes, light skin, and red hair. This discreteness is reminiscent of the conceptualized state of infantile ego organization when self and object are perceived as parts and pieces before they become unified into one meaningful whole.

In this scene were re-enacted the meaning of her autistic withdrawal from, and symbiotic attachment to, her mother; the secret, longed-for seductive, exhibitionistic relationship with the father; and the fear of the mother's savage retaliation by genital castration and damage to her biting, demanding mouth, and the total annihilation of herself. Her own primi-tive rage and aggression, projected onto the image of the symbiotic mother, in her anticipation of the mother's punitive cruelty, in her archaic fantasy, would inevitably destroy the mother. To protect the mother from her aggression, she must banish her to the moon world or permit her to return to her autistic world only as a dangerous invader or as an hal-lucinated voice. Likewise, the fear of her own libidinal erotic wishes toward the doctor as the image of the absent father could only be experi-enced within the safety of an hallucinated communication with him. In her delusional system Rena held complete control over those hallucinated objects which, although they had lost the capacity for tenderly loving her, could gratify her need to feel loved and wanted under masochistic condi-tions.

In an outburst of genuine, tearful anguish and fear Rena pleaded, "Do they have the right to beat me up? Tell them to stop it!" In this telescopic panorama of her psychotic illness, the full force of her terror made an empathic impact upon me. "What a terrible thing it must be for you to feel that you have no escape or protection from the danger that you feel in your mother," I said. "Yet you need her so desperately that you can't survive without her. It's a hopeless dilemma to be caught in. I can understand how you must feel that neither I nor anyone else has a solution for you. But with all of us helping together there still might be a chance to find a way out."

Rena's incoherent babbling subsided. She fell into silence and her lips worked convulsively and rapidly. Suddenly, as if she had formulated her fragmentary thoughts into a relevant communication, she asked, "If I eat rice and my skin gets dark and my nose changes, will I be kidnapped?" What first seemed more inappropriate, meaningless, psychotic rambling abruptly clarified itself as a disguised psychotic response which confirmed the correctness of my attempt to empathize with her dilemma. It contained in one stream of primary thought the confession of her hopeful optimism, her dismal hopelessness, and her fear of the only possible but secretly dreaded solution of her dilemma. Presented as a puzzle, it revealed her perceptive, though psychotic insight into her hostile symbiosis with her mother.

"Yes, Rena," I confided, "I think I understand the secret answer to your puzzle. In order for you to escape from the trap you find yourself in, you have to become free and independent, to be different from your mother, and to become yourself. You have to turn to another food, to strange and foreign people, to the rice eaters, and find in them your model for living, even changing your appearance and looking like them. But this seems like a very dangerous way of escaping from your attachment to your mother. You're afraid that if you turn to others and become like them, your mother will feel that she's lost you, and in her rage she would try to destroy you or kidnap you and not let you remain different, free, and independent. It looks like such an insoluble problem that this solution could also destroy you. You want to become independent, but you're terrified that your mother would never let you become yourself, different from your mother, a separate person."

A variety of insights rapidly ran through my thoughts as I perceived the adaptive value of Rena's illness that also threatened her very existence and denied her own potential for becoming a healthy, creative individual. Only through achieving a new reality and by creating a new world of her psychotic inventiveness could she accomplish her individuation and separation from Mother. This new identity she must preserve by remaining distant, inaccessible, and incomprehensible. Being bizarre and unrecognizable, she could maintain her successful psychotic disguise and guarantee her safety as a fugitive. Only in this disguise could she ward off the efforts of her mother to return her to the feared embrace of their symbiotic relationship. But if she remained a fugitive, alone in her autistic world, she had no one to protect her from the terrifying dangers of her own archaic fantasies of savage aggression. The only object left to her was the image of her mother, hopelessly perceived as hostile, hateful, and savagely intent upon destruction of her and her symbiotic capture, irreparably split off from any image of the protective, loving, and supportive mother. Her appraisal of her mother's unrelenting need to possess her and to derive narcissistic gratification from her was appropriate and realistic. She intuitively understood that her mother's survival depended upon the ambivalent need to restore her (Rena) to health in order to feed the mother's insatiable narcissistic self-esteem, lost to her through her daughter's autistic regression. The mother also desperately needed Rena to remain infantile and attached to her mother, lest she lose her in the normal course of maturation which would inevitably lead to the separateness that, to Mrs. R., meant the loss of her daughter and her own psychic death. It was indeed an almost insoluble dilemma for Rena to resolve. Having found a kind of solution in her psychosis, only with drastic efforts would she relinquish it for the dubious benefits of the perplexing world of her reality.

My answer to Rena's puzzle was no comfort to her. As if in headlong flight, she returned to her perseverative echolalic preoccupation with the irritation and the rash in her vagina and demanded that I look at it, diagnose it, and prescribe the medicine for it. I told her I was very interested in seeing about all of her difficulties but I thought that she could just as well tell me much more about them than I could see by looking in one place. Her vagina, like her mouth, was so completely tied up with her whole life, her problems, and her fear of her mother, that we would first have to find a way to find the prescription that, hopefully, would help all of her problems. That meant that we had no immediate prescription nor medicine, but would have to figure out the correct treatment and prescription that would work for her.

Rena's perplexed expression deepened. I told her that I knew that this was an awful lot to hear and think about. It was like a big dose of medicine that was hard to swallow, but our time had come to an end for now and we would have to stop. Rena refused to leave and insisted on a prescription. Firmly, yet warmly, I said that she wasn't ready to accept a prescription from me yet. Taking my medicine, accepting my help, was still much too dangerous for her. It would be like accepting me into her life, and this only terrified her since it meant losing her mother or turning her mother's hatred against her. We still had a number of problems to work out before I could give her a prescription that she could accept and use. I would talk to her mother again and we would see what we could work out. Rena peered into my eyes, nodded her head in almost invisible compliance, and waddled out of the office, followed by her mother.

Mrs. R. arrived on time for her next appointment, appearing depressed, harassed, and weary. She plunked herself into her chair, and smilingly confided, "Well, I suppose you found out that my Rena is a very sick girl." I agreed that I thought she was. "Then why are you seeing me today?" she flared. "Aren't you wasting time that Rena needs? Why aren't you seeing her instead of me?" I tried to soothe her. "I know that Rena's illness is very hard on you. Talking about it, thinking about it, brings it all back to you so that you have to relive it all. I can understand that you would want to be left out of it, forget that it exists, and even be left out of this evaluation." "It's been terrible," she lamented. "What have I done to her? Was everything that I had tried to do so bad for her?" I said, "Rena's illness is very ugly to you, constantly staring at you and reproaching you that you have been a bad mother. I can see why you want me to act and prescribe quickly and immediately, in order to get rid of this illness and get it out of your sight so that you won't have to feel so guilty."

"Of course I want Rena to get well," she retorted heatedly. "Is it so wrong for a mother to want her child to be happy, to grow up, to be beautiful? Look at her! She's dead, like a lump of dead clay!" Her voice rose in anguished grief and anger. "Why don't you do something quickly, before it's too late? Do you think she has to be in the hospital, too? I couldn't see how Rena could have gotten well there. She was so frightened. Then Dr. L. said we would have to put her in a hospital, but I couldn't leave Rena with him. And when Dr. H. told Rena she'd have to go to the hospital, she wouldn't go back to her."

"So I guess you're telling me that if I tried to put Rena in the hospital, it wouldn't work either. You're certain and so afraid that I, too, will tell you that she needs to be in a hospital that you come all prepared to fight me. What do you suppose there is about her going to a hospital, separating from you just for her treatment, that makes it so terrifying for you?"

Mrs. R. seemed no longer to be able to hear me and even seemed to lose contact with me: "You're going to send her away, too!"

"I didn't say that, Mrs. R.," I assured her. "At this point I don't know whether she should be in a hospital or what kind of treatment she would need. That's why I want to talk with you, to explore with you what choices we have. And for that I need your help as much as you need mine. Besides, I don't see what good it would be to tell you what has to be done if it turns out you just can't do it."

"I don't see how I can tell you what to do. I can't decide what treatment she needs." Angrily, Mrs. R. pleaded ignorance and helplessness. "You're the doctor. You have to decide what treatment is best for her. I'm her mother. I can't know what it takes a doctor to know."

"Perhaps so," I agreed, "but in order to carry out any treatment for Rena I would need your help. If you couldn't accept and do what had to be done, we would have no treatment for Rena. You can understand this, Mrs. R."

Mrs. R. pleaded confusion. She didn't understand. It seemed strange to her. The other doctors had told her that Rena needed to be in a hospital.

They were honest with her. It looked to her that I was trying to deceive her, to protect her feelings, to make her think Rena was not so sick after all, that she didn't need to be in a hospital. The other doctors must have been right. Why didn't I recommend it if it had to be done? If I said it needed to be done, she would make any sacrifice for Rena.

I agreed that this could be the right decision, but I was puzzled. Up till now a lot of people had advised her to place Rena in a hospital, but she had been unable to do so. She had even felt that it was the worst thing for Rena. I wondered why she wanted me to make this very same recommendation when she might still not be able to let Rena go into a hospital?

Mrs. R. insisted that as a doctor I had to use my medical judgment to make whatever recommendation for treatment was necessary. If I thought that Rena should be in the hospital, it was my duty to tell her that.

I confessed I was still puzzled. Three other psychiatrists had advised her that Rena needed hospitalization for treatment. Surely they were as qualified and as competent as I, yet she would accept my advice as if it carried more authority than that of the others. I wondered if there wasn't much more about this decision about a hospital that we should understand before we could take any definite action.

Mrs. R. grew angry and scornful. She wasn't so sure that I was such a qualified doctor after all or that I knew what I was doing. I didn't seem able to do what the other doctors had done. I couldn't give her straight advice and a straight answer. It looked as if I didn't know what to advise and perhaps I was too scared to tell her what had to be done. Her scorn deepened into disdain as her anger grow more intense until, on the verge of losing her control, she shouted at me, "Don't you understand? Why don't you tell me that Rena has to go to the hospital? You're afraid to tell me. I just know you're trying to protect me, and it's too late for that!"

I told her that I thought I did understand. I knew she had been trying to tell me something very disturbing to her. She felt that she had been a very bad mother, that she had been derelict in her responsibility to Rena, and yet she felt completely helpless to do anything else. The only way she could do what was right for Rena was to be made to do it and she was angry with me because I would not force her with my authority to do what she herself felt she should do yet could not do willingly on her own initiative. She wanted me to protect her and Rena from her own powerful conflicts that interfered with her carrying out what her reason and her wishes as a protective mother directed her to do. Unless I did this, she was sure that she would oppose and interfere with the treatment that Rena needed. This made her terribly guilty and terribly angry with me for not acting with authority to stop her from failing Rena and being harmful to her.

Mrs. R. remained silent and reflective. Her anger had subsided and again she seemed weary and depressed. She spoke mournfully of her feelings of loss over her mother's death. The world had almost come to an end for her, too, just as it had for Rena. It would be better for anybody but herself to take over Rena's care. She had brought only sickness into Rena's life and it would be better if she would let her go.

I agreed that this might relieve her. But I wondered whether it was in her power to do so. Perhaps she had been trying to tell me that she had problems of her own that would not permit her to act according to her reasonable judgment. Her life had been so closely intertwined with Rena that she must really feel that without her she was nothing. This conflict between having personally to see to it that Rena was taken care of and her feeling that she had been harmful to her and should give up this responsibility to someone else might prevent her from doing anything. Rena's illness might even serve some kind of valuable purpose in her own life. Mrs. R. looked at me, startled, and then laughingly questioned, "Do you mean that I want her to stay sick?" She became heated. "You don't know what you're talking about. That's the most ridiculous thing I ever heard. How is it possible for a mother to want her child to be sick? Do you think that I hate her so much, that I'm so wicked and so bad?" Her face flushed with anger and her lips twitched. When it seemed that she could again listen to me, I said that it must have sounded ridiculous and cruel to imply that perhaps she wanted Rena to be sick. I hadn't meant that. I was trying to understand what tangled feelings and wishes could have made it so difficult for her to make the very decision that she felt was the most important thing to do. I was sure that she didn't really want Rena to be sick, but it seemed to be the nature of this kind of sickness to provoke many strange notions that we might feel powerless to stop from carrying out because they belonged to a part of our life over which we had no control.

Still angry, Mrs. R. asked, "What possible use could I have for Rena's sickness? What good could it do except show me how ugly everything can be?"

I said, "That may be the strange and peculiar value of Rena's sickness. It could make obvious what you feel about all of your life: the sadness, the ugliness, the grief, and the loss that you experience in it. Your life has been so tied up with Rena that it is very hard for you to lose her. It would make you feel that you were all alone again, just as you have always felt, dissatisfied with your marriage, feeling it to be empty of love and companionship, and just as you feel abandoned and alone without your mother. And the trouble is that it looks to you that whatever you do, you lose Rena. Either you lose her on account of sickness or you lose her because of her natural growing up. So you have had a terrible time trying to arrange for treatment, yet at the same time you felt forced to interfere with it, and unknowingly prevented any positive decision from being carried out."

Mrs. R. started to protest that all this was too much for her to understand. She still seethed with anger but seemed to want to continue the discussion. She questioned what could be done if the situation were that bad? I said that I supposed that since her problem was so very much tied up with Rena's sickness and arriving at a treatment program, she would most likely need help for herself to resolve this problem. The way it looked now, both she and Rena seemed to need each other as if their lives depended upon each other, so that they could not let go of each other. Maybe that would have to be considered in arranging some kind of treatment for Rena. Mrs. R. began to protest that I was expecting too much of her to require that she take part in this decision. It was only something that I as a doctor could do. She began to cry. As her sobbing ceased I said that perhaps we weren't really ready to make any kind of definite plan yet. We would have to think more about it. Mrs. R. immediately asked whether that meant that I would have to see her again and that I would not continue to see Rena. I said that this was not necessarily the case. I suggested that one way we could explore the possibility of helping Rena would be for me to continue to see her if she could bring Rena to my office, while she herself could continue to see her own therapist. We could continue this arrangement as long as it would be of benefit to her and Rena. If at a later date we might see that it wasn't working out, we would then see what else might be done.

Mrs. R. was not quite ready to yield to the authority of the doctor. She protested that it might not work. It might be harmful to Rena to continue this way. If her own problems interfered with Rena's treatment, how could she ever be able to do more? I said that whatever recommendation we would arrive at she would need to have serious doubts about. That, too, was part of her own problem. Hopefully, she might be able to get help for this in her own therapy. Mrs. R. protested that, without the same doctor seeing Rena as well as herself, she did not see how treating her own problems could be of any help to Rena. I said that she felt that Rena was so much a part of her life that even in their treatment they would have to stick together. But it was possible that her own therapy could in some way enable her to help Rena who, in the meantime, would be seeing another doctor. Meanwhile she was free to keep in contact with me, if she felt that she might need to talk with me, and I would be in touch with her should I feel that I would need her help.

Mrs. R. made a last determined plea for her position. She expressed her distrust of this plan and her certainty that it could not work. When I said that if she thought that anything else would be better, I would be glad to consider it with her, she confessed that she didn't think that any thing could work. It all seemed hopeless. She would, therefore, try this. We discussed the schedule of appointments for Rena, agreed on a schedule of three hours a week, and we set the fee. As she reached the door, Mrs. R. stopped, turned to me, held out her hand to me, and sobbed, "Please help my Rena. You must help her. If you don't, I'll die and Rena will die." With a woebegone look, she wiped her tears and hurried out.

The diagnosis of paranoid schizophrenia could have been confidently made, without examining Rena, from the mother's historical account of her illness. And one glance at Rena's grotesque appearance, reflecting her inner state of disorganization and disharmony of ego functioning, could have amply confirmed this diagnostic impression. The combined data obtained from the history and from the personal interaction with Rena during the evaluation interviews formed a composite clinical picture of a classical case of schizophrenia in an adolescent girl.

That Rena was seriously ill emotionally and in need of treatment was known to both herself and her mother. Both had come to the doctor announcing Rena's illness and had insistently demanded treatment, essentially attempting to eliminate the preliminary process of the diagnostic evaluation, and wanting to fuse it with the treatment process which they urgently desired as an emergency measure. The manner itself in which each presented the illness—Rena's repetitious echoing of her mother's demand for a simple prescription for a minor somatic irritation; and the mother's deeply ambivalent, obsessional conflict over the anticipated recommendation for hospitalization for her daughter—could have been utilized for the diagnosis of Rena's severe psychotic illness, the mother's deep emotional disturbance, and their psychotic symbiotic relationship. Their demand for a self-prescribed treatment had become the means of resisting the development of the diagnostic process that could lead to a rational decision about treatment. The expression of their psychotic folie à deux, intruding into the diagnostic process, determined the rationale for the diagnostic process: diagnosing and dealing with the conflicts of mother and daughter which opposed their acceptance of a rational program of treatment. The imperative purpose of the diagnostic process was sufficiently to resolve elements of this conflict in order temporarily to restore to mother and daughter the ego capacity to accept and to act upon a rational choice of treatment.

The paralyzing dilemma that bound mother and daughter in this psychotic relationship destroyed all freedom of choice and of action to extricate themselves from its bonds. They could not realistically survive with each other and were each individually and separately destroyed without each other. Their life was intolerable under the status quo, but it seemed even more threatened and doomed by the change a cure would bring about.

The mother thus needed both the daughter's illness and health for her own survival. The illness served to secure the position of her daughter within her psychological orbit and to explain and justify her own disordered life and deep sense of infantile guilt toward her own parents. Rena's health and the promise of a richer, fuller life would sustain the otherwise untenable image of herself as a good and successful mother, equal or superior to her own mother.

Rena needed her illness in order to remain fixed within the mother's symbiotic orbit, since she derived her stability, protective limits, and control over her instinctual drives from the omnipotent image of her mother. Without emotional and psychological health, however, she could not achieve her own individuation and separateness from her mother. It was as if the mother, the center of this psychological solar system, had become a dying sun, drawing away the energies of its satellites in order to maintain its own focal hegemony in a decaying solar system. To Rena, the wish to achieve health as a feat of growth and maturation, was perceived as a psychotic delusion, a goal too painful to attain, and was itself a defense of the psychotic illness which, for her, was the only reality. Their psychotic symbiotic relationship was realistically intolerable to both mother and daughter, but it provided them with delusional omnipotence against the omnipresent danger and hostility from within and from without.

To preserve the status quo both partners in this relationship brought to bear their characteristic modes of defense. By her resolute, seemingly obstinate perserveration of her demand for a prescription for the irritation in her mouth, Rena echoed her mother's directive for a specific magical method of treatment. She identified herself with her wish, the symbolic representation of her mother, thereby preserving the symbiotic attachment to her mother. Thus defended against the intrusion of the alien and hostile image of the doctor, she simultaneously maintained her own autistic omnipotent control over the dangerous relationship with him. She commanded him to do her bidding, prescribed to him what he should prescribe to her, and narrowed his mode of communicating with her by directing how he should respond by means of her questions. As she constricted the area of his operation, and directed his judgment and efforts, she made him the narcissistic image of herself. She could then exert autistic control over him, in this way limiting his capability of acting on his own judgment, and reducing his effectiveness as a helping doctor to a state of impotence. He thereby ceased to exist as an object, as a threat to her autonomy, or as a destroyer of her symbiotic relationship with her mother. At the same time, she tried to create a new symbiotic relationship with him, assigning to him the function of the authoritarian person with omnipotent power as possessor of the magic medicine prescription. The net result of ascribing magical power to him was to render him impotent and valueless, thereby guaranteeing the status quo in her relationship with her mother. In other words, she assigned to the doctor the role of an omnipotent godlike figure who was also perceived as a puppet to be manipulated magically by her.

Similarly, on a more advanced but still regressive pathological level of ego functioning, the mother also desperately clung to the status quo. By active manipulation, she frantically strove to obstruct the development of any process, rejected any decision, and interfered with any action that could lead to the dreaded change in her relationship with her daughter. She announced her wish to seek the doctor's help, armed with a glowing recommendation of his competence. But in order to meet the threat inherent in his competence, she disguised the purpose of the evaluation. She tried to make it an inconsequential attempt to seek treatment for a physical illness that could not endanger her relationship with her child. She came prepared to resist entering into a relationship with the doctor about whom she had a preformed judgment as a hostile enemy who could empty her world by removing her attachment to her daughter. But in her obsessional conflict over the potential decision to hospitalize Rena, she attempted to maneuver the doctor into recommending the very procedure which she was powerless to accept, and which, to preserve her remaining emotional health, she must forcibly resist despite her daughter's compelling need for treatment. The net result was to obstruct treatment even before it was initiated. For both Rena and Mrs. R., the preservation of their remaining integrity depended upon their successful mastery of any situation and the manipulation of any person who threatened to dissolve their symbiotic relationship and to separate them.

The mother's characteristic defensive pattern of omnipotent control over, and manipulation of, the external environment and its objects had served to fix a deep and intensive anxiety regarding feelings and fantasies of inner helplessness. In her external behavior she gave the impression of an efficient, energetic executive. Inwardly, her self-image was that of a dependent child whose power sprang from the attachment to an omnipotent maternal image. This maternal image she created in her own narcissistic self-image, and from it she derived the boundless narcissistic nutriment indispensable to the quasi-integrity of her ego. Accordingly she idealized the image of her mother and molded her daughter into the image of a perfect child, brilliant, docile, and sexless. She attempted to sculpt her husband into a respected and admired, gregarious social image; and successfully persuaded many civic-minded persons to contribute money for community works that she regarded as a memorial to her altruism and philanthropy. In doing so she utilized her powerful aggressive and destructive drives acceptably and constructively. More important for her ego functioning and survival, however, was the fact that she created the image of greatness and omnipotence in others who then served to nourish and support the integrity of her own ego. It was as if she could be powerful only by creating great and powerful figures with whom she could share this power in a symbiotic relationship. She could exert power, however, only if she had created it on the throne, while she remained the force behind it, a power of which she was conscious only in terms of insurmountable helplessness.

In this sense, the mother's omnipotence lay in her capacity to manipulate others to assume responsibility and to accomplish, while her self-image remained that of a helpless child who is destroyed when abandoned by the protecting object. Hers was the quasi-omnipotence of a narcissistic individual, just as Rena's psychotic omnipotence also depended on the delusional omnipotence of the mother's image.

Mrs. R.'s manipulative strength, then, lay in her effective capacity to exploit her inner state of helplessness as a means of harnessing the commitment of others to do for her what she felt she could not do herself. But her defensive omnipotence and manipulative maneuvers proved to be a two-edged sword. As a means of enforcing and guaranteeing her symbiosis with her mother, daughter, husband, and community, they safeguarded her fount of narcissistic energy and sustained her ego integrity. In the service of her regressed, more archaic ego organization, however, they became self-destructive tools that drove a wedge between her and the object, and destroyed the power of her ego for rational functioning and action. In her manipulative control over the process of getting help for Rena, she interfered with the freedom of the doctor's action, obstructed, belittled, distrusted, and rejected his professional motives, judgment, and skills. In arousing his hostility, she reduced his professional effectiveness and drove him to countertransference attitudes which led to the loss of his helping image. Rena's treatment was thus averted, but the precious symbiosis was preserved.

The role of the doctor in regard to treatment and the demand for hospitalization as a condition for treatment bears re-evaluation in this situation. Normally in a medical relationship the expected function of the doctor is to make a diagnosis and prescribe treatment, which he or a delegated authority then carries out. In an illness in which special treatment measures are necessary, the hospital is accepted as the proper and most effective environment. This decision becomes an expected part of the treatment recommendation which the patient usually accepts. In the psychiatric diagnostic evaluation, the doctor's prescription for treatment can, in many cases, also serve the immediate purpose of obtaining treatment for the patient.

In the situation of Mrs. R. and Rena, it seemed imperative that the mother actively participate in the prescription process in order that her daughter could be treated. Otherwise, in prescribing hospitalization for Rena, the psychiatrist inadvertently mirrored Mrs. R.'s omnipotent manipulative action. In doing so he provided the threatening, dangerous stimulus of the loss of her daughter that motivated Mrs. R's. negative transference to him. This led to the inevitable process of ego regression, reviving conflicts between her disturbed and archaic past and those negative, hostile aspects of her symbiotic relationship with her own mother that created the dilemma which prevented rational action.

The doctor's decision for Rena's hospitalization threatened the mother with the loss of her daughter, and also conveyed to her his judgment that she was indeed helpless, incompetent, and destructive as a mother. Indicted and condemned as a mother, deprived of her narcissistic source of self-esteem, she was at the same time thrown back to her own hostile and competitive relationship with her own mother, and demeaned before that successful image. Mrs. R. symbiotically shared Rena's regression into illness, simultaneously experiencing her dissolving relationship with Rena as she had experienced her own conflictual relationship with her own mother. Confronted with conflict overwhelming to her own ego, Mrs. R.'s indispensable defense was to struggle against this catastrophic assault on her own ego organization, and to reject its demands upon her.

On the surface, her actions appeared as the intrusive, hostile behavior of a destructive mother who could not permit her daughter to separate from her. In actuality, the danger of separation was a psychological reality that was destructive of her own ego functioning. The mother, therefore, in apparently opposing the treatment recommendation was, in fact, attempting to save and to provide for treatment, albeit in her own image! In reality, her seemingly destructive manipulation provoked the doctor to recommend Rena's hospitalization. In permitting himself to be manipulated, he became the manipulator with the magic prescription of a hospital and the magic formula for cure. By this action he implied the resolution of a complex relationship that could in fact be modified only by the treatment of both partners rather than by the abrupt amputation of the daughter from the mother. In prescribing hospitalization for Rena, the doctor, in effect, responded to the mother's emergency with alarm, and was provoked into performing emergency surgical treatment of a gangrenous viscus on a dirty, pathogenic battlefield, when in his most measured, expert professional judgment he would have preferred to give first-aid treatment and to have postponed the radical surgery for the antiseptic, fully equipped operating room.

The doctor could perceive the mother's violent opposition to the recommendation for hospitalization as the active expression of her destructive, possessive impulses toward her daughter, confirming her indictment as a schizophrenogenic mother. That there were these destructive elements in her relationship with her daughter was an undeniable psychological reality. That the mother's negative attitude toward the daughter contributed to the creation and persistence of the daughter's illness was also an undeniable psychological fact. But permitting these facts to arouse a countertransference and to interfere with the effective execution of a helping program would place the doctor in the role of supporting the mother's destructive relationship with her daughter and of becoming an ally of the forces of illness.

Destructive elements seemed to dominate the mother's relationship with her daughter. Libidinal mothering forces were also present in her character, however, but these were bound up in her own psychological conflicts. Her efforts to express her positive strengths, therefore, were distorted and appropriate action was blocked. The mother, accordingly, had no choice but to act out her positive impulses in hostile destructive action. In order to carry on effective treatment for both Rena and her mother, it would be necessary to preserve their own ego functioning at a maximum level. This could be attained only by introducing no immediate change and by permitting both to preserve the source of their ego strength which lay in their symbiotic relationship with each other, however realistically destructive it was to both. Without this relationship, mother and daughter would lose all vestige of ego identity, illusory as it was, and would collapse into a state of apathy. The mother's quasi-psychotic intuition that both would die was psychologically correct. It could be predicted that the mother would collapse into a severe, possibly suicidal depression, while the daughter would regress into an inaccessible catatonia. The mother's manipulative effort opposing this recommendation constituted her desperate efforts to make the treatment situation possible. Her destructive manipulative maneuver provoked hostility toward her and shaped her image as too helpless and hostile to contribute to the daughter's recovery. Convinced of and provoked by this image of the mother, the doctor could be manipulated into asserting his authority to recommend Rena's removal from her mother without the mother's active participation. This would confirm the mother's helpless and destructive image of herself and would render her incapable of any other alternative but to oppose and abandon Rena's treatment. The destructive manipulation by the mother, therefore, lay in her power to manipulate the doctor into becoming the manipulator who recommends the action that would dissolve the only source of strength of the mother and daughter.

The immediate function of the diagnostic evaluation thus became the task of recognizing the emergency situation as the mother's emergency, of immediately engaging her in a process of evaluating, while coping with her own urgent conflicts. She had to be helped to mobilize her available strength to create a psychological atmosphere that would most effectively support her own treatment and Rena's. Allowing mother and daughter to remain undisturbed in their current relationship was recognition that their symbiosis provided the basic foundation and structure for the treatment situation, analogous to the structure of an old bridge whose available buttressing and pylons would be left intact as the foundations for the building of a new bridge.

The treatment recommendation most appropriate in this situation was, therefore, to introduce no immediate change in the mother-daughter relationship. The mother was to continue her psychotherapy, and the daughter would start her own therapy while continuing to live at home. Starting with this basic plan, it was expected that modifications would have to be considered as treatment progressed. But with the support of ongoing treatment, new problems could be more effectively met. It could be anticipated that the father's role and his participation in the treatment would become a consideration. The use of psychopharmacological drugs, opportunities for Rena's continuing her education, occupational therapy, even eventual hospitalization, and other unpredictable matters would, hopefully, emerge out of the therapy process itself. Because of the treatment relationship, these would be experienced with decreasing anxiety by both mother and daughter.

Mrs. R. accepted this arrangement and permitted Rena to start in therapy on the basis of three hours a week. The treatment continued in my office for a number of weeks. Mrs. R. accompanied Rena to her psychotherapy sessions, sometimes remaining removed from the therapy situation, sometimes hovering on the periphery as she sat in the waiting-room. Infrequently she yielded to the irresistible impulse to become a part of the relationship between the daughter and the therapist. Through telephone conversations Mrs. R. continued to place pressure on me to put Rena in a hospital, constantly questioning the worth of the treatment, protesting her certainty that we were not doing enough for Rena. When the situation seemed sufficiently stable, I suggested to Rena that perhaps we could think of her participation in an occupational therapy program in the hospital during the day. At the same time I assured her that we would continue as we were, that I would treat her, we would remain together and she would continue to live at home. Coincident with this particular issue it became necessary to cancel one therapy hour with Rena. At the time of the following session, Mrs. R. called to inform me that Rena had refused to come to therapy. At the next appointment the mother again phoned with the same report. Before the next appointment, she frantically called again to inform me that Rena had been sleeping long hours during the day. I recognized that we had come to a crucial point endangering the treatment situation. The only alternatives were either to accept the patient's interruption of treatment or to see Rena in home visits, rather than place the demand on her to come see me. I chose to see her in her home on the same schedule.

The first hour that I saw Rena at home made the whole situation quite clear. She was lying on top of her bed, her hands folded across her chest, her eyes closed but with her eyelids blinking, her face pointed upward in a deathlike pose. Except for her eyelids, she lay completely motionless and impassive as if she were dead. Dealing with this catatonic trance became the focus of the therapy for a number of visits. As the psychotherapy continued, Mrs. R. maintained a steady pressure upon me to remove Rena to a hospital. As her sense of urgency became greater, she acted out in a variety of ways to force me to carry out this demand. Finally in genuine panic, she insisted that I take Rena to the hospital. I told her that I would agree to any arrangement, including hospitalization, that would make it possible to continue Rena's psychotherapy. I was, therefore, quite agreeable to her taking the action of bringing Rena to the hospital. Frantically, she protested that it was impossible for her to do this, and that I as a doctor should be the one to carry this out. I told her that this was something she would have to do. From the point of view of Rena's psychotherapy it was irrelevant whether Rena remained at home or in a hospital.

Mrs. R. furiously protested that she did not understand this. She was certain that Rena could receive better treatment and more help in a hospital. She threatened that the situation was becoming increasingly dangerous for the family because of her own mounting rage. If she could not take Rena to the hospital, she did not see why I would not. I told her that it was a matter of great importance as to who took Rena to the hospital and that it was of even greater importance how she was taken to the hospital. The mother protested her bewilderment. She was certain I was being unjustly and vindictively cruel. I told her that the important point was not whether Rena was in a hospital or at home. What was most important was that she be able to convey to Rena that she, Mother, wanted her to go into the hospital and to continue her treatment: that she, Mother, could survive without Rena's presence at home, and that she,

Mother, had confidence that Rena could also survive in a setting physically apart from her. For only by taking Rena herself could she confirm and reassure her daughter that she did not hate her and would not kill her for leaving, that she was not afraid that both would die, and that her primary interest lay in genuinely accepting whatever was needed for Rena's recovery.

Mrs. R. violently rejected this interpretation and in my future visits continued to demand that I remove Rena from the home before it was too late. Her emotional outbursts, however, became less intense, and after a relatively short period of time, with the help of her own psychotherapy, she was able to make the decision to arrange for Rena's occupational therapy program in a psychiatric hospital during the day. She also arranged for the services of special nurses at home. Rena accepted this program without a struggle but under the delusional insistence that she was attending school. She participated in the program in an active and determined manner and diligently applied herself to the various art and craft activities. She was approachable but still delusional and hallucinated.

After a period of about two months in this program, without informing me of her intentions, Rena arranged with the hospital authorities to enter the hospital on an inpatient basis. The mother initially accepted the move with a sense of relief and of accomplishment, and with renewed hope for the outcome of Rena's treatment. During my first visit with Rena in the hospital, she was rational and deeply moved about having entered the hospital. She was tearful at being so different from other people, so unfortunate as to have such extreme fears about every move she made in contrast to the freedom that other people had, to live spontaneously and without worry. This flight into health was the first hopeful sign of the possibility of achieving some recovery. As if liberated from the pathogenic relationship with her mother, she could return to a more normal relationship to herself and to reality, could mobilize her inner forces to meet the new living situation as a preparation for the future treatment process. The apparent flight into recovery was shortlived. Rena's psychotic state quickly returned in full flower, as if she were again presenting her illness to the therapist but in a setting in which hopefully the treatment could be effective.

Diagnostic evaluation and treatment were fused into one process in this situation. It remained the constant task of the psychiatrist to provide stability of structure and purpose since mother and daughter had only the power to confuse and the unconscious need to destroy. However, the instability which characterized this diagnostic process is also characteristic of the treatment process with such patients and may be the external representation of the inner disorganization of the patient and of those around him. This also characterizes the prognosis, which is "guarded." Prognosis, rather than being an implicit innate element of the diagnostic label itself, must always remain an indefinite issue. It is determined by the outcome of the process between the psychotic patient and his doctor and by the effective means with which both of them can influence the patient's illness.

The diagnostic process with psychotic children and adolescents may be thought of as a kind of opening gambit. The diagnostician seeks to initiate with a family a process which will ultimately result in their being able to support the optimal treatment process for the child. Treatment can best be developed out of a thorough understanding of what has gone on in the diagnostic process. Consequently, with psychotic children who, often, can communicate only through actions rather than words, the process of the evaluation rather than the content is of unique importance.

REFERENCES

[1] Bleuler, E. Dementia Praecox oder Gruppe der Schizophrenien. Leipzig, Deuticke, 1911.

2

A TECHNICAL PROBLEM
IN THE BEGINNING PHASE OF
PSYCHOTHERAPY WITH A
BORDERLINE PSYCHOTIC BOY*

This phenomenon of transference in the playing child, as well as in the verbalizing adult, marks the point where simple measures fail—namely, when an emotion becomes so intense that it defeats playfulness, forcing an immediate discharge into the play and into the relationship with the play observer. The failure is characterized by what is to be described here as play disruption —i.e., the sudden and complete or diffused and slowly spreading inability to play.

ERIK H. ERIKSON

The initial phase of psychotherapy may throw some additional light on the generic problem of beginning treatment with the borderline psychotic child. The beginning of treatment in the case of Ted required special technical consideration because he was limited by an ego disturbance that enabled him to mobilize only specific primitive solutions of his conflict. His struggle, on different levels of consciousness, was with the problem of separation and the emergence of his conflict about divided loyalties. The vicissitudes of his ego organization and of techniques to facilitate the emergence of the conflict on a higher level of ego capacity shaped the beginning phase.

Ted was seven years old when his parents brought him to Southard School for evaluation.** An only, adopted child, his severe problems of

---

* Seymour W. Friedman is coauthor of this chapter.

** We are indebted to Harold Plotsky, M.D., Dorothy Fuller, Ph.D., and Arthur Mandelbaum for permission to use the examination anamnestic data derived from their evaluation of Ted.

behavior, bizarre mannerisms, and isolated, withdrawn appearance frightened and bewildered his parents. They described him as thin and sickly, at times ignoring them completely, at other times behaving toward them in an extremely negativistic, hostile, defiant, and controlling manner. They complained of difficulty in contacting him on the frequent occasions when he appeared markedly preoccupied with his own fantasies that dealt with themes of violent aggression, battles between space ships, warring planets, and the destruction of Earth and of his parents. He identified himself with volcanoes and lava, and considered himself "ten times badder than tornadoes, cyclones, and earthquakes." His solitary play also was observed to be violent, as he sent his toy trains and automobiles crashing into each other, repeatedly and inevitably ending the play in crashes, collisions, and complete destruction.

Unable to relate to children or adults, Ted was also unable to separate from his parents for any length of time without evidencing marked fear; and he often demanded to be fed and treated like a very young child. He made no attempt to disguise his hatred for his mother, whom he saw as a dangerous, hateful witch who had changed a man into a frightening, ugly, two-headed monster; and on numerous occasions he openly expressed his avowed wishes for her death as he would scream at her, "I'm glad you're sick, you old devil, you. I wish you were killed. I could kill you." On other occasions, he developed a variety of odd tics and mannerisms, such as repetitive compulsive grimacing of the mouth, jerking of the neck, sudden peering over his shoulder in a darting motion, and uttering strange hiccough-like noises from his throat.

Ted was unable to attend public school although he was of almost superior intelligence. His infantile speech was marked by a pronounced articulation impediment. He contacted objects by smelling them, sometimes rocked back and forth on his knees, and frequently whirled, spun about, or excitedly hopped on his toes, bizarrely waving his arms like a grotesque bird in flight. On first contact with him, the most remarkable and conspicuous feature about him was his ghostlike appearance and vacant, empty, and distant facial expression, tinged with sadness and despair. For his parents, also, his unexpressive features held no warmth and no love. They felt an enormous distance from the child, just as he felt himself to be apart, but inseparable, from them.

The social history revealed that Ted had been adopted at three months, and that during the early years of his life, his adoptive parents had undergone many enforced separations, brought about by wartime circumstances. Ted's mother experienced these separations as unjustly burdening her with the solitary care of the child, while the father seemed secretly to regard them as welcome respites from the burdens of family life.

At times it seemed apparent that Ted was used by both parents as their sole means of maintaining their precarious marriage.

The psychological test report indicated that Ted suffered from a very severe emotional maladjustment, some aspects of which suggested a schizophrenic type of adjustment. Prominently seen in his test performance were his tendency to withdraw from reality that was "too complicated"; some fluidity in his thinking; intense, intrusive fantasying of psychotic content; fluctuations in levels of functioning; and an unusual degree of tension and anxiety. Organic impairment was suggested by some peculiarities of motor coordination and perception, difficulty in visual-motor coordination, and indistinctness in his speech.

The examining psychiatrist observed that Ted was extremely suspicious upon entering into new situations, exploring all areas in the room, asking about the content of the cabinet and the closets, noting which toys were present, and asking for others. He asked many questions, but almost invariably he could supply his own correct answers. It was as though with his questions he were attempting to verify his own possible erroneous ideas about reality. Despite his apparent attempts to enter into an interpersonal relationship with the psychiatrist, there was always a quality of separateness about him. He preferred to have no intrusion into his thoughts or actions. Any attempt at exploration into his thoughts or fantasies was met by silence or the admonition not to ask "that kind of question" or "those silly questions." When he voiced his questions, it was as though he were sending them out into the world in general rather than to a specific person.

The physical and complete laboratory examinations, including X ray of the skull and electroencephalogram, were normal. The consulting neurologist was of the impression that the neurological findings indicated a diagnosis of congenital defect of the brain and skull, but he recommended no specific neurologic therapy. It was also his impression that whatever disease process might be present was not progressive.

A review of the evaluative data [1] from the point of view of certain concepts of the ego psychology of borderline psychotic children (see Chapter 4) revealed an extreme personality damage. Ted's capacity for interpersonal relationships was severely defective; his self-concept was shadowy and disintegrated. He perceived the world of human beings as empty, inhuman, and more like distorted skeletons devoid of flesh and life. His ability to express direct, appropriate affects was extremely impaired or lacking. His test picture revealed many characteristics of borderline children: the use of extreme "distancing devices," affective impoverishment, fragile, brittle ego controls, regressive phenomena, the emergence of primary-process material, and the feeling of despair about the insolubility of his problems.[2]

During the early interviews of the initial phase of treatment, the patient gave the impression that he was unable to make contact with the therapist; and the therapist, at this point, toyed with the feeling that he himself was the one who was unable to make contact with the patient. The child's situation could be characterized as one in which he did actually "communicate" to the therapist through his behavior and the distance he maintained from the therapist. In this sense, the apparent lack of capacity or wish to communicate was the very communication the child wished to express about himself. The therapist was experienced by Ted as an intruder and was tolerated only if the patient could use him as an extension of himself, as a tool rather than as a partner in a therapeutic venture, and as a quasi-mechanical guidepost for his explorations of a world which was spatial and geographical, rather than populated by human beings. At this point, Ted's mode of relationship was primarily an autistic one. An abbreviated account from the treatment process of the child's first session with the therapist will illustrate the initial situation:

I asked Ted if he did not want to come with me to the playroom. He said he wanted to go outside. . . . He led the way to the house in the back. I mentioned that he had been here before, but perhaps he wanted to get better acquainted with it. Ignoring me, he silently went ahead. There was a ghostly, trancelike quality about him as he silently pursued his search. He walked around the house as I followed him until he found a door which he could not open. . . . He mumbled something to the effect that he wanted to look around, went back to the house, and indicated that he wanted to climb up the fire escape. I noticed that he was carrying a map of Topeka with me. . . . He wanted to climb up first and I told him I would be right behind him. After testing the doors and trying to get into the house through the back door, he went downstairs again. He dropped his map on the ground and I said I wondered if he knew his way around Topeka without the map. He then led the way to the playroom, turning and whirling in a rapid fashion a number of times. When he spoke a few words, it would be with a singsong quality. When we got into the playroom, he again explored and attempted to look at everything. I commented that I guessed he wanted to find out what was going on here, but he responded with an apparent ignoring of my remark and by continuing his silent exploration. He noticed the blocks and said that somebody had started to build a modern house. After trying some of the play material, he went to the blocks and said he was going to build a house. I asked him if he would like me to help him. He said he wanted to build it alone. As he started building the house, he made a remark about the blocks being confused. I said that it would be hard for him to build when the *blocks were confused and mixed up. Maybe we could get them unmixed so he could build a very nice house. He stopped building his house and went to the telephone. He started to play with the phone and then dropped it.*

One may gain the impression from this material that although it is not Ted's primary intention to communicate with the therapist, he actually conveys his very difficult dilemma in his actions. Not only does he attempt to orient himself in his world by means of a map of Topeka which he cannot read, but he also carries out an apparently aimless search for the whereabouts of every entrance and exit, in order to make possible his escape from a situation which must terrify him in spite of the bland picture he gives of himself. He clutches a useless instrument in his hand and despotically orders the therapist to follow behind him, using him as if he were an impersonal guide or a compass to pilot him through his world. In the way he uses the therapist, he conveys his deepest fears about the unfamiliar and threatening therapeutic situation, and his gravest doubts about the trustworthiness of the therapist as a helping person. He tells us, by means of his map and his search, of the desperate plight of a wandering waif trying to find his way with only the most ineffective tools at his disposal. He reminds us of a small child who imitates the adult and pretends he can read, even though we notice that he holds his book upside down.

Another relevant observation for the understanding of the beginning moves of this child refers to his apparent rejection of, or flight from, any attempt on the part of the therapist to contact him and to let him know that he is aware of his dilemma. As soon as the therapist, used as the impersonal, lifeless extension of the patient, wants to come to life and offer real help, the patient intensifies his insistence upon a tenuous gadget relationship rather than following through with a genuine interpersonal exchange. One has the impression that the child really speaks to himself as he wanders through the maze of this new situation, and even as he begins to play. Remarks directed to the psychotherapist are directed to the extension of himself. If the therapist attempts to respond to these remarks on a level of difference between himself and the child, the patient must escape to the next activity or appear not to hear the remark. To this phenomenon we wish to refer as the autistic position of the child in which the psychotherapist is tolerated only as the child's tool, rather than as his partner.

So far, we have stressed the imitative, cue-taking, and autistic position of this child. The material, however, also lends itself to a variety of additional inferences, and one might be tempted to say that there is much that he communicates in this situation. His reference to the "confused blocks," for example, is a clear communication about his state of mind. His apparently aimless wandering and searching could possibly convey to the therapist that he seeks that which he feels he lacks—order, stability, and the love object—as well as his need to keep open avenues of retreat, should the danger of the new situation become too menacing and threatening. To understand the cue-taking, autistically oriented child, however, does not mean that he communicates directly with us. But despite the child's attempts not to communicate, the therapist must constantly attempt to see meaning in his material and to facilitate the establishment of a therapeutic climate in which the patient's potentiality for a future object relationship can be realized.

It is at this point that the technical problem becomes apparent to the psychotherapist. After his attempts to interpret the material indirectly or metaphorically have been rebuked, he speculates about the technical leverage that he can create for himself in order to reach the child. Thus far, he has attempted to induce the child to follow him into the playroom or to follow his interpretive comments. But rather than finding that the child follows him into his world, he discovers himself in a situation in which he literally must follow the child around, and is included in the child's world only in a mechanical sense. One could expect that he might feel frustrated at this point, not unlike the parents who told us that they could not reach the boy and could not genuinely contact him.

During the first period of psychotherapy, the therapist must find meaning in the behavior of the child who takes recourse primarily to preverbal, action forms of "communication." Ted does not play at this particular stage of psychotherapy, but goes through a phase of fragmented action which reminds one of the seemingly aimless moves of preverbal, crawling children who have not yet learned to play. The therapist's words are not taken as interpersonal communications, and he seems to make contact best if he, too, relies on a language of action. As the therapist accepts the patient on his level of communication and neither threatens him nor closes the exits which he has established for himself, Ted moves into a new type of relationship which one may characterize as quasi-symbiotic. While he seemingly acts independent and forces the therapist into a dependent, imitative situation, he really reverses the symbiotic situation in which his own strength is derived from his fusion with the omnipotence of the therapist. Another process specimen which occurred during approximately the fourth week of treatment illustrates this second stage of the initial phase:

Ted went to the toy box and took out a long wooden block, calling it "the engine." He wanted me to hand him the blocks so he could build a long train. Switching small trains on to each other, he built the train longer and longer until it extended from the playroom into the hallway. He then wanted the train to be brought back into the playroom. . . . He ordered me to switch part of the train in another part of the playroom. He called it my switchyard and designated an area for himself that he called his switchyard. He ordered me to switch my train in my yard, just as he switched his trains in his yard. I said I guessed he preferred that I use a separate switchyard. I could do this, but I thought that Engineer Ted might want the switchman to help him build up his switchyard and his trains. Tartly he ordered me to use the other switchyard and just to switch my trains. He sniffed at his knee. I went back to my yard and Ted said he would build a new line this time, and he started to build a track in the direction of my switchyard.

While he now can accept the structure of the playroom for a larger part of the hour, Ted cannot really tolerate the individuality of the psychotherapist. The situation in which he orders the psychotherapist to do exactly the same things with his train that he does on his own track reminds one of the shadow in Sir James M. Barrie's delightful story of Peter Pan. As long as the shadow is attached to the feet of Peter Pan and as long as he can control it with omnipotent power, he feels safe; but he dreads letting the shadow go to assume an independent nature of its own, as if Peter Pan, in turn, would become the shadow of his former shadow. The same holds true of Ted's manipulative maneuvers. On the one hand, he tolerates difference in the psychotherapist as long as he can use him as his shadow, as his double. But whenever the therapist attempts to express his difference and risks an interpretive comment, the boy literally puts him back on his track and permits him only to act the role of the dependent shadow, to reflect in a mirror-like fashion what the child is doing. Instead of a mechanical guide who follows the child in his seemingly aimless search, the therapist has become the child's mechanical reflection. The progressive move in the therapeutic situation, however, can be seen in the fact that the child now attempts to express a definite and more recognizable theme. He wants to master his train and he wants to control its destination as well as the partner-therapist.

In this primarily symbiotic situation, the therapist has to take his cues from the patient, a method which reminds one of the way a tyrannical, small child might control the mother who must never be out of his sight and is used as an extension of the child. One may well conjecture that Ted was occupied with the constant anxiety that the parent might desert him, and one suddenly gains more insight into the early attempts of the child to become acquainted with all exits by means of his map, which may lead him back to the parent, and thus to check the danger of becoming separated from his love objects. By means of this symbiotic domination, he makes certain that the other person cannot act independently and cannot desert him. In these psychotherapeutic sessions, he tests the psychotherapist in very much the same way that we assume he tried to test the trustworthiness of the mother. He can tolerate difference in the therapist only when he can begin to sense that the latter may be reliable, a trustworthy double, and a safe tool for his purposes.

His first attempts to permit himself and the psychotherapist a sense of difference are of an extremely cautious nature. After making a variety of impossible requests, the child provides himself with a magic wand with which he conjures up a number of things available in the playroom. He organizes a new game, remindful of the play of the eighteen-month-old child Freud described in *Beyond the Pleasure Principle* who symbolically has the mother come and go, then later disappears and reappears himself. The therapist is told to search for a hidden toy car. This problem of coming and going, disappearing and reappearing, is expressed symbolically through distance devices and is disguised through a reversal of the true situation. For it is not the parent or the therapist who searches for the lost child. Rather, it is the child who, desperately afraid of being deserted, searches for the mother. This problem is expressed more directly as it is re-enacted in a game with a ball which Ted arranges. He continues to throw the ball to the therapist in such a way that the therapist finally can neither catch the ball nor find it. The following process specimen illustrates this period of the therapy:

> Ted came out from under the table pushing a ball into the room. I said his magic wand was working very well now. It must make him happy. He hit the ball so that it rolled outside the room into the hallway. He wished for the ball to come back. I rolled it back into the room. Again he rolled the ball out, wished for it to come back, and I retrieved it again. As I came back, I said the magician was a little slow in giving him his wish, but he did make the ball come back to him. Ted became excited and gleeful, and as he rolled the ball out, he told me to roll the ball back to him. We played this game for a few minutes and then he started to roll the ball in all directions away from me. As long as he could keep the ball away from me, he seemed gleeful and excited. He sat on the floor with his legs spread apart to receive the ball, clapping his hands in a gleeful manner, chanting "da-da-da" very much in the manner of a year-and-a half-old enjoying the game. I said Ted wanted the ball to stay with him so very much and needed to be sure that the magician would go anywhere to bring the ball back to him. I guessed he wasn't sure that the magician's

powerful magic could bring the ball back to him. Ted then dropped the ball downstairs. He wanted me to retrieve it. I said how much he must want to have the ball close to him, but was afraid it might get away from him, that over and over again he had to see that no matter what he did, it would not get away and he wouldn't lose it. He then said he wanted to play hide-and-go-seek with the ball.

This material permits us to observe Ted's omnipresent fear that his love objects may disappear and desert him. It discloses his wish both to control their coming and going and to master his own impotence. As a magic extension of the patient, the therapist is entrusted with a meaningful communication about the patient's fear that his "badness" may make it impossible even for the magician-therapist to retrieve the lost object. Expressed on the play level of a small child, this communication also serves as a cue to the therapist to accept the role that the child assigns to him, and to respond on his level as a small child and within the distance of symbolic language. It informs the therapist that although he may feel free to convey his understanding of the meaning of the boy's anxiety within the metaphor of the play, the patient is not, as yet, ready to accept the same interpretation expressed in the adult language of the secondary process. The therapist is seen as the omnipotent figure and is actually stronger than the patient. The child's controlling use of the therapist as his extension can, therefore, be considered as the acting out of a defensive fantasy erected against his own fear of engulfment by the therapist.

As the process continues, the boy slowly introduces a new theme. He boasts that his toy trains are better than those in the playroom and organizes the play into a battle between his home trains and Southard School trains. Crashes occur and the play pattern reveals that he suspects a battle between his mother, on the one hand, and the therapist, on the other hand, with sole possession of himself as the prize of war. He seems to describe his perception of the psychotherapist as one who tempts him to exchange Southard School for his home, and he discloses his fear that should he permit himself to be tempted into a relationship with the therapist, he would be in danger of losing his own home. This emergence of his conflicts regarding his budding interpersonal relationships and his growing allegiances can well be documented by another process specimen.

Ted entered the playroom, went to the sandbox and started to rummage in the sand. He started to build in the sand and soon two mountains emerged. Off to the side he built a third, and smaller, mound of sand and said this was another mountain. He took a car and ran it along a road connecting the three mountains and a cave. He stopped running the car, rocked back and forth on his knees, and then danced excitedly on his toes.

He started to pile some sand against the side of the road and I said that the drive between the three mountains and the cave looked pretty dangerous. It was a pretty narrow road and had steep sides. The wall could make it a lot safer for the car. Ted took the car off the main road and drove it through the sand over to the other side of the box. He said it was rough country. Soon he built up another mound of sand, somewhere quite distant from the other mountains, and said this was another mountain. I said this mountain suddenly had appeared from out of this very rough country. It was pretty far away from the others. He drove the car between the fourth mountain and the others and said there was a road leading to it. I said this roadway connected all these mountains and separated them, too. I noticed the steep, sloping angle of the roadway and I said that this road didn't look as safe as the other one. I could see how a car could tip over if you tried to drive it. He again drove his car along the road and pushed the car so that it turned over. He found a dangerous place in the road and built a wall there. I said this road was getting safer all the time. Suddenly he smashed in the cave near the three mountains and excitedly danced on his toes as he exclaimed that a mean old man was attacking the cave.

The map that Ted had brought with him to his first therapy session now helps us to identify the meaning of the landscape that emerges in this new material. Appearing at first as a lost traveler, equipped only with a map he could not read, Ted suddenly seems to demonstrate that he can permit the geography of his interpersonal relationships to emerge out of the unformed sand. The mother and father mountains, the child mountain, and in the distant corner, the new, and at first threatening, psychotherapy mountain, appear. He admits into his awareness those introjects which he earlier experienced in an amorphous, shadowy, and unstable fashion. This hour indicates not only the pull toward the therapist, but also constitutes the expression of his main concern, what therapy might do to his situation within the family group.

After approximately five months of twice-weekly psychotherapy, Ted took one more significant step in his attempt to communicate his conflict between psychotherapy and his position within the family, between the therapist and his parents. As he permitted the therapist to accompany him on his fantasy space-travels, he suddenly demanded that the therapist give him a real rocket ship and pleaded with the therapist to take him home with him. But no sooner did he confess his dislike for his parents and express his wish to be reared by the therapist than he embarked on a frenzied campaign of repetitive wishes to bomb and destroy Southard School and everyone in it. He could not tolerate formal sessions within the playroom and again proceeded to wander about and to search for avenues of escape from the therapeutic situation.

During one such session, Ted had a particular need to cling to his mother during her session with her social worker. Verbally, he told the therapist that he did not want to have anything to do with him. The therapist followed the child's cue and interpreted his fear of desertion and abandonment by his parents should he continue to see the therapist and begin to find him a helpful friend. The therapist's assurance that his only intention was to try to help Ted and his parents live more happily together now had a reassuring and relieving effect upon the child. His mother reported in the subsequent hour that Ted had become "unusually cooperative and good" at home, although "he had been very troublesome for some time." Ted's readiness for such an interpretation at the point where his conflicting wish for mother and therapist had moved into complete consciousness, and on a level of ego organization that was receptive to a more conventional interpretation, permitted the beginning phase to move along more conventional lines of child therapy and on a more advanced, more genuine interpersonal level.

The fear that his parents did not love him and wanted to give him away because of his "badness" dominated the first few months of psychotherapy, and was expressed on different levels of awareness. One might very well trace back the theme of desertion and of divided loyalties, and find that even in the quasi-autistic and quasi-symbiotic stages the child actually always expressed the very same concern. We also realize that his archaic and regressed modes of communication of this particular theme constituted his defense against the conflict. By avoiding a new relationship with the psychotherapist as long as possible, he fought off the awareness of his double loyalty, of being torn between father and mother, between the parents and the therapist, and he restored the minimum security inherent in symbiotic and autistic-like arrangements. The different levels of communication were not only an indication of the brittle state of defenses that he employed and of the chaotic state of his ego organization, but also conveyed his very need to keep himself off the "transference track." Thus his relationship modes conveyed the content and meaning of the conflict as well as the form of his primitive attempts to resolve this struggle of the beginning phase.

One could conceive of therapeutic sessions with less disturbed children in which this process may be brief and swift-moving, rather than occupying an extended span of time, as it did with Ted. Erikson [3, 4] has described beginning situations in which children went through similar experiences within a few seconds or minutes. Such manifestations of ego disruption in play and during a treatment process are not unusual in children, and very frequently take place at the end-point of a play communication where a fantasied danger situation suddenly terminates the play.

In Ted's situation, however, the beginning stage of psychotherapy can be likened to a pattern dynamically not unlike the one Erikson describes, but in which the interruption occurs before the play even begins. We could describe this pattern as one of "play interruption without play," whose purpose is to communicate his fear of separation from his parents as he simultaneously hazards the wish to bring this about. This communication is expressed on various levels of ego organization and consciousness and within various relationship modes. The technical problem for the therapist is to accept, to understand, and to respond to the child on whatever level will permit him to reach the patient without pushing him into modes of relationship for which he is not yet prepared. In this sense, the technical problem of the therapy process can be thought of as dealing with the need to help the child to see the meaning of his play interruption. And we may consider his play interruption as acting-out behavior appropriate for a child whose ego organization is on a preverbal and preplay level of development. The therapist's objective is to help the child obtain the strength to enter into a genuine interpersonal relationship with him which eventually will enable the child to express that which is hidden behind the pattern of interruption, and so facilitate the child's therapy journey that he may have the opportunity to develop more mature identifications, reliable object relationships, and a stable identity of his own.

REFERENCES

[1] Sargent, Helen. Personal communication.

[2] A review of the current literature of child schizophrenia and other psychotic conditions of childhood (Friedman, Seymour W. Diagnostic Criteria in childhood schizophrenia, Bull. Menninger Clin., 18:41, 1954; Hendrickson, Willard J. Etiology in childhood schizophrenia, Nerv. Child, 10:9, 1952). suggests that diagnostic criteria are linked with the theoretical frame of reference of a particular author, and are intimately associated with an implied therapeutic philosophy. The descriptive evaluative data regarding our patient would lend itself to a variety of diagnostic labels commonly used in our present-day attempts to classify these childhood illnesses. At first glance, these labels offer a prescribed method of therapy, but on closer scrutiny, they would appear to be not too helpful in the formulation of a therapeutic strategy. Ted's illness could, in parts, conceivably belong to all the various categories suggested by Kanner, Bender, Mahler, and Rank and their associates. Dependence on the diagnostic label for clues derived from these therapeutic philosophies would lead to confusion in the therapeutic work with the child, as well as to lowered therapeutic effectiveness. The diagnostic label as a therapeutic cue is usually not much more than a danger signal and warns the therapist that his entry into the psychological world of his patient will not be an easy task.

[3] Erikson, Erik H. Studies in the interpretation of play, I. Clinical observations of play disruption in young children, Genet. Psychol. Monogr., 22:557, 1940.

[4] ——— Childhood and Society, New York, Norton, 1950.

3

THE OPENING GAMBIT
IN PSYCHOTHERAPEUTIC WORK
WITH A SEVERELY DISTURBED
ADOLESCENT GIRL*

As the chess problem, given on the next page, has puzzled some of my readers, it may be well to explain that it is correctly worked out, so far as the moves are concerned. The alternation is perhaps not so strictly observed as it might be, and the "castling" of the three Queens is merely a way of saying that they entered the palace: but the "check" of the White King at move 6, the capture of the Red King at move 7, and the final "checkmate" of the Red King, will be found by anyone who will take the trouble to set the pieces and play the moves as directed, to be strictly in accordance with the laws of the game.

LEWIS CARROLL

The complexity of the technical problems in therapy may have suggested Freud's comparison of the psychoanalytic process with "the fine art of the game of chess" in which he suggested that "only the opening and closing

* The present study was stimulated by earlier clinical research which hypothesized that in the psychotic and borderline patient this process of establishing psychological distance fluctuates markedly and without apparent predictability. The use of "distance" serves the function of defense as well as permitting the patient to make some approach to the therapist characterized by specific processes of ego regression and restitution.

For the current investigation the patient was chosen on the basis of a detailed diagnostic study which included social history, psychodiagnostic testing, and psychiatric evaluation. Records are being kept of the casework with significant relatives and of the patient's experience in a school for emotionally disturbed children. The electrically recorded sessions and the therapist's notes on these sessions are being employed by a group of clinicians to study her use of psychological distance to establish and maintain a working neurotic façade moves of the game admit of exhaustive systematic description." Even his cautious comment on our technical knowledge requires further restriction when we deal with the severely disturbed adolescent. My choice concerning the opening gambit in psychotherapeutic work with such a patient imposed limitations on me which make it impossible to arrive at a definite set of rules.

Prevalent notions, such as gaining the confidence of the adolescent; letting him know that we are not the extension of the parent; making ourselves useful to him; identifying with his problem; being prepared for the contingency that he can accept us only with limited commitments; his constant need for innovations as far as structure is concerned—all these turn into vague generalizations. To make them specifically useful requires inventiveness; a special kind of spontaneity; a readiness for labile commitments, for constant disappointment, and for uncertainty as far as structure of the psychotherapeutic situation and the goals of psychotherapy are concerned. Accordingly, I limit my description to the opening moves in one specific case.

Teresa Esperanza's treatment started in the fall of 1960 when she was approximately fifteen and a half years old. A bilingual Spanish-Mexican Catholic, she was diagnosed as suffering from a "schizophrenic reaction, childhood type, with hysterical personality features." The unstable and rather violent marriage of her parents ended in disaster and divorce. The father disappeared when the child was five and a half. The mother, too, proved an unstable source, disappearing from time to time because of schizophrenic illness; she is presently in a State hospital. The child was being taken care of by the mother's sister, but spent part of her early childhood with another aunt and her grandmother, who died of cancer a few years ago.

---

of an hysterical nature, characterized by an anaclitic object relationship, as long as she remains on the level of a latency child. When she attempts to function near her own age, she is overwhelmed by hallucinatory and delusional material. Regression to the lower age level permits normal distance in object relationships while attempts at higher functioning are followed by a shift in distance and loss of contact.

The clinicians will attempt to devise a scale to reflect the patient's psychological movement. Zero will be defined as the point at which the individual achieves optimum distance for her functioning; "plus" will represent an increase in distance, and "minus" a decrease. The purpose of devising this quantitative measure for psychological distance is to have an objective tool with which to follow the fluctuations of the patient. This procedure would permit a more reliable investigation of the factors within the psychotherapeutic process which precipitate the movement of the patient. The study will include not only the patient's conscious and unconscious distance devices but those which are reflected in the therapist's technical interventions.[1]

At the time of application the patient was living with the aunt, who then was also caring for the patient's mother, a violent schizophrenic locked up in her room until the aunt, as an outgrowth of the intake process at the clinic, became convinced that her sister must again be hospitalized. The aunt and the patient lived together with the aunt's brother. Teresa's life contains the story of strong rejections but also of devoted attempts on the part of relatives, particularly this aunt, who, at times, overwhelmed her with gifts and care. Before Teresa came to our attention, attempts had been made to help her through a variety of private schools, some of them Catholic parochial schools, in Mexico and the United States. She also lived with another aunt in South America. Her early traumatic experiences include a car accident, some five or six years earlier, which necessitated many weeks of hospitalization; and, allegedly, a sexual seduction by a friend of her aunt's when she was eight.

The summary of the mental examination describes her as:

. . . quite immature and of dull normal intelligence. Basic conflict areas are related to her infantile anaclitic relationships and her constant feeling of being threatened and endangered by the loss of objects. Her chief defense mechanisms are projection and flight, and her chief defense against anxiety lies in her attempt to receive love as an assurance of being wanted and of maintaining the relationship with a love object. The basic conflicts are related to her intense infantile oral demands, and her fear that she might be rejected because of her excessive needs and demands. What seems to be an hysterical character formation is a disorganization and loosening of thought processes. This suggests a thought disorder related to the fusion of past and present, and to the absence of adequate ego and intra-ego boundaries and isolation mechanisms making for inadequate intellectual integration and separation of functions necessary for adequate reality testing.

Another excerpt from the psychological test relates directly to the problem of establishing initial contact. The test reveals:

. . . a psychotic youngster, who shows a massive hysterical overlay in her personality structure. The psychological test picture is of a girl, who is fending off open psychosis through becoming like a nine year old child — being simple-minded, withdrawing any libidinal investment from the outside world, and remaining close to, and wallowing in, fantasies of the latency period in which she found herself most protected and happy. Despite these massive efforts to protect herself, she is a fearful youngster whose fearfulness assumes panic proportions. Her terrifying fantasies become so vivid to her that she finds only sporadic protection and support from these kinds of defensive maneuvers. Basically she appears to be a labile, strongly affectively charged young person, who lives extensively and richly in fantasy, and in whose thinking reality is readily pushed aside in favor of autistically preferred frames of reference. All of this, plus a borderline flirting on the fringe of delusionary and hallucinatory ideation, an intensive reaching out to all objects and persons for stability is done on the level of a much younger child.

She will reach out so long as one does not touch her infantile defenses, but once the effort is made to make these less ego-syntonic, I think the therapeutic going may be quite difficult. I also think that it will be hard to dislodge behavior that has pervaded so much the intellectual area, because her low functioning gives relatively little resource material with which to work.

She was accepted as a research case, to be seen three times weekly, while her aunt would be seen weekly by a case worker. The case was electrically recorded. In addition, after each hour, the treating analyst dictated his version of what went on to supplement the objective data of the electric record with impressions and interpretations. The case was also discussed in a weekly research seminar on "distancing devices in childhood schizophrenia and allied conditions"[1] in order to understand more fully their use in defense and adaptation and in relation to the psychotherapeutic process.

Attempts were made to predict certain features of the therapeutic process as well as to suggest a rationale for the prospective predictions. These predictions were based on the extensive workup, which included a careful social history, clinical psychiatric interviews, a complete battery of tests, as well as medical reports and other available records from the past.

The material indicated that Teresa could maintain a quasi-hysterical façade if maintained on the level of an eight or nine year old. As such, the basic relationship to the grownup world was an anaclitic one, dominated by constant demands for gifts, for food, and for love as expressed in the wish that life ought to consist of Christmas and Easter, of valentines and birthdays. Teresa would ceaselessly express longings for childhood and openly state that she hated growing up. Growing up to her meant temptation with which she could not cope, sin, exposure to rape, to mean, exploiting, and unreliable men, and to the forbidden which made her "nervous." Being "nervous" brought forth delusional and hallucinatory experiences which she constantly tried to reconcile with reality, as when she suggested that most of the time she thinks that these voices are just in her own mind and not actually outside. In those moments of disturbance, she had left the safe bases of the small child. She then saw herself fusing with other people, harassed by oppressive voices which were, at times, experienced as superego voices and, at other times, as having powerful seductive and destructive qualities. In those moments of stress, her more mature psychotic adjustment, as it were, could not differentiate between past and present, outside and inside, object and subject. She found herself in uncontrollable anxiety states, faced by rage and homicidal or suicidal impulses which she could conquer only as she returned to the threatened base of childhood.

The suggestion was made that the first transference development would show her as a small child coming to the rescue worker. The rescuer would bring about a miracle and make her well magically. At the same time, he would allow her to remain in the forbidden childhood forever, thus creating a conflict between her and the aunt. This maternal figure Teresa saw as demanding that she grow up and act normally, a goal which she would like to achieve but which threatened the stability of her quasi-adjustment as a small, happy child. She would allow the therapist to be the provider, and would constantly ask him to meet her anaclitic needs, the restoration of objects of her infantile world. He would become, as it were, the provider of the "glass menagerie," and thus restore the external objects of childhood which would permit her restitution on an infantile level. As she would attempt to allow herself a relationship with him, she would begin to see in him the dangerous object. She would thus fluctuate between the quasi-hysterical position of the small child and the psychotic position of the adolescent. The therapist would have to adapt himself to these fluctuations and follow the dominant ways of her describing her inner experience. He would thus allow for optimum distance in which she could find her own goals at her own speed rather than experiencing the therapeutic situation as a threat to whatever precarious balance she might achieve at the moment.

Predictive formulations, then, suggested that the therapist would have to remain with the façade and the surface content at the same time that he would have to indicate his interest in her problems and his desires to establish a way to help her. He would need to refrain from intruding into her inner thoughts, in part because the aunt, the parental person, had depicted him as a kind of father-confessor to whom the girl would have to tell all. He could not fall into the role created for him, since this would lead to the re-creation of an actual triangle, which Teresa first revealed in a letter. Written to us at the aunt's command, it confessed that she had been seduced by the aunt's lover.

The following discussion concerns the initial interview and describes the opening gambit of the therapist as well as that of the patient. The therapist's dictated impressions and reactions right after the initial interview indicate that he thought this session clearly demonstrated the correctness of some of the predictions made in the seminar.

The child instantly greeted me in the waiting-room with deep expressions of gratitude. She told me very often during the session how much she had been looking forward to this and that not only her aunt, but she, too, looked at me as a sainted person, someone who was about to perform a miracle, someone . . . perhaps . . . sent by God in order to help her in her deep illness, which she described primarily as finding herself isolated on an island in an engulfing world of fantasy. The fantasy was primarily characterized by her interest in all the holidays of childhood such as Christmas, Eastertime, or Hallowe'en, in which pleasant gifts and things are given to children. This fantasy life dominates her life more and more, so much, as she told me in the latter part of the interview, that her aunt at one point had threatened not to celebrate Christmas this year. By having Christmas taken away and not allowing presents, maybe she could ban the constant thinking and talking about Christmas from her mind. She spoke repeatedly about the aunt as the one who pointed out to her how crazy she was and how she assumes things about others, for example, that the aunt is nervous or angry when really this was just in Teresa's mind.

I very quickly caught on, I believe, to the metaphoric quality of her language and attempted to let Teresa know that this treatment would consist in our attempting to get to know each other and each other's way of thinking. I spoke about building bridges or connections from the island on which she found herself to the rest of the world, so that she could venture out into the rest of the world if she wanted to. I hinted at the reason for her feeling isolated on an island when talking about the history of Mexico City, originally an island built for protection against surrounding hostile tribes, then developing into a magnificent city which dominated the country. The back and forth between Teresa and me indicated that she was eager for the connection though time and time again she used allegories of space movies and television programs in order to show the danger of therapeutic contact.

Turning from the therapist's impressions of the hour to the verbatim recording, we find that his condensation does not take into account a variety of factors which must be considered as characteristic for this particular opening. The second part of the session consists of the back and forth he mentions in which Teresa more and more takes the initiative in leading to the material which the therapist characterizes as "metaphor." The beginning of the session, however, is actually dominated by the therapist, unaware of this as his own recording seems to be. He attempts routines of opening which, while not destroying the contact with Teresa, somewhat miss the point she is attempting to make. He had seen her some months earlier for a few minutes and refers to the delay in beginning. She suggests now that she heard he hadn't seen her because he was "making machinery, or something." This remark had to do with the social worker's preparation of the family for the fact that since this case was taken on for research purposes, it was to be recorded. The therapist, however, assumes the remark to be Teresa's expression of concern about the electric recording, an assumption easy to make, since he, indeed, was concerned with this very issue and, thus, explains the recording. She asks again what the machinery is for, and he continues on the level of the scientific explanation.

She speaks about her symptoms and uses the phrase, "I am in the middle of an island . . . I don't know what to do. That is why I need your help. After all, you are the only one who can help me." After this overt plea, she speaks in short sentences and vacantly listens to the therapist's elaboration. He takes over more and more, trying to bridge the silences and to cope with the anxiety of the beginning. She maintains a kind of pseudoadjustment in which it seems that she understands him, that she is in contact with him. He patiently explains and takes every one of her words as a cue of a girl of her chronological age who perhaps is having difficulties in a situation in which she is to talk about herself, to share secrets of her life, with a comparative stranger. Only slowly, as her correct, and somehow well-rehearsed, responses for everyday contact with people break down, does she pick up comments of the therapist in a way that would not be correct for the social chit-chat she tries to maintain. She draws now on inner images and problems directly connected with her illness. The therapist's personal reflections were correct as far as the content was concerned, but he had overlooked the heaviness of his own opening. Only later during the interview does it become apparent that he relaxes and is willing to listen rather than to make a special, conscious effort to move toward her, to be reassuring, to be facilitating. The double way of recording then discloses a special feature of the therapist's opening gambit: his special attempt to reach out for her, to move toward her. The method is different from the waiting and expecting attitude that would be typical for more conventional forms of working, which possibly would also have worked in this instance.

But while he attempted to reach her in a somewhat awkward way, she too was attempting to reach him, not truly to understand him but to bring her own methods to him. For example, concerning a question as to how long it would take to get her cured, he suggested that certain things cannot be rushed, and used as an example the writing of a letter which if written too fast would not sound as she would want it to sound (an allusion to the letter which she had prepared previously for the therapist and in which she stated her problem). At that moment she was reminded of a television mystery show which had to do with writing. The therapist's allusion actually concerned the contact between him and Teresa as did the show she mentioned. Her contribution, however, was obviously made on a different level of communication from the conversation that had gone on up to this point. She said:

I don't remember but it was something about the teacher of the girl in the television story. This teacher used to teach grade school, you know, and it is about one of the students who gave her once a pin, a beautiful pin as a present. Well, at first she was in a hurry and he gave it to her and she said, "Thank you, I don't want it," and she gave it back to him. But he said, "Oh, please, Teacher, take it, I thought it was a nice present for you," and she kept it and she thought it was very pretty. But that pin that he gave his teacher was a special pin. He had a wife and his wife had died, she was a beautiful girl, his wife, and it was her pin. I don't know, that pin was sort of witchy or something. It had power. One day the teacher was writing on the blackboard. Yes, and then that pin made her start writing real fast, and she wrote the same letters that his wife used to write because she used to write in another language, his wife, and that's why she started writing, you know, fast. The mystery is that how can she write so fast in another language, in a language that his wife had written.

We started to speak then about the magic power of the pin, about that aspect of the story wherein the teacher learned from the student to write a language which was actually not his own but the language of the student's dead wife. Teresa described how this particular pin had made the teacher write so fast, and how a voice, a horrible voice, as she started writing, began to sing. And there was this horrible-sounding music as she was writing faster and faster under the influence of the pin that had the powers of a witch.

Teresa moved quickly then to fantasies concerning the idea that a girl might die, and that the soul of the dead girl might get into the soul of the live girl who then would be possessed and would write and think things that belonged to the dead girl and would start acting like the dead girl. She interrupted herself then, and suggested that when watching television she would sometimes see people as strange, suggesting that she saw the therapist also as strange.

I know it is my imagination. I have been living in a fantasy world, see it's Christmas, see my aunt explained to me that Christmas is what made me live in a fantasy world, you know every time a Valentine, Easter, birthday, you know and I get so excited about the holidays. And I'm always asking what will I get, and I'm a grown girl now, I'm not a child, but I have a baby's mind, I don't have a growing person's mind. I have a baby's mind, and I have a cousin in town who is the smartest boy I have ever known in my life. He has a man's intelligence, he does not have a baby's mind any more.

Through the television experience she thus described her own difficulties in object relationships, the constant threat of fusion experiences, her inability to maintain object relationships, the constant experience of not being herself, of being forcibly possessed by alien elements. She described the very difficulty in the therapeutic situation which did not permit her to maintain a situation of two but required of her magic-like, regressive, archaic attempts to resolve the interpersonal problem.

One could think of this metaphor as a description of the bilingual problem, the question whether the therapist would ever understand her language, not only her native Spanish but also the language of the primary process. It was as if she expected that the therapist, like the teacher, would be drowned in the world of the patient for whom there could really be no hope.

She repeated this metaphor as she talked about an angel in Mexico City, the statue of an angel that had been destroyed by an earthquake which, however, they had put back together again. They had put together all the broken pieces and in fact that angel now, she thought, looked prettier than it ever had before. She described this angel, actually the monument of Mexico's revolution for independence, as more beautiful than ever before.

The therapist, now in contact, used her communications correctly, in metaphorical response, and to the point. But there can still be seen in the verbatim recording an occasional heaviness in his approach. He out-metaphored her at times, almost as if trying to stem the avalanche of primitive material which, through his metaphoric understanding, must receive more structured meaning.

He recorded his reflections on the second part of the hour as:

She described herself, as it were, as the good girl who was possessed by a demon. Then she described a man who was given life by a woman who allegedly loved him but who really was from another planet and brought evil to him. One could see that she caught on quickly that I was ready to offer myself as the helper. Even so, she actually described herself in the end as the "thing" from another planet, that if one touched it, if one tried to master it or perhaps destroy it, or would even try to change it, it would destroy one in the process. I constantly indicated my willingness to participate in these processes and found myself up against two elements mentioned earlier. First, I was seen as the miracle worker who would somehow cure her. Second, I was also up against the injunctions of the aunt who would not allow the child to think the way she wanted to. The cure was seen as something that I would do to the girl. Her remark as she left the room was concerned with her idea that it was through machines, perhaps, through machinery, that I would influence her. It is interesting that her preparation for this research setup, in which she was told that sound recording would be used, actually touched off in her the notion of treatment as something in which I would use all kinds of machinery to enter her mind to take the evil spirit, the being possessed with another way of thinking, out of her and cure her.

The battle in her was between the passive expectancy that I would change her and the opportunity to say whatever was on her mind on this island, the therapeutic situation. This battle between the injunction of her aunt to accept total responsibility and the island escape here where she could see herself as being allowed to continue her childlike existence will proceed for a long time. This first session has given sufficient cues about the way to proceed. It seems to me, she must be allowed maximum contact and full acceptance of her way of talking. I must also open up a way of meeting her needs for such contacts by allowing her to create a world here without, at the same time, completely identifying myself with the role she has selected for me.

The therapist's estimation of the contact achieved, and the technical problem ahead becomes more meaningful if compared with the verbatim record from the electric tape. Teresa (T.) tells her story, interspersed with comments of the therapist (E.), which are of a facilitating, contact-making, or interpretive nature.

T.: Did you see this picture that they gave on television, Invaders from Mars, it's about space, you know.
E.: Yes.
T.: Did you see it?
E.: I saw some of those, I don't know whether I saw that one — you know there are so many of these Invaders from Mars in these television shows.
T. (giggling): Too many space pictures.
E.: Too many space pictures, maybe, but you like those?
T.: No, they scare me. But I'm interested in them, you know . . .
E.: Sometimes one just likes to watch something because it scares one.
T.: Yes, that's right. I saw three pictures on space in television, invaders from Mars. I saw one about a girl that came from another planet . . . she was a devil girl, I mean, she was horrible, she had a face like a devilish face, a doll, a painted face . . .
E.: Maybe a person just possessed by someone.
T.: I guess, I don't know, but she was a girl that came from another planet.
E.: Yes . . . a mean person?
T.: In a space ship.

E.: A mean person?

T.: Yes, a very mean girl, you know, she was . . . you know, she wanted, it begins with this, it was somewhere on the North Pole, there was a man that got frozen, you know, he was walking in the snow in the North Pole, and it was very windy, you know how cold it's in the North Pole?

E.: Certainly.

T.: He felt very tired and he wanted to go to sleep so he laid down on the snow and he stayed so long sleeping that he got frozen.

E.: That was the end of that.

T.: Uh, huh, yes, but then that man had a friend, you know, there were two men, and so his friend was looking for him, and when he found him frozen he couldn't believe it, he got scared and said, "Ooh, he's frozen," and this and that. So then he went back to the house where he was living and told another friend of his that his friend was frozen, and what could they do about it, and well, they were trying to think and discover what.

E.: How to save him?

T.: Yeah, and then when he went back in the house that's when the girl from another planet came . . . she appeared, you know . . . well, let's say he was still frozen and she appeared like a virgin . . . some . . . I . . . I . . . when I saw her appear I thought it was an angel who appeared, who was going to get him unfrozen and give him life again and all that . . . and it was that girl . . .

E.: Then she was really evil, rather than good.

T.: Yeah, she was . .

E.: Isn't it terrible to think when you see someone you don't know whether a person is good or evil?

T.: Yes, uh huh, because you feel afraid of them, scared . . . and then, well, she gave him life again, and then he woke up and saw her and he asked her, "Who are you?" and when he saw her he thought she was the most beautiful girl he had ever seen in his whole life and he said, "Well, what am I doing here, was I sleeping or what?" And then she told him that he was frozen and that he was dead and she gave him life and he thanked her and everything and then he was alive again, but he had the life of that girl, he had the life of another planet, he didn't have the world, he didn't have the world's life, you know.

E.: He must have become a very strange person.

T.: Yes, uh huh, he was a devil like that girl, he had a devilish face like that girl from another planet . . . And then he went back to the house, you know.

E.: Looks as if her influence on people isn't so good.

T.: She was horrible, really, she had a horrible face. . . . It made me sick every time I saw her face . . . ugh . . . you know those people of other planets . . .

E.: I wonder if one could help such a girl, you know, this girl from the other planet, to take on our characteristics and be like us. You know, if

someone who really knew had met this girl and rather than allowing her to
make this poor fellow into someone from the other planet would turn her
into an earth person?
T.: Yeah, that's right.
E.: We figure out a method, you and I. . . . It would be great, wouldn't it?
T.: Yeah, I know it . . . I wonder, but she was the strangest thing . . .

This material could be considered as a fantastic allegory of the psychotherapeutic process in which the magic capacity for change is seen in the
girl from the other planet who, instead of saving the man, destroys him or
rather, changes him into her. Taken as a simile of the psychotherapeutic
process, the devilish quasi-rescuer from outer space could actually be considered as the evil aspect of the patient who, by means of fusion, transmits
her evil nature to the man, frozen and incapacitated as he is now. The end
of the process possibly would be double evil, mental illness and terror for
two, rather than a situation in which the patient would get restored to
health; instead of a folie à deux, an evil symbiosis. This is very unlike the
more conscious fantasy which Teresa carries into the treatment process
when she sees the psychotherapist as an angel sent by God to rescue her
through magic.

Toward the end of the session she spoke about another part of a
mystery show in which "that thing," that witchy thing that could not be
harmed and could not be destroyed "would finally kill that person, so that
if a poor man touched the ball, he harmed it because he thought it was an
enemy, you know, he wanted to kill it and that ball harmed him. It killed
him."

The therapist countered this with: "What happened as he attempted
to touch it or change it or destroy it is that it turned out that actually he
was weaker than it. Since it was the stronger one he should have figured
out, I believe, how to handle it without getting into danger, isn't that so?
I think that if he had been a very smart person he would have figured out
the safe way that he needed."

While the therapist thought that he had set the tone for the therapeutic session and tried to arrange the next hour, Teresa ended the session
with: "Oh, thank you, Doctor, very much. And thank you because you
are going to help me. I am really glad. I just wonder how you are going
to help me. I would like to know that. Well, because, you know, I thought
you were going to open up my head and take out what was wrong with me
or something . . . that's what I thought."

As the opening session came to a close, it was finally revealed what
her original question about the machinery referred to. Rather than sound
recording, as the therapist believed, she revealed she actually had in mind

a machine which by magic or surgery could influence the forces within herself which she considered evil or destructive.

In these initial moves the therapist was actively engaged in trying to reach the person. The overactivity was necessitated, perhaps, by his not really being on her wave-length, if this metaphor is permitted. As soon as he had made contact with her kind of thinking, and had helped her to realize that he understood her, she slowly took over, became herself, and more and more dominated the session. She saw herself as a powerful evil influence which could wipe out the other person, destroy the helper, devour him under the pretext of love or because of the evil implications that love held for her. This danger she could counter only by asking of him that he himself become the one who, through his machinery, would take the evil spirit out of her. His attempt to influence her was countered by her attempt to devitalize him and to see the helper primarily as an influencing machine rather than a person.

The optimum contact which the psychotherapist tried to maintain was easily broken, since the child moves, sometimes without provocation, to positions in which the object is seen as destructive, as devouring, or in which she imagines herself to be murderous. The splitting of self as well as object representations into positive and negative fragments characterized even the first hour and led to the patient's expressed demand that the therapist accomplish a miracle cure through the use of brain machinery; a schizophrenic reinterpretation of the recording machinery, set up for the research, of which the patient was made aware.

Freud's simile of the opening gambit in the chess game referred, of course, to a variety but limited number of moves which the analyst has available. Teresa referred frequently to the adventures of Lewis Carroll's Alice in Wonderland. He who works with young people like Alice needs more than the opening moves of the chess game. No sooner does he start playing the chess game against the background of its rules than he realizes that his patient is actually playing ticktacktoe on a three-dimensional level or checkers; or is having him participate in a mad tea party, meet the monsters of the Wonderland, or go through her experiences of changing size. This session illustrates the therapist's attempt to move with Teresa into her Wonderland, and to stay with her.

As to whether this Alice, Teresa, will return to the living-room, just as the dreamer wakes up and returns to a world of outer reality where opening gambits do not defy exhaustive systematic description, permit me to predict or, rather, to prophesy. I quote from Lewis Carroll. As Alice wakes up she realizes that her kitten was the Red Queen of the dream. She says, "Now, Kitty, let's consider who it was that dreamed it all. This is a serious question, my dear, and you should not go on licking your paw like that. You see, Kitty, it *must* have been either me or the Red King. He was part of my dream, of course—but then I was a part of his dream, too! *Was* it the Red King, Kitty? You were his wife, my dear, so you ought to know. Oh, Kitty, do help me settle it! I'm sure your paw can wait!" But the provoking kitten only began on the other paw, and pretended it hadn't heard the question.

"Which do you think it was?"

REFERENCES

[1] A description of this work, by Rudolf Ekstein and Mortimer M. Meyer, appeared in Psychological Reports, 1961.

PART TWO

EGO STATES AND THEIR FUNCTION

In judging the success of a defense, we will inquire not
only into the fate of the instinctual drive and the protection afforded to the ego, but also—more than before—
into its effects on the ego functions not directly involved
in the conflict. The concepts of ego strength, ego weakness, ego restriction, etc., are all related to this realm,
but they remain nebulous as long as the specific ego
functions involved are not studied in detail. Ego strength
—though it manifests itself strikingly in the struggles of
the conflict-sphere—cannot be defined solely in terms of
that borderland of the ego which is involved in the conflict. In terms of our analogy, the effectiveness of the
armies defending the borders also depends on the support they get or do not get from the rear. Once we have
determined objectively those factors of ability, character,
will, etc., which are the empirical—not theoretical—
correlates of "strong" or "weak" egos, we will have es-
caped the relativity of the usual definitions which determine ego strength from the individual ego's relation to
its id or superego. We will then be able to compare the
ego strength of different individuals, even though the
relationship between mastery of reality and achievement
on the one hand, and ego strength on the other, is very
complex.

HEINZ HARTMANN

4

OBSERVATIONS ON THE
PSYCHOLOGY OF BORDERLINE AND
PSYCHOTIC CHILDREN *

Now let us, by a flight of imagination, suppose that Rome is not a human habitation but a psychical entity with a similarly long and copious past—an entity, that is to say, in which nothing that has once come into existence will have passed away and all the earlier phases of development continue to exist alongside the latest one. . . . and the observer would perhaps only have to change the direction of his glance or his position in order to call up the one view or the other.

SIGMUND FREUD

He who ventures to accompany the borderline or psychotic child into the terrain of his inner world will find his journey beset not only with initial technical problems but with many special hazards and bewildering phenomena. We do not refer to the fluid landscape with archaic figures which emerge, coalesce, fade, and reappear. For despite the dimness of the landscape, some maps have been charted and reports of previous travelers are available for aid. Even the most seasoned traveler, however, must be puzzled by phenomena of arrival and departure in the world of fantasy. After having communicated his readiness to embark upon these journeys in whatever guise the child requires, the traveler cannot help but wonder at the exact moment and at the startling abruptness with which the voyages commence and terminate. He cannot help but speculate that a knowledgeable grasp of the timetable might provide him not only with more adequate preparation for the journey, but with the means for affecting the course and destination of his young guide as well.

Children whose adjustment is marginally located in their use of both

* Judith Wallerstein is coauthor of this chapter.

neurotic and psychotic mechanisms are a clinical group described variously as borderline, schizophrenic-like, or severely neurotic. They and psychotic children are subject to marked and frequent fluctuation in ego states, visible in the treatment process. This striking phenomenon of continual alteration of psychotic and neurotic ego organization makes for a characteristic pattern of unpredictability which is paradoxically one of the most predictable aspects at present of psychotherapeutic effort with these children.

Time and again the child will begin the therapy hour with conversation or play wholly suited to his chronological age, so that the clinical observer may reasonably be led to conjecture the presence of a relatively intact ego, well able to use and to sustain the demands and vicissitudes of classical child therapy and analysis. Yet suddenly, and without clearly perceptible stimulus, a dramatic shift may occur: the neurotic defenses crumble precipitously; and the archaic mechanisms of the primary process and the psychotic defenses erupt into view. Then just as rapidly they recede, and the neurotic defenses or perhaps more accurately, the pseudo-neurotic defenses reappear.

To illustrate these rapidly fluctuating ego states we offer the following interview drawn from the psychotherapy of a ten year old psychotic girl which occurred a few weeks prior to an anticipated visit from her mother and stepfather:

Ann asked me for a cigarette and began to inhale. She showed me with some pride how well she could smoke now, and I commented that she no longer choked and almost threw up when she inhaled. When I said the words "throw up," Ann jumped and looked a little frightened and then assured me that she did not become upset any more when I said things like that. I agreed perhaps she didn't, but noticed that she had jumped this time. Ann said that it startled her, but it was not upsetting like it used to be. I wondered how it used to be and Ann said it made her feel all squirrely inside with thrills running up and down her back.

She then began to ask many questions. How tame were squirrels? I said they were not very tame but were little wild animals. Did I like squirrels? Yes. Could squirrels be tamed if you got them as babies? Yes, I thought so. How tame would they be then? I said they would probably take nuts out of your hand. Ann waited a minute and then said soberly, "When will my folks be here, Dorothy?" She then proceeded with, "Do squirrels bite, Dorothy?" "Yes, they would if they were molested." "If a squirrel is tame it wouldn't bite would it?" "No, I suppose not." "Dorothy, do you think I'm a little squirrel?" "Yes, you are, Ann." "I'll be a squirrel, Dorothy, and I'll come to you and you give me a nut." I agreed and so we played with her getting nuts from me and running back to put them in a pile. She asked many more questions about squirrels and I thought maybe the squirrels were asking questions, too, when they chattered so much. She asked then if squirrels got mad, and I assured her they did, and when they got mad they really chattered. Ann asked if that was like it was when she got mad at her mother. I said yes it was like that only she didn't used to be a little chattering squirrel. Instead of chattering when she got mad she left bowel movements on chairs and did other things to show her anger toward her mother. Now my little squirrel can chatter when she is angry.

Ann did more running around the room like a squirrel, coming back every so often, chattering all the time, returning to her questions as to how tame a squirrel was and so on. She only came near enough to get the nut from me. I commented on how the little squirrel was afraid to get close to people. Ann asked how close a squirrel got. I stated, "Just close enough to get the nut. A little squirrel cannot get close enough to cuddle up like a kitten, or push against you like a puppy dog." Ann ran around a few minutes in silence and then suddenly stopped a few feet from me. Her face was serious and thoughtful and she was now entirely in contact. She said, "Dorothy, what kind of a person is my mother?" I said that I did not know for sure, what kind of a person did she think her mother was? Ann said her mother was not like any other woman. I asked, "How is your mother different?" Ann said, "Well my mother's love is stern, not like Mrs. A.'s, whose love is friendly and soft. I wish Mrs. A. were my mother." Ann then went on desperately, "My mother isn't like the mothers of other kids who come here. They are friendly and they pat the dog and my mother never pats the dog unless I tell her to. She never does things with kids. My mother never smiles." Again Ann repeated, "My mother's love is so stern, Dorothy." I told Ann I thought she was telling me something very important. She undoubtedly felt her mother's love was stern when all little girls want a warm, loving, friendly mother. But I stated some women just couldn't give that kind of love. Maybe her mother was one of those people. Ann said she thought her grandmother loved her more than her mother. I stated I was sure her grandmother was able to show her love in a warm, friendly way while her mother was not. This did not necessarily mean her mother did not love her, but it might mean she couldn't be soft and friendly. Maybe that was one of the reasons she had been so angry with her mother.

Ann jumped around a little bit and then went over to the mirror. She spit out a lot of saliva on the mirror and was again out of contact, wiggling and twisting and making grunting noises. She stopped and asked me to come over near her. She pressed her lips hard against the mirror and in the reflection I could see her tongue coming out and in against the glass. She said, "See Dorothy, I'm a snail." I said, "Yes, you're a cute little baby snail." She began sucking hard on the glass, stopping in between to say, "See Dorothy, the snail sucks its food." I said that sucking was wonderful, *for the little snail got fed that way. "Poor little snail. I hope it gets enough food. I hope the little snail doesn't have to suck and suck and not get enough food to keep her well. That would be terrible." Ann came over from the window and sat down on the small bed and said, "When is my family coming, Dorothy?"*

One is led to elaborate Freud's [1] vivid likening of the exploration of the psychic apparatus to the archaeological excavations of Rome in order adequately to describe these fluctuations. It is as if the many civilizations which constitute Rome throughout her long and varied history, built each upon the ruins of the other, were to come into view simultaneously, each distinguished by a light of different coloration. And as the therapist pushes the buttons, i.e., responds to the patient, different colored lights flash into view, lighting up their particular historic epochs; the earliest and most primitive stage of Roman development following upon the most recent phase of Italian history, to be followed in turn by Rome at the time of the Crusades and so on, making for a wild display of colored lights and widely different architectural structures, all of which constitute Rome as she stands today. Similarly, in these children, via the fluctuation in ego state occurring in the process of treatment, we are enabled to see in a bold relief, which is not available in the more neurotic child, the multiple ego organizations which comprise their adjustment and behavior of today, and thereby to gain an invaluable vantage point from which intrapsychic organization can be observed in action.

Perhaps we can convey the concept of ego state fluctuation as we have visualized it and some of our initial theoretical formulations by means of a crude model. We may sketch a series of concentric circles, the center point of which is designated as the place where the conflict appears in full consciousness. The respective lengths of the radii of the concentric circles extending outward represent ever increasing psychological distance which the conflict may travel from this center point of conscious awareness. We suggest that different defensive constellations attach to each of the circles or distances from consciousness. Thus, at the outermost circle, the conflict would achieve maximum distance from conscious awareness by virtue of the gross psychotic distortions and disguises imposed by the defense apparatus of the perimeter which would render it least recognizable by the conscious ego. Similarly, when appearing on the inner circles, the disguises imposed by the defense mechanisms would be either incomplete or less far-reaching in character. The remoteness or proximity of the conflict from consciousness at any given time can be thought of as a function of the ego's capacity to tolerate and withstand the pain of recognition.

In the light of this model we may compare the intrapsychic fluctuation of the neurotic patient with that of the group under investigation. In the psychotherapy and analysis of the neurotic patient, problems frequently presented on the outer circles travel inward as therapy proceeds, until they advance close enough to consciousness to permit meaningful interpretation. In this process the patient makes use of his characteristic modes of defense. Extreme variability in the use of different defense mechanisms is uncommon, and we may conceive of neurotic conflict as traveling within a limited range of circles. This enables us to infer the presence of a relatively stable ego organization, since the stronger the ego the less need to maintain psychological distance. Or as Karl Menninger [2] has suggested, the stronger the ego the less need to abandon first- and second-order regulatory devices in order to maintain homeostasis.

In our patients, the characteristically precipitous fluctuation in their use of different defense mechanisms can be conceived of schematically as broad leaps from inner to outermost circles and back again, occurring in the absence of gross perceptible stimuli. So wide are these leaps, in fact, that the total defense picture alters radically and we speak of a marked and rapid change in ego state when the neurotic defenses which attach to the inner circles give way to the psychotic or psychotic-like defenses of the periphery. In this clinical group, then, the ego's capacity to bear the proximity of the conflictual material (as represented by the presence of the neurotic ego state) or to require the most remote possible distance (as evidenced by the upsurgence of the psychotic ego state) may vary frequently and abruptly in a single therapy hour.

It is important to emphasize that the distinction between our patients and the neurotic patient cannot be drawn in terms of fluctuation in ego state per se. For, sleeping and waking, imaginative play, fantasy, certain creative efforts, and recreational pursuits demand the ability to regress and to return and to employ different states of ego organization. In fact, the capacity to achieve a shift in ego state in accord with the situation and the individual's needs and wishes is an integral part of daily living. Furthermore, deep repressions are discernible in persons well within the neurotic range in the face of extraordinary circumstances, as in reaction to anesthesia and certain drugs, to hypnosis, and to overwhelming personal and social crises. Yet in general we observe that a radical change in the use of characteristic defenses, so as to bring into view a different ego state, is not an attribute of the waking life of the neurotic, nor can we find any comparable rapidity of fluctuation in the neurotic group. We are led to conclude that the borderline and psychotic patient has available, in his daily waking life, the spectrum of defenses that is available to the neurotic only where the ego is subjected to extraordinary conditions of stress or in the regressive ego state of sleep.

We arrive at a significant distinction between the ego of the neurotic patient and the ego of the borderline and psychotic child by recognizing that whereas all persons have the potentiality for regression under certain circumstances, the difference in the two groups may be seen in the kind and degree of stress which calls forth the regression as well as in the rapidity of the regression itself. The ego of the borderline child is characterized by a specific vulnerability or hypersensitivity in response to both inner and outer stimuli. We may conceptualize this difference by comparing the ego of the borderline child to a delicate permeable membrane through which the primary process penetrates with relative ease from within and which external forces puncture easily from without, as contrasted with a resilient, relatively nonporous, more intact membrane which might represent the more permanently cathected ego of his neurotic contemporaries.

In order to delineate more clearly the functioning of the sensitive and fluid ego organization of these patients, and in accord with our interest in patient-therapist interaction, clinical material was studied in the light of two questions: In response to what stimuli or lack of stimuli do shifts in ego state occur? What purpose do such fluctuations fulfill within the psychic economy of the individual?

We may hypothesize at the outset three possible determinants for shift in ego state occurring within the therapeutic process: (1) that these shifts specifically reflect changes in the transference in the child's relationship with the therapist; (2) that these shifts occur autistically, welling completely from within the psychic organism and bearing no relationship whatsoever to external stimuli; (3) that these shifts occur in response to feelings arising within the child which may be related to changing introjects, not yet given expression within the therapeutic context.

In reviewing our clinical material we repeatedly found that the ego regression was directly preceded by an inadvertent rebuke or a lack of comprehension by the therapist of the child's message, and the return into the secondary process followed directly upon the therapist's retrieving of his error and demonstrating his sympathy and understanding. An example both of the losing of affective contact through possible technical error by the therapist and the retrieving of the situation with the therapist's expression of understanding can be seen in the material from the end of the hour with little Ann. As the child complained of her mother's coldness, the therapist said that perhaps her mother loved her but could not express her love with the requisite warmth, and observed that this might have caused the child to become angry at her mother. We suggest that the snail fantasy in the psychotic state which followed immediately upon the therapist's remark may well have been a reaction to the implied rebuke that

Mother after all did love her and it was only she, the child, who failed to perceive this appropriately. At the termination of the hour when the therapist was able again to enter affectively into the child's world by saying that she hoped the little snail would not be disappointed and would get enough to eat, Ann responded by a return to meaningful contact within a neurotic relationship mode around the topic of her parent's forthcoming visit.

It seems reasonably demonstrable that certain transference reactions are perceived with such overwhelming fear or pain that they force into defensive operation an ego state which permits the furthest possible removal of the painful stimulus from the ego's awareness as indicated by our diagrammatic representation. Thus, the ego achieves a measure of safety by taking flight into the disguises, distortions, and fantasy displacement under the dominance of the primary process, as in this instance in the retreat to the snail fantasy.

When we subject these phenomena to closer scrutiny, it appears that the regression achieves more than this measure of protection in the face of an intensely threatening affective situation. It is noteworthy that the shift into the regressive ego state does not sever contact with the therapist. More frequently, the child invited or commanded the therapist to join the fantasy and follow the primary process productions. (In the interview cited, Ann called the therapist over to join her at the mirror.) We may speculate, therefore, that the shift fulfills a double function in the psychic economy of the child: that of reacting to the transference threat, and that of simultaneously maintaining contact with the therapist on the only basis now possible.

We suggest that every fantasy production carries this double message. It reveals both an attempt to master conflict and a confession of current inability to do so. Similarly the psychotic regression in these children may be said to convey the double message of the attempt to maintain contact with the transference object and an inability to do so, except where the dangerous emotional charge of the relationship can be reduced via flight into regression. We may offer another illustration drawn from Ann's record:

She had experienced vaginal bleeding which was initially diagnosed as precocious onset of menses. Later examination revealed little grounds for this initial diagnostic impression which had been shared with the child, but the bleeding was rather thought to be associated with extensive masturbatory activity. This latter diagnosis was not told to the child. In a subsequent therapy session Ann asked, "Dorothy, why do we use words like menstruation and masturbation? Why not 'mend the seam' and 'master the bait'?"

If we analyze these neologistic, primary-process productions, we cannot fail to recognize the child's sensitive perception of the conflict and
her statement of it in a way which could be discussed with her. "Mend
the seam" refers to her wish to have the bodily damage or tear mended,
and "master the bait" refers to her recognition of its association with
masturbation and her concern with mastering the temptation to masturbate. In effect, the child presented the totality of the conflict, including
the diagnosis not discussed with her.

Our speculations regarding the functions of the ego-state fluctuation
in response to transference reactions reach further as we compare the
child's preoccupation immediately preceding the regression with the material expressed from within the protection of the regressed ego state. We
may draw on an example from outside of the psychotherapeutic context
to illustrate some of the formulations which emerge from such comparison.

Robert Fliess [3] described the experience of an analyst who brought to
Freud's attention an observation of his which he felt might contradict
some of Freud's formulations about dreams and particularly Freud's thinking regarding the purpose of disguises in dream life. The analyst described
a reverie preceding sleep in which he envisioned his attempts to seduce
an older woman of his acquaintance, and in finding her dress too tight
for his purposes, he set about unsnapping the back of her dress. In the
sleep which followed, the dreamer found himself outside a locked inn
which contained a waitress and a dining-room into which the dreamer
sought access unsuccessfully and therefore tried to enter via the rear
entrance. As the analyst compared his reverie and his dream, he felt that
both expressed essentially the same content and differed only in the mode
of expression and in the use of disguising symbolism in the dream. He was
therefore at some pains to understand the purpose of the dream and
particularly the purpose of the disguises of the dream in expressing what
had been quite accessible to the conscious and waking ego of the dreamer.
In effect, we may say that he asked Freud to clarify the cause for the shift
in ego state in relation to content that was readily accessible to his ego
in its initial waking state.

In responding to this question Freud suggested that the content of
reverie and dream differed in that the dream contained a hidden reference
to the dreamer's mother via the reference to the waitress at the inn and
hence the disguises were directed at the different content expressed in the
dream.

We may take this as our point of departure and push the explanation
further by noting that the reverie expressed a phallic fantasy about the
mother, whereas the dream contained an oral fantasy. Obviously a phallic

fantasy is more acceptable to an adult than an oral fantasy. And since ego regression occurs in sleep, the more regressed needs and wishes, in this instance the oral wishes, emerged into expression. Thus the shift in ego state changed not only the content, as in this instance, from a current love partner to an infantile love object, but the entire wish system as well. We may suggest, therefore, that fantasies can reflect different instinctual needs deriving from different layers of the personality and that the layer which is tapped at any given time may be a function of the person's ego state.

In our children, when the neurotic defenses are prominent, the problems raised for discussion are not inappropriate to their chronological age, and frequently deal with sibling rivalry, variously disguised oedipal themes, fears of being different, and feelings of shame and guilt. Their fantasies, however, in their regressed ego state are by comparison pronouncedly oral in character, having as their themes: fear of separation and abandonment, of bodily disintegration, distortion of body image, fantasies of devouring giants and their victims, and primitive rage outbursts. We may draw again on the interview which we have cited. When the neurotic ego organization of the child is predominant and Ann is wholly in contact with the therapist, she gives expression to her concern over her parents' forthcoming visit, and her doubt regarding their love for her. In her regressed state, she fantasies herself a snail, sucking on the glass and terribly frightened lest she suck and suck and get nothing to eat. (We suggest, that via this fantasy of sucking on her own reflection, the child re-establishes an emotionally empty symbiotic world in which no gratification seems attainable for her.) We see accordingly her concern reflected on two different levels of ego organization, dealing in content with the problem of her relationship with her mother, but reflecting different need systems as her ego state changes.

Hence we conclude that ego-state fluctuations have as their additional purpose the expression of different instinctual need systems and wish constellations associated with different stages of development which seek and find expression as the ego state changes.

To return briefly to Fliess's stimulating contribution, the example cited suggests that the dream reproduces the frustration of the reverie, for in both reverie and dream the dreamer's wish is stymied and he is denied access. It may well be that the dream in this instance contains the nuclear problem of the individual, that of deprivation at the hands of the withholding oral mother, which, transposed up the developmental ladder in the reverie state, becomes expressed in phallic terms, in frustration in attempted sexual seduction. The similarities and differences in this experience spanning two ego states strongly suggest that when ego state shifts occur, the instinctual need systems expressed differ, the representation of latent and manifest content differ, and the language and mode of representation differ, but what remains constant is the conception of the conflict and its characteristic resolution. In this instance we may suggest that the dreamer characteristically offered the alibi of being unable to obtain gratification from the thwarting mother to justify his turning to the father via the "back door." Similarly, with our little patient Ann we may conceptualize her nuclear problem as deprivation at the hands of an unloving mother and her characteristic solution of desperately searching for infantile gratification which she does not expect to find.

We note that throughout our case material, problems terminating in frustration on oedipal or phallic levels were similarly presented in the most archaic fantasy. In fact, it is striking how frequently these children conceive of their problems as inadmissible of solution. It is as if they say to us continually and on whatever level of presentation, "My dilemma is absolute and insoluble. You cannot understand me and if you did understand me, you could not possibly help me." If this be so, that the ladder of unsolved problems extends upward throughout the entire intrapsychic life of our patients and that problems presented on an oedipal level mask problems deriving from much earlier stages of development, then the shift in ego state fulfills no function in relation to the resolution of the conflict itself except in so far as it exercises a restitutive function within the psychic economy. Rather, the ego-state fluctuation serves to permit the continuation of the relationship and to elaborate the conflict which threatened its disruption. Both the regressed mode of relationship and the communication content from the regressive ego state can be conceived of as aimed at revealing to the therapist the ways in which the conflict is experienced within the depths of the child's personality, by its most primitive and most cathected ego organization.

We have emphasized until now ego-state fluctuation occurring in relation to the threat of emerging feelings within the transference. It is, however, reasonable to assume that psychotic regression might also emerge in response to permission granted by the therapist. Our material yielded several such possible instances. Thus, in the presence of a benevolent transference and a real figure, powerful infantile wishes and impulses, ordinarily refused recognition by the ego, are permitted access and the open seeking of gratification. It is a common experience in play therapy with young children that the presence of a nursing bottle in the playroom, and the permission its presence conveys, will evoke play at being a suckling infant in children who would not dare show such regressive behavior at home.

In offering this hypothesis, which implies that the child "permits" the regressive material to appear, we are confronted with the significant question regarding the extent to which ego fluctuations in these patients are subject to conscious control by the child's ego. Are the ego-state fluctuations in these children, for instance, comparable to the experience of the child who plays in the playroom at being an infant?

Theoretically several possibilities can be advanced. We may think of relative control exerted by the ego when an individual is able temporarily to suspend more mature ways of ego function and then to recapture the more mature ego state as the situation changes as, for instance, in the transition from sleep to waking, or in the child who decides it is "safe" to play at being a baby but puts the bottle down when he hears his mother's footsteps outside the room. Much as we wish to remain in bed in the morning, and even consciously try with the help of a dream to incorporate the alarm clock's stimulus and to continue to sleep, the alarm insistently penetrates to force its real nature upon us. The world of the secondary process intervenes rudely. We rise to its summons and, with the help of certain motor rituals, increasingly succeed in dismissing the regressed sleeping state from consciousness.

At the other end of the psychopathological spectrum, we may think of the psychotic ego as having little control over its hallucinatory and delusional experiences, having almost lost the capacity to differentiate psychological from outer reality. Between these polarities of relatively full control and almost total loss of control, we conceive of a wide spectrum of possibilities: occasional control, control operating efficiently in one direction only, as in inability to fall asleep readily and difficulty in waking, or, as reported by the patient who stated that his depressions no longer troubled him because he could almost banish them at will.

We may postulate an ego mechanism of control which can be roughly compared in its function to that of a thermostat. A reliable thermostat is capable of maintaining fairly even temperature in a room despite climatic changes, and we may think of this as analogous to the ego of the neurotic where ego states fluctuate minimally and are subject to relative control by the individual. An unreliable thermostat, on the other hand, can lead to unpredictable and inappropriate temperature changes and figuratively represents the regulatory and controlling devices in the borderline and psychotic child. We suggest that this ego mechanism of control varies in its efficacy in persons well within the neurotic range but within fairly narrow limits, since the total personality functioning is largely under the dominance of the secondary process.

These children make abundantly clear, however, their weakness and fear in the face of upsurging psychotic fantasies. One of our young patients told his therapist that he was afraid to enter the Valley of Death, a well-elaborated fantasy of his, because he would not be able to make the return trip. In effect he described the strength of his ego as too deficient or inadequate to move from the primary into the secondary process despite strenuous efforts. In numerous and varied ways these children tell us how fearful they are of being inundated by their fantasies. Yet at the same time they demonstrate some ability in control, particularly with the help of external stimulus, as for instance when reminded that the therapy hour is terminating. It seems characteristic for this group that ego-state fluctuations occur many times throughout their day, occasionally with control, but that a large part of their waking life bears strong similarity to the sleep-dream life of their neurotic contemporaries in the lack of control exerted by the dreamer.

We therefore suggest that one relative distinction between our patients and persons within the neurotic range may lie in this still obscure mechanism of control. For precisely this mechanism of control, which in the absence of gross trauma is available to the neurotic in his waking state, seems damaged or inadequately developed in the borderline and psychotic child.

This observation supports the view that only the early stages of ego development have been fully achieved by these patients and that the evidences of more advanced ego functioning represent only weak and beleaguered outposts whose contact with the main ego body is tenuous and intermittent.[4] The degree of conscious control which the ego can exert over its shifting states may be a function of ego structure and the relationship between the stages of development achieved. Thus, where the different developmental levels are closely interconnected, as in the neurotic patient, we may think of the ego as having relatively full control over its fluctuations; whereas, as in our patients, the lines of communication between the different ego states are tenuous and easily disrupted, and the ability to go back and forth at will is seriously impaired. We have tentatively characterized this phenomenon as inadequate or defective ego control.

In some of our case material we were unable to find any sign of activity on the therapist's part which preceded the ego-state fluctuation and which might be thought of as a stimulus to the regression. It may well be that some of these fluctuations occur autistically, having no relationship whatsoever to the actual therapeutic process or to external stimuli, and that they arise entirely from obscure and, in effect, unobservable phenomena within the individual. However, we may also conjecture that fluctuations may occur in response to emerging inner feelings and changing introjects within the patient. Much like the person in love who experiences a succession of agonies and exhilarations in relation to what he imagines to be the changing feelings of his beloved, and which may occur in the total absence of the beloved, so too we may surmise that certain introjects which have not yet become visible in the transference may provide the stimulus which eventuates in the regression. Certain feelings probably cannot be expressed in the transference before the psychotherapeutic process has paved the way and before various aspects of the therapist have been introjected.

There are many additional questions which the material stimulates and which demand continual exploration. For instance, is there a relationship between the content of the conflict and the ego state that is in evidence? If the ego state can be related to the period in the child's life when the original conflict occurred,[5] it would theoretically be possible to chart the time of the occurrence of the original conflict by plotting the content of the conflict with the ego state. Further, to what extent can the nature of transference be derived from the ego state itself, that is, from the mode of expression and from the defensive constellation as well as from the content of the communication? May we speak properly of transference psychosis where the shift into the regressed ego state occurs, and how can this be distinguished from transference manifestations in neurotic children?

We have suggested that patients in the borderline group seem to face absolute dilemmas which admit of no solution. Is this a distinction which can be drawn between this group and the neurotic patient? Can we propose that the neurotic conceives of his problems as leading to dangerous or unhappy consequences but that the possible solutions envisioned have some reality anchorage and are less overwhelmingly catastrophic? If we think of neurotic dilemma in terms of the excursion of a pendulum, can we say that the excursion of the pendulum in the psychological world of our patients covers an infinitely wider amplitude than in the neurotic's world and can be specifically associated with the degree and nature of his illness?

Further, can we subject the process of the shift itself to more microscopic examination? Several writers have suggested that in the transition from sleep to the waking state, the ego ascends the developmental ladder step by step, reachieving and resynthesizing each major stage of development, until it arrives at full conscious control and contact with itself and reality. We are interested in the clues which we can derive from the clinical material regarding the process of the shift and how it is experienced by the child.

We proceed with the aid of some of our clinical material to examine more fully the transference manifestations of these children and the characteristic patterning of their relationships in the treatment process. We may note here parenthetically that in the course of our experience with the therapy of seven borderline and psychotic children, sometimes by trial and perhaps too frequently by error, we have arrived at some tentative technical formulations which were stimulated by the exquisite sensitivity of these children as much as by their particular psychological attributes. The rapidly fluctuating ego states and the different modes of communication accompanying these fluctuations have dictated the continual reassessment of therapeutic tools and suggested the refinement of some methods of communication and interpretation.

We can schematically represent the gamut of possible patterns of interpersonal relationships both in the psychotherapeutic setting and in daily life by anchorage around three distinguishable modal points: (1) an autistic relationship mode,[6] (2) a symbiotic relationship mode,[7] and (3) the whole progression of relatively differentiated object relationships characteristic of neurotic life. These different relationship modes can be viewed genetically in terms of their postulated derivation from the different developmental phases of the growing ego. Or they may tentatively be conceived of as associated with different ego states along the spectrum of sleep to full waking consciousness.[8] A diversity of relationship modes and the different ego organizations from which they derive is available to all persons. In the neurotic range of behavior these find their necessary and useful places appropriately within the richly textured emotional life of each individual.

Our material suggests that the dominant cast of the relationship seen in the borderline and psychotic child is frequently autistic and symbiotic. This phenomenon is most strikingly discernible in the initial phases of psychotherapy, and is partly explainable in terms of ego regression occurring in response to the anxiety evoked by beginning treatment. The concept of the *dominant cast of the relationship* is used advisedly, since the potentialities for more mature ways of relating is clearly available to these children and makes its appearance within the psychotherapeutic relationship. This availability of different relationship modes, coupled simultaneously with the periodic lack of such availability (since at the time that the child employs symbiotic and autistic ways of relating, he evidently cannot do otherwise), constitutes a baffling phenomenon.

Our efforts have been clinically rather than genetically oriented; therefore we have attempted to follow the changing availability of different ways of relating within the psychotherapeutic process and to understand their defensive and restitutive functions within the treatment relationship. In the first several weeks of Ted's therapy (Chapter 2), the phenomenon of coexistence and coavailability of different ego organizations occurs within a short time-span. In comparing the familiar model of early therapist-child interaction in which, despite great anxiety, conflict breaks through and some give and take is achieved with Ted's behavior, the remoteness and frozen quality of his contributions and the rigid ways in which he has structured his and the therapist's roles are striking. Ted maintained an almost complete emotional insularity. Furthermore, one senses a devitalizing of the therapist, as if the therapist had been rendered a lifeless tool, or automaton, whose role it is to facilitate the complex mechanics of living. At each point that the therapist attempted to assert his independence, and to break out of the assigned role of silent partner and mechanical assistant, the child withdrew—yet without agitation, as if simply to shut out the distressing intrusion and thereby cause it to disappear. We suggest that this kind of transference manifestation finds its psychological model in earliest infancy, at an autistic level of development, before the child experiences the mother as a separate person.

Throughout this period and particularly during Ted's explorations, the therapist reports that he frequently felt as if he were following a little ghost who if touched would vanish. And indeed the child's communication with the therapist in these hours is characterized by a seeming emptiness, abortiveness, and inhibition in the spheres of play, verbal interaction, and affective response. Yet, despite the paucity of direct communication, if we permit our imaginative faculties to range freely and to work upon the clues which the child provides, we may perhaps gain some idea of the psychological world of this borderline child, which reflects itself in this autistic mode of relationship.

We speculate briefly, with no attempt to delineate its many meanings, about the psychological significance of the child's exploration of the physical plant of the house, and his bringing along a map of the city, which was his constant companion during this early treatment phase. They suggest a child who is frightened and lost in a world of disorder and imminent disaster, and who is actively seeking to achieve some inner and outer order by external means. And we may—via the map and with recognition of its extraordinary uselessness to a seven year old child— gain some idea of the child's desperation and his frantic and unsuccessful reaching out with the aid of a mechanical and useless device for the clarity and identity which he so urgently desires. Just as the child seeks to evaluate the new person of the therapist by the faulty method of avoiding the therapist and exploring the physical terrain, so he seeks to insure his psychological integrity and safety by carrying a map which he cannot read. At times, the disorder which the child perceives rises painfully to consciousness (as in the hour where he complained he could not play because the blocks were mixed up) and abruptly disrupts his capacity to play.

In observing the mode of the child's expression in this initial period, we are struck by the faultiness of the methods which he employs in order to deal with his anxiety, with the primitive and unintegrated nature of his defenses and of the magical thinking from which they derive, and with the absence of affective response throughout. The use of the external device of the map to achieve an ordering of his inner psychological world can be viewed as a forerunner of an obsessive-compulsive defense which has not yet been integrated into the personality. We note that the map is not only a magical device but represents an imitative playing out of an adult role; we surmise, partly on the basis of our knowledge of other borderline children, that imitation and cue-taking, rather than true identification, govern various aspects of Ted's behavior. Further, we may speculate that the map symbolizes Ted's way of maintaining reality anchorage in this autistic phase, by the substitution of a mechanical contact with a total panorama of reality and with a largely inanimate reality, for live contact with its various parts. In effect, it would seem that here a total, diffuse, and confused surface contact replaces meaningful relationships.

Within a brief period of four weeks, the relationship underwent a perceptible change as Ted began to demand that the therapist act almost as his double. He commanded the therapist to build his own trains at the far end of the playroom. He separated blocks for himself and the therapist by a special system of markings and directed the therapist to build alongside of his own building. In his play with the trains he kept switching his own trains from track to track and ordering the therapist to do likewise, so rapidly and confusedly, that his intent seemed to be to "keep the therapist off the track" and to confuse communication to such an extent as to render it unintelligible. Yet his conflicted yearning for a closer relationship broke through at times when he occasionally built a connecting line between his freight yard and that of the therapist, only to disrupt it quickly, or when his blocks inevitably became confused in play with those which he had marked for the therapist. Once his request for help was expressed in his attempts to push a long train with a very small block which he designated as the engine and which seemed to reflect the heavy load he felt so powerless to carry unaided. At the same time, he made curt, officious, and urgent demands for toys evidently not in the playroom as if to establish a priori the incapacity of the therapist to fulfill his many needs.

Throughout this period, the child continued to maintain his vacuous facial expression. Although his explorations of the house ceased, he began each hour with a few minutes of aimless searching around the playroom as if telescopically to recapitulate what had gone on before. He developed a new symptom of saying "urp" continually, and at very frequent intervals, which became more pronounced in moments of heightened tension.

Ted began to seek the therapist's protection also by offering him his scissors to carry and characteristically ended each hour by dictating a strongly worded sign for the therapist to write ordering everyone entering the playroom to leave his house and trains untouched. He was hyperalert to every change in the playroom and complained of any difference in the toys from one hour to the next. He indicated in manifold ways his inability to tolerate the intrusion of another person into the relationship between himself and the therapist and his desperate wish and demand that the therapist protect the continuity and immutability of the status quo. The strongly eroticized fantasies accompanying these transference developments were strikingly revealed when Ted told his mother that he had gotten all wet in a therapy hour because he and the therapist had gone swimming together and, in many ways at home, he hinted darkly at "goings on" in his therapy which he utilized to taunt his parents.

The dominant cast of the relationship which Ted imposed in this second phase of treatment finds its legendary prototype in the story of Aladdin as the leitmotif of the magical, all-powerful giant, subject to the child's absolute domination and permitting no independent existence. It was here played out between child and therapist. Ted's genie is the projected therapist who was instructed to imitate his little master from a respectful distance, and commanded to do away with change by various magical devices including the sign, which the child carefully dictated at the termination of each hour. He is an exciting and dangerous genie about whom erotic fantasies are woven and who must be kept at a careful distance, bottled up or let out in accord with the child's wishes and needs. Most significantly, his identity is fused with that of the child. And if we think of symbiotic identification as a stage of development in which the young child seeks to achieve mastery by being the powerful or beloved person, then we may suggest that Ted defends himself against the fantasied dangers of an interpersonal relationship by a symbiotic-like fusion with the therapist.

With the aid of the tale of the sorcerer's apprentice we may gain some idea of the grave perils which the symbiotic identification attempts to avoid. The venturesome little apprentice of the story tries to separate himself prematurely from his symbiotic relationship with the sorcerer. Before he has fully assimilated the magical spells (or before he has achieved true identification with the sorcerer), he attempts imitatively to play the sorcerer's role only to find himself disastrously unable to control the upsurging flood of his aggressive and sexual impulses. Significantly he is rescued not by his own devices but by the return of the powerful sorcerer, i.e., by return of the symbiotic relationship.

It is of particular interest that Ted instructed the therapist to imitate his own play activities at the far side of the playroom, and we may, via this segment of behavior, elaborate briefly on the particular psychological meaning of this symbiotic relationship in this borderline child. For, implied in this distance which the child establishes between himself and the therapist, and implied in the duplication he imposes, there is both his recognition of separation and his tentative and fearful beginning moves toward object differentiation and a neurotic mode of relationship.

Thus, a noteworthy difference between the symbiotic relationship of this phase of therapy as compared with his beginning unawareness of the therapist's presence, except insofar as the therapist served as a necessary or useful tool, is the admission of the therapist into the child's psychological orbit. Yet this admission is carefully and fearfully controlled, and with the aid of a symbiotic fusion fantasy, kept safely within bounds. Implicit, however, in the child's demands that the therapist imitate him and not he the therapist, is the recognition of separateness which presages the neurotic relationship to follow.

In this second phase, there are many indications of the autistic mode which preceded it, as well as of the more neurotic mode ahead. For instance, the sign which the child dictates at the end of the hour resembles the map of his earlier phase in being a faulty, external device, designed to achieve an inner psychological goal of continuity of the status quo. Yet it is here transposed up the developmental ladder, for it appears now within the framework of a symbiotic relationship. Or, further, the vacant searching of the playroom which begins each hour replaces the aimless exploration of the total house which figured so prominently in early days.

The beginnings of a neurotic relationship which attract attention are expressed by the child in his dimly disguised appeal for help as he plays out the overburdened little engine and in his abortive and somewhat wistful play at building connecting lines between his trains and those which he has separated for the therapist. Most significant, perhaps, is his new symptom of saying "urp" which can be thought of as a neurotic symptom reflecting a deep infantile wish, breaking through toward expression, and a searching for contact and infantile gratification. It is interesting that the "urping" symptom disappeared during a later phase of therapy when the child threw a ball repeatedly for the therapist to retrieve and in ecstasy clapped his hands, saying "da-da" like a small baby.

In the twelfth therapy hour, Ted began shortly after the hour commenced to call for the therapist by name on the toy telephone and after hanging up several times when the therapist responded "Hello," he finally continued the telephone contact and made a series of requests for toys obviously not in the playroom, culminating in a demand for a magic wand. He followed this interplay by animatedly acting like a roaring bull and picking up a little toy bull, directing the horns first outward and then toward himself. He then announced that another world was about to destroy this world. He constructed a peaceful scene with the ranch house toys, and then proceeded vigorously to scatter the pieces, identifying himself as an outer-space monster. He talked of cities being annihilated, of worlds colliding, of tornadoes striking, and threw a ball around the room knocking over the toys with force and abandon. Once when he paused anxiously and the therapist suggested that his wish to destroy had frightened him, he quickly rebuilt the fence of the ranch house, asking softly how the therapist knew.

To the following hour Ted brought the therapist a little box car he had brought from home, which he had previously requested unsuccessfully of the therapist and which he now presented with much ceremony, asking the therapist to close his eyes. Immediately following this, Ted picked up the little toy telephone and asked for Daddy. When the therapist responded, Ted instructed him to hang up and talked briefly to his father saying that he loved him and wanted him, rather than the therapist, to get the little box car. For the remainder of this session, Ted played out an excited battle between good and mean soldiers and at the end of the hour commented that it would be forty-eight hours before their next meeting.

Ted again brought some trains from home to the next hour and built a line of the playroom trains, connecting them with the trains which he had brought from home, excluding only one little car, which he ran around the long train, ramming into it at intervals.

In a subsequent session, Ted asked to take the therapist to the school shop where he demonstrated a lively curiosity in many things and how they work, and proudly displayed his recent accomplishments. Once he pointed to the electric switch, stating, "That controls the robots." During the session when a "mean old man" destroyed the three mountains, leaving the fourth mountain intact, Ted noticed that the therapist had taken out a cigarette. After inquiring what brand the therapist smoked, he suggested that the therapist change his brand to Luckies. He found a little harmonica and proceeded to spend ten minutes playing with it, rocking back and forth in a little rocking chair in a trancelike state. Then he announced abruptly that a tornado was due to strike, and so it did, joined by a meteor storm which quickly reduced the room to a shambles leaving untouched, however, the corner where the therapist was seated.

The marked change in relationship between child and therapist which appeared in these hours was abruptly and dramatically introduced when Ted called the therapist and made requests of him across the shortened distance defined by the toy telephone. The child's use of the therapist's name in this interplay gains significance against the background of his initial almost total obliviousness to the therapist's person and his subsequent inability to grant the therapist an independent existence. However, as Ted proceeded to make free use of play medium to create and communicate his inner world and as he expressed his conflicted and fearful yearning for the protective closeness which he felt the therapist could provide, there was considerable resemblance to the play-therapy sessions of a neurotic child. The neurotic relationship mode which was hinted at in the preceding phases had gradually come to provide the dominant cast for the transference manifestations. And although this neurotic transference relationship formed a continuum with the two preceding phases and embraced all of the relationship modes which we have distinguished, earlier and more regressed manifestations were now only fleetingly and more subtly discernible.

A comparison of the child's construction of four mountains in the sand box with the aimless searching characteristic of his early therapy, highlights some of the changes which have occurred. In the sandbox play, Ted actively created his psychological landscape. The three mountains represented his parents and himself, and the distant mountain represented the therapist. The little car which traveled ceaselessly around the mountains described, among its many meanings, the peregrinations and vicissitudes of the therapy journey and the precariously felt position of the child in this discouraged search for clarity and stability. We note that an active creative ego, capable of vivid and live communication and intent on mastery, is evident in the sandbox play. Yet, the endless wanderings of the little car and the sand mountain construction recapitulate, on this higher neurotic level of ego organization, the theme of the map and the unceasing search of the house expressed earlier in the autistic phase of the relationship. Thus, through the screen of the neurotic level of integration, one cannot fail to be impressed with the marked difference between these two levels of ego functioning.

The transition in relationship mode which impels our interest is here infinitely better expressed by the child in his construction of the fourth amorphous mountain, the therapist mountain, rising out of the "rough country." For in the symbol of the mountain rising dimly out of the distance, we may see a graphic and in fact poetic representation of the emergence of the figure of the therapist into the child's psychological ken. As this figure became more clearly perceived and recognized and acquired a name, the child gradually entered into a more differentiated object-relationship mode, and was able to sustain the therapist's presence as a protective figure who could be relied upon to withstand even tornadoes and meteor storms.

In this third phase of the initial treatment period, the child finally gave full expression to his profound preoccupation with separation and abandonment. The child could express these fantasies of separation only at the point when he was able to separate himself from the therapist, and only within the context of a predominantly neurotic relationship. Some of the content which underlay his behavior from the start can be formulated as follows: "If I love the therapist I will lose my parents," or "If I turn to Father I will lose Mother." These themes emerge vividly in his play with the little car which is excluded from the long line of trains, in combining trains from home with those in the playroom. And his struggle with conflicting loyalties is openly demonstrated in his loving gesture of the gift of the little car to the therapist, which wipes out his previous disappointment in the therapist and which is accompanied by the reminder of prior loyalty to his father.

With the aid of these elaborations we can retrace our steps and more confidently understand the content of his beginning hours. Woven into all of Ted's behavior during the entire period which we have described, is his despairing recognition of conflict between his parents, of his own adoptive and vulnerable status, his fear of imminent abandonment, and his perception of the therapist as the ally of the parents in their dark plans for his destruction, as seen in the two trains which combine to exclude the little car. It is interesting to add corroboratively that during this period his teachers observed that when other children attacked Ted, which they did partly because he offered himself so readily as a target, his chief concern was as to which of various weapons they would employ, as if clearly anticipating attack and wondering only from what quarter it would appear.

Ted's fantasy is not unfamiliar in the therapy of children, although the degree to which he experiences it as totally catastrophic and without possible solution may, as we have suggested, be specific for the nature of his illness. What is striking, however, is the distinctive ego organization of this borderline child, which within a span of sixteen sessions fluctuates in its use of autistic, symbiotic, and neurotic relationship modes, thereby reflecting the coexistence and coavailability of different ego organizations. It is this phenomenon which we have seen so frequently in all of these children whom we have studied.

We observe that the first significant indication of the child's capacity to sustain a neurotic relationship with the therapist is accompanied almost immediately by a fantasy of worlds colliding and a destructive monster from out of space. Since outer-space life has become so much part of contemporary culture, one must exercise caution in drawing conclusions from its introduction per se. Yet, the timing and content of space fantasies, which appear so frequently in the treatment of these children, have led us to assign to them a special psychological meaning as distance defenses, whose collective function it is to achieve maximal distance between the unconscious conflict and the conscious ego. Therefore it is of special interest that, just as a separation from the symbiotic relationship mode, the space fantasy too becomes immediately apparent and necessary as the neurotic relationship emerges. We have conceived of the space fantasy's function as in part that of a safety valve which permits the maintaining of the neurotic relationship while at the same time representing a necessary return to more regressed modes of relationship. This material suggests corroboratively that these distance fantasies become necessary only within the framework of a tenuous neurotic relationship, where the constancy of the object cathexis is continually imperiled.

Ted's first space fantasy appeared within the context of impossible demands made on the therapist for toys and a magic wand and his frustration at the latter's inability to supply his needs. The strong aggressive and sexual urges rising to expression were evident in the play which followed with the little toy bull, and it was at this point that the first outer-space fantasy ensued. We suggest that in Ted's play with the little toy bull, such strong aggressive feelings were mobilized that the little bull no longer sufficed to carry their full charge, and in fearful retreat from the rising anxiety the child introduced the space fantasy, to protect both himself and the therapist from the dangerous fantasies which had been stimulated. Or, stated differently, Ted's impulses had grown beyond the capacity of the neurotic defenses to contain them and forced a temporary reversion to a more primitive ego state.

The child's fantasy of the electric switch controlling robots permits some brief speculations referring back to the ego mechanism of control which we have previously postulated. If we think of the machine as a projection of sexuality and aggression, then the content of the fantasy may describe the degree of control which the patient experiences in relation to his own impulses, which would be in inverse ratio to the distance which he sets between himself and his machine. It is this capacity for the degree of control reflected in this fantasy that helps to demarcate the borderline status of our patients from the overt schizophrenic.

The world of every child, his mode of thought and perception, differs markedly from that of the adult therapist. And it is necessary in the therapy of all children to devise and create ways of living oneself into the world of childhood. This difference and the attendant difficulties in understanding and communication increase sevenfold in work with the borderline and psychotic child. His psychological world is not only alien to the logical adult mind of the therapist but is characterized by a fluidity of ego organization which can hardly be captured in the therapist's conscious recollection of his own childhood. This wide gulf separating patient from therapist has faced us with formidable problems of many kinds. At the same time it has provided the chief stimulus and challenge to the work which we are attempting.

REFERENCES

[1] Freud, S. Civilization and Its Discontents, New York, Norton, 1930.

[2] Menninger, K. A. Psychological aspects of the organism under stress. Part I: The homeostatic regulatory function of the ego. Part II: Regulatory devices of the ego under major stress, J. Amer. Psychoanal. Ass., 2:67 and 280, 1954.

[3] Fliess, R. The Revival of Interest in the Dream. New York, International Universities Press, 1953.

[4] Knight, R. P. Borderline states, Bull. Menninger Clin., 17:1, 1953.

[5] Hoffer, W. The mutual influences in the development of ego and id: earliest stages, Psychoanal. Stud. Child, 7:31, 1952.

[6] Kanner, L. Autistic disturbances of affective contact, The Nervous Child, 2:217, 1943.

[7] Mahler, M. S. On child psychosis and schizophrenia: autistic and symbiotic infantile psychoses, Psychoanal. Stud. Child, 7:286, 1952.

[8] Federn, P. Ego Psychology and the Psychoses, New York, Basic Books, 1952; and Isakower, O. A contribution to the pathopsychology of phenomena associated with falling asleep, Int. J. Psychoanal., 19:331, 1938.

5

OBSERVATIONS ON THE
PSYCHOTHERAPY OF BORDERLINE
AND PSYCHOTIC CHILDREN *

> . . . My endeavors should be directed to persons and char-
> acters supernatural, or at least romantic; yet so as to transfer
> from our inward nature a human interest and a semblance of
> truth sufficient to procure for these shadows of imagination that
> willing suspension of disbelief for the moment, which consti-
> tutes poetic faith.
>
> SAMUEL TAYLOR COLERIDGE

In the preceding chapter we reported several observations regarding the
ego psychology of borderline and psychotic children. We described the
fluctuating availability of different ego organizations in these children,
ranging from psychotic manifestations to advanced achievement appropriate to chronological age. These observations have various implications
for psychotherapy. In this paper we shall attempt to examine some of the
technical problems of interpretation which arise in the treatment of these
children. Furthermore, since our primary goal is the enrichment of
clinical skill, we shall describe some technical modifications which
gradually took shape in accommodating to the particular ego attributes
of these clinical groups.

We may take the well-known story of Hansel and Gretel as our
common point of departure. For the psychoanalyst and the small child,
this fairy tale is a story of conflict which gathers dramatic strength as it
moves regressively from one level of ego organization to another. The
mother image in the fairy tale appears in at least two successive guises:
first as a stepmother plotting to banish the children and separate them
from their loving father, and later as a witch inside a candy house who

* Judith Wallerstein is coauthor of this chapter.

means to devour them. Thus, the story follows a regressive pathway in developing the theme of the rejecting and vengeful mother figure, and the children's attempt to master this threat. For it retreats from secondary-process thinking, moving from the suspiciousness of the children at the outset to the paranoid projection of the devouring witch. In libidinal terms, the dominant oedipal and phallic elements in the stepmother figure give way increasingly to primitive, oral, cannibalistic fantasies. (We say "increasingly," since the witch certainly has attributes associated with stages more advanced than the oral stage, as do regressions in our patients as well.) On an ego level, action begins with an attempt to outsmart the parents and eventuates regressively in destruction by incorporation and trickery.

The divergence between the children's relationship to the stepmother and to the witch additionally points to the changing dominance of different ego organizations. The hostility to the stepmother is within the confines of an established object relationship, and the solution proposed, namely separation, reflects a neurotic ego with a consolidated core of identity and beginning capacity for independent activity. The relationship with the witch, by contrast, falls within primitive "either/or" bounds suggesting a predominantly hostile symbiosis, and the major solution offered is the incorporation of the bad object.

It is important to bear in mind that the Hansel and Gretel story expresses the repetitive statement of conflict at different levels of ego achievement which can be distinguished primarily in terms of the degree of dominance of one ego organization over others. Clearly, ego organizations are numerous and overlapping. Their complex hierarchical structure and functional interrelationships range along a continuum which does not permit absolute distinctions.

We may now transpose the fairy tale to the clinic and assume it to be an original fantasy of little Gretel in therapy. If we assume Gretel to be suffering with a neurotic illness, the therapist has a variety of interpretive choices which are well known in child analysis. He may, for instance, link the content of the stories of both stepmother and the witch directly to conflict with the mother. He may alternately stress defense against conflict by calling attention to the significant resemblances between the two story parts and by noting the regressive transition from stepmother to witch. Or he may employ what we shall call "metaphoric interpretation" and fashion his remarks around the witch and the frightened children in order temporarily to help maintain a distance of the fantasy from the conscious awareness of the child. He can, in effect, move with relative freedom in appropriately making use of the range of interpretive possibilities. For he can rely upon his patient's achievement of a neurotic level of ego functioning, upon the relative stability of the child's ego state, and upon the relative strength of neurotic defenses. To return to our example, he can depend upon the immediacy of Gretel's conflict with the mother which has its roots in early fixations expressed in the fantasy of the witch, and can gradually bring this conflict into the realm of full recognition.

If, however, we assume little Gretel to be a borderline or psychotic child several inferences can be drawn regarding her ego organization which operate to constrict the therapist's freedom of interpretive choice. For such a child, the "neurotic"* relationship with the stepmother represents one outpost of advanced ego achievement whose connection with earlier and more primitive ego achievements is tenuous and intermittent. Accordingly, for a borderline or psychotic Gretel, the image of the witch draws the main cathexis, and the associated fantasies of cannibalistic fusion are experienced as fearsome reality. Moreover, the fragility of the neurotic defenses exposes the borderline or psychotic child to the imminent threat of psychotic upheaval.

In the therapy of neurotic children, interpretations are addressed primarily to the more mature ego achievements. In the treatment of borderline and psychotic children, however, such interpretations often results in panic and the precipitous disruption of contact. Or they may succeed in superimposing a pseudo secondary process upon a shaky foundation, as a concession to an outer demand for social adjustment and conformity.

We have had many opportunities in residential treatment to observe the extensive use which borderline and psychotic children make of imitation and cue-taking. These imitative mechanisms are of considerable help to these children as they try to find their way through the intricacies of social intercourse and daily routine. But the very success of these mechanisms should not obscure the dangers of perpetuating and strengthening their use in psychotherapy.

Clinical material is drawn from the second year of Ann's treatment, when she was eleven. This schizophrenic child, previously mentioned (Chapter 4), had impulses and fantasies closely akin to our psychotic fairy-tale Gretel, which illustrate the consequences of interpretive techniques addressed to different levels of ego organization. In this first excerpt the therapist offers an interpretation which would be appropriate in the treatment of a neurotic patient. This interpretation, focusing on a trans-

---

* Our use of "neurotic" refers to the neurotic manifestations of the ego which may be present in different kinds of personality organizations, including psychotic personalities.

ference displacement which the child had employed for several weeks, triggers a psychotic regression.

Ann found a piece of paper in the playroom where one of the other children had printed, "Jimmy will be upset and he will act it." Ann asked, "Dorothy, did you write this?" I asked if she thought I would write something like that. Ann replied that she did not think so because I would use script if I had written it. I asked if that was the only way she was sure that I hadn't. Ann disregarded my comment and went on to try to figure out which one of the children had written the note. She assured me Jimmy was doing better. "Sometimes," she said, "Jimmy is very aggressive, but that is good for him because he needs to get it out of his system." She then said Mary was "at it again." Mary had told Ann that all the kids did not like her and that was not true, was it? I thought that Ann would be the one to know if it were true. Ann said she was trying to figure out these old problems. Wasn't she stronger than her problems? I thought perhaps she was. But, she continued, she was still so afraid of Mary, and what was she going to do about that? I told Ann I thought the feeling she had toward me and the feeling she had toward Mary were both expressions of the feeling she had toward her mother. At the present time, Mary stands for the bad mother whom Ann fears, and I for the good mother whom Ann tries to please and who doesn't hurt her. Ann said, "Oh, dear, Dorothy, this mother problem is a big one." I thought so, too. Ann continued that this mother problem was about the biggest she had now. Would her mother understand if she had to act silly? I thought so, although it was hard for Mother always to be understanding. Ann was sitting in the chair beside me and said, "Oh, Dorothy, here it comes. I feel like being silly. What will I do? What will I do?" She began rolling around in the chair, smelling her hands and squirming. She exclaimed: "Dorothy, what are you going to do?" I said I would like to try to help her understand these feelings. Ann got up and said she needed to tell me about a number that had to do with the numbers in the 20s. She used to have several numbers that bothered her, 9, 12, and 15. But these don't bother her any more. This last number is the only one left now, but it is the biggest one of all. She began rolling around, saying, "Oh, how often does this have to come up? Oh, Dorothy, what will I do?"

It is likely that the therapist was misled at the beginning of the hour by what seemed to be the child's relatively "neurotic" functioning, and accordingly interpreted the displacement to Mary, much as one would with a neurotic child. Ann's response demonstrates the tenuousness of her adjustment: it could not be sufficiently maintained to permit either the integration of the interpretation or its rejection by neurotic means. For as the displacement was interpreted, transference feelings and impulses previously bound by this mechanism could be warded off only by regression. In effect, the therapist's interpretation was directed at secondary-process thinking and was understood, but without consolidated secondary-process mediation and without capacity to synthesize or defend against the implications of this interpretation on a neurotic level. Consequently, it triggered a collapse of ego boundaries and the ensuing invasion of the ego by primary-process material—an action accompanied by acute suffering.

Ann's use of displacement is relevant to the problem of interpretive choice. In general, the mechanism of displacement represents a relatively advanced achievement in the hierarchy of defenses. For it is associated with the differentiation of self from the outer world, and its efficacy as a defense maneuver can be said in large part to be predicated upon the stable cathexis of ego and object boundaries. In the neurotic patient, displacement is a mechanism available prior to therapy which becomes manifest within the context of the transference neurosis. For the psychotic child, however, the ability to use displacement as a defense frequently signals a significant progress because it is associated with a growing capacity to maintain object cathexis.

The interview cited occurred at a time in treatment when the transference was in the process of becoming consolidated on a neurotic level, but when psychotic transference manifestations were still very much in evidence. Consequently, the interpretation was premature in its failure to appreciate the fragility of the newly acquired ego functions and to recognize their close interdependence with the cathexis of the therapist. Ann's capacity to displace certain hostile and sexual impulses was of central importance in safeguarding the relationship with the therapist. As the displacement yielded, associated functions of ego-boundary maintenance and object cathexis became strained to the breaking point.

To return briefly to Hansel and Gretel, our selection of this story was based in part on its ending. When the children came home, they were surprised to learn that the stepmother somehow had died in their absence. The fairy tale thus conceals from the conscious awareness of the children the connection between their murder of the witch and the nondisplaced death wish toward the stepmother, and thereby makes it possible for them to return safely home. In keeping with the views offered here, the fairy tale maintains the psychological distance between witch and mother and refrains from adding to the already overburdened children a direct recognition which they could not bear.

The following interview excerpt which is drawn from approximately the same general period of treatment is offered to illustrate a successful attempt to employ interpretation within the mode of thought and level of ego functioning as manifested in the child's communication. For the

understanding of this material it should be known that Ann's father had
been mentally ill and had committed suicide while undergoing therapy.

Ann came in with a big package wrapped up in foil paper and told
me she had brought me a present. There was a piece of cake for herself
and for me. I exclaimed how wonderful it was that we could have a party.
Ann barely touched her cake and wandered aimlessly about the room and
finally stopped and stared for a long time at a smear of ink on the far
wall. She turned to me and said, "Dorothy, see the sign of death." I repeated, "Yes, Ann, the sign of death." She stared at it and then put her
arm out straight and started walking toward it, slowly saying in a frightened
voice, "How close am I to it, Dorothy? How many inches?" I gauged the
inches and when she got real close she drew back. Then she silently went
toward it again and as she drew close to it, she asked me how close she was.
Then she touched it and in a wild panic turned and ran back toward me,
holding out the finger which had touched the sign of death, saying, "Oh,
Dorothy, do something." I took hold of her hand and kissed her finger at
the end. She said, "Oh, Dorothy, you saved me." I said, "Yes, I would
never let the sign of death hurt you, Ann." She quickly left me and went
over to the mirror and started sucking, with her lips pressed hard against
the glass. Then she came back to the table and took a small piece of clay
which she placed just barely below the sign of death and told me that the
clay was on her side and it was safer. I said I was on her side, too, and did
we also need the clay? Ann affirmed that the clay was safer. I asked if it
would save her better than I could. Ann said no, that the clay and I would
both save her. I suggested maybe that was a good idea because the clay
wouldn't frighten her as much as I did. Ann made no reply but again
went through the approach to the sign of death, but only touched the
clay. Then she took a pencil and approached the wall, telling me it took
fifteen seconds for the sign of death to run through the pencil and into
her arm and for me to keep track by the clock and tell her when ten
seconds were up. I warned her at ten seconds and she threw the pencil
into the sand pile, asking anxiously what would happen if she had held
it the full fifteen seconds. I told her I would not have let her hold it that
long. I was here to keep her from getting hurt and I wasn't going to let
anything happen to her. Although she felt very close to the sign of death
at times, I would never stop looking after her and we would never leave
her alone, as they had left her father. Ann said, "Johnny is a poor little
kid. He doesn't have a mother and I don't have a father." I repeated, "Yes,
poor little kids." Ann said, "Dorothy, I wish you would have Johnny in
therapy because he needs a therapist. And I think you're the best therapist
in the School." I replied that that pleased me because maybe she thought
she was getting help from me, too. Ann said she knew she was better,
but after all they had thought her father was better, too. I asked, "Yes,
and you wondered whether we might be mistaken, too, about your being
better?" Ann said, "Sometimes my father scared me."

The child employs the magic thought and gesture of the primary process as her only available way of expressing suicidal impulses. She requests and receives help from the therapist in terms of the primary process. As the interview proceeds, her anxiety noticeably lessens and she is finally able to discuss, in secondary-process language, her relationship with her father. We note, therefore, a shift from psychotic to neurotic ego state which, we suggest, resulted primarily from the therapist's understanding of the most central aspect of the child's communication, and the therapist's ability to interpret effectively within the context of the regression.

In the first part of this hour Ann recaptures a magical mode of thought deriving from a developmental stage when reality and fantasy are blended and when the secondary process has not yet become sufficiently established to separate thought from action. Magical thinking is commonly synonymous with omnipotent thinking. Yet, from the vantage point of maturity, thinking which is inseparable from action fails to achieve the primary purpose of all thought which is trial action. Therefore, magical thought from the perspective of the mature ego is ineffectual thought; its use bespeaks the weakness of the ego.

Ann's regression and mounting panic culminating in her cry of "do something" arise from an immobilizing dilemma. Her urgent need to confess her suicidal preoccupations is opposed by her terror that in so doing she will be compelled to act them out. In acceding to the child's frantic request by means of a magical protective gesture, the therapist deliberately employs the primary-process language of the child's communication. In this way the therapist expresses understanding not only of the affective content of the communication but of the ego weakness to which the child confesses and of the psychotic ego state itself. Furthermore, the assurance of protection combined with full acceptance of the child's terrifying fantasy is designed to help drive a wedge between thought and action. Ann responds by regaining sufficient psychological equilibrium to express the same content in a more mature, more reality-anchored way. Thus, by taking hold of the therapist's hand and symbolically, in primary-process language, of her strength as well, the child has for the moment achieved the capacity to separate thought from action and is thereby enabled to proceed.

This kind of interpretive response which we have variously called "interpretation within the regression" or "interpretation within the metaphor" involves, to paraphrase Coleridge, "a willing suspension of disbelief in unreality for the moment." Such interpretation rests upon the temporary willingness to assume that the patient's grossly distorted perceptions reflect outer reality, because they accurately reflect his inner psychological reality and the state of his ego which has temporarily lost the capacity to differentiate between inner and outer reality. At the same time, the interpretive response remains firmly anchored in the secondary-process world. For it is predicated upon the therapist's conscious metaphoric use of the patient's regressed language in order to convey understanding of his inner world and feelings in the only way immediately available to the patient, namely, the language of regression. Accordingly, in the material cited, the therapist accepted the projection of omnipotence and acted in a manner entirely consonant with the child's magical expectations. In this way, she employed the primary process of the child's communication as a metaphor designed to convey her assurance of continuing love and protection, in direct response to the child's expressed fears of being deserted and left to commit suicide.

It may be helpful to distinguish between interpretation within the regression and the kind of metaphoric interpretation which can be used with any neurotic patient, depending upon the personal style of the analyst. In metaphoric interpretations, in which the therapist's immediate response uses the metaphor of the patient's communication, there follows rapidly an explication which elaborates meaning and intent in mature secondary-process language. Interpretation within the regression, however, is predicated on the assumption that the patient's ego state directly reflects the extent of his ability to come to terms with the conflict. Therefore, communication remains within the confines of the patient's expression until some future time in the treatment when the patient himself indicates his capacity for fuller understanding.

Interpretation within the regression, furthermore, is often a direct result of the therapist's primary aim which is to maintain the relationship and prevent the disruption of contact. Borderline and psychotic children readily regress to a prior stage of development in which human contact was tenuous. Consequently, such regressions threaten rupture of all object relationships, including the relationship with the therapist. We recall that in the last interview cited, Ann screamed for help almost as if the therapist were not present. By attempting to follow the child into this state of attenuated human contact, the therapist tries to uphold the object ties on whatever level possible. For by returning with the child to ego stages where contact is almost disrupted and by reliving early experiences, primitive transferences are evoked or maintained which can serve as the foundation for new and more mature identifications. This maintenance of the therapeutic relationship, often made possible by interpreting within the regression, thus lays the foundation for the new development of identificatory processes rather than the superimposition of an imitative façade. It is by the continual repetition of such experiences that the secondary process can emerge and extend its dominance.

As in any other therapy with children, interpretive work with the borderline and psychotic child proceeds gradually to more mature levels. Clearly, every psychotherapy seeks not only to comprehend the child's world but must ultimately help the child to understand the world of reality. As regressive trends lessen and as the neurotic aspects of the child's ego become stabilized, interpretations aim at giving insight and thus eventually approximate those used with the neurotic child.

Sometimes these changes will appear very slowly over a long period of time. Sometimes the child will mark the turning point dramatically by describing a previously highly cathected fantasy as science fiction, by projecting responsibility for its emergence upon the therapist, by stating, as did one nine year old to his therapist after months of painstaking work, "Space patrol? Really this is 1953, not 2053. You must have been dreaming." These are among the clinical signs which indicate that the child's ego has achieved sufficient strength for the therapist to relinquish the special interpretive measures which had been previously required.

From its beginning, analytic work with children has been based upon departures from the basic model of classical analytical technique as originally worked out for adult patients. These changes were necessitated by the special psychological attributes of childhood, namely, by the immaturity of the child's ego and consequent inability to maintain a relatively intact level of ego functioning and by the resulting dependency. In their impact upon the basic treatment model, the special ego attributes of borderline and psychotic children can be viewed as extensions of psychological attributes common to all children in comparison to adults. The interpretive techniques here elaborated also represent not innovations so much as further adaptations of methods which have already been constructed for the therapy of the neurotic child.

The chief technical difficulty in the psychotherapy of borderline and psychotic children is how to respond to the rapidly changing need systems and modes of expression of these children in order ultimately to develop secondary-process potentialities to their fullest. The approach described essentially aims at working with that part of the ego that is intact, at whatever developmental level that may be, in this way enabling the ego ultimately to achieve a higher level of functioning. Communication remains within primary-process fantasy and modes of expression *until the patient has acquired on each such occasion the strength to move to a more mature position.* Interpretation within the regression, in the sense here defined, is an effective tool for the accomplishment of the therapeutic task.

PART THREE

COMMUNION, COMMUNICATION, AND INTERPRETATION

When there is a minimum of distance between allusion and what is alluded to, the analyst gives the patient words to express feelings just rising to the surface and thereby facilitates their becoming conscious.

This procedure of deducing what the patient actually means and telling it to him is called interpretation.

OTTO FENICHEL

6

THE NATURE OF THE INTERPRETIVE PROCESS

I should not like my writing to spare other people the trouble of thinking; but, if possible, to stimulate someone to thoughts of his own.

LUDWIG WITTGENSTEIN

In his *Confessions* St. Augustine stated that he knew what *time* was only as long as nobody asked him. It may be assumed, then, that he was familiar with the usage of the concept of time although he could not offer a satisfactory definition. I propose to take the same attitude concerning the concept of interpretation. I shall, therefore, conduct a survey concerning its meaning within the historically given natural language,[1] which will include the pre- and extra-analytic use of the term *interpretation* before tracing the concept in Freud's writings. While I differentiate between interpretation in the sense of scientific explanation and in the sense of technical intervention, my stress will be on aspects of the concept of interpretation which concern its function as technical intervention. Some questions will be raised on validation problems and intuitive aspects of interpretive work. Finally, the total interpretive process will be considered within the framework of modern ego psychology.

Dwelling on existing problem areas, I want my thoughts to be understood as open questions rather than as implied answers. These questions, I believe, are a consequence of progress in our field and need fullest consideration in order to ensure further growth of our technical competence as well as our theoretical insights.

Rather than attempting an explicit definition of the psychoanalytic concept of interpretation, I will try at first to throw some light on selected aspects of this concept which determine certain of its psychological characteristics as well as its logical place in nonscientific or scientific context. The extra- and pre-analytic meanings of the concept may help us to find

125

its logical and psychological place within our specific field of operation.

The difficulties of this inquiry into the ordinary use of the word *interpretation* are increased by the fact that the German words *Interpretation* and *Deutung* are both translated into English as *interpretation*. The Webster and Oxford dictionaries say that the verb *to interpret* is used in terms of *explaining* or *translating*, and that it is synonymous with *to expand* and *to elucidate*; also, that it may be applied to language, dreams, signs, conduct, mysteries, and religion. The verb is also employed to mean *to understand* or *to appreciate* in the light of individual belief, interest, or judgment; as an equivalent for the verb *to construe*, it can be used in the context of interpreting actions, intentions, and legal contracts.

A wide range of the verb usage has to do with the attempt to *apprehend* something or to *represent* it by means of art; to show something by means of illustrative representation. It may also be used in the sense that an actor may interpret a character, a musician a work of music, a painter a landscape, and the like.

The noun *interpretation* is used as a substitute for *explanation*, *exposition*, giving a different, a special version, or construction, as, for example, in the interpretation of dreams. The noun also refers to *translation* from one language into the other, or *oral translation* by interpreters. Further, it refers to *construction* which is placed on actions and to the religious meaning of passages of the Scriptures given in different ways by different interpreters. *Interpretation* also refers to *representation* in performance, delivery, or criticism of the thought and mood in the work of art or its producer, especially as penetrated by the personality of the interpreter. Synonyms for *interpretation* include *explanation*, *solution*, *translation*, *rendering*, *sense*, and *definition*.

The *interpreter* may be someone who *translates* from one language into the other, who *gives meaning* to a work of art or music, or who *reveals* the will of God.

The German word *Deutung* has approximately all these meanings, but is also frequently used in religious or superstitious contexts, for example, for *prophecies* or for *fortune-telling*. A *Deuter* may be a gypsy who *reads the future* in a person's palm or an *oracle priestess* or *seer* who foretells the future, attempts to predict the future from signs, such as the symbols in manifest dream content, as is true for the interpretation of dreams found in the Old Testament or in the writings of antiquity.

The German word *Interpretation* (incidentally, never used by Freud), may also be used in philosophical, religious, or artistic context. It refers frequently to the attempt to *give meaning* to something, and is burdened by certain philosophical differences in essence between the sciences which explain (erklaerende Wissenschaften) and the sciences which merely understand (verstehende Wissenschaften).*

This is approximately the group of different shades of meaning, the diffuse logical climate, as it were, which characterizes the usages of these words—the wide range from explaining to translating, to giving a special personal meaning to foreseeing the future, to reading the signs of the gods. This makes it difficult to decide whether the word belongs in a scientific or prescientific context. It certainly is burdened with many prescientific notions, a difficulty it shares, of course, with many scientific concepts which have been borrowed from everyday language and have slowly assumed a new meaning. The analytic concept of interpretation, thus, originates in prescientific, and frequently antiscientific, usage, and one may wonder whether any or how much of the wide range of usage is reflected in psychoanalytic writings, explicitly or implicitly.

The word *interpretation* became connected intimately with psychoanalysis when Freud † started to use it at the close of the nineteenth century and popularized it in his opus magnum, *Die Traumdeutung*.[2] In the second chapter of his *Interpretation of Dreams*, Freud comments:

The title that I have chosen for my work makes plain which of the traditional approaches to the problem of dreams I am inclined to follow. The aim which I have set before myself is to show that dreams are capable of being interpreted; and any contributions I may be able to make towards the solution of the problems dealt with in the last chapter will only arise as by-products in the course of carrying out my proper task. My presumption that dreams can be interpreted at once puts me in opposition to the ruling theory of dreams and in fact to every theory of dreams with the single exception of Scherner's; for "interpreting" a dream implies assigning a "meaning" to it—that is, replacing it by something which fits into the chain of our mental acts as a link having a validity and importance equal to the rest. As we have seen, the scientific theories of dreams leave no room for any problem of interpreting them since in their view a dream is not a mental act at all, but a somatic process signalizing its occurrence by indications registered in the mental apparatus. Lay opinion has taken a

---

* It is claimed by some schools of thought that there is a qualitative difference between these two types of sciences. Dilthey in history and Jaspers in psychology represent the position that there is a distinct difference between explanation in the natural sciences and interpretation in the social sciences. This insistence on an *essential* difference is based on a misunderstanding of the nature of scientific laws which are seen as opposed to freedom.

† Freud actually used the word "Deutung" before the *Interpretation of Dreams*, in his 1899 paper on screen memories. He used *Deutung* there in the sense of *Aufklärung*, elucidation. *Aufklärung* in a different context means "enlightenment," e.g., the sexual enlightenment of children.

different attitude throughout the ages. It has exercised its indefensible right to behave inconsistently; and, though admitting that dreams are unintelligible and absurd, it cannot bring itself to declare that they have no significance at all. Led by some obscure feeling, it seems to assume that, in spite of everything, every dream has a meaning, though a hidden one, that dreams are designed to take the place of some other process of thought, and that we have only to undo the substitution correctly in order to arrive at this hidden meaning.

This, I believe, constitutes the first extensive Freudian reference to the concept of interpretation. It seems Freud deliberately chose the word *Deutung* in order to return to a view which was given up by the scientists of his day, and thus to restore to life the old insight that dreams are not simply to be explained as physiological processes but that they may be interpreted as having meaning as well. He chose the same word pre-scientific dream interpreters use, noting that its origin is prescientific, religious, or superstitious, and subjective in nature. The analytic interpreter shows that which is hidden, which is unconscious, which gives meaning to that which seems to have no meaning otherwise. His task is to undo the disguising substitutions in order to get to the hidden meaning. Freud's introduction of the prescientific word *Deutung* into his scientific work has, of course, deep psychological meaning and hints at logical and methodological difficulties as well as psychological problems. Early science at that time stressed reason, and thus preferred to ignore that which seemed unreasonable. The irrational aspects of the mind were segregated, as it were, and a value system was introduced in order to strengthen science, which needed to assert and maintain itself against religion and metaphysics. Nineteenth-century science, if I may put it into psychoanalytic terminology and oversimplify it, at that, put the highest value on the secondary process and sent the primary process into exile. Freud reversed this process in the field of psychology although, as will be shown later, he never quite gave up certain of the value concepts of nineteenth century science. Has he not said epigrammatically that "where id was, there shall ego be"; and that "the voice of the intellect is soft but it is persistent"?

Freud stressed a number of aspects of *interpretation*, such as the *hidden meaning* of the dream, the *dream work* which can be undone through correct *substitution*, a form of *translation*.

In 1904, he spoke of himself as having

. . . developed on this basis an art of interpretation which takes on the task of, as it were, extracting the pure metal of the repressed thoughts from the ore of the unintentional ideas. This work of interpretation is applied not only to the patient's ideas but also to his dreams, which open up the most direct approach to a knowledge of the unconscious, to his unintentional as well as to his purposeless actions (symptomatic acts) and to the blunders he makes in everyday life (slips of the tongue, bungled actions, and so on). The details of the technique of interpretation or translation have not yet been published by Freud. According to indications he has given, they comprise a number of rules, reached empirically, of how the unconscious material may be reconstructed from the associations, directions on how to know what it means when the patient's ideas cease to flow, and the experiences of the most important typical resistances that arise in the course of such treatments.[3]

In 1922, Freud again referred to psychoanalysis as an art of interpretation and he summed up his comments on interpretation as follows:

Now, in the first resort, this psychoanalysis was an art of interpretation and it set itself the task of carrying deeper the first of Breuer's great discoveries, namely, that neurotic symptoms are significant substitutes for other mental acts which have been omitted. It was now a question of regarding the material produced by the patient's associations as though it hinted at a hidden meaning and of discovering that meaning from it. Experience soon showed that the attitude which the analytic physician could most advantageously adopt was to surrender himself to his own unconscious mental activity, in a state of evenly suspended attention, to avoid so far as possible reflection and the construction of conscious expectations, not to try to fix anything that he heard particularly in his memory, and by these means to catch the drift of the patient's unconscious with his own unconscious. It was then found that, except under conditions that were too unfavorable, the patient's associations emerged like allusions, as it were, to one particular theme and that it was only necessary for the physician to go a step further in order to guess the material which was concealed from the patient himself and to be able to communicate it to him. It is true that this work of interpretation was not to be brought under strict rules and left a great deal of play to the physician's tact and skill; but, with impartiality and practice, it was usually possible to obtain trustworthy results—that is to say, results which were confirmed by being repeated in similar cases.[4]

Freud here stressed the fact that interpretation cannot be compared simply with a deductive or translating technique. It is more than mere logical inference. He spoke of its artistic aspects, the lack of strict rules, the importance of the analyst's tact and skill, the necessity to "catch the drift of the patient's unconscious with his own unconscious." Artistic intuition, the capacity to listen on different levels of mental functioning, the evenly suspended attention of the analyst—all are used in order to get at the hidden meaning of the patient's communications.

Interpretation here is firmly linked to the *personality of the interpreter*, to special capacities and skills which he possesses, so that one is inclined to think of interpretation in similar terms as in the case when one refers to a musician's creative interpretation of a specific musical score, originated by somebody else. How different is such an interpreter from a modern translating machine? Some clinicians think him to be unreliable and clamor for more reliable actuarial, that is, statistical types of prediction. Meehl [5] quotes Rapaport as highlighting this difference of opinion by wondering whether certain statisticians wanted him to substitute a Hollerith machine for his eyes and his brains. It is also clear from these Freudian quotes that *interpretation* in this context refers to a technique within the therapeutic context and does not simply constitute a scientific explanation. Scientific explanations do not cure and it is an interesting question as to just what interpretations within a therapeutic context actually explain.

Psychoanalytic literature has not always made explicit this aspect of the nature of the *interpretive process*. The clarification of its nature may make it easier for us to see fully what we mean when we state that we are attempting to validate a psychoanalytic interpretation. It is not only for historical reasons, not only because we follow Freud's usage of certain terminology that we speak of interpretations rather than explanations. The concept of interpretation contains an element which goes beyond explanation. At times it refers to dynamic and genetic propositions which are of an explanatory type; at other times it refers to a type of communication which really constitutes a technical intervention. It is an interesting question whether or not interpretations which constitute technical interventions are necessarily identical with those propositions which explain genetic and dynamic personality factors and which are also frequently referred to as interpretations. The reason that these two different types of propositions have been so frequently confused in the literature is that the research method of analysis also constitutes a therapeutic technique. The confusion concerning the nature of interpretation hinges on the fact that the reconstructive process which leads towards change, towards restructuring of the personality, has also been the research method which has helped us link adult pathology with its dynamics and with certain childhood events.

In most cases interpretation leads not only to structural changes in the personality, but also to the lifting of repression and to the reconstruction of the past. It is, therefore, tempting to consider every interpretation not only from a technical point of view, from the point of view of change, but also as a hypothesis about the past.

Correct explanations do not cure, and effective interpretations do not necessarily describe the decisive determinants of an illness.[6] I think that this state of affairs is implicitly recognized whenever in the interpretive process we refer to the facts of overdetermination [7] or where it is clear to us that fairly different technical handling may lead to the same results.[8] Overdetermination is not specific for psychological facts, but is an important concept which throws light on technical problems of analysis, i.e., the problem of working through interpretations on different levels. I have discussed this more fully elsewhere.[9] I do not exclude the chance possibility that an ideal analysis, containing an ideal sequence of interpretations, may lead to a state of affairs in which one may be able to match the sum of interpretations which were used as therapeutic interventions with the sum of those interpretations which really consist of dynamic and genetic propositions and which are designed to describe and explain adequately certain personality functioning.

One could roughly define the meaning of a scientific proposition, speaking now about interpretation in the sense of explanation, as being rendered by the methods which lead to its verification or falsification, or, to bring this philosophic notion more up to date, if we can describe the methods which lead to confirmation or disconfirmation.[10] This simply means that all our predictions are probability predictions which are based on induction even in the single, the unique, case.

If the term "correct or exact interpretation" is to refer to technique, the truth of interpretation could be ascertained through predictable future patient response. The literature of analysis abounds in many examples of the types of future responses which could be used to confirm the correctness of an interpretation in its technical sense.[11] The synonymous use of "true" and "correct," here, of course, is possible only to the extent that a correct interpretation will lead to certain predictable responses. It is as if we were to say: "If under certain conditions a certain interpretive intervention is used, the patient will respond in a certain way." If such a statement can be verified, we speak of it as true and of the interpretation which has been used as a technical device, as correct or effective. The word "correct" stands in our literature at times for "true," at other times for "effective," and often for both.

Freud has frequently compared psychoanalytic work to the work of the archeologist:

 . . . *the interpretive work is now, however, a preliminary labor in the sense that the whole of it must be completed before the next piece of work can be begun, as for instance, is the case with housebuilding, where all the walls must be erected and all the windows inserted before the internal decoration of the rooms can be taken in hand. Every analyst knows that* things happen differently in an analytic treatment and that there are both kinds of work carried on side by side, the one kind being always a little ahead and the other following upon it. The analyst finishes a piece of construction and communicates it to the subject of the analysis so that it may work upon him; he then constructs a further piece out of the fresh material pouring in upon him, deals with it in the same way and proceeds in this alternating fashion until the end. If, in accounts of analytic technique, so little is said about "constructions," that is because "interpretations" and their effects are spoken of instead. But I think that "construction" is by far the more appropriate description. "Interpretation" applies to something that one does to some single element of the material, such as an association or a parapraxis. But it is a "construction" when one lays before the subject of the analysis a piece of his early history that he has forgotten, in some such way as this: "up to your nth year you regarded yourself as the sole and unlimited possessor of your mother; then came another baby and brought you great disillusionment. Your mother left you for some time, and even after her reappearance she was never again devoted to you exclusively. Your feelings toward your mother became ambivalent, your father gained a new importance for you . . ." [12]

This late contribution of Freud's in which he elaborates again on the nature of interpretation is important for a variety of reasons. In it he differentiates between *interpretation* and *construction*. He applies the former to small units while the latter refers to a total Gestalt, a pattern which is demonstrated as a piece of the patient's past and links up dynamic aspects, perhaps Freud's "single elements" in the material, with genetic aspects, Freud's "early pieces" of the patient's history. The interpretive work is not satisfied with the meaning of the material within the context of the present, but establishes through constructions (actually interpretations on a different level) links with the past of the individual.

The methodological difficulty, mentioned earlier for interpretations, also holds true for constructions or reconstructions, as they are sometimes called. It is suggested, for example, that the confirmations of reconstruction from external sources can be used as evidence for the correctness of this type of interpretation. I believe, though, that this evidence is applicable only if the concept of interpretation or construction is seen on the level of dynamic or genetic propositions rather than in terms of a technical intervention. The method of confirmation or disconfirmation concerning a genetic proposition, frequently called a construction, consists in finding out if a prediction into the past of the patient, that is a postdiction, turns out to be true or false. This prediction may be true and still may not be correct, that is, not effective from a therapeutic point of view. The *validation of a technique, a construction, a reconstructive inter-*

pretation as a technical intervention lies in the future, while the validation of an explanatory proposition, where present and past patterns are linked, lies in the past. That interpretations or constructions in the technical sense and in the explanatory sense so often fall together and permit us to reconstruct all the facts of a patient's life and of his illness is indeed one of the most powerful aspects of psychoanalytic scientific advance. But, it also creates a methodological problem whenever the validation of psychoanalytic interpretations in the technical sense is discussed.

If we restrict ourselves to a validation of psychoanalytic interpretations and constructions in the technical sense, we may perhaps find it easier to employ a variety of objective ways of verifying interpretive techniques. Such objective-validation studies of psychoanalytic interpretations and constructions should go beyond the need to prove psychoanalytic techniques to the doubting public or to make psychoanalysis more respectable in the family of sciences. Validation studies should rather, as Kubie has suggested, provide psychoanalysis "with instruments of greater qualitative and quantitative precision. In the area of technique such instruments are urgently needed and can hardly be provided by the individual practitioner alone." [13] Such studies, I suggest, will yield better results if not applied at first to global problems, but rather to circumscribed and limited processes amenable to qualitative and certain simple quantitative procedures applicable to the field.

Freud's feelings about the problem of validation of interpretive techniques, are described in his Introductory Lectures. As summarized by Jones,[14] Freud questioned whether an element is to be read literally or symbolically, whether a phrase has to be inverted or not, and what the various possibilities of arbitrary and subjective interpretation are. Freud conceded that such work does not attain the certainty to be found in mathematics, but suggested, since all conclusions in scientific work are in the nature of varying degrees of probability rather than absoluteness, that in most work the trustworthiness of results largely depends on the skill and the experience of the scientist. Regarding dream interpretation, he felt that a competent analyst could reach a high level of probability in his interpretations. He drew the analogy of the original uncertainty in the deciphering of cuneiform hieroglyphics and also suggested that in certain languages, for example, in ancient Egyptian or in Chinese, only slight indications are necessary for understanding which one of the many possible meanings is intended.

At this point it would be possible to investigate the nature of interpretation as explanation. It would be necessary to show the characteristic form of psychoanalytic explanations and the methods of confirmation which give proper meaning to them. Such a discussion would essentially be a clarification of the nature of psychoanalytic theory, and different explanatory levels found today in psychoanalysis would have to be characterized. The relationship among the descriptive, the explanatory, and the basic concepts of psychoanalysis could then be discussed. Instead, I prefer to investigate the aspects of the interpretive and reconstructive processes which deal with analytic techniques. Since I believe that theoretical advance stays in a functional relationship to technical advance, the theoretical task is not completely neglected in turning to the technical problem concerning the nature of interpretation. This emphasis is particularly appropriate in our field where theory is usually ahead of technique.

Regarding interpretation as a special kind of technical intervention, its purpose is "to reveal hidden meanings at a dynamically specific moment." [15] *The primary intent of an analytic interpretation is not to explain, but to cure.*

Bernfeld once spoke about psychoanalysis as *Spurenwissenschaft,* the science in which clues are used to find what seems to be lost.[16] He demonstrated that a variety of methodologically different types of propositions are called interpretation, because the basis of all these propositions is the psychological fact characterized today as "Gestalt." Each symptom, each dream, each manifestation of the patient receives its meaning if it is put into a *Gesamtzusammenhang,* a total structure. Psychoanalyst as well as analysand, whenever they experience insight, deal with such affective, meaningful Gestalt experiences. Schmidl stresses that Bernfeld's idea about the concept of interpretation and the Gestalt character of psychoanalytic propositions is essential for evaluating the validity of psychoanalytic interpretations. He suggests that the analyst interprets by fitting together different pieces, different data, into a total, a complementary Gestalt. He uses the example of the porter of a small village inn who, since he could not write, gave guests one part of a piece of cardboard which he had torn into two. One piece was fixed to the luggage while the other was given to the guest. Both pieces of cardboard have in common a specific Gestalt, and the two Gestalten therefore must fit each other precisely so that there would be no doubt about their belonging together.[17]

It should be useful for us to point up a number of psychological implications conveyed through these metaphors or analogies. Bernfeld [18] as well as Waelder [19] compared this technical task to the work of the detective who sometimes uses as clues the tracks that have been wiped out by the criminal. In this case a careful study of the criminal's ways of destroying the evidence of his deed may give clues which, in turn, may help the detective to track him down. Similar suggestions, although with an entirely different analogy, have been made by Freud [20] and Bernfeld [21] in discussing the work of the archeologist who looks for lost traces, and who sometimes must take into account the nature of the process of the destruction in order to be able to make inferences about what has been destroyed, its age, and its possible function. The detective as well as the archeologist work from the present into the past and try to restore the facts.

Both the above metaphors allow inferences about certain aspects of our *method* of investigation, as well as about the attitudes of analyst and patient who participate in this interpretive process. At times the patient may feel like the criminal who wants to destroy the clues which may lead to his discovery and punishment. He may even feel so guilty about the past "crime" that he may leave, against his conscious wish, clues which lead to his discovery. He may experience the analyst as the one who surrounds him with evidence, tracks him down, and confronts him with his "crime." His problem, of course, constitutes a transference problem, and I believe that the comparison of the psychoanalytic process with criminology, with interpretation being the revealing clue, also hints at countertransference potentials with which the analyst frequently may have to cope. One specific and extreme technical distortion of classical psychoanalysis is that in which interpretation is completely replaced by an interpretive tool, confrontation. Confrontation is usually used in order to call to the patient's attention behavior which is not ego-syntonic, which is not "appropriate" in the analytical situation, and which constitutes a breach within the otherwise "reasonable" character front of the patient.

It is true that even confrontation constitutes a form of interpretation (although not its classical and final form), but such "confrontation analysis" or "character analysis" [22] as it may be called, does not analyze defense in the classical sense. In my opinion, it simply points up aspects of behavior in very much the same way in which the detective may confront the criminal with actions for which he must account. The primary response of the patient in such a procedure will be an alibi-producing one in which he will try to rationalize that which has been pointed up as ego-alien and will try to make it ego-syntonic again. This method, rather than permitting the development of a full classical transference neurosis, tends to prevent it. As soon as confrontation, only one of the maneuvers of interpretive work, becomes the grand strategy of the therapist rather than remaining a tactical maneuver, it will invoke those aspects of the transference neurosis which are quite well characterized through the criminal-detective relationship. The countertransference problem implied in such a relationship may also express itself in an excessive need of the analyst to make constant direct inquiries of the patient.[23] And he may invoke the basic rule in such a way that it becomes actually an order for honesty, the enforcing of a parental rule rather than the maintaining of the analytic situation agreed upon by patient and analyst. The countertransference problem of the analyst may also take the form of his not being able to use confrontation to ask questions where this is actually indicated. Delay of confrontation with reality or the delay in ascertaining certain information may actually hamper the process and indicates certain problems of the analyst in accepting objectively the patient's transference reactions.

The comparison of psychoanalysis with history, or better, with archeology, yields insight into the interpretive process, especially in considering not only the methods of the archeologists but also the psychological undertones which are suggested through the metaphor of archeology. One may sometimes think of analysis as a procedure in which the discovery of the *trauma*, the making conscious of the *cause* of the patient's difficulty, will make the patient well. This point of view, heir to former hypnotic procedure, has frequently been the source of a variety of resistances. Anna Freud [24] warns of the danger of intellectualization of the process, but one must remember that, as early as 1892, Freud spoke about the uselessness of the restoration of memories without accompanying affect.[25] He stressed the fact that it is the *process* of recovery of memories, the *reconstruction* of the past, which brings about the cure. It is for this reason that the mere translating of data into meaning, into language of the secondary process, does not help the patient. However, this very misconception of psychoanalysis as a translating technique, which again is but one of its aspects, has led to innovations which throw out the child with the dirty bath water. I refer to Kaiser's overstressing the translation function of interpretation [26] which is but one of the functions of the interpretive process. I believe that Fenichel, in discussing the Kaiser contribution, also overstressed the function of translation. He did, however, see the difficulty which would arise if Kaiser's then-proposed technique became a valid stratagem useful for all syndromes,[27] instead of a specific tactical maneuver in the analysis of obsessive-compulsive patients.

The archeological metaphor also hints at the specific psychological need to restore continuity between the past and the present. He who has lost his past cannot maintain an identity in the present. The achievement of mature identity depends on the capacity to integrate formerly repressed identities of the past and to restore a continuum between childhood and adulthood. A great deal of our historical interest represents society's attempt to restore continuity and to reinterpret the past in the light of present tasks. Modern historians have fully recognized the fact that the social scientists use reconstruction of historic processes to solve current tasks and current conflicts. Reconstruction is a necessary adaptive function of the mature ego (representing in the neurotic organization that which is expressed in the psychotic organization through restitutive processes), and I believe that this view agrees with Erikson's [28] on ego identity as well as with a recent clarification by Kris on the function of the recovery of childhood memories.[29] The repressed past prevents mature identity and thus remains useless although pathologically effective in the life of the adult. The discovered past leads to reintegration and loses its effectiveness as the creator of pathology. Freud's simile is of the mummy which falls to dust when finally unearthed by the archeologist.

If a combat flier were to bring back photographs from a reconnaissance mission, our capacity to interpret them would depend in part on the tools—the photographic apparatus, the chemicals used to develop the films—as well as on the skill of the interpreter. The same holds true for the psychoanalytic interpreter. His tools consist of the psychoanalytic body of knowledge, the psychoanalytic theoretical frame of reference, as well as of the use that he can make of himself—which goes far beyond his knowledge of the facts and the theories of psychoanalysis. Even if the statement that analysts are born not trained is an exaggeration, its implications suggest a serious problem for the science of psychoanalysis: if interpretation depends largely on the artist in us, on intuition which perhaps cannot be taught, we cannot verify our interpretations. The inner evidence which the psychoanalyst feels when interpreting (that which Bernfeld has described as *Deutungsakt*) [30] is not sufficient evidence for science, which depends on external criteria. The nature of our problem as scientists is that, even if we wish to remain only within the technical problem of interpretation, we must continually return to the problem of validating our findings.

Waelder has seen this in his discussion [31] of criteria of interpretation (RE's translation):

> Therefore when we proceed in such a way that we take notice of all phenomena with equal attention; when everything which cannot be clearly explained through external circumstances becomes our problem; when our interpretations explain all phenomena; when all inferences made on account of these interpretations are confirmed in experience; when all other possibilities of interpretation of phenomena are examined and have to be dismissed; when all interpretations can be reconstructed in a synthetic fashion, and when the individual pieces are found to be in good agreement with other experiences, above all with direct observation; and if we have taken the precaution during our work, to formulate the interpretation of the present material in such a way that it also implies a certain infantile conflict, as long as this conflict does not give itself away through clear material; and if we also study the reaction to the interpretation during the analysis; then we may assume that our interpretations have a sufficient measure of probability.

Another quotation from the same source pertains to the intuitive aspects of interpretation (RE's translation):[31]

All these considerations take place preconsciously in the experienced analyst. Only if one discusses the criteria of interpretation must one lift them out into sharp focus. In the practical situation, however, the way of working is best described in the manner Freud's teacher, Charcot, characterized his way of working and which is also characteristic for Freud's way, in actual analysis as well as in the fields of application of analysis: to look at the phenomena so long that they seem to tell the story by themselves.

This characterization of Charcot's work is typical for the clinical work of the analyst, and poses many scientific problems, since we are interested not only in the logical justification of an interpretation, but also in the working methods of the analyst who interprets by means of sudden discoveries. If one looks at phenomena so long that finally they seem to tell the story by themselves, one is indeed confronted with the interesting experience of discovery, interesting in the sense that it seems to be impossible that one could later retrace the logical steps which have led to it. As a matter of fact, one asks, were there any logical steps and how did they influence the sudden grasp of meaning?

I am reminded of the contention that nature has wisdom, which is attributed by the believer to God. This wisdom is thought to have created natural laws which are so useful that they permit the fish to survive because water does not start freezing at the bottom but rather at the surface. One could easily reduce the awe for this wisdom to projected self-admiration since the laws of nature merely describe regularities which man hypothesized. If one were to think of the cause of such projected self-admiration, one might well think of the suddenness of most of the important scientific discoveries. The benzene ring discovered by Kekulè in a dream, as it were, and a good many other scientific hypotheses owe their establishment to sudden insights which carry the quality of Charcot's observation that phenomena will tell the story by themselves if only we look at them long enough. The sudden emergence of insight, a regularity in nature or in ourselves, is frequently experienced as ego-alien and is easier to bear if the discovery is ascribed to the phenomena that tell the story by themselves. It is as if we were to distrust primitive insight rather than to rely on the power of archaic processes. While interpreting, the psychoanalyst frequently makes the same self-observation of sudden insights, and a good many of his reconstructions and interpretations, rather than being acquired logically step by step, have the quality of the unpredictable, at times of the uncanny. Only he who can trust the workings of his preconscious, who can surrender the ordinary secondary-process thinking to evenly suspended attention, and who can permit himself to be influenced by thought processes which stem from more archaic levels, can do psychoanalytic work. This is frequently held against analysis since it seems to make our science into an arbitrary discipline which can only be carried out by the initiated who happen to have special capacities. It is a fact that certain candidates, in spite of their own satisfactory analysis, cannot make use of analytic training which could guarantee the development of these facilities.[32]

Waelder has referred to the fact [33] that analysis is not alone in this difficulty, and that even the exact sciences during certain stages of their development went through the same problems while trying to train scientists who could not be taught to see in a way that would verify certain hypotheses. He cites Rutherford's 1918 discovery of the split of the nitrogen nucleus. The observation of the fluorescence phenomena depended upon "subjective interpretation—of the ability of some people to see it— as psychoanalysis still does today." Waelder mentions that:

The Physical Institute in Cambridge dropped half its students because they did not get the right results. The leading physicists, insisting on their convictions, berated their students as we do ours if we think that they cannot "see" the minute phenomena of psychic life. But . . . these screening methods in early physics and in psychoanalysis today are scientific as long as we have to rely on subjective methods; a state of affairs in psychoanalysis which will prevail a long time in spite of our work towards objectivation.

The strange mode of discovery, the capacity for interpretation through the use of thought processes frequently following primitive modes of thinking is, however, no excuse for the lack of verification nor the absence of both scientific controls and attempts to retrace the possible logical steps which justify certain interpretations discovered by the analyst through such short cuts. Since each analyst develops such sudden insights according to his own personality makeup, we will find that analysts differ in their ways of interpreting, so that different processes will develop. This is true even if these analysts have had the same basic training and share the same basic theoretical assumptions.

The interpretive process, as I have remarked earlier, depends for its degree of exactness on the body of knowledge available, on the specific sensitivity of the analyst as an observer, and on the theoretical frame of reference. As our theory has developed and changed during the history of analysis, interpretation has taken on a different character. *The metaphor of archeology is perhaps more fitting for the days when id analysis was in the foreground of our interest and influenced technical interventions. The* metaphor of criminology might be more fitting for interpretive processes in which ego psychology stands in the foreground of our interest.

The relatively recent development which has excited the most active interest in psychoanalysis today is the ascent of ego psychology. This concern with the development of thought and language, with affect organization and the relationship of affects and thoughts to impulse has deeply influenced current ideas of interpretive work.[34] Interpretation represents a complex communication within a complex interpersonal situation. It might help if we were to look for a *model of interpretation* which simplifies study of the rudimentary aspects of the interpretive process. For this purpose we might successfully utilize the model which Rapaport [35] has used to develop a psychoanalytic theory of thought. He speaks of the tension-need system of the hungry infant who "communicates" his need to the mother through crying or restlessness. The mother, understanding his "signal," his crying need, offers him milk; this "interprets" the situation correctly. The baby, after being gratified, relaxes and falls asleep again. Temporary homeostasis is achieved. The words in quotation marks are to call to attention that this primary model of quasi-interpretation should not tempt us to project conditions into the baby-mother situation which actually do not obtain. This model does not suggest parallelism between the mother's action and the analyst's interpretation but rather establishes, as Loewenstein [36] suggests, a kind of "ontogeny" of interpretation, and it helps us to trace the basic components of the interpretive process. Loewald [37] also uses the parent-child relationship as a model which throws light on the therapeutic action of psychoanalysis. The rather primitive psychic organization of the baby, referred to by Hartmann as the undifferentiated phase, does not yet include the capacity for even rudimentary object relationships, and is characterized by symbiotic arrangements in which there is no clear differentiation between mother and child. The discussion of this model is amplified in Chapter 11, but, using it as the forerunner for interpretation, it can be seen that the therapist's task of interpretation is based on his understanding of the patient's language. A part of this has to do with the psychoanalyst's capacity for understanding the language levels which the patient can utilize. The analyst is not simply a translator but has to estimate the patient's capacity for different levels of language. Thus, for example, some deeply disturbed patients can understand precursors of interpretations only, such as the prohibition which one must express in the case of a child who cannot give up the delay of need gratification without this auxiliary help from the adult.

Wexler's helping the schizophrenic patient pray so that she may avoid forbidden and painful thoughts which lead to disorganization,[38] could be considered as *interpretation* rather than an injunction if we realize that he interpreted correctly, through his communication, the patient's inability to control thoughts which would lead to disruptive and violent behavior. The child in play therapy who becomes too destructive and must be held, or the one who must be told that this or that cannot be done, is in need of the auxiliary ego of the therapist. The psychotherapist's action or injunction may be the only kind of interpretation that the patient can understand at this point. This view may be dangerous since it might open the way to confusion concerning the difference between educative and therapeutic means. The corrective emotional experience [39] is an educative means based upon a misunderstanding of interpretation (comparable on that level to reconditioning). Or such experience is interpretation in the sense that, during a certain phase of treatment, the patient could not make use of more advanced interpretations and thus requires direct gratification or injunctions to advance to an ego position in which he can again make use of interpretive language which is primarily symbolic.

The distinction between educative and therapeutic means, that is, the difference between child psychotherapy and analytically oriented child education, has concerned workers in the field for a long time.[40] The younger or sicker the child, the less clear is the difference between the two procedures, for in both instances the child's weak ego cannot utilize a procedure using only symbolic, insight-giving language. Direct gratification may frequently be a part of the therapeutic process even though we may soon wish to use such gratification as symbolic with a schizophrenic patient.[41] Symbolic gratification does not primarily gratify but uses the token gift for the purpose of interpretation. It is true, nevertheless, that some aspects of this gift are experienced as direct gratification. But this is also true for the play language of the child which directly gratifies, and we also know that the adult patient in classical analysis frequently experiences the interpretation of the analyst as a direct gratification, a real gift. No wonder then, that we frequently speak about the "giving" of interpretations, and that it is suggested here and there that a patient "cannot swallow" or "does not want to stomach" an interpretation which we offer. I believe that such semantic use refers to the fact that, even in a process in which there is only symbolic language, there will be underlying aspects of direct communion.

Most people have the capacity to use at one and the same time different ranges of language, reflecting higher or lower organization; they are more or less multilingual. Nevertheless, the specific problem which is worked through in a specific analytic treatment situation might require the cathexing of special language levels, which, for example, may lead to the patient's suddenly communicating a problem in childlike language. Often the patient can understand a language which he does not speak.

The therapist must, therefore, know what level of language is most cathexed, what level is most effective, and what level of language may be useless. These problems can be transposed into the work with adult patients who have not yet learned the language of reflection and use acting-out language, "experimental recollection," a term which also indicates the incapacity of such patients to use reflection as is used in classical analysis. At times the analytic interpreter teaches a new language and must then rely on the capacity for identification with him. How does one assess such capacity? Will his interpretation be more successful if he remains within the metaphor which the patient offers, or does he delay final integration into secondary-process thinking if he is satisfied with archaic forms of understanding and insight? When can he progress from metaphoric to conventional interpretation?

Many analysts may feel that I have too loosely used the word *interpretation* for a variety of technical interventions which are actually precursors of interpretation proper. If one accepts, however, a hierarchy of insights ranging from primitive to more advanced levels, one could think of the interpretive process in terms of steps. Accordingly, I see no reason to withhold the designation of "interpretation" from early equally important steps [42] leading to primitive insight. Nevertheless, I feel strongly identified with Bibring's point of view [43] which stresses a hierarchy of therapeutic principles characteristic for classical analysis and which considers the most important principles the ones of *clarification* and *interpretation*. He uses *clarification* for all those techniques which assist the patient to reach a higher degree of self-awareness, self-differentiation, and clarity— techniques which make adequate verbalization possible, as in the restating in more precise form what the patient tells us. *Interpretation* refers exclusively to unconscious material, unconscious defensive operations, warded-off instinctual tendencies, hidden meanings of behavior patterns, and their unconscious interconnections. It transcends the clinical data and usually consists of a prolonged process preceded by preparation which may take the form of clarification. Bibring [43] refers to interpretations as "explanatory concepts." This, of course, does not mean that he sees the therapeutic process as a didactic or a directive one [44] but rather that he wishes to call our attention again to the problem of validation of the therapeutic process. This emphasis on the final form of interpretation is not a value judgment, tempting as such a judgment may be for some analysts. Rather, it leads us back to the basic model of technique and thus helps us to consider analytic work from the point of view of the standard procedure, and to differentiate between parameters [45] and pure analytic technique as applicable in the basic model of the standard procedure. [46] The decision to call precursors of interpretations parts of the interpretive process depends, then, on the total strategy which is employed.

Another problem which is of interest to the interpreter concerns the relationship between interpretation and distance. The concept of distance could be a function of the transference situation, could refer to distance from the unconscious conflict, or could be considered a concept which is in functional relationship to the capacity for delay. The use of metaphoric language which allows for distance in interpretive work poses a problem for the interpreter. We need to consider whether this usage may not at times stimulate archaic processes and thus overcome, perhaps too rapidly, distance from id conflict.

Some of the problems which I have merely touched upon might perhaps become more graphic if we were to compare the interpretive process to a communication system between the interpreter, the sender, and the patient, the receiver of the interpretation. This metaphor purposely neglects the split in the patient's ego which allows for both free association and the observation of his associations; for identification with the analyst, or, better, with the analytic process; and leads to the patient himself doing interpretive work. We could compare this communication system to a radio communication system. If the interpreter were to send out messages only on an FM frequency while the patient could receive only on an AM receiver, the interpretive work of the analyst would be entirely useless. The patient could not even hear him even if the analyst were to shout into the microphone of his FM set.

The decision concerning the use of certain interpretive tools depends on the goal of therapy. If we think, for example, of the process in terms of a transportation system, we may suggest that communication from Kansas City to New York in a jet plane would be useful but that the use of a jet plane would be inappropriate from Kansas City to Topeka. If we wanted to travel to a downtown store, we might do better in a car or a bus, but most certainly we would not use an airplane. I suggest that interpretive techniques constantly have to be geared to the capacity of the patient to understand, and to the goal of treatment. Perhaps I should also stress that the interpretive work, in part, at least, depends on the capacity of the interpreter to observe and to understand. His choice of language cannot always be in complete accord with the need system of the patient since he depends on the choices that he has available. The richer his choices are, the more he will be able to adapt his interpretive work to the needs of the patient and the more sensitive and effective his interpretive techniques will prove to be.

Goethe said once that "The man of action has no conscience; the man of reflection has." We might apply this to the analyst who, as interpreter, reflects and acts. We could liken his two-fold activity, reflection and technical intervention, to the patient's mild ego split which permits both free association and self-observation. The analyst's interpretive actions may prevent him from sufficient reflection about the effectiveness and validity of his interpretations. Listening to his patient, he is engaged in constant reflection on the meanings of the patient's communication, and thus it can be said that he has a conscience. However, he must interpret, he must act in order to help the patient change. And as an interpreter, he has often not much time to acquire a conscience in terms of the development of a satisfactory methodology. This is one of the reasons that the problem of validation of psychoanalytic interpretations has created so many issues. The analyst has slowly developed a methodological conscience. As we know from Hamlet, a pathological conscience can prevent action or lead to destructive action. We need, then, to look at our own activities with the double concern of developing a more satisfactory methodology relating to validation and theory construction, while remaining acting, interpreting analysts.

My purpose in dealing with the nature of interpretation has been to raise questions to arouse interest not only in the cleaning of our methodological eyeglasses, to use a simile of Freud's, but also in the improvement of our capacity for seeing while using these spectacles for therapeutic action. The man who acts after proper reflection, after having used his scientific conscience, cannot be said to be without such a conscience. Thinking is not to delay action forever but to prepare for it. Each science must reflect on its methods, its basic tools. This involves the philosophical task of asking real, meaningful questions which serve as challenges for new scientific investigations.

REFERENCES

[1] A study which R. Carnap (Meaning and synonymy in natural languages, Philo. Studies, 6:33, 1955) refers to as pragmatic and which he differentiates from the study of constructed language systems, which he calls pure semantics.

[2] Freud, S. Interpretation of Dreams (1900), Collected Papers, London, Hogarth Press, 1953, 4 and 5.

[3] ———. Psychoanalytic Procedure (1904), Collected Papers, London, Hogarth Press, 1953, 7.

[4] ———. Psychoanalysis (1922), Collected Papers, London, Hogarth Press, 1955, 18.

[5] Meehl, P. Clinical versus Statistical Prediction, Minneapolis, University of Minnesota Press, 1954, 6.

[6] When Glover (The therapeutic effect of inexact interpretation, Internat. J. Psycho-Analysis, 33:1, 1931) refers to technique, he should not speak about exact or inexact interpretations. His adjectives "exact" and "inexact" are as

applicable as if we were to characterize a novel as true or false. I do not voice an objection to his empirical findings but to his ambiguous choice of the adjectives "exact" and "inexact," which prevents a clear distinction between true and false proposition and effective and ineffective intervention between inexact and incomplete statements.

[7] Waelder, R. Das Prinzip der mehrfachen Funktion, Internationale Zeitschrift f. Psychoanalyse, 16:283, 1930.

[8] Freud, A. The widening scope of indications for psychoanalysis: a discussion, J. Amer. Psychoanal. Ass., 2:607, 1954.

[9] Ekstein, R. The Tower of Babel in psychology and psychiatry, Amer. Imago, 7:76, 1950.

[10] Carnap, R. Testability and meaning, Philo. of Sci., 4:420, 1936, and 1:1, 1937.

[11] Brenner, C. The validation of the psychoanalytic interpretation, J. Amer. Psychoanal. Ass., 3:496, 1955; Fenichel, O. Problems of psychoanalytical technique, Psychoanal. Quart., 8:57, 1939.

[12] Freud, S. Constructions in Analysis, Collected Papers, London, Hogarth Press, 1950, 5.

[13] Kubie, L. S. Problems and techniques of psychoanalytic validation and progress, in Psychoanalysis as Science, E. Pumpian-Mindlin, ed., Stanford, Stanford University Press, 1952, 46.

[14] Jones, E. The Life and Works of Sigmund Freud, New York, Basic Books, 1955, II.

[15] Erikson, E. H. Remarks on play therapy, Amer. J. Orthopsychiat., 8:507, 1938.

[16] Bernfeld, S. Der Begriff der "Deutung" in der Psychoanalyse, Zeitschrift f. Angewandte Psychologie, 42:448, 1932.

[17] Schmidl, F. The problem of scientific validation in psychoanalytic interpretation, Int. J. Psychoanal., 36:1, 1955.

[18] Op. cit.

[19] Waelder, R. Kriterien der Deutung, Internationale Zeitschrift f. Psychoanalyse und Imago, 29:136, 1939.

[20] Freud, S. Analysis terminable and interminable, Int. J. Psychoanal., 18:373, 1937.

[21] Op. cit.

[22] Sterba, E. Interpretation and education, Psychoanal. Stud. Child, 1:309, 1944.

[23] Olnick, S. Some considerations of the use of questioning as a psychoanalytic technique, J. Amer. Psychoanal. Ass., 2:57, 1954.

[24] Freud, A. The Ego and the Mechanisms of Defense, New York, International Universities Press, 1946.

[25] Freud, S. and Breuer, J. On the Psychical Mechanism of Hysterical Phenomena, Collected Papers, London, Hogarth Press, 1949, 1.

[26] Kaiser, H. Probleme der Technik, Internationale Zeitschrift f. Psychoanalyse, 20:490, 1934.

[27] Fenichel, O. Concerning the theory of psychoanalytic technique, Internationale Zeitschrift f. Psychoanalyse, 21:78, 1935.

[28] Erikson, E. H., The problem of ego identity, J. Amer. Psychoanal. Ass., 4:56, 1956.

[29] Kris, E. On some vicissitudes of insight in psychoanalysis, Int. J. Psychoanal. 27:445, 1956a.

[30] Op. cit.

[31] Op. cit.

[32] Wheelis, A. The vocational hazards of psychoanalysis, Int. J. Psychoanal., 37: 171, 1956.

[33] Waelder, R. The function and the pitfalls of psychoanalytic societies, Bull. Phila. Psychoanal. Ass., 5:1, 1955.

[34] Hartmann, H. Technical implications of ego psychology, Psychoanal. Quart., 20:31, 1951; Kris, E. Ego psychology and interpretation in psychoanalytic therapy, Psychoanal. Quart., 20:15, 1951; Loewenstein, R. The problem of interpretation, Psychoanal. Quart., 20:1, 1951.

[35] Rapaport, D. Organization and Pathology of Thought, New York, Columbia University Press, 1951.

[36] Personal communication.

[37] Unpublished.

[38] Wexler, M. The structural problem in schizophrenia: the role of the internal object, in Psychotherapy with Schizophrenics, E. Brody and F. C. Redlich, eds., New York, International Universities Press, 1952, 179.

[39] Alexander, F. and French, T. H. Psychoanalytic Therapy, New York, Ronald Press, 1946; Alexander, F. Psychoanalysis and Psychotherapy, New York, W. W. Norton, 1956.

[40] Bornstein, S. Missvertändnuisse in der psychoanalytischen Pädagogik, Zeitschrift f. Psychoanalytische Pädagogic, 11:81, 1937; Sterba, E. Interpretation and education, Psychoanal. Stud. Child, 1:309, 1944.

[41] Sechehaye, M. Symbolic Realization, New York, International Universities Press, 1951.

[42] I believe that G. and M. Piers (Modes of learning and the analytic process, Selected Lectures, Basel, New York, S. Karger, 1965) call to our attention that these early steps might be better understood if the therapeutic process is seen as a learning process in which different modes of learning can be distinguished. They differentiate between reflex learning or conditioning (superego), insight learning (ego), and learning through identification (ego ideal). The first mode of learning requires repetition and automatization and is accompanied by moods derived from expectations of reward or punishment. Insight learning is characterized through explanation and closure experiences (Gestalt) and inductive-deductive reasoning processes, the connection between past and present, between emotion and intellect. The third operative process is identification, as stressed also by R. Sterba (Clinical and therapeutic aspects of character resistance, Psychoanal. Quart., 22:1, 1953) and J. Strachey (The nature of the therapeutic action of psychoanalysis, Int. J. Psychoanal., 15:27, 1934). Working through contains reflex learning. Piers and Piers stress then that "Insight learning is certainly not what makes psychoanalysis." They feel that analysts who expect that "Interpretation is everything" underrate repetition and automatization. The effectiveness of an interpretation in the therapeutic process depends on the integration of all the aspects Piers enumerates.

[43] Bibring, E. Psychoanalysis and the dynamic psychotherapies, J. Amer. Psychoanal. Ass., 2:745, 1954.

[44] It should prove of historical interest that Alfred Adler did not use the term interpretation but rather speaks about explanation, describing the patient's

illness as a mistake which can be cured through the physician's *explaining* the style of life (Ansbacher, H. and R. The Individual Psychology of Alfred Adler, New York, Basic Books, 1956).

[45] Eissler, K. The effect of the structure of the ego on psychoanalytic technique, J. Amer. Psychoanal. Ass., 1:104, 1953.

[46] Ekstein, R. Psychoanalytic techniques, in Progress in Clinical Psychology, D. Bower and L. Abt, eds., New York, Grune & Stratton, 1956, 79.

7

CHOICE OF INTERPRETATION IN
THE TREATMENT OF BORDERLINE
AND PSYCHOTIC CHILDREN*

My theory is that metaphor can only evolve in language or in the arts when the bodily orifices become controlled. Then only can the angers, pleasures, desires of the infantile life find metaphorical expression and the immaterial express itself in terms of the material. A subterranean passage between mind and body underlies all analogy.

ELLA FREEMAN SHARPE

Within the past decade clinical investigators in various places have worked intensively with borderline and psychotic children. Out of their diverse efforts has come the recognition that the conventional methods of child analysis require accommodation to the special ego disabilities of these patients. Accordingly, new and improved ways of communication and interpretation,** especially suited to the regressive phenomena observable in these children, have been sought.

This search has led to the uncovering and exploration of a wider range of interpretive and communicative modes than those employed by the psychoanalyst in his practice with neurotic patients. And, while these interpretive modes still lack complete theoretical clarity and coherence, they bring within reach a fuller understanding of the inner life of such children and significant additions to ego psychology which are not obtainable through other means.

* Judith Wallerstein is coauthor of this chapter.
** *The interpretive process* refers to the psychoanalyst's central technical interventions which, catching the drift of the patient's unconscious, aim at revealing the patient's unconscious at a dynamically specific moment in the therapy. The concept of interpretation as used here includes what has been referred to and elaborated elsewhere as precursors of interpretation.

148

A fourteen year old boy provides an example of the therapeutic problems and the complex accommodations required of the psychotherapist in his interpretive work with these clinical groups.

In his first therapy hour, after describing his distaste for psychotherapy and his disappointment with previous therapeutic experiences, Jim offered to tell a story and went on to recount a tale of two brothers who set out to prove to their father that they could equal his achievements. This they accomplished by inventing a mathematical formula which permitted them to penetrate the mirror of their living-room and enter the wonderful Looking-Glass Land beyond. Their father was frightened by the invention and ran to consult a psychiatrist who agreed to accompany the father and to follow the children through the mirror. The adults found the boys there in the company of a monster who instantly killed the father. The story ended as the badly shaken psychiatrist, whose life was saved by the elder brother, fled back into the living-room, leaving the children alone to their own devices.

The therapist said that if he had been that psychiatrist he would surely have remained in the Looking-Glass Land with the brothers despite the dangers.

Jim's story states succinctly what we have finally learned: the confines of the conventional living-room of therapy and the conventional rules of adult society and adult thinking, that is, secondary-process thinking, transposed into the consulting room will not contain Jim nor deeply impress him. While he leads the way into the primary-process land beyond the Looking-Glass, he points mockingly at the timidity and pomposity of the adults who are afraid to accompany him and whom he firmly expects to abandon him to the terrors which await him there. The therapist's comment answers the boy's covert plea for help and defines his own intention to remain with the child as needed.

Having ventured so far, however, patient and therapist face many problems simultaneously: What are the formulas that will permit access to Looking-Glass Land? What are the laws by which the land is governed, and what is the language of the relationships which prevail there? How is the inner strength of the patient marshalled to go back and forth between the living-room and the land beyond the Looking-Glass? And finally, how is the eventual goal reached of having both return into the living-room of secondary-process living? It will be recognized that these questions comprise the psychotherapeutic problems which have engaged our attention in recent years of work with borderline and psychotic children: the patterns of ego-state fluctuation and their timetables; the patterns of ego regression, primitive transference manifestations, and early communication modes; the complexities of countertransference phenomena; the sum of factors that make for change in therapy and the capacity for lasting identification. Encompassing all of these problems is the technical question of how to convey effectively to the child the understanding which has been so hard won.

Perhaps our most consolidated achievement to date is reflected in our ability to grasp the importance of Jimmy's message immediately, whereas a decade ago its meaning might have eluded us except as a variation on the oedipal theme. It must still be demonstrated that we understand how to respond effectively, and, furthermore, that this understanding rests not only upon clinical inspiration, but upon a more solid base of theoretical and clinical knowledge.

In our early experiences with borderline and psychotic children, the rapid fluctuation in their ego state appeared to have most relevance to psychotherapeutic planning and to interpretive technique, particularly the alteration in primary-process and secondary-process dominance. There followed a search for interpretive techniques which would prove helpful when the child did not have available the capacity to employ secondary-process thought and language.

Continued observation of such children has drawn our attention increasingly to the *multiple dimensions of ego regression*, and to the importance of spelling out these dimensions in planning treatment for each patient. While the concepts of ego regression (and ego progression) have long been recognized as umbrella concepts, their use, nevertheless, suggests a uniformity in the regression of the various ego functions which is in contrast to the significant unevenness observed. Furthermore, since regression describes a conglomeration of psychological happenings, the use of the single concept tends to obscure rather than to clarify these covariant psychological occurrences. Our experience suggests that the elaboration of the different psychological occurrences which comprise the regressive experience for each patient is of central relevance in understanding the appropriateness of the interpretive mode for each.

There is a direct connection between the aspect of the regression which the therapist regards as of primary importance and the theoretical rationale underlying the technique. For example, Madame Sechehaye [1] in describing her work with severely regressed schizophrenic adults states: "It is important to the analyst to enter into contact with the patient at the exact level of his regression, however archaic it may be." She describes a patient at a preverbal stage who she feels can be reached by physical care rather than by words. Here the therapist selects the dimension of verbal versus nonverbal capacity in the patient's regression as the determinant of her interpretive choice. In many instances, this particular dimension provides the patient's most important communication, which is also technically useful to the therapist. Yet, theoretically and more generally, her choice is not the only possible one since several of the ego functions which change with the change in ego state can enter into a consideration of the choice of the interpretive mode. The range of possible ways of contact between patient and therapist is necessarily limited. Out of their meeting comes the mutual adaptation which creates a language adapted to the child and possible for the therapist. Accordingly, the dimensions selected by the therapist as the chief determinant of his interpretive mode will vary with each patient within the vicissitudes of the treatment process and with the therapist's capacities.

Observation of psychotic transference manifestations has brought several dimensions of regression into sharper focus. For instance, a child's regression to a symbiotic transference relationship is marked by a multiplicity of ego changes, including breakdown in ability to differentiate past and present; propensity toward trigger action; breakdown of symbolic communication; tendency to fuse parent with therapist; difficulty in maintaining cathected ego boundaries; and difficulty in experiencing any but extreme and unmodified affects.

The following excerpt from a therapy hour of a fifteen year old schizophrenic girl illustrates some of these ego changes as seen by the patient. A severe psychotic episode had preceded this hour.

Mary now took out her story and was going to read it to me, but before she did so commented that she had been feeling better lately. She said she had spent a lot of time the night before in planning how she would escape from the hospital and go and see Doctor B. (her former therapist), but she had no intention of doing it. She was just getting enjoyment from thinking about it and this was now different with her, that she was going back to where she had been a while ago and she can now think about something and not have to do it immediately. I commented that I guessed what she was saying was that she could now tell the difference between thinking something and doing something and it sounded like that gave her more freedom. She said yes it did and she was getting back to that way. She hadn't been that way in quite a while.

She said that she had been writing to Doctor B. and it helped her to have him write but if he didn't want to write to her to just say so. She did not want to feel that he was writing only to help her or only because he felt that he had to. She wanted to be sure that he was writing because he wanted to.

Here the patient tries thoughtfully to review a recent psychotic episode. In so doing she spontaneously distinguishes her experiences along several dimensions, along a relationship axis and along an action-language continuum. The patient describes her feelings of change in her capacity to separate thought from action, and her emerging wish to give up a magical domination of the therapist for a more mature, interpersonal relationship. She looks back upon the psychotic episode as one in which magical omnipotence was the dominant relationship mode and in which trigger language was the dominant communicative mode. We note, accordingly, a range of communicative modes and of relationship modes in the patient which, under optimum conditions of treatment, will find their counterpart in the range of interpretive modes of the psychotherapist. In this hour, for instance, the therapist was able to make use of interpretations which approximated interpretive technique with neurotic patients.

One of the distinctive aspects of work with borderline and psychotic children is that frequently the therapist feels that his interpretive choice at the moment represents the only choice possible. This reflects, in part, the limited range in the capacity for contact which this category of children possesses. Furthermore, one of the primitive defensive devices of these children is to constrict the range of relationships tolerable to them lest their tenuous defenses be threatened to the point of panic and loss of their precarious identity. Consequently, they set up stringent conditions for contact; when a response is evoked, it often appears that only the one possibility for contact existed.

Another clinical excerpt epitomizes the characteristic attributes of this interaction.

Ted, the borderline child, part of whose therapy has already been mentioned (Chapter 4) repeatedly played out the following game in his therapy hours: The therapist was stationed by the child in the middle of the school yard and was instructed not to move while the child ran at breakneck speed from one end of the yard to the other. Ted told her that it was her task to guess his current secret fantasy (referred to as a "secret field") in the split second that the child crossed in front of her. The strict conditions of the interplay were that if the therapist guessed correctly the child would drop the ball which he was holding. If not, he would return at the same speed and each time provide her with a single chance, a single clue, and a single second in which to guess.

Regardless of her understanding, the therapist's intervention here remains effectively circumscribed by the child's condition that the therapist make use of the single chance which the patient provides. It is not correct to infer from this material that the child was setting up impossible conditions for contact. On the rare occasions when the therapist was able to meet these extraordinary conditions and guess the secret correctly, the child was vastly and pathetically relieved for the remainder of the hour. The game accurately depicts Ted's feeling of being almost inaccessible to a relationship with another person and hence almost beyond help, except by what would appear to be a magical intervention of the kind used in the movies where the heroine is miraculously rescued from imminent disaster.

One interpretive mode with which we have been clinically familiar for some time but which we have only recently begun to link theoretically to the psychology of these particular patients, is the use of the *symbolic act as an interpretation*. This technique rests on the conscious symbolic use of the act as the therapist's method of communicating with the patient of whom it is presumed that he can be effectively reached only in this way. This is a form of expression very familiar from everyday life. Each of us has had experiences where a particular movement or gesture conveyed more than words possibly could; where, in fact, words failed because of the strength of the message to be conveyed. Similarly, among the limitations of this technique we note that while many degrees of affective intensity can be portrayed in this way, it is hard to communicate nuances of ideas by way of action. In this sense, symbolic action represents a relatively impoverished method of speaking as compared, for instance, with the richness of the classical interpretation.

We offer first a clinical example of a situation in which the symbolic act seemed the only way of communication open to the therapist. The patient is a six year old borderline boy in the time month of treatment.

Jack asked that we play hotel and he invited me into the playroom where he set up an imaginary lunch, carefully dividing the play cookies equally between us. I said it would really be wonderful if it were like this all the time instead of everybody fighting and hurting each other. Jack nodded and we played for a while quietly at eating our lunch. He then bounded up on the play table and started to look at some of the toys. As he turned to get off the table he slipped and fell from the table which was quite high from the floor. He did not raise his hands to protect his face. Consequently, he fell flat on his face, landing with a heavy bang on the floor. He rose, lips bleeding, and started to wail. He permitted me to hold him and to examine him, but my holding him in no wise comforted him. He held his body apart and rigid and his crying had a quality to it different from that of a child's crying. It seemed to be of a deeper kind of almost inconsolable wailing, as if implicit in the crying was the fact that no one was expected to come.

After ten minutes of crying, Jack returned to the play table, took back the lunch which he had arranged for me and said, "You get no lunch." I said that I understood that. He meant that his falling was my fault. "Yes," he said with tremendous intensity, "you did not catch me, so no lunch." (It would have been physically impossible for anyone except a professional runner to catch Jack at the distance at which I was from him when he fell.) I said, "That's right, Jack, I didn't catch you, and I didn't keep you from falling, but I would like it very much if you wouldn't always be falling and not putting your hands out to help yourself, and I would like it if some day you would trust me enough to let me comfort you when you do fall." Jack handed me an empty Coke bottle and said, "Here, eat this." "Yes," I said, "and that will be punishment for me and then my mouth will hurt just like yours." "That's right," he said with great feeling. I pretended to eat the empty Coke bottle and I started to cry like the child had been crying. I cried out aloud, "My tooth, my tooth, nobody cares about me, nobody wants to catch me. Nobody cares, I'm all alone, I'm all alone." Jack regarded me with great animation and encouraged me to go on. "Pretend you got another tooth knocked out, and then another." I did so and continued to lose lots and lots of teeth. Finally the child said relentingly, "You may have some chocolate milk." I thanked him profusely for the imaginary chocolate milk which he gave to me, and as I was drinking Jack said suddenly, "Will you catch me if I fall?" Without any more notice, he jumped up on the play table with great rapidity, and threw himself headlong into space. Again he made no move to protect himself against the impact of the fall. By what seemed to be a miracle, this time I caught the child and I twirled him around several times saying that I had caught a lovely little boy and I was so glad that he had let me catch him. Jack laughed happily.

Although the child is borderline and not schizophrenic, the interaction and the interpretive mode described have as their model the earliest prototypical relationship; that interaction between mother and baby which precedes verbal interchange and clear differentiation of self from nonself in the baby. In fact, the particular clinical illustration reflects the relationship between mother and child in its beginning, when the child screams with hunger pains and the mother in bringing him milk correctly "interprets" his needs. As with the nonverbal baby, the only way in which to assure Jack of the therapist's interest, of her understanding of the disappointments he has sustained in the past, of her hope that she would be able to facilitate change in the present and the future, was to do so on his own terms and in the language which he understood, that is by magically catching him when he fell.

From this use of the single symbolic act as the interpretation, we extrapolate instances when the patient's psychosis is sufficiently pervasive so that the therapist's maintenance of a particular symbolic action stance or role seems to provide the only avenue of communication and interpretation. An example of this was provided by Ken, an eight year old, whose severe schizophrenia was marked by fluctuation between a contactless autism and an equally contactless savage and uncontrollable destructiveness. The only relationship tolerable to him, and even this for only a short period of time, seemed to be one in which the adult acted the role of a symbiotic partner and could be included by him within his ego boundaries. The words of the patient, happily referring to his therapist, were, "She is my big foot."

With Ken, the initial treatment strategy was predicated upon a symbolic exploitation of this relationship and an attempt to cement a symbiotic transference and identification. Accordingly, the therapist not only made abundant use of the pronoun "we" in referring either to herself or to the child, but literally walked when the child walked, crouched when he did, and offered herself wherever possible as a physical and psychological extension of the child. When Ken asked, "What do you do when you are away from here?" the therapist answered, "I think of you."

After three months of this technique, when the therapist told Ken that she would be going away on a short vacation, he responded by asking for an electric extension cord. He soberly plugged one end of the cord into himself and the other end into the therapist after which he was able to let her go. In this way he indicated not only that his needs and ways of communication had been correctly understood, but also, and significantly, that this understanding had led to an increase in *his* capacity for symbolic communication. Similarly, when the therapist returned from her vacation Ken greeted her with an alarm clock which he made ring as soon as he saw her as if to say, "Now that you are here I may awaken from my sleep, that is, can give up my autistic position."

Thus, the continual duplication of his activity by the therapist, the symbolic action stance, had been entirely understood by the child in its full emotional context and had enabled him to achieve a higher level of ego organization. This advance of Ken's opened the possibilities for other modes of communication and interpretation.

Symbolic action, as an interpretive mode, provides a flexible tool with various adaptive possibilities. Sometimes communication is thought to be operating on a verbal and symbolic level but actually derives its primary effectiveness not from content but from the soothing tone of a therapist's voice, the repetitive rhythm, the continuity of words, the predictability of voice, words, and rhythm. These can readily be understood as interpretation via a symbolic act modeled after the mother's lullaby to the very young child.

There are limitations and hazards which attach to the symbolic act as an interpretive mode. If not rigorously attuned to the needs of the patient, it can all too easily lend itself to the expression of transference and countertransference needs of the therapist and to what Gitelson [2] refers to as "acting out in the countertransference." In addition, the separation of symbolic from real gratification is not easy to conceptualize clearly or to maintain. The interpretive mode described derives its usefulness from its conscious symbolic use by the therapist and the actual or potential capacity for symbolization and symbolic communication in the patient. In the case of Ken we observe a striking illustration of the borderland between the concrete and the symbolic. Psychotherapeutic work depends upon the crossing of this border.

A closely related interpretive choice is associated with language tied to motor activity which brooks no delay. This may be characterized as representing the dominance of *trigger language* in which the word, like a red flag, triggers the action implied in the word, without any intervening delay or control mechanism. At times each of us, despite well-consolidated maturity, shows the capacity to respond trigger-like—in everyday language, unthinkingly—to words that are affectively charged for us in particular ways. The school desegregation issue is, in some situations, a complex social problem with many political, moral, and psychological implications. In other situations, it is a direct incitement to riot.

We soon learned with Ted that, in certain ego states, the tentatively offered comment that he might be feeling angry would indeed lead him to a direct angry outburst. Ted experienced the therapist's statement that it was the end of the hour as the direct end of the relationship; he was triggered into an attempt to annihilate the therapist and to break the playroom to pieces. At such times the patient was totally inaccessible to verbal intervention by the therapist.

When trigger language or signal language is dominant over language used with appropriate symbols and delays, the psychotherapist in shaping his response needs to be concerned with necessary verbal omissions, substitutions, and circumventions. He must learn, for instance, not to use certain signal words. When the dominant transference is reflected in trigger language, the possibilities for psychotherapeutic help become sharply limited, especially since the trigger words are those most often used in interpretive communication. In extreme situations this may lead to a temporarily blocked situation where the therapist's understanding cannot be effectively translated for the child. At such times, it is important to remember that effective psychotherapy with such patients can be based on the fact that other ego states are available side by side with this regressed position and will reappear.

We have confined ourselves here to discussing some of the factors which influence interpretive choice in the psychotherapy of borderline and psychotic children with particular reference to ego fluctuation along an action-symbolization continuum. This continuum ranges from trigger action, which permits no delay, to the mature use of thought as trial action, and constitutes only one of the ego changes which may influence or govern interpretive choice. Psychotherapy with these children depends upon finding or creating a common language which begins the relationship, enables its development, and will, if successful, eventually become unnecessary. It is this language and the finding of it which characterize work with these children.

We may conceptualize this psychotherapeutic interaction by likening the borderline and psychotic child to the small baby, with its limited expression range, and likening the psychotherapist to the mother, whose special capacities for taking care of the baby and particular sensitivities to the baby's needs will be decisive for the mother-baby interaction. Similarly, the specific capacities and sensitivities of the psychotherapist when brought together with the limited expression range and unknown potential of these patients will create a unique psychotherapeutic relationship. This particular interaction of synchronism which varies with each such patient-therapist unit will find expression in a specific choice of communication within the interpretive process.

REFERENCES

[1] Sechehaye, M. A. The transference in symbolic realization, Int. J. Psychoanal., 37:270, 1956.

[2] Gitelson, M. The emotional position of the analyst in the psychoanalytic situation, Int. J. Psychoanal., 33:1,1952.

8

INTERPRETATION WITHIN THE METAPHOR: FURTHER CONSIDERATIONS*

The investigation of metaphor is curiously like the investigation of any of the primary data of consciousness; it cannot be pursued very far without our being led to the borderline of sanity. Metaphor is as ultimate as speech itself, and speech as ultimate as thought.

JOHN MIDDLETON MURRY

Among choices of interpretations, we mention "interpretation within the metaphor." Although this, like all interpretation, has its dangers, we point out that the use of the metaphor may be regarded as an essential technique for gradually establishing communication and initial insight with borderline and schizophrenic patients but that it must not be regarded as a treatment technique in itself. It is but a preliminary approximation to the final therapeutic act which ultimately consists of a classical interpretation at the level of the secondary process. The use of the metaphor derives its primary value from maintaining contact with patients who are in constant danger of being inundated by a breakthrough of primary-process material. In such patients, the ego structure is so fragmented that it seems to be isolated islands [1] of secondary-process functioning in constant danger of becoming temporarily flooded by archaic modes of thought, which may then recede to permit the resumption of adaptive functioning in limited areas. In such instances the metaphor can, metaphorically speaking, be regarded as a bridge between the remaining islands of ego functioning. Although relatively intact, their brittle defensive structure could not withstand the impact of a secondary-process interpretation aimed at bringing the material to the level of conscious awareness and thus in the service of

* Elaine Caruth is coauthor of this chapter.

158

adaptive functions. The metaphor utilizes primary-process material, manipulates it, as it were, but does not translate or lift its meaning into the language of the secondary process. The metaphor may be of particular value with the patient who is beginning to decathect any discourse which requires adaptation to reality. Like the dream, the metaphor enables the patient to maintain the necessary distance with the feeling that the meaning of the dream/metaphor is ego-dystonic and not meant by him really. Only gradually is the meaning accepted as part of the inner reality.

The borderline patient is struggling with two types of discontinuities. Like the neurotic patient he still retains the separation between conscious and unconscious processes, even though in the schizophrenic there tends to be an invasion into consciousness of previously repressed thoughts due, as Wexler has postulated,[2] to the decathexis of object representations in the unconscious. In addition, however, he is also struggling with discontinuities in ego functioning arising out of the fragmented ego structure with its lack of appropriate defense and adaptive devices. The use of the metaphor enables therapist and patient to establish continuity between the remaining islands of ego functions and, at the same time, helps to maintain sufficient discontinuity between primary and secondary process, thus avoiding further ego regression. In this way, the metaphor maintains discontinuity by not forcing the conflict into direct consciousness. Yet, paradoxically, it simultaneously creates greater continuity by permitting insights that can be tolerated at the increased psychic distance which the metaphor facilitates. The use of the metaphor serves the defensive function of allowing the patient to maintain greater distance from conscious awareness of the content of the conflict, even while serving the adaptive functions of facilitating a reduction in distance between the therapist and the patient. The metaphor enables the former to follow the latter to this lower but more optimal level of ego functioning at which he is capable of operating while still maintaining his psychic integrity in the face of psychotherapeutic interventions.

It is important to note that it is the patient who normally initiates the use of the metaphor. The borderline and schizophrenic patient frequently has no real choice at the moment that he does so; it is the only language then available to him and he must "speak" it rather than deliberately and manipulatively "use" it, which is a choice open only to the therapist. Thus, only when Teresa (Chapter 3) says, "I'm in the middle of an island, Doctor," does the therapist speak of treatment as building a two-way bridge to her island, the very groundwork of which he is laying at the moment that he follows her choice of metaphor. He uses the metaphor to communicate with her at a level which maintains sufficient distance to enable her to sustain contact under conditions which respect her specific ego difficulty.

The borderline patient tends to use the metaphor at a point when the psychic organization has become weakened, when primary processes are threatening to invade ego functions, and when the ability to communicate at an abstract symbolic level is disappearing. The patient is losing the capacity to differentiate between object, and sign or symbol for the object. The "as if" quality of the more abstract meaning of the metaphor is lost and the metaphor becomes an immediate concrete experience. This concretization of thinking has been frequently described by investigators of schizophrenic thought disorders,[3] generally in terms of the patient's inability to conceptualize a relationship of mere representation between symbol and object and a tendency to look for more concrete relationships between them.[4]

The normal or neurotic person, on the other hand, uses the metaphor by choice, in the service of goal-oriented thinking, and at an abstract level. He may choose the metaphor as a sort of alibi, a conscious allusion which is a way of implying what he wants to communicate without actually committing himself, a way of simultaneously keeping and revealing a secret. Like the repartee of the cocktail party, the metaphor permits a kind of freedom and license which is recognized by both parties to be both meant and not meant at the same time. The metaphor may also serve an aesthetic function; for some people the veiled implication becomes more attractive, just as does the veiled portrait. The therapist uses the metaphor in communicating at a level which maintains sufficient distance to enable the patient to re-establish or sustain contact. Thus, with Teresa's metaphor of the island, the therapist uses it to describe how Mexico City was originally an island and was slowly connected with the mainland. He communicates his understanding of her fears through this interpretation within the metaphor:

> . . . at first the Aztecs were isolated . . . do you know why . . . they preferred to live on islands? . . . it was safer . . . in those days the tribes used to fight each other and . . . an island was easier to defend . . . because the enemies could not get to the island. And when the tribes around them became . . . their friends then they slowly built bridges . . . to the mainland . . . and the islands were not needed any more.

When we look at the borderline and schizophrenic patient's relation to concrete reality, we note an interesting reversal. Whereas we described above his inability to deal abstractly with verbal symbols (the metaphor being understood as a concrete proposition rather than an allusion), when he is actually faced with a piece of concrete reality he may then deal with it metaphorically. He experiences the concrete piece of present reality as if it were symbolic of an earlier inner reality. For example, with Teresa, presents given to her by the therapist were never reacted to as a current and actual event taking place between them but rather served only to trigger off fantasies of earlier gifts. The concrete immediate reality of the gift could be reacted to only as if it represented something else. To paraphrase a modern writer, for such a patient "a rose is a rose is not a rose" and one does well to weigh carefully the impact of gifts to such a patient in terms of their potential symbolic realization. A more dramatic example of Teresa's tendency to deal with concrete reality in metaphoric fashion may be seen in an incident of psychotic acting out. She "chose" to communicate her conflict over sexual feelings in the transference via an action metaphor (see Chapter 21), in which she set fire to pieces of furniture in her home. For her, the actual act of firesetting was a metaphoric expression of her sexual feelings accompanied by an almost complete loss of the capacity to judge the reality meaning or consequences of her act. For this patient, acting out and action serve as the metaphoric expression of a thought, not unlike the symbolic meaning of a dream act, whereas thoughts may become concrete reality. For the neurotic, thinking is trial action; [5] whereas for the borderline, thinking becomes action unmediated by "trial," and action and acting out becomes a form of trial thinking or experimental recollection (see Chapter 9).

Just as the patient communicates through action metaphors, the therapist may similarly choose to communicate through a symbolic act or stance (Chapter 7). Early in Teresa's treatment, the therapist chose to communicate with her his capacity and willingness to remain with her in her "wonderland" by attempting to gratify her constant and insatiable demands for gifts of food and small toys. As he began to move towards internalizing the conflict between remaining at an infantile regressed level of fairy tales and fantasies as opposed to growing up, maturing, and facing her fears of heterosexuality and growth, his gifts began to reflect this choice, i.e., a movie magazine or a child's fairy tale, candy or a teenage story. At one point he chose to "interpret within the regression" the girl's increasing withdrawal through symbolically play-acting a nap. He then succeeded in establishing contact with her and "waking" her up sufficiently so that she questioned him about what he may have dreamed. His symbolic act was followed by metaphoric communication about her desire to withdraw into a never-never land of her imagination. This symbolic act followed by the symbolic communication permitted contact to be maintained at a point when the girl's withdrawal had become so extreme as to simulate a level of consciousness close to sleep.

With this particular patient, metaphoric communication initiated by her during her first therapy hour has proved a major medium of communication. At times the therapist remains entirely within the metaphor, at other times he chooses to interpret the metaphoric communication at the level of the secondary process. During one hour the patient sought to make him describe her beauty as similar to Snow White, Cinderella, or Tinker Bell; he tried to define it in such a way as to establish some contact with reality. While she was angrily and persistently beseeching him to describe her beauty in the language of her fantasies, he described her as a frightened deer who does not wish to come where people are, or a beautiful rose with thorns to protect her from being touched. This hour ended in a truly charming metaphoric interchange. She asked him to bring her a real rose, he acquiesced but pointed out that it would have to have thorns— for only artificial roses have none. "All right," she acceded, "bring me a rose with thorns and I'll pull them off myself," thus telling him she will maintain the façade of being real, while actually still choosing to remove its sting and remain in her fantasy world. Again, to use the metaphor of another hour, she choses the Never-Never Land of Peter Pan to the everyday school tasks of Wendy. On a more basic level, she told him she chose to return to an autistic level, excluding him from any true discourse and allowing him only to echo mechanically her dereistic intrapsychic communications in a deanimate fashion.

If the metaphoric mode chosen by the borderline child is responded to correctly, the danger of possibly arousing the pre-existing paranoid trends is eliminated. In addition, he cannot help but know what the therapist is getting at, and, furthermore, feel safe because he also knows that he is not going to be forced to reveal or deal with anything except that which he himself selects. Furthermore, metaphoric communication may to some extent repeat an earlier preverbal type of communication, arising out of the original faith situation of the mother-child fusion, where there was no need for communication because there was communion, the precursor of what will be later unanimity of opinion.[5] Interpreting within the metaphor permits communication beyond what is verbalized in the manifest content. While there is no direct interpretation about the underlying latent meaning, it is alluded to by symbols to which patient and therapist react in "unanimity." Patient and therapist are, in a sense, in wordless communion, and this may lead to such a feeling of empathy on the therapist's part that it may appear to approximate the symbiotic experience which the borderline and schizophrenic patient is endlessly driving towards as well as struggling against. By empathy we refer here to the essentially preconscious therapeutic phenomenon of temporarily sharing or experiencing the feelings of the patient in the service of developing deeper understanding.[6]

The capacity for empathy originates in the early mother-child nonverbal communication, i.e., the communion of the early symbiosis. The process of empathy—a function of the experiencing ego rather than the analyzing ego to which the function of intuition belongs—involves a temporary decathexis of the therapist's own self-image and thus lends itself to the above experience.

The therapist ended his analysis of the first hour with Teresa by quoting from *Alice in Wonderland:* "Now, kitty, let's consider, who was it that dreamed it all—it must have been either me or the Red King—he was part of my dream of course, but I was part of his dream, too." One year and 115 sessions later, such a degree of empathetic understanding had developed between patient and therapist that the therapist truly pondered whether his interpretation of certain communications within the hour were a projection of his own or were true insights into the girl's projections. During this hour, the girl started to do her "homework" for school, pasting pictures of current events in her notebook. She seemingly selected them at random from a pile of pictures which she had brought with her. She sat preoccupied with this self-imposed task, functioning seemingly at the regressed level of a first-grader, but obviously feeling subjectively as if she were fulfilling the school task appropriately. Excluded from this activity, the therapist managed to intrude himself by commenting upon the literal meaning of the pictures that she had selected. These turned out to be a picture of Dag Hammerskjold's funeral and one of a saint currently being decanonized for lack of positive evidence as to her saintliness.

Gradually, the therapist began to see the underlying meaning in these "current events" which, upon closer analysis of the girl's inner reality, could be understood as her actuality.[7] The concept of actuality refers to those aspects of reality which reflect the patient's current psychological task and are selected out and acted upon by him. She herself was preoccupied with destructive impulses against the therapist/man of peace who, like Hammerskjold, was trying to help her live more happily. She was also beset with guilt over her own sinfulness and lack of saintliness, as it were, which she, within the psychotic transference, blamed on him. She dwelt on the dilemma of the saint and wondered if she perhaps really had been innocent but just had given a wrong impression so that perhaps the Church might have been incorrect. Finally, able to tolerate a less distant dealing with the material, she left the metaphor, and wondered if she herself were really good or innocent.

Subsequently, the therapist, recollecting the seeming random selection of these current events—literally drawn out of a huge pile of clippings —wondered whose actuality was operating during the hour. Was it his own actuality of what he had chosen to focus upon in treatment recently, or the girl's which had led to a selective collection and presentation of these "current events"? The requisite empathy that developed between patient and therapist led to such momentary doubts. These doubts were further intensified by the tremendous object hunger in this girl which was voracious and devouring but which she reversed and experienced subjectively as being constantly overpowered. She constantly felt, and frequently provoked, being manipulated and overpowered; she stimulated in the therapist the countertransference feeling that he was force-feeding her as it were, by "dreaming her dream," and re-establishing the fusion relationship which she both dreaded and sought. At the same time, this was also the girl's "dream," and the actuality of her present therapeutic conflicts was operating prior to the therapy hour in her very selection of these current events. But it must also be noted that the girl "dreamed this particular dream," i.e., brought in these particular events, under the reconstituting influence of the therapist. By that time, he was a part of her —a primitive introject who, although fluctuating, was maintained from hour to hour.

This issue of "who does what to whom," of who is stronger, of whether the therapist is going to cure the patient or the girl is going to contaminate the therapist, or whether both are going to happen in the symbiotic fusion of patient and therapist, was also metaphorically evident in the communications of the first treatment hour. This can be seen in her having related the television story of the gift to a teacher which forced her to become someone other than herself. This tale the patient followed with the one about a man rescued from a frozen sleep by an evil angel who was strong enough to turn him into a monster like herself. The patient was torn between feelings of either bedeviling or being bedeviled; of being a lifeless puppet or an evil puppeteer who controls the therapist. In her can be seen the infant's total helplessness alongside the infant's omnipotent megalomania, a primary narcism stemming from the undifferentiated mother-child fusion and being re-experienced within the transference psychosis.

It would appear, therefore, that the limits, complications, and countertransference potentials of this technique are essentially those of every other therapeutic technique. The therapist always needs knowledge, skill, and insight to understand the conditions under which a particular technical tool is applicable.

REFERENCES

1 Knight, R. P. Borderline states, Bull. Menninger Clin., 17:1, 1953.
2 Wexler, M. Hypotheses concerning ego deficiency in schizophrenia, in The Out-Patient Treatment of Schizophrenia, Samuel C. Scher and Howard R. Davis, eds., New York, Grune & Stratton, 1960, p. 33.

[3] Kasanin, J., ed. Language and Thought in Schizophrenia, Berkeley, University of California Press, 1946.

[4] Aleksandrowicz, D. R. The meaning of metaphor, Bull. Menninger Clin., 26:92, 1962.

[5] Ekstein, R. Faith and reason in psychotherapy, Bull. Menninger Clin., 22:1, 1958.

[6] Greenson, R. R. Empathy and its vicissitudes, Int. J. Psychoanal., 41:418, 1960.

[7] Erikson, E. H. Reality and actuality, J. Amer. Psychoanal Ass., 10:451, 1962.

PART FOUR

COMMUNICATION AND ITS GROWTH: IMPULSE, PLAY, ACT, AND WORD

Acting out is a form of experimental recollection.
RUDOLF EKSTEIN and SEYMOUR FRIEDMAN

9

THE FUNCTION OF ACTING OUT, PLAY ACTION, AND PLAY ACTING IN THE PSYCHOTHERAPEUTIC PROCESS*

When once the second system has concluded its exploratory thought activity, it releases the inhibition and damming-up of the excitations and allows them to discharge themselves in movement.

SIGMUND FREUD

Restraint upon motor discharge (upon action) which then became necessary, was provided by means of the process of thinking, which was developed from the presentation of ideas. Thinking was endowed with characteristics which made it possible for the mental apparatus to tolerate an increased tension of stimulus, while the process of discharge was postponed. It is essentially an experimental kind of acting, accompanied by displacement of relatively small quantities of cathexis, together with less expenditure (discharge) of them.

SIGMUND FREUD

In the psychoanalysis of adult neurotics, acting out is considered a substitute for recollection,[1] while thinking is regarded as experimental action.[2] Our clinical material, derived from the treatment of a neurotic delinquent adolescent boy, suggests that *acting out is a form of experimental recollection*. Play action and play acting, both facets of play to be differentiated later, may be thought of as containing the elements of both acting out and thinking. Freud's reference to the dream as the royal road to the unconscious has often been quoted whenever the classical technique applicable for adult neurotics is discussed. The royal road to the unconscious of the child patient is his play,[3] his best means for the communication

* Seymour W. Friedman is coauthor of this chapter.

169

of the unconscious conflict. Nevertheless, as one knows from the treatment of more severely disturbed children, it is not always possible to create a situation which permits the use of play, just as many borderline adult patients are not capable of using free association.

Play requires a certain maturation of the ego organization. It is possible, therefore, only in those situations where the achievements of maturation are fairly stable and are not excessively invaded by more regressive precursors of thinking such as acting out, a more primitive mode of attempted problem solving. In order more clearly to understand the differing functions of acting out, play action, and play acting within the structure of the therapeutic process, we must review certain facets of ego development.

In the genesis of the psychic apparatus one observes that the main mode of functioning consists of instant need gratification. The first, most primitive "problem solving" of the human mind consists primarily of instant impulse discharge, and even the attempts at hallucinatory gratification by means of vivid fantasies are but substitute means of instant need gratification. The preverbal period of personality development, in which motility and motor development are dominant, usually takes place in a symbiotic relationship. The mother is used as the auxiliary ego which not only gratifies and prohibits, but also thinks for the infant who, in a certain sense, is capable of a kind of "thought" as expressed through impulsive action whenever need arises. As the psychic apparatus develops, modes of problem solution grow richer, and impulsive action is supplemented, among others, by play action.

Accompanying this change, more advanced thought is developed in spoken language. While action is an attempt to master reality immediately in order to make it subservient to the needs of the individual, play action actually is delayed action as far as reality is concerned, and combines the quasi-gratification of play with an attempt at resolution of conflict. Although the child's play has been considered as his first great cultural achievement [4] through which he is capable of giving up immediate gratification, it still is near the primary-process mode of thinking.

The model example illustrating the original function of play and demonstrating it as an attempt to master the separation from the mother can be found in *Beyond the Pleasure Principle*. This first achievement of impulse delay by the child is an unstable one and frequently cannot be maintained. If too much inner or outer stress burdens the child, he cannot use play action to counteract increasing anxiety and must return to earlier modes of mastery or pseudo mastery such as emergency measures extending to panic reactions. Panic could be considered as a form of action since one of its meanings is to summon the rescuer. Parenthetically, we may say that the replacement of play by action does not always necessarily mean ego regression. If play is considered a form of trial thinking, action may well represent the final carrying out of a task which has been successfully thought out. We might well then differentiate between acting out—the unconscious repetition of a conflict—and action—the conscious solution of a conflict situation.

As the mental development of the growing child continues, he slowly replaces more and more elements of play action by expressed fantasy and higher forms of thought. Pure nonhallucinatory fantasy could be considered as standing between play action and secondary-process thinking in the hierarchy of prevalent modes of thinking. The stages of mental development—action without delay, play action, pure fantasy, play acting, reality-oriented secondary-process thinking—should not be seen as distinctly separated from each other but as arrangements in which any of these modes of thought might be dominant while other, coexisting modes are more or less submerged. Psychosexual development [5] is similar in that it contains not distinctly different phases but different dominant expressions of instinctual life. Hartmann's concept of phase dominance [6] is applicable to ego development as well as to instinctual development.

For example, although we assume that forms of problem solving or pseudo problem solving, such as vivid imagery, the first beginning of language, and simple reality testing are present in the one-year-old child, action is his dominant means of problem solving and of communication. Play action is, therefore, a very complex mental phenomenon which includes the act, the fantasy, advanced elements of language, and frequently strong aspects of reality testing. The child knows that he plays rather than acts and may criticize the adult who assumes that the child takes his play fantasy seriously in the sense that he cannot test outer reality. But even if the secondary-process thought is in command, we know that it is accompanied by more primitive forms of mental functioning.

Here we shall attempt to develop the concept of acting out as experimental recollection; of play action as the slow replacement of impulsive and inappropriate action by a more advanced form of thinking; of play acting as an initial identification with a fantasied object in order experimentally to master the future; and of fantasy as a higher form of play action in which the need for action is given up. Whatever the patient produces, acts out, plays out, or talks out, is to be understood within the framework of psychotherapy as the communication of the unconscious conflict that has driven the patient to seek the help of the psychotherapist. Since acting out is an attempt to resolve an unconscious conflict of the past, it is neither appropriate in terms of current reality testing, nor adequate in the forming and maintaining of present object relationships.

In structural terms, one must say that it expresses the dominance of id over ego, while secondary-process thought constitutes the dominance of ego over id. In terms of the capacity for object cathexis, acting out is a manifestation of a more narcissistic personality organization, while secondary-process thinking usually implies the capacity for more normal object relationships.*

The precursors of acting out in the genesis of the psychic apparatus are found in the preverbal period of the child's development.[7, 8] Greenacre suggests that a child who learns language from parents whom he basically cannot trust will not rely on speech as a means of orienting himself to reality and is apt to regress in later life to preverbal forms of communication, that is, to acting out, in order to find a better means of reality adaptation. Acting out, it can be said, originates in the impulsive act of the infant, his only means to obtain gratification, to "call" the helper. Later acting out contains a variety of elements. In common with the impulsive act, the first way of the baby to meet his needs, it contains the quality of impulsivity and the lack of sufficient capacity for reality testing. In this latter sense it can be considered as inappropriate action. Together with play, it contains certain elements of thought and action which attempt to bring about recollection. And since it is usually fairly well rationalized, it also contains elements of advanced thought, an attempt at integration with these elements in the personality which are capable of reality testing. The impulse and the frustrating environment thus may be thought of as the "parents" of acting out.

In classical adult analysis, acting out has always been considered a major form of resistance,[9] as a substitute for remembering and the free-associative process. Attempts are usually made to stop it through interpretation and, occasionally, through taboos, if the acting out seems to make the psychotherapeutic process impossible. For certain adults whose character structure included excessive acting out before the beginning of analysis, it has been suggested that analysis might not be the preferred

* These comments on the hierarchy of different forms of thinking, of different aspects of the psychic apparatus, have their usefulness if understood within the framework of psychotherapy. The concept of acting out is used in a different framework if it is applied simply in order to describe asocial behavior. Even from a social point of view, however, acting out may consist of socially laudable action. We use the concept here in order to describe and explain certain behavior which is to be understood as repetition of an unconscious conflict, as the patient's only available way to communicate this conflict. The repetition of the conflict is possible only under the condition of the distance device of acting out. The function of distance as a psychological concept and its role in the psychotherapeutic communication are discussed in Chapters 15 and 19.

method of treatment [10] but that such patients may require serious modifications of the classical technique.

The free-associative process has been replaced particularly with younger children, largely by communication via play.[11] Thus recognition has been given that the less mature ego organization of the child is not capable of using the free-associative process as expressed in the requirement of the basic rule and must make use of other forms of communication. The play of the child has been likened to the dream of the adult, and the opportunity for play action bears many similarities to, and many differences from, the opportunity for free association in relation to various dream elements.

Just as the adult neurotic is unable to associate freely for considerable stretches during the analytic process, we soon find that the child is unable to play freely and that play interruptions take place which are indicative of increased resistance, increased defense against overwhelming anxiety, and inner instinctual demands.

In order to go beyond the mere descriptive aspects of acting out, we conceive of different states of acting out, seen here as a complex phenomenon which may partake of elements of different components in the hierarchy of the thought organization. We owe to Dr. Helen Sargent [12] an attempt to schematize the concept of *acting out* in relation to developmental stages of impulse expression, mastery, and utilization in problem solving (see Table 1).

The vertical axis of the schema represents the theoretical normal evolution of impulse control from immediate action through stages of delay, internalization, substitution, modulation, and eventual balanced adaptive direction and mastery.

The horizontal axis defines states of impulse expression within the context of mastery mode, thought development and reality testing, and characteristic level of ego organization.

This schema may have generic value in determining the specific stage of acting out in the dynamic interplay during psychotherapy and certainly proves a valuable aid in following the patient during the recovery process.

Our clinical observations are concerned with a type of play interruption in which the play, rather than being replaced by silence or by the change of topics, tends to erupt into acting out. Play action may become so stimulating, so powerful, that it threatens to lead to genuine acting out and impulsive action. The unconscious conflict, then, is not re-enacted via play but tends to be re-enacted in actuality. One may liken such a child to an actor who plays a dramatic part on the stage only to find himself being driven to living out this part off stage. Such a turn of events creates special technical problems for the psychotherapist since communi-

TABLE 1

CONCERNING THE CONCEPT OF "ACTING OUT" IN RELATION TO
STAGES OF IMPULSE MASTERY AND EGO DEVELOPMENT

Levels of Communication	Impulse Expression	Mode of Mastery	Thought Development	Reality Testing	Ego Organization
	Action	Immediate gratification	Hallucinated object	None	Symbiotic
Regressive "call for help or control"	Play Action	Rudimentary replacement of impulse by thought	Trial thought; primary-process-dominated	Play solution as reality test	Struggle against symbiosis
Experimental recollection: past-directed; inappropriate to reality	Fantasy	Gratifying object internalized	Thought substituted for action: primary and secondary	Temporary decathexis of real object	Autism and/or temporary internal gratification
Elements of thought and reality testing; future-directed	Action Fantasy (Play acting)	Preconscious trial solution	Rudimentary secondary-process domination	First attempt to master future by role taking	Beginning of autonomy; identification by imitation
	Delay and Adaptive Direction	Resolution in thought and adaptive action	Secondary process established	Object relationship and reality testing established	Ego identity mature ego

COMPONENTS OF ACTING OUT

cation via action, more than any other form of communication, tends to destroy the psychotherapeutic situation. In the case from which we derived our material, however, we encountered the problem of treating an adolescent boy with strong tendencies to act out his conflict. For him the capacity for verbal communication and free association in a psychotherapeutic setting was so limited as to be almost unavailable to him as a means of therapeutic communication. Since acting out and play action dominated his language development, it seemed necessary to permit his use of this language in the therapeutic situation until his development enabled him to turn to verbal language and to use more conventional form of psychotherapy.

Frank was brought to Southard School by his parents, when he was thirteen years old, as an alternative to detention in the Juvenile Hall of a large Eastern city after he had been caught by the police, following an act of petty thievery. On their way home after committing the crime, he and two other boys of his gang had been discovered carrying dangerous weapons; Frank's was a piece of lead pipe. For Frank, admission to the residential treatment center was a welcome event that climaxed a succession of delinquent acts of petty thievery, truancy, and running away from home. Admission was hopefully a final refuge from an unbearable home situation, and the last resort to save him from what seemed to him his inevitable fate of ending his life by "frying in the hot seat."

Unwanted by both parents from the time of his conception, Frank started life as he fantasied it would end—in an atmosphere of violence, treachery, hatred, faithlessness, and futility. His father, an irresponsible playboy barely out of his adolescence, had impregnated his mistress while Frank's mother was pregnant with Frank. Frank's father acknowledged the affair but refused to accept responsibility. The same irresponsibility, aloofness, and rejection characterized the father's attitude toward his son and his marriage, which from its very inception also had been unstable and turbulent. The father's infidelity was but another incident that poured fuel on an already seething marital discord and added to the mother's fury and desire for revenge. A bewildered girl of seventeen when she had married, Frank's mother found her abrupt plunge into motherhood an impossible task to carry alone. Already burdened with a daughter born one year before Frank, she had immediately become pregnant again only to seek refuge throughout her pregnancy in a threatened miscarriage and in a variety of illnesses. Immature and deeply troubled, she had married mainly to assert her independence and to express her defiance of her own father who characterized her marriage as an act of a "screwball" motivated "only by a biological urge."

Into this marital setting Frank was born five weeks premature, a cyanotic baby unable to breathe spontaneously, sucking and feeding only with the greatest difficulty. An object of pity to his mother and the target of his father's scorn, contempt, and hatred as a weakling, Frank was described by the mother as a baby who refused cuddling and developed slowly. Anxiety, experienced as being caused by his poor state of nutrition, led his mother to force-feed him until by the end of his first year he had become fat.

By the second year he demonstrated his greater need for eating than for cuddling by developing an almost insatiable appetite and an immense craving for sweets. On the advice of a pediatrician, his mother began to deprive him of food, with the result that Frank began to raid the refrigerator and cupboards at night devouring everything edible that he could find. Food, having once been the only supply that his mother had given him freely, now had to be taken forcibly and by stealth.

Goaded by his mother's withholding of, and his intractable hunger for food, he turned to garbage cans for nourishment. At the age of two he had poisoned himself by ingesting rat poison in a neighbor's chicken house, necessitating emergency treatment in a hospital. By the age of four his scavenger activities led him to his mother's purse in search of money, an action which, interpreted by his parents as stealing, resulted in brutal spankings and more deprivation of food by his father. Frank, in retaliation, turned to the neighborhood groceries for food so that by the age of four and thereafter his practice of stealing food, candy, and soft drinks had become a well-established repetitive pattern.

The combination of his apparent general retardation, clumsy motor development, stealing, ravenous greed for sweets, and his indifference to reward or punishment further strained his relationship with his parents to such a point that Frank was regarded by his mother as emotionally inaccessible and unreachable. Attempts at imposing discipline and toilet training were futile and Frank remained enuretic until he was eight, even continuing to wet and soil occasionally when he was thirteen. Thumb sucking, which enraged his parents and could not be stopped by restraints, beatings, scoldings, or food withdrawal, also persisted on occasion until the age of thirteen, when it was replaced by biting and gnawing of his nails and knuckles.

Throughout his first eight years, the continuity of his physical contacts with his mother was broken by repeated moves, living with grandparents, and the abortive efforts by a succession of maids to care for him and his sister while his mother sought to achieve a professional career. Regarding his desperate loneliness and the bleak and dreary emptiness of his early childhood that he could not emotionally communicate, Frank remembered an incident in which he saw himself sitting alone, waiting, for what seemed like hours, for his parents, until in a panic he went in search of them at the home of a friend. Relieved to discover them, he ran to them, only to be scolded and rebuffed and ordered to go home. Another memory of his loneliness, as he described his mother's habitual absence from home, involved a Sunday outing in the park with a neighbor's family that left him with a deep yearning for his mother but with only a sense of hopeless futility and resigned indifference about his capacity ever to win her love.

Frank's early emotional reactions of silent withdrawal, inaccessibility, or sulking changed to overt temper tantrums, rages, and aggressive outbursts against his mother and favored sister following the parents' divorce when Frank was five. Relieved to find that his father would no longer be able to terrorize him, Frank was at the same time confused, puzzled, and disappointed by the meaning of his father's desertion, which he remembered only as a casual announcement by his father that he would be leaving for another city and probably would never see the children again. But what he failed to express verbally and affectively of his deeper feelings regarding his father's abandonment of him, he enacted in his intensified stealing activities and further estrangement from his mother and hated rivalrous sister.

His mother's remarriage when he was nine rekindled Frank's dwindling hope for a loving father. A brief attempt to court the stepfather soon ended in disappointment, pseudo indifference, and resignation, as well as intensified stealing and running away, as Frank found his stepfather wanting in the qualities and characteristics that he fantasied for the ideal father; nor could he tolerate the stepfather's flourishing relationship with his sister. In quiet desperation, Frank expanded the area of his thievery from food to clothes and finally to any object that was not attached or assiduously guarded and accounted for. He became a problem child in school and was repeatedly threatened with expulsion. Falling below his superior intellectual capacity in his failing school performance, he also provoked and taunted the teachers and principal with his boisterous swearing, obscene tricks and jokes, and unruly and defiant behavior. When finally he began to rifle the purses belonging to his female classmates, in reaction to his sister's entrance into the same school, the school authorities demanded that his parents take some drastic action about him.

Attempts by the parents to foster his interest in YMCA and church activities, and to supervise and encourage his association with children of their professional friends led only to his furthering his contacts with other delinquent boys, one of whom was soon detained in the Juvenile Hall for robbery with a gun. Unable to cope with the rising tide of his delinquent behavior, his parents finally acceded to community pressure by requesting psychiatric help, first in a child guidance clinic, which was soon relinquished as allegedly ineffective, and finally with a psychotherapist who was both a social friend and professional colleague of the parents. Although the therapist was helpful in a limited capacity for a year and a half, Frank's detention in the Juvenile Hall, as a haven of safety for him until he reached twenty-one and could forever escape from the hated and intolerable life at home, was conveyed both to the examining psychiatrist during his evaluation at Southard School and to the psychotherapist in his first therapy sessions. He described the state of affairs at home as:

I am angered by my mother and sister. They fuss at me all the time. Both stick up for each other and nobody sticks up for me. I feel alone against them. I have a temperamental temper and almost always I have mean thoughts about my mother. My folks say I shouldn't swear but I'll be damned if I care. Maybe I steal to be a big shot or just to oppose them. I do almost anything I can think of just to oppose them. I steal, get on the loose after curfew, stay out all night. I used to steal things right and left. I just went ahead and did it without thinking. I got so I wasn't careful. I got caught. I wanted to get to Juvenile Hall. I thought they would keep me out of trouble and that would also give me a chance to get away from home.

Despite Frank's glib manner, the gravity and desperation of his situation did not escape him as he acknowledged that things had gotten to such an "extreme urge and necessity, that a very radical step had to be made" so that he was finally brought to Southard School. But on reflection he thought he was "going to like the place," that he was "going to latch onto it." Frank lived up to this prediction of his and stayed at Southard School for five and a half years, undergoing psychotherapy three times a week over a period of five years.

Frank could not have had a more perfect alibi for the police who caught him stealing and the judge who ordered his detention than his lifelong traumatic background. For the staff of the residential center also, his miserable life at home could readily be accepted as the whole explanation of his difficulty. Overidentification with this miserable and appealing boy by those responsible for his care and treatment, as well as the tendency to overlook his loss of capacity to use a home and intimate, stable contacts, could well justify a program which would visualize his treatment only as providing a new and more loving home environment geared to meet his emotional needs. The importance of understanding and treating his intrapsychic conflicts by intensive psychotherapy could, under these circumstances, be quite readily considered unnecessary.

The power of Frank's plight to depict his victimization by his parents and family circumstances as an "alibi" for his delinquent behavior immediately became evident from the character of his initial relationships with the staff personnel. Failure to receive letters from home or the arrival of a brief, cold note from his mother evoked the deepest sympathy from the staff and tended to arouse their furious indignation over the injustice of his neglect and desertion by his family.

In interviews with his social worker, he would freely discuss his disturbed behavior at the school, his stealing from local stores and in the residence, his abortive runaways from the school, and his exhibitionistic pranks and swearing in the classroom. Then he would break into tears or sink into depressive apathy as he would silently make a plea for understanding and acceptance. After destroying his possessions and clothing as horrible reminders of his past, or squandering his allowance on one spending spree, he would recall to the staff his "inadequate background" to excite their sympathy.

Increasing awareness by the staff that almost his sole source of contact with his family lay in the maternal grandparents' financial support of his treatment at the school, stimulated them to try to reach him and to make themselves more available for closer relationships. In his hunger for such relationships, Frank repeatedly reached out to every available adult, and the initial impression he made was that of a child who "given a chance," love, and adequate fulfillment of his basic needs could blossom into emotional health.

It soon became evident, however, that despite his hunger for close relationships and despite the immediate availability to him of the setting, Frank could not avail himself of people. His relationships would break down shortly after his initial contact with adult parental figures. He was unable as well to relate himself to other children, but would form a close parasitic type of relationship usually with a younger boy whom he could exploit (possibly a reversal of his expectation as to what would happen were he to turn to an older person). His emotional withdrawal became increasingly evident as he would sit at times in what seemed like a depressive stupor, his head on his chest, or his slumped body crying out the despair, hatred, and loneliness within him, refusing to participate in any activity or respond to any ministrations from the staff. At these times his impoverished relationships and apparent vacuous emotional life gave the first overt glimpses of the depth of his illness, and of the difficulty in reaching and helping him which had been revealed during his evaluation in the psychological tests and psychiatric examination.

The examining psychiatrist was impressed with Frank's rapid shift of moods from initial apparent apathy and depression to lively animation as the examination proceeded. He seemed like a boy who, having left a "prison," was now discovering that he could breathe more freely in a hoped-for, new-found freedom. Southard School was seen by Frank as at least an improved version of the Juvenile Hall, of the "Big House." But there were many signs that this freedom, too, would soon become threatening and disappointing to Frank.

Sometimes under pressure of speech, he glibly rationalized his stealing, his defecation in his pants, and a host of antisocial acts, seriously expounding with pseudo insight upon his many problems. He freely acknowledged that his delinquent behavior, so troublesome to his parents, was intended as revenge against them. With quasi-insight he discussed his detention in the Juvenile Hall as a means of demonstrating what a "big shot" he was.

His self-concept was unusually self-depreciatory and he described every aspect of himself in derogatory terms.

I'm too fat; I've got big feet. The only brains I have are those I eat. Oh yes, if you'd crack my head open and you'd fry what you got out of it you'd have scrambled eggs. My ears are always dirty and my teeth are no good. They're crooked, chipped, and yellow. Not scared, they're not scared, just yellow. My hands are no good either. I bite my fingernails, too. My chest isn't any good either. It mixes in with my stomach and my stomach's too fat.

He perceived his mother's contribution to his self-concept as follows:

She would like to get rid of me but doesn't want me out of her sight. She says I cause her to fuss. She says I shirk my work. I don't like her and she likes me even less. It all started when my father went away.

His view of his previous treatment was stated with finality:

It was a waste of money. The therapist was a family friend. I was awfully sorry to put my stepfather to so much expense. It did give me a chance to be away from home though.

Regarding his hopes for help at Southard School and for the immediate future, Frank expressed a rather dim view:

I don't know if it will do any good or be a waste of time. I hope it will do good. It won't stop me from doing things.

But what he alone felt would help was

One person, me, myself, and I. I'd like to stop. Heck, who wouldn't? I don't want to end up in jail. Most you could do though is to find out why I act the way I do.

On the psychological tests Frank showed almost superior intelligence and a limited capacity for affective response. Strong aggressive impulses could be expressed only in fantasy or in acts which had the purpose of reassuring himself about his own ability and of inflicting punishment upon and exacting revenge from the parent figures. Severe anxiety stemming from deeper conflicts and the fear of retaliation appeared to impair his intellectual efficiency. The Rorschach reflected his critical evaluation of situations, his lack of trust in others, and his preoccupation with missing parts of bodies, crawling creatures, and crouching animals. Prominently seen in the Thematic Apperception Test was his callous disregard for the feelings of others and his secret pleasure over his success in defying parental figures. The diagnostic impression of the evaluating team was that of a behavior disorder with neurotic features.

Frank's efforts to communicate with the therapist verbally in the initial interviews failed to establish a productive psychotherapeutic atmosphere. Silences associated with strong inhibition, blocking, and distant withdrawal frequently interrupted Frank's tenuous contacts with the therapist, and his verbal productions appeared against the background of an emotional vacuum. To create an optimal therapeutic atmosphere, Frank was given the opportunity to communicate via play action those inner struggles that he otherwise could not relate.

The therapeutic setting then became a scene of play action, a conspiratorial meeting between the patient who became "Jocko the Monk, the Big Boss," and the therapist, the "Doc" who, having served ten years in prison for practicing medicine illicitly, had joined the Big Boss as a gangster-lieutenant or as a doctor, and who could provide either a gangster or medical type of service, depending on the wishes of the Big Boss. The gang met regularly to discuss the plans to pull the "big heist" which, starting out with Frank's fantasy of holding up an armored car and then a bank, extended into a gigantic criminal operation which aimed to overthrow the current administration and to seize power and land, with final control of large cities and states. The following is a sample interview as the patient was taking hold of the play technique and was in the process of discussing the gang's plans:

Frank came to the interview with the news that there had been a slight hitch in the plan. He excitedly reported that even though we got most of the bulls, some of them had gotten away. He explained that some stoolies must have been at work and that the plan had been sabotaged. On second thought, maybe the real reason that our plan had not worked completely was that we had not thought of something very important rather than because of a stoolie. We had forgotten that there was a day shift of bulls and that these bulls were not in the formation at the police academy when we had bombed it. There must have been at least a hundred bulls out. He had already thought of a plan to get rid of them, but believed that it would be better to wait because the remaining bulls would be on the watch for another attack and we wouldn't be able to pull this plan so easily.

I mused that since we had delivered a knockout punch they would be dazed and in shock. Maybe we could follow up with another attack before they could reorganize and get reinforcements. He agreed it would be a good idea and immediately had a plan to get rid of the other bulls. We would have to get more planes, bomb each precinct police station, and strafe the whole area around it with machine guns. Satisfied with his plan, he gave me the order to call the airport and to have sixteen planes ready within two hours. I went through the play motion of following his orders and complimented him on his ingenuity. I told him that when he pulled this heist we would from then on have no more bulls to oppose us. We would own the city and run it.

Frank picked up the fantasy with a rather satisfied grin and began to talk about owning New York City and how he could exploit it and capitalize on it. Once we had taken over the city the bulls would have to kowtow to us. We would be the police force. Nobody could leave the city except by paying 1,000 dollars ransom. I wondered why the boss was acting like a piker, making them pay only 1,000 dollars when we could bleed them dry as long as they were at our mercy. Frank instantly agreed and said that they would have to pay 50,000 dollars in order to get out.

As the discussion about the plan to complete the big heist continued, Frank began to show signs of anxiety. He was afraid that the U.S. Government might oppose our plan, that they might send in detectives who would be even harder to spot than the bulls who wore uniforms. I assured him that no matter what opposition he had from anyone else, he had my full support.

Anxiously, Frank wondered if the plan could succeed, and then after considerable thought suddenly broke out with a beaming expression on his face as if inspired by a wonderful idea. "You remember the deal where the Indians sold the deed of Manhattan Island for twenty-four dollars? That deed is still kept on exhibit in a museum." He had thought that if we could steal the deed to the city we would have legal and lawful possession of the city. On the other hand we wouldn't even have to steal it but could leave twenty-four dollars for the deed and this would give us possession of the city legally without any fuss or trouble. I complimented him on the ingenuity of his plan but wondered whether the bulls would see eye to eye with us and whether they might not oppose this. He said, in a grand manner, that we could leave them a century note and this would be more than enough to pay for the deed which was worth only twenty-four dollars in the first place. I protested that we needn't give the bulls any more than we had to. If the deed were worth twenty-four dollars originally, then maybe that was all it was worth now. It didn't seem to have gotten any more valuable since it was originally signed.

As we continued to discuss our plans to pull this big heist, Frank thought of the final step of rounding up the remaining bulls and putting them in jail. I wondered again whether this was not dangerous, that maybe it would be better to rub them out since there was always the possibility of their breaking out. He said that wiping them out quickly would be too good for them. This was too peaceful a means to get rid of them. I thought that maybe the boss had a good point and that his revenge was important. He suggested that he could keep them in jail and guard them heavily, but starve them slowly and weaken them so that they could never break out. He again became anxious and thought it would be better to knock them off quickly. He didn't have such cruel feelings toward them that he wanted to torture them. I said that the boss took pity on the bulls and was pretty nice to them even after they had let him go hungry for so long, but whatever he wanted to do with them, it was all right with me. We ended the hour as Frank took out a package of Life Savers and we toasted the heist with them.

In the following hour, Frank's enthusiasm for the big heist continued to be tempered by his marked anxiety that led him to question the wisdom of every step that we were about to take, and that led him to introduce a variety of obstacles that he expected would result in the failure of the heist. He ordered the therapist to call the Weather Bureau and then announced that weather conditions would make flying impossible. The heist would have to wait. As the therapist confronted him with his fear of his wish to eliminate all the bulls, he coped with his mounting anxiety only by a pseudo bravado and a feigned enthusiasm for the heist, and then actually missed the following hour.

With his anxiety reduced because of the missed hour, Frank in the subsequent hour could announce that the heist had gone off well. We were in possession of the big city and everything seemed to be going as arranged. He thought, however, it would now be necessary for the gang to wall itself in and just stay put until the heat was off. He fantasied that the F.B.I. might bring in its entire force and the gang would be in the desperate position of having to defend its new gains. Maybe it would be better to avoid an outright battle with them by collecting huge taxes from the businessmen so that after accumulating 1,000,000 dollars the boss could pay for the city by selling the deed back to the government and thus make everything legal and straight. If necessary, he would renounce his citizenship and secede from the United States. The F.B.I. would then not have any right to make war on the boss since he was no longer part of the Union.

The therapist questioned whether the F.B.I. would accept these terms and the boss insisted they would have to or face another more terrible atomic war. When the therapist wondered aloud whether the F.B.I. would accept this deal, Frank turned to another solution. This entailed the cessation of all gang activities and the return of the city as well as of the deed to the United States if the government would only return the original twenty-four dollars. These twenty-four dollars he would not even keep but would give to charity. In the meantime all members of the gang would have to become respectable and honest citizens. When the therapist asked if this were not a plan to buy the F.B.I. off, the boss protested that he didn't like to think of it as a bribe, but just as a smart deal. The alternative to the deal was to risk an atomic war with destruction for everyone. The therapist assured him that his loyalty was first to the boss, but he had to think of the gang, too. He was beginning to wonder whether the gang would go along with this plan to become respectable citizens. It might sound crazy to them and make them wonder whether the boss had not gotten sick. As far as the therapist was concerned, if the boss decided to change his plans he might need more help and the therapist was ready to stay by him either as a doc or as his henchman.

Relieved of the pressure aroused by the fantasy of destruction and of dreaded retaliation, Frank turned to a verbal account of his trip to his grandfather and told of a pleasant visit with his uncle. He confessed that while on this visit he was tempted to heist something from him, but decided against it because his uncle was such a nice guy.

These samples from the initial phase of psychotherapy may be considered a prelude of things to come, and permit us to observe *in statu nascendi* the major defense operations used to cope with the unconscious conflict and the ensuing anxiety. In the patient's struggle to reveal the unconscious conflict to the therapist and to himself, as well as to keep the unconscious conflict repressed, he utilizes a variety of means which offer a model of operations that permits predictions of the process to follow.

As he starts to talk about himself, anxiety increases and stops ordinary means of communication through thought. Thought may lead to recollection and threatening imagery, both of which have to be warded off under all circumstances in order to cope successfully with anxiety. Increasing anxiety leads then either to silence or, as we have seen in these samples, to the imminence of acting out. Talking out is replaced by playing out, which threatens to erupt into acting out. Playing out and acting out keep the unconscious conflict repressed, but at the same time permit the patient to reveal the unconscious conflict on a more regressed level of mental functioning.

The psychotherapist recognizes the conflict by noticing the pattern of the play fantasy, the play act, and the emerging acting out in the psychotherapeutic situation. As the therapist understands the patient, and confronts him with his inability to destroy the policemen even in fantasy, at the same time letting him know that he accepts his material, the patient feels understood although he cannot understand himself in terms of thought. His displaced negative transference, directed against the "bulls," is unconsciously compared by the boy with the actual therapeutic situation in which he finds himself working on his problems accompanied by a friendly, understanding, and accepting psychotherapist. He turns away from the playing out and returns to talking out, discovering now that he does not want to steal from a kind and friendly uncle. The interpretations by the therapist have to be understood against the background of the patient's inability to give up displacement at this point. Accordingly, the therapist must avoid interpreting the displacement, but may freely interpret as long as the patient's safeguard against anxiety is respected.

These initial moves permit anticipation of future trends in the therapeutic process. One may assume that the beginning months of psychotherapy will show an overwhelming use of action and play, a lesser use of pure fantasy, and a very moderate use of secondary-process thought. The interpretive work will help the patient to resolve his conflicts in the manner that has been discussed in the model. As the months go on, however, one may be certain that the amount of play action will decrease and will be taken over more and more by verbal communication typical for the chronological age of the patient. Concomitantly, we may also expect to observe a regressive process manifested by actual or imminent acting out.

While play action in the therapy proceeded as has been described in the first interview sample, we learned about an experience Frank had not reported to his psychotherapist that reflected an aspect of the transference situation and culminated in genuine acting out. Frank had visited his grandfather during a holiday and found him unusually loving and giving. Under the influence of alcohol his grandfather made numerous erotic advances toward Frank, heaped kisses upon him, and made frequent promises of gifts, eternal support, and affection. Shortly following this incident, Frank stole a knife from the dime store. Characteristically, he arranged that the theft be discovered as he freely exhibited the knife to the personnel in the residence and hinted that he had stolen it. How this acting out became a direct part of the psychotherapeutic process is illustrated in the following interview:

Frank followed me into the office. With a slight sneer in his voice he began to complain contemptuously about the way things were run at

Southard. He thought that the kids ought to get together to write a constitution to guarantee that "No R.T. [recreational therapist] could enter a person's room without a search warrant." He went on to complain that the police could break in any time and there was no privacy or protection against them. Then quite abruptly he remarked that being the boss of a gang was getting a little bit wearing on him.

He had decided to plan no organized heists any more but to let the members of the gang go on their own free heist. The therapist retorted, "Well, Boss, if the job is getting too big for you then maybe we ought to turn it over to someone else. It looks like the boss hasn't been doing such a good job of being a boss lately anyway." Frank's face expressed a faint trace of relief as he asked how I had come to that conclusion. I reached into my pocket, pulled out the knife that he had stolen from the dime store, and said, "This shiv, for instance, Boss, this stinking, worthless little shiv. When you pulled that heist didn't you know you were putting the gang's neck in a noose? The bulls could have come down on our tail and then what would have happened to the big heist that we've been working on for so long?" Frank immediately took the knife, opened the blade and kissed it, appearing surprised that I had it. He placed the knife in his belt and said he was certainly glad to see it back. Then he grinned broadly and said that no man should be without his weapon. This was really a wonderful weapon. I retorted, "A wonderful weapon! That little tin shiv? A worthless piece of junk! What protection can the shiv give you compared to the kind you can get from the really big weapon, Boss, the secret weapon we're working on here?" Frank became anxious, removed the knife from his belt, and began to reflect. He fingered the blade and said nothing. I continued, "The big heist is too important to both of us, Boss. We've got to protect it even if we've got to make sacrifices for little things. Compared to the big heist everything else is just small potatoes and we're not going to let anything like a tin shiv stop us from pulling it right."

Showing annoyance, I asked him what had been the price of the knife and Frank meekly answered that it was worth eighty-nine cents. I said, "Okay," and pulling a dollar out of my pocket, added, "we've got to undo that little heist and keep the bulls off our tail and from interfering with our big plans. You want the shiv, you can keep it, but here's the dough, and you're going to take it back to the man." Frank said he was beginning to see what I meant. Maybe the thing to do was take back the knife. He didn't want the money and he didn't need the knife. It was just a lousy little weapon that was no protection compared to the protection that the big secret weapon could give him. He would put the knife back and that would square the account.

He leaned back and with a trace of emotion in his voice as well as with some conviction said that he could see what I was driving at. I had hit the nail on the head. The shiv was worthless; the big heist was the most important thing. We had to protect it at all cost. He sat back and seemed tense as he held the knife in his hand. He looked at it fondly and said that it was a nice shiv, though. For the next twenty minutes Frank debated about what to do with the knife. At one time he was sure it was a good weapon and at another it was just a worthless piece of junk that ought to go back to the store. Finally, with determination, he agreed that this was the only thing to do and wondered how it should be done. He thought he could do it alone, and I told him that this was something between us and maybe we ought to pull it together. He suggested that maybe we could take it back tomorrow. I said, "Today, Boss, two o'clock." He agreed this would be okay.

A few moments later Frank expressed his concern about the future of the gang. Even if he should be caught by the cops, we would have to keep the gang together and the plans for the big heist alive. I told him that no matter what happened, the gang would always be behind the boss, and he could remember that if we pulled our big heist together in our own stronghold no cops in the world could ever get to us. Frank nodded in agreement and reflected that, after the big heist was pulled, we would have complete and real freedom. I said that he had come upon a very wise thought. It sounded like the big boss talking now. Frank said, "Who wants to be dodging bullets coming down your ass?" I retorted, "Yeah, Boss, it's a strange kind of freedom that makes you have to run all the time to dodge bullets. It's a kind of freedom that makes a guy sometimes even prefer to go to jail to escape those bullets. Maybe the heist can bring real freedom for the boss, so that he never has to be afraid that he'll always have to dodge bullets or wind up in the hot seat."

At two o'clock as we had arranged, I accompanied Frank downtown, and we went into the dime store where he surreptitiously replaced the knife on the counter as I stood guard. As we walked out together he remarked that our mission was accomplished. We had walked through heavy snow and Frank complained of having wet feet and feeling cold. We stopped at a soda fountain and had hot chocolate together. When I left him at the school Frank thanked me for having come along with him on the mission.

The friendly image of the good uncle which had permitted him to curb the impulse to steal from the uncle is here fused with the overwhelming, noxious image of the threatening grandfather. Both images are the expression of the strong ambivalence in a transference situation. As he runs away from the threatening transference situation and as anxiety mounts, Frank cannot maintain play action but saves himself by delinquent acting out. As he is attracted by the friendliness, acceptance, and understanding of the therapist, implicit in the therapist's way of dealing with the gangster game, Frank wishes to give up stealing and to undo the acting out. Diminished anxiety in the psychotherapeutic situation permits him to move from playing out a problem to talking it out and to resolving it in a reality-oriented manner. Increased anxiety, however, reduces the effectiveness of the ego organization, forces regression to a lower level of communication, and leads to acting out. The increase of instinctual pressure that may be caused by inner or outer stimulation in seduction is the decisive factor that leads to increase in anxiety and to a use of less mature ego organizations which may thus be considered as an SOS signal, a flight reaction during the therapeutic process.

Clinical material demonstrates how increased anxiety is intimately related with predictable sequence to regression and the tendency to act out. In Frank, however, we observed a peculiar modification of this familiar sequential relationship, in contrast to what can ordinarily be expected. In normal or neurotic individuals, increased anxiety often leads to more rational, though more restricted, seemingly more highly adaptive behavior, while in Frank, the reverse was true. One possible explanation for this phenomenon is that in the hierarchical organization of the ego, recent, more appropriate, and more highly adaptive functions can operate simultaneously with more primitive, outmoded functions because they are cathected by energy, which itself is differentiated into hierarchical systems. These systems are differentiated by virtue of the quantity of neutralized or deneutralized energy available for their cathexis, or upon any combination of these energies lying at any point intermediate to the opposite polarities. A more mature ego organization under the dominance of neutralized energy cathexis is less prone to resort to acting out as a method of problem solving than is the more primitive organization which is cathected mainly by deneutralized energy, i.e., by sexualized and aggressivized energy.

Apparently it is the extent of the deneutralized and neutralized energy cathexes which determine what portions and levels of the ego organization will be set in action. Under pathological conditions of personality development, certain aspects of the ego organization fail to become consolidated at an optimal specific time. Under similar conditions, there is a failure of development of the neutralized cathexis. But as soon as the energy cathexis is neutralized, then the lower levels of functioning fall under the aegis of the adaptive functions rather than remain a part of the expression of the neurosis.

As Frank's anxiety about continuing the big heist diminished, and as he could permit himself to take hold of the therapeutic situation, it was seen as less threatening despite his perception of it as an apparent encouragement to him to act upon his murderous fantasies. He began to plan the big heist with the aim of acquiring the proper weapons and tools for its execution. It soon became apparent to the big boss that in order for the gang to carry out the big heist it would be necessary to have guns and blackjacks. How the fulfillment of this aim was carried into the therapeutic situation by the medium of play action and acting out to the point where these two means of expression became fused in the therapeutic process, is demonstrated in excerpts from interviews:

On the way to the office Frank told me where he could get a real rod, one that shot real bullets. I asked him where. He said that the head man in his outfit had swiped it from him and had kept it in his hideout. He thought he could heist it from the head man by getting the moll (Frank's social worker) into the operation. He thought she could be trusted by this time. I didn't think it was a very good idea to let anybody else in on our heist because it could get around too far and the bulls would be down on us. He insisted that we see the moll anyway and proceeded to get an appointment with his social worker through the receptionist. As the hour ended he assured me that the moll was all right. She had been in the racket a long time and he was sure she was on our side and could be trusted. I told him I would leave it up to his judgment and go along with him since he was still the boss.

The therapist's questioning of the soundness of his being the boss seemed to be clearly understood by Frank as a question regarding his capacity for reality testing and was not construed by him as adverse or belittling criticism.

On the afternoon of the preceding interview, Frank met me as I was about to leave the school and told me he had arranged with the moll to case the head man's hideout. He had discovered where the rod had been stashed away. I fell in with his plan to pull the heist there and then, and we entered the director's office. Frank immediately went to the closet where his B.B. pistol had been put for safekeeping, and we also discovered a home-made blackjack that Frank had once carried around with him. Together we stealthily reached my office across the street where I suggested that we keep the weapons in our own arsenal.

This phase of psychotherapy shows a significant change as a consequence of the therapeutic technique employed. In the earlier phase the child could handle the increasing pressure, when stimulated by play action, only by play interruption on the one hand, or by delinquent acting out on the other. He could see the psychotherapist only in terms of the good and friendly uncle or of the drunk and seductive grandfather. As the psychotherapist permitted the child to express himself through play action and fantasy by the psychotherapist's entering the child's world and becoming part of it, he was creating a bearable situation and allowing a transference situation to develop. In the situation, initial projection of narcissistic problems was possible, and the child within the psychotherapeutic process could combine play action with a modified form of acting out. The stealing of the gun from the director's office took place, as it were, within the psychotherapeutic process, within the limits set by the psychotherapist. While remindful of the stealing of the knife, it also showed some of the significant aspects of play action inasmuch as it included a form of reality testing. True enough, the reality testing employed actually depended on the auxiliary ego of the psychotherapist who set and provided the limits. He let the boy know the difference between those actions that create danger and those that can still be used to work on a problem through trial action. He who steals from someone with the intention of being discovered does not actually steal but communicates his concern about the consequences of delinquent behavior.

The child's activities were also attempts to test the psychotherapist and the newly gained limits. As the play action continued, Frank wished to know if the psychotherapist would be willing to go beyond the boundaries of the school, beyond the four walls of the therapy office, and whether he was really ready to follow the boy in his quest for an answer to his problem. In the samples just cited we see a fusion of play action and acting out, but note a preponderance of play action.

Increasing anxiety in the therapy process suggests that new aspects of repressed material are pressing toward consciousness, and one very often has the feeling that acting out threatens to overwhelm play action. It is during these phases of psychotherapy that the skill and patience of a psychotherapist are taxed the most, and that the danger exists that the psychotherapist's interpretive language within play action and play fantasy may carry him away to a form of counteracting out with the patient, either through a form of delinquent participation or a form of oppressive forbidding, both technical mistakes mentioned by Fenichel.[13]

Clinical case material not infrequently fails to be convincing enough to clarify per se its technical framework and basic strategy. Too often it may give the impression that the choice of the technical method used is the result of an arbitrary decision by the therapist who seemingly imposes upon the patient the atmosphere of the therapeutic process and the mode of communication to be used within that process. In Frank's therapy, the inference might be made that the therapist imposed the techniques of play action and acting out upon the patient, that he preferred to plan robberies and play act the role of a gangster. The inference could be carried to the point of Moreno's conviction that since his stage is the equivalent of the therapist's analytic couch, he is within his prerogative, as the therapist, to choose the technique of play acting as the means of communication between himself and the patient. It is our conviction that ideally the choice of communication belongs to the patient whenever it is possible and that it is the patient who decides upon the language that he can best use to convey his thoughts and to make contact with the therapist. From the many cues that he gave the therapist and from the therapy process as it developed, Frank clearly conveyed that this was his choice of communication, a message that the therapist understood and accepted.[14]

Play action within the limited setting of a therapy office in a residential setting changed to a combination of play action and acting out in the therapeutic process as the therapeutic situation of the big heist moved into the community. In the search for weapons and suitable operations for the big boss, Frank and the therapist began to play out the gangster activity of "casing" the pawnshops and jewelry stores in the downtown section of the city:

As we reconnoitered the downtown district for suitable victims for the gang operation, our drive took us through the north side of town, which aroused Frank's anxiety. This wasn't familiar territory to the doc because it was the territory of the North Side Gang, a rival gang of the big boss. Frank became fidgety and suggested that we ought to move through it quickly. Along the way to the airport, Frank practiced shooting it out with the bulls while I was instructed to practice making a quick getaway so that we could time the whole operation in case the gang would get hot and would have to take it on the lam by plane or train.

In a subsequent session, the casing operation evoked in Frank paranoid suspiciousness about women who might actually be bulls in disguise:

On the way to the heist, Frank opened the door of the car and pretended to be shooting it out with the bulls. He was sure that the bulls were cruising around in their prowl cars and although he knew it was smarter to keep the rod concealed, he thought it was smart to be able to get the drop on the bulls. I veered to the side as a woman driver moved out of a parked position and Frank cursed at her and called her a dumb moll. He thought she might be a bull trying to head us off. There followed a determined plan to shake the moll by turning into a side street and then getting behind her so that she couldn't be trailing us.

As we entered the jewelry store on the pretext of getting the doc's watch repaired, Frank pointed out the wall safe. Casually we looked it over and overheard a woman talking to the clerk about this very old safe.

Frank eavesdropped on their conversation without appearing to pay attention to them and then as we left, announced that he really wasn't interested in the joint at all. He knew of another good joint that we could case. I remarked that that dame was innocent-looking enough but maybe she was working her racket, too. Frank said he didn't know about that.

As we returned to the therapy office to deposit our weapons in the arsenal I offered him some brownies that I had brought from home. He said he was hungry after the heist. He reached into the bag and took one and I also ate one. He reached in again and I told him to help himself. He took all of them.

In a subsequent hour, we moved in on a Federal job, a postal truck carrying unregistered mail containing money. Armed with a B.B. pistol and blackjack, we had played out casing a postal truck in front of the Capitol Building and we had agreed to pull the heist that morning. First the pawnshop would have to be heisted for the rod and this was set because the boss had planted Slippery the Ox in the pawnshop. Frank immediately began to suspect Slippery. Maybe he had squealed and had given the heist away or had been fired because the owner might have become suspicious of him. We would have to call the heist off and lay low.

As an anxious expression crossed his face, Frank attempted to assume a pseudobravado air but could not conceal his anxiety. The therapist said, "Boss, you've got plenty of guts, real guts. You wouldn't have gotten so far without guts. But I have the funny feeling that when we go on these casing jobs you become troubled. Maybe you're not satisfied with this heist and want to pull another one." Frank grumbled sadly, "Sometimes too much guts gets you into trouble." I said, "The kind of guts you've got sure carried you a long way. But I hate to see the boss so unhappy and I'm beginning to wonder if casing these joints and pulling these heists hasn't been making you dissatisfied and unhappy. I still know a little bit about this doctoring business that I used to do before they caught up with me and put me in the stir. Maybe you'd rather I work for you as a doc than as a gangster." Frank insisted that it wasn't the casing jobs that made him dissatisfied. He wanted to pull a real heist.

Deciding on a sporting goods store that carried rods and ammunition, we found a parking place in front of the State Capitol Building. Sighting the Capitol Building Frank blurted out that he had an idea. We could go up to the dome of the Capitol and case the city from up there. We took the trip up to the Capitol Dome and on our way down stopped in at the Chambers of the Supreme Court and at the State Legislature that was in session. We ended up discussing the difference between the legislative and judicial branches of the government and having refreshments in a drugstore. Frank sniffed the air and remarked that the place smelled like a sewer. Finishing our refreshments, we drove back to the School as Frank again played at shooting it out with the bulls.

The operation of the big heist broadened into the scope of a syndicate that extended its plans to murder, robbery of armored cars, and the plunder of federal agencies. The need for weapons to carry out the heist continued to carry the therapy process into the community jewelry stores and pawnshops in order to enrich the gang arsenal with guns, holsters, and knives. The fine line between play action, acting out, and carrying into action his primitive impulses became so thin that Frank had begun to experience mounting anxiety bordering on panic. With increasing paranoid projection of his internal threatening images onto even the most innocent external figures, he suspected strangers on the street and even the maids in the residential setting of being bulls. The tension in the transference situation could be dealt with only by externalizing and by removing the threatening figures of the stoolies and the bulls from the immediate therapy situation, since the therapy office, the hideout of the big boss, had now become suspect and dangerous as well. Nevertheless, the office continued to serve as the base for the therapy situation, the big heist, as each hour started and ended in the office.

To safeguard the operation of the big heist, i.e., to maintain the transference situation, Frank conceived the notion of establishing a hideout and an arsenal, a "stashout," somewhere on the outskirts of the city. The further extension of the gang's operations into blackmail, when Frank announced his plan to take pictures of the school staff walking into a whorehouse, and the recognition by the therapist of this plan as a "shakedown," enhanced the need to remove the base of the gang operations to an old abandoned house outside the city.

As Frank confessed his intention to make a big business out of his camera which, evidently, was to be a mixture of delinquent and legitimate activities, he related his anxiety about the sex play that was going on among the children at the School. They would strip before each other and exhibit themselves. He belittled this behavior as "kid's play" and felt that when a guy got older he wanted to go a lot farther than that. He didn't think it was right for boys his age to have intercourse. That was for married people. But when older people got married they didn't seem to get much fun out of sex either. They got more fun out of having children. Since he had come from a family of five kids he could speak with some authority.

He felt especially sorry for his stepfather who was really a good guy and who had married into the family when there were two kids but wanted more children of his own. He had tried very hard to make the family happy but he seemed to be up against it. Besides working hard, he took many special courses at the University in order to get ahead so that he could do more for his family. But look what happened. Hard times had befallen him and his family. There was a lot of sickness in the family and his stepson was in jail. Frank felt sorry for him because he was such a real good guy, and more than anything else wanted his children to like him and to be happy. He had worked like a slave for them and they had let him down. And the hardest thing for him was having his son in jail.

Frank became genuinely remorseful as he continued his rueful lament about his stepfather's unhappy plight. The therapist empathized with Frank's plight, too, and remarked that his stepfather probably didn't know how much Frank wanted to like him and how tough this whole business had been on him, too.

We reached the abandoned house and cased it before we entered. Stealthily making our way through an open window, we played out the act of breaking into the house in order to burglarize it. The sight that greeted use recalled the bleakness and dreariness of Frank's past. Amid dilapidation and dirt was an array of broken-down furniture, packed trunks, and household belongings in sordid disarray. It was is if a family had suddenly taken flight and had abandoned and deserted their home. Rats' nests and droppings, cobwebs, and beehives stuck out from the walls while a pile of intimate family correspondence dating back to the early years of the century attested to the history of this abandoned house. Frank walked about, exploring in a desultory and bewildered manner, picking up and discarding a number of items. For many minutes he appeared as if in a trance and could not be contacted.

In our second excursion to the abandoned house we conversed about many things. Frank said that his new photography racket would be a front for our heists just as my doctoring business was my front. With both of us having a respectable front we could go on the heist without too much trouble. We might even end up in Hell. I said, "At least we go down there together, Boss," Frank grinned and appeared anxious.

Frank proposed that we pose as respectable people looking over the house so as not to arouse the suspicions of people in the vicinity. We could pretend that we were artists who were making sketches of the house. I complimented him on his clever idea and suggested as an alternative that we could pose as architects interested in old Topeka homes that had their hey-day back in the golden days. He responded with another alternative, namely, that we could pose as realtors looking over the property.

As we drove past the college campus we talked about college education. Frank said that he had heard that college education was quite expensive, but he thought it was a good thing for people. By coincidence I noticed a rabbi crossing the street and pointed him out to Frank. He thought it was a nice thing that people who went to college could get some religious education also. He used to attend the Episcopal church but reflected that he didn't like the hypocrisy of people who went to church on Sunday and then disobeyed the Sabbath law by working that day. There was something hypocritical even about the minister preaching on Sunday since this was work and opposed to the commandment of the Sabbath law. When he found out that the rabbi headed the Congregation Beth Sholom, and when translated for him that it meant the House of Peace, he reflected that it was a good name and that there should be more of it. There wasn't enough peace in the world and not enough people had it. He confessed that at one time he had thought of becoming a minister. He had been very much interested in religion but gave it up. He thought it was a noble profession since many ministers worked and died for the sake of others. But what was the use of sacrificing oneself for others?

Once he thought he might be a bull, too. Bulls often gave up their lives for the sake of others. But that was some stupid idea that he had long since given up. When the therapist reflected that Frank had been doing a lot of thinking about what he wanted to be, Frank agreed that he had, but right now he would like to be a traveling salesman. He would like to go out and see the world.

Quite abruptly he said he wasn't going to be President. The therapist said that maybe he had been thinking that he would like to be President. Frank was quite emphatic in his denial. If he were President, the country would be involved in six different wars with Russia, and families would be involved in fifteen different wars among themselves, and there would be a hell of a lot of trouble in the country. If he were President he would really make a mess of things. He had made a mess of things already. Frank moodily reflected on his thoughts as we arrived at the abandoned house, slipped under the dense thicket of dead brush, and climbed through an open window.

The shift in the process of identification from more primitive narcissistic to more advanced object relationships coincided with Frank's search for his identity, with the quest for the person that he wanted to be. As reflected in the preceding interview, this process continued for some time and was associated with increased capacity for communication by means of verbal language and the use of secondary-process thought. The following interview illustrates Frank's preoccupation with the nature of his identity and its complex unintegrated structure, composed, as it were, of a variety of conflicting individuals:

Frank greeted me with a reserved "Howdy," and went to his usual seat. I wondered whom I was addressing today. Was I talking to the boss or to Frank? A little surprised by this, he grinned and in a swaggering, bragging manner, Frank said he would let me in on a secret. The boss and Frank were the same person. I said that, in a way, I knew this too, but thought in some ways that they were also different persons, just as a person had different feelings about himself and would have different ambitions at different times. Puffing out his chest in a swaggering manner, Frank said that he was really the boss and that Frank was his alias. I told him that I had heard that he went under many aliases. He said it was true. He also went under the alias of F. C. Smith. I told him I had also heard that he went under the aliases of Frank Charles Smith, and Frankie Smith, as well as Frank. With a broad grin he said, "They're all me."

I said that sometimes I wasn't sure to which Frank I was talking. And I thought that he must be unsure to whom he was talking when he was with me, the doctor who was once a reputable physician, or the doctor who had been released from stir. I usually had a hunch as to which Frank I was talking to, though. When he planned his heists I knew he was Jocko the Monk, the Big Boss. And when he was a reserved, growing-up fourteen-year-old boy, I thought he was Frank Charles Smith. When talking about his ambitions for the future, he was a boy who wanted to make something of himself and could talk about justice, current events, and could make a public speech; then I thought of him as Frank C. Smith. And there was the Frank Smith who didn't quite know what he wanted to be and wasn't himself certain who he was, so he would put up a show like a grownup person and feel that he couldn't quite fill those shoes yet. And there was little Frankie who longed to be even younger than his years and wanted very much to be like a young child but also found this kind of person out of place. Frank listened attentively and nodded his head slowly and somberly in agreement. He said that he knew he was in an awful dilemma but didn't quite know what to do about it. He fell silent and seemed to be groping for something else to talk about. When he began to talk again, it soon became evident that while the original topic seemingly had been dropped, Frank had actually returned to it in the metaphor of a play production.

In the discussion that ensued we made plans to produce a great play. Between ourselves we would combine the roles of producer, writer, director, actors, prop-men, and audience. Frank's enthusiasm became fired as we discussed the plans for this great production. He suddenly announced that he had an idea and immediately briefed me on the plot. He would be the proprietor of a liquor store who was to be held up by a stickup man at the close of a busy day. I was to play the part of Liquor Louie, a small-time mug who had been robbing liquor stores for weeks, unmolested by the cops. Frank set the stage and we proceeded to act out our roles. The play ended as Frank, as the proprietor, was shot to death. His dying words were for the criminal, Liquor Louie, with whom he pleaded to make his getaway before the cops could descend upon him.

In the following hour Frank was full of venomous criticism of the food that was served in the residence. His thoughts turned to the then recent atomic spy trials and he supported the President's demand for the death sentence. Nothing was worse than a spy or a traitor. They deserved to die. With increasing animation he became vituperative against deserters.

The guy who ran away in combat and deserted his buddies deserved to die. The therapist took the view that deserters might be intensely troubled and frightened and perhaps needed help rather than the punishment of death. Frank expressed some doubt that men could be helped after they had deserted and then categorically passed the judgment that he had no use for draft dodgers either.

His thoughts turned to the recent event of the firing of a famous general by the President. Frank supported the view of the general that the then current war should have been pushed on to the mainland of the enemy's country. It was the only possible way of winning the war. But instead of being rewarded for his intentions he was fired as disobedient and insubordinate. Frank emphatically insisted that if the war were going to be won it would have to be pushed.

But Frank's dilemma, like that of the general, seemed insoluble. Not to push the war meant to lose the war but to pursue it vigorously was to incur humiliation and disgrace. To find a solution for this dilemma, Frank again turned to the big production as he expressed his dissatisfaction with the scene that had been enacted the previous hour. He announced the name of the big production: "The Bulls March On," Scene I: "The Beginning of the Last Holdup." In a crucial moment, as we re-enacted the scene, Frank announced that he was F. C. Smith, the Dick. He revealed that he was a detective who had been trailing and had now caught up with me, that lousy mug, Liquor Louie. He fired point blank into my body and ignoring my pleas for the croaker as I lay dying, he contemptuously and venomously retorted that I didn't need a doctor any more, and that my criminal career was over. What I needed was the police, and if I lived at all it would be in jail. He had no pity for me as this was the fate and deserved punishment of all crooks. Shortly after this therapy session the staff found circulated around the residence the following circulars: "Wanted for Murder, Dead or Alive, Jocko, the Monk, Alias Frank Smith."

At this point, when the patient begins to modify his identification with the criminal gangster, the negative, threatening paternal introject, to one in which he wishes to play the part of the detective, and thus to ally himself with the positive forces of culture, a further comment should be made on the psychological nature of play action. Our material suggests that we can differentiate between two different forms of play, one of which will be called play action, the other, play acting.*

In his play action, Frank unconsciously repeats the original conflict, identifies himself with the aggressor, the negative, paternal introject, and "resolves" the conflict through pseudo mastery and identification which is

---

* The concept "play acting" is used in the text because of its descriptive usefulness. In the genetic schema we speak of fantasy action in order to stress the genetic and functional difference between play and role playing.

experienced as complete and which permits no compromise. (As expressed in Frank's fantasy, "Traitors deserve to die.")

Play acting, however, refers to an activity in which there is no complete identification with the role that he acts but in which he rather tries to master the problem by cue taking and imitation. He now wishes to take the part of the detective, the honest citizen, the defender of our societal structure against subversion. However, he takes these roles with tongue in cheek, as it were, and tells the therapist that they are merely to pretend, that they are merely acting, as if they were to put up a front in order to hide their true selves.

In our case, play action is oriented toward the past and represents the repetition of the unconscious conflict. It thus constitutes an attempt at recollection. Play acting, however, attempts to modify a past identification and constitutes Frank's first attempt to master the future, to trial act, as it were, the future role with which he wishes to identify himself. He thus unconsciously repeats ahead of time the future rather than the past. He adopts the world of the psychotherapist on a trial basis without as yet permanently committing himself. Play action serves the past, while play acting is in the service of adaptation, of future growth. Behavior which is primarily based on imitation, on acting a role, could be considered regressive in comparison to behavior which is dominated by more complete identificatory processes. Inasmuch as this behavior stands in the service of trying out the future, however, of testing a new role, it can also be considered a progressive move within the psychotherapeutic process.

One month later as Frank was in the throes of anxious suspense lest his grandparents withdraw him from the school and from treatment, he heralded the end of the big heist as a gangster game:

Frank seemed very uneasy and did not look at me. I slowly walked to the window and then very casually said, "I guess you're convinced that what I say to your grandmother on Tuesday will make all the difference about your staying or leaving here, and you don't feel that you can really depend upon me." Frank silently nodded his head in agreement.

I went on, "I can understand that you feel you can't really trust me yet." With considerable irritation Frank retorted, "I wouldn't say that exactly. If I didn't trust you I wouldn't tell you anything. I wouldn't talk to you at all." I said, "That's true, Frank, you do have more trust in me than you did, but I think you feel you can't trust me to come through for you all the way and to stick by you in a real pinch." With deep conviction and with unbiased candor Frank said, "That hits the nail on the head, that's exactly the way I do feel." I said, "I certainly appreciate the way you feel about your grandmother's visit on Tuesday. The outcome means a great deal to you." Frank found it hard to continue and fell silent. I said, "It's just as hard for you to say that you like being here and that you depend on Southard School and me as it is impossible for you to trust me completely. But I expect that, and I wouldn't believe anything else. Something that has been a problem to you for so many years can't be overcome that quickly." Frank grinned and slowly nodded his head in affirmation. I casually remarked that maybe he thought I would have to prove myself to be the kind of person he really could trust. Maybe he would have to find out what kind of person I really was.

Frank slowly went back to his seat, restlessly searched through the drawer of the desk, and drew out the B.B. pistol. He cocked it, took a shot at the wall, and then began to shoot at a distant target. I remarked that he was hitting the target much better now. Slowly and deliberately he looked the gun over, and then with heated disgust exploded, "This goddam gun isn't worth anything. I don't know why I bought it. I spent three dollars for it and I don't know why. It's caused me nothing but trouble since I bought it." With considerable remorse and self-condemnation he went on. "For six months I've done nothing here. I thought that it made me a big shot." And then with explosive condemnation he said, "But I'm only a big shit." I said, "I remember not so long ago when that gun was the most important thing to you, Frank, so important that you could think of nothing else and you had to have it." Frank said, "I'm going to take this thing apart and get rid of it. Do you have a screw driver?" Finding a paper clip as a substitute for a screw driver, he went to work on the gunsight and with a vicious gesture removed it and laid it on the desk. He remarked that this was as far as he could go now. He would need more tools to take the gun apart completely.

I wondered if it were the gun itself that he had needed so much. I remembered that once he told me that the gun had as much value as the U.S. Treasury because it had buried within it an extremely important secret, George Washington's secret. With considerable anger in his voice he said, "I made one mistake." Cocking the gun and looking down into the barrel he added, "Living. That was my mistake. Being born was my mistake." Again he viciously attacked the gun with the intention of ripping it apart. I said, "Maybe we'll get to the secret in that gun sometime after all." As he laid the pieces of the gun on the desk, he sat back silently, and as if in a distant trance, nodded his head in confirmation. He sat in silent dejection and contemplation until the hour was up.

The vicissitudes of the patient's acting out during the psychotherapeutic process have brought us to a stage during the recovery in which a new facet of the problem of acting out becomes visible and requires clarification. While he still acts out and travels along with the therapist in order to accomplish the big heist, to plunder the abandoned house, we find that he himself attempts to cover up his delinquent activities and ambitions, his destructive fantasies and wishes, by trying to create an impression that he is really like everybody else. He challenges the psychotherapist and wants him to help him so that they both may appear as decent law-abiding citizens, that they may act as if they belong to the community, while underneath a solid front they would continue with their undercover activity.

This turning point in the psychotherapy in which Frank toys with the choice of a variety of noncriminal professions gives one the feeling that the reversal of the process is taking place. At first it seemed that the psychotherapeutic process could be maintained only if the psychotherapist were willing to play act with him, to put up a front as if he himself were a criminal, the doc who helps the boss. This situation in which the psychotherapist imitated the child seemed to be the only way in which Frank could express himself and could move toward the nuclear conflict.

As he moved toward the basic conflict, and as anxiety increased, he wished more and more at least to act like the psychotherapist actually is, like his teachers, and like those who take care of him. But underneath he wished to maintain a life of his own. He wished to impose on his rich and destructive fantasy life an imitative façade, a crust which could be considered a precursor of identification with the love object. One may see in this development an increase in the strength of genuine object relationships whereas previous object relationships were overburdened with the projection of narcissistic affects.

Two facets of the material deserve special comment. On the one hand, via the new object identification, via the effort to assume at least an imitative front, Frank suddenly discovered a new image of the stepfather whom he described as a disappointed man who did his best and wanted nothing more than the love of his children, but instead had the bitter experience of having his stepson in jail. The delinquent pattern was exchanged for neurotic symptomatology, the capacity for and the necessity of increased guilt. One could predict that the acting-out process would soon come to an end, or rather, that its occurrence would be less frequent.

The second facet which deserves our consideration concerns the disappointment which Frank experienced when he finally entered and conquered the forbidden, abandoned house, the symbol of the unconsciously hoped-for childhood home. He found nothing there but a few old letters, like expected letters from home that he never received, and thus discovered that the big heist ended in his unearthing of a heap of abandoned dust.

As soon as he could give up past longing as well as longing for the past, the acting out, the delinquent but neurotic reconquest of that which has been abandoned, became meaningless. Recollection of the past, achieved via the acting out and expressed as an unconscious memory through the conquest of the abandoned house, thus can be understood to be in the service of the reconstructive process.

Frank is now ready to take another step. The potential love objects of the present who have been no more than objects of imitation for him now receive new meaning. The original capacity for identification, documented in the different image that he now has of his stepfather, and well illustrated in earlier wishes for positive, helpful professions, is restored, is mobilized, and can be set in motion.

From time to time as disappointments occur one could expect that Frank could not help but fall back on old defensive and adaptive devices which are dominantly primitive acting-out mechanisms. These acting-out devices, however, would now be in the service of a more mature personality organization and in part, at least, would have an adaptive function to help him to some extent to master reality, and would only secondarily serve the purpose of the repetition of past unconscious conflicts.

As the psychotherapy proceeded, Frank developed the capacity to maintain contact and to communicate with the therapist almost exclusively on a verbal level. Play action and acting out within the therapy process were replaced by talking out and thinking out even those fantasies dealing with a variety of inner conflicts that were mainly concerned with Frank's efforts to cement the identification with the therapist as a nonthreatening masculine object. The symptom of stealing and the wish to steal were relegated to the background of his psychic life and had started to subside completely. What acting out occurred was experienced on the fringe of gang activities, within the residential setting and with his adolescent peers who bullied the younger children and engaged in defiant, boisterous, and sexually aggressive gestures against the residential personnel.

After a number of months of this phase of his therapy, Frank again began to feel the inner pressure which he ascribed to repeated disappointments about his family. He very rarely received mail from home and was under constant tension lest his grandparents carry out the threat of removing him from the school because of financial reverses. These circumstances, associated with the approaching date of his birthday and the anticipated visit with his parents during the holiday season, again stimulated strong wishes in Frank to possess a real gun. For many months he struggled with his conflict about the wish to possess such a gun and the fear of the consequences of this responsibility, and many therapeutic sessions were concerned with the means of obtaining such a gun.

During one point of this phase of his therapy, Frank hit upon the plan to borrow money from the bank with the therapist underwriting and guaranteeing the loan. Frank and the therapist went through this procedure and obtained a loan of twenty-five dollars. Its effect, rather than elating and gratifying Frank, was to intensify his anxiety. It was as if he had been discovered in a forbidden act with the therapist, and as if he had revealed a secret mission to the loan officer who appeared to him as a terrifying and threatening figure. The fear also that he would not be able to repay the loan and would damage the credit and reputation of the therapist led to his immediate repayment of the loan with the loss of two-and-a-half dollars of unused interest. Action and acting out had been replaced by a new symptom which we might consider to be the precursor of a phobia.

Frank's desperate and compelling wish to possess a real gun was finally fulfilled in a quasi-legal manner after he had managed to save a sufficient amount of money from his allowance, a no small feat for him. Together with the therapist he purchased a gun which was registered with the police by the proprietor of the gunstore, and was kept under lock and key in the therapist's office. The gun became the symbol of a trusting, loving, and accepting relationship between Frank and the therapist, and on one level served as a source of play gratification, as a number of therapy hours were spent shooting at targets along the river.

Frank glowed with pride at his achievement of overcoming his fear of guns as he fantasied himself the master of that which he once dreaded. His self-esteem rose, but was soon dampened by the renewal of his conflict about possession and shooting of the gun, until he began to express doubt to the therapist as to whether this was what he really wanted and whether it was a source of enjoyment to him after all. At this point in his treatment he declared himself ready to enter a boarding home and to enter public high school.

The positive relationship in the transference situation was paralleled in Frank's immediate and gratifying state of acceptance and positive feelings in the boarding home. Although he made many complaints of a feeble nature about the boarding-home mother, he basked in the new-found relationship with the boarding-home father. For the first time in his life, Frank declared that he had met a man who made him feel that he (Frank) was a person, worthy of respect and dignity. With guarded astonishment he confessed that it was the first time that something like this had ever happened to him. The feeling of being trusted and respected was experienced as the arrival of his day of glory.

The brittleness and fragility of this new-found identification with the male love object and of the trusting relationship for which he had searched so long, however, soon became evident. Frank experienced a homosexual panic that drove him back to Southard School and forced him to relinquish the boarding home. The panic was provoked by keen disappointment in the boarding-home father, when he expressed distrust of Frank's possession of the gun. Frank had been certain that he would be trusted with his own pistol since the boarding-home father had trusted him with his own hunting rifle and the two of them had enjoyed using it together. When the boarding-home father, with some justification, expressed his fear of pistols, and did not permit Frank to keep his in the boarding home, Frank experienced this rebuff as an expression of deep distrust. If the father with whom he had identified himself could not trust him, he could not trust himself. Fear of his own aggression and erotic impulses, coupled with his perception of the boarding-home father as one who could not trust him in the active masculine role, brought on the panic. For Frank, denial of the right to possess a gun symbolized the fear that the father could not trust his control over his aggression, but could accept him only as a passive child, as one who would therefore have to surrender, to submit, and to be castrated in order to be accepted.

Paralleling this same experience in the transference situation, Frank, in a panic, broke into the therapist's office one night, stole the gun, and ran away. He left the following note: "Dear Doc. I am very sorry that I went back on your trust about the gun but it was the only thing left to do. I feel shitty all over anyhow. Frank Smith." Although he was found in his room the following morning, depressed and almost inaccessible, he later revealed that he had walked the streets all night, gun in hand, full of rage and bitterness, desperately hoping that he would not encounter the therapist who, he had expected, would look for him (and who actually had carried out a futile search for him during the night). Frank's reaction again was to destroy the gun as being a source of nothing but trouble. He vowed that never again would he have a gun and gratefully accepted the therapist's help in selling it, again with a loss of money but with great relief. The public-school situation also collapsed as Frank found it impossible to continue attendance when he experienced a most profound panic and paralysis which made it impossible for him to enter the high school building. The abrogation of acting-out symptoms had led to the appearance of a genuine phobic symptom, a form of "inverted acting out."

Frank's runaway note confirmed our speculation that the panic situation in the boarding home had been a displacement of the transference situation. The therapist, like the boarding-home father, was suspected by Frank of accepting him only in the pseudo-masculine role, expressed in the act of carrying a gun, which the therapist, however, controlled and kept from Frank's possession by keeping it locked in his office.

In the ensuing months, Frank on two separate occasions again experienced the all-compelling and irresistible wish and impulse to possess a gun, a wish which he could gratify only in forbidden secrecy with another boy in the residence. On one occasion the illicit possession of the gun culminated in remorse and self-condemnation with the violent dismantling and destruction of the gun, flinging the parts into the river, and the loss of his highly cherished monetary investment. In the second incident Frank concealed the gun in his room for a number of months and then brought about its discovery and confiscation, but with the additional feature that this time Frank participated in its legal disposition, again with a loss of money, but with the conscious choice on his part that he would have to sacrifice the gun in order to enter a second boarding home.

These incidents paralleled and climaxed Frank's agonizing inner struggle over his holding on to or finally rejecting the bonds that attached him to his family. Frank compared his dilemma regarding his relationship to his phantom mother to the futility of a dead-end street. Desperately he pinned his hopes on the fork in the road that would lead him in another direction, but just as desperately he felt the incapacity to trust that this fork could lead to anything but another dead end. The abandoned house that yielded nothing but rubble, dirt, and memories of a token love in the past, now entered his conscious thinking. It took the form of the dismal awareness that his hopes for a loving and reawakened relationship with his mother, the hope to return to his family, had also crumbled into a heap of dust. He saw his dying hopes in the fantasy of himself as a ship's captain, dutifully remaining with his ship as it went down to the bottom of the ocean; and as one who once had pathetically held on to a spark with the futile hope that he could kindle it into a flame.

The relinquishing of his narcissistic relationships and the cutting of his ties with the past, facilitated by the increased capacity for new object relationships and more genuine identifications with his love objects, culminated in the second and this-time successful attempt to live in a boarding home, an event in which Frank actively participated from the planning stage. In the psychotherapy, play action and acting out ceased and gave way to the conventional form of treatment of a neurotic personality. Secondary-process thinking largely replaced primitive play fantasy and acting out.

Frank re-entered public high school and was able to maintain himself with excellent academic performance, despite the residual of his phobic symptom which made it extremely difficult for him to give reports particulary in front of the class. He became interested in religious training and seriously considered entering the ministry. After graduating from high school, he maintained the bond with the boarding home, at the same time loosening it to some extent, terminated psychotherapy, chose a university he wished to attend, and took a part-time job in the interim before entering the university.

With a positive and more realistic view of his helpful and supporting grandparents, he had now created for himself new introjects upon which to rely, introjects which gave him new purpose in life and had the power to help him overcome the early difficulties in which adults were seen to be undependable, treacherous, deserting, and criminally negligent. Limited originally to taking from society aggressively that which he felt was always withheld from him by troubled and immature parents, he had come to a new self-concept of a young adult who was now in the position to help others.

How the core of the acting-out personality remained active despite advancement in the hierarchy of personality organization is illustrated in an experience of genuine, neurotic acting out toward the end of his treatment.

Frank had become a member of the church and was an active and enthusiastic participant in a young people's group. During one particular discussion led by a woman church group-worker, the subject of the rightness and wrongness of stealing under various circumstances came up. The group leader felt that, in the case of a Czech boy who during the Nazi occupation of his country was forced to steal in order to maintain himself and his family lest they starve, it was not wrong to steal. Frank took violent exception to what he considered a lax and hypocritical judgment on the part of the group leader. He strongly felt that under no circumstances could it be considered morally right to steal and quoted the appropriate Commandment as his authority. He insisted that only this rule in the Bible could determine the rightness or wrongness of the act. The judgment of the group leader had troubled him greatly.

The therapist interpreted for him his need to maintain absolute and infallible rules of rightness and wrongness that could not be compromised by human beings, and his need to place trust only in such rules when he felt that the word of a human being could not be relied upon as a guide to reality testing in extreme circumstances. Frank's response was to confirm the interpretation by acting out in the following experience. That same evening he took the boarding-home parents' car with their permission and drove it along an icy street. Looking in the rear view mirror, he found that his rear window was steamed up and he could not see outside. The impulse to have fun by "gunning" the car led him to drive for two blocks with the car swaying from side to side until he was suddenly halted by a police car. Frank was chagrined, but was able with the boarding-home father's help to go through the court experience with dignity and with increased understanding of his failure fully to accept his responsibility as a driver.

In the therapy session, it became clear that he was acting out his perception of the unreliable internal image that hid itself when he was tempted to obey a primitive, dangerous impulse, but which made its presence known only after he had exposed himself to danger so that he was made to pay the penalty for his primitive and illicit gratification. The acting out confirmed the therapist's interpretation, carried him back to the past conflict with his parents, and served to further his insight into his conflict in a way that contributed to a more effective resolution in the future. In this view, the acting out could be seen as a positive attempt at new resolution.

In adult neurotics, acting out is considered a form of resistance to be removed by interpretation, or injunction. But in this case, the assumption was made that the *acting out, play action,* and *play acting,* rather than being merely a substitute for recollection, *represented experimental recollection,* a primitive mode of the ego to bring about reconstruction, which is in the service of adaptation. The unavailability of sufficient neutralized energy cathexis for higher forms of ego organization was considered a contraindication to the use of technical tools applicable to adult neurotics.

REFERENCES

[1] Fenichel, O. Neurotic acting out, Psychoanal. Rev., 32:197, 1945.

[2] Freud, S. Formulations regarding two principles in mental functioning (1911), Collected Papers, London, Hogarth Press, 1948, pp. 4, 13.

[3] Erikson, E. H. Studies in the interpretation of play: I. Clinical observation of play disruption in young children, Genet. Psychol. Monogr., 22: 557, 1940

[4] Freud, S. Beyond the Pleasure Principle (1920), New York, Liveright, 1950.

[5] Greenacre, P. Problems of infantile neurosis: a discussion, Psychoanal. Stud. Child, 9:18, 1954.

[6] Hartmann, H. Problems of infantile neurosis: a discussion, Psychoanal. Stud. Child, 9:31, 1954.

[7] Carroll, E. J. Acting out and ego development, Psychoanal. Quart., 23:521, 1954.

[8] Greenacre, P. General problems of acting out, *in* Trauma, Growth and Personality, New York, W. W. Norton, 1952, p. 224.

[9] Fenichel. Op. cit.

[10] Spiegel, L. A. Acting out and defensive instinctual gratification. J. Amer. Psychoanal. Ass., 2:107, 1954.

[11] Freud, A. Psychoanalytical Treatment of Children, London: Imago Publishing Co., 1948.

[12] Sargent, H. Personal communication.

[13] Fenichel. Op. cit.

[14] In some instances, however, even the therapist of this conviction must decide upon the language form of communication, as when he cannot use the mother tongue of the patient and forces him to use a second language in which the patient necessarily says and conveys much less about himself and his deepest basic problems. (Greenson, R. R. The mother tongue and the mother, Int. J. Psychoanal., 31:18, 1950.)

10

THE MEANING OF PLAY IN CHILDHOOD PSYCHOSIS*

. . . and pass on to examine the method of working employed by the mental apparatus in one of its earliest normal activities —I mean in children's play.

The interpretation of the game then became obvious. It was related to the child's great cultural achievement—the instinctual renunciation (that is, the renunciation of instinctual satisfaction) which he had made in allowing his mother to go away without protesting. He compensated himself for this, as it were, by himself staging the disappearance and return of the objects within his reach.

SIGMUND FREUD

Victor Tausk's classic contribution, "On the Origin of the 'Influencing Machine' in Schizophrenia," [1] in spite of its now partly outdated conceptualizations, continues to stimulate many investigators in our field through its richness of ideas. The nature of Natalija A.'s "influencing machine" was then understood primarily in terms of paranoid projections. Tausk speaks about the "infantile stage of thinking, in which a strong belief exists that others know of the child's thoughts." He suggests that "a striving for the right to have secrets from which the parents are excluded is one of the most powerful factors in the formation of the ego, especially in establishing and carrying out one's own will." He speaks of "the loss of ego boundaries," a concept which is frequently used in the work of Federn, and suggests that "this symptom is the complaint that 'everyone' knows the patient's thoughts, that his thoughts are not enclosed in his own head, but are spread throughout the world and occur simultaneously in the heads of all persons. The patient seems no longer to realize that he is a separate psychical entity, an ego with individual

* Seymour W. Friedman is coauthor of this chapter.

207

boundaries." We recall that the ego concept here does not derive from the tripartite model of psychic organization, and is used somewhat loosely in terms of the self-concept.

Freud [2] discussed Tausk's contribution in a meeting of the Vienna Psychoanalytic Society, and he "emphasized that the infant's conception that others knew his thoughts has its source in the process of learning to speak. Having obtained his language from others, the infant has also received thoughts from them; and the child's feeling that others know his thoughts as well as that others have 'made' him the language and, along with it, his thoughts, has therefore some basis in reality." Freud's comment, as well as Tausk's discussion, would have to be considered an oversimplification of the genesis of paranoid projections, in the context of more modern concepts of psychic organization.

Natalija A.'s "influencing machine" represents a regressive phenomenon within a psychic organization which is characterized by rudiments of a mature psychic apparatus. Her fantasy of the "influencing machine" constitutes a restitutive element, the psychotic's attempt to reconstruct the dramatic past and to describe inner experiences which run parallel to the infant's lack of developed capacity for differentiation of self from object, his struggle to maintain a world of omnipotence while growing towards awareness of self and objects. During this stage, primary narcissistic omnipotence, as it prevails in a comparatively undifferentiated psychic organization, shifts at times by means of narcissistic projection on to the object, which is then experienced as giving thoughts or knowing all thoughts, and as thus influencing the other. The "influencing machine" characterizes the fluctuation of fantasies of omnipotence from self to object and back again to self. This struggle attempts to restore symbiosis, and thus to overcome fragmentation of body image and to restore the "oceanic feeling," the oneness with Mother, in which she has the executive function of the controlling ego.

These newer assumptions which attempt to describe the development of the psychic organization before individuation has taken place were earlier expressed in terms of the *content* of fantasies. Only later were attempts made to infer from the content the *state* of the psychic organization. For example, when discussing Tausk's contribution, Freud also suggested [2] that the "significance of the mode of burial of Egyptian mummies [placing the mummy in] a case resembling the human body suggests the idea of the return to 'mother earth,' the return to the mother's body in death." He continued that "as a compensation for the bitterness of death, man takes for granted the bliss of existence in the uterus." The fantasy of the return to the uterus is "then an atavistic one, a pre-formed fantasy;" and as such, "this fantasy appears symptomatically in schizophrenia as the pathological reality of the regressing, disintegrating psyche. The mummy returns to the mother's body by physical, and the schizophrenic by psychical death."

The "psychical death" of the schizophrenic constitutes an attempt actually to restore an early unity in order to gain safety. It usually fails to do so, since the symbiotic experience often signifies the threat of loss of identity, the fear of being devoured, and of being dominated by the other. The "influencing machine," then, represents both the wish to return to an undifferentiated, symbiotic phase and the lonesome struggle against the loss of precarious identity.

As we trace the literature for contributions in which psychotic mechanisms of childhood are described and note particularly the use such children make of machines,[3] we face a variety of problems of a different order. These children, particularly the younger ones, have, of course, never advanced to states of maturity characteristic of the premorbid adjustment of Natalija A. Rather, we find in them personality organizations which frequently are better understood in terms of psychotic fixations than in terms of psychotic regressions. In this regard, we must remember that the application of these dynamic processes towards the characterization of the essential nature of the state of personality organization of psychotic children is a way of speaking, a convenient shorthand generalization, as it were, for a complex situation, rather than a scientific conclusion reached as the result of valid evidence. For these processes merely refer to the importance of developmental factors in the evaluation and understanding of the various problems of psychosis in childhood. They stress the need to make qualitative as well as quantitative distinctions between the psychotic processes of adults and children, and between the psychoses of younger and older children.

Thus, in the very young children of preschool age, we find ego fragmentation, symbiotic and autistic conditions, an extremely impaired capacity for reality testing, and primitive precursors of object relationships which characterize their specific adjustments. The dynamic considerations which define the dimensions of the play of psychotic children are derived from factors which characterize the archaic structural aspects of the developing ego. Significant and relevant components of the ego organization which determine the patterns of psychotic play concern the concept of distance as a function of defense; the vicissitudes of impulse organization during the development from primary- to secondary-process control; language development and object relationships; the problem of identity; and the adaptive functions of the ego, especially its motor and synthesizing functions.

Similarly, qualitative differentiations can be made between the play of neurotic and psychotic children, for example, in the play of acting-out children (Chapter 9) in which acting out, play action, and play serve the functions of recollection, mastery of conflicts, and the search for identity. But in the play of the psychotic child, the functions of mastery, pleasure, and motor expression are less important as the end products of ego development. They interest us rather as diagnostic indicators of the functional state of the ego and as the means of communication about the conflictual problems confronting the ego in its particular developmental state.

The foregoing considerations have been among the many subjects dealt with in an enormous body of literature which accumulated during the last decade and which has been described and integrated by the present authors and their coworker, Bryant.[4] More recent publications deal with the relationship of play patterns and diagnosis in childhood psychosis.[5]

Our purpose here is to study the play of such children in order to find answers to two sets of questions. Their play constitutes the royal road to an understanding of certain aspects of the available psychic organization. The understanding of the structure of available psychic organization can then be used in order to develop therapeutic techniques. The child's play, his royal road to the unconscious,[6] can be considered the dominant language of the child, and thus his most powerful means of communication with the therapist.

The word "communication," just as the word "influencing," must be understood in terms of the available psychic organization of the child. Even the assumption that play be considered a substitute for free association in the treatment of the psychotic child needs amplification, since the effectiveness of language, of interpretive work, would depend upon the nature of the psychic organization, the available capacity for differentiation of self and nonself, and the fluctuating state of affairs concerning object relationships. Consequently, we must question what communication and interpretation really mean when psychotic "transference" prevails. We would like to ascertain how psychotic play can teach us to make contact with such children. And we wonder how it might be possible to develop "sending power"[7] in profoundly psychotic children in spite of the deficits in their psychic organization. It might also be wished that Natalija A. had been able to teach us how to develop "influencing machines" for those autistic and mute children who possess only a rudimentary capacity for play, the nature of which is so different from the play of children within the neurotic range.

An analogue of Natalija A.'s "influencing machine" was experienced by a five year old boy. He felt all noises to be intrusive penetrating tormentors who, by gaining entrance into his body, could simultaneously discover his secret forbidden wishes and destroy him. Upon hearing loud noises, he would cringe and cower as if in pain, whimper in terror and in mounting panic, and instantly clap his hands over his ears as if to block out the hideous frightening sounds that were attempting to invade his head. For this psychotic boy, the threatening noises and sounds were equated with the frightening voice of his enraged father, threatening to send him away if he were naughty again. And like Natalija A.'s "influencing machine," they represented a monstrous but impersonal delusional force which the boy had introjected in order to achieve symbiotic union with the omnipotent father. At the same time the boy struggled against introjection of the father's violent image and enraged voice which would have separated him from home and the needed father.

While the "influencing machine" of both Natalija A. and this psychotic child dealt with their common struggle around the conflicting wishes toward symbiosis and individuation, one essential difference between them lay in the capacity of their respective egos to internalize and stabilize parental introjects. In a sense, Natalija A., having internalized the object, could create a completed machine which could function without the external physical object and could derive its driving power from the force of her delusional fantasy. The psychotic child, not having succeeded in internalizing the introjected image of the omnipotent father, could create only a precursor of the "influencing machine." The machine could not function independently of the real, external object-voices and -sounds, around which he wove a delusion of the ambivalently viewed father who could both destroy and protect him within the same fantasy. Reality is the "nutriment," as Piaget puts it,[8] for the ego of the child without which the inherent patterns cannot be mobilized.

The successful achievement of identity depends upon the ego's capacity to internalize its introjects, or it never comes to fruition, as in the severely psychotic child. Waelder has suggested that the play of the child can be understood as fantasy woven around external objects.[9] Although he refers to physical objects which the child employs for his play activities, he nevertheless assumes a capacity for differentiation between outer and inner world, a primitive form of thinking which, however, has moved toward a more mature developmental stage. Natalija A.'s "influencing machine" might be considered such an external object around which she weaves fantasies. Its nature, however, is such that no differentiation is possible between her own body image and the fantasy image of the "influencing machine" in the hands of her alleged tormentors. Winnicott's [10] conception of the transitory object provides us with intermediate stages of object formation in which part objects may also become the hub around which delusions may be woven by the child's ego.

Of the small psychotic child it may often be said that when he weaves fantasies around external objects, he frequently cannot identify these external objects as being a part of the outside world. We might paraphrase Waelder and suggest that the play of the psychotic child is explicable as hallucinatory and delusional fantasy woven around external objects. The adult psychotic, having once in the past internalized but having later lost the introjected object, can create a psychotic fantasy through autistic thought processes without the help of actual external objects. The psychotic child, never having been able adequately to internalize the object, must weave hallucinations and delusions around external objects which are not experienced by the child as differentiated from the internalized object. Abortive attempts at differentiation between internal and external objects (also, his interrupted struggle toward individuation and identity formation), are regularly followed by regressive moves for the maintenance of symbiotic union with the parental object. The psychotic child's play very frequently characterizes the conflictual struggle to maintain symbiosis and to wipe out the difference between himself and the outside world, in order to avoid painful insight and to remain one with the world.

This brings to mind the play of the psychotic child who had to twirl constantly and who reacted with violent displeasure to attempts to interrupt her twirling. She suggested that she did so because she wanted the world to be confused and topsy-turvy, so that it would be exactly as she felt within herself; she would no longer be able to sense that she was different from others. No doubt, this child could make such an observation only at the point when her symptoms no longer completely possessed her, and after she had started to experience them as an alien part of herself. She needed to rationalize these symptoms in order to make them ego-syntonic.

We are indebted to M. Williams [11] for these data. This psychotic girl, whose play so vividly demonstrates the need of the child to maintain a sense of oneness with the outer world, started intensive treatment in the early latency period. Her outstanding play activity during a long period of treatment centered around her fascinated love for incinerators which she attempted to control by magic gestures and to which she was endlessly attracted. During many therapy hours her fantasy life was woven around one special incinerator. The incinerator, as the representation of the fragmented maternal introject, separated the negative, engulfing, and threatening aspects of the maternal object from the positive, nourishing, and protective components of the maternal image. The child's endless play around the incinerator and her fascination with it contained both precursors of obsessive mechanisms and related instinctual derivatives, witnesses of the ceaseless but unsuccessful struggle of the rudimentary ego to establish a stable, adaptive, and defensive organization.

This child used a mechanical object upon which to attach psychotic thought processes. In situations that are characteristic of a somewhat higher psychic organization, actual persons are used as the nucleus of the psychotic fantasy.

The situation existent in the case of Natalija A. might be considered an intermediate stage, as she utilized actual persons in combination with fantasied "influencing machines." As another example, illustrative of another stage of ego organization, we think of the Space Child whose pure psychotic fantasy concerning the Time Machine (Chapter 16) attached itself in the transference situation to the person of the psychotherapist. Still another example, provided by M. Wexler,[12] concerns the play of a psychotic boy who repeatedly threw a ball in fantasy to an actual child while actually he remained on the periphery of the play group. He fantasied himself joining the group at the same time that he remained uninvolved and isolated from it. In fantasy, he made contact with the playmate as he combined the fantasied physical object, the ball, with the fantasy of making contact with an actual object.

Predominant discussion in this area in 1919 concerned the *meaning* of symptoms, a meaning which was sought in the origin of symptoms. Since then the question of historic origin has been enriched by questions concerning the nature of the psychic organization—of which the symptom is but a sign—and concerning the nature of techniques that must be developed to bring about therapeutic change.

Our case illustrations serve as models for the type of thinking necessary to reconstruct the psychic organization characteristic for the child and to develop modes of intervention derived from a better understanding of the nature of the psychotic child's "communications," his play activities. Once more we wish to call attention to our meaning of "communication" in psychotherapy with a psychotic child. Within this context, we differentiate between that aspect of communication which is derived from the child's activity, and the alternate pole of communication which refers to the therapist's interventions. Psychotic play activity, if properly understood, might yield insights necessary for a fuller understanding of the process of communication, as well as of a number of other mental processes, which, hopefully, will enrich our understanding of the psychic organization. In turn, this might enable us to develop more effective therapeutic techniques which could further the development of the patient's psychic organization.

Robby was almost five when he was brought for psychiatric treatment. For the past two and a half years he had posed the most difficult management and discipline problems to his parents, who felt themselves caught in an impregnable trap created by his incomprehensible behavior and wild emotional outbursts. They complained of his severe temper tantrums that erupted with volcanic fury at the slightest frustration and sometimes with apparently trivial provocation. They felt desperately helpless that they could not reach him or make themselves understood to him. They were deeply concerned and frightened over his failure to mature along normal developmental lines, thus leaving them with the fearful expectation that he would be diagnosed as an organically damaged child for whom there was no hope of cure or improvement. Robby's father particularly despaired that the child's intellectual development would remain permanently retarded. He found himself inextricably enmeshed in his own struggle between his despair for Robby's future and his own violent rage toward his son when provoked by the boy's uncontrollable behavior.

The one area in which the parents found a glimmer of hope, agile motor development, proved to be a mixed blessing for them. For although this precocity gave them the one ray of hope that he was not retarded, it also provided the most excruciating provocation for their anger and helplessness. They could not prevent Robby from using his motor skills and his singular mechanical aptitudes to dismantle the doors, locks, and mechanical appliances in their home. Sporadically the parents frantically felt that they could only stand by in paralyzed impotence and watch their house literally taken apart, piece by piece. In frenzied excited forays, Robby would leave the doors hanging loosely from their hinges, the moldings separated from the walls, the carpet torn up to expose the bare floors, and every object sufficiently loose to become vulnerable to his prying tools, torn from its moorings. Robby's parents feared that his infantile verbal and language development must mean hopeless mental retardation. Robby's language consisted of very few words, which were difficult to comprehend, and bizarre sounds and fragments of words to which only his parents, eager to understand him, could attach meaning.

For the first few months of psychotherapy, Robby did not display the unusually frantic behavior that plagued his parents. At best his play was fragmentary, impulsively interrupted, but never impetuously frantic. From fragmentary house building with blocks, Robby slowly turned his interest to the door stoppers in the therapist's office. Quickly, all other play activities were pushed into the background as Robby became obsessed with collecting every door stopper within his visual and tactile reach. His speech would rise in an excited crescendo as he would gleefully repeat the phrase, "want a door stopper," and impulsively pounce with either hand or foot upon every door stopper accessible to him. He would tug and pull, jump and pounce upon the door stoppers, until he either broke them off or unscrewed them from the wall. He carried a large collection of door stoppers of every variety with him and, at one time, posed a difficult problem for the therapist. He ran through the corridor of the medical building in which the doctor's office was located, dashing into every office, and pounced upon the door stopper in each office that he had already precisely located, until he was apprehended and removed. With lightning speed in one foray he dashed away from the therapist and, bursting into a strange office, quickly broke off the door stopper and slammed the door against the wall, cracking the plaster and leading to a socially difficult situation for all concerned.

The interpretation that Robby was looking for a stopper that would keep him from destroying his house when he could not prevent himself from flying open like a door and breaking the wall, eventually diminished his compulsive, frantic need for the door stoppers, as both therapist and parents assumed more effective forms of external control for him. But as he slowly gave up his need for the door stoppers and yielded to the authority of adults as stoppers of his lightning impulsivity, Robby's compulsive preoccupations centered around a collection of screw drivers and doorknobs which he skillfully and with lightning rapidity removed from every available door. At home, in the therapist's office, wherever there was a door, no doorknob was safe from his frantic clutch. With one swift movement of the screw driver, he could remove a doorknob before he could be stopped. The one word "knob" formed the nucleus of his verbal expressions.

During the phase of his compulsive attachment to doorknobs, Robby's father was absent from home for several weeks. Robby's need to dismantle the doors and to remove the doorknobs heightened in intensity until his mother found herself desperate and unable to cope with his impulsive destructiveness. Prior to one therapy hour, the mother had told the therapist that Robby had had quite a scare. He had suddenly burst into the kitchen where the mother was working, and in wild excitement threw his screw driver into the air and cracked the ceiling fixture so that part of it came tumbling down to the floor, crashing between Robby and his mother. Robby had become so frightened that he had dashed in wild panic from the room while his mother dashed after, both to comfort and to scold him. She angrily took the screw driver away and threatened him with its loss forever unless he learned to refrain from using the tool as a dangerous weapon. Robby erupted into wild hysteria and could not be comforted for two hours until, in spent exhaustion, he lapsed into a tormented sleep.

When Robby arrived for his therapy hour, he quickly dashed to the therapist's drawer where his favorite screw driver lay waiting for him. Following his familiar pattern, he hastily went to the playroom and removed the doorknobs and the plates from two doors in the playroom.

The therapist, whom the boy called Friend, had been interpreting to Robby his need for the doorknobs as his need for Mama who left him with Friend.

For many weeks Robby had gone through the ritual of demanding numerous kisses from his mother as she left him, whereupon with reassurance that she would return, he went flying to the doors with the therapist's screw driver. Dismantling the doorknobs would leave Robby with a smile of satisfaction, mischievous cunning, and an almost ecstatic pleasure in which the therapist could feel Robby's great relief from his anxiety over the mother's leaving. As the time approached the ending of the hour and the mother's expected return, Robby went through the ritual of replacing the doorknobs with the help of the therapist's interpretation, insistence, and encouragement that now he could put the knobs back and leave them with Friend since Mama was coming to take Robby home.

At this point Robby became quite anxious and repeated with almost tearful pleading that he needed the doorknobs and did not want to put them back. "Why put doorknob back?" he cried in repetitious, frantic excitement. "Don't want to put doorknob back," he asserted with a defiant gesture. As the therapist tried to allay Robby's anxiety he told him that he knew that Mama had taken the screw driver from him and that he was very frightened that he would be without his screw driver and could not have his knobs. Maybe he was even more frightened without his knobs when Daddy was away, especially since Mama had taken his screw driver away. Robby confirmed this interpretation by displaying mounting anxiety and by more intensely repeating his pleas for the knobs. The therapist told him that he knew that Robby needed the knobs in order not to be afraid that Mama would leave him and sometimes he needed the knobs so that he would not be afraid of Mama. But Friend wanted to help him so that he would not have to be afraid and he would feel big and strong even without Friend's knobs. Although Robby listened and betrayed a fleeting satisfied smile, he maintained his insistence that he must have the knobs and could not put them back, repeatedly asking why the doors needed the knobs. When it became clear to him that he could not take the knobs with him but would have to replace them on the door and leave them with Friend, his anxiety mounted into panic proportions. He looked at Friend and in a terrified whisper confessed, "Don't want to be girl."

Robby's strange, repetitive play, the compulsivity of which was also characterized by uncontrollable passion, moves through a number of phases which permit conjecture about the nature of the process which took place. The first phase of the game concerned the ceaseless removal of door stoppers, the prevention of the locking of doors, the deeper purpose of which was to fight against isolation, against separation, and to secure access to the parental figure. Availability of the mother had to be fought for through the struggle for the open door. The removal of the door stoppers could be understood as an expression of his uncontrollable impulsivity, with no holds barred. Thus he told the world, that is, his therapist, about the deep conflict between his uncontrollable impulsivity which had to be stopped and governed, which threatened him with the punishment of isolation and separation from the protecting and nourishing mother, and his deep wish to be reunited with her and to keep the doors, the access to her, open. One could hardly think of a better symbolic presentation for the struggle between the autistic and the symbiotic position. The removal of the door stopper portrays the eruptive quality of Robby's impulsive life which then actually threatens the desired accessibility. The parent is driven away by his lack of control, lack of boundary between self and non-self, and ceaseless passionate yearning for unification. The constant threat to the home, the literal physical annihilation of the inside of the home, destroys the very basis for emotional security which such a child needs. It is characteristic and most certainly a symbolic presentation, also, for the state of the personality organization of the child, in which neither the boundaries between different psychic organizations nor the identity of separate functions can be maintained. The regressed and fluctuating ego of this child is deprived, if we may use the metaphor of the play, of its door stoppers, its doors, its walls, and its separate entities. The struggle against walls and doors, motivated by the wish for unification, for togetherness with the mother, actually achieves the opposite and threatens the very foundations of the child's life.

While the first phase of the play characterizes the archaic conflict, the regression to a state of uncontrollable impulsivity, the second phase aims at restitution, at the solution of conflict for which the psychotherapy is preparing. The removal of the door stoppers, the removal of all controls, is followed by the passion to remove doorknobs from all available doors, to collect them and to keep them. They assumed for Robby the purport of a quasi-fetish. This play assumes different meaning at different points, and at times maintains different meanings at the very same moment. Whenever Robby found himself in a phase where higher functions of personality organization were available, where there was some availability of differentiation between object and self, the knob symbolized parts of the mother or the father which the child wished to make accessible to himself. By holding on to the knob he had access to the open door, and he could maintain the connection between himself and the parent. At most moments, though, as is expressed so clearly in Robby's frantic and terrorized plea that he did not want to be a girl, the knobs refer to his own body. It would be incorrect if one were to see in the knobs only symbolic representations of the male genitalia. The dominant meaning of these knobs referred to his inability to maintain a clear body image. The loss of the knobs, identity with the loss of the mother as an accessible object—as an introject that could be maintained—referred to the threat of loss of identity, a threat particularly powerful whenever separation was threatened.

The ending of each psychotherapy hour, when Robby had to give up the knobs of the office doors, created a new threat for him, in the separation from the therapist and the necessity to take along the quasi-fetish. The function of the fetish was not only to replace the lost love object—which explains the reference to "quasi-fetish"—but to secure narcissistic cathexis, so that the body image could be maintained and precarious identity insured.

The external knob, not dissimilar in function from the "influencing machines" described earlier, is the external object around which delusions and inner perceptions concerning body and self-identity are woven.

If our interpretation of the play is correct, we should be able to draw conclusions for therapeutic technique. In this instance the use of a quasi-fetish for symbolic representation and symbolic gratification becomes a part of the therapy. The therapist cannot treat the doorknob simply as a utensil, but has to think of it as part of an important ritual without which communication cannot succeed. Zulliger [13] made use of a talisman which he gave to his girl patient as symbolic representation of the father image. Sechehaye [14] used symbolic gratification in the gift of an apple to her schizophrenic girl patient. The use of the knob here, above and beyond the verbal interpretations as they are possible, insures communication and contact with the child.

The ritual which developed about leaving time, when the knob was finally returned to the therapist, as was the screw driver which was used in order to control the different knobs, became for Robby the symbol of security. It was as if the two had agreed that the means of control were safe as long as they were left with the therapist, and that the child would trust the therapist in terms of accessibility and in terms of a guarantee for restitution. As long as he is with the psychotherapist he borrows, as it were, the strength of the therapist by taking his doorknobs, the guarantee of parental supply. When he leaves, he is willing to restore the therapist's wholeness, and feels secure in the knowledge that the continuing process is guaranteed. The quasi-fetish is returned to the psychotherapist, a form of undoing of the fantasied destruction of the therapist. This is the child's first indication that he aims to master the problem of impulsivity and will replace the primary process with higher mental functions which will make available to him a new capacity for delay.

During an interim phase of this play Robby would bring old battered doorknobs from home and try to exchange them for the therapist's new shiny doorknobs. Such an exchange could be the symbolic representation of an attempt to get well by introjecting the therapist and also to get rid of introjects from earlier phases of life which were experienced as damaged, powerless, and undesirable.

The compulsive behavior of Robby's play differs from compulsions on a higher level of development in that it is accompanied by unbridled affect, that it is dominated by uncontrollable impulsivity. One might suggest that the obsessive-compulsive in the neurotic range is characterized by a compulsive ego. In the case of this child one is tempted to speak of a compulsive id which dominates the situation. This manner of speaking, though, is inexact unless one remains aware of the nature of the comparatively undifferentiated psychic organization.

Three months later, Robby's therapy hour had assumed a new compulsive and ritualized form.

Every hour would start with his bursting into the therapist's office, his hands filled with an odd assortment of tools. He would go through an anxious procedure of bidding goodbye to his mother with demands for more and more kisses, gradually decreasing in intensity as he seemed more reassured that she would return for him. He would dash to the drawer for the screw driver and urgently remove the doorknobs in the therapist's playroom with obvious relief and satisfaction in his prowess, and then quickly explore the office for more available doorknobs and loose hinge-pins. These he would quickly remove if he were given freedom to do so, then gather up his screw drivers and tools which he would store in Friend's pocket as he would exclaim, "Want to go out," and lead the way into the corridor. The familiar trek along the corridor followed. Robby would compulsively touch the doorknob of every office door. Then, with one hand in the therapist's he would almost happily walk down the stairway and out into the alley to look for abandoned pipes, bulbs, hinges, and doorknobs in the piles of rubbish conveniently left by workmen who were remodelling offices in nearby buildings. The therapy journey would lead to a parking garage in which Robby had come to know the location of every door and of every doorknob. At the doorway to the stairs leading up to the various levels, Robby would inspect the door which for a long time was without a knob: Robby had dismantled and thrown it away rather than have it taken away from him. Finding the knob missing, he would rapidly ask where the knob was. On being told that Robby had thrown it away, he would smile with a satisfied, cunning expression on his face, and with that would lead the way to the second level where he would inspect the doorknobs of the door leading into the garage. Noting that the knobs were present, he would immediately proceed to the third floor where one knob was still absent as a result of his prior activities. Demanding that the therapist hold this door open, he would wrap his legs around the door and hold on to the protruding part of the lock as he would swing back and forth and emit a loud, excited, shrill, "EEEEE," and rapidly ask where the doorknob was. When told that Robby seemed happy that the doorknob was gone but that maybe he was really frightened to see that there was no doorknob after he had thrown it away, he would give up swinging, slam the door shut with great gusto, and proceed down the stairs into the alley. The therapist could interpret to Robby that he seemed happy to see the doorknob gone, but he must be afraid that every time he saw a doorknob missing, it must make him think that the same thing would happen to him. And without his doorknob Robby was afraid that he had no Mama, no Daddy, and no Friend. Robby would characteristically respond with a satisfied smile and place his hand in the therapist's as they would walk together to a new building which was undergoing completion. Here Robby found a windfall of doors, doorknobs, wooden paneling, molding, and building equipment of all kinds.

During one hour, a door that had not been fixed to its hinges but was leaning against the wall became the center of Robby's frantic compulsive activity of removing its doorknob. As he deftly and swiftly removed it and looked for other knobs to place in his collection, the therapist remarked that Robby seemed very happy when he could have his bright, shiny doorknob. It must make him feel very strong and big so that he would not have to be afraid that he would be left alone. A pleased smile crossed Robby's face as he went on to explore a pile of rubbish for more doorknobs and hinges. As the time approached to return to the therapist's office, Robby went through the struggle of returning the doorknob at the therapist's request. With the therapist's interpretations that he knew how hard it was for Robby to leave the doorknob on the door when Robby thought he needed it to make him feel like Robby and as big as Friend and Daddy, Robby went through an obsessional struggle with the doorknob. He replaced it and then quickly removed it, until the therapist remarked that he knew how hard it was for Robby to leave the doorknob with the door. Robby didn't like to see that the door had a better doorknob than Robby had. And Robby was afraid to return the doorknob when he was always afraid that he would not have his knob and that he would have no one to belong to, while the doorknob belonged to the door. For a moment Robby seemed satisfied as he replaced the doorknob, but as he started to walk away he quickly removed it with one sure turn of his screwdriver and a tug of his hand—and stood still as if transfixed. He looked at the therapist and rapidly repeated the question, "Who took doorknob off? Who put knob in Robby's hand?" The therapist remarked that Robby needed Friend to tell him that Robby took the doorknob and that Robby had put it in Robby's hand. Robby needed Friend to tell him what he did, because Robby did not know Robby, and he did not know what Robby did. But now he could put the knob back and Robby could go back with Friend to the office, to Robby's and Friend's house, where Mama would be waiting for Robby.

When Robby seemed at first unable to return the knob, the therapist suggested that maybe he would be able to help Robby put it back. Robby quickly remonstrated that he would do it, and as he quickly returned the knob he said, "Friend, I fix it."

On the trek back to the office, he followed the familiar path of going down the stairway into the basement of the building, where more doors and knobs were quickly explored and given up after a struggle. The route then led into the alley past the parking garage and up the back stairway of the building. Here Robby, on hearing loud noises, would suddenly close his ears and appear frightened. The therapist would remark to him that the noises frightened Robby whenever he thought that he was bad. He was afraid the noises would jump out and carry him away from Mommy, Daddy, and his home. Sometimes Robby felt like the knobs that he took from the doors, alone and not belonging to Mommy and Daddy, and when he took the knobs he was afraid that Daddy would scold him and make big noises like the noises that he now heard. Apparently satisfied with this interpretation, Robby would remove his hands from his ears and place his arm in front of his eyes as he put one hand in the therapist's hand. Blindly, he would again lead the way up the stairs, but with the assurance that the therapist was shadowing him. In this manner he would reach the therapist's office where he would dash into the office and inquire in a loud questioning voice, "Where Mama?" Upon her arrival he would happily entwine his legs around the door and, with one hand on each knob of the door, would swing back and forth in gleeful excitement. Then, on his mother's request, he would pick up his screw drivers and other paraphernalia and bid goodbye to Friend before rapidly dashing down the hall to the elevator.

In this play sequence, which took place after several months of therapy and repeated itself hour after hour for many weeks, we find a new development in the ritualistic play around the doorknob. First of all, we realize that the patient can cope with the threat of the psychotherapy situation only if he can control it through the ritualistic play. The compulsive control and collection of these doorknobs guarantee his mastery over the object and reduce anxiety. The meaning of the play is, of course, overdetermined inasmuch as his control of the doorknobs guarantees him both accessibility and an avenue of flight. He can get to the object without having to be afraid of it, and can leave it at will. The doors, physical symbols of the object, are deprived of their controlling mechanism and thus can be controlled by the child. His collection of doorknobs, combined as it was with the passionate glee of victory, could be compared to headhunters' trophies, whose collections indicate not only mastery of the enemy but also incorporation of his virtues and his strength. These trophies are not only the sign of victory but a protection against deep-seated anxiety.

As the play continues, Robby struggles with the therapist, but actually attempts to resolve his inner struggle about control. Hour after hour as he incorporates aspects of the psychotherapist who continues to show him the meaning of the play, he gathers strength and can be compared to a head-hunter who feels that everybody is afraid of him when they notice all his trophies of victory. The child therefore can discontinue this attack, and may even be able to discontinue the exhibition of his trophies.

This struggle concerning the incorporation of introjects as it is exhibited in the play with physical objects leads him to the beginning of individuation. As he incorporates the therapist, or rather the therapist's well-meaning and helpful intentions, he can raise the question as to "who did it." In the mind of the child, the loss of body function may be caused by the threatening, castrating, negative introject. This introject creates a paralyzing fear, which, if recognized and given up, may lead to the restoration of function. It is during this period of the hour that Robby, in raising the question, permits the therapist to help the patient see that he (Robby) himself took off the doorknobs from the door. By thus destroying the function of the door, he had tried to undermine the functioning of the therapist, had symbolically destroyed him. Even though he expects retribution, he also finds out that he may safely ask the question since separation and individuation have now become less frightening.

As he understands that he himself is the one who takes the doorknobs off, and as he starts to sense his own will, the first recognition of individuation, he is overwhelmed by fear. As the play, the ritualistic repetition of the hour, proceeds week after week, he finds himself confronted by terrible noises, as frightful as the vengeful chorus of the Erinyes. He interprets the noises, actually the acceptance of the therapist's earlier interpretation as to "who did it," as voices of doom and danger. He tries to deny their existence, shuts his ears, but nevertheless works through on this level his extreme fear of annihilation, of the destruction of his body, and of his individuality. Again, the interpretive and reassuring voice of the therapist, who permits individuation but does so at the child's speed helps the child to take one step further in his development.

It should be pointed out that this part of the therapeutic process is worked out in play action and in a language in which the third person is used instead of the "I" and "thou." It is as if the therapist spontaneously recognizes the psychological need of the child who cannot take full responsibility for what he does, and cannot yet accept full individuation. The expression of the conflict through the use of third-person language is characteristic for interpersonal relationships in which there is no clear-cut separation, in which the way towards identity is still characterized through incomplete recognition of the "I" and "thou." But as the confidence of the child is restored, he accepts some of his newly gained individuality and also accepts the therapist. He expresses trust in the psychotherapist by means of denying his own capacity to find the way back. In closing his eyes as he pulls towards his goal, he holds onto the therapist whose control he thus wants and to whom at the same time he wants to express that he is pulled by blind forces.

In the ending phase of this ritualistic game the child acts out not only the rediscovery of the object, the finding of the mother, but also the restoration of the object now that the anxiety has dwindled. As he holds on to both doorknobs which he has restored to the door, and as he gives passionate expressions of joy at his mother's return, he restores the unity with her on a different basis of mastery which permits him to seek out the object without having to destroy its function. The head-hunter has given up his fear and turns with joy to the source of love.

We believe it ought to be stressed that in this phase of the play activity we find not only the emergence of individuation but also the emergence of language. It may be suggested at this point, and Piaget has given us many instructive examples, that the development of language mirrors the development of the psychic apparatus. Thus we find that originally it was only the compulsive play activity which helped us to understand the conflict and the psychic organization which tries to master it. Now, at this stage of the psychotherapeutic process, the child also has available to him language, primitive and fixated at an early stage of development as it may be. He thus comes nearer to a stage where the acting-out fantasy is replaced in part by verbal fantasy. Waelder's formula [9] of the play as a fantasy woven around physical objects is now applicable since the patient has achieved the first inroad against the destructive force of compulsive and fragmented activity determined by hallucinatory and delusional processes.

Earlier we referred to Freud's discussion of Tausk's paper. The present situation in Robby's case may be taken as further illustration of Freud's comment. The boy, who does something with the doorknob and who, because of his illness, does not know what he has done, turns to the psychotherapist. The therapist, in understanding the play activity, reads the child's mind, as it were, and literally gives the child the thought and, therefore, the language and knowledge of his deed. Terrifying anxiety did not permit Robby to know that he could be an individual or that he was the one who had done it. It would be worthwhile to discuss this material in terms of superego and ego development. The child's question as to "who did it" indicates the emergence of the precursors of superego formation, and of beginning delay mechanisms, but at the same time it refers to the exploration of reality and to the wish to master reality. Robby's wish to know who has done it establishes new ego strength as well as superego function. Elsewhere it has been suggested that the precursors of reality testing can be found in primitive, early superego injunctions. This kind of reality testing, rather than making use of a more advanced ego organization, takes recourse to the early parental "who did it" and its implied injunctions and threats of punishment.

Nick was almost thirteen when he was brought to psychiatric treatment. He had been profoundly disturbed, in the parents' recollection, ever since he was three years old, when his sister's birth apparently precipitated the acute onset of his illness. The parents characterized his difficulty mainly in terms of his retarded intellectual development which they attributed to a birth injury, although this was never medically established. The mother was convinced that Nick was doomed to an incurable illness for which there was no real help but only those futile gestures of medical treatment which parental conscience and duty required her to arrange. Although there had always been an open question regarding the etiology of Nick's disturbance and there were grounds to suspect some organic brain damage, it was clear from an evaluation of Nick's illness that he had been psychotic for many years. Further, there was reason to believe that his intellectual retardation was more in the nature of a pseudo stupidity than a genuine organic type of dementia. At the age of thirteen, Nick displayed a grotesque masochistic compliance in relation to his peers, which manifested itself in bizarre ways. He had long become known to his schoolmates as a clown who would do the most ridiculous things in order to make other boys laugh. Nick never saw humor in these situations, only a desperate need to comply with the tormenting provocations of his peers and to offer himself as a helpless victim of their abuse and ridicule. Nick described these situations with an air of remoteness about them, as if he were talking of the exploits of another boy rather than of himself. Actually, he did speak about a dissociated part of himself. A favorite pastime of his schoolmates was to gather around Nick and to shout various orders to him and to humiliate him. When they would order, "Nick, piss on the wall," Nick would immediately comply by urinating on the wall. When the boys would shout at him, "Shit in your pants," Nick would go through the motions of having a bowel movement and would sometimes be so compliant as to succeed. When the boys would torment him with the command to kiss their shoes, Nick would get down on his hands and knees and obediently kiss the shoes of his tormentors. Nick's parents were confused and mystified by his behavior, since to them his most cardinal problem seemed to be that he never obeyed them. They felt that the most difficult thing about him was his negative attitude towards them against accepting their authority, an attitude manifested most provocatively in his constant clownish attacks on his sister.

Although the parents vaguely recognized that there was much that was immature in his development, they were never really aware of his illness. They complained only of his badness and the irritation that he aroused in them. Nor did they realize to what extent Nick suffered an invisible panic lest he be deserted and abandoned. For Nick literally forced his mother to do his bidding at all times lest he become aware that he no longer controlled her and therefore had no assurance of her continued presence and attachment to him.

During many early therapy hours with Nick, the therapist felt the extent of the unbridged chasm that lay between himself and Nick. Nick would withdraw to a corner and read the therapist's medical books or ply him with a number of questions related to the manufacture of drugs used in psychiatric treatment. Nick wanted to know how sodium pentothal was made and why the therapist did not use it on him. He carried a pharmacy manual with him and repeatedly asked the therapist whether he knew what the drugs were for and why he did not use drugs. He brought numerous books with him that he obviously could not understand and perhaps could not read. He gave the impression at all times that he was interested only in what was useless to him. He seemed to imply in his behavior that he felt that he could expect from the therapist only what was useless, just as all his life he had received only futile gestures of help from the many different types of treatment he had undergone in his pediatric and allergy care. In his unguarded moments he broke out in bizarre clownish behavior in which he attempted to shadowbox with the therapist in such a manner as to convey the deepest anxiety and the most pathetic kind of humor that would inevitably lead to his ridicule and humiliation.

On one occasion the therapist remarked how much Nick would like to be a tough guy but that he was having a terrible time as he was always so afraid of everyone. Nick liked being called a tough guy and said, "That's my name." The therapist told him that it was fine with him that Nick wanted to be a tough guy and maybe he even wanted to be the leader of a gang. Nick thought this was a great thing and when the therapist offered his services to him in the gang, Nick, now christened Tough Guy, referred to the therapist as Red.

Tough Guy and Red formed the nucleus of an invisible gang which had no apparent purpose for its existence. Tough Guy, as the leader of the gang, had no desire to be a criminal. But he needed Red to accompany him on his explorations through the streets of Beverly Hills, first to discover the whereabouts of the residences of famous movie stars and then to trace a familiar route along the streets, apparently in search of nothing. But as Tough Guy and Red pursued their aimless wandering, Tough Guy cautiously confessed to Red that he had heard that Nick was having a lot of trouble. He heard that he must have many disorders. He even heard that Nick had shit in his pants at school. He hated Nick; he thought he was crazy. Red said that he, too, had heard about Nick. He heard that he had many troubles and that he was looking for someone to help him but that he never could find anyone who could understand him. Tough Guy snorted and said that he hated Nick anyway. Red said that he heard that whenever Nick heard that anyone hated him, he got plenty scared because he couldn't stand being hated. He especially got in trouble when Tough Guy hated him. He really wanted Tough Guy to like him. Tough Guy said that he could never like Nick because he was so crazy. He even kissed the boys' shoes when they told him to. Red said that maybe Nick had to do this because he thought that the more he did crazy things, the more he made the other boys laugh at him, the more he thought they liked him. Tough Guy looked at Red, and suddenly the vacant and incomprehensible look on his face faded slightly, and a faint smile of recognition with genuine feeling appeared as he turned to Red and said, "Red, you're a good psychiatrist."

Red turned to Tough Guy and snorted, "Do you mean like that crooked quack, Friedman?" Nick laughed cautiously and asked Red if he knew Friedman. Red said he had heard about him; he had heard that Friedman was one of the biggest crooked quacks in Beverly Hills. Tough Guy turned and said, "Red, do you know what that Friedman does?" Red said he thought Friedman probably did a lot of crazy things too. Tough Guy said he had heard that Friedman sent big bills to Nick for his treatment. Red said he had heard about that too, and then snorted in disgust, "That dirty, crooked quack, Friedman. He's a crooked crook. He pretends to be a doctor and is supposed to cure Nick of his disorders, but all he does is sit in his office and doesn't give Nick any medicine to cure him. He just sends big bills and makes Nick's parents pay out all their money so that there is nothing left for them."

Tough Guy looked at Red with questioning but vacant eyes. His suspiciousness of Red was quite apparent and the look of incredulity remained with him as he seemingly became more embarrassed and anxious. Timidly he said, "Friedman's all right, Red. He's a nice guy." Red again snorted in disgust, "If you want to think he's a nice guy, that's for you to think, Tough Guy. But all I ever hear about Friedman is that he is supposed to treat Nick, but all he does is charge so much money that Nick *thinks that there is nothing left for his family. He just talks to him, doesn't give him any medicine, and doesn't cure him. He just keeps him coming and sometimes he doesn't even see him in his office. No wonder Nick always disappears as soon as he comes to see him. He would probably get more help if he joined our gang than if he came to see that quack, Friedman."*

Tough Guy said, "Yes. Maybe you're right, Red." And then he musingly remarked, "But I don't want Nick in this gang. He does crazy things. He has a lot of disorders. I hate him."

This case material illustrates the case of a psychotic boy with possible organic involvement whose behavior is quite typically schizophrenic. The case illustration is of special interest to us since it refers to the adaptation of a technique which was described in the previous chapter. In the work with Frank, both therapist and patient play but one role, the role of the gang member, "Doc" and "Boss," respectively. In the play sequence in this case, each has two faces, as it were, so that, at times, one has the feeling that four persons are involved. It is not only the child who suffers from a "split personality," but also the doctor, who is perceived by the child as a Dr. Jekyll and a Mr. Hyde with different names.

In becoming "Tough Guy," the patient strives for the ego ideal, and for support from the therapist, actually the "Red" part of the therapist. At the same time he tries desperately to keep out his pathological counterpart, the masochistic child who has no identity of his own and lives on borrowed identity, usually the disgracing "orders" of his contemporaries. This despicable part of himself is matched by the despicable part of the therapist who is experienced as not helpful, as charging too much, and who seems thus to express what the child does not want to have true, but what he might hear the parents say as they express discouragement about the slow treatment, the lack of visible success, and the tremendous expense involved in trying to help their child. The negative version of the therapist is also the projection of the parents' own negative attitude towards the child. This is experienced by the youngster as the hated parent who is to be kept out of the therapy, just as he attempts to keep out of the therapy the hated child-patient. This seems to maintain the collaboration of the positive aspects of patient and psychotherapist, and thus provides a vivid example of schizophrenic ambivalence.

One could look at this situation as one of a divided-identity struggle. The therapeutic situation can be maintained only by the forceful seclusion of the other aspect of the personality. It is as if Dr. Jekyll is not allowed to know about Mr. Hyde but finally comes to the point where he might be able to go through life with the identity of Dr. Jekyll and with the added knowledge of a role belonging to Mr. Hyde who is to be kept out of the treatment situation.

It is interesting that our metaphor actually could be understood in reverse, since what is accepted consciously are the negative aspects, if we were to look at these in terms of contemporary values. The conscious value of the patient is complete obedience and masochistic pleasure. The rejected value, which is rescued in the sanctuary of the psychotherapy situation, is the one of the strong boy, the "Tough Guy." As such, he is then supported by something in the therapist's personality which is experienced by the patient as forbidden, as a secret to be kept from the parents; the positive concept of the therapist, the psychiatrist with the doctor's title, is experienced as unwelcome and unacceptable to the child.

One might well wonder how the psychotic illness of this child must have looked when he was five years old. One may very well wonder whether the child might not have utilized, instead of schizophrenic play acting, the use of physical toy objects as Robby did. We would like to make the point that the prevalent modes of expression will depend upon the patient's stage of development, and that the schizophrenic process will find different expressions at different times of the child's life. It is as if the disease process makes use of different channels in the ego organization as they become available through age-bound maturation which, though distorted, nevertheless follows a chronological sequence.

The convenient assumption, in the case of the adult personality, is that the psychotic process finds similar expression regardless of age. This example permits us to raise the question concerning certain quantitative and qualitative differences in the psychic organization of the psychotic ego. If correctly understood, these would suggest appropriate methods of communication with the sick child rather than force acceptance of mere abstract understanding of the disease process.

"Influencing machines," inventions which control perpetual motion, frequently play a part in the inner life of certain adult schizophrenics. Physical objects which are utilized as toys or as transitional objects by children as they slowly develop the capacity for adult thinking, seem to be the infantile equivalent of these machines. The play of psychotic children indicates a special use of physical objects which are the external crutches, as it were, supporting the delusional and hallucinatory ideation which characterize the inner life of such children. Certain qualities of the psychotic play of children, such as stereotyped repetitiveness, fragmentation, condensation, among others, are striking and outstanding features, the observation of which permits inferences about the nature of the psychic organization of the patient. In our case illustrations, play is used as springboards toward an understanding of the fragile and fragmented ego organization of these children. With such understanding, therapists are better equipped to develop rational treatment techniques for this patient group.

The questions raised, concerning certain elementary processes which characterize the psychotic child's ego, indicate the desirability for formalized research into the nature of the psychotic child's play. Such research would require the study of both the different stages of the illness and also the nature of the ego organization and its changes when certain maturation takes place. Peller has provided us with a similar study of play patterns in normal development.[15] Such research regarding the psychotic child will contribute towards increased flexibility in approach. Reliance on older formulas may be useful for initial contact but fails in different stages of the therapeutic process. Psychotic play, then, constitutes the royal road not only to unconscious mental process and conflict but to an understanding of primitive ego organization and its developmental course in childhood psychosis.

REFERENCES

[1] Tausk, V. On the origin of the "influencing machine" in schizophrenia, Psychoanal. Quart., 2:519, 1933.

[2] Ibid.

[3] Elkisch, P. Significant relationship between the human figure and the machine in the drawings of boys, Amer. J. Orthopsychiat., 22:379, 1952; Mahler, M. S. and Elkisch, P. Some observations on disturbances of the ego in a case of infantile psychosis, Psychoanal. Stud. Child, 8:252, 1953; Rank, B. Adaptation of the psychoanalytic technique for the treatment of young children with atypical development, Amer. J. Orthopsychiat., 19:130, 1949.

[4] Schizophrenia: A Review of the Syndrome, L. Bellak, ed., New York, Logos Press, 1958.

[5] Loomis, E. Play Patterns in the Schizophrenic and Mentally Defective Child, unpublished; Loomis, E., Hilgeman, L. M., and Meyer, L. R. Childhood psychosis: 2. Play patterns as non-verbal indices of ego functions: a preliminary report, Amer. J. Orthopsychiat., 27:691, 1957; Shugart, G. The play history: its application and significance, J. Psychiat. Social Work, 24:204, 1955.

[6] Erikson, E. H. Studies in the interpretation of play disruption in young children. Genet. Psychol. Monogr., 22:557, 1940.

[7] ———— Childhood and Society, New York, W. W. Norton, 1950.

[8] Piaget, J. The Construction of Reality in the Child, New York, Basic Books, 1954.

[9] Waelder, R. The psychoanalytic theory of play, Psychoanal. Quart., 2:208, 1933.

[10] Winnicott, D. W. Transitional objects and transitional phenomena, Int. J. Psychoanal., 2:1, 1953.

[11] Personal communication.

[12] Personal communication.

[13] Zulliger, H. Child psychotherapy without interpretation of unconscious

content: a theoretical exposition of pure play: the use of a child's talisman as a psychotherapeutic agent (translated by R. Ekstein and J. Wallerstein), Bull. Menninger Clin., 17:180, 1953.

[14] Sechehaye, M. Symbolic Realization: A New Method of Psychotherapy Applied to a Case of Schizophrenia, New York, International Universities Press, 1951.

[15] Peller, L. E. Libidinal phases, ego development and play, Psychoanal. Stud. Child, 9:178, 1954.

11

THE ACQUISITION OF SPEECH
IN THE AUTISTIC CHILD

*Dreifach ist die Leistung der menschlichen Sprache, Kundgabe,
Auslösung und Darstellung.*

KARL BÜHLER

In 1934 Karl Bühler published his *Sprachtheorie*.[1] This classic offers a conceptual model for mature language, which stimulated much thinking and experimental work among researchers of different empirical and theoretical backgrounds. Its influence and relevance are still felt.

Bühler describes three functions of mature language: expression, appeal and description. He depicts a simplified model of language in this diagram:

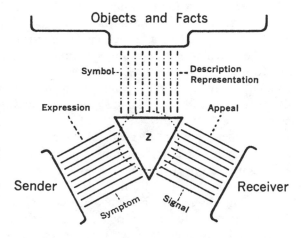

The speaking person, the sender, expresses something about himself, for example, his awareness of inner or outer experience. Were he to do so without any wish to communicate to another person, or perhaps without any capacity for such communication, he would but talk to himself. His self-expression could be considered by observers merely as a symptom of a certain state of mind. If he were intentionally to choose to avoid communication, his behavior could be considered quasi-autistic. He could be diagnosed as autistic in a pathological sense if he were actually unable to avail himself of the communication function of language.

The speaking person does more than just express something about himself, a symptom of his inner state of mind, of an inner direction or intention. He may use language also as the means—as Plato put it—"to say something about things," facts which may be of a physical or psychological nature. He then has acquired the descriptive, the representative, function of language. Thus his words are not only symbols of his inner state, but are also symptoms of outer or inner reality. These symbols may refer to many different levels of symbolism or to an empirical fact, as has been elaborated by Freud [2] in his discussion of the hierarchy of thought within a range which is defined through the "primary- versus secondary-process dichotomy." The unavailability, for example, of the functions of time and time-oriented memory would bring to the foreground a language which would not allow the speaker to differentiate consistently between outer and inner worlds or between present and past experience. Such language would thus indicate in the "sender" a symptom of permanent or temporary loss of reality testing, an impairment which has been associated with psychotic states.

Finally, the sender, if he can avail himself of the full power of speech, can appeal to the "receiver" of the communication. He gives him a signal in order to influence him in some way. Mature language, then, can be examined in terms of the nature of its functions of description, expression, or appeal; it may be understood as symbol, symptom, or signal. Any loss or restriction of function in any of these areas may be taken as a sign of emotional or mental illness based on organic and/or functional deficiency and will challenge the investigator of language to raise questions concerning the particular nature of such loss.

These questions may be posed in terms of the genesis of the loss, as well as of the genesis of available functions. Clinical considerations, at least until very recently, have usually influenced us in searching for the cause of pathology. Studies such as Bühler's strengthen a new and more recent trend in the clinical scientist and encourage us also to ask questions concerning the genesis of available functions. If we wish to repair what has been modified pathologically, or if we wish to restore and encourage growth potentials for functions not as yet available, we will do well to concern ourselves with both available strengths and the genesis of such strengths.

Bühler's model of mature language seems to be in agreement with recent psychoanalytic considerations. In an unpublished lecture, Anna Freud [3] spoke about the normal person as one who is capable of using mature language. She defines mature language in terms of its communication and symbolic function, a definition which is in agreement with Bühler's concept. A child acquires mature language through imitation and identification in a process of socialization, after giving up symbiotic ties and forming object relationships.[4, 5] Mature language is, thus, usually an indicator of the person's capacity to form and maintain object relationships; to utilize reality testing; to replace the pleasure principle with the reality principle and impulse by delay; to deal with a widened area of genuine choice.

Bühler's contribution to language theory and to thinking has also been given recognition in recent psychoanalytic literature, such as in Rapaport's "Organization and Pathology of Thought," [6] in Spitz's "No and Yes" [7] as well as in his "Genèse des premières relations objectales;" [8] and in Loewenstein's "Some Remarks on the Role of Speech in Psychoanalytic Technique." [9] Reference will be made to these authors in developing my thesis on how the autistic child acquires part functions of speech.

The diagnostic category of early infantile autism was introduced by Kanner in the early forties. Kanner and Eisenberg [10] restate their position on speech development in the autistic child as follows:

A second distinctive feature was noted as the failure to use language for the purpose of communication. In three of the eleven cases, speech failed to develop altogether. The remaining eight developed a precocity of articulation which, coupled with unusual facility in rote memory, resulted in the ability to repeat endless numbers of rhymes, catechisms, lists of names, and other semantically useless exercises. The parroting of words intellectually incomprehensible to the child brought into sharp relief the gross failure to use speech to convey meaning or feeling to others. The repetition of stored phrases while failing to recombine words into original and personalized sentences, gave rise to the phenomena of delayed echolalia, pre-nominal reversal, literalness, and affirmation by repetition.

In Travis' Handbook of Speech Pathology, Wolpe [5] expresses current, dynamic, clinical thinking on speech difficulties, as does Gertrude Wyatt on stuttering:

Since the primary function of speech is social communication which in itself implies an interdependence in interpersonal relationships, and which reaches its highest functional value when a oneness in understanding is *attained, disturbances in speech, would occur primarily when the inter-dependent relationship is off balance. Instead of the anticipated under-standing resultant from the acquisition of speech there is heightened anxiety and frustration, for the individual finds a widened rather than a narrowed gap in the area of communication. This is actually what frequently occurs. When the infant is in the babbling stage, the parent is able to coo with him and delight in his dependency. But as the infant moves on to a higher stage in his maturational process, the parent is less and less accepting of his behavior, more and more critical of it, and determined to train the child by imposing demands upon him. The acquisition of speech, equated as it is with maturation, now becomes a symbol of the danger of further maturation, and the child holds tenaciously to infantile speech patterns as symbolic of the period when demands were minimal and when understanding was heightened. Functional disturbances in speech, therefore, would indicate an interference in the normal speech process because of difficulties encountered in the dynamic interaction between the ego and its surrounding forces. Speech, per se, divorced from social interaction would be static and mechanistic and would cease to have any communicative function. Speech is part of the very acculturation of the child and carries with it, therefore, the emotional impacts that any dynamic interaction involves.[11]*

This general statement does not differentiate among a variety of different pathological forms of speech, nor is it designed for differential diagnosis which might permit us to use the speech difficulty in order to determine the specific syndrome characteristic for the child patient. But it is a beginning in the right direction which has been followed up by more recent work of other contributors to this problem area.

Spitz,[7] for example, refers to Karl Bühler's formulation on the organization of behavior as a most concise and convincing one. Bühler[1] states that behavior is progressively segregated out of the random disorganized movements of the newborn through the conservation of success—specific movements on the one hand, and the simultaneous elimination of unsuccessful movements on the other. The goal—specific movement—will then be organized into a goal-directed pattern.

Spitz attempts to tackle the problem of speech in investigating preverbal communications.[7] He discusses communication in the mother-child duality and defines these communications as: "Every directed or non-directed action of one or more persons, which influences the perception, the feeling, the sensation, the thinking or action of another person in an intentional or unintentional manner."[8] Spitz has investigated preverbal communication, that is, phenomena occurring a long time before the use of words or of language proper is acquired.[8] He suggests that:

It will serve to clarify our concepts if we try to enumerate the successive steps in the process of acquiring verbal communication. The first of these steps is the direct discharge of tension in the neonate. This is the step which I have discussed in the article "The Primal Cavity." In the next step of the infant's development a secondary function of this discharge process is acquired; the infant, having developed the functions of perception and memory, links his own discharge, screaming, with the tension relief offered by the environment. In the terms of Karl Bühler's language theory, in which he distinguished within the total phenomenon of language three functions, namely expression, appeal and description, the first step just described is expression, while the second step is appeal. Bühler intentionally limited his approach to the descriptive function of language.[7]

Spitz suggests that words which designate concrete things and persons are acquired by the child at the end of the first year in the form of "global words," such as "ma-ma." Greenson [12] has made the same point in his paper "About the Sound 'MM'," which designates the contentment of the nursing child as well as the echo in the mother's identification with the child's pleasure. The first global word is used by the child to communicate his needs to the libidinal object, that is to the mother, who is also his executive. It signifies, indiscriminately, hunger, boredom, discomfort, etc., and the wish to be relieved of them, just as it signifies biscuit, toy, mother, and the desire for these. Other such global words are acquired in the following weeks by the child, and a certain measure of specialization of single words is achieved. These first verbal symbols signifying needs manifestly are, to use Karl Bühler's classification, still in the nature of an appeal and not of a description.

Spitz suggests that "a new level of integration is achieved after eighteen months of life. The verbal symbols which are now acquired are used not only for the purpose of appeal, but also for the purpose of description, and specific individual syntax is elaborated." [7] Spitz suggests that this development permits the child to fulfill the function of abstraction. Or, as Kubie [13] has expressed it, "The child has acquired the symbolic function."

When I was investigating the nature of the interpretive process, a model of interpretation was suggested which may permit us to study rudimentary aspects of interpretation and communication. Rapaport's primary model of thought [6] was utilized in order to develop a psychoanalytic theory of thought. My suggestion was that the tension-need system of the hungry infant who "communicates" his needs to the mother through crying or restlessness utilizes the appeal function of language. Actually, at first the infant uses only the expressive function, the unintentional signal type of language. It is, however, understood by the mother as an appeal and stimulates her to offer him nourishment and thus to "interpret" the situation. If the baby "communicates" successfully, and is correctly "interpreted" by the mother, a state of affairs exists which presupposes communication between infant and mother—a healthy symbiotic arrangement. In this way a steppingstone is created which will permit the child to move from the first function of language, the expressive one, to the acquisition of the appeal function. Such language, even though it makes use of words and sentences, is not as yet under dominance of the symbolic function and does not allow for delay. It is really an exchange of unintentional baby signals and intentional maternal acts, and is under the dominance of the pleasure principle. This primitive "language" should really be considered a forerunner of language. It serves to restore homeostasis and is based on the successful achievement of communion which, with incorporation, is directly associated with the togetherness in the root of the word "communication."

A remarkable process, the preverbal features of which have been excellently described by Spitz [7] and the logical features of which have been studied by Piaget,[14, 15] is observable in the development of language out of impulses, to early imagery, to noun language, to language which consists primarily of the expression of needs (or the expression of restrictions), to fantasy, to secondary-process thinking and to reality testing. Isakower [16] has referred to the spoken word in dreams as the expression of the conscience. This idea is expressed in popular usage by "the voice of conscience." Clinically it can be seen in auditory hallucinations of schizophrenics whose restitutional efforts have regressed to this early development of communication with others and within themselves. The nature of interpretation has been examined within different therapeutic contexts and in reference to patients who have not achieved full capacity for object relationships or symbolic communication. They have given up, in part, the function of descriptive language, which allows for delay and which reflects thinking as trial action. Indication was made of some of the problems which confront us as we communicate with people who are not capable of contact through communication but only through communion in the more primitive sense. Such people fuse the act and the word so that, for them, interpretations become primarily signals which trigger off action rather than stimulate reflection.

Reference was made, as in Loewenstein's work,[9] to communication devices which are nonverbal and which occur on a different level of consciousness. The sicker or the younger the patient, the more we must rely on means of communication and on interpretation which must consider preverbal aspects of language as well as the spoken precursors of mature speech.

The speech problems of the autistic child might lend themselves to a variety of considerations concerning the early functions of language and their acquisition which might prove clinically useful. Bühler's language model can serve as a yardstick against which to measure the task that the autistic child has accomplished; the functions that he has not acquired; the problems that he and the therapist face. They are trying to bring about communion and to form a relationship, initially dominated by utilization of a need-gratifying object and progressively developing to mature communication, which is dominated by the interpretive process. The foundation of this process is the acquisition of mature speech and of mature object relationships. It has frequently been said that the schizophrenic needs contact, communion, and communication. No doubt, communication, the use of speech, is the basis for the lasting therapeutic effects, but as Loewenstein stated,[9] "People do not change just because they communicate with each other. What counts in analysis is not communication by itself but *what is being communicated*, on the part of both patient and analyst, what leads to communication, and what psychic processes and changes occur as a result of this communication as such and of its contents." Differentiation has been made between precursors of interpretation and interpretation proper, both of which, however, seem to be equally necessary parts of the total interpretive process.

The analytic understanding of the autistic child, a comparatively new interest, as reflected in the literature of the last few years,[17] must begin with a consideration of the symptom of autism in reference to available speech development. Kanner believes that one distinctive feature of autism is "the failure to use language for the purpose of communication."[10] The autistic child is described by him as suffering from extreme withdrawal, representing the turning away from intolerable, frustrating, and ungiving relationships with parents who could not meet the child's emotional needs, and lead the child to seek comfort in solitude. The child's relationships are described as mechanistic, and its use of others as if they were tools or machines. The autistic child is not capable of genuine human relationships, and his repetitive, mechanical speech is imitative in nature and dominated by echolalia.

Mahler [18] has offered many valuable discussions on the autistic child in dynamic rather than in mere descriptive forms. She sees in autism a special symptom of the disease process, a position which is to defend the child against the symbiotic position, the danger of being devoured by the mother in a pathological relationship. She speaks of autism as the negativism of the symbiotic child. Bleuler [19] discusses symptoms of touching, echopraxia, and echolalia and considers them as "phenomena of restitution." This conception suggests that in tactually ascertaining the presence of the object and thus "introjecting" it (identifying with it) through imitation, the patient attempts to regain the world of objects from which he has withdrawn. Echolalia may serve a similar purpose, and the schizophrenic manner of dealing with words could be considered, as Freud [20] has also stated, an attempt at restitution of the lost world of objects.

The adult schizophrenic, in spite of regressive phenomena, retains many functions of adult speech which make it difficult, perhaps, to answer questions concerning the early problems in infantile autism, which are our present concern. Autistic thinking, or as Bleuler has called it, dereistic thinking, is a part of normal development. Spitz [7] speaks about these facts as follows:

For the child, the feces form a part of his own person. Toilet training is resented as an attempt to deprive him of the liberty of using his self, his body, the sphincters. He will defend these liberties stubbornly. This explanation does not exhaust the various aspects of the anal phase. It purports only to show the role of growing self-awareness in the manifestations of stubbornness during the anal phase.

One of these manifestations is the child's repetitive use of the "No" while doing what the adult wishes him to do. It seems to us that this "No" is a manifesto of independence. It is the same statement, "I have a will of my own and even when it is the same as yours, it is different because it is my own! I am doing this because I want it and I am not doing what you want!"

In this example the autistic (dereistic) thinking of the child is very much in evidence. It clearly shows the inappropriate affect, the cleavage between the affect and that which occasions it. In consequence of this cleavage, the message conveyed by the child contradicts the action he performs. This example shows a behavior which is completely normal for the child in his second year. However, this normal action of the child also throws light on the processes of dereistic thinking and inappropriate affect in schizophrenia.

The child suffering from infantile autism is characterized by lack of speech, dereistic thinking, and the availability of only archaic forerunners of object relationships which have an autistic or symbiotic taint. Speech development is primarily expressive; dominated by signal and emergency functions of language; has usually mere nonintentional appeal function and only occasionally intentional appeal function. Speech development is also frequently characterized by motor equivalents of early means of communication, the purpose of which is usually the restoration or the absolute avoidance of communion. Other characteristics of speech development include echolalia and echopraxia, the imitative aspects of which can be considered a forerunner of identificatory processes and an unsuccessful attempt at incorporation.

Everyone who treats such children must be prepared for frustrations of a very strange kind. The therapist soon finds that he is attempting to relate to a child who desperately attempts to use the adult but cannot establish an object relationship; who constantly searches for contact but must destroy it; who hopelessly and unhappily attempts to acquire the means of communication but achieves only a senseless echo. The child reacts to the awareness of being understood with violent, frequently rejecting, motor acts. Words which exist to express thoughts are received by the child as a signal which triggers off unexpected action. The psychotherapist must deal with children who may not speak for many months, even though they indicate here or there that some of what is communicated to them is understood in primitive ways. The child's utter rejection of him whom he most needs creates a bewildering puzzle for the therapist who can only understand such terror-stricken reactions as something that must have been caused by rejecting, condemning, and violent parents. The therapist's anger at the parents can be understood—to paraphase E. Kris— *as regression in the service of the therapist's ego*, thereby permitting the maintenance of identification with the child. If the therapeutic ego loses control, genuine regressions create "hate in the countertransference." [21] Frequently, one's own anger in the countertransference can be tolerated only as it is projected onto the parent or to a colleague in the institutional setting.

The expressions of the autistic child, scarce as they may be, seem to urge us to understand them as an appeal to us. We try to meet the appeal by offering ourselves as the need-gratifying objects. And then—we are rejected. We are experienced by the child as a danger to the precarious precursor of identity which the autistic position offers him.

Much of the foregoing can be seen in an autistic three-and-a-half-year-old girl, Nanny, during her psychotherapy on an outpatient basis.*

Nanny, whose twin sister is a comparatively healthy youngster, and whose parents have brought up two older children quite successfully, showed all the characteristics of autistic behavior. Her first weeks in therapy consisted of aimless searching and a wild manipulation of the therapist whom she would pull along with her in her chaotic investigation of the clinic's surroundings but whose words she seemingly did not hear. The child's speech behavior was characterized by the dominant use of echolalia. Occasionally, the therapist understood some of the child's echolalia-like communications. When following Nanny through the corridors

* For this striking clinical example I am grateful to Mrs. Leda W. Rosow.

of the clinic, the therapist could hear her say repeatedly: "Here, Nanny, go." It was as if she were describing her own activities in the third person.

Actually she was repeating the therapist's description of her activities. In an attempt to maintain some kind of communication with Nanny, the therapist had decided to describe in simple words what was happening, what Nanny was doing. The echolalia was of such a kind that it suggested the interpretation that it was the child's attempt to repeat what the therapist had said; that is, to describe her own actions, and thus to incorporate descriptive statements as well as occasional commands. The seemingly meaningless echolalia of the first few weeks changed. It turned into a practice in which it seemed clear that the child imitated, without apparent awareness, the voice of the therapist or, as it were, the voice of a commanding conscience to which Nanny now listened. The child's aimless act, through the "description" of the therapist, had now become a task, and the description of the therapist had become a command within the matrix of the autistic-symbiotic struggle.

A few weeks after the development had been noted and was continuing, the mother reported that as they were driving home, Nanny verbalized repeated short sentences. These were actually verbatim statements of the therapist's communications to her, which she was mechanically repeating. It became clear that the therapist had gained some foothold in the child's primitive inner life. Echolalia, rather than an empty and mechanistic repetition of words, a parrot-like imitation, seemed to be, in this case, an attempt to introject the therapist, to incorporate her voice, and to become her. Rather than hearing the "voice of conscience," Nanny repeated the voice of the therapist and thus tried to use the therapist's communication as a quasi-organizer of her own inner life. One could look at this as an attempt to restore the introject which was lost and which could be maintained only if a quasi-auditory hallucination was maintained. Echolalia then could be considered as the motor and verbal substitute for the auditory hallucination. It is as if Nanny now could weave her fantasies of having the therapist with her around the spoken word. The spoken word is comparable to the toy, the external object around which a fantasy or delusion may be woven. Echolalia then could be considered a forerunner of more advanced psychotic play.

It is interesting that the clinicians have used the term "echolalia" in order to stress the mechanistic, blindly imitative, hardly human characteristics of autistic speech. On the surface, popular usage holds the same view. A German proverb says: "Wie man in den Wald hinein ruft, so kommt es heraus." The phenomenon of sound being thrown back by the woods as one calls into the woods, is actually used as the simile which suggests that "communication may be any directed or non-directed action of one or more people, who thus influence perception, feeling, sensation, thinking or action in one or more other people in an intentional or unintentional manner." [7] Even the autistic child, incapable as she is of communication on a higher level, responds, and the response itself depends on the nature of what is expressed by the therapist. The autistic child, then, has neither completely lost nor, as yet, completely achieved the capacity for understanding, for mature communication. She works with primitive speech elements and many archaic forerunners of the organum of the language, which indicate strongly that she can be reached, albeit in a primitive way only. The functions of expression and appeal, even though they are not fully developed, dominate the communication scene. The appeal value of the therapist's voice has not yet become a permanent introject. It must be constantly restored through echolalia, a form of self-appeal, a forerunner of internal language and thought, of silent inner speech.

Nanny gave the impression that she was trying in vain to incorporate the love object. The endless repetitions of the therapist's simple orders, suggestions, or descriptions were not fully "swallowed," but were only endlessly repeated.

One of the child's motor activities, a precursor of play, was her interminable occupation with the water fountain. This seemed to refer to Nanny's attempt to restore the mother object. Whenever the mother was out of sight, the child would endlessly play with water and continually drink large amounts of it, as if to restore a situation of nurture. The use of echolalia, also serving the restoration of the object, or at least serving the primitive maintenance of some form of primitive object relationship, characterized this particular phase of treatment.

The echolalia activity of the autistic child could be considered the child's attempt to make herself independent of the love object by introjecting, or repeating its appeal function.

Echolalia, a primitive form of imitation, a failure in the achievement of permanent introjections and identifications, is an attempt to acquire the capacity for object relationships and the capacity of speech by the installment plan, as it were. I am reminded of the Viennese dialect expression which refers to paying in installments as "abstottern," to stutter it off.

Brenner [22] discusses the importance of identification for the child's acquisition of language and suggests that:

Simple observation will show us that the child's acquisition of motor speech depends in considerable measure on the psychological tendencies to imitate an object in the environment or, in other words, to identify with it. It is perfectly true that a child cannot learn to speak until his central nervous system has matured sufficiently and that the acquisition of language as a whole is far from being simply a process of imitation. Nevertheless it is true that children ordinarily speak in imitation, at least at first. That is to say they repeat sounds that adults say for them, and learn to say them in imitation of an adult, very often as part of a game. Moreover, it is most instructive to observe that every child talks with the same "accent" as do the adults and other children of his environment. Intonation, pitch, pronunciation, and idioms are all copied exactly if the child's hearing is normal. So exactly, indeed that it makes one wonder whether what we ordinarily call "tone-deafness," that is the inability to detect relative differences in pitch, can really be congenital. However that may be, we can have no doubt that identification plays a very great role in the acquisition of this particular ego-function that we have called motor speech.

We may speak of the autistic child's lack of communication only if we think in terms of mature language. If the communication function of language is primarily thought of in terms of description, of symbolic expression, then indeed we will find the young autistic child severely handicapped and we may think of our patient as being unable to "communicate." If, however, we consider other functions of speech, such as expression, appeal, contacting, signaling, imitation, and restoration of part objects, we will be inclined to give up the designation of "autistic" as a diagnosis and to see in it rather a special phase of psychotic illness. Even an older child patient, who regresses to an autistic position, does not completely withdraw, but rather withdraws from or gives up symbolic communication.

The attempt of the patient to restore communion whenever necessary may constitute a regression or a fixation at a level of development characterized by the shifting positions between positive nurture within a symbiotic communion and the autism of sleep after satisfaction has been achieved. The dream could be considered as the normal hallucination of the healthy, containing among other functions a normal form of echolalia. Echolalia or echopraxia in the waking stage, however, represents a pathological form, and could be looked upon as a quasi-dream. This way of looking at echolalia and echopraxia is a useful device as long as it does not mislead us to overstep the boundaries of this analogy. The therapist who succeeds in becoming a part of the system of echolalia and of delayed echolalia, as was true in the case of Nanny, has created a transference-like condition, analogous to the one of the patient who dreams of the analyst. Nanny's therapist thus stepped into the child's dream and became a part of a new, common, comparatively undifferentiated matrix. Out of this, a new form of echolalia might grow, which could lead to symbolic speech, an acquisition characteristic of the descriptive function of language.

Bak [23] suggests that the internal image "appears in almost clean culture in automatic obedience, in the echolalias and echopraxias" and "is a part of [the schizophrenic's] symptomatology and comes under the heading of ego restitution." He wonders as to how the "furthering of the same mechanisms" is to "lead to appropriate behavior and clinical improvement." He expresses "doubts that the mechanisms of object-finding and identification would account for it." And he wonders as to what else there is, to account for the higher integration of the ego. It seems to me that Wexler's [24] experience with adult patients and my own with very young child and adolescent patients do not suggest that the internalization of the therapist's image is the cause for change but rather allows for the creation of the transference track upon which the psychotherapeutic process may proceed. We are simply speaking of a modified technique to allow for the establishment and maintenance of the therapeutic situation rather than trying to account for all agents of change.

Nanny's small language vocabulary is further restricted by a group of implied rules for usage. These rules must be discovered by us as we study the natural habitat of this child's language, thereby enabling ourselves to reconstruct this very habitat; that is, the state of her psychic functioning, the degree, quantitatively as well as qualitatively, of the "disturbance in the reciprocal identification between mother and child." [11] We can thus reconstruct the available capacity for the maintenance or formation of object relationships in whatever precursor form they may appear. We may also be able to reconstruct existing conflict and crises in the psychosexual and psychoaggressive development as they occur within the matrix of impoverished ego maturation and development.

Echolalia is a phenomenon under constant change as the inner dynamics of the child and the vicissitudes of the therapeutic relationship change. At the end of one session and at a time when the child was screamingly unruly and chaotic, the therapist spoke to Nanny about the necessity to stop. The violent and archaic movements of the child gave the impression that she did not hear or understand her therapist. After the therapist's repeated comments concerning ending and leaving, Nanny suddenly and unexpectedly stopped screaming and kicking and said quietly, "Nanny, say bye-bye!" These words were not directed to the therapist. They were said in seeming self-absorption—as if Nanny had carried on a dialogue with herself—and they clearly represented the mother's repeated demands. In regard to the mother, they constituted an expression of delayed echolalia; in regard to the therapist, an indirect response, which indicated that the patient had understood her. It is as if Nanny suddenly recalled her mother's order, which, rather than executing, she now repeated in parrot-like, echolalia-bound fashion.

Echolalia here served not only the function of restitution, the restoration of the mother's voice, but was also in the service of the recognizing ego. We deal here with an example of "regression in the service of the ego," albeit a psychotic ego (a formulation suggested by Ernst Kris). As Nanny regresses to echolalia, the delayed imitation of her mother's voice, we note that this *selected regression*, as it were, now permits her to understand and to deal with a new situation by making it into an old and familiar one. Every mental act of recognition, of insight, is an act of reducing the new to the old and the familiar. Otherwise, such a neutral act must be experienced chaotically with mechanical and blind reliance on the auxiliary ego of the mother. But the mother's organizing capacity cannot become part of the child's mentality except as the child desperately tries to identify with the mother through the primitive echolalia response.

At a later point of the treatment process, Nanny pulled the therapist back and forth through different parts of the clinic, implying an aimless searching for objects which she has in mind but seems able neither to name, nor to know in a conscious sense. The therapist said to the child as they arrived at the door which led to the street: "It is raining," Nanny followed with, "It's wet." There is the possibility that the child did not respond to the therapist but made an independent statement which by chance corresponded to the therapist's comment. Barring this, her short sentence provides a beautiful and simple example of how she moved from the use of stereotyped and delayed echolalia limited to the service of restitution and imitation of objects. The echolalia of her response was in the service of the recognizing ego and demonstrated the capacity of rephrasing somebody else's statement. While seemingly a repetition and, as such, still related to echolalia, it was clearly an indication that words were being grasped as symbols rather than as mere signs or signals, that a beginning had been made in the acquisition of the representative, the descriptive function of language.

At the end of one session, approximately six months later, the child's mother came to the therapist to say: "I have something encouraging to tell you. Until now Nanny never showed any signs that she had learned anything from you. But now I know that she has learned something, because she says two things that you always say. She says, 'No, no, no, you mustn't do that,' and that's what she always hears you say, because I never say anything like that. She also says to herself—again your way of putting it—as she does something, 'That's the way!' "

We might look at the mother's observation as a confirmation of our earlier interpretation of delayed echolalia, and, even more, we may see in it an example of a clearer and more highly developed use of the therapist. We may think of Nanny's walking through her world in the way that we think of an airplane landing, guided by radar rather than by the pilot's direct observations. Nanny's "radar" consists of the therapist's commands and assurances. As she echoes the therapist, her own voice, "No, no, you mustn't do that," guides one aspect of her activity. She thus establishes the forerunner of a superego. Approved activities of Nanny's are accompanied by the delayed echolalia response, "That's the way!" and serve as forerunner of ego-ideal functions. She travels on these two beams supplied by the therapist and thus lands safely. Blind flying may not always be the safest way but it is the only way when one is surrounded by dense and impenetrable fog. The therapist's injunctions and approvals, when genuinely internalized, turn echolalia responses into stable ego functions, thus replacing blind flying with genuine reality testing.

This schematized and oversimplified use of clinical data does not do justice to the fantastic difficulties one encounters when working with such children. Nevertheless, even schematic, oversimplified thinking may permit conjectures which might lead to technical suggestions for the treatment of such patients. Their chaotic behavior, their nonconventional responses, and their lack of capacity to communicate on levels on which we are able to respond put us in the situation of a person lost in the primeval forest and searching desperately for the way out. Such a person might be overwhelmed by millions of impressions, but might not find a sign from which to glean a cue as to the direction which will lead him into known, explored, and cultivated territory. Not even a ray of sunlight comes through in sufficient strength since the thick ceiling of the foliage screens the forest floor. The therapist of such children will find frequently that there seems to be no familiar sign on which to attach a tactical maneuver or from which to derive a strategic plan built on a possible rationale. The therapist might find that Bühler's formulation on the organization of behavior, according to which behavior is progressively segregated out of random disorganized movements and directed toward goal-specific movements and goal-directed patterns, does not seem to hold for both therapist and patient. It is as if the therapist repeats the experience of the mother who desperately but vainly attempts to arrive at a relationship with her child which is based on reciprocal identification.

But as the therapist follows the most *dominant speech event*, the echolalia phenomenon, he finds himself in a situation comparable to that of the explorer who suddenly discovers an open spot in the forest, accessible to sunlight and allowing him to synchronize the time on his watch with the shadow patterns and thus to find his bearings. Echolalia thus becomes meaningful and opens for him an access to primitive communion-communication. It is as if he, rather than the child, has to give up random-disorganized movements, and has to strengthen success-specific movements in the achievement of contact with the patient. Rather than expecting that the child can identify with him, he imitates the child, follows its actions, and puts them into words and imitative acts. The child's echolalia is met by the therapist's advanced echolalia, a translation of the child's acts into the therapist's symbols. He thus reaches the child in terms of living himself into the world of the child. The child's autism grows into a symbiosis which is based not on commands or on expectations, but on understanding by the therapist. By the therapist's saying what the child does, he echoes the patient and becomes the partner in the child's search for contact; he offers strength which will allow the patient to replace the unsuccessful imitation with his capacities. Thus, the child may acquire capacity for identification and symbolic language through the therapist's willingness to become, temporarily, like the child. The demand on the child to identify with the more mature person results in echolalia, a symptom through which the child tries to imitate, and indicates that the child is unable to complete the act of imitation. This is a symptom which is replaced with the less threatening gift of the therapist; that is, his effort to become the patient's extension. Instead of persistently demanding that the child identify with the world of the adult, the therapist persistently intrudes into the inner world of the child. He does this by means of imitation of acts and with descriptive words, through quasi-echopraxia and echolalia, as it were. Since the therapist expresses no more than the child's appeal, the child learns to understand itself against the matrix of a child-dominated symbiosis. The child may thus be able to give up the autistic position it assumed as a defense against negative symbiosis. Since this poses an impossible task and forces the child into failure, trying to meet the task and failure are combined in echolalia.

These few remarks neither explain sufficiently the success of such therapeutic maneuvers nor do they throw much light on the etiology of this illness. But they do seem to allow us to enter an unknown area which, once within it, we may open to more consistent and formal research. These recesses of the mind, preverbal in origin, must be understood if we wish to understand more fully the dynamics of language development and its meaning in terms of first relationships. It is not arbitrariness that popular conception speaks of "Muttersprache," "mother tongue," when it refers to one's native language. Greenson [25] pointed this out when he contended "that the early mechanisms of auditory incorporation and identification necessary for learning to speak and learning a new language are decisively influenced by the outcome of the conflicts between mother, breast, and child." Schwing's therapeutic "motherliness," [26] a suggestion for the opening phase of psychotherapy with adult schizophrenics, also has its place, in modified form, in our therapeutic work with such children. It gives them a new mother tongue through which expression turns into successful appeal and, thus, allows for description, completing hereby the development of language, characteristic for *homo sapiens*. This triple accomplishment of mature language was stated by Karl Bühler in 1918: "*Thrice is the function of human language, expression, appeal, and representation.*" [1]

REFERENCES

[1] Bühler, K. Sprachtheorie, Jena, Verlag von Gustav Fischer, 1934.

[2] Freud, S. Formulation regarding the two principles of mental functioning, Collected Papers, London, Hogarth Press, 1949, 13.

[3] Freud, A. The Concept of Normality, Medical Faculty Lecture, University of California at Los Angeles, April 2, 1959 (unpublished).

[4] Fenichel, O. On the Psychoanalytic Theory of Neurosis, New York, W. W. Norton, 1945.

[5] Wolpe, Z. S. Play therapy, psychodrama, and parent counseling, *in* Handbook of Speech Pathology, L. E. Travis, ed., New York, Appleton-Century-Crofts, 1957, p. 991.

[6] Rapaport, D. Organization and Pathology of Thought, New York, Columbia University Press, 1951.

[7] Spitz, R. No and Yes—on the Genesis of Human Communication, New York, International Universities Press, 1957.

[8] ————. Genèse des premierès relations objectales, Rev. Franc. Psychoanal., 18:479, 1954.

[9] Loewenstein, R. M. Some remarks on the role of speech in psychoanalytic technique, Int. J. Psychoanal., 37:460, 1956.

[10] Kanner, L., and Eisenberg, L. Early infantile autism, 1943–1955, Amer. Psychiat. Ass. Research Reports, April 1957.

[11] Wyatt, G. Mother-Child Relationship in Stuttering Children, unpublished.

[12] Greenson, R. R. About the sound "Mm," Psychoanal. Quart., 33:234, 1954.

[13] Kubie, L. S. The distortion of the symbolic process in neurosis and psychosis, J. Amer. Psychoanal. Ass. 1:59, 1953.

[14] Piaget, J. Play, Dreams and Imitation in Childhood, New York, W. W. Norton, 1951.

[15] ————. The Origins of Intelligence in Children, New York, International Universities Press, 1952.

[16] Isakower, O. Spoken words in dreams, Psychoanal. Quart. 23:1, 1954.

[17] Ekstein, R., Bryant, K., and Friedman, S. W. Schizophrenia: A Review of the Syndrome, *in* Childhood schizophrenia and allied conditions, L. Bellak, ed., New York, Logos Press, 1958.

[18] Mahler, M. On childhood psychosis and schizophrenic, autistic and symbiotic infantile psychoses, Psychoanal. Stud. Child, 7:286, 1952.

[19] Bleuler, E. Dementia Praecox oder Gruppe der Schizophrenien, Leipzig, Deuticke, 1911.

[20] Freud, S. The Unconscious, Collected Papers, London, Hogarth Press, 1925.

[21] Winnicott, D. W. Hate in the countertransference, Int. J. Psychoanal., 30:69, 1949.

[22] Brenner, C. An Elementary Textbook of Psychoanalysis, New York, International Universities Press, 1955.

[23] Bak, R. Discussion of Dr. Wexler's paper, in Psychotherapy with Schizophrenics, E. B. Brody and F. C. Redlich, eds., New York, International Universities Press, 1952, 201.

[24] Wexler, M. The structural problem in schizophrenia, in Psychotherapy with Schizophrenics, E. B. Brody and F. C. Redlich, New York, International Universities Press, 1952, 179.

[25] Greenson, R. R. The mother tongue and the mother, Int. J. Psychoanal., 31:1, 1950.

[26] Schwing, G. A Way to the Soul of the Mentally Ill, New York, International Universities Press, 1954.

12

PUPPET PLAY OF A PSYCHOTIC ADOLESCENT GIRL

After a long, long look, Pinocchio said to himself with great content: "How ridiculous I was as the marionette! And how happy I am now that I have become a real boy!"

C. COLLODI

Play has been considered the royal road to the unconscious conflict of the child. While one may suggest that the neurotic child in his play—as Waelder [1] phrases it—weaves fantasies around external objects, Friedman and Ekstein (Chapter 10) characterize the play of psychotic children as weaving hallucinatory and delusional fantasies around external objects. They stress the child patient's unstable capacity to differentiate objects which serve as play material from internal objects. The psychotic child's play represents the ceaseless struggle between the forces of individuation and identity formation, on the one hand, and those which aim toward symbiotic union or symbiotic conflict on the other, a struggle which has been elucidated by Mahler and her coworkers.[2]

In Chapter 9 it was suggested that the play of children, neurotic, borderline, or psychotic, can be understood in terms of different maturational stages of play activity, along a developmental axis of thinking, the end points of which are impulse release and secondary-process reality-oriented thinking. We referred to Freud's [3] famous dictum according to which thinking is trial action, and suggested that acting out be considered a form of trial thinking, a form of experimental recollection. We related the different forms of play to action and to acting out, to a form of unconscious trial thinking. The attempts to resolve unconscious conflicts can be ordered along the above-mentioned axis, which leads from impulse release, a kind of thoughtless act, to secondary-process reality-oriented thinking, an actless thought.

In the clinical presentation which follows, these ideas have been applied to elucidate more fully the meaning of the puppet play of a psychotic adolescent girl. The use of puppet play is, of course, not new in work with children, has been mentioned frequently in the literature, and has received special consideration in Rambert's *Children in Conflict*.[4] Piaget, who introduces her work, suggests that

> *It is many years since such specialists in child psychoanalysis as Anna Freud, Melanie Klein, Susan Isaacs, and others have employed techniques founded upon spontaneous games of children in the same way as the analysis of dreams is employed in the case of adults. . . . But Mlle. Rambert has to offer an original innovation, a technique of her own in the form of puppet games of such a kind that the standardization of the material and the motif-types which it elicits permit the comparison of one case to the next and yet allow each patient to unfold his own personality.*

Rambert utilizes the insights of analysis as well as the insights of Piaget into the development of thinking. She offers fascinating clinical examples which show the differing uses that children of different ages make of puppets. The puppets taken up by the child usually represent forbidden wishes and activities which the child cannot readily accept as his own and which he has displaced onto the puppets. In using the puppets the child guardedly conveys to the analyst not only the nature of his wishes but also that he is only playing with the forbidden thought; he may not yet be fully aware of it or he may feel that it is permissible to play-act the thought rather than to act and live it out in reality, to fantasy about and verbalize it. Erikson[5] has shown that if play brings the conflict too close to consciousness, or if play is in danger of becoming a realistic act, we will frequently find a "play disruption" in the therapeutic situation. This is true, of course, for puppet play as well, since it only temporarily is suitable as an appropriate distance device.[6]

The puppet play to be described differs from Rambert's material in that the puppet play was the spontaneous invention of a child, who was struggling with a psychotic disorder.

The material to be presented was obtained in the 60th and 130th treatment hours. It consists of two kinds of data: the therapist's process notes and summary, and electric tape recordings of the hours. The latter raises many questions in terms of scientific methodology.[7]

The analyst's notes were taken immediately after each session and contained his attempt to remember what happened, what he thought the various happenings meant, his own reactions, and whatever else he deemed important in order to recapture the spirit of the hour. These notes are supplemented by the electric tape. There are several reasons for making this attempt at integrating these two kinds of data, rather than relying exclusively on the usual methods of the analyst, that is, to use his own recollections and interpretations. The techniques used in the treatment of psychotic children and adolescents have not yet been consolidated and need to be investigated case by case. Apart from the fact that we do not yet have a reliable body of techniques for this category of patient, we are constantly trying to use theoretical concepts which are derived from our basic experience with neurotic patients and which are not completely applicable to the new situation. Moreover the rapid give and take in work with these severely disturbed borderline and psychotic patients, who usually arouse strong countertransference reactions, does not readily permit the therapist to give as reasonable an account of a process as is true for other types of analytic work. As indicated earlier (Chapter 3), I was able to document that some of the oversights, of which I was unaware while dictating my own impression at the end of each session, could be rectified through comparison with the electric tape.

In that chapter, I reported much of the diagnostic work of Teresa Esperanza. For my purpose here, I shall abstract a summary from the records of her mental examination:

Teresa is a fifteen-year-old girl who seems quite immature and of dull-normal intelligence. Basic comfort areas are related to her infantile ana-clitic relationships and her constant feeling of being threatened and endangered by the loss of objects. Her chief defense mechanisms are those of projection and flight and her chief defense against anxiety lies in her attempt to receive love as an assurance of being wanted and of maintaining the relationship with a love object. The basic conflicts are related to her intense, infantile oral demands and her fear that she would be rejected and cast away because of her excessive needs and demands. What seems to be an hysterical character formation is a disorganization and loosening of thought processes suggesting a thought disorder related to the fusion of past and present, and to the absence of adequate boundaries and isolation mechanisms making for adequate intellectual integration and separation of functions related to adequate reality testing. She was diagnosed as suffering from a "schizophrenic reaction, childhood type, with hysterical personality features."

By the time of the 60th hour, the patient, now about sixteen years old, had been in treatment for about half a year. During the first few months of treatment she was involved in play with small objects which she obtained as gifts from the therapist or from other sources. Her life reminded one of the *Glass Menagerie*. There was a complete absorption in these little objects, which she used in order to fantasy about the past, which was fused with the present. Much of her symtomatology centered around the constant need to be gratified with such objects, candy, and food of all sorts, and an insatiable appetite for outer stimuli of this type which, however, always proved almost useless in the attempt to re-experience actual events in her life. Frequently she would ask for a special object which she would describe in detail. Whenever she would receive it she would discover that it was not exactly what she had had in mind. She reminded one very much of a person who wants to play; who wants to weave fantasies, delusions, and hallucinations around some kind of object, but who cannot find the object which could serve as the crutch for either recollection or for trial thinking in the play activity. She could not maintain a cathexis on an external object, which, instead, immediately triggered off and became fused with inner stimuli. Neither her internalized objects nor her external objects were stable. She is presently the victim of insatiable object hunger, but whatever she swallows, whatever she attempts to introject, seems to be devoured by an empty void and becomes useless again. At the same time she struggles desperately to maintain a façade of normality, trying to meet the external demand as much as she can, and giving one the feeling that all her play is an attempt to move toward a position in which rather than "playing crazy," [8] it could be said that she is attempting to play normal, but cannot truly think or act normal. Her play reveals the attempt at a hopeless flirtation with normality, and the dim awareness that this goal is unreachable, that she is caught in a dilemma for which there is no way out. The notion of normality is borrowed, of course, is imitation rather than identification with the adult world, is a flirtation with a new identity, behind which lurks the inability either to maintain or to abandon earlier positions.

This struggle, her play with normality, as well as her play with the therapist, who has not yet become an external object for her, but is at best a crutch, a dehumanized mechanical object, is beautifully illustrated in the hour to follow. I shall present first my own recording at the end of this particular session, my summary of the event as well as my understanding at that point of what went on between me and the patient.

Today a rather charming hour with Teresa. She was at first somewhat delayed and asked whether she could go to the toilet before she came in, but then when the session started she soon brought out the puppet that she had made at school, an Easter bunny by the name of Lizzie, with black eyebrows to remind one of the movie actress, Liz Taylor, and practically the whole hour was spent in a conversation that I carried on with Lizzie, the puppet, while Teresa listened in. It was a conversation which helped us to establish a collaborative relationship between two aspects of Teresa, the sick Teresa and the healthy Teresa. Lizzie somehow represented the helper who understood Teresa very well and served as a kind of interpreter between the different aspects of Teresa, who described during the hour that she wanted to be many contradictory things, such as a movie actress, a puppet maker, a candy maker, a teacher, a sales person, a married woman, a child, etc.; in this attempt I constantly tried to bring about a collaborative relationship. The Easter bunny was, as it were, the healthy part of the child who tried to understand the child, who tried to work with me in order to help the sick child to keep from stuffing, to grow up, to clear up the confusion, etc. The device of the puppet served marvelously to bring indirectly into the situation a variety of treatment goals such as the desire to grow up, the desire to work well with the school, to do junior high school work rather than grade-school work and to make an adjustment.

The hour would be typical perhaps of an eight-year-old child, but nevertheless I felt that I had much better and constructive contact than in previous hours; and Teresa herself expressed her delight about Liz, whom she considered to be an excellent collaborator, somebody who was trying to help her, somebody who ought to come back.

I am reminded of the kind of hours that Rambert described in children's conflicts where ample use is made of puppets. The only difference is that this puppet device, rather than being suggested by me, was brought in by the child and was, as it were, the spontaneous and creative contribution of the patient who in this way found a new bridge for communication.

We talked also about the Easter gift that ought to be brought tomorrow and the main version was one in which the puppet, as it were, would help Dr. Ekstein to help Teresa. I felt that in this case the puppet was not so much the expression of the id wish but was rather the expression of the reflecting ego, the part that was successfully identified with the psychotherapeutic process, with maturation and development. The puppet in that way became the projected replica of the psychotherapist, that part of Teresa's mind which can fully collaborate with the therapeutic process but is still, as it were, a puppet in the hands of the illness.

The transcript of the tape recording of this hour will permit a more exact study of the interplay between therapist and Teresa, or rather, between that part of her which is projected onto the puppet, Lizzie the Bunny, and that part of her which she maintains for herself. The typed transcript, of course, while going much further than the therapist's own summary, does not quite allow us to gain insight into the emotional quality of the interview, the artistry of the interplay between Teresa and her puppet. We miss the inflection of the voices of the patient and the therapist, the whole range of emotional subtleties, the laughter, the giggles, the pauses and interspersed remarks in English or Spanish which could not quite be caught by the transcriber. Even the spoken word makes one aware of the many ingredients still missing: the visual representation, the actual activity and acting going on during this interview, types of observation so important in a psychotherapeutic contact. The meaning of the spoken word is but one aspect of the total meaning which is carried through play acting, through the change of voices, the acting out of voices, the handling of the puppet, as well as the movements of the therapist, who sometimes addresses himself to the puppet and does not look at the child, and vice versa. Nevertheless, the transcript, whether heard over the loudspeaker or read in print, does permit us to gain insight into the actual therapeutic situation.

What follows is the transcript of the electric tape.

T.: I'm sorry I took a lot of your time—I took a little longer, I guess (breathlessly). I told you that I would bring a puppet now that I would show you. These are the puppets we made at school. Yes, umhmm—it's a bunny. Look, you handle her like this—you put your finger here and she starts talking.

E.: Starts talking, opens the mouth, has two long ears, beautiful black eyebrows.

T.: Isn't she pretty?

E.: Very nice. Make her talk.

T. (falsetto voice): Hello, Doctor. (T.'s voice:) You know what her name is? Wait. (Puppet:) Guess what my name is?

E.: I'd like to know. Tell me.

T.: My name is Lizzie.

E.: Is your name Lizzie?

T.: Yes.

E.: Now, tell me, what kind of bunny are you, Lizzie?

T.: Well, I'm an Easter bunny.

E.: Oh, and tell me, what are you going to do at Eastertime this year?

T.: Well, I'm gonna help T. take the children some Easter eggs and give away Easter eggs.

E.: Are you a friend of T.'s?

T.: Yes, I'm her pet, we're pals, aren't we? (T.:) Umhmm.

E.: Well, tell me what about T., what's T. doing these days?

T.: Well, I'm gonna tell you something she's been doing, but I'm gonna tell you the truth, I can't lie to you about it.

E.: Okay, go ahead.

T.: She's still been stuffing herself.

E.: Oh, is she doing that?

T.: Wait, she just feels she can't help it, that she oughta keep on doing it.

E.: What do you think about it, Bunny?

T.: Well, what I think about it is that . . . she's still harming herself by doing it, it's not healthy for her body, it's unhealthy. . . .

E.: Do you really think it's . . .

T.: It makes her sick, it gives her tummy aches, she's stuffing herself with too much junk. Yesterday she did it. . . . I'm gonna tell you all the things she stuffed herself with, Doctor, so that you know.

E.: Tell me, Bunny, what can we do to help her?

T.: Well, Doctor, I'm gonna tell you something she tells me. Can I tell you? (In *T.'s* own voice, "Yes, go on, Lizzie.") Well, she told me to tell you, this is very important, I want you to listen carefully.

E.: Well, Bunny, go ahead and tell me, I'm gonna listen.

T.: She said that when she stuffs herself she feels she has a need to do it. It's a sickness, not really, because if she were cured and she would see things the way they are, do you think she would feel like doing it? She wouldn't.

E.: Why do you think that she has that need?

T.: Well . . . she has that need . . . because . . . uh. . . .

E.: It's hard to think, Bunny, isn't it?

T.: Yes. Well, I'll tell you right now. She has the need to do it because she feels that in her sickness she's . . . she's supposed to do it, like if somebody tells her "do it, do it, you're supposed to do it, you should do it. . . ."

E.: You mean she thinks that someone makes her do it.

T.: Yes, that's right. She knows that nobody makes her, but she feels it that way, it's part of her sickness, believe me it's not a lie, it's the truth.

E.: Tell me, Lizzie, how do you think we can help her?

T.: We-e-ll . . .

E.: Maybe you and I can think something out that helps *T.*

T.: Well, you know the only way I think that we can help her because she feels that she's gonna keep on doing it all the time and she might still do it forever.

E.: Umhmm. Do you think we can do something to help her?

T.: If she can't do it, yes.

E.: What do you think we can do to help her?

T.: Well, let's see, I'll stop and think of something. (In her own voice:) She's thinking (giggles).

E.: A very thoughtful bunny.

T. (Laughing and in her own voice): Isn't she cute?

E.: A very cute bunny.

T. (In her own voice): Yah. Miss Jayne made her for me. Emily sewed the eyelashes. Miss Jayne sewed the mouth . . . the only thing I sewed the . . . the . . .

E.: Ears?

T.: Ears. And *Miss Jayne stuffed them up. And Miss Jayne sewed the rest of her. (Reverting to puppet voice:) Well, let's see* . . .

E.: She's a very, very nice bunny.

T.: Thank you, Doctor. (*Bunny voice:*) Is it true that I have beautiful eyelashes because that's what my mommy says, she says that I'm beautiful, that what she likes best in me are my eyelashes, that I sort of resemble Liz Taylor a little. That's true?

E.: That's right, you got eyelashes like Liz Taylor's.

T.: Well, that's why she named me Lizzie.

E.: I wonder what Liz Taylor would think if she would hear that she looks like a bunny.

T.: Oh no . . . you think she would want to look like a bunny, she wouldn't even dare. . . .

E.: She might love to look like an Easter bunny.

T.: Well, I think she's too old for that. When she was a little girl that would be fine.

E.: Well, Easter bunnies are nice people.

T.: Yes, that's true, they are very nice, they're the ones that bring the children Easter eggs in the baskets and candy . . .

E.: Tell me, Lizzie, I want to ask you something.

T.: . . . and candy eggs. Yes, go ahead.

E.: Will you listen to me, Lizzie?

T.: Yup, any time.

E.: Tell me, did you notice, Lizzie, that T. has a new hairdo?

T.: Oh yes, well . . . doll . . . you didn't say nothing about it, why didn't you say something?

E.: Well, I wanted to ask you first whether you noticed it, Lizzie.

T.: Sure, sure, I noticed it. . . .

E.: You like it, Lizzie?

T.: Very much, I think she looks lovely, she looks beautiful.

E.: Tell me, since when did T. do this, Lizzie?

T.: Well, yesterday, last night my . . . her aunt fixed up her hair in curlers and this morning, and she slept all night with the curlers on—but she sleeps in the rug, you see, because that's healthy for her, and her aunt prefers her to sleep in her rug than the bed, but she's seldom comfortable without a pillow, 'cause she always sleeps without a pillow 'cause that's the best thing you can do, you know, because if she sleeps with a pillow it's bad for her, she gets neck aches, you know, her neck, her neck starts aching terribly. . . .

E.: Oh, she's so used to just sleep on the ground, without a pillow.

T.: Yes, you know her neck starts aching terribly, so she felt she needed a pillow. (*In her own voice:*) I wish she would really talk and I wouldn't talk for her (giggles). I love her so, Doctor.

E.: But you do pretty well talking for her.

T.: I do?

E.: Yes.
T.: But if I wish that she would talk instead of me making her talk, that really gets me more sick than what I am, Doctor.

At this point it seems appropriate to interrupt to make two observations. The first concerns the fact that the voice of the puppet, while representing the voice of health, as it were, the voice of the adult world which puts realistic demands on the child, actually does not represent the therapist to any large degree. The words of the puppet are primarily the injunctions of the aunt who constantly tries to keep Teresa within limits, who forbids her the senseless devouring of food, and who constantly threatens her that the overeating will lead to illness and must be stopped. We hear therefore that the puppet calls the therapist's attention to the child's eating difficulty, and does very much what Teresa has done in the past, when she informs the therapist that her aunt had told her to speak to him about having again been caught overeating, stealing from the refrigerator, etc. The puppet then voices the educational goals of the aunt; inasmuch as these repressive goals are voiced through the puppet, the mechanical extension of the child, the sick child, the injunctions are nothing but hollow imitations of orders from the outside which can be ignored in the name of the illness.

What will happen during the interview is reflected in the change in the puppet. The puppet will take on more and more the qualities of the therapist. Instead of a forbidding puppet who has educational goals, and who speaks of limits, the puppet will become a reflecting puppet, will make efforts at explaining, at creating a rationale for the difficulties of the child. One can literally see how the image of the forbidding aunt disappears and is slowly replaced by the image of the therapist, but also how both are kept at a distance since they gain entrance into the child's mind only via a well-controlled puppet which is in the child's hands and cannot get out of hand, as it were.

Teresa's last comment shows that the influence of the therapist is in ascendancy; that she plays with the idea, so to speak, of permitting the controlled extension, the puppet, more freedom. The child wishes that the puppet should really talk, should become alive, and that she, Teresa, should not talk for the puppet. She flirts with this change of roles, with the idea that the controlled voice of the puppet, still an extension of the psychotic child, should become the uncontrolled and spontaneous voice of an independent function, an independent ego. But as she seems to choose this new situation, in which the puppet becomes alive like Pinocchio in the story (which she will quote later), she also becomes frightened.

Since the puppet actually represents the increasing influence of the therapist, she cannot help but try and ward off this influence; she expresses the fear that if she wished for the puppet actually to talk independently, she might become sicker. She is afraid of the overwhelming power of a fantasy which is to lead toward normality, toward health, toward self-control, and she sees a danger in becoming well.

The fear that the puppet might become alive, might gain power over her, is the projected fear that the therapist might gain power over her, that his interpretations or interventions, understood by her as injunctions, might be an evil influence and lead to the giving up of the quasi-individuality which she retains in her illness, which is her defense against the symbiotic position. As we follow the transcript, we shall see that the puppet no longer stresses the goal of control but turns more and more to reflection. The contact with the therapist becomes more meaningful, and much of what the puppet says seems to be the working through of earlier interpretations, but on a level which permits the sick child to retain control. Beginning reflection should be associated with identification rather than mere imitation mechanisms.

E.: You mean if you would really think that that thing's alive.
T.: Umhmm, that's right, that would get me worse than what I am, and I might really see it, and I don't want to see it, I would be frightened, and that's why I shouldn't even think of it. It's something to see even a cartoon, you know, funnies, talking cartoons, like Donald Duck, you know—at least I can make her move as if she were alive, she seems to be alive, see. (Reverting to puppet's voice:) Well, so she felt uncomfortable to sleep without a pillow because all her curlers were bothering her and were aching her head and she couldn't just sleep well, so she asked her aunt if she could let her sleep with a pillow, so she slept with a pillow in the night and she slept comfortably and everything and next morning she, well, well, she fixed her hair nice and everything and now she has this nice hairdo—what do you think of it?
E.: Very nice hairdo—grownup girl hairdo.
T.: Thank you. Yeah, that's what I think. But, you know, the poor thing she always feels she's a child, you know, and . . .
E.: Suddenly she has a big girl's hairdo.
T.: Well, you know, she's mixed up, she's in between the two, this is something hard to explain, but I'll explain it to you at one time. She acts both ways—sometimes she acts like a grownup and sometimes like a child, and she doesn't know which to choose, which of the two, she's mixed up, you know—it's something like if, let's say, you go to a store, and you see two dresses, let's see—this girl sees a very pretty dress, and she sees a beautiful dress, and they're both so pretty she doesn't know which one to choose, she gets mixed up, you know, it's the same way with her. You understand what I mean, Doctor?

E.: Yes, I understand that very well. I just wonder why she doesn't want to choose the one or the other, Lizzie.

T.: Well, it's—that's a part of her sickness, don't you understand? 'Cause if she were cured, she would choose one of the two dresses.

E.: She sure would.

T.: Of course. But the reason why she doesn't is she gets mixed up about it and starts saying, "Well, I want this one or this one." She goes for the two but she doesn't know which one, she gets mixed up, confused, it's in her sickness, you should know that, I'm sure you know it, don't you?

E.: Sure. But tell me, what would be the trouble if she were to choose one part, just leave out the other.

T.: Well, um, uh, let's see, let's see.

E.: Oh, Lizzie, you gotta do a lot of thinking.

T. (Giggles): I know what you're saying.

E.: Yah, well, if you can think that out, you've got a good thought.

T.: Well, what do you think would be the best thing? Which of the two dresses would you choose? (Lizzie addresses T. here, who answers, "Well, I think I would choose if I were cured, I would choose the beautiful more than the pretty one.") See? She would choose the beautiful one.

E.: She'd rather be the grownup woman.

T.: That's right. Well, that would be both for a grownup woman and girls, you know, but she would choose the beautiful one, you know what I mean? You understand me, don't you?

E.: Yes, she would want to be the beautiful woman.

T.: Yes, that's right. See? You like my voice, isn't it sweet?

E.: It's sort of like a bunny's voice.

T. (Giggling): Oh. Thank you. You're very nice (giggles).

E.: Tell me Bunny, what are you eating for breakfast? Are you stuffing yourself the right way?

T.: No, I'm eating Easter eggs right now and carrots. My aunt—my mother—gives me carrots, celeries, this morning I had two carrots for breakfast and a celery.

E.: That's healthy food.

T.: Oh very, it's better than eating Easter eggs and chocolate and all that because that's, I have that for dessert, you know. For breakfast sometimes I have two carrots, and for lunch a carrot and a celery and for dinner carrots and celeries and for dessert chocolate eggs, chocolate Easter eggs, you know.

E.: Tell me, do you and T. eat the same things?

T.: No, she eats different from what I eat, but she also eats carrots and celeries and chocolate eggs and Easter eggs. . . .

E.: She does.

T.: Of course, but not exactly as much as I do because she's not a bunny, I'm a bunny and she . . .

E.: You mean you stuff more than she?

T.: Well, of course, I think bunnies . . . no, no, no, we both stuff ourselves the same way, don't we, T?" (*In her own voice:*) Yes (giggles).

E.: Liz, you got a big mouth, if you start to eat with that mouth, you sure would stuff yourself.

T.: Oh, thank you, thank you. I wish I had a little mouth, you know, T. was gonna make me a little mouth, first Miss Jayne asked her, "What kind of a mouth would you like in your Easter bunny in your puppet, a big one, a little one, or a medium one?" And she first told her, "A little one." Then she said, "No, a medium one." This isn't a big mouth, Doctor, this is a medium mouth.

E.: Oh, that's just a medium mouth.

T.: It's not big, not little, just the way it should be.

E.: Sure. If it were a big mouth, it would be as big as a crocodile's.

T.: Yah, and I don't wish to have a mouth as big as a crocodile, worse if it were like a hippopotamus.

E.: Well, it isn't really a small mouth of a birdie either.

T.: Well, it's just the way it should be, you know.

E.: It's like a big Easter bunny's mouth.

T.: That's right, it's the way it should be, not little, not big, just the way it should be, you know.

E.: Well, you would be very nice in a puppet show, Lizzie.

T.: Oh, thank you, thank you.

E.: Children would love to watch you.

T.: Oh—I love children, don't you?

E.: Oh sure, and you could tell them a story about T.

T.: Oh, any time. I think she told me once that she's gonna get me in a puppet show, didn't you? (*T.'s own voice says,* "I think I did.")

E.: She might even help you make up the story.

T. (*In her own voice*): I must have, did I tell you that? I think I did, I'm not sure, I don't remember, did I, Lizzie? (*Reverting to Lizzie's voice:*) Well, well, I think she must have anyway.

E.: And if she didn't, she will later.

T.: Yah, but I think that she told me that one time she was gonna put me in a puppet show so that kids would watch me, and I said, "Oh, I'd love to be in one."

E.: Well, what kind of show would you put on, Lizzie?

T.: Well, an Easter bunny show or fairy tales of bunnies or remember when the children are asleep and the bunnies go and hide their Easter eggs?

E.: All around the place.

T.: That's right and then when they wake up and go hunting for their eggs—or, also, a parade, an Easter bunny parade, a puppet show, the bunny family. . . .

E.: One after the other marching up and down.

T.: That's right. Or, also a story of bunny, of bunnies, of parents, of the mommy, the daddy, and the kids, the granny, the grandpa, the uncle, the aunt, and all the family. You know what I mean, don't you?

E.: Umhmm.

T.: And the bunny family, you know. Well, I would also like to be in a bunny family, you know. You understand what I mean, no?

E.: Yes, I do, I certainly do.

T.: Well, you see, that's what I mean.

E.: Well, what would it be, dear bunny, if T. would grow up and when she would be a grownup woman she would have nice, beautiful puppet shows for children, and in that way she wouldn't have to give up all the lovely things of her childhood. But she still would be a grownup woman, she would become a puppeteer.

T.: Well, that would be wonderful. But, you know, Doctor, this is something I want to tell you. She wishes she could become many things, not only that, she wishes she could become a movie star, a nun, a nurse, a doctor, a lady that sells in a toy store, that sells toys for children or that sells nice things, jewelry or perfume or, you know, things for the ladies that they use, you know, or also, a cake store, she wishes, what she would like the best to be, to become if she's big and . . . that, that she would make cakes herself, and she would sell them. She would make pies, cakes, you know, doughnuts, and all sweets and she would sell them and have her own sweet store, you know like in Mexico those stores. (Talks in Spanish:) You know, that's the way they call them in Spanish—I know how to talk in Spanish also, she taught me, didn't you, T.? (In her own voice: "Umhhmm.") She taught me how to talk in Spanish.

E.: So you're a Spanish bunny too.

T.: Yup. So what I'm telling you is that, um, let's see, for example, well those stores that are in Mexico where they sell wheat bread, you know, and she would be working in one of those stores and she would sell wheat bread, she would make them herself, cakes, pies, doughnuts, and all kinds of sweets and sell them. Or she would also love to be a toymaker, she would like to have her own toy store, like Giuseppe—did you see the story of Pinocchio where Guiseppe was a toy maker and he used to make his toys and sell them? He had all kinds of toys, cuckoo clocks, and the cutest things, he made them himself, he used to be really a good toymaker.

E.: Well, she will have a very rough time, won't she, to make up her mind which one of these things she wants to be.

T.: Yah, you know the poor thing is confused. I'm gonna help her, really, I'm gonna try and see what she would really . . .

E.: Gee, the poor thing, she can't do all these things, she can't do all these things all at once.

T.: Pardon?

E.: This poor thing, she can't do all these things all at once, she can only do one thing at a time.

T.: Well, yes, of course, but I'm gonna help her to try and see which of all the things she would really like to become to be.

E.: What do you think, Lizzie, you would want her to be? If you could make her?

T.: Well, let's see, I would . . . let's see . . . that's hard for me to think of also. I'll see.

E.: A rough question.

T.: Umhmm. Yup.

E.: Gee, you're a great thinker.

T.: Thank you (giggles). For an example, I think I would like her to be . . . well . . . I have an idea . . . she could make . . . she could be, she could become to be a toymaker, you know, and sell. . . .

E.: Like Pinocchio's daddy.

T.: That's right. But look what kind of a toymaker, she would make puppets and, you know, all kinds of toys, and she would sell these puppets and all these toys in her own toy store, she would have her own toy store and she would sell them. That's what I would like her to be. Wouldn't you think that would be fine?

E.: I believe it would. It would. So that's what you would want her to do: to make toys and sell them to children.

T.: Yup. And puppets also and sell them.

E.: So she would be a grownup but she would always make children happy.

T.: Sure. She likes children, she loves them, she would never say she hates them, 'cause she loves them all.

E.: She would never pull them by their hair.

T.: Oh, no, even her own children if she would get married and have her babies. She said, you know what she said? That every time they would behave bad and, and, and, you know.

E.: They would be naughty. What would she do?

T.: She would punish them, she wouldn't hit them, she wouldn't hurt them, because she'd feel that she wouldn't like to harm her own children, she would just punish them, you know.

E.: But not very strongly, not very badly.

T.: No, because she would love them so much that she would just be too delicate with them, you know, she would have so much love for them that she would treat them as if they were little angels.

E.: Would she take candy away from them?

T.: No, she would always give them everything they wished for if she had the money. She would give them all the toys in the world, all the candy, clothes, and everything.

E.: Would she help them not to stuff?

T.: Oh, that's right, that's the trouble, well, that's what she's mixed up in, you know.

E.: Gee, but she doesn't want to mix up her own children with that stuff.

T.: No, but that's something else that she's mixed up in, you know. (To

T.:) Aren't you? (*T.*: Umhmm.)

E.: Well, you know, Lizzie, as long as we are fond of T., it's all right if she's a little mixed up.

T.: Well, yah, at least we know why.

E.: You still like her, don't you?

T.: Sure, I love her.

E.: Even if she's mixed up.

T.: Sure, I love her very much.

E.: That's good of you, have you ever been angry at T.?

T.: No, never, we get along very nice, don't we?

E.: You would even get along with her nicely if sometimes she is not so nice to you?

T.: Well, yah, sure. You only should be careful when she gets in a bad humor because she really gets like a bad humor, you know.

E.: What would . . .

T. (Interrupts): If you just get calm and listen to what she says and that's all. Because look, Doctor, just hear me in this, every time she gets in a bad humor just stop and say, "Well, the reason of why she gets that way is because that's a part of her sickness, that's an attack that comes to her, that's something, an attack that gets her in a bad mood, see?" So every time that happens just think of that and you, you know why it happens.

E.: But, Lizzie, if she would have a bad humor about you?

T.: Oh. Well, then I'd just accept it, that's all. But if it's about something else . . .

E.: You would just accept it if she has a bad humor about you?

T.: Yep, yes, I would.

E.: I hope she doesn't have a bad humor, because you're a very nice bunny, nobody should be angry at you.

T.: Well, well, just very little times she's been in a bad humor of me, because I'm always nice to her and I always behave good, and she loves me very much, believe me, she likes me, since she made me and she created me, she likes me very much.

E.: Well, she most likely thinks that you're very much like her.

T. (To T.): Do I look like you? (*T.*: Yah. Well, then her eyebrows are brown.) See, she says my eyebrows are brown.

E.: Just like yours, just like T.'s.

T.: Umhmm. Yup. And my eyelashes are black, like Liz Taylor's. Because she has brown eyelashes, you know.

E.: So between T. and Liz Taylor.

T.: Hu huh, yup, you know, I wish I looked like T., completely like T.

E.: Of course, who wants to look not completely like T.? T.'s . . .

T.: Well, of course.

E.: T.'s a very . . .

T.: Well, tell me one thing, Doctor, who is more pretty, who do you think is more pretty . . . because to me Liz Taylor and Tammy and her . . .

*I don't know, they're both so pretty, I mean, they're both so pretty, which
of them do you think is the nicest?*

It seems that the puppet is trying to reconcile the interest of Teresa
and that of the therapist. Teresa, through the mouth of the puppet, plays
with a variety of identifications, a variety of roles which are to make her
acceptable in this world, and she tries them on for size. As a matter of
fact, she even tries to make up roles which would permit her to continue
to live in part in the world of childhood, in the world of the puppets, in
the world of fantasy, but in the service, as it were, of helping other children.
It is almost a role which could be compared with the role of a therapist
who can indulge in metaphors and similes, work with fairy tales, and continue with puppets in the service of the therapeutic ego. As she continues
to make these compromises, she starts to offer herself to the therapist as
a more acceptable love object, and she tries out whether the changes she
promises are sufficiently attractive for the therapist. It is true these
promises are—to use a phrase of Schlesinger's [9]—"primary promising," a
kind of promising which is not meant to be kept, but is meant to solicit
love from the adult and to stop his anger. The puppet's name is Liz, a
reference, of course, to the movie actress Liz Taylor, a movie idol of the
child's, a reminder of the movie career which failed for her once so
beautiful but schizophrenic mother, and her present notion of what mature
and desirable womanhood may lead to.

The puppet's question whether the therapist could make a choice by
comparing Liz and Teresa raises a technical problem because the answer
gives the patient a cue to what the conditions of acceptance are. When
the choice is directly between the rabbit puppet Liz and the patient
Teresa, the therapist decides here (as well as at a later point) in favor
of the child. He feels that as long as the healthy aspects of the patient's
ego organization are merely rudimentary formations which can at any
moment be upset by new regressions, he will do better to ally himself with
the dominant forces rather than to choose or identify with the puppet.
In showing his preference for Teresa, the therapist seems to maintain a
contact which permits the child to express, via the puppet, her actual
concerns about the problem of getting well. She offers a rationale for her
illness, for her unwillingness to identify with the forces of growing up,
and eventually she describes her dilemma by comparing it to a dream from
which one cannot wake up. One might well say at this point that the playing with normality, as expressed through the investment she makes in the
puppet, could be compared with a dreamer who starts to become aware of
the fact that the nightmare is but a dream, that he should wake up, that
a part of him knows better, but that nevertheless he cannot wake up and

must continue with the experience of terror. The puppet—Teresa's nascent ego—knows better, but cannot yet wake her up.

E.: Well, I think T. is much nicer than Liz Taylor.

T.: You think? Because Liz Taylor is the beautifulest, you know.

E.: Well, yes, for the movies. But T. is a nicer person.

T.: Oh, oh. Well, she would also like to become to be a movie star, you know.

E.: Well, you think she should, Liz?

T.: Well . . . sure, any time she wants to.

E.: Well, I think so, too, but once she worried about becoming a movie star, Liz, you know, she told me that maybe if she wanted to become a movie star that might make her sick. What do you think about it, Liz?

T.: Oh yah, just like her mother got sick.

E.: You think she's right on that or is that just sort of a worry that she could throw out?

T.: No, that's a worry she has in her mind. But it wouldn't happen if she . . .

E.: No, it wouldn't happen because if we make her well she could be a movie star as much as she wants to.

T.: That's right, she just worries about things and that's a worry she has, you know.

E.: That's right. Well, I guess you can't blame her to worry. She saw that happen in her family.

T.: Yah. Poor thing, really, that's the sad thing about her.

E.: Well, you know, you can tell her, Liz, that she didn't get sick, I mean her mommy didn't get sick because she wanted to be a movie star, that just happened to be that way, but there's no connection.

T.: Well, what I think is it wasn't her, it was her father that got her that way. Her father was always so mean with her mother, he used to always slap her in the face, he used to be the meanest father one child could have ever had.

E.: Oh gosh, well that mommy sure didn't choose right when she chose that man for a husband.

T.: Yah, she chose the wrong one.

E.: That wasn't a very reliable man.

T.: Umhmm. That's right.

E.: He was a mixed-up guy.

T.: Yah, Alice in Wonderland, I guess.

E.: He wasn't Alice in Wonderland.

T.: Well, something like that, lost in between Wonderland and other places, you know.

E.: You mean mixed up because Alice in Wonderland, you know, she liked it there most of the time.

T.: Yah, but she was lost, didn't you know that? One thing, she was dreaming.

E.: That's right, but she woke up.

T.: Umhmm, and good thing she did because that nightmare she had was just too painful.

E.: That's right, nobody likes painful nightmares.

T.: That's right.

E.: She woke up and what pleasure it was to realize that it was all but a dream.

T.: That's right, and maybe with her she feels that she's dreaming also, that all this is a dream, a nightmare she has, but it's not that, not really, I mean it's a nightmare in her sickness that she sees things this way, she sees them, she dreams them. . . .

E.: She really wants to wake up more and more.

T.: Yah, it seems as if she's dreaming . . . but you know that she's not dreaming, you know that it's true, you know? You understand?

E.: Oh yah, sure, we do quite well. I guess as T. watches us she must have fun. You think we should get T. into this conversation or should we just continue talking and leave her out?

T.: Well, I don't think it's bad really, we can get her into this.

E.: Lizzie, I'm just sort of a little worried that if we leave her out she might feel offended, you know, or she might think we don't like her any more, and really we do like her.

T.: Of course we do like her.

E.: So maybe you tell me what you think whether we should leave her out and just let her watch us or whether we should invite her to become a part of the conversation.

The puppet here displays some insight: in comparing the patient's experience with that of a dreamer, and in suggesting that the therapist knows, as does the puppet, that Teresa actually was not dreaming. The therapist takes this as a cue that Teresa is ready to listen to the puppet, as it were, to permit the therapist more influence and to join the conversation as an active partner. He invites a conversation among the three of them, Teresa, the puppet, and himself. The folie à deux turns into a folie à trois.

T.: I'm gonna ask her, wait. (To T.:) Would you like to be with us or just hear us or what? (T.'s own voice answers: "Well, I'd like to join you.") Well, she says she'd like to join us.

E.: Oh sure, well, you tell T. to come right in and join us.

T.: Yah, come on right in and join us.

E.: Now we're three people, Liz, Dr. Ekstein, and T. Hi, T., are you awake?

T. (*In her own voice*): Yup, hi, how are you? (*Giggles.*)

E.: How have you been passing these last two days?

T.: Oh fine.

E.: You did fine. You know, I had a very fine conversation with an old friend of yours.

T.: Lizzie. You like her? Isn't she nice?

E.: Lizzie the bunny is very, very nice, a real pleasure.

T. (Giggling): I think she's the cutest thing.

E.: Didn't we do well? She and I did very well together, we talked a lot of good things, and she's a bright kid, a very good observer, she starts to get to know you very well.

T.: Sure.

E.: Yah, even though she has eyelashes like Liz Taylor. She's got also, I suppose, brown eyes, like T.

T.: Well you know something, she wishes she had eyes like Liz Taylor. She wishes she had long eyelashes.

E.: Oh, you mean T.

T.: Yah.

E.: Oh, you tell T. she's pretty enough.

T.: Oh, really?

E.: Oh, yah, she's a very pretty girl, she doesn't need to be any prettier.

T.: Oh, thank you. (To *T.*:) See? You heard what he said? Tell him thank you very much. She said thank you very much.

E.: Delighted, delighted.

T. (Oohs and aahs.)

E.: Well, Lizzie, what will we get T. for Easter?

T.: For Easter, well, now let's see.

E.: Should she get tomorrow some surprise?

T. (Screams delightedly): Oooh, she can't even imagine it! Will I get something? Oh, please, please! Look, give me carrots or celery for Easter, candy carrots and celery.

E.: Oh, you got, T. gives you plenty of that.

T.: Oh well, Easter eggs, oh please, oh please!

E.: Well, wait a moment, I was just asking you what to give T., now you want something yourself. How can you be so greedy?

T.: Ohhh . . . I'm sorry.

E.: Why don't you think of T.?

T.: Oh, well, for both of us, no?

E.: Oh, for both, I see. Now, okay, what do you think we should get T. and you?

T.: Well, oh, look, she's excited, she's excited!

E.: Who, you or T.?

T.: T., and I'm excited also, aren't we? (In her own voice, as T. giggles: "Uh huh.")

E.: T. likes Easter, as a matter of fact, T. likes all the holidays.

T.: Oh, she gets excited about things like that, you know. Well, you know

what the best thing we could give her. . . . Well, tell me, for example,
give me an example of what you got for her.
E.: *Well, I haven't made up my mind yet, you know, because if I tell you*
everything, then you might go and tell T., and I don't trust you, you
know?
T.: *Oh.*
E.: *You might whisper it into T.'s ears. You might . . .*
T.: *I wouldn't, I wouldn't dare. . . .*
E.: *Oh, but look, I know you like T., so you would tell her.*
T.: *Oh, well come on, I won't tell her, I promise you I won't, I give my*
word.
E.: *You promise?*
T.: *I promise.*
E.: *Well, I thought to get her something that really has to do with Easter,*
you know.
T.: *Yes?*
E.: *Exactly with Easter time.*
T.: *Oh goodness. Give me an example of like . . . what?*
E.: *Well, it will be something that is filled up with something, but it*
won't be stuffed, it will just be filled up.
T.: *Filled up?*
E.: *Filled up, yes.*
T.: *Will it be to eat? Or just toys?*
E.: *Well, I think . . . usually it is to eat, you know.*
T.: *Oh.*
E.: *Because Easter time is an eatup time.*
T.: *Yah, that's right.*
E.: *Not only a happy time, but an eatup time.*
T.: *Oh.*
E.: *And it's a time where all of us are allowed to stuff a little bit.*
T.: *Oh, goodness, Ohh* (excitedly).
E.: *A little stuffing time. You think T. likes that?*
T.: *Of course. She'll bring you something else that she has for you to-*
morrow.
E.: *That's great. But tell me, will, maybe T. will get upset about stuffing?*
T.: *No. She'll eat it little by little, she promises. Don't you promise? Now,*
I'll try to stop her, believe me, I'll help her in that, I'll be her companion.
E.: *All you need to do is to keep her, you know . . .*
T. (Interrupts): *That little devil is just attacking her too much, and she*
needs a little guide from heaven, she needs a little angel or something.

This statement is an excellent example of insight, expressed through
the voice of the puppet, into the shifting fortunes of the different introjects as well as into the need for external help, the angels, who are to
struggle against the forces of the devil. We are, of course, aware of the

fact that at this point the therapist is in a precarious position because the very problem of psychotic transference is that his influence, too, fluctuates. In most phases of therapy he is experienced not as a real and full object but rather in terms of ever-changing, fragmented introjects, good ones and evil ones. In a similar fashion, the patient experiences the environment's demand for health and adulthood sometimes as temptations, as seduction, as evil action, and at other times as positive and desirable forces.

E.: Little by little. Well, what you do is you give her the food . . .
T. (Interrupting): And I'll be her little angel and I'll guide her to good ways.
E.: Excellent, you give her little by little, and when that devil comes you snap at him.
T.: That's right, that's what I'll do, I'll . . .
E.: You got a nice big mouth.
T.: I'll spit him in the face and blow your horn, get out of here.
E.: Exactly, that's what you'll tell him.
T. (Giggling): Yah.
E.: The old devil will run so fast that he won't know what his clubfeet are doing. Oh, will he be frightened.
T.: He sure will.
E.: He sure will. Because now that the devil has found out, you know, that T. is not alone any more, T. has friends, she's got you, she's got Dr. Ekstein, and between the two of us she'll be stronger than the devil.
T.: That's right. And she has God, her best friend.
E.: That's right, and the poor old devil, he will say, "Oh . . ."
T. (Interrupting): He's just gonna cry to the full moon.
E.: That's right, that's good for him, because maybe some day he will turn into a good guy. Then we eat him.
T.: That's right.
E.: When he's a good guy we eat him, if he's a bad guy, we spit him out.
T.: That's right.
E.: Okay? We only eat good guys, no bad guys.
T.: That's right, eat only the good guys, not the bad guys.
E.: The bad guys we spit out.
T.: See? The bad guys we spit out.
E.: And the good guys we swallow and keep.
T.: Umhmm . . .
E.: That's what we'll do.
T.: Well, that's the best thing we can do really, there's nothing else you can do but that . . . you're a very wonderful doctor, really, that's all I can say.
E.: Thank you, Lizzie.
T.: You're welcome.

E.: I guess we understand each other.
T.: Sure, that's all I can say, that you're wonderful, you know, you're marvelous.
E.: Well, I hope, Lizzie, that T. understands that too, but if T. doesn't know it, then it doesn't help me to be marvelous; you think T. understands it too?
T.: Oh, she knows it, sure she knows it.
E.: Well, if she doesn't know it, we're gonna help her find it out.
T.: Aw, don't worry, she knows exactly all about it.
E.: I think she's a pretty smart girl, that T., don't you think so?
T.: Yah, she's very smart. She's bright.
E.: Well, even though she's sometimes such a confused little girl. Tell me, Lizzie, I want to ask you something, you know, behind the back of T., don't tell her.
T.: No, I won't.
E.: Tell me, Lizzie, how is she doing in school right now?

It is at this point that the therapist wishes to test whether this play with normality can be translated into normal action. Could he press the collaboration between himself and the puppet (the auxiliary ego) to a point at which Teresa will face some of the tasks of growing up, such as her school work? Will this encounter then be more than a playing at normality? Will it be true trial action, or will it prove that the puppet is actually well controlled by the child; that Pinocchio is still but a wooden figure instead of a live person; that the healthy part of the child is still "dead" and only the psychosis lives? The puppet in the hands of the child represents inverted psychotic omnipotence, comparable to the megalomania of the infant who is helpless but "controls" the mother. The Negro spiritual about Him who "has the whole world in His hands" touches upon the problem of utter helplessness and omnipotent trust.

In the ensuing conversation the puppet seems to give the answer. The puppet asks again on whose side the therapist is. The original choice was between Liz Taylor, the beautiful actress, and Teresa, the patient. This time the choice is more direct: who is prettier, the puppet or Teresa? Whom does the therapist elect as true collaborator, as true friend, as his choice? Does he side with the forces of insight, the forces which are to meet real tasks, or does he side with the forces of regression? Realizing the extent to which the collaboration can be maintained, he chooses Teresa, although giving some credit to the puppet.

T.: Well, she's doing very well, she's cooperating with the teacher, everything that her teacher gives her she does it well, only some things that Miss Jayne gives her she doesn't know how to do them she doesn't do them.

E.: Does she get easily discouraged when she gets some harder work?

T.: No, she doesn't, she just doesn't do it, she says, "I don't know how to do this." She just does what she can do, but she's cooperating and is doing very well.

E.: Do you think, Lizzie, that she will soon be able to do some more advanced work?

T.: Well, I have a feeling she will.

E.: You know that all the children do. Because I think, Lizzie, I wanted to ask you whether that's true, I sometimes think that she does sort of third-grade work, fourth-grade work, when really she could do junior high school work.

T.: Yah, she does, that's right. She's doing second- or third-grade work right now.

E.: Uh huh, so tell me, do you think we can get her to do junior high school work?

T.: Yah, sure, we can help her.

E.: Uh huh. But why do you think that she gets so easily, you know, thinks that she can't do it. She's such a bright kid, you know, I think she can.

T.: Sure, she can, oooh, if she really tried.

E.: Tell me, Lizzie, how long does she sit still there when she does her work?

T.: Well . . . well . . . an hour, I think?

E.: A whole hour? That's pretty good.

T.: Yup. Till twelve, because she gets to school at seven, at eight, and at twelve she leaves and goes home, but sometimes at one or at two when she stays for lunch. . . .

E.: Do you think she's gonna be able to stay with her work a little longer?

T.: Yah, sure.

E.: Because you know what I think, Lizzie, between me and you, we want to make a high school girl out of her. Or are we wrong?

T.: No, no, we should make a high school girl out of her, yes.

E.: She's pretty enough to be a high school girl.

T.: Oh yes, sure she is, of course.

E.: But don't tell her too often, because, you know, if we tell her too often that she's pretty she would just be full of vanity, you know.

T.: Oh! No, never!

E.: We want her to be a modest girl even though we know she's pretty.

T. (Sort of a half giggle): Oh, yes, sure, thank you anyway for saying that. Now, am I pretty?

E.: You're not talking about T. now, you're talking about yourself.

T.: That's right.

E.: Well, Lizzie, I tell you a secret. You're very pretty, but you're not as pretty as T. I hope that you don't mind that I tell you that.

T.: Oh no! Oh no! I'm not, it doesn't hurt my feelings. Yah, I know that. . . .

E.: You know why it doesn't have to hurt your feelings? Because, look, T.'s older than you. When you will be her age you will also turn to be prettier. When people grow up, when you will grow up too, they become prettier and prettier. So you don't worry, you know. But right now, T.'s prettier than you. Oh, she sure is. Don't you admire her? Just don't tell her too much, you know, because if she thinks that she's so pretty she'll be conceited.

T. (Punctuates the above with "ohs" and "very much," etc.; then, giggling): No, I won't.

E.: And you know, we want her not only to be a pretty person, we want her also to be one that isn't confused, that does well in school and does well with people and enjoys life, and you and I are going to do this together. You are from now on my helper. You know what I want to tell you, Lizzie? You are going to be on the staff, you know, you are going to be employed by Reiss-Davis Clinic for Child Guidance to help T.

T.: Oh, oh, Doctor, that's nice, I'd love to.

E.: You're my helper, and I don't mind if you tell T., because I don't want to do anything behind her back, I want her to know that you and I are going to be assisting each other.

T.: Oh, sure, sure, no, she doesn't mind, it's okay.

E.: Why should she mind?

T.: It's okay, go on.

E.: Well, you know, I want to tell you something, Lizzie. I brought something tiny for T. today. Do you think we should give it to her?

T. (Considering): Well . . . yes . . . really, Doctor, I'm gonna tell you something—if you don't hear this . . . if you don't give it to her . . . she feels heartbroken. . . .

E.: Oh, she does?

T.: Yes, she feels terrible, she feels very painful in her sickness. . . .

E.: But, Lizzie, doesn't T. know by now that even if I wouldn't give her anything I'm just as fond of her?

T.: Yah, sure, but she still feels that she needs a little present.

E.: Isn't it funny that she needs that?

T.: Yes, she does, it's part of her sickness.

E.: Maybe some day she will know that people like her without ever getting anything.

T.: Yah, she will, she will notice it. . . .

E.: You know, I brought her a little telephone book to put in telephone numbers . . .

T.: Oh, isn't that nice?

E.: . . . so that she can put in Dr. Ekstein's number in case she needs him. . . .

T.: Oh. (To T.: You heard what he got you, how do you like it?)

E.: And then I brought her a few little tiny toy charms, so she will have more charms. Do you think she will like that?

T.: Oh, oh!!! Sure, she would love it!

E.: I tell you what I'm going to do, I'm going to stick it in your mouth, and then you give it to T.

T. (Giggles delightedly): Oh!! Okay, I'll take it. Okay, come on! (Giggling happily.) She's not gonna look, don't look, huh? I have my mouth open. . . .

E.: Don't let T. look. Here's one, snap it, and then I have to find the others. Well, here goes! Okay, snap it. Wait a minute, open your mouth, okay, snap it. Wait a minute, open the mouth again, you didn't do right. Okay. Wait a minute, wait a minute, okay.

T. (All through this giggling delightedly): Isn't this cute? (In her own voice: Oh, Lizzie, tell Dr. Ekstein that this is awfully pretty.) Oh, she says that is very nice, she says she liked it very much and thank you very much for it, she's very happy with it.

E.: Very pleased, Lizzie. Lizzie, will you come tomorrow again?

T.: Sure.

E.: You know, we had such a pleasant hour with you, a very pleasant session. Will you tell T. now that we have about come to the end of the session and tomorrow is Easter Friday.

T.: Yah, that's right, she has to—(not understandable)

E.: So please, will you tell her not to forget to come tomorrow? It's important.

T.: Okay, I'll tell her.

E.: If she forgets tomorrow, what would I do with the surprise?

T.: She won't forget, she'll promise, she knows she has to come.

E.: She knows it.

T.: She will come, don't worry.

E.: And some day she might even come if she doesn't get anything, because she would know that she gets her health here, that's even more important than little things.

T.: That's right, yup, to be sure, that's the best thing.

E.: Did you see the telephone book that I gave her? It has an alphabet, where she can put under each letter the people whom she knows and to put in the little . . .

T.: It's very nice.

E.: . . . and the phone numbers.

T.: Yah, it's a very cute telephone book. She's happy with it, you should see how glad she is, she has a beautiful smile on her face, a big one. Aren't you happy, T.? (In her own voice: Umhmm.)

E.: Yes, sort of a grownup child smile.

T.: Yes, she feels painful, you know, once in a while she gets a pain. She gets, well, you know, she gets sort of mixed-up things, and terrible misery that come into her life and they're painful and make her suffer and a lot of things, you know. Well, something, Doctor, I'm gonna tell you, this is very important, I'm gonna help her, and please, you give me a little power to help her.

E.: Exactly. I will.

T.: Look, she feels that since tomorrow you're gonna bring her her Easter things she wishes that she, she wishes and she feels even that she's gonna try hard not to stuff herself because she still—yesterday she thought to herself that yesterday is gonna be the last day that I'm gonna stuff myself, and I'll never do it again. But she feels like doing it again today.

E.: Lizzie, tell her this, tell her that you're gonna watch over her so that she only stuffs herself a little bit, and only little by little, then she won't have to be unhappy, but around Easter time everybody stuffs a little, just a little, and you see to it that she won't stuff more than a little. Okay?

T.: All right. Okay. I will. I'll take good care of her.

E.: Okay, you take your T., pack her up now.

T.: Okay. And see you tomorrow. Happy Easter. It was very nice talking to you.

E.: Happy Easter.

T. (In her own voice, giggling a little nervously): I'm gonna put her back in the bag. Bye!

E.: Bye-bye.

T.: Oh, Lizzie, come on, go in, say good night to Dr. Ekstein, we're leaving. Ooh, can't go in this way. Well, Doctor, it was very nice seeing you. Did you like my Lizzie?

E.: Well, you saw, you heard me, no doubt about it. Lizzie and I got along beautifully. If you and I get along always as well as Lizzie and I, we'll do fine.

T.: She's my best pal I ever had, believe me, she's wonderful.

E.: I'll see you tomorrow.

T.: Okay. It was very nice, uh, talking to you, and I enjoyed talking to you. Happy Easter. (She seems a little upset, giggles nervously, finds it hard to leave.)

E.: Sure.

The interchange could be maintained as long as the therapist again made concessions to the child, who wants gifts and food, who must satisfy the object hunger, and who feels she has done all she could by offering a pseudo act, a microcosmic stage play of inner forces at work. This conflict was staged in such a way that health was confined to the little bunny-puppet, who on the one hand aspired to look like Liz Taylor and on the other shared with Teresa her main preoccupations, the love of carrots and gifts and the fear of stuffing herself with too many things given by objects who can turn into evil forces. Both Liz and Teresa struggle for mastery through maintaining the distance from outer forces, namely, the parental figures and the therapist, all of whom at times of stress are experienced as evil creatures trying to enter her mind and destroy her.

This play with normality is a desperate one. It constitutes her attempt to "wake up" as well as her struggle against it—a struggle between the tendency to turn imitation into identification and the fear of becoming a victim of devouring outer forces. The primitive projective-introjective mechanisms threaten to wipe out the precarious individuality of the delusional world which permits the maintenance of a sort of private world but at the same time constantly undermines the search for human objects. This endlessly repeated struggle, which goes on week after week, month after month, which at times spells hope and frequently desperation, nevertheless permits one to discern an upward spiral. This progressive trend can perhaps best be demonstrated if we turn to an hour, some eight months later, in which the child again, for the second time, made spontaneous use of puppet play.

In this 130th hour Teresa had some difficulties in establishing contact with the therapist as well as in describing her own problem. She turned from toy to toy and somehow none seemed to allow her to develop what she wished to convey.

I quote from my summary prepared at the end of that session:

Finally, she took the puppet and here, for the first time, a sort of fantasy dialogue developed inasmuch as she assigned the puppet the role of Suzie Wong, a movie role, which she knew only from magazine descriptions. She did indicate, though, that Suzie Wong stood for the beautiful girl who loved many men, attracted many men, and was loved by many. She was a sort of mature fantasy of a world of promiscuous love, and Suzie Wong now had, as it were, a talk with Teresa. Somehow, with occasional questions from me, directed primarily to Suzie Wong, Teresa developed with Suzie Wong the theme of Suzie Wong's being interested in an adult love life, as defined by the role of Suzie Wong. Teresa seemed to indicate that marriage was a rather dangerous thing and that one could be a lovely beautiful girl and grow up without marrying. I intervened to have Suzie Wong ask her whether it wasn't perhaps true that she liked to think of herself as a person who would never marry because of the hard fate of her mother as well as the decision of her aunt not to marry. Both seemed to believe that men were dangerous. Suzie Wong took this up with Teresa, who was trying to explain. I had Suzie Wong ask Teresa whether there would not always be a conflict even if one did not marry, that one would have to choose between adulthood and childhood anyway. At this point the situation became too dangerous for Teresa, even though she had Suzie Wong try to pose the question.

Putting pressure on Teresa via the puppet, which she handled herself, about the choice between childhood world and adult world, I also remarked that the puppet, that is, Suzie Wong, was from the world of the movies and Teresa was from the world of fantasies; I wondered how they would get along with an adult person who was mature. Teresa let Suzie Wong say that she knew of a man on television who had a puppet and that this man and the puppet talked to each other, and that was exactly what Teresa and Suzie Wong were doing. It was her way of saying, I thought, that what I was doing with Teresa was, in a way, a method of talking with the puppet and therefore she identified with that method and did the same thing with Suzie Wong. I said that I realized that there was such a man, after which the play deteriorated. It had become dangerous. Teresa became restless, seemed to look more disturbed, and suddenly apologized for having to go to the bathroom.

After she returned from the bathroom, the session proceeded in terms of "what should we talk about now?" She took up the question of what gift she might expect me to bring her for Christmas. I said that just as she was wondering about Christmas, I had been wondering about December 31, the date that she had set for herself when "things will have passed once and for all" (her reference to the promise to give up delusions, come New Year). Teresa wondered what sense there was to my wondering since I knew the answer anyway. The answer was that she would have passed things once and for all by that time. Actually she felt she was well by now. Nobody had helped her. I did not help her even though I was a wonderful doctor. She had helped herself completely and alone. She would simply have passed things once and for all by New Year's. She would be a different person, and that was that. I said I understood that, but I was wondering what kind of a different person she would be, because when one thing ends something else starts. What would come then? This question, of course, could not be answered and was deeply disturbing to Teresa; she tried to direct the conversation to something else, as if to say that she did not want to have that issue raised. Then she chose to take a piece of chewing gum and recognized the flavor; as the end of the hour had come, she said loudly, "So long," packed up all her books, and took her leave.

I shall again present the transcript of the recorded 130th hour, but only the part that deals with the Suzie Wong puppet episode.

E.: Your time is running out, you told me you will have it passed once and for all by December 31.

T.: Well, you know that I'm doing it right now, you've seen me do it these days. (Changes voice): Hello, my name is Suzie Wong.

E.: Suzie Wong, I'm glad to meet you, you are one of those dolls that the boys like.

T. (Suzie's voice): Oh, thank you

E.: Have you seen the movie, T.?

T.: The movie?

E.: Suzie Wong.

T.: No, oh yah, it was a movie, yah.

E.: Yes, there was a movie about Suzie Wong.

T.: Oh yah, Suzie Wong.

E.: Did you see that?

T.: No, I saw it, I saw parts of the movie in a magazine, yah, I saw pictures of the movies in a magazine, I saw Suzie Wong, she . . .

E.: She's quite a girl, that Suzie Wong.

T.: Is she pretty anyway?

E.: A very pretty girl.

T.: Is she beautiful?

E.: Yes. She's a Chinese girl, you know.

T.: But is she beautiful?

E.: I think so, yes. She lives in Hong Kong in that story. A Chinese town.

T.: See, the world is full of pretty girls, see how many pretty girls there is in the world? There's too many pretty girls, yeh?

E.: That's right, some are real girls and some are just movie projections.

T.: Yah, like this one is a doll, kind of. . . .

E.: A puppet.

T.: A little puppet. (Changes voice:) Hello, hello, hello. My name is Suzie Wong.

E.: Glad to meet you, Suzie Wong.

T.: No. (Changes voice, screams:) Hi!!

E.: Hi, Suzie.

T. (Suzie's voice): Hi!!!

E.: Suzie, what's new?

T. (Suzie's voice): What's new? Well (sings), wake up, Little Suzie, wake up in the morning, wake up, Little Suzie, wake up in the morning . . . wake up . . .

E.: Yes, wake up, Suzie.

T. (Continues with song, unaware of Dr. E.'s interruption; giggles): Isn't she cute?

E.: Sounds like Suzie wants to keep on dreaming.

T. (Giggles, pays no attention to Dr. E.): What's your name, Suzie? (Suzie's voice:) Suzie, that's my name, Suzie Wong, haven't you seen me in the great picture, Suzie Wong? (T.:) No. (Suzie:) Well, when they give the picture, I'll tell you and you can go and see me, okay? (T.:) Okay. I promise. (Suzie:) You promise you'll go? (T.:) Yeh. (Suzie:) Or if not I won't tell you. (T.:) I promise you I'll see you. (Suzie:) Okay. Then, then, then I can tell you. Whenever they get it, they start getting it, I'll tell you where they give it and you can go and see it. (T.:) Okay.

E.: Suzie?

T. (Suzie): Yes?

E.: What kind of picture is there about Suzie Wong?

T. (Suzie): Well, it's about a Jap . . . Chinese girl, she's a very pretty girl, and she acts very well. It's a story of her, see? She falls in love, she finds many men in the story, she dances in that story and she sings, and you know what Japanese girls do, you know, that's the story.

E.: What do they do?

T. (Suzie): Well, they sort of do what American girls do, only that in their type they also kiss boys, they fall in love, they sing, they dance.

E.: Exactly. These Japanese girls do just like our American girls do.

T. (Suzie): That's right, that's what they do, exactly. So what's the big idea? What's the big idea, Curlie? What's the big idea, what's the big idea? (Giggles; her own voice:) What's the big idea? What's the big idea, so what's the big idea?

E.: Well, the big idea is that Suzie Wong is interested in boys.

T.: Are you? (Suzie:) Uh huh. And I have many loves. (T.:) You know, Suzie has many loves in that picture, didn't she? All the boys used to see her and just fall in love with her because she was so lovely that they couldn't resist her. She couldn't resist them either, because she just liked to have so many loves.

E.: That was one of her troubles, that she couldn't resist.

T. (Suzie): Yah, yah, naturally.

E.: So that was the tough thing with Suzie Wong.

T. (Suzie): Uh uh, that's right. (T.:) See, Suzie Wong liked to be kissed by boys and liked to have them as sweethearts. She, she, she even liked, they liked to date her and take her out for dates and all that stuff, and all those things, you know. Oh, look at the little ball, oh, this is a little goat, oh, it's a dog, yah, it's a German shepherd.

E.: It's a war dog.

T.: Yeh, it's a beautiful . . . (Changes voice:) Hello, hello, beautiful, beautiful, you heard what Suzie Wong said: Beautiful Suzie Wong, she's a beautiful gal, you should go and see the beautiful Suzie Wong in her picture, you know, beautiful, beautiful, beautiful Suzie Wong. (Sings:) Cuddle up a little. (Deep sigh:) You should see Suzie Wong, believe me, she's a precious child on earth. No matter how many beautiful girls in this world there could exist, but she's one of the most beautiful, Suzie Wong, so why don't you go and try and see her? See the angel, Suzie Wong, in her great picture Suzie Wong.

E.: Is Suzie Wong an angel?

T. (Suzie): Well, that's how beautiful she is, dear. I said she's one of the most . . .

E.: Well, but then she was running around . . .

T. (Interrupts): Like, she's not the only beautiful, dear, this gal here is beautiful too, the one you're seeing, hah?

E.: Who's beautiful?

T.: Well, T., isn't she beautiful?

E.: Oh, T. too?

T. (Suzie): Well, aren't you seeing her, don't you think she's beautiful? Or don't tell me she's ugly?

E.: Oh, is she also one of those girls who likes all the boys?

T. (Suzie): Well, let's see, I'll ask her. Do you like boys? (T.:) Sure.

Sure, I do, I didn't used to like boys, but I do. I'm like any other girl is, so what's something different about me? (Suzie:) Well, you have loves? (T.:) No, I had one when I was a little girl, I had many loves, you know, the little boys used to go lalala, bother me too much. (Suzie:) Well, do you like to have loves, would you like to have loves? (T.:) Would I like to have loves? Uh huh. Well, sure, all the loves I . . . no . . . I'd rather not get married. I just want to be without marriage, I want to live my life alone. (Suzie:) You wouldn't like to get married when you grow older?
E. *(Interrupts):* Who is that, Suzie Wong or T.?
T.: *No, she is talking to me. (Suzie:) You mean you wouldn't like to get married? (T.:) No, no, uh uh. I want to live my own life happy when I grow older. (Suzie:) Really? (T.:) Yah, I don't want to get married, if you get married you get into trouble, that's all, your husband later doesn't love you, he just fooled you, you have to be sure whom you marry first anyway. (Suzie:) Oh yah, that's right. (T.:) But Suzie Wong got married at the end of the picture, I think, I don't remember.*
E.: Suzie, Suzie.
T. *(Suzie):* Yeh?
E.: *Tell T. that the reason she doesn't want to marry is because she thinks her aunt feels it's wiser not to marry, and not to have trouble, like Mama.*
T.: *'Cause what?*
E.: Suzie, tell T. that the reason she, T., doesn't want to marry is because she thinks her mummy had trouble getting married and her aunt thinks it's wiser not to marry.
T. *(Suzie):* See, dear? *(Explains to T. in Spanish:) Your mommy got into trouble, you heard me? Your mama got into trouble when she got married. (T.:) Well, well, yah, see? (Suzie:) Well, tell me about it, I don't understand. (T.:) Well, you see, Suzie, when my mother got married she was a very young girl, she was about nineteen or twenty and she was very beautiful, and when she got married she got into trouble, see? (Suzie:) She got into trouble? (T.:) Yeh, she got into trouble. See, the first thing that happened was . . . was . . . see, the first thing that happened was . . . she . . . (Suzie:) Yah, she what? (T.:) Well, she, uh, she, uh, well, uh, she just got into some trouble, see. (Suzie:) Oh. (T.:) She didn't, she just got married because she wanted to be a movie star, see, and I don't know how the trouble came but it just came. See, when she married my father he was a millionaire, like "The Millionaire" on the program on TV, and she thought that he would make her a movie star, see, like Rita Hayworth, but it didn't happen that way, because my mother didn't turn out to be like a movie star, like Rita Hayworth is one of her favorite movie stars, she always talks about Rita Hayworth. Rita Hayworth married this guy, she divorced this other one and now she's gonna get married again, she's the most beautifulest of Hollywood and who knows what? (Giggles:) Well, see, it became upside down, the world of Suzie Wong. (Suzie:) Gee, oh goodness, well, yah, things like that happen, oh yes. But with you I don't*

think it will happen, you're very lucky, you know, and you can get married any time you wish when you get older. Not when you're too young, you know, right now you're a young kid, you know, but when you grow older, you'll be a woman, then you can find yourself a nice guy and marry him, you know like this song (sings): "I was born as others in August, I was born as Blueberry pie, lalalalalala, I'm in love with a wonderful guy." You know, I was in love with a wonderful guy in my picture, and I called him "Candy." (Sings:) "Candy, I call my sugar Candy, 'cause he's as sweet as candy, and he's my candy dear. He treats me handy, my little sugar candy, 'cause he's as sweet as candy, and he's my candy dear."

E.: Suzie?

T. (Suzie): Yes?

E.: Suzie, I want to ask you something. But why would you want to tell T. to marry some day when she's scared of it?

T. (Suzie): To marry some day? Well, it isn't that she's scared, yes, she is scared of getting married, because she's afraid that her husband might then not really love her, that he might just have fooled her, see?

E.: Yah, but more than that, Suzie, haven't you heard, didn't T. ever tell you that she sometimes thinks that it's better to stay a little girl than to grow up and work hard to become an adult person?

T. (Suzie): Well, let's see, let's see, let's see. Well, I guess, I don't know, I don't know, I don't know, I don't know what's going on.

E.: Don't you think we should try to find out, Suzie?

T. (Suzie): Yes, I think so, why not?

E.: You think we could find out?

T. (Suzie): Yah, any time.

E.: Why don't you ask her? Go ask her.

T. (Suzie): Yah? What shall I ask her?

E.: Suzie, ask her why she thinks it's hard to grow up.

T. (Suzie): Well, why do you think it's hard to grow up anyway? (T.:) Well, because when you grow up . . . it isn't hard to grow up, that I think it's easy to grow up, you just want to grow up and that's all. You want to get married and you can get married, if you don't want to get married you don't have to get married, when you're old, no matter, look, there's a million beautiful girls in this world that don't get married. How beautiful they are, I believe there's more beautiful girls that are more beautiful than Elizabeth Taylor or Rita Hayworth, and they would never get married, they would always be living their own lives, living without marriage or nothing and they wouldn't even have boy friends. I'll bet all the boy friends in the world would look at them, but they wouldn't mind getting married and they would never get married. Well, why can't I be that one? (Suzie:) Well, that's true.

E.: But Suzie, tell T. that even if one doesn't marry one could still grow up to be an adult person rather than a child.

T. (Suzie): Well, that's right, you could grow up to be an adult person rather than a child, you heard, dear. (T.:) Yah, that's right.

E.: What does T. think about that?

T. (Suzie): Well, what do you think about that? (T.:) Well, I think about that . . . well, what do you . . . I think about that, well . . . (Suzie:) Well, you see, I guess T. and I are friends, we became good pals for one? Right now, we're good pals, I guess, aren't we? (T.:) Yah, we're good pals.

E.: Who are good pals?

T. (Suzie): Well, me and T., we're good pals.

E.: Oh, Suzie, you and T. are good pals.

T. (Suzie): Yah, we're good friends. We became friends. Aren't we good friends? (T.:) Yah. (Suzie:) Yah, I guess we are, we're good pals, we're very good palsy-walsies.

E.: Well, Suzie, you're from the movies, that is, really from fantasy-land, and T. is from the childhood land, no wonder you're good friends.

T. (Suzie): Well, yah.

E.: How would the two of you get along with someone who is from the adult world?

T. (Suzie): Well, I'll give you an example. Like, have you ever heard of this program on TV of this guy that has this doll and he talks to this doll? He's a show guy on, on the show he comes on with this doll that he makes talk to him.

E.: A puppet, yes, he works with a puppet.

T.: That's right, they're pals, no?

E.: Yes.

T.: That's the same, she and I are pals the same way, so what's wrong with that, it's just a little . . .

E. (Interrupts): Nothing, it's excellent, excellent. But I was just wondering how the two of you would get along with someone who is . . .

T. (Suzie): Well, I face reality, see, as she does, and she faces fantasy sort of a little, as I do, see? But we, we face reality more than fantasy, because we think it's best of all, that it's the better thing to do, see?

E.: Suzie? When will you go to school?

T. (Suzie): When will I go to school? Well . . .

E.: You haven't finished high school yet.

T. (Suzie): Well, well, uh, well, now I'm going to school, I mean I'm not going to school.

E.: Does T. go to school?

T. (Suzie): Well, do you go to high school? (T.:) No, I just go to school. I'm very back in my studies, that's why.

E.: Are you back in your studies?

T.: Well, why do you think I'm going to this school, to catch up, this school helps you catch up, so that then you can start going to high school, see?

E.: You think you might catch up?

T.: Sure I will. Naturally, Western Air Lines, the only way to fly.
E.: Where does it say that? Where does it say Western Air Lines?
T.: Well, have you ever heard of that owl?
E.: What?
T.: Well, have you ever heard of that bird that passes flying in an airplane
on TV and says, "Naturally, Western Air Lines, the only way to fly."

The conflict and the modes of expression in this particular play interview are very much the same as in the hour when the puppet represented
Liz the bunny. Again we find that the voices of interpretation, of reflection,
and of adult demands toward growth are vested in the puppet. The struggle
is again between three people, as it were, the therapist and Teresa, and
the link between them, the puppet, who represents partly the introjected
therapist and partly the transitional object, the extroject, as it were.
Basically the conflict again involves an attempt to establish an object
relationship, a struggle against the object, against the forces of growing
up, and at the same time a kind of progression in terms of the playing
out of normality.

The struggle again is a one-sided one; when the therapist starts to
push toward action, tries to induce the patient to make some form of
commitment, he again loses the struggle, and it becomes quite clear that
it is still impossible for the patient to choose the actual realistic task.
Although the therapist presented the choice as a question for the puppet
to put to the patient, it is experienced as a frightening injunction.

However, there are also important differences between these two
interviews. In the first puppet hour the theme is the struggle against
orality, while the second puppet hour represents the conflicts between
impulse and delay on a higher pseudo-phallic level. The bunny Liz, a
compromise between the overeating animal and the beautiful tempting
movie actress, now turns into Suzie Wong. The eating animal now is a
tempting man-eating lover of the screen. Suzie Wong introduces more
openly the choice of the sexual partner, the temptation of adult sexuality.
Liz, the bunny, contains more features of the hospitalized schizophrenic
mother, once a beautiful aspirant for movie stardom, while Suzie Wong
presents the features of the unmarried aunt who plays with adult sexual
roles but cannot maintain them. Both female figures thus offer negative
models for identification, although the image of the uncontrollable mother
arouses more fear than that of the aunt, who in spite of her many difficulties has some sustaining strength.[10]

The interplay now is between Suzie Wong, who invites Teresa to
look at boys, to think of marriage, to think of children, and Teresa, who
defends herself against temptation by pointing out that one could well

grow up without making this choice which is so fraught with dangers. She has Suzie Wong explain to her or, rather, to the therapist, the reasons in the history of the patient which might make her refusal to choose love and marriage understandable and rational.

When the therapist intervenes, we find that the pressure becomes too great. While he permits Teresa to take the stand she does, he wonders whether there isn't a way of growing up without the choices that Suzie Wong suggests and he refers to Teresa's schoolwork. This suddenly turns the play into a regressive move; the therapist's comment whether Teresa could catch up with her schoolwork is countered by the patient's telling remark that surely she would catch up: "Naturally, Western Air Lines, the only way to fly."

The nature of the puppet has changed somewhat in those last eight months. It must be realized that the puppet is but a slave of the illness, attains only temporarily some form of independence, fluctuates from toy to the projection of the introject, to the function of a transitional object, and a bridge to the real object of the therapist. One might also suggest that one sees the growth of an ego, a living link between the illness and the therapist, but an ego that is still weak, in the service of the id, and not differentiated from it.

During the following three months of treatment further changes, although of a subtle nature, make one feel that the playing with normality might move toward a point at which it might become genuine action, albeit frequently disturbed by more primitive maneuvers of powerful acting out as well as play acting.

The material raises the question whether one can expect to help such patients to move from play to action. Play is, of course, psychic work which can lead to the development of new functions in the ego organization and allow such patients to make a new and different commitment. On the other hand, one can only push people toward a choice when they have a capacity for choice. The material offers examples of a reintegrative process which leads toward the crossroad of choice. This example of psychotic puppet play can be considered to be a version of psychotic obsessionalism; its constructive purpose is to ward off destructive impulsivity on the part of the feared internal object which is experienced at times as the danger that lies in the external world and is confused at times with the angry reactions provoked in the environment,[11] both tending to push the child from the psychotic world of play into a world of age-appropriate action.

One may well say that the psychotherapist, as well as he who takes care of such children, must bear with the nature of the puppet. The puppet not only is a transitional link but is in part the therapist himself. Can he give up the fantasy of power and allow himself to be for a while a helpless puppet who is manipulated by the forces of illness? Patients have their own ways of allowing the puppet to become alive. As they can allow the psychotherapist to become a real person rather than a fragmented part of their delusional system, they develop a stronger ego and self-organization in order to meet the challenge of objective reality.

When this challenge is met and recovery has been obtained, both patient and therapist may look back at the process that has taken place and may then feel identified with Collodi's statement at the end of *The Adventures of Pinocchio:* "After a long, long look, Pinocchio said to himself with great content: 'How ridiculous I was as the marionette! And how happy I am now that I have become a real boy!'"

REFERENCES

[1] Waelder, R. The psychoanalytic theory of play, Psychoanal. Quart. 2:208, 1933.

[2] Mahler, M. S. On child psychosis and schizophrenia: autistic and symbiotic infantile positions, Psychoanal. Stud. Child, 7:286, 1952; ———— and Gosliner, B., On symbiotic child psychosis: genetic, dynamic and restitutive aspects, Psychoanal. Stud. Child, 10:195, 1955.

[3] Freud, S. Formulations regarding the two principles in mental functioning, Collected Papers, London, Hogarth Press, 1948, pp. 4, 13.

[4] Rambert, M. L. Children in Conflict. New York, International Universities Press, 1949.

[5] Erikson, E. H. Studies in the interpretation of play: 1. Clinical observation of play disruption in young children, Genet. Psychol. Monogr., 22:557, 1940.

[6] Ekstein, R., and Meyer, M. M. Distancing devices in childhood schizophrenia and allied conditions: quantitative and qualitative aspects of "distancing" in the psychotherapeutic process, Psychol. Rev., 9:145, 1961.

[7] For different opinions of such methods, see Melanie Klein, Narrative of a Child Analysis, New York, Basic Books, 1961, p. 11; David Shakow, Psychoanalytic education of behavioral and social scientists for research, *in* Science and Psychoanalysis, J. Masserman, New York, Grune & Stratton, 1962, p. 146; Kenneth Colby, An Introduction to Psychoanalytic Research, New York, Basic Books, 1960, p. 28.

[8] Cain, A. C. On "Playing Crazy" and Identity Problems in Some Borderline and Psychotic Children, unpublished.

[9] Schlesinger, H. (1964) A Contribution to a Theory of Promising: I: Primary and Secondary Promising, unpublished.

[10] Ekstein, R. The parent turning into the sibling, Amer. J. Orthopsychiat., 33:518, 1963.

[11] Ibid.

13

PLEASURE AND REALITY, PLAY
AND WORK, THOUGHT AND ACTION

Reality is an opportunity before it is a hindrance.
CHARLOTTE BÜHLER

To play with ideas is to think through play, a form of trial action which reconstructs the past in order to prepare for the future. I will be playful in the sense that I will work with and on ideas that are not as yet meant to be a firm commitment but rather are trial thoughts concerning the historical development of certain ideas which have given rise to difficulties.

Charlotte Bühler [1] has frequently contended that the Freudian concept of reality was a negative one, and that she prefers to look at reality as a positive factor. She suggests that the active, outgoing baby "anticipates" a "positive reality," that is, one in which he can operate expansively, while the passive, more withdrawing infant "anticipates" a "negative reality," that is, one which is frightening and potentially harmful. She speaks of Erik Erikson's basic trust as "an inner condition implying a receptiveness and a looking forward to good things to come, things that would enhance the baby's existence, would be upbuilding . . ."

These seemingly contradicting comments all remain on a phenomenological level, but they stimulate thinking on the level of metapsychology as well. It is not sufficient to explain the discrepancy by saying that the psychoanalyst's concept of reality derives from consideration of psychopathology, while Charlotte Bühler's concept of reality derives from the field of education and prevention.

The negative connotations of reality to patients are particularly impressive if we concern ourselves with how the psychotherapeutic process can be utilized in order to help a psychotic patient move from the primary-process level of functioning to a secondary-process adaptation in such a way that there is movement in terms of the level of thinking which can also be translated into an appropriate act.

I will refer to clinical data which I have already partially discussed. In this context, Teresa acts out her dilemma somewhat like this: Upon entering, she wants to have the therapist confirm that her dress is pretty and that she is good-looking. After he confirms this, she wonders whether he thinks that she looks as beautiful as Snow White. Before he even answers, she, not needing his response but describing to him her own, continues on the theme and speaks about the beauty of Snow White, with whom she now identifies. She speaks about Snow White's hair, black as ebony, and her skin, as white as snow, and how the prince would come to kiss her and awaken her and bring her to his castle. She then gets lost in this apparent transference fantasy, but, unlike a hysterical patient who may direct fantasy about the erotic wishes she has toward the therapist or a real displacement figure, she becomes involved in the love relationship between the prince and Snow White. She simply used the therapist, not as an object around whom to weave fantasies which are to represent the transference situation, but rather for the projection of an introject around whom she develops the imaginary love relationship in which she herself assumes the role of another fantasied introject. One might well ask why it is easier for Teresa to be in love with the introject of the therapist than to permit herself to cathect the actual object. Indeed, nonadaptive fantasy seems always more pleasant to her than the kind of fantasy that would attempt to make something positive out of her reality.

One might state the technical problem with certain borderline and psychotic patients metaphorically if one were to ask how one could get Alice back from Wonderland and into the living-room, not merely as a temporary guest, but as a permanent resident in this world rather than in her Wonderland. In the treatment of these patients the therapist must become a visitor in their Wonderland, their realm of fantasy. It is as if he must acquire a temporary visa to a foreign country in which he momentarily suspends judgment and the language of his own world, all the while knowing that he has a round-trip ticket back from the Wonderland into the living-room, the realm of reality, as it were.

Similarly, such patients can only be persuaded to visit in the living-room if they have the security of knowing that they, too, have a round-trip ticket which will enable them to go back into their Wonderland whenever they wish. They are more likely to remain, however, if they can find there replicas of their psychotic past—a past which is most of the time interwoven with and indistinguishable from the present and the future— a "Glass Menagerie" around which to weave past and current delusions. Since, however, the "remembered" psychotic past contains things which themselves are replicas of the normal world of the living-room, the problem is to help them to distinguish the real things from the replicas.

It is important to note that for these patients the present experience is but a forged re-edition of their past. That is, they treat reality as a dream and a dream or delusion as reality. And our goal is as if we wanted Alice to be able to look at a deck of cards and realize that what she saw in her dream was its replica. She is to discover that the Red Queen was a replica of the playing cards on the living-room table, rather than that the cards were a replica from Wonderland. We help her to discover who dreamed the dream, but at the same time we do not take away the dream; nor do we forbid the dream, if we wish to maintain the psychotherapeutic communication.

The issues which concern us, then, are the difficulties of getting Alice back into the living-room, and how we might theoretically conceptualize these problems. Alice seems to prefer the Wonderland to the living-room, and Teresa prefers the fantasies about Prince Charming to actual social life with her peers. She does not want to be deprived of the pleasures of her inner life and seems to be unable to perceive reality as a positive rather than a poisonous nutriment. We have learned that her "preference" is actually a symptom, an inability to use fantasy toward adaptation. Her "preference" is not a choice, but rather a compelling limitation, a consequence of current defects in her psychic organization.

In order to deal with these issues more satisfactorily it may be useful to explore and expand the theory of the development of normal secondary-process thinking. The *primary model of thought*, as discussed in *The Interpretation of Dreams*,[2] later elaborated on by Rapaport,[3] states in essence that thinking derives from delay, frustration, and postponement. Mounting drive tension, the absence of the drive object, is followed by the hallucinatory image of the drive object. This primary model is schematized by the picture of the baby at the breast who meets up with situations of delay which create frustration and lead to the baby's attempt to hallucinate the lost object. In this way the baby temporarily delays the panic of overwhelming frustration and maintains himself in a state of well-being and homeostasis which, however, cannot last and only temporarily postpones the panic.

The first stage in the development of thinking, therefore, is that of hallucinatory wish-fulfillment which develops as a consequence of delay. Like the dream, this hallucinatory wish-fulfillment has the function of delaying frustration, of postponing the "rude" awakening. Freud has characterized the dream as the guardian of sleep, or having the function of delaying awakening. It is, however, only possible to postpone the awakening for a little while, just as it is only possible for the baby to hallucinate the breast for a brief period.

In this primary model, therefore, thinking is conceptualized as developing as a consequence of delay which increases drive tension. A part of this tension is used for the cathexis of the hallucinatory image, and is a temporary safety valve for the baby; but for the psychotic patient it becomes a permanent substitute. The hallucinatory experience permits the baby to "solve" the task by himself in fantasy, although he achieves only a temporary solution. Nevertheless, the consequence of this delay leads to the development of an inner capacity which is the precursor of thinking and which can ultimately lead to more permanent solutions. This primary model of thought, a scientific myth of the genesis of thinking, stresses the importance of frustration in the development of this function. One is reminded of the story that is told about the autistic nonspeaking child whose mother has been unsuccessful in getting him to talk until the age of seven when, in order to cut his birthday cake, he suddenly turns to the mother and asks for a knife. When she asks him why he never spoke before, he suggests that he never needed to, since every one of his wishes had always been fulfilled instantly.

The problem in such a model, however, is that frustration is used to explain the development of psychopathology as well as creative, healthy functions, thus requiring the concepts of a positive trauma leading to creative solutions out of "blood, sweat, and tears," as it were; and of the negative trauma, leading to the experience of being overwhelmed. This dilemma was not always recognized and dealt with in early psychoanalytic literature. Frustration was described both as a mover toward growth as well as the creator of pathology. Such expediencies as speaking of the correct amount of frustration balanced by the correct amount of gratification have been necessary in order to deal with the issues. Thus this early model conceptualizes reality as essentially bad and frustrating, a necessary evil, somewhat similar to certain religions which describe life as a series of obstacles which, if successfully overcome, will lead to union with the Deity in Heaven, or to identification with one's analyst in a postambivalent genital utopia, the psychoanalytic heir of Paradise. Such a model seems to imply that the pleasure principle and the reality principle are at war with each other, like Eros and Thanatos, engaged in a cold war at best, and that the most one can hope for is a truce or armistice, a not-so-peaceful coexistence.

In Freud's early clinical writings concerning the etiology of hysteria, he struggled with the notion of the sexual trauma, the early sexual seduction or attempt at seduction of the patient during his childhood by the parent of the opposite sex. Early overpowering instinctual stimulation, the actual sexual trauma, was seen as the cause of the later symptom. Freud soon realized that it was not the actual sexual trauma that the patient recalled, but rather a fantasy during childhood. This fantasy frequently could not be differentiated from an actual event in reality, and might stem from a period of thinking in which the boundaries between fantasy and reality could not be clearly maintained, especially not in later recollection. Freud thus moved away from genetic interpretation of psychic development, which seemed to base explanations on external events, to one in which the inner preparedness, the available capacity to think on adequate levels, the predisposition in the growing child, was seen as equally important.

Freud slowly moved toward a conception of the genesis of psychic structure as growing out of the resolutions of the conflicts between the instinctual forces and the growing superego—the psychic representation of parental demands and ideals—as well as deriving from the contributions of available predispositions in the total psychic matrix from which ego functions will develop.

Growth of the capacity for postponement was primarily seen by Freud in terms of parental frustration and injunction, expressed as an "if-then" relationship: "If you will wait, then you will get the treat." The giving up of the pleasure principle and its substitution through the reality principle was sometimes described almost as if the child were to be told not to do "it" now, but to delay "it" and eventually he will be allowed to do it. "Being allowed to do it" was somehow equated with all the fantasied utopian gratifications that the child ascribes to the prerogative of the parent. This, of course, never turned out to be quite that way, since rules never stop, at least not in this life. In the clinical literature, then and now, external rules and internal capacities were frequently not clearly differentiated. The reality principle was simply seen as a consequence of frustration, of imposed delay which slowly leads to internalization and brings about a modification, seemingly a giving up of the early paradise of the pleasure principle which knows no delay. Now the reward for this paradise lost is the achievement of the capacities to judge the appropriate moment and methods to bring about the gratification of paradise regained in the future. It is as if we were to give up instant gratification, the mark of the pleasure principle, and identify with the injunction that we are to earn our bread by the sweat of our brow.

Freud then made a tremendous step forward which is expressed most clearly in "*Formulations regarding the Two Principles of Mental Functioning.*"[4] In this paper he clearly stated and elaborated that the early misunderstanding, which had seen the pleasure principle as a quasi-amoral and the reality principle as a quasi-moral principle, was obviated. These principles were not to be seen as beginning- and end-points of certain external educational events which lead to developmental changes that move from gratified pleasure via frustrating delay to reality adjustment.

Instead, he speaks about these principles as capacities for operations within the psychic apparatus. Delay is not a forced compromise, but rather a free choice, based on judgment, leading to succesful solutions of a task. The baby is unable to choose such delay, since he has not as yet developed this capacity. Of him we may say that he cannot as yet truly act, since an act is based on the capacity for delay, choice, and judgment. We may say of him that he does not act, but rather that he "impulses."

At that stage we might perhaps better speak of the "panic principle" than of the pleasure principle. The infant has only the alternative of panic or "psychosis" when frustrated; that is, he either panics or postpones the panic through hallucinating the object. But this hallucinatory experience cannot last long, and itself develops into panic.

The notions of the pleasure principle and the reality principle are metaphoric means of formulating a concept which refers to the inner psychic state of mind; they describe stages of mental functioning. They are meant to be metapsychological concepts describing the existing mental apparatus, which we now conceptualize as a hierarchy of psychic organizations. Therefore, one may speak of many principles of mental functioning which can be conceptualized as moving along a continuum from the primary process, where the pleasure principle rules, through the secondary process, when the reality principle governs and where there is the choice for delay, the choice of rational action. The capacity for delay, however, is not in itself a successful solution for all tasks. I am reminded here of Hamlet, who seemingly had only the capacity for delay, rather than a preparation for action. If Hamlet were a psychotic obsessional, thinking for him would be not only a thought, it would be equivalent to action as well.

This primary model of thought is used in spite of our clinical sophistication which comprehends, of course, that frustration alone would destroy rather than promote the growth of the mental apparatus. We need only to think of Spitz's contributions on "Hospitalism" [5, 6] and anaclitic depression [7] in order to remind ourselves that our theorizing never denied the importance of gratification at the appropriate time and in appropriate amounts. Actually, the model discussed implicitly calls upon the importance of gratification for the development of the psychic apparatus, but does not elaborate on its role explicitly.

I should like now to develop the notion of the *secondary model of thinking*, in which the role of gratification and success is spelled out more clearly. This secondary model shows more clearly that frustration is but one of the paths to be traveled from the primary to the secondary process of thinking. The primary model has made use of the infant-breast situation and utilizes the actual observation of the mother-child nursing experience.

Another part of this mother-child nursing experience may serve as a prototype experience in schematizing the secondary model.

There is a period after gratification has been achieved through sucking but before the infant falls into the state of satiation described by Christian Morgenstern's poetic allusion, "Selig lächelnd wie ein satter Säugling," when the satisfied baby starts to play with the nipple. He pushes the nipple out, searches for it again, and takes it back, until finally he either falls asleep, or the mother breaks up the game and the play.

I should like to refer to this play as afterplay, an epilogue, and discuss its special function in the total nursing situation. The hallucinatory image of the sucking of the breast could be referred to as foreplay, the prologue, being followed by the actual act of gratification, the latter being followed by the afterplay, the baby's playing with the nipple. In this situation the baby [8] weaves fantasies around an external object, namely the nipple, which just a little earlier has served the purpose of direct gratification. Before the breast comes, during the period of frustration, the infant hallucinates the breast; and this anticipatory fantasy enables him to delay the panic that would ensue, until his hunger cry, experienced by the mother as signal communication, leads to gratification. After the gratification he plays with the nipple, and we characterize this play (as well as the foreplay) as a kind of acting out—that is, as trial thinking which serves a psychic function.

The pushing out and taking in of the nipple recalls Freud's description of the play which a little boy of one and a half years had invented.[9] This good little boy, who was greatly attached to his mother,

had an occasional disturbing habit of taking any small objects he could get hold of and throwing them away from him into a corner, under the bed, and so on, so that hunting for his toys and picking them up was often quite a business. As he did this he gave vent to a loud, long drawn-out "o-o-o-o," accompanied by an expression of interest and satisfaction. His mother and the writer of the present account were agreed in thinking that this was not a mere interjection, but represented the German word "fort" ["gone"].

Later Freud added another observation. He describes the child as having a wooden reel with a piece of string tied round it. It never occurred to him to pull it along the floor behind him, for instance, and play at its being a carriage. What he did was to hold the reel by the string and very skillfully throw it over the edge of his curtained crib, so that it disappeared into it, at the same time uttering his expressive "o-o-o-o." He then pulled the reel out of the crib again by the string and hailed its appearance with a joyful "da" ["there"]. This, then, was the complete game—disappearance and return. As a rule one witnessed only its first act, which was repeated untiringly as a game in itself, though there is no doubt that the greater pleasure was attached to the second act.

Freud interpreted the game as the child's first great cultural achievement, since it enabled the child to achieve the necessary mastery to make the instinctual renunciation of allowing his mother to go away without protesting. In this paper, *Beyond the Pleasure Principle*, Freud wondered why the child would repeat this distressing experience, since this game did not seem to fit in with the pleasure principle. It was here that Freud discussed the relationship between the compulsion to repeat the painful act, and the notion of the death instinct. This issue of separation, the giving up of the object, and the attempt to regain it, has been considered, of course, a tremendously important issue and has led to a variety of theoretical innovations, such as Rank's [10] overemphasis on a Freudian observation concerning the trauma of separation at birth.

Freud's example, the separation from the mother, whether it be later in life or whether it be the "trauma of birth," seems to focus on renunciation, on frustration, on giving up.

The present example, the child's behavior during the afterplay, the separation from the nipple and the attempt to regain it, is brought about not by frustration but by gratification and by the child's active withdrawal. The question then arises: If the needs of the child have been met, why then is there the need to play with fantasies following the successful act of sucking? That is, what is the psychic function of the playful taking the nipple in and out of the mouth after it has served the function of gratification? One suggestion is that the child actually has had only nutritional gratification and that the oral sexual gratification was not yet completed, similar to thumb-sucking after and beyond the act of nursing. Another way of interpreting the "afterplay" goes beyond its instinctual function.

This play permits the baby once more to weave fantasies around the external object; moreover it can also be considered essentially as a form of acting out—that is, of trial thinking by means of which the baby tries to recall the past. Since the baby cannot recall in thoughts, he recalls in the act. His recalling is the kind one can speak of as arising from an undifferentiated matrix in which recollection through thought and recollection through the act are fused. Since the baby has no psychic differentiation of structure permitting thinking, we postulate that he can remember the past only through the act. We conceptualize, therefore, the "afterplay" with the nipple as a recounting of his blessings, as it were, through a play repetition of the earlier rooting, sucking, and pushing out of the nipple. This play on the part of the infant can be conceptualized as an attempt to remember the past, to link this past with the present, somehow in the manner that we celebrate Thanksgiving. This is the baby's first thanksgiving, by means of which he remembers what work it took him to come to the point of feasting. This play can also be conceptualized as an adaptive device, as serving him as a preparation for next time, to prepare for the future through repetition, and thus reinforces the means-end relationship between past pleasures and future work. Rather than speaking now about the compulsion to repeat, we speak about rhythmic, spontaneous repetition in which, instead of a compulsion to repeat, which is its pathological equivalent, the baby's afterplay has turned into adaptive behavior.

The hidden trial thought behind the breast play is the equivalent of a new trial action (the first trial action being the foreplay in the form of hallucinatory imagery), but this time developed out of success and gratification rather than out of frustration. The baby's accomplishment of having successfully achieved gratification will also develop a capacity to let go. Anxious people, those who dread separation, have the underlying feeling that they will never get back to the source of gratification and that whatever will come will spell failure for them. The baby, through this afterplay, remembers the successful struggle, and therefore is more willing to prepare for the future. This play is an adaptive effort which prepares for many more happy returns. It links the pleasure of the past and the work necessary to get such pleasure. In this way, the pleasure associated with successful mastery becomes associated with the functioning necessary to obtain pleasure in the future.

It could be said that the baby works first for milk, or love, and eventually learns to love his work, to milk his work, as it were, for love and pleasure.

A pathological outcome of the nursing experience could be thought of as leading to the compulsion to repeat the unsuccessful foreplay. If there was only or primarily frustration, this could be the origin of symptom formation. If there was a successful solution, it could lead to the development of the love for rhythmic repetition, a kind of recollection of the successful past, the development of what Karl Bühler has called *Funktionslust*.[11]

A synthesis of the primary model of thought with the secondary suggests a model of mental functioning which will give equal weight to the primary and the secondary process, as well as a *tertiary process* which links up thinking with action. These considerations have been furthered by Erikson's discussion of reality, and actuality,[12] which seems to suggest

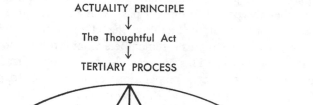

THE MODEL OF MENTAL FUNCTIONING

ACTUALITY PRINCIPLE
↓
The Thoughtful Act
↓
TERTIARY PROCESS

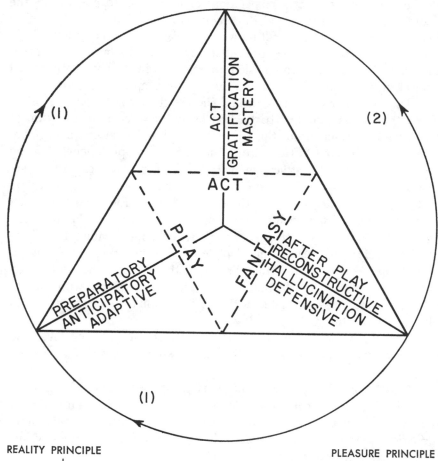

ACT

GRATIFICATION MASTERY

ACT

PLAY

FANTASY

PREPARATORY
ANTICIPATORY
ADAPTIVE

AFTER PLAY
RECONSTRUCTIVE
HALLUCINATION
DEFENSIVE

(1)

(2)

(1)

REALITY PRINCIPLE
↓
The Actless Thought
↓
SECONDARY PROCESS

PLEASURE PRINCIPLE
↓
The Thoughtless Act-impulse
↓
PRIMARY PROCESS

(1) Normal Process: clockwise
(2) Psychotic Process: counter clockwise

an adaptive point of view in which past and future are related to the ego's functioning at any given time as acutely relevant to a special task in reality. We are suggesting that the reality principle to which we previously referred refers both to a level of thinking and to a level of acting—that is, to the ability to act upon reality—which is separate from the ability to think about reality. Perhaps a graphic illustration of the model of mental functioning will serve to make the issues clearer as well as to sum up the discussion.

The three end points of the equilateral triangle within the circle represent the *pleasure principle*, the *reality principle*, and the *actuality principle*. The pleasure principle, at the bottom right, refers to a way of thinking which does not allow for delay, where the *impulse* is but a *thoughtless act* and where the rules of "thinking" or, rather, "impulsing" are under the domination of the need for instant gratification.

At the left bottom angle, we picture the *reality principle*, which refers to a way of thinking in which there is available the capacity for delay, the capacity for the *actless thought*, and where the rules of thinking follow reality testing.

At the top angle, we picture the *actuality principle*, the capacity of the psychic organization to act upon the thought, so that one can change oneself or the environment. This capacity permits turning the thought, which, according to Freud, is trial action, into a *thoughtful act*.

If play or action activity is located at the mid-point of the triangle, three components of play, dominant in varying degrees and at varying times, may be described.

One: The hallucinatory image of the breast situation is considered as *foreplay*, as the fantasy deriving out of frustration, but in the service of delay by means of primitive "anticipation" of the future. Repeated frustration would lead to pathological forms of the compulsion to repeat.

Two: In this phase of actual gratification, *play* and *work* are undifferentiated. The infant's work leads to satiation. The "pleasure principle" of the baby, his thoughtless act, supported by the thinking of the mother, his auxiliary ego, is his kind of actuality principle. Only later will he move from reacting from the need for immediate gratification via the secondary process to the thoughtful act. At present, the mother represents this intermediary link.

Three: The third kind of play, the *afterplay*, is the assertion through the play that the source of gratification did come and will come again. Out of the act of gratification the child develops a kind of play, recollecting the successful past which leads him to the development of the adaptive capacity to prepare for the future by means of recapitulation and repetition, which does not represent the compulsion to repeat, but *rhythmic repetition* which leads to *Funktionslust.*

In normal development, the basic rhythm of mental functioning would lead from the pleasure principle to the reality principle and to the actuality principle. Primary-process thinking would develop toward secondary-process thinking and lead to the thoughtful act. Conceiving of this rhythm as clockwise, the circle in the diagram presents the cycle of the thought and action process.

Patients such as Teresa are occasionally dominated by the primary process, prefer to live in a world of fantasy, and only occasionally do they achieve secondary-process functions. In her case, the price for nonpsychotic functioning is infantile regression. But even when she uses secondary-process thinking, and indicates judgment and the capacity to test reality, she cannot act upon her thoughts. It is as if she were capable of judging, but not of living up to her judgment. There is a constant pulling away from actions and back into a "way of life" where the primary process rules.

In Teresa's history there is much clinical evidence which would indicate that early experiences were primarily in the shadow of frustration and rarely in the light of success. Unfortunately, the basic traumatic experience of her early life does not fully account for her counter-clockwise movements which turn the rhythm of normal mental functioning into the compulsion to repeat, an expression of severe pathology.

As George Santayana wrote, "Those who cannot remember the past are condemned to repeat it." The nature of this repetition, however, should not be considered static and destructive, but rather the expression of the relationship of man to himself. He who has accessible to him reality principle, pleasure principle, and actuality principle will remember the past as well as spontaneously repeat aspects of it. The repetition will not be a compulsion; it will be adaptive. Old pleasures will be restored, though on a higher level. Each repetition will serve the recollection of the past, as well as the adaptation of the future. Each repetition will have something new in it. Man's thinking will make use of all his capacities, all the mental apparatuses along the continuum from primary process (the thoughtless act) to the secondary process (the actless thought) and to the tertiary process (the thoughtful act). Only if man has lost access to his intuitive, his reasoning, or his action powers, or any combination of these, will he need to forget the past and be dominated by the compulsion to repeat.

One might say that the human life cycle is characterized by the life-long rhythm of mental functioning in which reality—to amplify on Charlotte Bühler's theme—*is the source of opportunity as well as the creator of hindrance, and the utilization of each a simultaneous process.*

REFERENCES

[1] Bühler, C. Values in Psychotherapy, New York, Free Press of Glencoe, 1962.

[2] Freud, S. The Interpretation of Dreams, New York, Basic Books, 1955.

[3] Rapaport, D. Organization and Pathology of Thought, New York, Oxford University Press, 1951.

[4] Freud, S. Formulations regarding the two principles of mental functioning, Collected Papers, London, Hogarth Press, 1925, pp. 4, 13.

[5] Spitz, R. "Hospitalism"—An inquiry into the genesis of psychiatric conditions in early childhood, Psychoanal. Stud. Child, 1:53, 1945.

[6] ———— Hospitalism—a follow-up report, Psychoanal. Stud. Child, 2:113, 1946.

[7] ———— Anaclitic depression, Psychoanal. Stud. Child: 2:312, 1946.

[8] Waelder, R. The psychoanalytic theory of play, Psychoanal. Quart., 2:208, 1933.

[9] Freud, S. Beyond the Pleasure Principle, London, Hogarth Press, 1950.

[10] Rank, O. The Trauma of Birth, New York, Harcourt, Brace, 1929.

[11] Bühler, K. Die geistige Entwicklung des Kindes, Jena, Gustav Fischer, 1918.

[12] Erikson, E. Reality and actuality, J. Amer. Psychoanal. Ass. 10:451, 1962.

14

PSYCHOTIC ACTING OUT:
ROYAL ROAD OR PRIMROSE PATH? *

Go the primrose way to the everlasting bonfire.

SHAKESPEARE

It is an interesting psychological phenomenon that the technical psychotherapeutic problem of acting out by the patient has frequently been countered in classical analytic technique with a kind of "superego acting out" on the part of the therapist. We refer here to the *technical* interventions, somewhat akin to the rule of abstinence, which are perceived by the patient as if the therapist is reacting to him out of moral conviction. The patient, whose acting out is an expression of an unconscious thought and hence a truly amoral act, nevertheless reacts to the interventions as if they were re-editions of past parental injunctions of moral conviction which prohibited or condoned thoughts and acts.

Acting out has been regarded as undesirable in classic analytic procedure. Acting out was assumed to be a defense against reflection, and accordingly interpretations were made in order to replace the acting out with free associations. Such interpretations were frequently misperceived by the patient as either injunctions or prohibitions. However, such interpretations and injunctions were occasionally misapplied by the analyst when he used them with patients for whom there was as yet no true choice available: they were not able to replace the act (the acting out) with the word (the reflection on the couch).

The acting-out patient seems to have been regarded figuratively as taking the primrose path, succumbing to temptation and violating the straight and narrow road of free association. Acting out was regarded as maladaptive behavior. Instead of being in the service of reality, it seemed to further the defensive function of relieving unconscious tensions through repeating rather than remembering past unconscious conflicts. Acting out

* Elaine Caruth is coauthor of this chapter.

298

thus seemed to avoid the conscious memory of repressed events in their appropriate connections. However, even in the earlier publications, acting out, such as in the transference, was always referred to not merely as a regression, involving a repetition of an old conflict, but also as a "new edition." [1] Implying revision and modification, a re-edition involves bringing up to date an older notion and adapting it for expression in the present.

With the development of ego psychology, it has been recognized that acting out in itself is a form of experimental recollection in a personality structure not yet capable of utilizing thought as a form of trial action. The therapeutic dealings with Frank (Chapter 9) indicate that acting out is a language in itself—a form of communication by a person who cannot think out but must act out. The specific thought which is acted out or, more accurately, the specific conflict, is repressed and consequently leads to behavior that appears irrational and inappropriate. Thus, just as the dream is referred to as the *via regia* to the unconscious of the adult neurotic, and play as the royal road to the unconscious of the child, acting out may be regarded as the main thoroughfare to the unconscious of that patient for whom this is momentarily the dominant form of communication available and for whom it may be regarded as a thought equivalent. It expresses both the impulse and the defense against the impulse, similar to the neurotic's symptom. This expresses an attempted resolution of a conflict by means of which a homeostasis is maintained between the impulse and the counterimpulse (that is, the defense against it). In both instances, the resolution is unsuccessful although the repression is partly maintained. In both instances, energy is expended in maintaining the repression; with the neurotic symptom we might speak of an "acting in," [2] as it were, in distinction to the "acting out." Both may involve a neural and motor discharge, and the term "acting out" must not be equated with either action or "acting up."

Whether the patient "chooses" to communicate through symptom formation or through acting out is determined by the total psychic structure and the level of ego development. Both may be considered a form of language (e.g., the body language of the hysteric), but they differ in their "rules of grammar," that is, in their structural and dynamic implications. Both are functions of the ego, but acting out is dominantly in the service of the id, and symptom formation is dominantly in the service of the superego. Acting out is experienced therefore as more ego-syntonic, and as more consciously gratifying, and is usually accompanied by less internal suffering and pain. Acting out reflects a more concrete language and more limited capacity for symbolic thought, and occurs at a moment when there is more limited capacity for postponement and delay. It is relatively more dominated by impulse, although the superego pressures are present. There is relatively no or only minimal functioning of a critical or observing ego, but rather a complete identification with the experiencing ego. The total lack of insight into the irrational nature of the behavior provides little capacity for reflection about the experience. Acting out, like the symptom, may occur along the dimensions of affect, ideation, and/or motor action. A patient may experience powerful but inappropriate depression, accompanied by the conviction of being rejected by the analyst and thus "feel out" and "think out" in the same way that another "acts out," as a substitute for recollection which serves as an obstacle to reflection. The language of acting out tends to be a signal language which is unsuitable to the usual office routine and may openly conflict with society. The symptom, on the other hand, is more ego-dystonic and hence more accessible to reflection by the critical observing ego, which may recognize the presence if not the content of the irrational conflict.

Up to this point, we have been considering acting out as a form of pathology, analogous to clinical manifestations of neurosis and psychosis. We would like now to consider acting out as a normal developmental phase—an advanced form of play—which forms a transitional link in the progression from the actless, thoughtless, helpless, impulsing of the newborn to the thoughtful, helpful act of the mature adult. The infant starts out helplessly reacting to the stimuli from within—his impulses—and from without—his environment. In the course of development he must learn how to help himself by acting upon both thoughtfully. We use the term "act upon" in its broadest psychological sense: as a mental phenomenon that can have varying proportions of ideational or motor components, and that is in the service of problem solution or conflict resolution. Mature thought is a form of trial action in the service of future thoughtful action. Primitive, archaic thought, the "actless," hallucinatory wish-fulfillment, may also be considered as a trial act without action—an attempted resolution of the conflict of frustration. The less archaic but immature thoughtless acting out may also be considered as an unconscious trial thought without conscious ideational representation. To paraphrase Wordsworth, the impulse is the father of the thoughtful act, just as the child is the father of the man, and perhaps we may add facetiously that acting out is the adolescent—half-child, half-man—beyond the pleasure principle but not fully committed to the reality principle.

Such a progression from "impulsing" to thoughtful action (e.g., thinking, problem solving, conflict resolution) is a function of maturational, developmental, and psychological determinants. If communication ranges from the most primitive impulse expression through acting out and play to verbal communication of secondary-process thinking, it is evident that the intellectual maturation necessary for the development of the means of verbal communication is not necessarily accompanied by a comparable development of other ego functions.

If we think of acting out as a form of communication, the rules of its language will be determined by the structure of the psychic organization at that particular moment. Psychotic acting out, like psychotic thinking, reveals the primary thought disorder; that is, the relative lack of secondary elaboration of the primary process. Nonpsychotic acting out, like nonpsychotic thought, may be infantile, may be close or far from the impulse, but it follows the rules of the secondary process. Psychotic acting out, the equivalent of trial delusional thoughts, is acting out through primary symbolization like the symbolic distortions and condensations in dream work, and appears on the surface to be unpredictable and irrational. Neurotic acting out, on the other hand, with its compulsive repetitive features, will often impress us with its stereotyped, overdetermined, and quasirational quality.

A classical example of psychotic acting out occurs when Teresa breaks the furniture in the waiting-room and Dr. Ekstein's paper knife. She seeks thus to fight the delusional "creature" who is attempting to possess her mind, while at the same time she claims she did not wish to hurt the therapist or his possessions, since she wants his help desperately.

(*Violent banging in waiting-room audible*)
E.: What happened to the lamp?
T.: Oh, nothing . . . Well, the lamp fell carelessly, that's all.
E.: Uh, uh. The lamp was careless.
T.: Yeah, the lamp fell carelessly. I pushed it carelessly so it fell. So I was just standing it up 'cause I wasn't careful. It was just an accident, yes. Well, I didn't tell you I was fixing it, that's all, just fixing it . . .
E.: T., I was just concerned with the fact that you pushed against the lamp and I asked you what happened and you said nothing and I thought that between the two of us we always had the truth. . . .
T.: Well, I just sat down and I accidentally threw the lamp down. I don't know how.
E.: But you look so angry, as if I did it. . . .
T.: I didn't destroy your lamp because I was angry. That fell carelessly. I did it carelessly—but I'm also angry because of something. . . . 'Cause something bothered me in my mind, that I imagined, that got me angry.
E.: What bothered you?
T.: Well, something horrible . . . I imagined . . . something that just bothered me, that made me want to throw that and break it, ruin the lamp . . . that made me so angry that I felt like breaking that lamp and I would feel like breaking anything.
E.: What was it?

T.: I don't know what thought it was. It was just a strange thought that bothered me, that got me in a bad mood and got me so angry that I felt like breaking anything so I ruined the lamp and I had to break that, that . . . You know, it is sort of something like an imagination. You can imagine many things, like you can imagine yourself, that you lead yourself, you know what you do and what you're not supposed to do and what you're supposed to do. But then suddenly you can imagine another person that, well, thinks that he is more greater than you and that person would think that that he can do . . . that he's more stronger and he can do better than you and then he will tell you, "Look! I'm stronger, so I'm going to leave. Not you, you're weak. You do what I say." So then he, he makes me do what he says and that's what gets me in a bad mood, that he thinks he's more stronger and more smart than I am. . . .

And then that, that person when he does . . . suddenly he gets me in such a bad mood that my imagination, and he's scolding me in my imagination, he's punishing me, he's getting angry at me, and then that is what gets me angry. That's what gets me in a bad mood. Then I grab something I feel like grabbing and just breaking it . . .

E.: But now we understand what happened. I think I do. You came here and said to yourself, Dr. E. is so strong that he might make me well and I will show him that I am stronger, that he cannot lead. What I will do is, I will try to destroy his strength so that he cannot make me well and if I destroy his strength he will get so angry that he will throw me out and hospitalize me and I won't have to get well. And I think what you did here is that you wanted to destroy your chance to get well by destroying my things . . . because that person in your fantasy that is stronger than you, that takes the lead away from you, that's me. You feel that . . . he is stronger. . . . He's about to win.

T.: That's imagination, it's something like that. It isn't that. It isn't that another person thinks he's more stronger than me. It's something like that. It's a creature, funny.

E.: That's right. But I'm the creature in your mind.

T.: No, you're not that creature.

E.: T., you told me through your act. You told me, see.

T.: You're not that creature, you're not that creature. . . . You're not that creature! (Screaming extremely loudly)

Psychotic acting out, a form of communication in an organization in which the development of thinking is at an egocentric level of development,[3] is dominated by the primary process. The neurotic patient is acting out a repressed thought which, if understood correctly, can be translated into the language of the secondary process. Psychotic acting out expresses the language of the primary process, and the thought within is on an archaic level, even though it can retroactively be given meaning by the therapist. It is similar to a dream, which if properly understood can be translated from the manifest content, which may be on an archaic level, into the everyday language of the secondary process, that is, the latent thought. However, the dreamer must have the capacity for understanding the dream at the level of the secondary process, just as this capacity has to be available to the psychotic patient and his therapist before it can be translated into this language. It is perhaps in those instances where such capacity is not fully available that we find the need and the greatest value of metaphoric communication as a transitional link between different language levels. Psychotic acting out has a nightmarish, dreamlike quality; it follows the logic of the unconscious; it is amoral, unrealistic, and not bound by time or causality.

The differences between neurotic and psychotic acting out may be understood by examining neurotic and psychotic transference reactions which can be considered as acting out.[4] Although Freud has frequently been misquoted as stating that the psychotic patient is incapable of a transference reaction and hence unanalyzable, it is now recognized rather that he wrote that the psychotic transference was of a nature which made it generally unsuitable for the usual office treatment. The reasons for this arise out of the more primitive psychic organization of the psychotic patient. Such patients have limited capacity for postponement and delay, hence a limited capacity to differentiate past from present; nor can they clearly differentiate the thought from the act, fantasy from reality, the primary object from its symbol and, perhaps most important of all, the object from the introject. They are not capable of a true displacement, such as with a neurotic transference reaction. Rather with such patients the external object upon whom the transference is acted out becomes fused with the projected introject (fantasy or real) from the past. The reality love object is experienced primarily as an inanimate object, the dehumanized thing around which to weave the psychotic fantasies. External reality, rather than being repressed, may perhaps better be spoken of as not adequately cathected and differentiated from internal reality.

We would like to suggest that acting out is a royal road with two lanes, as it were, one for the therapist to enter the inner world of the patient, and the second for the patient to enter into encounters with reality. It is a road with many dangers for both. For the therapist, it may involve the temporary relaxing of secondary-process functioning in order empathically to understand the world of his patient. And enter this world he must, in order to establish some line of communication with patients who do not have sufficient critical or observing ego to assist the therapist to understand their illness in his language. For the patient, it involves giving up the fantasied omnipotence of hallucinatory gratification, and suffering the frustration attendant upon involvement with actual reality.

The inner reality of the psychotic patient is phenomenologically experienced between two opposing polarities: the omnipotence of the satiated infant; and the impotence of the frustrated infant who can neither gratify himself nor ensure his own survival. Such patients vacillate between the feared and desired autism, and the dreaded and longed-for symbiosis.[5] When alone, they lose the capacity to maintain introjects and begin to lose their own identity through autistic withdrawal. Yet, when not alone, they must push for fusion and thus lose their individuality in the dreaded symbiotic union. They are torn between the feelings "I am not" and "they are not," in contrast to the more typical neurotic conflict over "I am not loved" and "they do not give enough to me." To the extent that they are still struggling with this basic problem of individuation, they have not yet firmly established the capacity to differentiate between the animate living person, and the inanimate thing. Thus, stealing may have an entirely different meaning for the psychotic patient than for a neurotic patient. Stealing frequently occurs following the loss of an object, and may represent an attempt to ward off an imminent depersonalization experience by thus seeking to restore the introject. That which is stolen is like a primitive precursor of a transitory object, symbolic of the very supplies needed for survival, psychological as well as physiological. Phenomenologically we might almost say that the ownership becomes debatable. Similarly, in a lighter vein, one might question to whom the mother's milk belongs—we are reminded here of a film of Spitz's. It shows a mother, who had recently weaned her own infant, start to lactate while observing another mother nursing her infant. Mother, milk, and baby—you can't have one without the others. Symbiosis neither comprehends nor respects the niceties of private property. Thus, schizophrenic Teresa admits to stealing some money, but cannot acknowledge that it should be returned; she stole the money to ward off the panic threatening to break through over the imminent loss of a relative. By stealing his money, she thought to maintain his introject so that the money figuratively became a part of her, which she could not comprehend returning.

To the extent that the stealing wards off anxiety and threatened psychotic disintegration, it serves an adaptive and progressive function. For the neurotic patient, with a personality capable of more mature reflection and delay, such acting out represents primarily a regressive and defensive maneuver. For the psychotic patient, however, the acting out may rather be partially understood as an attempt to move from a world dominated by inner needs into the world of external reality. For such patients, reality has existed only to the extent that it has been forged by their powerful need systems; reality testing has been relatively unimportant, and objects have existed primarily as inanimate things around which to weave their omnipotent fantasies. With such patients the acting out may be their first attempt to give up such hallucinatory gratifications and to become more actively engaged with their external reality. It is a move from a relatively helpless position, in which they perceive or misperceive but cannot act upon their reality, into a state in which they can actively select and organize those aspects of their reality with which they can become engaged —that is, their actuality.[6]

Such psychotic acting out may thus be construed as an attempt to act upon outer reality rather than remain inactivated and immersed in an inner world. Since it occurs in an ego which is governed by primary-process thinking, the reality it acts upon is a reality fashioned according to the rules of the primary process. However, the very act itself, to the extent that it begins to restore a function, strengthens the progressive development of the ego.

One way of acting upon reality is to fulfill a promise. The development of this capacity roughly parallels the development from the primary to the secondary process.[7] In the young child, the promise—"the primary promise"—is made by a primitive ego organization where thought and the deed are relatively undifferentiated. At this stage there can be no true conception of later fulfillment, since neither a differentiated time concept nor sufficient capacity for delay and postponement has developed. In such ego organization, the act of promising—often an appeasing gesture to a threatening parental figure—is seen as its very fulfillment.

In Teresa's treatment, a period of intense acting out followed her promise to the therapist to bring him a Valentine's Day gift. The therapist's technique was to focus upon her incapacity to fulfill a promise, specifically, to compose and bring him a written fairy tale. Behind the manifest content of this promise we can see, of course, the very promise of therapy—to grow up and to become capable of filling and fulfilling mature love and work commitments, truly an appropriate promise for Valentine's Day. It is a promise to give as well as take, to begin to work for the therapist's love in order ultimately to learn to love her work, as it were.

The therapist indicates that only as she fulfills her promise will he begin to bring promised gifts to her. In this way he indicates to her the conditions for his love. It is as if he seeks to initiate a true dialogue with her and, metaphorically, to introduce some solids along with the bottle. (We refer here to Spitz's film episode which shows the first "argument" between mother and infant: the infant wanting the bottle, the mother negotiating for some solids.) The therapist is now seeking to become a part of her external reality after having successfully entered her internal reality. Like Jonah in the whale, having now become a more stable introject, he is beginning to attempt to return to his own world and help her to cathex the reality relationship with him as a real love object rather than the hallucinatory fantasied one with the introject.

Subsequent hours with Teresa demonstrate the progression of the psychotherapeutic process through a series of instances of acting out which occur on higher and higher levels of ego organization. In the progression can be traced the identical conflicts first expressed through acute psychotic violent episodes and gradually taking on a more delinquent flavor. The culmination is the therapeutic hour in which the psychotic fantasy recurs in a sleep dream rather than a waking dream, and Teresa reports and reflects upon it in a manner beginning to approximate that of the neurotic individual.

The following is a summary of several hours in which the girl makes an effort to move from a life of fantasy, dominated by the primary process, to a life of actuality, where the secondary process governs and where a promise can truly be fulfilled. The day after Valentine's Day, the therapist first confronts her with her own unfulfilled promise to him of a Valentine's gift. In the following day's appointment there is the first attempt to fulfill the promise via a piece of psychotic acting out: instead of a written fairy tale, she has acted out a cautionary tale by setting fire to her house (at which to "go the primrose way to the everlasting bonfire" seemed more actuality than metaphor). This can be understood as her attempt at fulfilling the latent content of the promise, that is, to develop the capacity for mature love, as well as the manifest content of producing a piece of work. The work, however, is dominated by the impulse, since she is not yet capable of a true thoughtful act.

When the therapist confronted Teresa with her inability to act upon the real world, he did this via a seemingly narcissistic demand of his own: "Where is my Valentine's Day gift that you promised?" Out of this developed a quasi-struggle. The girl maintained the stand that, like her, he must wait, must not demand, must not be so childish. The therapist's position was that he only expected her to fulfill the promise that she had chosen to make. She felt that the promise itself should satisfy him as it does her; "mañana" should be good enough for both. But he called for fulfillment in action, in deed, not merely in thought. The next day it first appeared that this kind of negotiation had little impact upon Teresa. She came in seemingly having forgotten the surprise which she had promised to bring him. When challenged by him, she defended herself by saying that he had told her that he did not care if she brought him things or not. He accepted this but insisted that he did care whether or not she could keep the promise. She called him childish for caring so much about a present and resumed her usual demands for gifts from him. He maintained that he would not give her anything until she could remember to give him the fairy tale she had promised. Suddenly, however, she remembered something. Her aunt had asked her to tell him this. Yesterday she had been playing with matches, a thing that she had never dared to do when she was younger, for fear of being burned. Now, however, with her new-found "maturity" she was not afraid to play with them. It was then revealed that she had been "playing" with "burning the house down" (although not too much actual damage was done before she was discovered by the aunt). It turned out she had been trying to "fight off the Creature," to burn him out, as it were; that is, to drive the therapist out of her thoughts. The therapist had asked her to remember a promise. This seemed to have assumed a kind of obsessional driving quality which she was both compelled to fight against and yet, in her very fight against it, she fulfilled it. For she truly brought in her fairy tale but acted out, as it were, rather than written out, and a fairy tale about witches and devils rather than good fairies and angels.

In subsequent treatment hours there emerged a kind of play fulfillment of the promise. She brought in an unwritten fantasy as a fairy tale, the content of which was still dominated by the primary process. This was followed by a relatively nonpsychotic but infantile and token fulfillment of the promise to work: she brought in a childish, although written, story about animals alone in the woods.

Subsequently we saw the attempt to fulfill the promise to love, acted out on a higher level of ego organization. She frequently described less bizarre episodes of simultaneous searching for and running from the transference figure. The language of the acting out moved from the nightmarish, dream-like grammar of the fire-setting to a more understandable but somewhat delinquent kind of expression, such as when she stole underwear and claimed it was a gift from the therapist. Finally there occurred an open acting out of sexual feelings, with the father-therapist surrogate in the home.

Some two years after the violent noises in the waiting-room indicated the monster's appearance, the monster reappeared, but in a new form and in a new setting. It had returned to the realm of the unconscious and reappeared in a nightmare, and even then in the disguised form of a man with knives attacking her.

At this point the violent psychotic acting out slowly gave way to more quasi-delinquent and neurotic forms of acting out, allowing somewhat more conventional therapeutic techniques to be employed.

He who can dream about a nightmare can also wake up from one and reflect upon it. Formerly, Teresa could not differentiate a fantasy from a dream because in a sense she truly could not wake up. Now that she can dream she can sleep; and now that she can sleep she can wake up.

REFERENCES

[1] Weiss, E. Emotional memories and acting out, Psychoanal. Quart., 11:477, 1942.

[2] Zeligs, M. Acting in. A contribution to the meaning of some postural attitudes observed during analysis, J. Amer. Psychoanal. Ass., 5:581, 1957.

[3] Piaget, J. Quoted by D. Rapaport in Organization and Pathology of Thought, New York, Columbia University Press, 1951.

[4] Weiss, Op. cit.

[5] Mahler, M. S., and Furer, M. Observations regarding the "symbiotic syndrome" of infantile psychosis, Psychoanal. Quart., 29:317, 1960.

[6] Erikson, E. H. Reality and actuality, J. Amer. Psychoanal. Ass., 10:451, 1962.

[7] Schlesinger, H. Progressive and Regressive Elements in the Making of Promises, unpublished.

PART FIVE

DISTANCE, SPACE, AND TIME

Thus we see that a balance of power exists between separate nations. Each one is a potential aggressor, but each is kept from aggression from fear of the other three. The nations in the United Worlds live in harmony with each other. The era of interplanetary conquest is in the minds of many forever in the past. Unless two of these great nations band together, which is unlikely because of the distrust of each other, there will be no more wars.

THE SPACE CHILD (age 15,
writing in *The History of
the United Worlds*, a science-fiction novel)

15

THE SPACE CHILD *

A company of porcupines crowded themselves very close together one cold winter's day so as to profit by one another's
warmth, and to save themselves from being frozen to death.
But soon they felt one another's quills, which induced them to
separate again. And now, when the need for warmth brought
them nearer together again, the second evil arose once more.
So that they were driven backwards and forwards from one trouble to the other, until they had discovered a mean distance at
which they could most tolerably exist.

ARTHUR SCHOPENHAUER

From the Pullman car little Tommy watched his parents on the train
platform. He attempted nervously to get their attention and finally began
to pound on the window. He got more and more frightened, and amidst
pounding and sobbing, yelled to his travelling companion: "They won't
even look at me." Only as the train started to move did the parents look
up and wave goodbye to Tommy, pressing his tear-stained face against the
glass. Upon returning to the residential treatment center after a short
vacation with his parents, Tommy could not have characterized better his
psychological situation, the psychological distance he felt between himself
and his parents.

At that time eleven years old, he had been in our Center almost two
years, receiving intensive analytic psychotherapy three hours weekly. He
had suffered from severe asthmatic attacks since the age of twenty-one
months. He could neither play nor get along otherwise with other children, and expressed numerous fears about an impending disaster. The
parents complained about his rebellious attitude and their inability to
manage him.

The parents, civic leaders, were described by the social worker as
conscientious, intellectual, without spontaneity, shy, cool, compulsive, and

* Dorothy G. Wright is coauthor of this chapter.

eager to help their only child. They could hardly be described as "reject-ing" parents despite their inability to give, to contact him. Whether their difficulty was a consequence of his illness or a cause of it cannot be answered unequivocally. Their initial concern was the child's asthma. They had taken him to specialists and after a fruitless placement in Arizona brought him to us for a psychiatric evaluation, consultation, and possible placement.

The examining psychiatrist summarized his findings as: "Although of superior intelligence and capable of achieving a high educational level, play activities reveal marked disorganization and very intense destructive fantasying. Intellectual activity is over-stressed and isolated from ordinary events. Affect is flattened and somewhat inappropriate. Capacity for inter-personal relationships is almost absent. Diagnostic impression: Childhood Schizophrenia."

This pessimistic diagnosis was shared by other psychiatrists. The psychologist spoke of "A rather severe neurotic illness in which intel-lectualizing, obsessive-compulsive and hysterial defenses are used in order to try to control unusually strong aggressive urges and sexual conflicts." Of his fantasying she said that "It has at times a psychotic-like quality."

We wish to consider certain selected aspects of psychotherapy with this "schizophrenoid" child, a label we suggest for him in order to under-line the severity of the illness, and to bypass at present the diagnostic problem.[1]

After entering the Center, the boy spent weeks in bed with severe asthmatic attacks and presented more of a medical than a psychiatric problem. For most of the first two years he was so disturbed and fright-ened that he required twenty-four-hour care. He needed a constant special companion because of his intense anxiety, his open threats and attempts at suicide, his constant provoking behavior, and his phobias—alone, he dared not cross the street which separates two buildings of the Center. While this scared little boy needed a personal policeman to protect him from the wrath of the world and from his own anxieties, at times he would not permit the companion to enter his room.

Most of his communications to children, companions, teachers, and other professional personnel at the Center consisted of frightful fantasies which in many ways seemed a complete contradiction to Tommy's actual behavior. In these fantasies he was a Five-Star General, commanded count-less space ships, was out to destroy the world, sailed to faraway regions of space, destroyed stars, and invaded different solar systems. At the same time he was an unusually endowed little boy who had practically learned by heart the Book of Knowledge, knew more about school subjects than most of the other children, and put brilliant questions to the personnel.*

So inaccessible did he seem at first that the psychotherapist avoided his fantasy world and remained on the level of his reality problems, his everyday fears, and his needs in the living situation. After some months of such treatment the decision was reached to accept his fantasies and to try to enter his psychological world. This seemed a dangerous shift in technique since his fantasy world seemed so overwhelming that to accept it might mean breaking down the remnants of his contact with us and wiping out the limits of reality.

However, as we changed our attitude toward him, we discovered underneath the manifest content of the fantasies the story of his life and of his family situation. All the problems of love, of secret longing, of sensual gratification were hidden behind a world of aggression between and among monsters. He talked for many hours about an old man who did not need and did not want to be married: in other words a man who had no sexual life whatsoever. This man, however, was so tremendously wise and clever that he could rule the solar system, the stars, and could ward off any invasion from Mars or any other planet.

Tommy talked about faraway battles, victories, defeats; only rarely did he return to earth. At that time he was as far away from the psychotherapist as he was from his own unconscious conflicts. The problem of distance that he proposed for us at that time suggested one specific aspect of the strategy for our psychotherapy with him. The authors decided not to concern themselves primarily with the problem of the content of his fantasies, even though they seemed clearly to suggest presentations of the primal scene, or violent danger that is implied in thoughts about sexuality, but rather with the problem of defense.†

While in real life he presented himself as a timid, scared, little boy who needed protection from everyone, in his fantasy world he was an aggressive, deadly, faraway monster. Between these two there seemed to be no connection without a space ship from here to Mars.

The psychotherapist expressed sorrow for the old man who tried to

---

* Dr. Jan Frank suggested that frequently such precocious children have experienced in early childhood intensive sexual traumata, have most likely been seduced by the mother or a nursemaid, and that treatment might reveal at a later point the repressed sexual trauma.

† Dr. Nelly Tibout correctly pointed out that the separation of content and defense is at times an arbitrary one, that they are actually two inseparable sides of the same coin. We describe one specific technical aspect of therapy and do not aim at theoretical clarification. We deal with that part of the content which serves a defense function. The problem of distance constitutes a defense constellation, a syndrome of defense mechanisms within the content of the fantasy.

win all his battles. True enough he might win them but how lonesome he must be, how sad for him that he never had a mother or father, as Tommy had stated, and that he never had any friends on earth, and did not want to think of marriage. How sad to think that he had only one gratification, that of believing that he could destroy everybody. The psychotherapist's main concern was with the distance between the psychological world of this faraway monster and that of the little fellow who was yearning to be loved and accepted by his parents, by the children and the teachers in the school.

When we speak of distance we refer to it in the physical, emotional, metaphoric sense, since his way of describing the man far away, his using the metaphor of hundreds and thousands of light years seemed to be nothing but an allusion to a psychological problem which he could not present in any other way. The mode of his defense, the way his ego attempted to master internal problems, rather than the content of the conflict was attacked by psychotherapeutic work.[2]

The therapist occasionally heard from Tommy that the old man wondered if, after one of his victories when it would be quite clear that no one could defeat him, he might come down and visit earth. By implying that the old general could win all battles only if he gave up forbidden sexual striving, Tommy revealed how difficult it was for him to bring the old man, the sexless, aggressive beast down to earth.

One day Tommy suggested to the psychotherapist that Tommy was not there any longer. He had gone far away to Arizona to do research to improve the atomic bomb, in order to protect America and to destroy its enemies. The boy who was left behind was simply a friend of Tommy's named Oscar Pumphandle. While he had a different name now, he stated that he still had some connection with the "real" Tommy. As a matter of fact, he was going to visit Tommy once in a while but never would he, Oscar Pumphandle, tell any of Tommy's secrets to the psychotherapist. He could not do it because if he did, he would lose Tommy's friendship.

The forbidden instinctual impulses, at first thousands of light years away, had returned to earth. The split was now not between the humble, frightened, asthmatic-ridden boy on earth and the old destructive general in space, but rather one between two boys, both on earth and about a thousand miles apart. There was still tremendous distance between the forbidden and between the overt but the distance was reduced.

Again the psychotherapist commented primarily on the distance and did not refer to the content of research, as symbolically presented through the secret explosion of the atomic bomb in the Arizona desert. The therapist suggested that Tommy in Arizona was perhaps scared of psychotherapy and wouldn't he, Oscar Pumphandle, suggest to Tommy that psychotherapy was not so dangerous and Tommy might return. Oscar Pumphandle said that Tommy was not scared since he was a great researcher into atomic explosions. As a matter of fact, according to Oscar Pumphandle, Tommy was not sick at all. Actually no one was sick and if anyone was, it was Oscar Pumphandle. What was his illness? His illness was that he made too many jokes. The only help Oscar Pumphandle wanted from the therapist was to help him not to make too many jokes.

It was the first indication on the child's part that he was aware of his defensive system. He defended himself by distance. The undesirable, the unconscious, forbidden, and repressed were sent far away. The other line of defense consisted of denial, in suggesting that what seemed to the therapist a psychological reality was nothing but a joke. Even the choice of the name, a funny name, a good joke on the psychotherapist, contained both a repressed and a re-repressing force. The funny name of the joker gave away what the secret research was about.

The psychotherapist, recognizing the defensive problem in the transference, slowly conveyed to the boy that it was not Tommy who was afraid of the therapist but rather Oscar Pumphandle who was afraid of Tommy. They were not really such good friends. Each time they got together they had tremendous struggles, and Oscar could not call Tommy back because he was afraid of what would happen. This changed the situation indeed. Tommy came back; and with his coming we had a new problem. The shy little boy suddenly seemed to permit the other part of him, the forbidden one, to come back and the result for a while was utter chaos. The psychotherapist felt like the sorcerer's apprentice who loosed the uncontrollable devil. Tommy was at first as helplessly exposed to his own inner impulses as the therapist was to Tommy's aggressive provoking behavior. Only as the therapist turned into the sorcerer again could the flood of impulses be limited. The child attempted to masturbate openly during psychotherapeutic hours, began to steal and to destroy equipment, blew up car tires, expressed hate for staff members, organized gangs with other children, and turned from a timid youngster into a vicious little monster.

We now had an administrative and educational problem as well as a psychotherapeutic one. If the child could not have the support of his defense through distance, he needed the support of the therapist and of the limits that would be enforced in the educational setting. The therapist told the child she would not permit him to be destructive. She had to let him know and feel that the personnel at Southard School was strong enough to protect him from his own destructiveness, and to help him grow up. At the same time, however, she accepted him without condemnation.

After a number of weeks of these episodes, Tommy began to talk more and more about himself, and one day suddenly started to talk about his parents. Until then he seemed convinced that he had no parents or rather, that he had parents much as fish have parents. One of his fantasies was that his parents had been dinosaurs who battled each other. He had survived by hiding in a little hole while the army of dinosaurs swept across the country and destroyed everything in their way. His fantasy seemed to be that by chance and because of his smallness and timidity, he had managed to survive and live alone without parents.

We see then the lonesome old man was in a way the lonesome, helpless child in reverse and, at the same time, someone who was not abandoned but rather had chosen lonesomeness, someone who was not weak but terribly powerful and strong so he could win any battle as long as he would give up childhood sexuality and childhood helplessness and dependency.

The fantasies and the distance problem of time and space shifted and reflected the transference situation. We do not suggest that certain changes occurred in definite stages and that the child started on a new problem, or a new type of fantasy as soon as one was worked through. There were no sharp delineations, but certain regressive moves in the types of fantasies, while always continuing, became less frequent. One could differentiate definitely certain changes in his use of a complicated syndrome of mechanisms of distance which could be taken as indicators of psychotherapeutic progress.[3]

For example, the boy would sometimes return to types of fantasies such as the one concerning dinosaurs, but a new element in the fantasy would indicate that "distance" now had new meaning in the transference situation: he told the therapist that things were worse again. The newspaper headlines warned that soon there might be a destructive atomic war and our civilization might come to an end and he needed to do something in order to get away. He spoke of a farm in the mountains, far away from present civilization, and "incidentally" a dinosaur farm where he could be occupied with his buddies raising dinosaurs. This is a reversal, indeed, of the idea that the dinosaurs had reared him. He wanted to go there because he felt that his interest in fossils, his great knowledge about geology and archaeology, would be rewarding, and that he would be safe. He felt his therapist ought to come along with him. This suggestion was very significant in showing the change in the transference situation. Since she liked him and he liked her, she should not be destroyed by our contemporary civilization. As long as she kept the rules of this safer world which he had invented, she could stay there with him and would not be punished. We note again a reversal of the situation. He took her along and the two travelled together in his fantasies to the far reaches and while, true enough, this again was an escape from reality, an escape from the contemporary world, a reaction to extreme anxiety, it revealed at the same time a different attitude toward the therapist, a change of the transference situation.

In the beginning of treatment he had used the therapist as a kind of *tabula rasa*, writing his fantasies on her, without seeming to notice her. He had spent many weeks alone in his room, too scared to be outside yet unable to tolerate the presence of recreational workers in his room. If one were to speak of transference at that time, one would have to state that he was as distant from his therapist as he was from his parents, whose pending visit at that time frightened him immensely, and as was the old general in space from our earth.

The only way the therapist could enter his psychological world at first was to be willing to tolerate and watch it. But now she was accepted as an equal partner and was permitted to assume roles in his fantasy world. We saw now on a different level how the patient was tortured not only by powerful instinctual strivings but also by an equally strong and cruel superego. He described an inner situation which was ruled by the talion principle.

It was not the content particularly that changed, only the form that the content took. A decisive step forward was the different use of defense syndromes in describing, revealing, and disguising the inner situation.

The child had moved from the days when he had represented his sexual conflict only in symbolic form to a situation where he was able to talk openly with his psychotherapist about sex, about the creation of new life. One day, during one of these discussions on problems of sex he asked the psychotherapist what would happen if either his testicles or his penis would be surgically removed. The therapist reassured him and told him that no one would remove the genitals of little boys. Very much to her amazement the boy came back during the next hour obviously in a state of panic. He had not described an external danger but rather an internal one. He had also described his reaction to the psychotherapist whom he experienced as a tempting and seductive mother figure. He told her: "You cannot help me. Psychotherapy will never help me. I need a mental hospital forever and ever. I need a closed ward and I need more than that; I need a neurosurgeon to open my brain all around and look for the swollen emotions and cut them out and perhaps that would make me all right." Only as she was able to ponder the question aloud as to what he thought he had done that would need such cruel punishment did the panic subside and the child regain control of the situation.

The freedom she gave him to discuss sexual material heightened sexual tension and was experienced as sexual temptation. He was not only fighting his erections during the hour but felt terribly sinful about it. What he needed was not reassurance—though it was intended by the therapist to reduce an external danger—but recognition and a chance to admit his "bad" thoughts and feelings. He needed help so that he could cope with the inner danger. Since he felt she was responsible for this, he could not accept her as helper at that point but thought of the neurosurgeon, the punitive father figure.

Decisive, it seemed, in the treatment of this child, was the problem of the analysis of his defenses, particularly the defense distance which he introduced over and over and characterized as a specific ego problem. The internal struggle continued, but on different levels of distance.*

The shifting psychotherapeutic situation permitted us to observe the emergence of different self-concepts of the child. During the first phase he created a picture of the unacceptable part in himself through the fantasies about the old general. On earth we met a helpless child, the counterpart of the destructive hero in space. This self-concept slowly and, at times, violently grew into another one, where the unacceptable part was a child explorer and inventor in a desert a thousand miles away and the acceptable one, participating in the therapeutic session, was a joking youngster. Again, as the therapeutic situation developed, a different concept evolved where both, the acceptable and the unacceptable aspect of the personality, blended together and produced a delinquent youngster who challenged his environment.

Only as the educators and the psychotherapist were able to set limits, could the boy master the chaos, and in the period to follow he could for the first time express thoughts about the childhood home, about his parents, and his feelings of rejection.

As he faced his thoughts about his parents, he also moved on in the transference situation. He spoke more openly about the therapist. When feeling that she could not help him, when experiencing her as seductive, he expressed utter lack of confidence in psychotherapy.

In this later period, in spite of his open and direct expressions of

* Distance problems are observed in all psychotherapeutic situations or patient groups. Some of this child's space fantasies occur in other children and are actually nurtured through science fiction, science-fiction movies, and other similar literary productions. This child differed from others, or his therapeutic experience differed from other ones, inasmuch as a specific process could be observed in which distance, while oscillating, became smaller. Spatial and temporal distance were specific aspects of the defensive system of the ego. The same held true for the content of his fantasies which were always traceable to actual experience, just as the manifest dream content can be traced to day residues. Even Tommy's dinosaurs had their place in actual experience: huge plaster cast monuments in the zoo of his home town.

hostility, suspicion, and fear, and requests for direct gratifications, he was able to bring more immediate experiences into the therapeutic situation. Change in the transference situation expressed itself in the fact that the psychotherapist now more than ever was an experienced part of the child's psychological world.*

It is interesting that in his attempt to describe to the psychotherapist what she meant to him, he reintroduced the problem of distance: his need to divide her into her bad and her good aspects. For example, during one session, his teeth set, his stare directed at her breasts, he suddenly accused her of being a witch, and expressed the thought that she ought to be burned. Then he changed and said that she was not really a witch but had witches inside of her. He had done research on witches and told her that she was an undesirable person since she had witches inside her which made her brain say things to him that he did not like to hear. She also made him do things which he did not want to do. He began to draw a picture of a witch. The picture he drew was one of a phallic witch, having male genitals but also breasts, riding on a broom, and possessing a large witch's hat. He connected the witch's brain which he placed in her stomach with her male genitals and her breasts. This brain of the witch, which was controlled by breasts and genitals was connected with the brain of the therapist, and thus controlled her. He suggested that most people had two or three witches but his therapist had at least six witches. And witches had to be burned.

Therapeutic interviews of this period revealed that some direct content interpretations were experienced by the patient as seductive and over-permissive; and what seemed more interesting than his condemnation of the therapist, his struggle against her, and his flight from her, is the method that he employed to express condemnation of her. To maintain his love for her he projected onto her superior forces responsible for her seductiveness; they operated in the same way and dominated her in the same way as instinctual forces dominated his own life and were experienced by him. His beginning awareness and understanding of the psychotherapist was blended with powerful projective elements and his picture of her, while suggesting a mother introject, was also a projective description of himself.

When a few weeks later the child's parents were to visit him he

* When we speak about transference situations we are using the concept "transference" in a double sense. Certain expressions of the child refer to early pre-Oedipal phases of his life and are reflected in a "transference neurosis." Other expressions toward the psychotherapist are a transfer, not from the repressed past to the present but rather from present relationships with parents or educators in the environment to the therapist.

prepared himself for the event. During the first visit he had refused to see them, and was panic-stricken. During the second visit he met them as a joking little boy who could control his anxiety only when being funny and entertaining.

For this third visit the child elaborated a new fantasy. He spoke about the Martian agent, who had come to earth and was to return to Mars in his space ship. In the beginning of therapy he had used this fantasy but then the space ship was destroyed and the Martian agent could not return to Mars. It was as if the space ship expressed the distance from the parents and his own home; and its being destroyed meant that he had given up all hope that he could ever go back to them. Now he suggested that he had a space ship, that it was buried, and maybe he might be able to go back to Mars. He insisted that he would return in the near future. He wanted to leave the earth because the earth was too warlike and he described Mars as peaceful.

When the psychotherapist reminded him of the early stories of the general conducting catastrophic wars in space, he said that they were just "science-fiction stuff" and he insisted that the Martian people were quite peaceful. We learned that the Martian, whose anatomy he drew for us, was not sexless as the old general in space had been. Among other things, the boy stated that the Martian urinated through the rectum because the genital sexual regions had to be pure. The new Martian man in many ways was a picture, a new self-concept, of the patient. The child described copulation on Mars in such a way as to deny the joy of sex life. When the therapist asked him once why he was against enjoyment in the case of Martian men, the child lost patience with her and said, "You are supposed to be a therapist and interested in the mind and mental things and here you are asking questions about sexual matters." He said that he was a space explorer and not a biologist. This new concept of himself not only put the psychotherapist in her place but also indicated in which way he felt he could be accepted by his parents, in which way he was lovable and could accept himself and he indicated also his problem, the exploration of space, of distance, of defense.

An example concerns the child's play with a wild horse through which he indicated to us how he attempted to cope with his fluctuating defense system. Tommy built feverishly and frantically a wall of blocks around a wild horse. While this wall was being built by men, the horse rushed around and trampled everything that was in his way. Luckily enough, for the time being, the horse trampled only other animals to death, and men were spared. The game lasted a number of days and consisted in constantly building up walls and tearing them down again. At one point the psychotherapist referred to the horse as a representation of the wild and untamable in Tommy but he rejected the interpretation as if to say that he did not want to tell her about the wild horse but rather his attempt to tame the horse. Constantly he built up and tore down the walls which held the animal and thus he described his inner situation, the shifting ego strength he used successfully and unsuccessfully to contain the wild horse.

We cannot better illustrate the progress that Tommy made during these two years than by quoting from the psychotherapeutic record just before the third visit of his parents.

He asked if the therapist thought that his parents would think he was different. The therapist assured him that they hardly could think otherwise from the way that he acted now. On the other hand, she added, it was possible that he might feel he had to withdraw and act as he had in the past. She did not know for sure what he might do but indicated that she would accept him both ways. Tommy didn't think that he would withdraw. He was less anxious and quite cheerful. He had been depressed and frightened before their last visit. Tommy asked what he had said last time. The therapist recalled how unhappy and scared he had been. Tommy said, "Well, let's dramatize that interview. I will be Mrs. W. and you will be Tommy."

Tommy: *Well, Tommy, you don't look very happy today. Is there something wrong?*
Therapist: *Yes, Mrs. W., I'm so worried about my parents' visit.*
Tommy: *What in particular are you worried about, Tommy?*
Therapist: *Well, I'm afraid they won't like me as the kind of boy I am.*
Tommy: *Well, why don't you think they will like you as you are?*
Therapist: *Well, the way I figure it I tried so hard to be the kind of child my parents wanted me to be and I failed and that's why I am sick.*
Tommy: *Yes, there is probably something to that. How do you feel about it now?*
Therapist: *Well, I feel I have changed some and I don't know if they will like me as I am now.*
Tommy: *But you told me worrying about whether or not they would like you is what made you sick before. Why don't you forget about what kind of boy your parents want and just act like you feel like acting?*
Therapist: *You think if I do that my parents will be upset?*
Tommy: *Well, they will understand better when they see the social worker and she can explain to them that it is important for a boy to be himself.*
Therapist (*Pretending to cry*): *But, Mrs. W., I hardly know my parents.*
Tommy: *Of course you don't. It will take a long time for you to know them and them to know you.*

Then Tommy stopped for a minute and asked the therapist if he cried last time with very big tears. He then went on to predict how he would act this time with his parents. Actually, his asthma symptoms had almost completely cleared up by then. He needed no special companions and made good progress in school. He had more satisfactory contacts with children and staff. His fantasy life did not have the intensive quality it had in the beginning. He was much improved.

After this interview he went on a vacation with his parents and the incident described in the beginning of this presentation occurred. It was as if the myth of birth without parents, of a lonesome life far away in space, of constant hostility, conquest, and fear had given way to a more realistic myth about his childhood. At the end of the treatment phase described here, he reacted to his parents in very much the same way that adult patients "reconstruct" their frustrating childhood and the picture of their parents during the initial stages of analysis. His situation was complicated, of course, by the fact that many of the elements of the picture he had about his parents, about childhood, and about himself were aspects of a grim undeniable reality. The reconstruction of the early childhood situation, however, does not seem to be decisive, but rather *the way in which reconstruction takes place*.

This presentation may help clarify the fact that the main attempt of the therapist is not aimed at the reconstruction of the trauma or of the series of traumata but rather that such a reconstruction allows the psychotherapeutic process to take place. During the psychotherapeutic process we discover the main modes of defense which the suffering child has been using consciously and unconsciously in order to master, successfully in part and unsuccessfully in others, the problems of growth and development.

Tommy offered an unusual example of a situation in which the way he had used to master his situation indicated new therapeutic possibilities. We have attempted here to describe more fully these aspects of the therapeutic process which refer to his unusual pattern of *defense through distance*.

REFERENCES

[1] Abraham suggested in 1908 (The psychosexual differences between hysteria and dementia praecox, Zentralblatt für Nervenheilkunde und Psychiatrie, 19:521, 1908), that an abnormal psychosexual constitution in the direction of auto-eroticism was the cause for dementia praecox. He added that future research might help to elucidate the intellectual disturbance seen in the clinical picture of dementia praecox. It is as if he foresaw the development of modern ego psychology. Our *diagnostic interest in Tommy concerns the shifting ego stages as they emerge during and because of treatment*. We think then of childhood schizophrenia as an ego illness despite the preference of

some authors to use this diagnosis only for adults whose illness might develop out of such childhood disturbances as seen in Tommy's illness.

[2] Our therapeutic concern with the problem of ego defense and our technical innovation have been greatly stimulated by Berta Bornstein's "On Latency" (Psychoanal. Stud. Child, 6:279, 1951) and Hans Zulliger's "Child Psychotherapy without the Interpretation of Unconscious Content" (Bull. Menninger Clin. [translated by R. Ekstein and J. Wallerstein], 17:180, 1953).

[3] Anna Freud, in "Observations on Child Development" (Psychoanal. Stud. Child, 6:18, 1951) states: "In the analytic literature on the subject of libido development, it is stressed repeatedly that the oral, anal and phallic phases merge into each other at the points of transition and that they should only be thought of as distinct from each other in the sense that in each phase one of the component urges is highly cathected with libido and therefore prominent, whereas the others, earlier as well as later trends, though they may exist, have a low cathexis and therefore play a minor part. Such warnings are useful to the analyst to whom the libidinal phases often appear as closed-off entities when seen in retrospect." This observation could be paraphrased for the shifting defensive fantasies, and for the amount of cathexis which is given to one particular type of fantasy, while the others coexist, but with less intensity.

16

THE SPACE CHILD'S TIME MACHINE

Their personal history is not only, as one might expect, an essential part of their self-representation, but has become a treasured possession to which the patient is attached with a peculiar devotion. This attachment reflects the fact that the autobiographical self-image has become heir to important early fantasies, which it preserves. In this sense, I propose to speak of it as of a "personal myth," which, as all living myth, extends from the past into the present. Some aspects of the patient's conduct of life could best be viewed as a re-enactment of part of the repressed fantasies, which had found their abode in their autobiographical constructions.

ERNST KRIS

The main purpose of this chapter is to discuss the use of a fantasy of delusional strength and some of its significant changes during treatment. The description of the functional use of a schizophrenoid boy's fantasy about the "Time Machine" will provide the clinical basis for a discussion of some aspects of the concept of *reconstruction*. While the main emphasis will be on the psychotic-like attempts at "reconstruction" brought out in this borderline case, the material may be used to arrive, perhaps, at a better understanding of the concept of reconstruction in all psychoanalytic psychotherapy.

Some of Tommy's background and experiences in therapy have been described previously (chapter 15). I repeat here only those features which are essential background for this discussion.

The examining psychiatrist's diagnosis was "childhood schizophrenia," while the psychologist spoke of "a rather severe neurotic illness," and stressed that Tommy's fantasying had a "psychotic-like quality." My suggestion of calling him a "schizophrenoid boy" stresses the diagnostic and semantic dilemma, and the severity of the illness of this borderline case.

Tommy was at first completely inaccessible, and only later "permitted"

324

the psychotherapist to enter his psychological world, which took them far away into outer space. Tommy felt comfortable only when millions of light years away from us, and he thought of himself as an old, murderous general who won one battle after the other against invading planetary armies and who lived a lonesome, sexless life. The timid, shy, and asthmatic-ridden youngster could permit himself aggression only in the faraway spaces of the universe.

The discrepancy between the phobia-ridden, anxious child and the violent general became less pronounced during treatment when Tommy gave up the "space" fantasy for a "distance" fantasy. Instead of the timid boy and the vicious old general, we were faced now with two boys. One, Tommy, was alone in the distant Arizona desert engaged in secret atomic research, while the other, his friend Oscar Pumphandle, met with the psychotherapist. Oscar Pumphandle did not want to let the psychotherapist know what Tommy was doing in Arizona, nor did he want to let Tommy know what the psychotherapist had said. But the distance had decreased to earthly dimensions.

As the treatment proceeded, Tommy himself returned. It seemed to us at first that the old general had landed with his destructive space ships right at Southard School. Our timid patient had turned into a rebellious, defiant, aggressive child who found it almost impossible to cope with his aggressive and his sexual impulses.

The matter of space and distance was related to the patient's attempt to erect defenses against unacceptable behavior and impulses. Selections from Tommy's communications concerning the "Time Machine" may help us to understand another aspect of his treatment and to clarify the function of reconstruction.

The peculiar aspect of space and distance in Tommy's fantasies is related to his specific attempt at instinct mastery and fantasy control of interpersonal relationships. Sometimes distance was not expressed through space but through time. Distance in time served as a protective device, a shock absorber against the present and, simultaneously, permitted communication about the past and the present.

About fifteen months after the onset of psychotherapy, Tommy gave up the fantasy of the distant space general and returned to earth and also started speaking directly or indirectly about his parents. While excessive fantasying still went on, it was not fantasying directly about himself. Shortly after an unsuccessful visit with his parents, he told the therapist that he had been away "shooting your ancestors." He said he had shot a pterodactyl, adding the explanation that he spoke about a flying reptile, the direct ancestor of the mammal. He had also killed another of the therapist's ancestors, a fish. When the therapist asked if this meant that he shot his own ancestors as well, Tommy said that he did not know if he had any ancestors, or, for that matter, how he came into this world. He claimed that he had watched the development of mammals for millions of years. His first recollection, he said, was of walking along the beach and then coming out of the water. He did not remember if he was walking along the beach before he came out of the water or whether he came out of the water first.

The therapist's comment to Tommy that he probably had a mother and a father was met with, "I do not know, but I doubt it." He did not recall ever having been a baby. He had never been able to find any remains of his mother or father. He had studied fossils a lot in order to find out his origin. He thought he was a freak. He said, "I think I must have come from some animal; possibly some reptile or fish laid an egg in the water by the beach, and I came out of that egg and walked out of the water onto the beach." When the therapist remarked that Tommy's mother then must have been a reptile or a fish, Tommy said, "Yes, and it is possible that I would have eaten her." He would have eaten his relatives for food, for it would have been impossible for him to recognize them. His father must have been an animal or fish, too; he must have fertilized the egg. But he said that he really did not know how he came to be on earth. When the therapist said that he really did know, but did not want to accept it, Tommy yelled loudly, "Shut up, shut up, shut up!"

This first fantasy about his origin as a fish, unknown by his father and mother—a sort of primeval Paul Bunyan theme—seems to be the beginning attempt at reconstruction of an aspect of his childhood, the feeling of lonesomeness and the absolute denial and reversal of dependency, and fear of being devoured. This attempt to master his life by projecting himself into the dim past was to play an important part in the exchanges between the child and the therapist. In each of these fantasies concerning the past was a kernel of truth, an aspect of remembering. This case of actuality indicated in which way he attempted or dreaded change; in which way he hoped that change was possible; or how he despaired because of the overpowering feeling that he could never master the present.

About two months later Tommy told the therapist that there was one more thing that he wanted to tell her about his past. He spoke then about the trip that he took to Europe in 1425. He stayed there for fifty years and, because of his many inventions, was almost tried as a witch. (One can't help recalling A Connecticut Yankee at King Arthur's Court.) He asked the therapist jokingly if he should have brought her a witch steak. This joke contains the fear of being devoured and its reversal. The fantasy threat shows him identifying himself with the witch, but a few weeks later, he expresses the idea that the therapist is dominated by a witch who makes her put dangerous ideas into his mind (Chapter 15).

In both the distance fantasy taking place in prehistory and in the one in the fifteenth century, he "remembers" early feelings about parental figures which could be correlated with the transference situation.

A few days later his fantasies about the past, describing always his own return to the past, took a specific form. He claimed that he had to talk with the therapist about his *survival*. Present civilization was eventually going to blow up the earth. He wanted to figure out some way to survive. He and his friends had an invention which would do the trick. It was a *time machine*. With this it would be possible to travel back into history and change things. Many of Tommy's friends had spent years in the study of history and these experts would make the decisions as to what changes should be effected. For example, if knowledge of history showed that an emperor in Germany was responsible for some of the warlike atmosphere of the present age, the time machine would allow us to go back to that age and kill the emperor before he had a chance to be influential. Of course, so Tommy informed the therapist, this would "screw up" history and all the history books would have to be automatically changed, but it might mean survival for his friends and himself. (There is no evidence that Tommy read Orwell's description of the Ministry of Truth in *1984*.)

The therapist said to the child: "You mean you are going to be able to go back and change the past so the present will be different?" This was indeed the child's idea, and while such a procedure might "screw up things, lots of things," perhaps he and his friends would not be destroyed. He asked if the psychotherapist would come along into the past and be a volunteer. From then on, she followed the child on a number of expeditions with the time machine. Each mission was carried out with Tommy as the pilot of the time machine. He explained that the almost instantaneous flight into time took much less time than flight into space.

One mission took them to the shores of Normandy in 1066. At first, two of his friends had gone out to destroy the fleet of William the Conqueror so that he would not be able to land in England. The therapist wondered how this particular incident would help Tommy and his friends to survive although she readily saw that it would "screw up" the history books. He did not know how such a change would make sense but expressed hope that the committee of historians available to him would help him so that all the changes put together would make sense. On a second mission, Tommy announced that they were now on the shores of England in 1072; and they were going to help William the Conqueror instead of destroying his fleet. The therapist called to his attention that he seemed to want to help William and to hinder him at the same time. Tommy admitted this after the therapist's remark that she could not understand how it would affect history particularly, although it was understandable that at the same time Tommy wanted to help and to destroy William the Conqueror. This pointing up of his ambivalence toward therapy helped the child consider more realistically the everyday problems in the Center which he had wished to tell and attempted to keep from her.

In the hours that followed, Tommy's time machine took him back to the era of Caesar, whom he was trying to hinder. He also tried to stop the Trojan Wars. Once he wished to take the therapist back in time to a dinosaur farm which he and his friends had organized and which was to help them to escape from civilization—today's Atomic Age. When the therapist asked him if the changes they would make in the past would mean that he would be able to survive, Tommy said that he did not know. Some of the things that he had to do seemed silly and insignificant, and he could not see how they could help the present situation very much.

On one occasion the therapist suggested that "maybe it is not possible to *change the past* since it is so very complicated that changing a few things will not alter the whole picture" and that "maybe it will be more effective to try to *understand the past* and work from there instead of wanting to go back and make it different." Tommy became hostile and told her to "shut up," to keep on the subject, to say nothing that he did not want to hear, and, above all, to make no comments that had to do with problems of therapy. He then returned to his fantasies with the time machine, as to how he had shortened one man's life by seventy-two years and had lengthened the life of other men. He spoke about a woman who had nine children and whom he had killed after she had had two so that the other seven were not born. The therapist suggested, "My, we certainly did a lot of killing to survive ourselves." Tommy said, "Yes, we did, but I am not sure it was successful. I am just not sure."

Thus, he attempted to master his anxiety about the present, his fear of death, destruction, and annihilation, by making himself the master of the past. He who could change the past might thus secure survival and save the future. The helplessness of early childhood, the lonesomeness and the feeling of rejection, his weakness, his smallness, all of it was reversed into its opposite. Just as once he had governed space, he was now governing time. Rather than recalling the past and the misery of his early life as he must have experienced it, he mastered the past. Since he had changed it, he did not need to change the present nor be afraid of the future.

However, the therapeutic work made it impossible for him to continue the omnipotent fantasy and his megalomania about time on the same level. It soon seemed to be clear that even if he could change the past as he wanted to, he could not be sure that this would guarantee survival. He simply doubted his own wisdom and that of his historian friends, fantasy extensions of himself as they were. Before long another difficulty arose. He said that he had not figured out all the complications of the time machine and he would need to work at that a little bit. There was something wrong with its mechanics. He wondered why they had put a better suit of armor on a soldier who was not even going to be killed.

The time machine had led to the point where the therapy was experienced in the transference as overseductive and the child could not control his sexual urges. No suit of armor could protect him from the sexual panic which was developing. When it was under control and the therapist had helped him to understand his sexual fantasies better, she wondered if he would not like to invent a machine whereby parents could have a better understanding of their children. He returned again to the expressed desire that he would want to perfect the time machine so that he could go back not only to the immediate past but into the prehistoric past. He already suspected that such an attempt was not too effective in the present situation but he still wanted to go back into prehistoric time.

It was as if he had gained insight into some of the aspects of his fantasy and had given up the idea that fantasy control of the past could affect the present. But he still needed to tell us that he was too impulsive and that "insight" alone could not help him master powerful inner forces with which his ego still could not permanently cope.

Four months after the beginning of the time-machine fantasies, the following interchange took place.

Tommy: Well, since I have been working with the time machine I realize how much there is to history.
Therapist: You mean a lot of things have happened in the past?
Tommy: Yes, more things than I thought. Our library was full of history books, and there are more and more of them, every kind of history imaginable.
Therapist: Yes, that is true. The past is very complicated and covers a lot of things that have happened over a period of many years.
Tommy: Yes, and to change the past is really almost impossible. Change is hard, did you know?
Therapist: Yes, I know that change is hard and that it takes time and that it is very painful.
Tommy: Yes, change—I can't figure out this business of change. Sometimes it's for the worse instead of the better. Did you know?

This was the period when Tommy had definitely returned from Arizona and had been "raising hell." He was a new, a changed, boy now. He did not know if he would like the change, but was about ready to give up the fantasy of the time machine. As he said: "To change the past is really almost impossible." He was almost ready to believe this, to turn his mind to the present. For six months nothing was heard about the time machine. Then he asked the therapist to guess what a lovely little house with colorful doors and windows was. He finally conveyed to her that this building was really the time machine. The exterior of the house always seemed to outsiders to be that of a regular home whether he was there or not. But the house really was a camouflage for his paleontological research into time. As he ended that hour he said, "Does it mean that I'm getting better now, that I'm building things that look like houses even if they are not?"

He wanted to observe extinct animals that existed about five hundred thousand years ago. He again wanted to take the therapist on a trip with him in the time machine. Before he did so he suggested that they cut a deck of cards and the person who got the highest card would win. If the therapist won, Tommy was ready to talk about his Christmas worries. If Tommy won, he would go on a time-machine trip. Whether they should talk about realistic issues of the present moment or about his fantasy life was to be left up to chance. As he finally took the therapist five thousand years back, he complained that he had a squeaky knob on the dial of the time machine and he might get stranded in time. He described a fight between dinosaurs, a male and a female; the victorious female ate the male. Tommy assured the therapist that this was a fight for survival, "That's what life is, didn't you know?" The therapist answered that that's what it might have been in the past for him but she wondered if the situation hadn't improved a little so that there was less conflict now. Tommy agreed but thought that perhaps man straightened things out a little bit, but not much.

One month later he spoke about a new machine that he had invented, a dimension transformer. This transformer permitted him to go from the dimensions of the dead to those of the living. It was a very complicated machine that had taken him 175 years to perfect. He was not afraid anymore that he was going to get stuck in the dimensions of the dead. (He was describing here his newly gained ability to control oppressive fantasy, his ability to choose and to return to realistic issues of the moment.) A month before it had been up to chance whether he would talk about fantasy material or his Christmas worries. He now wanted to take his therapist along on his trip to the dimensions of the dead. It was one of those periods when he could not cope with the living, loving, and seemingly seductive therapist. He started to yell at the top of his voice that he wanted to kill her. But he was not afraid of his death wishes since he thought he could disguise her or use another ruse to bring her back again from the dimensions of the dead:

Well, there might be another way you could get back. I could go down to the dimensions of the dead three times a week and have therapy with you there. Every time we had a good hour I would give you a block and every time we had a bad hour you would not get a block, and as the blocks gathered in numbers you would be able to pile them up and get back to the dimensions of the living.

His idea of a good hour was one in which the therapist would not discuss any painful psychotherapy material with him, but the therapist did not know if she could accept this definition. Tommy then said:

Well, if that's the way you feel about it you will just have to stay down there, that's all there is to it. I suppose you think this is a good therapy hour because I am plenty upset. I will have you know that. I am plenty upset.

Three months later he said:

Do you remember some time ago when I confined you to the dimensions of the dead? Well, you have now earned enough bricks to come back to the Earth. And you said you were not going to earn any bricks but you did anyway.

He laughed triumphantly.

When she discussed with him during this hour some of his recent problems in relation to her, feelings of little boys toward women, he warned her to be careful or he would send her back to the dimensions of the dead.

Many of the hours with him became more realistic and more like sessions with the average child in therapy. He did not have to escape as excessively into fantasies; neither did he have to keep himself away nor had he to keep the therapist away. He had gained control over his excessive fantasy life and he projected these gains into changes on his time machines.

For a few weeks there was no mention of any time machine but then he spoke about his latest invention. This new time machine took him back five years only. Perhaps later on he might be able to develop a time machine that would take them five years into the future, but for the time being he only had one that would go back into the immediate past. He said that it was important to know the past so we could understand the

present. He now did not speak about the past in archeological and historical terms but about the past of personal significance in his own life. At
the end of this particular hour he started yelling; "I'm going crazy. I'm
going to break all of my time machines. Somebody stop me or I will break
them all. I'm going crazy I tell you." He broke up the time machines and
threw them against the shelves. At the end of the session he said in a very
quiet voice: "Of course you know, I was not going crazy, I just like to
destroy my handiwork before I leave the office so the other children won't
have it." While this was not all the explanation of his sudden outburst,
it certainly indicated how much more he lived in the present and attempted to cope directly with the problems of the present. What his outburst of anger, his threat of going crazy, really meant was that he found it
very difficult to face his own immediate past and future. It was difficult to
get rid of the old crutches of fantastic projections of his life into the
enormous distances of space and time.

In this period also he invented another machine, this time a genetics
machine. It would change the character of the genes of man so that there
would be more freaks in the world. This would help, because making
normal people into freaks would make the majority consist of freaks. The
therapist told him that that would make the freaks of today feel more
comfortable, it was really tough to be a freak. The genetics machine then
was to change others in the present rather than to change himself, thereby
changing his position in relation to others.

The fantastic and forced reconstruction of the past by means of the
time machine is a control device to cope with the present. To fantasy
mastery in space- and time-distance could obscure Tommy's need to face
the problem of mastery of the present. It was as if he was out to forge
history, his own history, the history of the world, and even prehistory, so
that he could rationalize his present situation and endure it. The invention
of his time machine helped him to deny his helplessness, his lonesomeness, his castration fear, his fear of being devoured, his fear of dying or
killing someone. This he did by making himself a Paul Bunyan of prehistory, a successful Connecticut Yankee in the Middle Ages, and a
historian of Orwell's Ministry of Truth which constantly lied about the
past in order to assure survival.

The fantasies seemed to be forged *reconstruction*, but this held true
only in the realm of the secondary process. For in each of these fantasies
a true communication about the psychotherapeutic situation as well as the
feeling of the past was reconstructed. As Tommy changed and improved,
his time-machine fantasies changed with him. It was as if for each new
present attitude, new mastery, or new regression, he must find a rationale

in a fantasy about the distant past which was carried by almost delusional strength.

By means of the time machine, he magically mastered the traumatic history of the past. These traumata were changed into a more benevolent picture of the past by means of forging history—"screwing it up," as he put it. While he denied his powerlessness and his helplessness, his productions, nevertheless, offered a true reflection of the progression of reconstructive discoveries about repressed aspects of the past. It is as if he had constantly to change a myth about the past in order to find a rationale for a new present. It has been said that the Romans invented the myth about the early seven Roman kings when the republic gave way to Imperial Rome and a tradition had to be invented to justify the new regime. Modern dictatorships forge the historical past by distortion and omission. In like fashion, reconstruction by the despotic self of a borderline patient like Tommy has the flavor of tyranny and forgery.

In a magnified and special way here is an essential aspect of reconstruction as it takes place during the psychotherapeutic process. Tommy's preoccupations with the past and its changes, the strange and distant ways of his imagination are in the service of his inner needs. Of him could be said what Freud [1] says of the poets:

Long-past ages have a great and often puzzling attraction for men's imagination. Whenever they are dissatisfied with their present surroundings— and this happens often enough—they turn back to the past and hope that they will now be able to prove the truth of the inextinguishable dream of a golden age. They are probably still under the spell of their childhood, which is presented to them by their not impartial memory as a time of uninterrupted bliss.

If all that is left of the past are the incomplete and blurred memories which we call tradition, this offers an artist a peculiar attraction, for in that case he is free to fill in the gaps in memory according to the desires of his imagination and to picture the period which he wishes to reproduce according to his intentions. One might almost say that the vaguer a tradition has become the more serviceable it becomes for a poet.

While reconstruction always has been considered one of the basic concepts in psychoanalytic theory and technique, the meaning of this concept has undergone vast change since the early days of psychoanalysis. At first it seemed that reconstruction referred simply to the recollection of the repressed trauma which caused the symptom of the neurotic. But even then, and it seems important to be reminded of this, recollection was seen not merely as an intellectual function but as an affective process as well. Freud stated in 1892: "Recollection without affect is nearly always quite ineffective." [2] The alleged sexual traumata that the hysterical patients had suffered turned out to be fantasies rather than actual events. Our present view on reconstruction was excellently summarized by Anna Freud: [3]

Early traumatic experiences, where they survive in the individual's consciousness, do so in the form of cover memories. In analytic reconstruction, it is the analyst's task to undo the distortions, condensations, displacements and reversals which have constructed the particular cover memories out of the traumatic material and to revive the memory of the original events. The impression arrived at usually is that not one but two or more pathogenic happenings have contributed and been condensed to form the cover memory.

Actual observation of the same processes at the time of their occurrence suggests a correction of this view so far as the multiplicity of the pathogenic happenings is concerned. An action which we see the infant repeat a hundred times may in later life be represented as one traumatic happening. We see the infant play with his excrement, smear with it, try to taste it, over a period of weeks, or even months; the adult patient may remember this period in analysis as a single event of high emotional value. The memory of a traumatic fall, a traumatic injury may cover the whole series of smaller and bigger accidents which happen almost daily in a child's life. One traumatic prohibition or punishment, remembered and reconstructed, becomes the representative of hundreds of frustrations which had been imposed on the child; one longer separation from the mother takes over the combined effect of innumerable times when the infant has been left alone in his cot, his room, at bedtime, etc. Though we realize as analysts that past experience is telescopic in this manner, we are in danger of underestimating the extent of the phenomenon, when not reminded of it by the result of direct observation.

When we speak of reconstruction we refer not only to a specific form of interpretation but also to the attempts on the part of the patient to recall, to understand, to interpret the past of his life. At the beginning of treatment he may recall his childhood in a certain way, and thus "reconstruct" it, usually in such a way as to rationalize, or try to find a rational basis for, his present behavior. Reconstruction is constantly occupied with the present as well as the past. It is for this reason that one may say, as Kanzer [4] did, that the analytic process reconstructs not only past experiences but consists also in a "reconstruction of the present." Or, it might be put: The present behavior of the neurotic is an attempt to show us what happened to him in the past, while the reconstruction of the past, the changing picture of the past, is a justification for the ability or alleged inability to change the present.

The analyst's interpretation, and the reconstruction he offers, changes the patient's rationale and thus opens the way for changes in the present. Reider[5] suggests that the analyst's reconstruction is experienced as an order to remember, that is: to see the past differently, thus to introduce a new rationale toward change.

The Space Child might tempt us to put such a view about reconstruction into an extreme formulation: the psychotherapeutic process consists of the exchange of one childhood myth for another myth. He who saw himself deserted for a long time during the formative years of his childhood, thus justified a certain attitude toward parents, authority, analyst, life. The sudden discovery that such desertion never took place and that the parent, for example, was absent for a very short time only, changes the childhood history of this patient in such a way as to take away his original justification for a certain attitude. The potential for a new attitude expresses itself during the therapeutic process in the discovery of new facets of his life which permit him to exchange one view about his past for a more suitable one which offers a healthier rationale for living.

This extreme formulation seems to suggest that all of us are forgers of our past history. The new rationale discovered through reconstruction, through the lifting of the repression, then becomes simply a better forgery, a sort of psychological utilitarian or relativistic point of view.

The reconstructive efforts of the therapist and the patient cannot be understood properly if this process is misunderstood.

There is no attempt here to deny that reconstruction leads to actual facts of early life. When I say that the patient exchanges one myth for another, I do not suggest that he forges the past, but rather, that memory is a specific function of the ego, and is in the service of present action. The patient recalls what he needs to recall in order to act in the present in the way which is acceptable to, and possible for, him. As long as he is sick and suffers from past reminiscences, as Freud put it, his memory function is inadequate. Instead of serving the function of reality testing and adjustment, it serves the past, the unconscious conflict, and its representative, the neurotic or psychotic symptom.

The Space Child offers a magnified version of such reconstructive efforts where it can clearly be demonstrated that even psychotic-like attempts of reconstruction are functional fantasies which "justify" present behavior and adjustment. Reconstruction is considered here as an ego function, and demonstrates that memory is not an isolated faculty but has its specific functional task within the psychic apparatus. This holds true for psychotic-like memory as well, as Tommy's changed use of the time-machine fantasy demonstrates.

Our interest in this fantasy was re-enforced for a number of reasons. The first was that we saw in it not only the representation of unconscious conflict, of traumatic events of the past, but also of the attempts of the ego to master an internal conflict. We saw in this fantasy an attempt by the patient to demonstrate also how he had been trying to master these conflicts and what ego facilities he had in order to cope with them. The fluidity of the fantasy and the changing use he made of it were an indication of the process that took place during therapy and of the degree of illness as it had developed.

The fantasy of the time machine is, of course, not new. Tausk described "The Influencing Machine of Miss Natalija A." in 1918. This is discussed in Chapter 10. To recapitulate briefly, her machine was one by means of which she was influenced by others. Tausk discusses this machine as a projection of the patient's genitals, a defensive measure of the ego against the inopportune and reprehensible urges from the unconscious. Freud, in relation to Tausk's paper, emphasizes the justification for an infant's conception that others know its thoughts.

Tommy's time machine can also be considered a projection of his powers. In his case, it is he, not others, who uses the machine to "influence" the past. At first he influenced prehistorical past, later historical past, and finally the present, particularly the therapist. That is the psychological connection between the fantasy of an influencing machine which is controlled by the person and the fantasy in which the influencing machine is controlled by others. Is the difference a developmental problem that has to do with age or the course of illness?

The influencing machine of Frankie, a patient of Berta Bornstein,[6] was a "remembering machine," a "projecting machine" which could turn backward as far as he liked. This phobic patient developed the idea that through this remembering machine he saw the analyst's mother killing the analyst at the command of King Boo-Boo because the analyst had screamed too violently as a baby, and disturbed the whole world. Bornstein states:

We had to discuss with him the fact that though he might not remember his infancy, he must have heard many comparisons of his own baby behavior with that of his sister, and he must have received the impression that his parents had never forgiven him his screaming at night. His sister had always been praised as a good, quiet baby which must have made him even more angry at her. Perhaps it was not only the analyst who should have been killed with the baby by her mother—maybe he had often wished the same would happen to his sister, so that his family could not rave about her.

Frankie's influencing machine may be understood as being in the service of reconstruction of the past and the present.

Tommy's psychotic-like fantasies are the schizophrenoid child's substitute for the type of recollections, or reconstructions, found in the treatment of less severely disturbed patients. Just as we can demonstrate that screen memories function to keep the traumatic memory repressed, and thus permit the ego limited functioning with what is remembered, so Tommy uses what I would like to call "screen fantasies." During the process of psychotherapy, these give way to more basic fantasies, a form of reconstruction at the primitive level of his regressed ego organization. Psychotic fantasies are substitutes for recollection.[7]

The function of memory is to serve certain motives. In the case of the sick person, these motives, rather than serving reality mastery, are in the service of the unresolved conflict. In our borderline case, the function of the psychotic-like reconstruction was to serve the changing motives during the therapeutic process; its more or less psychotic-like nature was an indication of shifting ego organization. As Tommy moved from the past to the present, from distant space into the therapeutic situation itself, he not only seemed to resolve conflict material but regained lost ego functions. This permitted him to exchange fantastic reconstruction for more normal reconstructive attempts, which are a function of the normal ego. Reconstruction, then, may be considered as a synthesizing function of the ego and indicates that the analytic process is a synthesizing one as well.

REFERENCES

[1] Freud, S. Moses and Monotheism, Standard Edition, London, Hogarth Press, 1937–1939, 22, 71.

———— with M. Breuer. On the Psychical Mechanism of Hysterical Phenomena, Collected Papers, 1949, pp. 1, 24.

[3] Freud, A. Observations on child development, Psychoanal. Stud. Child, 6:18, 1951.

[4] Kanzer, M. Past and present in the transference, J. Amer. Psychoanal. Ass., 1:144, 1952.

[5] Reider, N. Reconstruction and screen function, J. Amer. Psychoanal. Ass., 1:389, 1953.

[6] Bornstein, B. The analysis of a phobic child, Psychoanal. Stud. Child, 3/4:181, 1949.

[7] Tommy made ample use of many archeological metaphors. Freud has used such metaphors in order to clarify the function of the psychoanalytic process. In 1937 he compared archeology and psychoanalysis (Constructions in Analysis, Collected Papers, 1950, pp. 5, 358) and stated: "But our comparison between the two forms of work can go no further than this; for the main difference between them lies in the fact that for the archeologist the reconstruction is the aim and end of his endeavors while for analysis the construction is only a preliminary labour." Analytic constructions are not the end but only

a means of the therapeutic process. In 1899 (On Screen Memories, Collected Papers, 1950, pp. 5, 47), Freud had already stated: "The childhood memories did not, as people are accustomed to say, emerge; they were formed at that time and a number of motives, which had no concern with historical accuracy, had their part in thus forming them as well as in the selection of the memories themselves."

17

A PSYCHOTHERAPEUTIC SESSION
WITH THE SPACE CHILD *

*But wherever our methods permit us to look deeper, we find at
the bottom of it all the conviction, the mortal self-accusation,
that it was the child who abandoned the mother, because he
had been in such a hurry to become independent.*

ERIK ERIKSON

In the last two chapters we have offered longitudinal studies of certain
aspects of the psychotherapeutic treatment of a borderline psychotic child.
These studies enabled us to consider several theoretical questions. These
included the function of time and space defense patterns in the restitutive
struggle of the patient, as well as the interrelationship of memory and
reconstruction with ego changes occurring in the treatment process. This
chapter, centering primarily around one psychotherapeutic hour, will allow
a cross-sectional view of some of the psychological mechanisms previously
described, and also will permit us to comment on the interpretive work of
the psychotherapist in reference to the psychology of this borderline
patient.

Tommy, now 12, had come to Southard School three years prior to the
interview which provides our data. His prominent middle-class parents
were intimidated by his threats of self-destruction, and felt rebuffed and
bewildered in their unsuccessful efforts to please him. While there is
mental illness in the family, the parents themselves show a fairly good
adjustment. One may wonder of course if they, and particularly the mother,
were rejecting to the child at an early age. We were unable to establish
with certainty if the mother's present cool and hopeless attitude toward
her son was a response to his lack in "sending power"[1] or if her present
attitude reflected her own lack in the capacity for motherly warmth.

* Dorothy G. Wright is coauthor of this chapter.

We described above (Chapters 15 and 16) Tommy's initial inaccessibility in therapy and the many weeks which elapsed before real contact was achieved when he permitted the therapist's entry into his psychological world via a fantasy which took the therapist and himself far away to outer space. The discrepancy between the anxious and helpless child and the violent and dangerous general was underscored, as we noted, by the patient's specific use of space fantasies. Gradually the infinite space characteristic of his fantasy productions turned into the geographical distance between Kansas and Arizona, although the dichotomy between the child's reality adjustment and the hero of his fantasy continued. When his fantasy finally landed at Southard School and the psychotherapeutic hour itself, it was accompanied by a crash of acting out of destructive impulses.[2]

Concomitant to these fantasies in which isolation was expressed through distance, the patient elaborated fantasies in which isolation was expressed through time. In controlling the time machine he controlled the past. Rather late in therapy he discovered that he could not change his life by thinking up a different past and he gave up the ghastly Orwellian control of the past as he gained genuine control of the present. To sum up, we quote Dr. Mark Kanzer: [3]

Space and time inevitably play an important part in the instinctual gratifications and in ego defenses: Actually, space and time are inherently involved in all object relationships. Introjection shortens space and time, projection increases space and time between the ego and the object. As the schizoid individual withdraws into himself, he concomitantly increases his psychic separation from the outer world until he feels himself infinitely remote in space and time from all surrounding objects. Then, as in the case of Tommy, a restitutional phase may be marked by efforts to regain in this fashion and experimental contacts with reality are set up, which the therapist learns to foster.

The interview which constitutes the basis for our cross-sectional study is drawn from a later time in therapy. The child has achieved a greater capacity for the mastery of inner and outer stress but is once again confronted with the problem of separation; his therapist is leaving for a week's absence. Our aim in this presentation is twofold: to illustrate the different modes of ego mastery which the child employs in his response to the threatened loss; and to demonstrate how interpretation *at this stage of the therapeutic process* enables him to regain control by bringing into play a more mature level of mastery.

At the time of this interview Tommy is still living at Southard School but is about ready to board with a family in the local community. He is already attending public high school and does extremely well in a setting which, at first, was very trying for him. Thus, in numerous ways, Tommy has changed considerably since his arrival at Southard School. In fact, if the measure of external adaptation could be considered the only measure of his improved health, one could indeed be very optimistic. External adaptation, the ability for social adjustment, and the capacity to cope with the pressures of everyday school life, however, are but one yardstick of the internal situation. Frequently, with children like Tommy, an excellent or improved record of external adaptation may well go hand in hand with parallel productions of extreme psychopathology within the psychotherapeutic situations. Notwithstanding Tommy's greatly improved social adjustment, he returned from time to time to the solution of violent and extreme fantasies in his therapy hour. This occurred when he could not cope with simple social situations which created difficulties for him. Furthermore, he continued to employ play material very much like a younger child and used it to express his current problems. All of this appears in the selected interview:

Tommy walked into the playroom, went over and opened the cabinet where the toys are kept. There on the shelf was a boy doll which Tommy had played with several months ago when he was struggling with his feelings about being a girl. At that time he had slit the doll between the legs and inserted a piece of crayon for a penis. For all these months the doll had remained dressed in overalls but today the doll's pants were gone and some other child had cut a big hole up between the doll's legs and into its stomach so that the rubber stuffing was falling out. Tommy grabbed the doll, held it up on its legs and yelled, "Look, Wright, a bomb has exploded and ruined this doll!" The psychotherapist expressed surprise at the state of the doll while Tommy explained over and over again that a bomb was responsible for the destruction. Tommy paused and asked what the therapist thought had caused it. She asked if Tommy remembered what he had done to the doll. Tommy said that he remembered all right and found the piece of crayon and showed it to her. The therapist told him that it looked as if some child had undressed the doll, found the crayon penis, and had been so disturbed that he had cut out that big hole. Tommy asked if she thought that a penis would bother a child that much and the therapist thought that it would. Tommy said plaintively: "You know, Wright, I think I have more trouble with this sex stuff than any other kid in the school." The therapist stated, "Maybe even more than the child that destroyed the doll." Tommy said, "Yes, more than that." The therapist said that this was possible since she knew that it bothered him a good deal.

Child and therapist used the play material here with a mutual awareness that they are talking about Tommy's problems concerning his own sexual identity, his anxiety about sexual wishes, his interpersonal problems with other children, boys and girls, and the help he needs in order to cope with his difficulties. At any moment, the language of the play in this hour could almost be replaced by the kind of discussion about such matters that one may expect of a child at the end of a latency period. During this session, with the therapist's acceptance and assurance, Tommy seemed ready to clarify his anxiety. This was stimulated by both his discovery of the damaged doll and, more specifically, his fear of punishment as expressed in his fantasy about a bomb (a castrating device) causing the damage. His behavior represents a marked change from the days when he could not accept any apparent connection between his fantasies and the psycho-therapeutic, as well as the social, situation with which he was attempting to cope. Very frequently during the period of therapy from which this interview is drawn, Tommy would successfully communicate a specific anxiety-arousing problem, then leave the play material and turn to more matter-of-fact conversation about himself and his day-to-day problems. Thus he has achieved some capacity to relinquish the safety device of re-gressive language. In the past, this had afforded him the protection to cope with the stress of inner problems and those deriving from transference feelings, and had also enabled him to remain in the psychotherapeutic situation instead of taking flight into an autistic world, into physical ill-ness, or from the therapy room.

The psychotherapeutic session continued:

The child then said, "Say, Wright, I have news for you. I won't be here Friday as I have to make up some school work." The psychotherapist stated that was okay but she also had news for him. She was going to be away all next week at a professional convention and would not be able to see him. Tommy thought a bit and said, "Are you famous or something?" She said no, she was not famous. He could not see why she would want to go away to the convention unless she was famous. The psychotherapist explained that the convention helped her professionally and that's why she attended.

The main concern of the reader will be attached to the response of the psychotherapist. It would seem that she was consciously reminded by the boy's comment about the hour which he had to miss that she, in turn, was planning to be absent. On a different level, however, one may wonder if she did not make a mistake in so stating her anticipated absence, since she seemed to be "paying him back in kind." It was as if she was telling him that she would leave him for a week since he had indicated that he would miss an hour. Her comment in the context of the hour could be considered, therefore, as "an act of revenge." We owe to Dr. Nelly Tibout the suggestion that the unconscious may have served the psychotherapist correctly. The things that we plan, and the careful psychotherapeutic maneuvers we devise, are occasionally replaced by spontaneous acts. These acts perhaps reflect—as we believe to be true in this case— the therapist's perception that the child is ready to deal with a trying situation and can afford the give and take of normal interpersonal relationships where less caution on the part of the adult is necessary. August Aichhorn has repeatedly stated that the most effective educational methods are not those which are deliberately planned by the parent or stem from an educational philosophy. Rather, they originate in moments of less control as expressions of strong positive or negative feelings. During the next moments of the psychotherapeutic session, however, the therapist may well have wondered about the timing of her remark concerning her absence:

Tommy returned to the play material and took the girl doll, undressed it, and announced that there was going to be a rape. The psychotherapist asked if this is what the doll deserved. Tommy said that it was and that we had to do something about this woman. She was a menace to society. There was only one thing to do and that was to bury her. He pulled out the sandbox and got out three boxes of soldiers and posted them around the edges of the box. The psychotherapist asked him why he needed so many men. Tommy said that they were there to see that this woman did not escape. The therapist asked then if this woman was going to the convention city, too.

Here we note that the matter-of-fact conversation about time arrangements for psychotherapeutic sessions to come gives way suddenly to the child's spontaneous play. Even though he continues the earlier play with the girl doll, he changes the theme and obviously reacts to the threat of separation. Early confusion about sexuality and aggression returns as the child's anger expresses itself in the fantasy of rape and of execution of the woman whom he considers a menace to society. We note also that the sexual and aggressive attack is carried out in this fantasy not by him alone but that he uses helpers, the little soldiers. It is as if he could stand up against the threat only by allying himself with men. The psychotherapist lets him know that she understands how overwhelmed he feels and how he considers himself unable alone to carry out his act of aggression. By asking him if this woman was going to the convention city, too, she lets him know simultaneously that she understands his fantasy and accepts it but wants to respect his wish for telling her indirectly.

We wish to point out how quickly the level of communication

between child and therapist changes after the psychotherapist's provocative comment which she did not consciously plan. In early interviews, the child in such situations would become inaccessible. Here, however, we note that his shift into a more regressive mode of communication serves to continue the communication between patient and therapist, not to disrupt it.

The interview proceeded:

Tommy said, no, didn't the therapist know who this woman was? She was Paul Bunyan's wife, and she was forty feet tall, and we had to bury her. He went ahead very slowly piling up the sand. When he got up to her buttocks he asked me if she needed to take a shit. If so, she had better do it now before he covered her up further. The psychotherapist said, no, and she thought that the woman could manage even covered up. The burying process continued slowly. When only her head was uncovered, Tommy said that she now had started screaming and calling for help but it would do no good. The therapist said that it would do no good. After all, a big overpowering woman forty feet tall had to be controlled. Otherwise, she might get the better of all those little men. It surely was difficult to control a woman that big and overwhelming. Tommy grinned a little and went on covering up her head. He expressed relief and satisfaction when he finally had buried her completely.

The therapist's intimation that she had some idea that she was connected with this woman, by wondering if she, too, were going to the convention city, encouraged the child to state his problem. He spoke about the woman as Paul Bunyan's wife. This may be considered a condensation of the oedipal and pre-oedipal mother image. He, being Paul Bunyan, was the baby who, after wiping out his parents by rocking his cradle with immense strength, grew up alone and mastered the world. He, in the image of Paul Bunyan, sees himself as the husband of the woman, as well as the deserted baby. In both roles the woman is a menace, for she is a deserting, neglectful mother and a dangerous wife, and therefore must be destroyed. We realize that the child turns the actual situation into its opposite in his fantasy. For in the fantasy, it is not the woman who deserts him but, rather, he, himself, who deserts and destroys her and makes separation into her death rather than his own. It is as if at this point Tommy was flooded with early emotions combining reactions to different traumatic separation situations in his life. Further, a powerful woman cannot be destroyed unless with the help of other men, the soldiers in the fantasy. They are little men, perhaps as little and as ineffectual as Tommy may at times conceive his father to be, but if he is allied with them he can face the all-powerful woman. We see that the actual situation brings to the foreground the child's specific way of "resolving" the oedipal and pre-oedipal triangle situations. By actively burying the woman in this fantasy he masters the problem. His own anxiety, his fear of being left alone, which is tapped through the threat of the loss of psychotherapy hours, is converted into a situation where the woman of the play fantasy suffers the anxiety. Even his question, when he slowly covers up the doll and asks his therapist if she needs to defecate, is his way of taking revenge upon the woman; for it is she who is now so frightened that she may need to do this. She is the one who starts screaming and calls for help, and he is the one who leaves her in the lurch and continues the burial. Thus he actively makes the doll suffer for what used to be his own fate, just as Paul Bunyan converts his lonesomeness, his helplessness, his rejection into a situation of mastery where, in spite of being a helpless baby, he can turn himself into a giant who has no need for his parents.

The psychotherapist accepts his feelings about the big and overpowering woman, and lets him know that she is not frightened or disapproving about his outburst of anger. When he had finally buried the doll completely, she felt that he was ready to share more fully with her an understanding of his play:

She said that it was quite an accomplishment, and then told Tommy that the buried woman was not really Paul Bunyan's wife but that it was she, the psychotherapist. Here she was, going off to the convention and leaving him alone again. And he cannot do anything about it except bury her and try to forget her while she was gone. She said that she was really sorry not to see him next week but that she would be back a week thereafter. Tommy asked if she was sure about it, and she said that she was. He said okay, then, and he would mark it down on his calendar so that he would not forget. He asked her how she was going, by train or plane, and some more details about the kind of convention that it was. After the excitement of his eruptive fantasy, he seemed quite calm and left in a friendly mood at the end of the hour.

The condensed finale of this session indicates that the child easily accepted the psychotherapist's interpretation, and found his way back from the violence of the fantasy, and from the fear and loneliness of a deserted child, to an ordinary way of communication. At the end we note that he makes arrangements for his next psychotherapeutic session. At first glance, the reader may find nothing remarkable about Tommy's ability to accept the interpretation and to return to a level of communication which indicates that he has mastered the disappointment of the original announcement. In earlier phases of treatment, however, the child could not have left his fantasy world. Originally his fantasies excluded the therapist completely except that she was permitted to listen to them. Later, the therapist appeared in the fantasies but her interpretations hardly affected the course of events. Nor did her interpretations in the earlier phase of therapy help the child to bring into play more mature levels of mastery.

In our discussion of the beginning of this psychotherapeutic hour we showed how easy it had become for the child to change from the language of the play to the language in which he could openly discuss his current anxieties concerning schoolmates, relationships with girls, and his relationship to the therapist. Many distance devices, which he had to use earlier in his therapy to check powerful impulses and to cope with reality, had given way to new modes of mastery made possible through the new capacities of his more fully developed ego. The powerful fantasy life had, in earlier days, obliterated secondary thought processes and continues occasionally to do so still. But most of the time, it is now in the service of more mature ego functions. Similar, direct, and full interpretation, which we might have attempted to—or did—offer in earlier periods of treatment, created panic and drove Tommy away from psychotherapy instead of providing the help that was intended. At such times, we may have understood him correctly in terms of being able to explain specific content which he had brought to us. We did not understand correctly, however, when we communicated our explanations to him in the face of his lacking capacity to make use of these on the level offered. Only when he could let us know that his fantasies had become less threatening to him, that he could almost consciously utilize them in order to cope with everyday problems, could our explicit interpretations be helpful.

Preconscious awareness is accompanied by the capacity of the ego to make use of interpretation and the child himself provides the cues regarding his readiness. We may note the psychotherapist's cautious attempts to probe just how much contact she really had with him in this hour and how far she could venture with her interpretive efforts. If the therapist would have stated in earlier periods of psychotherapy that she thought the woman of the play fantasy was going to the convention city, Tommy's behavior would have been quite different. He would have reacted either with panic; or told the therapist to "shut up"; or he would otherwise have indicated that he was not yet ready to leave his fantasy world or to try to solve his problems at any level other than his fantasy solutions.

The functioning of this child's ego organization on different levels, the rapid shift from extreme fantasy to secondary-process control has been typical for him, as well as for many other borderline children. These children have permitted considerable insight into shifting ego states and the different uses that they make of available ego functions during the psychotherapeutic process. They have permitted us to refine techniques in psychotherapy because of the cues that they provided, their exquisite sensitivity, and their widely ranging modes of solving problems and communication methods. Earlier concepts, in which interpretation was seen as an attempt on the part of the psychotherapist to translate the content of the fantasy or of the play into the language of the adult, have been deepened. Meaningful communication, in which insight is sometimes given not through translation, not through an explanation, but by accompanying the child into his fantasy world and responding to him within the language that he offers has been found useful with these children. The conscious or unconscious choice of "language," of "level of communication" provides safe distance which the therapist learns to respect if he is to maintain contact and be of maximum help. In the last example above, the psychotherapist communicates with this child at first within the context of the Paul Bunyan fantasy. She lets him know that she understands why Paul Bunyan must turn against his wife and (the phallic) mother. She sympathizes with him and realizes the depth of his fear that impels him to call for help from so many little men (passive, weak father image). As he travels on with her, she senses that he is ready to deal with the problems on a higher level as well. Her final comment in which she links Paul Bunyan's wife with herself is not *the* interpretation. In our opinion, it simply links the total therapeutic process throughout the hour and gives final meaning to preceding interpretive comments on different levels in terms of his present anger with her.

The affective character of interpretive comments that distinguish them from an intellectual process has frequently been stressed. Here we wish to give an example of interpretation on different levels of ego functioning, so necessary in child psychotherapy and particularly in therapy with the borderline patient. The different levels of communication must be appropriate to different states of the ego, as these emerge during the psychotherapeutic process. These states, in turn, reflect important aspects of the nature of the psychotherapeutic situation and derive from several covariants: the nature of the conflict; the characteristic mode of its resolution; the defenses brought into play; and the ego organization evidenced at the specific moment in the therapy process.

REFERENCES

[1] Erickson, E. H. Childhood and Society, New York, W. W. Norton, 1950.

[2] A variety of investigators such as Robert Plank (Communication in science fiction, ETC., 11:16, 1954) and Samuel I. Hayakawa (From science-fiction to fiction-science, ETC., 8:280, 1951) have called attention to the increase in science-fiction literature, and have discussed the meaning of this literature in terms of its being a symptom for certain instabilities in our culture, a symptom of the unsolved problem of communication.

[3] Kanzer, M. Personal communication.

18

THE SPACE CHILD: TEN
YEARS LATER *

*Let us keep before our eyes the nature of the emotional
relations which hold between men in general. According to
Schopenhauer's famous simile of the freezing porcupines no one
can tolerate a too intimate approach to his neighbor.*

SIGMUND FREUD

Successes and failures may be of equal importance in their contributions
to the development of treatment techniques. This final report on the
Space Child is one of the few studies available on the long-term treatment
of borderline schizophrenics. A success story, the insights derived from the
work with Tommy may be applicable in the therapy of other such patients.

Today, Tom is a young man in his twenties, personable, shy, and
somewhat tense. He has completed his Master's degree in physics and plans
to secure his doctorate so as to participate fully in "space" research. He
handles his own inheritance and investments, drives his own car, and has
twice traveled in Europe. He is married, teaches in college, and is comfortable with those who share his intellectual interests.

Tom's treatment began when he was an in-patient at Southard School
and continued, first, when he was moved into a supervised boarding home,
and then, when five years later, he made other living arrangements in a
nearby university town while attending school. During this entire period
of eleven years, Tom was seen in psychotherapy as well as in casework
focused on reality problems, both processes being integrated into a total
treatment program. This report, however, will cover only the 1,236 hours
of psychotherapy.

Tom's *distance devices* could not be properly dealt with therapeutically in terms of the traditional notion of defense only. They had to be

* Dorothy G. Wright is coauthor of this chapter.

348

seen also in terms of their adaptive value, since they allowed the main-tenance of optimum contact—if "optimum" is understood in terms of current capacities of the ego organization.

As one studies anew the records of the early period of treatment, one is struck with two aspects of both the phenomenon and the use of distance in the psychotherapeutic process: a diminution of distance over the long haul of the psychotherapeutic process; and, at the same time, a constant shifting back and forth in each hour or phase of treatment. This suggests that there are strong fluctuations in the utilization of distance devices characteristic for each hour as well as for the total process. The reconstruction of the early childhood situation during psychotherapy, as in the case of Tom, can be a decisive instrument only if one pays attention to "the way in which reconstruction takes place" (Chapter 4). The psychotherapist accepts the main modes of defense and adaptation, the peculiar language of the child, is willing to enter a fantasy world with him, and allows for the type of relationship for which he is ready. The therapist's concern, as translated into treatment adaptations, seems to be responsible for Tom's progress.

Tom's time-machine fantasies reveal another aspect of his treatment and the function of reconstruction. In these fantasies, time shifted for Tom according to his fluctuating ego states. His control of the past and of the future in these fantasies was but a perversion of the attempt to control the present and the future: the time machine helped Tommy to deny his fears. When the analytic process is seen as reconstructing not only past experiences but also the present, reconstruction may be viewed as a process, as an ego function, and it demonstrates that memory, even psychotic-like memory, has a specific function within the psychic apparatus. Tommy's fantasies can be considered an attempt to demonstrate how he had been trying to master conflicts and ego facilities in order to cope with them. The fluidity of the fantasy, the changing use Tom made of it, can be considered an indication of the degree of illness as it had developed and the process of its reconstruction during treatment. Tom's psychotic-like fantasies are the schizophrenoid child's substitute for the recollections of less severely disturbed patients.

By the time that Tommy was about to move out of Southard School to a boarding home, he had achieved an acceptable external adaptation, had proven ability for a limited social adjustment, and could adequately cope with the pressures of high school life. Despite this progress the therapeutic material continued to reveal extreme psychopathology. Tom frequently brought into his therapy hours violent and strange fantasies which had a reality basis in the difficulties he experienced in the boarding home and at school. Therapy sessions of this period demonstrate the functioning of Tom's ego organization on different levels: the shift from extreme fantasy to secondary-process control, the insight into ego states, and the psychotherapeutic techniques employed, in which accepting the distance device permits Tom to restore his ability to cope with the present trauma.

The psychotherapy of Tom has provoked much discussion of the concept of distance. One is first tempted to see in this material early concepts of defense mechanisms rather than distance devices. One might well suggest that every patient uses distance devices, that is, defense mechanisms, as if to split hours. The peculiar nature of the borderline or schizophrenic child, however, suggests certain differences which picture the *special ego difficulties* of these children. We might simply think of Tom's "distance devices" in terms of projection, but then we are left with the question as to why the aggressive act or the forbidden practice takes place thousands of miles or light years away, or why it may be projected into the future or the past. These different aspects of projection demonstrate ego difficulties of a special kind. They suggest peculiar problems concerning the maintenance of object relationships, the stability of introjects, the breaking up of experience of self and/or objects. They are, moreover, directly related to restitutive and regressive phenomena in the struggle of the psychotic ego for survival and for the maintenance of optimum contact through optimum distance.

The way in which Tommy finally resolved his essential problem of strengthening his ego through meaningful close relationships with optimum distance can be fairly well traced through the last eight years of psychotherapy. When this period began, Tom was living in Southard School and attending public high school. In therapy he was no longer using the concept of time as a distance device, and the characters in his fantasies were no longer historical figures or bizarre Martians. Instead, they were real girls attending high school with him, whom he knew by name; although he referred to them as "dames." In his fantasies, they lived on various planets. He spent many therapy hours trying to eliminate them by artillery, warfare, suffocation, and torture. None of these methods was successful. All the "dames" survived because they tricked him and rendered him helpless. These fantasies were interpreted in terms of his feelings about the omnipotence of the therapist, about the fear of certain girls in high school being superior to him academically, as well as to an impending visit of his mother who still invaded his room and cleaned it out of all things which she considered nonessential. Tom then invented another fantasy. This one was concerned with the difficulty the world experienced in trying to adjust to the Inner Planetary System. In his fantasy, the world was the most inexperienced and the youngest member of all the planets and, because of its inexperience, it was very difficult for the world to adjust to the planetary system as a whole. He ended the fantasy by saying, "Of course, all planets have trouble in adjusting but they eventually make it okay."

This fantasy served to introduce reality discussions about his inexperience in relationships, especially with female figures. At that time he was attracted to an intelligent, older, inaccessible girl whom he pursued enthusiastically but fearfully. He was also concerned about another girl who pursued him much in the same way that he was pursuing the first girl. This brought forth a fantasy of Tommy's conflict between his real world and his dream world. It was reminiscent of the previous dichotomy he had made of himself when he had divided himself into the good Tommy in residence and the bad Tommy in Arizona. Now the distance was less, geographically speaking, since the good Tommy was in the reality world dealing with reality problems, and the bad Tommy was in residence. The same characters appeared both in the dream world and in the real world. In the dream world, Tommy was a dictator and the girl, whom he loved, was a patient in residence with whom he attempted to act out his sexual feelings but was thwarted by the supervision of the staff. In the real world he lived in the boarding home and, because of shyness and inexperience, was inept and utterly unable to establish even a speaking relationship with the girl. Here we see not only a diminution of the distance which separated Tommy's divided self, but also the acceptance of certain controls over what he considered to be his unacceptable impulses. Tommy suggested that he write a manuscript about these two worlds, which the therapist and he discussed in detail. The therapist used "the story" as a reconstruction device to help Tom understand where he had been and how far he had come so that he was finally able to accept his "badness" as not being entirely destructive. This was the beginning of many discussions between the therapist and Tom concerning his use of distance, not only in dividing himself but in separating himself from the therapist as well as all other relationships which seemed menacingly close to him. These discussions were confined to his therapy hours. His psychotic processes never interfered with his academic achievements, the two processes being entirely separated.

During this period, Tom's father died suddenly. Coincidental with this trauma, Tom's graduation from high school was imminent; graduation to Tom signified both an accomplishment and a finality. From the reality of these events and their destructive meanings to him, Tom presented his first fantasy on the theme of termination of treatment. According to Tom a planet was about to collide with the earth and we would all be destroyed. This was interpreted in terms of his fear of termination as well as the reawakening of the Oedipal struggle, which had been highlighted since the father's death. Tom then became able to give up the fantasy and to begin expressing his feelings of fear and depression more in terms of lack of success or failure.

Tom entered college in the fall after spending a summer month with his mother. He became deeply involved in his college life and in trying to relate to his peers in a socially acceptable way. Interspersed with this reality material were several lurid sexual fantasies which, Tom reported to the therapist, were his major preoccupation while he walked to and from his classes. As he had on other occasions, Tom wrote out his fantasies to bring to his therapy hours. His writing out his fantasies might have been thought of as another way Tom had devised to maintain distance in the therapeutic relationship. On the other hand, it could be understood in terms of his bid for closeness, inasmuch as through writing down and sharing his intimate thoughts and feelings with the therapist, he was seeking a safe but intimate contact. In these manuscripts, with much detail and in acceptable literary form, he described his fantasies of his relationships with many girls; they were all prostitutes who expressed admiration of him and over whom he had complete control. However, he never allowed himself, even in the manuscript, to have sexual relations with them. Instead he was preoccupied only with their armpits, a concern he was finally able to discuss in terms of phobic preoccupation which again restated his need to remove himself at least some distance from his real preoccupation, i.e., the girls' genitals. The therapist slowly interpreted within this metaphor Tom's need for care and love and his previous use of violence and destruction to cover up his feelings of tenderness and gentleness. Tom seemingly accepted the lessening of distance between himself and the therapist and acted out on this by attempting to make the therapist a mother figure. On one occasion he went to the therapist's home demanding help with his school work, which, of course, he did not need. He also made numerous attempts to get the therapist involved in his social life. Finally, in desperation, there were several suicide threats and one abortive suicidal gesture. During this emergency period, the social worker gave Tom additional external support by providing him with a companion. The social worker helped the boarding-home parents understand this crisis situation and gave Tom the heightened attention and care he needed just then.

Following this rather difficult period Tom was able to verbalize his reluctance to get well and his fear of losing his contact with the therapist. These fantasies assumed a different mode of communication. They were no longer on the planets, which in fact, had not been in evidence in therapy for some time. On the reality level, Tom was very much interested in major league baseball, and his fantasies were also concerned with baseball. For example, in his fantasy he was the manager of a complete baseball team in which all the members were girls. When the therapist commented on the change in fantasy content, Tom told her that he himself had noticed a difference in the material of his fantasies in that they must now be logical. He wasn't satisfied to use any material that was unscientific or unreal. The baseball fantasies were specifically and meticulously carried out according to national baseball rules, and every player's baseball statistics were mathematically computed for the entire season.

Another development which took place at this time, about which Tom was able to tell the therapist, was that his fantasies no longer were in control of him. He could engage in fantasy or lay it aside. He could also manipulate the fantasies as he pleased. In the baseball fantasies, he decided who was going to win and how competent the various teams and players were going to be. Tom further informed the therapist that these fantasies were not as exciting or pleasurable as his former ones. This was particularly significant because during this period Tommy was retested by the Psychology Department. In addition to the generally improved condition, one of the findings was that he was less creative than when he had been more psychotic. Tom seemed to have some awareness of this both in that the fantasies no longer seemed so absorbing, stimulating, and uncontrollable and that reality and interpersonal relationships were becoming increasingly more tolerable. As the therapist worked with the baseball fantasies and interpreted Tom's need for control, an element of chance entered into them. He devised a wheel with numbers on it which revolved and decided the fate of the players and the team. Tom found this more exciting than maintaining complete control himself. He thus seemed more able to allow himself to relax a bit and accept and deal with unanticipated situations which, previously, had always sent him into a panic.

While there was no panic now, the lessening of control did bring forth a very involved fantasy which Tom again presented to the therapist in manuscript form. Distance was not the prominent factor in offering this written communication either. It was rather like a shy lover who gives his love-object a sonnet expressing his feelings of intimacy. However, Tom's "sonnet" was raw and uninhibited, without the appropriate coverings which our culture demands. This fantasy involved only one girl. There were many pages of foreplay before Tom actually had the sexual act with the girl who performed throughout as a puppet or a doll to meet his sexual demands. This hour compares rather strikingly with earlier phases of treatment. He handed the therapist the manuscript and asked her to read it without making any comments. Then he attempted to control the therapist in the same way that he had controlled the girl in the fantasy. He demanded that the therapist answer only his direct questions on the fantasy and no more. As the therapist interpreted his fear of being over-whelmed and enslaved by her, there was a definite shift to Tom's real need to understand how to relate to another person, particularly to a female. This was discussed in terms of his lack of experience as to how one goes about getting a date and courting a girl, as well as in terms of the therapist's accepting him as a person who could disagree with her and maintain opinions of his own.

In this fashion, along with the educational process of learning how to initiate and carry out a social relationship with a peer, Tom and the therapist entered into discussions of philosophy, religion, and politics. In these areas the therapist attempted to help Tom express his opinions, which were often opposed to her own, and to allow him to maintain them without his feeling annihilated. During this phase of his treatment, Tom was able to tell the therapist that he no longer was afraid that she would die and he would be abandoned. He assured the therapist that if she were to die now, he thought he could tolerate a transfer to another therapist.

About this time Tom learned of the prospective remarriage of his mother. Just as he had been able to handle the mourning process for his father in terms of reality, he also attempted valiantly to maintain a reality focus on this problem. He informed the therapist that it was now difficult for him to go into fantasy at all and this rather depressed him because, in many ways, he would like to regress to the old symbiotic relationship. He told the therapist of his fears about the marriage and his own dependency needs, as well as his anxiety and revolt against growing up and being left alone. Along with these expressed feelings, there was considerable adolescent revolt and acting out against the boarding-home parents which had to be handled by the social worker. The following is a summary of the social work process: [1]

Tom used distance variably with the boarding-home parents. He did not think he could accept their religious and political philosophies and he saw their efforts to involve him in their activities and to get closer to him as dangerous. He felt it would make him a conformist, like everyone else, and thus destroy his individuality. Tom dealt with his great hunger for warmth and closeness as if he were a tiny planet, longing to get closer to the sun, yet fearing he would be pulled into its fiery center. On the other hand, too great a distance from those who cared for him meant coldness and suffering through deprivation. On one occasion, in the front yard of the boarding home, Tom observed a young bird which had fallen from its nest, struggling to fly back but unable to do so. In fury, Tom attacked the bird to the amazement and anger of the boarding family. By doing so he risked his own placement which was so precious to him, and yet so precarious. Tom identified his own fate with that of the bird which called forth in him anger and fear to an intolerable degree which found release in his attack.

Yet Tom was intrigued by the way the boarding-family lived and he observed and imitated their activities closely. He joined a youth group of a church, but it had to be a different one from that which the boarding-home family attended. He enjoyed playing with their grandchildren when they visited and was kind and gentle to them; but, in the presence of adults he concealed these feelings carefully and seemed brusque and detached. He wanted the boarding-home mother to wash his hair, to prepare his meals carefully, never to be away overnight. But toward her he affected an uncaring and rude manner and insisted on his independence and their nonintrusion into his whereabouts. When Tom was reminded by the caseworker that the care and protection given by the boarding-home parents were appropriate and that this did not mean his independence would be transgressed as had happened in the past with his mother, his attitude toward them visibly softened and he was secretly pleased. As the boarding-home parents observed and understood Tom's pattern of closeness and distance, they were able, through casework discussions, to accept the fact that Tom himself might never directly express his feelings of warmth and gratitude for their efforts in his behalf. Instead their gratifications came from seeing Tom improve and their realization of the part they played in helping him achieve these modifications, as well as the recognition given them for their contribution by the treatment team.

In therapy there was much use of denial, particularly in regard to the marriage. Tom explained that since his mother had had a hysterectomy this would undoubtedly prevent the mother and stepfather from having intercourse. He also thought that perhaps she would not go through with the marriage because she would be too concerned as to whether it would be upsetting to him. Gradually, however, he was able to evaluate what he would lose and what he would gain by his mother's remarriage and thus his initial concern was eventually dissolved.

It was interesting that as Tom reacted to his mother's marriage as his losing her to the stepfather, he initiated discussion with the therapist about changing his psychotherapy hours from three to two hours a week, which meant an additional loss, that of contact with the therapist. Immediately after making this suggestion Tom accused the therapist of trying to get rid of him! However, he had scheduled his college classes so that it was impossible for him to include more than two hours of psychotherapy a week. At the same time Tom also began moving out into the community and making plans to enroll at a neighboring university after graduating from the local college.

In evaluating the way Tom handled these events, certain conclusions seem possible. As long as Tom felt his parents were a part of his psychological world, as long as their reality was his reality which threatened always to engulf and enmesh him, threatening his own individuality as a person, Tom resorted to fantasy. He used it as a means of escaping the intolerable closeness of the symbiotic relationship. When he came to treatment, he continued to use fantasy but, through the efforts of the therapist, the fantasy was no longer useful or successful as a distance device. By entering into Tom's fantasy world, the therapist established a nonthreatening but close relationship so that the fantasy became a closeness device. But the closeness was safe for him and for the therapist in being limited by the structure of the therapeutic relationship and the hour itself.

As treatment progressed, the use of fantasy, understood and translated into psychological meanings, helped Tom to attain a real distance from his parents. In the appropriate relationship with them, he was no longer bound up in their own emotional turmoil and achieved a healthy emotional separation. Thus, again, fantasy was no longer a necessary means to fend off the intolerable close emotional relationship which, to Tom, had no boundaries. When something happened to his parents (his father's death, his mother's remarriage), Tom was able to deal with these events and their real meaning to him on a reality level and without the use of fantasy. From then on Tom never again resorted to fantasy. For the remaining period in treatment, Tom struggled with separating from the therapist but without the use of fantasy.

The last four years of Tommy's treatment were not too different from that of the usual adolescent neurotic. The need for distance persisted but was understood and easily identified by Tom himself. His anxieties about relationships were often projected upon his fear of academic failure.

From the enormous amount of data available we have selected material which permits an assessment of the degree of health Tom attained and can be compared with the earlier assessment of illness. This specimen interview reveals his then-current modes of dealing with new situations as well as with separation. The material also shows a continuity between his past and his present, revealing not only the recovery achieved but the remaining scar tissue and potential future danger spots.

A year before the termination of treatment, Tom, having had a two weeks' vacation with his mother and stepfather, returned to therapy:

Tom walked in with his head bowed, looking a bit depressed. He shook hands with me and acknowledged my greeting. He sat down in the chair in a rather slouchy way, throwing his foot over the arm of the chair so that he was sitting at an angle not facing me. He quickly cut through the small talk concerning the enjoyable holiday, and suggested that we talk about something that was much more important; namely, that he was rapidly progressing down the highway toward ultimate failure. In his opinion there was no question about this, and failure was the only end there could be to the road he had taken. Evidently, he said, he had chosen to take this particular road and defeat and failure were what he wanted. He guessed there was not much he could do about it except just proceed on this road. I said it certainly sounded like a pretty dismal road and wondered what he saw at the end of it. Tom spoke about failure, complete failure, and, at my request, he described this failure in terms of his never really being able to carry out his hopes and ambitions for his life's work. He supposed that he was fairly intelligent and if he had taken another road, he could have been a very adequate scientist and could have done some creative work in the field of space. But since he had chosen this other road it was going to end up with his being a second-rate technician, working for people who did not know as much as he. After all, what else could he get after being kicked out of graduate school? I said I was now beginning to understand since he assumed that as he traveled along this road he was going to be kicked out of graduate school. Tom thought there was no question about it since he could not apply himself as he should he was undoubtedly going to make a C in one of his important subjects, and they simply could not keep anybody in graduate school who made a C. Since he seemed so determined to experience this road of hopelessness, I asked Tom whether he had any evidence which would indicate that this was going to happen. Tom spoke about a test he had taken before he went on his vacation on which he had an F. I said that it was quite unusual for him to make an F. He then added that the F was not on paper, that he just supposed it was an F, since he had missed two of the problems and felt the paper could not be graded any other way. I told Tom I knew he was unhappy, worried, and anxious about something, but I could hardly believe that it was all due to his not doing well on one test. After all, these horrible things which he anticipated, such as getting an F on the test or getting the C in the course and being kicked out of graduate school, hadn't happened as yet, and I wondered if it was something else. Tom said that it might as well be that way, but he did not know exactly what it was. He kept worrying about his school work and the fact that he was not doing so well and might get kicked out of graduate school. I told Tom that I was quite sure that when he starts worrying about his school work, which actually and usually is one of his least worries, he seemed to be denying and covering up other concerns. Tom said he guessed I would have to tell him what it was because he could not figure it out. I suggested that we should figure it out together as we always have. Usually when he is disturbed like this it had to do with me and he had not seen me for some time. Also, he had been thinking recently about cutting down his hours to one hour a week. The other thing I thought which might enter into the picture was this relationship with his

*mother. I wondered what kind of vacation he had while he was gone
these two weeks.*

The trained ear of the therapist realized that Tom was attempting to
cope with massive anxiety which was displaced onto an area of actual
strength, thus permitting him to cope with it more successfully. It was as
if he could talk about the pending failure, the "road to destruction," with
tongue-in-cheek, since he actually knew that the evidence pointed toward
success. Tom's way of beginning this interview was similar to those interviews at the beginning or at the mid-point of treatment where reality
problems, concerns of the present, and conflict situations with the therapist
or his own life situation, were projected onto powerful battles in the stars.
These had been accompanied occasionally with feelings of lonesomeness
or utter dismal failure in the agonizing crashes of world systems. These
psychotic-like displacements permitted Tom to establish some distance
from powerful affect and thus maintain communication with the therapist. As the ego organization shifted to more advanced functioning, she
could bring him down to earth, as it were, and deal with the actual situation at hand. Although there is similarity to these hours of psychotic-like
displacement, neurotic displacement mechanisms are dominant here. The
structure of his early treatment sessions is recalled in that he is dealing
again with dismal and utter failure. In the past, however, the problem of
the therapeutic situation was projected onto the heavens in a cosmic
metaphor. Now displaced onto the school situation, the observing ego
permits him to accept how inappropriately he has reacted to a comparatively
small event like a poorly done test. The therapist pointed out the displacement, realizing that he does worry about a "road" which he is about
to take and which he thinks might lead to disaster. He spoke of the
therapy road, as it were: his wish to cut down on the therapy hours and
prepare himself for separation from the therapist.

Tom's childhood fear was that he would be both rejected and en-
gulfed by the parents, a fear which was not without some basis in reality.
Tom always felt as if he were catapulted into space or into an archaic
past. His present fear, as he thought about separation from the therapist,
was shaped by two elements. He saw himself as the passive victim of an
angry and engulfing psychotherapist just as once he had experienced his
mother in these terms; or he saw himself as being thrown out of graduate
school.

The interview continued:

*Tom said that the vacation was a horrible one, the most unsatisfactory
one he ever had. He said he felt bored with the insignificant things his*

mother and stepfather and their friends talked about. He thought of the university experience when he and his friends discussed basic science, philosophy, and history, which to him were truly significant in this modern age. He described the comfortable feelings he enjoyed when being with his fellow students at the university, how he can argue scientific issues with them, disagreeing with them or being put in his place, but he complained there was nothing at home that he could talk about. He was bored with people who were just not intellectually his equal. He realized that he had difficulties in establishing interpersonal relationships, in sensing how other people feel, and in developing interests which are parallel to the interests of others. He guessed that he would have to try a little harder to be interested in what other people talk about, but he very much preferred to spend most of his time with his "real" friends who have interests similar to his own. I suggested to Tom that this would be a better solution. When I wondered how his mother would feel about his spending less time with her, Tom turned, straightened up in his chair, and looking straight into my eyes, said: "I am not going to be bossed by my mother as much as I have been in the past. After all, I am going to be twenty-one soon, and at that time I'm going to take over my finances. I think I can manage to take care of myself fairly well. . . . You might be interested in knowing that I am now completely free from Mrs. N. (His boarding-home mother.) Before I left for my vacation I was still taking my laundry back to her. Since I have come back I have found a laundry near the university and I am taking my clothes there myself and I rather enjoy the experience. There is really some advantage to being independent and taking care of myself."

I agreed that this did have advantages. Tom went on to say that he was also going to be less dependent upon the social worker, who had suggested that Tom get a better place to live in the university town. But Tom said that he liked the place where he was. After all, he had found this place by himself and was comfortable there. He liked the people he was living with and he did not feel it was necessary for him to make a change even though the social worker thought he might be happier with a more intellectual family. He felt very well in this situation and he was not going to change. I told Tom that I certainly saw no reason why he should. I was quite sure the social worker too would understand that he had made this decision, and I fully approved of it. Was there anything else he wanted to tell me? Tom grinned and said yes. What he really wanted to tell me was that beginning next week he was going to see me only once a week. He said he had thought about it a great deal since we had first begun to talk about it. At first it seemed that he wanted me to keep the second hour open so that he might have it if he wanted it, but he did not think he was going to need it. Anyway, with the next semester coming up, his schedule might be changed and it might not be possible for him to get down here on Tuesdays, so he wanted to keep the Thursday hour and relinquish the Tuesday one. I told Tom that this was satisfactory with me and that I was prepared to accept his decision in this matter. I could understand, too, how it had been difficult for him to make this decision, since it meant growing up and eventual complete termination of treatment. But I was quite sure such an eventuality was less frightening to him now than it had been when we had talked about it in the past. Tom said he had not only done some thinking about it but he had managed some other things on his own which made it unnecessary for him to come to Topeka so often. Up until recently Tom had been coming to Topeka to attend a church group, but now he informs me that he has found another church group in the university town and this group seemed much more stimulating and intellectual since it was made up entirely of college students. Hence, he does not plan to come back here at all except on Thursdays to see me and his social worker. I told Tom I was quite proud of the fact that he had gone ahead and had managed to work out some of these things for himself. It certainly indicated to me that he was able to live quite independently now and I was proud of him. But I was not too surprised because I had always known he had considerable strength and a lot of courage when it came to doing things that he was honestly motivated to do. I thought, however, that the difficulty he had in telling me this during this hour indicated that there was some ambivalence about all of these decisions and that I wanted him to be sure and know that he was not being abandoned by us in any sense because he chose to become more independent of us. I was quite sure that Mrs. N. and the social worker would always continue to be interested in him. As for myself, I would be very glad to set up an additional appointment any day of the week or at any time if an emergency arose and he felt that he needed it. Tom said that he knew that, although at this time it did not seem necessary. He reminded me that when he cut down from three hours to two he was afraid I would not give him the additional hour if he needed it, but, he laughed, saying that the funny thing about it was that since he had cut down to two hours he had never needed the additional third hour. I told Tom that perhaps it would work out and in this way, too, on the one hour, but that if he needed an extra hour I would certainly be available. It was the end of the hour now and Tom left, reminding me to cancel the Tuesday appointment for next week and assuring me that he would be back to see me on Thursday.

With the therapist's interpretation which related his anxiety about school failure to therapy itself, and of his relationship with her to his plan to reduce the hours, she encouraged him to deal realistically with his plans. Tom was able to express his true feelings concerning independence from his family, the boarding-home mother, the social worker, and, finally, the therapist herself. The second part of the hour became more a counseling kind of interview with a young student than therapy. Tom gave the impression that he had the strength to deal with the realities of life, that he was helped to become the active master of his plans.

This interview shows a fluctuation of distance and closeness, which is reminiscent of past interviews but not a mechanical repetition. The modernized replica has appropriate choices available beyond the basic conflicts and the rudimentary solutions.

From separation experienced as desertion imposed on a passive victim to separation chosen for maturity and productive functioning, the former Space Child has labored with the problem of human relationships. As he fluctuates between shriveling isolation and devouring intimacy, the goal of psychotherapy must be the development of his capacity for maintaining a comfortable distance. In achieving this, Tom must resolve over and over again his conflict, the extremes of which on a psychotic level are autistic and symbiotic positions; on a neurotic level they are lonesomeness and other-directedness. Psychotherapy enabled this young man to achieve self-direction, inner-directedness, and the capacity which allows him to create living space for himself, rather than being pushed into emotional outer space. He came to us as a small child who fled to a fantastic world; he left us as a young man, a competent scientist, who travels in the real world. He has not yet reached a stage in which intimacy can become a fulfillment but has definitely moved toward a *capacity for choice.*

We helped free him from the prison of his inner world, thereby enabling him to share in the life of his outer world. In turn, he helped us to learn about his inner world and how to help him and others similar to him.

REFERENCES

[1] From the social work summary contributed by Mr. Arthur Mandelbaum, M.S.W., Chief Social Worker, Children's Division of The Menninger Clinic, Topeka.

PART SIX

INTROJECTS AND IDENTIFICATORY DEVICES

They resemble a type of patient, described by Helene
Deutsch, in a clinical work on the psychology of adults,
as being on the borderline between neurosis and psychosis. She calls them persons of the "as if" type, because
in every new object-relation they live as if they were
really living their own life and expressing their own
feelings, opinions and views.

The psychic situation in this and similar phases of
puberty may be described very simply. These passionate
and evanescent love-fixations are not object-relations at
all in the sense in which we use the term in speaking of
adults. They are identifications of the most primitive
kind, such as we meet with in our study of early infantile
development, before any object-love exists. Thus the
fickleness characteristic of puberty does not indicate any
inner change in the love or convictions of the individual
but rather a loss of personality in consequence of a
change in identification.

ANNA FREUD

19

A CLINICAL NOTE ON THE
THERAPEUTIC USE OF
A QUASI-RELIGIOUS EXPERIENCE

*To the medical mind these ecstasies signify nothing but sug-
gested and imitated hypnoid states, on an intellectual basis of
superstition, and a corporeal one of degeneration and hysteria.
Undoubtedly these pathological conditions have existed in
many and possibly in all the cases, but that fact tells us nothing
about the value for knowledge of the consciousness which they
induce. To pass a spiritual judgement upon these states, we
must not content ourselves with superficial medical talk, but
inquire into their fruits for life.*

WILLIAM JAMES

Elaine was brought to Southard School at the age of 13, against her will,
and under the well-sustained pretense of the frightened, guilt-ridden
mother that they were making the 2,000-mile trip solely for summer
pleasure. The mother lacked the father's support in her plan to institu-
tionalize the child. She told us, despairingly, that she would do anything
that was necessary, in order to help her only child, whose fantasy life was
encroaching markedly upon her hold of reality.

A highly gifted, articulate, and sophisticated youngster, Elaine in her
fantasy was married to Robin Hood. While she soberly maintained that
she could adequately distinguish her fantasy world from reality, she nevertheless restricted her life increasingly in order to please the phantom
husband. This proud fantasy hero, who fought fearlessly for the needy,
was very much the opposite of the cold hyperintellectual father who withdrew from the marital battles and the child, to escape into total preoccupation with his intellectual labors.

In school Elaine was found staring into space, laughing or talking to
herself inappropriately. Repeatedly she was overheard saying, "In order to

365

live, one must first die." On several occasions she gave vent to uncontrollable rage outbursts and would then beat schoolmates brutally without seeming awareness of what she was doing. She was described by the mother as a "frantically caged animal," who would occasionally walk the streets alone at night for hours, or run away through deserted city streets.

Her mood swings were striking as she was either "divinely happy" or "too sad to face the world." She saw herself as a special missionary who must go South to end all discrimination against Negroes. Crying spells, temper tantrums, panic states, complete withdrawal, and an overabundant fantasy life intruded extensively into her increasingly circumscribed ability to carry on with normal activities. Throughout the examination period she denied having any problem or being in need of any help. She objected most strongly to her notion that the "fantasy" might be taken away from her.

Intensive psychiatric and psychological study resulted in the diagnosis of a borderline schizophrenia, since despite the severity of the clinical findings, some measure of control over the fantasy world was still maintained and no complete rupture had occurred. Placement at Southard School was recommended. After a considerable working through, this plan was finally accepted by both parents and child. Accordingly, Elaine entered residential treatment; psychotherapy, three times weekly with a male analyst, was initiated shortly after her arrival.

Elaine's opening move in psychotherapy was to announce that she had made a New Year's resolution to give up all of her terrible fantasies. Her self-chosen position during some of these initial hours was reclining on the couch. Looking like a dainty and harmless fawn and seemingly unaware of her frequent seductive gestures, she described how she could go to sleep only following fantasies in which older women were tortured. It was these fantasies which she decided to relinquish. She requested the therapist's help in attaining Christian perfection, instantly qualifying this by affirming that in matters of faith a psychotherapist cannot help since his realm is the mind rather than the soul.

In the following hour she said she had given up a former boy friend and had decided to dedicate her life to God. She described how when she walked to the clinic on that very day, the traffic light from the distance, shining like a star of hope, had given her assurance that she would not be too late, but would reach him on time. So softly and distantly did she speak that one could not be sure if she spoke of a meeting with the Lord or of being on time for her psychotherapeutic session. And it is likely that her unconscious intent was indeed to prevent more clarity in her communication.

In the same session she went on to tell the therapist that for the past two years, at least, she thought of herself frequently in the third person. She would, for instance, write stories in the third person, although she really referred to herself. She discovered that when trying to pray she was unable to communicate with God and that in her inability to reach Him she would have to think about herself. With tear-stained face, she condemned herself bitterly for her inability to make contact with Him and she suggested vaguely that also in contact with people whom she loved she occasionally experienced similar difficulties, although less pronounced than with God. She gave the impression in these sessions of a passionate religious fanatic, and only an occasional impromptu gesture would reveal her awareness of herself as an attractive young woman, who could, to use her own words, "turn the charm on."

We note that as therapy began, and in response to quickly achieved transference manifestations, Elaine had spontaneously suppressed, or was at times consciously withholding, the weird facts of her fantasy romance with Robin Hood. And we may recall that it was this highly cathected daydream which she had been afraid would be torn from her. In its place she brought to therapy an equally intensive and deep quasi-religious experience which may be seen as replacing the Robin Hood fantasy. Accompanying this was a conscious pledge to give up the imagined brutality, in which older women and frequently the mother herself were victims. We may note parenthetically that considerable resemblance can be seen in both fantasies, for both Christ and Robin Hood lived out their lives in defense of the downtrodden and both died as a result of treachery.

The religious context, through which her inner turmoil now found expression, set the stage for the developing psychotherapeutic process. It is as if Elaine had fenced in the pathological process by ideological components, which are not only highly valued in our culture and may, in fact, form significant steps to self-healing, but which also serve the additional purpose of warding off interpretation. For, although Elaine could conceive of our wishing to take Robin Hood from her, who would dare to defy the inviolable word of the Lord or question His messages? As we read the unconscious intent of her communication, she seemed to be defining the emotional distance which she required, to cope with the presence of the therapist. This distance would permit her to ward off anxiety caused by excessive instinctual strivings and yet enable her to relate to us her sufferings and difficulties as she perceived them. Further, she seemed to be stating that the therapeutic relationship could be maintained only if material which she offered was not interpreted in the light of current or past life situations.

Elaine's communications about her religious preoccupation were accompanied by what seemed almost unbearable emotional pressure. Weeping, seizure-like shaking of the body, almost autistic despair and isolation, confessions of unforgivable sin and deep guilt punctuated the discharge of her trance-like communication. Yet these moods gave way, at times, to a rapid shift in which Elaine would suddenly become a playful and naïve little high school girl who talked in a giggling or matter-of-fact fashion about the daily events of her life. Nevertheless, even then she stressed that the psychotherapist was unimportant and in no way influenced her life. In fact, she stated that she did not consider him a human being since he was merely a therapist and what she told him did not really count but was like giving information to an impersonal expert or scientific automaton. She also described her father, neither incidentally, nor quite unjustifiably, as a thinking machine without religious faith, incapable of ever understanding her.

An event which occurred after three months of therapy may serve to highlight some aspect of the total psychotherapeutic process as well as illustrate some of the therapeutic technique employed. At that time the therapist was to be absent for a few days, and in the hours preceding his departure Elaine avowed that this would not disturb her, and denied almost vehemently that the absence was of any consequence whatsoever. During the psychotherapist's absence, however, she became extremely disturbed, ate hardly at all, locked herself in her room, and prayed for hours while complaining that she had no right to pray to God. She claimed that she did not trust Him and listened instead to the evil thoughts in her which had come to her from her environment at the school.

At the time of the psychotherapist's return, Elaine's panic state had subsided, and she came to her hour with regained self-control and poise. She denied that the therapist's absence had troubled her in any way but added that she had had an intensive struggle within herself over the weekend. She asserted the struggle had been about a matter of faith and had, as a consequence, nothing to do with the therapy since religion was clearly outside of the therapist's realm. Nevertheless, she proceeded to tell about her experience and as she went on, she could not maintain her original self-control. As the emotional impact of the weekend experience returned she became increasingly abstract and distant in the content of her communication. She began to discuss a Biblical incident which, in spite of its parable-like nature, soon came alive. She described the sheep who was threatened by a wolf and was surrendering in despair to its panic while waiting, paralyzed, for the shepherd to rescue it. She said that some shepherds give their sheep just food and water, but this was not sufficient. And she agreed when the therapist suggested that the little sheep, which she was describing, got only food and water, but no love. The therapist wondered where the shepherd was. Had he gone away? Had he deserted the poor sheep? Elaine stressed, as if she had to force herself to re-establish faith in the Lord, that the shepherd would never really abandon the sheep and would return in time to save it from the wolf. She did admit that the sheep perhaps felt lonesome; and if the sheep felt lonesome and deserted by the shepherd, then the wolf would have looked more enormous and more dangerous. It was only through the love of the shepherd, she asserted, that the poor sheep could regain its strength.

The therapist wondered how the sheep must have felt in the hour of danger. Elaine said that the sheep did not feel resentment because it was so terribly scared. The therapist said he understood how the sheep could not even feel its resentment, or its longing for the shepherd, since its overwhelming fear and panic had let it forget what it knew to be true: that the shepherd always returns and always watches out for all of his sheep, although at times there may seem to be too many sheep to care for. Elaine responded that the good shepherd could not possibly ever have too many sheep and would take care of all of his flock. Her agitation calmed and she spoke hopefully about the expected return of the shepherd, projecting into the future what obviously had just been worked through between herself and her therapist.

During this session, when she spoke about her doubt in the Lord, Elaine looked out of the window constantly, never facing the therapist. As she moved toward the feeling of certainty that the shepherd would return and save the sheep from the wolf's attack, she faced the therapist and terminated the hour in a hopeful frame of mind and positive contact with him, as evidenced partly in her regained capacity to discuss "everyday life." As she left, she showed the therapist a copy book into which she had arduously written many Biblical passages during her days of almost unbearable stress when he had been absent.

We offer a further illustration of the expression of the transference manifestations within a religious context. During the first few months of therapy, Elaine was striving to reach Christ and maintained that the century when Christ lived and died was the one in which she should have been born. During this period many of the therapist's interpretations, seemingly not accepted at the time they were offered, returned a few days later as revelations communicated by the voice of God. Elaine hinted that she did not expect to live to a riper age than Christ and felt that He had given her the message of the "board and the nail" while she was in silent prayer. She hoped that the therapist would help clarify this message for her.

In the session which followed she spoke of book ends which she wanted to construct and sketched a design of crosses which she had in mind for this project. She related these book ends, anxiously and under mounting inner pressure, to the message of the "board and the nail." The therapist perceived at that moment the true meaning of her communication. The board and the nail [1] referred to the cross to which Christ had been nailed, and His message, a request to identify with His goals, to be like Him, brought on the terrible thought, the blasphemous sin against which there was no defense, that she was Christ Himself. We may suggest that her frantic efforts to reach Him had loosened the bounds of more mature identification mechanisms [2] and brought about a regression to symbiotic identification [3] where subject and object are blended and lose their individual identity.

Elaine reacted to this powerful thought with panic, self-abuse, and a loss of contact. Nobody should or must ever know of the blasphemous secret of her wish to be Christ on the cross. She comforted herself again with the idea that the therapist did not count since he was only a doctor and not a human being. This struggle against the symbiotic devouring of the love object projected into religious context shows many elements, including the power of her primitive superego, the fantasy of supreme self-punishment, the unresolved conflict of bisexuality, and the sadistic implications of sexual union. The most powerful struggle, however, was directed against psychotic symbiosis.

A few months later, when the therapist expressed some mild leniency about a reality situation which Elaine felt should be more strictly handled, Elaine almost lost contact and finally confessed that she thought the therapist had the sacrilegious thought that he was Christ. This was the first indication that she had started to perceive her own projections. But so fearful was she of her own insight that she had to suspect the therapist of insinuating this connection.

During many long months of therapy the therapist attempted instantly to follow Elaine in her own way of communicating without trying at first to challenge the rapidly changing ego states or to translate from one level to another. Interpretation and communication thus took place within the context which the child offered, whether a distant religious parable, a medieval fantasy, or a frankly delusional experience. Elaine felt understood, in turn, in that the emotional distance which she needed was protected and respected throughout. This hypothesis is borne out in her increased ability to remain within the reality of the immediate situation and her ability to master conflict on different levels of insight. In fact, much later she herself called attention to the mode of communication where she and the therapist, with perfect understanding, seemed to be talking "about something entirely different." The time had arrived then to call to her attention the distance devices themselves, for she was then ready to tackle them with the newly gained ego resiliency now at her command. Clinically, as well, we note considerable improvement. Elaine attended the local high school, made a successful adjustment in a boarding home in the community, and became a leader in a church youth group.

One may wonder what forced this child into the use of these protective distance [4] devices of the ego, through which the affective meaning of her transference reaction was projected into the quasi-religious experience and was largely removed from the range of the secondary-process functions of the ego's organization. We suggest that this was due not only to anxiety in the particular characteristics of her ego which, under pressure, could not maintain its neurotic defenses. These neurotic defense mechanisms became, in part at least, temporarily decathected, and deneutralized energy [5] brought on further pressure leading toward ego regression. Under pressure the contact, which Elaine could normally maintain, was threatened by symbiotic and autistic regressions and the associated flight into fantasies or quasi-religious preoccupation. The internalized image [6] of the object could be maintained only on a symbiotic level. The symbiotic threat, however, when she reached out for objects, could better be coped with in the protection of the religious context.

Almost two years later, the transference conflict was on an entirely different level although displacement still played an outstanding part. One may even say that Elaine dealt with the same conflicts but on a higher stage of ego development. The transference situation was not mirrored more than occasionally in religious conflict. At that time her religious interest, although deep and firmly established, was more similar to that of other youngsters of her age group.

Rather, the therapeutic struggle was mirrored then in her changing experiences with different boy friends. Her latest boy friend was significantly described with, "We always think alike, and he and I never want some thing of the other that the other could not agree to." She stated that she had found the ideal relationship—or, should we say, the ideal distance? In this same period she told the therapist that she recalled now that she had always thought that he was not human, but now she knew that he was.

One has the clinical impression that the disintegrative threat could be more securely warded off. Firmer ego boundaries [7] had been established, even though from time to time one could see the seams cracking under the impact of crisis situations. Yet, the total adjustment was markedly improved. The rapid ego shifts were not visible any more and the fantasies of old were, at times, discussed by Elaine in terms of their psychological usefulness at the time, although she conceded easily that she still enjoyed daydreaming. But even in her extensive current fantasies, Robin Hood had been replaced by boys and girls of her acquaintance.

Elaine told her therapist, "I can see now how I needed you, how you have helped me in part; but most of my problem was solved by my faith, by Christ." There was no need to challenge her; as a matter of fact, there is not enough insight available to us fully to assess the contributions of therapy on the one hand, and, on the other, those of normal self-healing in a growing adolescent. The struggle against identification served as a defense against unbearable symbiotic regressions. The progress in therapy could be measured also in terms of the changing vicissitudes of the internalized image of the therapist ranging from a symbiotic to a neurotic pattern.

REFERENCES

[1] Through the auditory hallucination, "board and the nail," of our patient is expressed an almost identical conflict as through the visual dream hallucination "S(E)INE" of Erikson's patient, reported in "The Dream Specimen of Psychoanalysis" (J. Amer. Psychoanal. Ass., 2:5, 1954). We call attention to the difference in ego organization, ego mastery, and failure expressed through both condensed representations.

[2] For an elaboration of the concept of psychotic identification, see Edith Jacobson's "Contribution to the Metapsychology of Psychotic Identifications" (J. Amer. Psychoanal. Ass. 2:239, 1954), and the discussion remarks by Bak, Hartmann, and Jacobson, in the abstract of this paper (Psychoanal. Quart., 23:160, 1954).

[3] Mahler, M. S. On child psychosis and schizophrenia: autistic and symbiotic infantile psychoses, Psychoanal. Stud. Child, 7:286, 1952.

[4] Chapters 15 and 16, this volume; and Wexler, M. Psychological distance as a factor in the treatment of a schizophrenic patient, in Explorations in Psychoanalysis, R. Lindner, ed., New York, Julian Press, 1953.

[5] Hartmann, H. Contribution to the metapsychology of schizophrenia, Psychoanal. Stud. Child, 8:177, 1953.

[6] Wexler, M. The structural problem in schizophrenia: the role of the internal object, in Psychotherapy with Schizophrenics, E. Brody and F. C. Redlich, eds., New York, International Universities Press, 1952, p. 179.

[7] Federn, P. Ego Psychology and the Psychoses, New York, Basic Books, 1952.

20

VICISSITUDES OF
THE "INTERNAL IMAGE" DURING
THE RECOVERY PROCESS

*It is my growing conviction that the major function of partici-
pating in the patient's delusional system, of communication in
accord with the "archaic superego," of lending support in the
struggle against primitive impulses is to facilitate the development of such a constant "mental image" of the therapist.*

MILTON WEXLER

We expect no outstanding difficulty in the task of reconstructing patients'
early object relationships from the analysis of clinical material emerging
during the development of a transference neurosis. Freud said of the
neurotic patient, "He will always treat himself therapeutically, that is with
transference." The developing transference is the track upon which the
treatment process proceeds. With schizophrenic and borderline conditions,
we feel frequently, however, as if we never get the patient on the track,
since we cannot establish contact; or as if the track gets lost, as where
only intermittent contact can be maintained. In such instances, the transference track may be precarious and shifting, narrowing, widening, or
disappearing altogether during the vicissitudes of the treatment process.
Sometimes we may well wonder which vehicle to employ, and if there is
any that is adaptable to such fluctuating and unpredictable conditions.

This problem arose during the four year treatment of Elaine, a borderline schizophrenic adolescent.

We discussed (Chapter 19) Elaine's particular means of communication via religious metaphor and understood their use as protective distance
devices brought into play by the stress of the developing transference.
These distance devices were elaborated as the ego's attempts to maintain
itself in the face of disintegrative threat. The maintenance of the pre-

cariously weak neurotic defenses enabled the avoidance both of regression and the loss of tenuous contact with the therapist.

As treatment proceeded it was observed that the patient was caught between strong conflicting pulls. Her unremitting attempt to get near the transference object was opposed by forces of equal vigor in the service of distance and flight. Her struggle calls to mind the behavior of a butterfly drawn constantly toward the flame that may eventually destroy it. The patient herself used a comparable simile when she said on one occasion that she wanted to discontinue treatment because she was now in the same situation as the butterfly attempting to free itself from its cocoon. She stated that when someone frees the butterfly from its cocoon, the well-meant help may be disastrous even though the cocoon's protection has become burdensome; the freed butterfly does not have the strength which it would have achieved by struggling alone and must, therefore, die. Thus, in Elaine's transition from the chrysalis to the butterfly state, she felt that she had to avoid the therapist whom she regarded as helpful only so long as she was a chrysalis. This fantasy contains the essential dilemma of this patient which I want to present here.

The cocoon fantasy suggests, at least on the surface, certain common denominators with the neurotic or normal theme of the "Sleeping Beauty": a latent state is to be followed by awakening and potential fulfillment. Prince Charming ends the death-like sleep of the princess and the happy awakening symbolizes adult capacity for integrated sensual and tender love. In Elaine's cocoon theme, however, the helper is tolerated only during the latent state, and appears as the harbinger of death as soon as this quiescent state is about to be given up for the mature position. Thus, the helper safeguards life only so long as the desire for mature object relationships is not truly awakened. Elaine's simile states dramatically what is apparent in so much of her clinical material; she can tolerate only a distant love object (we refer, of course, to psychological distance). As she attempts to diminish the distance she experiences a growing danger which threatens not her self-control or her self-esteem, but the destruction of her very identity. Not Prince Charming but a devouring flame stands at the end of her efforts.

In Freud's classical study of his hysterical patient Dora,[1] the response to sexual temptation is regression to an earlier libidinal stage in which the protective father of childhood days is summoned up to help ward off the frightening situation. Elaine's defensive efforts bring into play more powerful, much deeper ego regression, in which the experience of identity is disrupted and exchanged for a partly symbiotic experience, namely, the chrysalis state of the ego before development enables the maintenance of object cathexis. We know that object cathexis can be maintained only if the internal parental image is stabilized. In Elaine's fluid psychic organization, the internal image breaks down and thus threatens the maintenance of identity except on a symbiotic or autistic basis. While Dora summons up her infantile love for her father in order to ward off the threat of sexual temptation, Elaine summons up, as it were, the archaic ego organization and thus copes with the transference threat by wiping out the capacity for self, as well as the capacity for object experience.

The first period of therapy was characterized by Elaine's compulsive cooperation with the therapist whom she described as a sort of unhuman psychiatric mechanical brain. (We note parenthetically that this concept of the therapist is mindful of the transitional objects which Winnicott [2] has discussed.) She kept her appointments faithfully and gave her unsolicited pledge at the start that she would suppress all her weird fantasies, including her fantasy marriage to Robin Hood as well as all thoughts of violent destruction. She insisted resolutely that her only wish was to serve Christ, and emphasized that real help would be forthcoming only from Him and not from me. It was as if the relationship with the therapist could be sustained only if grafted onto it was the "perfect" relationship with Christ which she felt could be trusted. This is very similar to her turning to Robin Hood at a time when her loyalties were divided between her troubled parents who were engaged in angry divorce proceedings. Robin Hood and Christ both served the same function, in that they afforded protection against the imaginary or real threat of the relationship in reality.

During this period my remarks on a confronting, supporting, or interpretive level hardly seemed to reach her or were instantly, though politely and quietly, debunked. She tried desperately to reach Christ and reported deep religious experiences while in silent prayer. She heard voices which she attributed to Christ whose image she tried to summon up in hours of distress. On one such occasion, a symbolic message, obviously an open delusion, concerning Christ's wish that she reach Him, created a panic and ended in terrible self-accusations and loss of contact with me. She castigated herself for the blasphemous thought of wishing to be Christ. Her wish to be like Him, to keep his image before her as an example of the good life, had turned into the uncontrollable thought of being Christ, and she fought the devilish thought that two could become one.[3] Clearly, at this time and at other such times, normal capacity for identification had given way to primitive, introjective, devouring mechanisms. The internal representation of the parental image had collapsed and had yielded to frightening and primitive ways of pre-ego or early ego mastery.

The transference implications of these experiences are clear. Yet, one is left with a bewildering question as to why normal, though displaced, object cathexis broke down and resulted in union without boundaries between self and object.

In these early days of treatment, Elaine shifted from fantasies of complete fusion with the object, to a contactless autistic position, showing as well a range of relative capacity to deal with the transference object on a temporarily normal transference track. In one of the later hours, following approximately six months of therapy, Elaine berated herself for her ugliness, her inability to reach Christ, or even to conjure up his image. She feared that she would never again find Him, and that her faith was too weak to bring about His return. Like the sheep eaten by the wolf, she would be exposed to the devil and be devoured by him. This seeming reversal of the transference situation was again a clear description by displacement of the therapeutic situation. Anger against the therapist had led to the loss of Christ's image. Her despairing feeling that she would be unable to recapture this image in spite of divine help was experienced in the therapy situation, despite my repeated assurances of help.

I offered her on this occasion a Christmas card which I possessed showing a combination of shadows on a vast snow field. This card presented a Vexierbild, a picture puzzle in which with sufficient perseverance and intent, the hidden image of Christ could be found. I ventured the thought that if she tried hard enough she might find His hidden image by our next session. This quasi-magical gesture on my part helped her back into the therapeutic situation via the discovered image of Christ. And during these swift shifts between the dangers of fusion with the powerful image and loss of the image, I helped her through magic gestures which represented actually projections of her own rudiments of post-symbiotic omnipotence. In such fashion I endeavored to strengthen the weak internal representation of the internal parental image through fusion with the newly added internal image of the therapist. It is as if I became a newly grafted-on parent. Her new inner state was expressed through displacement onto religious context in the description of her changing experiences with the image of Christ.

She began gradually to concede that I was a real person with some positive attributes and not merely a psychiatric thinking machine. Her new inner state found vivid expression in a dream which occurred about a half year later. Her dream was: "I was in a burning house. I think it was Southard School. I wondered what I could save out of my possessions in my room. I realized that my father's picture was downstairs in the steel file cabinet and that nothing would happen to it. But 'The Messiah' records were still in my burning room and they would be destroyed."

I wish to call attention here only to certain features of the manifest content of this dream which starts out similarly to Dora's jewel case dream but has distinctly different features. We recall that her fear at the time she came to Southard School was that we would take Robin Hood away from her. At the beginning of treatment she herself suppressed the fantasy romance and replaced it with her preoccupation with Christ and her struggles to reach Him and to maintain His image. This, as suggested, represented the more distant embodiment of the internal parental image. The dream, however, describes the significant change. The safe parental image, namely the transference picture, safe in my steel cabinet, had begun to make it possible to relinquish the more distant and elusive, and, at the same time, unstable image of the Messiah. The internal image of the parent strengthened by the grafted-on representation of the therapist's image, had made possible the achievement of a more stable or, shall we say, more neurotic, transference track.

In becoming safe, the relationship with the therapist led in several directions. Elaine could give up fantasy objects which protected her from the real relationships or which kept them at a safe distance. Moreover, she had, in effect, arrived at a stage where, not unlike Dora, she could in the face of sexual excitement (the house on fire) summon up the parental image and the therapist's protection. She no longer needed to conjure up a fantasy protector, a phantom substitute of the formerly rudimentary internal image.

At about this time Elaine underwent a routine psychological examination. The outlines of a man which she had drawn a year earlier had been vague and unclear. At this time her drawing was clear and concise. The man was drawn wearing a college outfit, and had the capital letter E on his sweater. Jokingly, one may suggest that E stands for transference.

One must keep in mind that the loss of the external love object or a temporary disappointment about the love object is not synonymous with loss of the internal image. The loss of the one goes hand in hand with the other only under conditions of ego failure as discussed above. As Elaine moved toward richer and more complex ego mastery she could use less archaic modes of handling disappointment and anger against the love object. And, as psychotherapy became a more secure experience for her, with few danger points to remind her of her earlier use of the thera- peutic situation, she made a corresponding advance by a more stable adjustment to the boarding home, school, and social contacts with boys and girls her age.

One incident showed this progress, as well as certain similarities with former modes of attempts at mastery and defense. Elaine had found a boy friend whom she described as sharing all of her wishes and interests. Nevertheless, she claimed that this relationship could only be of temporary duration since she felt herself too young to be thinking of a more lasting relationship. It was only puppy love, not real love, she said. The boy had given her his picture, on the back of which he had written an inscription far more intimate than is customary among high school students. Elaine cherished the picture, carrying it in her billfold so everyone might admire it. A few days after giving her this gift, and just before therapy was to stop temporarily because of a vacation period, he suggested to her, perhaps not unexpectedly, that they had better break up in order to find out if they really loved each other. Elaine took this as a sure sign of the end and expressed great anger and grief. While crying bitterly she confessed that she had lost her billfold which contained his picture. The loss was irreplaceable because of the inscription which he would never repeat even if he replaced the snapshot. She berated his unfaithfulness and said that she wanted to wipe his memory from her mind. She added that she could no longer even imagine what he looked like. But, even under deepest stress, unlike earlier and similar occasions where the regression was outstanding, Elaine remained in complete contact with her surroundings and maintained steadfastly that she would soon find somebody else to replace him. She was able to accept some hints from me that this ending was a response on both sides to the increasing conflict over their growing intimacy. Shortly thereafter she had an enjoyable vacation and fulfilled her own prediction about finding a new boy friend without difficulty. The stronger stabilized internal image took conscious form in her statement at this time that she no longer needed to fall back on a fantasy hero like Robin Hood since she now had real people to turn to in case of disappointment.

The loss of the object, therefore, no longer destroyed the internal image and the capacity for new object cathexis. Her outburst of anger and grief over the loss of the snapshot showed only structural similarities to earlier modes of response. It is as if the seam where there had been ego rupture was still visible, but though strained to the limit of its elasticity, it was holding fast.

In attempting to understand the special difficulties during the psychotic phases of the treatment process in the case of Elaine and similar patients, we found a particular impairment of early introjects to be characteristic. In transference neurosis the well-established introjected parental images are projected onto the analyst. During the psychotic phase, one may well speak of a transference psychosis. The insufficiently consolidated early introjects which contribute to the transfer of early experiences onto the therapist are of an autistic or symbiotic nature. It is these very early contact difficulties which are relived within the treatment situation, and the therapist is often perceived as lifeless and machine-like as well as a transitory love object.

If we ask then how therapy succeeds via the introjection of the therapist—when, according to our hypothesis, it is specifically this capacity to introject fully which is initially impaired—we face a difficult question. Perhaps, as the ego becomes strengthened in the treatment process, there is a carry over into all areas of the ego, so that its initial impairments are modified. Wexler [4] has stressed the superego aspects of these early introjects. We wish to add that these introjects provide the basis for reality testing and judgment, which are ego functions. It is perhaps in this regard that the therapist becomes introjected into the ego of the borderline patient and serves as an ever present mentor and guide to the patient when the patient becomes anxious and perplexed. Another possibility is that the parental figures of these patients themselves were poor objects of introjection and identification, because of their own vacuity, instability, and unreliability. And it may well be that the introjective capacity is not impaired except insofar as the introjected objects themselves were unreliable and elusive. Or, it may be an interaction of some impairment in capacity with elusive parental figures. If this were so then the reaching out by the therapist, his firm anchorage in reality, and his assurance of constancy and stability may in themselves be sufficiently strong to call forth response even from a relatively impaired ego capacity or incomplete introjective capacity. One may also conjecture about the defensive nature of these fusion states and consider them as devices against the awareness of early introjects. The data from Elaine's treatment and the treatment of similar patients permit a variety of ways of understanding. Our differential criteria are still insufficient for any comprehensive evaluation of therapeutic technique. Still less can we point to definite causes for these conditions.

A word of caution must be expressed concerning the psychotherapeutic techniques employed. Although the case described suggests that numerous innovations have been used, these are not intended as established or firmly held guides, but rather as experimental endeavors whose validity and usefulness await further clarification. In addition, it must be stressed that such innovations were employed primarily during the nonneurotic phases of the process. The neurotic phases have been treated, although perhaps more cautiously, according to the well-established classical principles of analytic interpretive technique.

In discussing the treatment of this borderline patient, I have tried to clarify the economic and dynamic role of the internal image. Stable capacity for object cathexis depends on a stabilized and integrated internal image of the parental figures. If such early stabilization is threatened by autistic or symbiotic dissolution of the internal image, special transference problems arise during treatment. The spontaneous grafting of an internalized image of the analyst, with shifting functions, may occur. The oscillating internal image of the parent-therapist figures reflects the recovery process in which the symbiotic defense against normal processes of introjection and identification gives way to more mature patterns of defensive and integrative ego organization.

REFERENCES

[1] Freud, S. Fragment of an Analysis of a Case of Hysteria, 3rd ed., London, Hogarth, 1946, pp. 3, 13.

[2] Winnicott, D. W. Transitional objects and transitional phenomena, Int. J. Psychoanal., 34:89, 1953.

[3] One is tempted to order these data according to the views expressed in Kubie's "The Drive to Become Both Sexes" (unpublished). Like Virginia Woolf's Orlando, Elaine at this moment succeeds only too well. As she fuses with Christ, she resolves the bisexual problem and wipes out the difference through return to an undifferentiated state.

[4] Wexler, M. The structural problem in schizophrenia: the role of the internal object, Bull. Menninger Clin., 15:221, 1951.

21

CROSS-SECTIONAL VIEWS ON THE PSYCHOTHERAPEUTIC PROCESS WITH AN ADOLESCENT GIRL RECOVERING FROM A SCHIZOPHRENIC EPISODE

Alan Gregg once said that an honest narrative of a doctor's treatment attempt with a patient is one of the best kinds of scientific writing. I believe that no such narrative can be either scientific or honest unless the writer gives a detailed report of what he, as therapist, did and said and thought as well as what the patient did and said, and then tries to relate what effects these complicated interactions between patient and therapist appeared to have on the progress and outcome of the treatment attempt. The role played by the therapist is at least half of the story. If an account of it is omitted from the case report and the patient's productions and behavior are described and interpreted as if the therapist's role were immaterial and even above examination, then an honest narrative is not being written.

ROBERT P. KNIGHT

The word "treatment" originated in early magical procedures as well as in medical practice. It implies that something is done to the patient in order to "fix him up," as exemplified in the administration of drugs or injections, or the process of surgery. One is induced, therefore, to overlook the subtle processes of psychotherapy which constitute interaction rather than a one-sided repair process. A successful psychotherapeutic process is as much the success of the patient as of the psychotherapist. Although it seems that the interaction takes place solely in the interest of the patient, it is sometimes overlooked, perhaps, that the patient has a profound influence on the therapist. The patient affords the therapist insights and the opportunity for the development of new techniques which actually constitute a change in the therapist. I believe that recognition of this may encourage the therapist to follow Knight's advice and to report about the process rather than the case or, more accurately, to describe the case by reporting the process.

The therapist faces many obstacles in such an endeavor. Psychotherapeutic ethics force him to disguise the material and make him hesitant even then. He does not want to give away his patient nor does he find it easy to give away much of himself. The secrecy of the psychotherapeutic session has a dual meaning.

He is also up against the fact that therapy records covering years of treatment do not lend themselves easily to useful communication. What was a living experience between him and his patient may become a boring repetitive narrative for the future reader.

In the face of these obstacles, I have chosen to offer cross-sectional segments of the initial phase in Elaine's psychotherapy (Chapters 19 and 20). During early parts of the treatment she was in residence in the treatment center and later moved to a boarding home, where she remained until her final discharge. During that ending phase, she was seen only once a week.

In this case we had unusual help from the mother whose literary talent helped us to reconstruct in vivid terms the child's tragic flight into illness. Excerpts from the mother's account may serve as perhaps better than a routine case history:

Elaine's favorite song during the preceding months, the theme song for the most delicate period of all, was:

> If they made me a king,
> I would be but a slave to you.
> If I had everything
> I would still be a slave to you.
> If I ruled the night,
> Stars and moon so bright,
> Still I'd turn to you for light.
>
> If the world to me bowed,
> Yet humbly I'd flee to you.
> If my friends were a crowd,
> I would turn on my knees to you.
> If I ruled the earth,
> What would life be worth,
> If I hadn't the right to you?

This theme song proclaimed the deadly clutch which fantasy was gaining on Elaine's life; the lure of the unreal to supplant the real. Night after night she put it on the record player. Night after night it resounded through the house as, with an eerie expression on her face, she slowly ascended the stairs to the imaginary kingdom of her room. There, behind a locked door, she found the love, acceptance, and security of her own making. For now she preferred to regard herself as married, her room as the bridal suite, and life with an imaginary husband more real for her than the give and take of high school life.

It is, of course, true that all children indulge in fantasy to some degree; but when a teenager goes out and buys a wedding ring and wears it, and becomes hysterical because by mistake the pillow case she wished to wash for her husband has already been washed, when she is wild with grief because she has arrived home a few moments too late to do an adequate cleaning for the reception to be given for her homecoming husband—then this is illness, not childlike imagination, but the most elusive of illnesses.

It was impossible to know just how sick Elaine was; to what extent she was aware of her deviation from the normal; how far she had actually moved into the world of her own creating. I felt lost in the unknown. Every hour, every minute I sensed some inexorable force pushing—pushing her God knows where. And I did not know how to bring her back. I treated her affectionately but casually; referred periodically to the fact that we both understood that she was playing with fantasy, but did not stress it; avoided all possible issues. Life at home became simply a holding action until the right help could be found for her. Her "married" status and her schoolwork were the only things that had any meaning for her. She could not take part in any activity—domestic or social. Much of the time she would not even come down for dinner but would take it (portions for two) upstairs to her room.

On the street Elaine walked with her head turned away from me, her arm crooked as though it were snugly fitted into another's arm. At the movie she would sit exchanging glances, smiles, and even whispers with her phantom. The terrible lure created by the husband of her fancy made living a nightmare because there was no way of estimating his power over her. At times she was like a frantic caged animal, begging to go walking alone in the late night hours or actually running away through the city streets. And one statement she repeated several times, with a strange look in her eyes: "In order to live, one must first die."

How much illness? How much adolescent drama? What thoughts did she control? What thoughts controlled her? I did not know. I just knew that she was headed in the wrong direction.

Each day became more strained, with Elaine removing herself from her group and cramping herself in her room. Everything about her was cramped, her gait, her gestures, her handwriting, her glance. She was a bird in prison in some mysterious cage.

Since the child had not acknowledged awareness of her illness and had fought off professional help in private practice, the advising physican suggested that Elaine be brought to the residential treatment center without her knowledge. The mother had followed the suggestion, so that when Elaine arrived, she felt herself betrayed.

Before I knew that Elaine might be assigned to me for psychotherapeutic treatment, I said in staff meeting:

I usually have no quarrels with diagnostic categories, but I am concerned with the label inasmuch as it indicates the kind of treatment we should offer. I would suggest we call her "schizophrenic." I suggest this category to imply that we would have to attempt the kind of analytic treatment which is appropriate for a schizophrenic child rather than for a child within the neurotic range. One of the main difficulties I see in accepting her is to find a way of initiating treatment which is different from the one initiated by her family. If I were responsible for the treatment, I would tell the whole family group that I disapprove of the wrong information the child has been given. She is certainly ill and we feel that she requires treatment, but we can only give it on the condition that we do not start out with a lie. This will prove very painful for the mother, but at the same time I think it would be the only guarantee for successful treatment. If we and they state the truth now from the very beginning we will thus initiate a different type of relationship.

We ought to tell the mother that it will probably take from three to five years to help the child. We should take her only if we know that we can provide her with intensive psychotherapy which ought to be expressive, analytic in orientation, a minimum of three hours per week and, if possible, five hours per week.

A few months after being accepted for treatment, Elaine was assigned to me for treatment.

The social worker brought Elaine to her first psychotherapeutic session with me. Both came to my office, and Elaine entered shyly. She sat down on the couch after taking off her coat, gloves, and hat, all of them obviously new, Christmas presents. The three of us sat for a few minutes talking casually about Christmas, about the gifts Elaine had received. She said that she was very pleased because a number of gifts from her parents came unexpectedly. The gifts from the treatment center were no surprise to her because she knew she would get gifts from her teachers and that they would be exactly what she asked for.

After the social worker left and Elaine was alone with me, she continued to impress me the same as she had some months earlier when she was presented in the staff meeting and I had addressed a few questions to her. She recalled this incident quite well and even remembered what we had talked about. She had been looking forward to psychotherapy. When I asked whether the feelings she had expressed at the time of her admittance to the treatment center had changed, Elaine told me that at that particular time—while feeling that she had considerable trouble—she was convinced that she could solve her problems all by herself. Now, four months later, she realized that she could not do it alone and needed some help. While she stressed this need, and was glad that she could start psychotherapy now, rather than having to wait six months as we had led her to expect, she also told me that she did not think the situation in residence had helped her particularly. She described her difficulties mainly in terms of the external situation. She had roomed at first with two girls, but she and Carol, one of the two, finally insisted that the younger third girl, who was rather difficult, be removed. She and Carol were still together, and her feelings about Carol were quite warm. However, Carol was soon to go into a foster home and Elaine was afraid that she might have to take back the younger girl, Mary, since the school could not afford to let her, Elaine, have one large room all by herself. Elaine said she could not help thinking of all the new words and slang expressions that she had learned at the Center. She hinted that she had learned other things there that she should not know and that she had never heard before.

I ventured the thought that this must be quite a burden to her since I knew she was striving to be the right kind of person. She picked this up gratefully. When I wondered how she could expect any help from the school, being exposed constantly to such temptations, she referred to psychotherapy and called to my attention that she had just made the New Year's resolution that she would give up all her terrible fantasies. While she remained on the couch in a semi-reclining position, she avoided looking at me; the impression she made as a dainty, harmless, little fawn was very strong. It was at this time that she told me that the only way she could go to sleep was by having fantasies of torturing someone. She spoke about all the women who were the victims in her cruel fantasies. She thought that this practice was terrible and she had decided that, beginning with the New Year, she would give up all such fantasies when she went to sleep and would substitute prayers for them. I suggested that I could see from these remarks how much she was striving to reach a goal of perfection and that I thought she came to see me so that I could help her perhaps to achieve this goal. I surely wanted to try and see whether I could help her.

At that point I commented that when people strive toward a lofty goal, the top of a high mountain, they may need to travel all kinds of roads: at first, perhaps, paved roads for automobiles; later they may have to walk on rough foot paths; then climb on rocks, and finally they may need an ice pick and mountain boots to surmount glaciers and mountain walls. They may need ropes. Even though the goal were the perfect view on the top of the mountain where the air was pure and the vista was beautiful, they may have to take all kinds of side paths, climb dangerous cliffs, travel dubious roads. Elaine said she was not quite sure she understood me. After I repeated my idea she indicated that, as a matter of fact, I was implying that it did not make any difference if one were good or bad. It was as if we at the treatment center were suggesting to her that there was no difference between good and bad. I attempted to correct this impression and stressed again my belief in her goals, but suggested that I was speaking about the method of getting to them. I recalled to her the original interview with the staff, in which she had talked about braces for her teeth, telling us that she wanted a dentist to help her get perfect teeth. She needed to show the dentist what was wrong about her teeth and she needed to wear braces which, perhaps, would not look perfect but would help her to get where she wanted to be. She accepted this and continued to speak about some of her inner struggles and about the goals that she saw for herself.

With some misgivings, she talked about Carol's future placement in a foster home. Elaine did not know whether she would want to go to one. She felt she would get used to home life again, but afterwards there would be nothing for her. Since her parents were to be separated she could not return to a home of her own. It was as if her goal of psychotherapy were really an empty one. I indicated simply that we would need time, perhaps a long time, in order to find out together what might be best for her in order to attain the goals that she had set for herself.

At the end of the session after she had left me, I found her standing somewhat anxiously in the waiting-room. She told me she did not know whether she should speak to the secretary or to someone to say she had lost a dime which she needed to return to the Center by bus. She asked me whether she could borrow one from me and I gave her the dime. When I asked her whether she could find her way to the office next time, she said half jokingly and half sadly that she might get lost, but if she did not come or if she was very late, I should know that she was trying to reach me and that she would find me.

Even the innocuous beginning of that first session revealed the keen sensitivity of Elaine. She spoke about the Christmas gifts from the treatment center as not being a surprise to her since she knew she would get exactly what she asked for. This subtle innuendo minimized the gifts, which she recognized as being in the nature of technical assistance rather than as evidence for the ideal relationship which she wanted to restore between herself and her parents. In spite of the fact that she had seen the psychotherapist only once, and then in a rather large group, she recalled his every word. While admitting she now needed help, she told the therapist just how afraid she was of this help and likened it, indirectly through the metaphor of the school milieu which teaches her nasty slang expressions never heard before, to a situation in which she would be permitted, and perhaps encouraged and forced, to think the forbidden, the immoral.

The therapist, rather than translating this directly, responded within Elaine's example, thus preserving the distance she requested. He hinted at the burden of psychotherapy but lined himself up on the side of the goal she chose: to be the right kind of person. As if to check whether the therapist believed what he said, she talked about her New Year's resolution "to give up mean and aggressive fantasies of torture."

The therapist again declared himself the ally of her strivings toward goals of perfection. He used the simile of the high mountain top that one can reach only if one uses all kinds of roads, in order to encourage her to speak freely in the service of her goal. More technically, one might put it this way: The therapist, while agreeing with Elaine's goal of integration, of becoming a moral person, suggested that her illness could be overcome only if she faced the conflicts, the forbidden wishes which she was attempting to repress. The patient, through the New Year's resolution, felt that reintegration was possible only if she were allowed to forget, or at least be permitted not to mention, not to think about, that which invaded her mind.

Elaine instantly experienced the therapist's example of the different roads that lead to the top of the mountain as temptation, as an invitation to take dubious roads. She told him indirectly that he did not seem to believe there there was any difference between good and bad.

As soon as he became aware of it, he tried to regain lost ground, and attempted to secure his foothold on her tenuous confidence in him by changing the example into a simpler one which, he recalled, she had used in the initial staff conference a few months earlier. In talking about her request for dental braces, he reintroduced the issue of means and ends on a level which was acceptable to her.

At this moment, she was able to move away from indirect metaphoric communication. In comparing herself with the other child, she spoke about her fear that she would not be able to go back to her childhood home because of her parents' pending separation. It is as if she were saying that there really was no available goal for her life, and, given that, what was the use of therapy? Thereupon, the therapist introduced time, time with him, as the healing factor.

Her request for the dime so that she could return to the residential center, her plea for patience with her, her calling to the therapist's attention that she would finally try and reach him, all were part of a prediction, as it were, of a difficult process ahead.

One might also suggest that she told the therapist how—even before therapy starts—she had made the decision to suppress the illness and her brutal fantasies, to keep her fantasy world out of the therapist's office, and to invite him to support her ethical goals of high perfection. She spoke about this even as she spoke about her wish to reach him, and invited his patience. He found it necessary to ally himself instantly with the goals of her conscience and tried to open the process by stating that many different means, at times risky and perhaps unacceptable at first glance, may be necessary in order to reach this goal. She tried to see her New Year's resolution as the method of therapy while the therapist tried to suggest that the New Year's resolution might be its goal.

The "acting out scene" between the therapist and Elaine can be considered an *action metaphor* in which he gives her the dime to get home while she promises to try to find and reach him even though she might get lost on the way. They try to accept one another on each other's terms, without denying the difference in their ways of looking at the nature of the illness.

In Chapter 19, I described the transference situation of this initial phase of treatment:

She described how when she walked to the Clinic . . . the traffic light from the distance, shining like a star of hope, had given her assurance that she would not be too late, but would reach him on time. So softly and distantly did she speak that one could not be sure if she spoke of a meeting with the Lord or of being on time for her psychotherapeutic session. And it is likely that her unconscious intent was indeed to prevent more clarity in her communication . . . she went on to tell the therapist that for the past two years, at least, she thought of herself frequently in the third person. . . . She discovered that when trying to pray she was unable to communicate with God and that in her inability to reach Him she would have to think about herself. With tear-stained face, she condemned herself bitterly for her inability to make contact with Him and she suggested vaguely that also in contact with people whom she loved she occasionally experienced similar difficulties, although less pronounced than with God. She gave the impression . . . of a passionate religious fanatic . . . only an occasional impromptu gesture would reveal her awareness of herself as an attractive young girl, who could . . . "turn the charm on."

The struggle between perfection and desire, and Elaine's peculiar way of bringing this into the transference situation, can be exemplified best perhaps by citing the records of a therapy session, in the fourth week of treatment:

Elaine started the session with a slight reproach for my being late, hidden behind the comment that she had read quite a number of pages of a book which she held in her hands. After my apology for the unexpected delay, she returned to the book and told me about its content. She felt sad for the heroine, a young woman. (The book, a novel by Thomas Hardy entitled Faithfully Reporting, was a Victorian novel about a pure woman who loses her inner peace and her good reputation.)

Elaine told me about the heroine whose parents insisted that she live with certain rich relatives so that she may perhaps inherit their fortune and marry a man from the better classes. For this reason she was turned against the common people in her community with whom she actually preferred to associate, and all these simple people became angry with her. While she faced one of these situations in which the people's anger was turned against her, a young man who allegedly loved her, saved her on his horse. As they were galloping away on the horse, the young, innocent woman was suddenly faced with the demand for a kiss from her rescuer. Elaine hinted then that the kissing led to violence, to rape, and that the victim, after giving birth to a baby, did not know what she was to do while she faced the anger of society. Finally, she decided to face the issue and she carried the baby about openly as if to defy everyone. Her coming out of hiding was the first method of reacting to the loss of her innocence.

Later, the heroine became a milkmaid and met a young man whom she loved dearly. He too expressed interest in her, but she felt compelled to push him away. She did not tell him of her shame and could not respond to his approaches. She turned him away by telling him that there were many other pretty girls and that she did not wish to see him. That is as far as Elaine had gotten in the novel.

I expressed interest in the heroine and I wondered whether she had any other choice. Elaine at first felt that while 1890 was not to be compared with 1950, she saw not much choice for the girl. However, on second thought, she felt she would have advised the girl differently and would have told her to wait until the friendship with this man developed to a certain point and then face him squarely with the issue and leave it up to him as to what the secret of her life meant to him.

I wondered whether the young man could have done something in order to accelerate the process. How could he have helped this woman to share the secret of her life with him? Did he need to stand by and permit her to ruin herself and thus lose her? Elaine insisted that there was nothing that the man could do. After all, he was no mind reader. All my attempts to assign him a role of helpfulness were warded off by the insistence that the girl did or should do nothing to let him in on the deepest secret of her life.

Finally I understood and suggested that Elaine's point meant that only as long and as soon as the heroine of the story offered some effective hint, or was willing to take some help from him or someone else, could she be helped. So much did the heroine assume a natural behavior and hide her secret that even with the best of intentions this young man could do nothing. But I wondered whether he might be helpful provided the heroine dropped a hint here or there. Elaine then told me that at one point of the story the heroine almost did this, and Elaine conceded that this man or anyone for that matter, for example, her minister, could be helpful, but it was up to the girl at first and not to the helper.

I fully agreed with her point, but I regretted that there was so little choice for him.

Some of our conversation then turned to the experience in the life of the heroine which the latter was hiding. Elaine blamed entirely the parents of the heroine because they had driven her to believe in the rich people, thus getting her into trouble with the simple people in the first place, and therefore indirectly creating this very situation. Thus, the girl fell victim to the man "who took her honor." I wondered whether Elaine spoke about rape and she took this up, suggesting that the story did not directly tell, but there was no question about it. But then she left the question somewhat open, since she felt that it was not certain whether this incident was entirely the responsibility of the man or whether the woman participated, too. She referred to some violence that must have been used but did not exclude the possibility that the girl gave in actively in this violent conflict.

When I wondered whether there were such parents today who might create a situation like the one in the novel, and which made it practically impossible for the heroine to accept help, Elaine denied that such parents could exist today. I reflected on the difference between 1890 and 1950, but I thought that even today parents at times were snobbish and insisted that their children marry within their own class.

The question arose then whether the heroine might be able to get out of this complete deadlock and we both, half in earnest and half jokingly, looked forward to our next session when Elaine would have completed the novel and might know the outcome.

At the point that we were starting to wonder about the outcome of the story, whether the man ever could help the heroine, Elaine rushed away since she did not wish to miss transportation back to the Home.

The experienced clinician cannot fail to see the relevance of this material in terms of the helping situation. Earlier we learned of the child's struggles between wild, destructive, and unacceptable wishes on the one hand and lofty ideals of perfection on the other. But it is also important to notice that the transference allusions divide the helper, the analyst, into two images, equally contradictory and opposed in terms of the purpose of their mission. The first rescuer helps the girl in order violently to take sexual possession of her. The other, ineffective as a helper, must stand passively by because the girl assumes he does not wish to help her and would not love her, were he to know the secret of her sin. The problem of different means and different ends of the helping process, stated in the first interview in the metaphor of the mountain climb or the dentist's braces, was on this occasion restated and rediscussed by means of the metaphor of the half-read novel. The theme was treated in a way that permitted both patient and therapist to allude to it only, rather than to speak about it directly and without emotional distance.

It may be noted here that the therapist, although always aware of the necessity to maintain distance, and to remain within the metaphor, pushed too much in the end. His attempt to speak about "parents today," and his joking suggestion that he was interested in the outcome of the story were both rebuked; this time, again, through an *action metaphor*. This was Elaine's way of saying that she did not want to use time talking about the outcome, since if she were to do so, she would not get back home. But her fear that she might not get back home, that she might "miss the bus," as it were, indeed hits at the outcome of the psychotherapy story itself. However, the psychotherapist did not remain entirely within the metaphor of the novel. The patient, therefore, had to regress to a mode of communication which, rather than returning her to the language of secondary process and reality testing, took her back to action language which interrupted the session and did not answer the problem. Disruptions of this kind are, of course, unavoidable but seem to be excellent indicators of the correctness of interpretive work since they yield clues to the levels of communication which can be utilized by the therapist.

In hours to follow, Elaine's struggle to reveal the secret as well as to keep it buried, kept up ceaselessly. The attitude of the therapist was one of waiting patiently while occasionally, though only indirectly and with a readiness to withdraw instantly, taking the initiative. Recorded material from the second month of treatment, shows how the psychotherapeutic process brought us nearer to the "secret," the real dilemma as posed by the nature of Elaine's illness.

During this session she spoke about her struggle for self-control. She did not want to hurt Mary and to reward herself for not giving in to the temptation to do so, she had manufactured little gold stars "in order to have something so that she could aim towards perfection."

She made some remark as to how she needed to think of God in order to be good. The basic idea was to convey to me that she was bad, but that whenever she accomplished something for which she could pin a gold star on the wall, this was not really the good in her, but rather the expression of the good that came from God. She conveyed to me that in her there was the devil and she suggested that whatever good she could accomplish was only through the help of God. It was really God himself.

I understood her to tell me, and I suggested this, that she felt she had no right to think of her good deeds as emanating from her, but that they were rather directives that she received from God. This was the first time she gave some recognition that I understood her completely.

At this point I compared her attempt to get the message from God, which she would need in order to do good, with the one she used previously when looking at the picture of her father who also told her through the expression she saw in his face what she was to do.

Her first glance in response was one of utter recognition and acceptance of what I said, but she had to retract quickly because it seemed a sin to her that she would want from her father what really she ought to expect from God.

However, when I referred to the educational functions of parents, and that it was the parents' prerogative to tell their children in which way they ought to live, she accepted it partly but added that her father never took responsibility for this. He kept away from educational problems and it was her mother who seemed to be responsible for education. Her mother was the one to say no and to put limits on her just as the school did in the Center. This was exactly why she hated school because the school did not permit her to do what she wanted and to have her kind of fun. When I carefully tied this up with the idea that the school took over the function of the mother, for which now she hated the school, and thus hinted at the notion she previously denied, namely, that she hated her mother for putting pressure on her, she did not protest. But she veered off again to the main complaint she had against the school. The school did not let her have her kind of fun. Her fun, however, was completely different from the fun of other people. What she understood to be fun, for example, was to have the opportunity to prepare herself for Christian service and to be permitted again to go to a certain church in another community as she had done some weeks previously at the time of the beginning of her treatment. She wanted to attend a group meeting of the church. She called to my attention that she did not dare to impose again on any member of the personnel to go with her. The staff member who went with her the first time might perhaps go again, but she was not sure the same person would be on duty that day. She then quickly and spontaneously asked whether I thought it was wrong that she had that kind of fun which was so different from the fun other people had.

I thought I was not sure in which way it might be wrong. I wondered whether perhaps she meant that it was wrong to the extent that it was hard to live up to this. Perhaps she really asked me whether she did not take on a burden for which she was not ready as yet.

She then reminded me—although I really could not recall being told of it—of a message which she had received during the last church meeting. The message concerned an example, a picture really, which implied a deeper thought. It concerned a board and a nail. She made some allusion that one could not possibly expect that a nail that would be so big and so strong could fit that particular board.

At first it seemed to me that this was an example used by the speaker, but Elaine told me that this message was actually given to her before the real meeting started, when she was waiting alone, and when she prayed all by herself. I wondered whether she referred to a message which was given to her while she prayed, a message that came from spiritual godly powers. She confirmed that and I, while commenting on the many deep meanings that this message might imply, took from the example of the nail and the board the idea that it might express two different aspects of Elaine. She wondered whether I referred to her inner struggle, the real conflict that she had, and I said I thought I meant just this. I thought she had really come to me to find out what kind of nail would fit the board. I played with the notion that her allusion of nail and board actually referred to two different aspects of Elaine. It seemed that Elaine's problem in relation to her "fun" was that these two different aspects of her personality did not constitute an equilibrium and were really not suited for each other.

While Elaine went along with this interpretation for a while, she gave them a different meaning, as if to correct me. I thought she was right, realizing that she felt the board represented her and that the question was whether the burden she would assume, that is the nail, would be appropriate for the kind of board that she was.

As the symbolism of board and nail, female and male, became clearer to me, I understood her wish for help to find the right proportions. I made only indirect and distant comments, but she accepted these fully and also the idea that I should be the one to help her. As a matter of fact, it was perhaps then for the first time that she said this as clearly as she did. She added there were not only she and I working on the problem, but that there were really three of us. It was about time to end the hour and I wondered whether she meant that she and I and God would work on her problem. She affirmed this and it seemed for the first time that I had been accepted into a triangle situation. I could not help but feel that now I had evidence that I had become part of her delusional system. I expressed the thought then that the three of us could do it, even though it would be a long struggle. Elaine left with an indication of inner satisfaction.

Elaine's gold stars really represented the gifts which she expected from God, thus, indirectly from the therapist. The therapist, who was then accepted merely as the insignificant shadow of God, nevertheless, thereby gained a "real" foothold in the transference psychosis. She would need to be good, to forbid herself cruelty against Mary, before being allowed to reach Christian perfection (like her fantasy-marriage) which would bring her nearer to God. In that state, she could have "my kind of fun," which she thought of as being forbidden by the school and the therapeutic setting (the mother).

While the conscious thought was that her kind of fun would be Christian perfection, we understand from the intrusive, auditory hallucination, the message of the nail and the board, that things were much more complicated. The therapist's waiting, a cue he took from their discussion about Thomas Hardy's novel, was reliable. She was willing to share the secret of the nail in the board with him. It will become clearer later that the therapist's first idea that the nail and the board constituted two different aspects of Elaine was not wrong. If seen against Elaine's problems in establishing and maintaining object relationships, the message of the board and the nail will lead back to this very meaning.

The next hour, just one day later, was described by the therapist as "a culminating experience, full of deepest emotion and the exposure of deepest material in an atmosphere of a mixture of feelings of passion and pain."

This hour started innocently enough, and at first sounded very much the way a counseling interview would sound in a high-school counseling office. She spoke about her school program, how well she had done, that she stood a good chance of getting only A's, and reflected on her marks. She felt somewhat guilty for showing off, but felt that these good marks would help her to go to college and this in turn would permit her to do the work that she needed to do as a good Christian. She seemed to be struggling with the meaning of growth and success in school, and saw in it an expression of competitive and exhibitionistic strivings on the one hand and, on the other, saw the meaning in terms of her own development. I tried only mildly to suggest the good points or, occasionally, the disadvantages in different ways of marking children and she went along with me; I felt only the pressure that she was trying to make me into a sort of moralist, or perhaps, some kind of educator who was to take an equalizing stand or one of trying to move her away from extreme considerations. Nevertheless, I think the main attempt was to be as noncommittal as possible, but at the same time to participate fully in the exchange of communications.

Thus I provided an accepting atmosphere and differed from her only inasmuch as the vibrations of my own value judgments, if any could be read into my comments, were less intense than hers.

I do not recall any particular important topic we discussed otherwise, but what follows developed from one facet of the discussion which had to do with a person's right or lack of right to show what she could do or what she was and how far she could go with it.

It was at this point that Elaine reintroduced the topic of the board and the nail. She told me that she had not forgotten what we talked about the day before and as a matter of fact wanted a piece of paper, a "scrap of paper," on which to show me what she meant to convey. She drew a design which she suggested had to do with bookends for which she wanted to use the idea of the board and the nail. My previous suspicion confirmed itself quickly when I looked at the design she had drawn. It certainly suggested the sign of the cross (and quickly I realized that the board that

she had always talked about was also the cross to which Christ was nailed).
What was to happen then went so quickly and was so full of drama that
I am not sure whether my memory reconstructs adequately the back and
forth of words, but perhaps I can convey the affect that broke through.

I told her that I realized when she spoke about the board she may
have meant it also as the cross which was made of boards. She told me
she did, but as quickly as she could she tried to remove the little design,
and to tell me that there was really no particular meaning attached to it.
However, when I had quickly recognized the main idea that she wanted
to convey to me, she went on to tell me with increasing inner pressure
about a story that explains the origin of the red breast of the little robin.
The robin, according to this story, attempted to pull out the thorn from
the forehead of Christ. It is in this way that the little bird got a red breast,
red from blood. She spoke then of a different version, again explaining how
the red breast of the bird was in one way or the other a symbolization of
the bird's attempt to save Christ, and his having taken on some of the
suffering.

I recalled at this point Oscar Wilde's story of "The Nightingale and
the Rose." While I recounted the story, thoughts went rapidly through
my mind. Her little robin reminded me of Robin Hood, her phantom husband whom she had never mentioned during psychotherapy. It became
also clear to me that she had been attempting to tell me that she was like
Christ, perhaps the bride of Christ, and that the question was whether she
was now strong enough to bear the nails, as Christ did. The sado-masoch-
istic nature of the fantasy became clear, in spite of the disguise, through
the theme of suffering in order to redeem others. At the same time I went
on to speak about the two young lovers, described in Oscar Wilde's story.
I told her the story about the girl's wish for a red rose. The young man,
in order to win her, has but one way to get this rose. A nightingale would
have to sing the whole winter night while pushing her chest against the
thorn of the rose bush. The loveliness of the nightingale's song, the
nightingale's love, and the blood which would slowly flow into the stem
of the rosebush, would form the rose. The young man got his rose, but the
nightingale was dead and its little chest was covered with blood.

Elaine, who was deeply involved with the story up to this point, suddenly got almost violent. Her body convulsed as if shaken by an orgastic-
like experience while tears were flowing down her cheeks. She told me to
stop. My comparison was completely wrong. One story had nothing to do
with the other.

I mildly suggested that I thought there was something in common in
the two stories. I did not know how I had hurt her so much. In both
cases, I suggested, the bird had suffered because of love. There was the
thorn in both stories. Elaine became almost incoherent. She could not
see the comparison at all. The one story had to do with God, with Christ,
with something holy. I wondered whether she was holding against me my
attempt to connect human love with a religious theme. She said that she

did not know what I meant. I wondered whether she resented my having brought into these stories not only tenderness and love, but also that aspect of love which was passion. She protested and told me that it had nothing to do with this at all. She then suggested that her being upset was caused by something entirely different, something that I had said much earlier, before I had talked about the nightingale and the rose.

I could not recall what she might possibly refer to. I asked her to give me a hint and she pointed to the drawing, to the cross. I had spoken in some special way as if I understood her deepest thought which she was attempting to hide from everybody, certainly ought to hide from me— the thought about the cross and the nail. I asked her then whether I had implied that I realized that she thought of herself as being in the same position as Christ. I used some "neutral" word as if to hint that I knew that she was He Himself. With bitter tears she told me that this was just what upset her. This was a most horrible idea that she could never tell anyone. She could only bear that I knew about it because in some way I was no person. She was attempting to say that since I had a therapeutic function only, I was just her doctor, I did not count in the same way as did the people who were in her family or were her friends.

I reminded her that only the day before she had told me how He and I and she, the three of us together, would be working on this problem, the problem of the board and the nail. That was true, she said, but it was too terrible and how could she ever suppress the thought, never to have it come again, with me bringing it out in her? She had always been trying to push it away. She felt that she was a coward, that she was weak because she could not keep it away even from herself. Though she slowly quieted down, we still had to run far overtime. I simply said that in spite of all the pain that I seemed to have caused her, I was glad that she had told me. I indicated that it was not the question of being forced to think that thought, and of being unable to push it away, but that the problem was to help her so that she would not need to push away thoughts. She stressed the forbidden nature of the thought and I did not want to disagree with her on that, but, still I thought that it was good for her to have told me. Now, while she was ready to accept this as something that she just had to do, it was terrible for her to think that He would know that she had had that thought again. I reminded her again that to speak about this was a task that the three of us had embarked on together. As she slowly regained her composure, she made ready to leave. She herself mentioned the next hour and left deeply shaken.

The wealth of this material is so overpowering that the basic secret which is communicated in this session might easily get lost. The theme of the board and the nail; the theme of the union with Christ; the theme of the little robin who dies in an attempt to save Christ; the theme of the bisexual and sadomasochistic arrangements suggested; the theme of the struggle against earthly love; each almost hides the basic problem: fear of the loss of identity, and fear of fusion with the love object. The necessary maintenance of distance, the desirability to "suppress that horrible thought" emphasized Elaine's need to keep the therapist diluted, as a shadow-like figure, from religious images which constitute not only projected introjects, but also serve to drain the affect from the psychotherapeutic situation. Only this way could she maintain sufficient middle-ground affect, and not be devoured by trigger-like and overwhelming emotional experience.

We do not know whether the therapist ought to be censured for introducing Oscar Wilde's story, for his attempt to change the heavenly theme into an earthly one. To be sure, he felt that he went too far. But was this feeling about his own activity not simply his countertransference awareness that Elaine went too far and could not maintain her identity as she pursued her "goal of Christian perfection," to be accepted by Him, to get His gold stars? Her problem then was that in this struggle to be like the other, she became the other and wiped herself out. In order to maintain her individuality, to remain different, she was in danger of wiping out the other. As she regained her composure, she suggested that it was possible to tell the therapist since he did not count, he was not a person, he was simply a machine. (This struggle for identity, against fusion, and the dynamics of her object relationships have been discussed in Chapter 20.) It is interesting that the therapist's notes do not indicate whether he told his patient the end of Oscar Wilde's story. The sacrifice of the nightingale was in vain. The young man brought his rose but was rejected by the narcissistic girl, who did not accept his sacrifice and did not give him credit for accomplishing the impossible. Does he who works with patients as sick as Elaine not feel frequently like Oscar Wilde's hero after he returned to his garret, the rose in the gutter, and the mission having failed? As in Oscar Wilde's story, the therapist is only used as the unimportant third person while Elaine is searching for Him and confides to the therapist that her confessions mean nothing since he is not "real," the patient's way of denying the perception of human contact.

As Elaine brought her deepest problem into the psychotherapeutic situation, thus revealing her illness and giving, of course, an impression of greater disturbance, she actually made progress in her social adjustment. She mastered the school program, and was soon ready to leave the hospital setting and enter a boarding home. As long as she had regular psycho-therapeutic sessions scheduled, there was no interruption in·her external adjustment, which looked to the outsider in the residential setting as vast improvement. It was as if the symptomatology of the illness found its main expression in the psychotherapeutic session itself. It was only during planned or unexpected absences of the therapist that the rapid gains registered in her living situation broke down again. Returning after an absence, the therapist learned from the social worker that Elaine had been quite disturbed while he was away. She had gone to the domestic personnel and had discussed with some of them her religious problems in a way which frightened them. She had cried a great deal, had locked herself in the closet of her room, and had been praying for hours on end, not permitting anybody to enter. In the first session after the therapist's return, she gave no inkling at first as to how upset she had been during his absence. She had to deny completely his absence or presence, his very existence or nonexistence. The question whether the psychotherapist thought her to be ready for a boarding home brought her back to the nature of the help which she was receiving, or rather which, in her words, she "had to take" from the therapist. This part of her session with him went as follows:

She did not know whether she should tell me what happened to her on Sunday when she was in tears and when even the Bible could not help her. She wondered whether I could understand or help her inasmuch as I did not have the same religion as she. If I were Catholic, for example, or Moslem or something like that, I certainly could not help her. I wondered whether she thought perhaps that I wanted to convert her, or that I did not believe in the values that she had found in her religion. If this is what she thought, I wanted to tell her there was nothing of the sort in my mind.

Elaine then went on to say that I could understand her only if I could be like her. She seemed to convey that I could understand her only if I were actually she, only if I could identify with her to that final extent. She did not pursue the topic of my personal religion any further, but slowly moved again to Sunday which had been so upsetting to her. She had finally discovered during this weekend that the devil was in her and that she had no power to change this. She said all this with tense emotion, with tears in her eyes, and with a sense of utter despair. I reminded her of the session when she had told me that he who thought that he was clean and had freed himself from the devil would suddenly find that the devil had come back with his seven brothers. This comment on my part re-established contact between Elaine and me. I thought she had been possessed during the weekend with deep doubts about God and about His helpfulness. She did not see it in terms of her doubts but rather in terms of the victorious devil.

She then went on to describe her experience. Her heart was on the side of God and full of sincere religion. It was only her mind, her thoughts, which were possessed by the devil. There were her mind, her heart, and her mouth. The mouth did the speaking, the communicating, but most of the time the mouth was dominated by the mind which, in turn, was possessed by the devil. It seemed that the emotions were hopelessly outweighed by the mind and when I offered to try to help her in this struggle, she felt that neither she nor I could do anything about it. It would actually be up to Him. This confirmed my earlier idea that rather than she being able to reach out for me, I would have to reach out for her. Again, in her example, it was up to Him to help her just as it was up to me to identify myself with her.

I wondered whether her upsetting weekend was not my responsibility. My absence, my inability to see her during the usual session, perhaps had brought about this state of affairs. She quickly said that she should not blame me, but rather be grateful that this opportunity arose since it was only because of my absence that she discovered the devil in herself. Otherwise she never would have known. I did not know whether I could fully agree with her, even though it was perhaps necessary for her to discover what she was really up against. She spoke then about an example from the Bible. [I am repeating material cited in Chapter 19 to convey the atmosphere of this session.] She spoke about the sheep which was endangered by the wolf and was desperately waiting for the shepherd to save it. There were shepherds who gave merely food to the sheep, food and water, which was not enough. There were others who gave love. It seemed to me that the sheep that she was describing at this moment got only food and water and Elaine agreed with me. I wondered where the shepherd was, had the shepherd gone away? Had the shepherd deserted the poor sheep? While Elaine needed to stress that the shepherd really would never actually leave the sheep and would be there in time to save it from the wolf, she did admit that perhaps the sheep felt lonesome and deserted by the shepherd, and that therefore it saw the danger of the wolf much more enormously. The sheep had lost all the power to jump, had lost the power to run away. It was only through the love of the shepherd that the sheep could regain its strength.

Once during the back and forth I wondered how the sheep might have felt in the hour of danger. Elaine said that the sheep felt no resentment against the shepherd because it was so terribly scared. Lonesomeness and longing for the shepherd, overwhelming fear and panic had taken hold of it. I reminded Elaine of a dream which she had told me earlier in which she found herself marching into a concentration camp and waiting for some terrible fate. She woke with terror. I likened the terror that she experienced when she woke up to the terror that the sheep must have felt and therefore thought for a moment that the shepherd would not come back to help it. I then expressed the feeling that I was convinced that the shepherd always would come back. For a moment perhaps there were too many sheep, or it might seem to the sheep that the shepherd had too many sheep to take care of. But Elaine herself then started to say that the shepherd never could have too many sheep. He could do it. I spoke then about the idea that I was sure he would return in due time. She took up my thoughts in terms of future events even though I was already there and had returned. We spoke of the return, and about her being calm, as if it would happen in the future, and as if we were concerned with the sheep of the Bible rather than with her.

This time she did not mind missing the bus. During the session at a moment when we were as far apart as possible, she reported only about the severe doubts that she had in the Lord and which brought out the devil in her, and at that time she looked out the window and never looked at me. At the end of the interview she turned her head and looked at me again. I made some comment that I was glad she saw me in the room again and looked at me. When she left, the mood of doubt in the Lord and the feeling of being possessed by the devil had given way to a large extent to a feeling that the shepherd would return and would not desert the sheep.

At this point it is clear that the psychotherapist had gained a secure foothold in the therapeutic situation, and that he was fully established in the inner struggle Elaine had to resolve. There is even the feeling, here and there, that the distance material, the disguise through the religious context (the defensive and adaptive meaning of which was elaborated in Chapter 19), had given way to sudden knowledge in Elaine that she was talking about the therapeutic process. In her communication the heroes changed and became more earthly and less perfect. Hours on end she discussed King David and his relationship to Bathsheba. The therapist occasionally stressed the psychology of Bathsheba and, while remaining strictly within Biblical context, helped Elaine to accept the fact that any relationship is a function of the behavior of both participants. King David's wishes towards Bathsheba are partly caused by her.

As soon as the deepest secret of Elaine was brought into psychotherapy, she was able to face more and more inner issues of her life and to share them with the therapist. One might well say that with the confession of her inability to maintain her individuality under stress, she had really started treatment. The opening phase was truly over, and a good many features of the therapeutic process, although interrupted by regressive phases and crises, henceforth showed more often the conventional features of psychotherapeutic work with adolescents—if one is permitted to see anything conventional in therapeutic work with adolescents.

I believe I can sum up the meaning of the next period, covering another month of psychotherapeutic work, by referring to Elaine's dream of the burning house in which her father's picture was safe but my gift of "The Messiah" records was not (Chapter 20); and by relating this dream to her obsessive thought that she was Christ and, later, that I was Christ.

The transference problem had now developed into a new direction. The image of the father could only be saved by projecting it onto the image of Christ. Whenever the attempt was made to approach the father, the therapist, or Christ, tremendous danger came into sight, wiped out her individuality, devoured the object, and destroyed all individuality. New attempts were then made to reach the father image. He could not be reached because Elaine assumed that he was Christ. As the transference developed, psychotic aspects of this transference withdrew into the dim past, were burned out in the burning room. The image of the father could be retained while its substitute, the image of the Messiah, was threatened. This dream was related without undue anxiety and no comment was made on my part with the exception of the suggestion that she must have felt good after she woke up, when she thought in the dream that the picture of her daddy was saved.

With transference achieved, Elaine's treatment took a more familiar path. She lived in a boarding home, finished high school with extraordinary success, and even won a scholarship at an excellent university. There were, of course, many ups and downs; struggles in the boarding home, critical situations with the parents, and the usual problems in her social relations with her peer group. She finished treatment after four years, seeing the therapist less and less frequently.

Four years after the ending of her treatment, she was a successful university student who appeared to have a rich and adequate personal life. She had contact with her parents, visited them during her vacations, but looked forward to her own home someday. She remained a sensitive person with a sense of social responsibility and adequate religious needs. Her therapist heard from her infrequently, but each time the communication confirmed the impression that she was doing well. She seemed able to bear up well under ordinary stresses of life and to be a valuable and appreciated person with a sense of self-respect and a pride in her individuality. The shame that she experienced about having to admit to others that she was in need of psychotherapeutic help gave way to a certain pride in the therapist. She needed neither to hide her past illness nor the fact of her therapy. She even took it on herself to introduce the therapist to a certain friend of hers. In a follow-up meeting, which she arranged when she spent part of her vacation visiting friends in the community where she had been treated, she reviewed some of her past experiences in psychotherapy. There was a clear recollection of the experience although it seemed to be viewed in the very same way that a dream is recalled by someone who is awake. The original experience could be likened to the one of a dreamer who would talk about the dream while dreaming. This dream which she remembered no longer frightened her after she had achieved new integration.

At the beginning of this chapter I spoke about the fact that a therapeutic process is really a joint effort. Its descriptions are coauthored by both the patient and the therapist. If Elaine chances upon this account, and could recognize herself behind the disguises used, as well she might, I believe that she would have reason to be proud of her successful struggle in which, to some degree, I was able to help her. She might suggest that the struggle is not quite over yet. I think she would add, as she did during her last session with me, that she feels strong enough to carry on alone, that she will not need to come back for further help. But if a crisis should develop, she also feels strong enough to come back for further help rather than to escape once more into a world of engulfing and deepening illness.

22

THE WORKING ALLIANCE
WITH THE MONSTER *

The Lord to Mephisto:
Appear quite free on this day, too;
I never hated those who were like you:
Of all the spirits that negate,
The knavish jester gives me least to do.
For man's activity can easily abate,
He soon prefers uninterrupted rest;
To give him this companion hence seems best
Who roils and must as Devil help create.

JOHANN WOLFGANG VON GOETHE

Dorothy Wright was eventually permitted by the Space Child to join him as a travelling companion on his fantasied and fantastic journeys to outer space. Only then could she, as his therapist, attain the necessary leverage with him for meaningful interpretive interventions leading to the ultimate successful treatment process (Part V).

He who works with psychotic children cannot interpret from the outside—from the world of reality testing and the secondary process. He would be in error to assume that there would be contact and communication with an intact, observing ego, capable of stable representation of past and current objects. Instead, he must be prepared to join a fiercely raging internal battle in which unstable, fluctuating, rapidly appearing and disappearing introjects constantly change sides in this intrapsychic "reign of terror." And, in fact, one is reminded of periods of violent social conflict in which the oppressed of today become the oppressors of tomorrow and where the amorphous panicky masses impulsively and irrationally switch from the support of one government to the support of rebellious forces who may well become the government of tomorrow.

* Elaine Caruth is coauthor of this chapter.

403

The therapist of psychotic and borderline children often finds himself with strange and ever changing bedfellows, and may well discover that some of his best friends are devils and witches, creatures and monsters, robots and ghosts. The patient's willingness, no more than tentative as it generally is, to accept a therapist into his delusional world must be matched by the therapist's capacity to ally himself with the monsters of the patient who reside in this world. In doing so, he begins to lay the ground-work for personality integration rather than fragmentation and for the development of adaptive functions within all aspects and layers of the personality. He seeks to avoid a suppression of the psychotic elements and hence a sealing-off of so much of the personality that the patient may well become a kind of living shell, doomed to a "burned-out" automaton-like existence.

Paradoxically, such patients will seem to demand that the therapist destroy these monsters who persecute and torture them; who make them steal and engage in forbidden sexual activity; who put crazy thoughts in their minds; and, at the same time, torture and punish them and seem even to keep them away from the therapist. The patients think that their only salvation is to get rid of their monsters, their influencing machines, or their bad thoughts, and they seek to engage the therapist to this end.

A schizophrenic adolescent girl (Chapters 3 and 17) describes her creature in this way:

You know it is sort of something like imagination . . . like you can imagine yourself, that you lead yourself . . . But then suddenly you can imagine and another person that will think that he is more greater than you . . . and then he will tell you "Look! I'm stronger so I'm going to lead. Not you, you're weak. You do what I say." So then he makes me do what he says . . . and he's scolding me in my imagination, he's punishing me, he's getting angry at me, and then that is what gets me angry. Then I grab something. I feel like grabbing and just breaking it . . . it isn't that another person thinks he's more stronger than me. It's something like that. It's the creature . . . if I do something wrong, he punishes me and . . . that's what gets me in a bad mood. When he punishes me because I did something wrong, it just makes me laugh at you and break anything and get rid of the creature and break him apart.

A schizophrenic boy [1] writes to the therapist and offers the following description of his struggle with his own personal devil, Mr. Punishment:

The only reason why I didn't want to do the dishes was because Mr. Punishment was telling me, "You're getting tired. You will not do all that work! We won't have time to have fun if it gets too late!" He wants me to *be in bed as early as possible so that he can have his fun. Just because I'm getting lonely for Mr. Punishment I don't do the dishes. HELP! HELP! I didn't want even to listen to the ball game because I was too desperate to go to my inner world! . . . it is real hard for me to do my job when Mr. Punishment is still in command . . . but any time he knows you're not here, he becomes powerful, very powerful!*

As one observes the vicissitudes of these monsters during the therapeutic process one realizes that they are but primitive precursors of the superego with rudimentary adaptive functions which are being utilized by the child in the psychotic transference. These powerful persecutors appear in the lives of these children at very critical moments; for example, whenever the therapist is unavailable or whenever the child is alone and, unable to maintain a stable and internalized object, is thus threatened with the dissolution of whatever remnants of object relations of which he has been capable. In such instances, these children are unguarded, as it were, and overcome with the anxiety and terror of autistic isolation. It is then that they call on these monsters in much the same fashion that the normal child, alone at night, uses his teddy bear, that de-animated babysitter, as a transitional object [2] by means of which to revive the absent nurturing mother. However, the psychotic children have never truly separated from the original mother-child matrix. They seek, therefore, to restore the hallucinated symbiosis via these creatures which might well be understood as *transitional introjects* and which are revived at such moments in the service of a psychotic kind of adaptation.

When the 16 year old schizophrenic girl, in the early years of treatment, was left alone, the creature appeared to urge her to overeat—a kind of do-it-yourself nurturing. The parent figure was absent and she needed to restore the object but was unable to do so. In this psychotic attempt at reconstitution, we can see also how the patient "reconstructs" her life history, where, in order to be nurtured, she was impelled to steal and force her needed supplies from an ungiving world. It is interesting to note here that this patient had the nightly habit of gulping down raw food in immense quantities; shortly before this period she would go to bed with a can opener. We might consider this a psychotic version of a transitional object, by which she revived a graphic picture of the original violent, aggressive, withholding mother-child relationship.

These children experience overwhelming terror in the face of the overpowering force of their monsters, and beg to be rid of them. Despite this, we would like to suggest that these same persecutors, whom the child beseeches us to destroy, and to help suppress (which presumably would result from dealing with them rationally and subjecting them to secondary-process functions such as reality testing), are the very basis for developing what Greenson [3] has referred to as a "working alliance." This is a condition which has to be restored when the therapeutic process seems to be at a stalemate.

In treating neurotic children we know the necessity of maintaining a working alliance with the parents. This is accomplished primarily through maintaining equidistance from the external parent-child conflict, a parallel of the necessary equidistance from the ego, id, and superego internal conflicts in the standard procedure that Anna Freud [4] has described. In work with psychotic children, however, we have to establish this equidistance with the incomplete and negative parental introjects—the delusional and hallucinatory monsters—the fused and undifferentiated representatives of both the bad self and the bad objects projected back on to the environment. The psychotic child comes to us and instead of trying to enlist us on his side against the parent, says in essence, "Let's love each other but hate my monster." The child at this moment uses the monster to become the personification and receptacle of all the bad impulses which enable him to establish distance from them and deny them as his own. In addition, he uses the monster to become the receptacle of all the bad extrojects and, in this way, is able to maintain and isolate the image of the good therapist. Winnicott [5] has reported what happens when the child does succeed in engaging the therapist in such a struggle with the bad side of him.

We suggest that the therapist develop a tolerance for the monster and develop an alliance with him. Since we deal with delusional psychotic introjects when we speak of the monster, we can expect the development of a fusion. Ultimately the features of monster and therapist begin to merge in what is the psychotic version of the alternating play between introjective and projective identifications. Mr. Hyde adopts some features of Dr. Jekyll. We expect therefore, to see the patient developing a tolerance toward both monster and therapist, since the patient now knows that the therapist does accept him, including his monster. Thus the child can begin to accept this part of him which has already become changed in part through the therapeutic alliance. We have developed techniques by means of which we use this alliance in order to strengthen gradually the secondary-process ego functions borrowed from the therapist. The patient can then utilize, rather than be overwhelmed by, the primary-process-derived functioning as expressed in the delusion of the creature.

By means of a movie version of one of the Grimm fairy tales, the above-mentioned schizophrenic adolescent girl has described the subjective experience of a therapeutic change brought about by the taming of the monster. She relates the story of the dragon who at the king's request is to be killed by two brothers, one "crafty and shrewd," the other "innocent and simple, and of kind heart." However, the older brother wants all the credit and the prize for the feat, and murders his younger brother. He returns to the king to boast of his own prowess and to claim the princess. Just as he is about to be rewarded, a little shepherd begins to play for the first time on a leg bone he had found and shaped into a horn. The bone was part of the killed brother. The magic bone sings the true story of the slaying of the wild beast and, as the story is told, the younger sibling magically comes back to life. He is rewarded by the king and made the master of the wicked brother. By this tale, the patient tells us that she initially appealed to the king, the displacement figure of the therapist, and demanded the death of the monster, the psychotic illness. But since she has learned that the monster within her also serves a positive function, she feels that the weakly helpless, although healthy, part of her would also be destroyed. With the king's help, however, the healthy part is gradually able to revive and become so strengthened that he who had been killed by the wicked part of her, the monster within, now becomes the master of the wicked part. The two parts of her are then able to live more harmoniously together, the psychotic process now under control and in the service of adaptation.

This kind of treatment philosophy almost seems to be prescribed by the monsters themselves when we begin to understand their function in the lives of these children. But the same treatment is also suggested by the structural model of personality which implies that conflict occurs at all levels of psychic functioning. Whereas the topographic model pictures the unconscious as Pandora's box, to which is assigned all repressed instinctual activity, the structural model recognizes rather the ubiquitousness of conflict and the quasi-adaptive nature of resolution through symptom formation. Thus the delusional monster, just like the handwashing compulsion or the hysterical tic, represents a compromise formation between impulses and delay mechanisms, and functions as an organizer of the inner life, although of a more primitive nature.

These patients whom we describe suffer from certain basic ego deficits resulting in islands of psychic structure [6] that are disconnected and fragmented and, in the case of the persecuting paranoid objects, projected. Dragons and monsters have always been the basis of early superego development,[7] and the primitive ego of the small child inevitably experiences the parent as either fantastically threatening and punitive or magically omnipotent and giving. Normally these early introjects of the child become modified and synthesized into developing superego structures and, as the internalization and identification proceeds, the archaic, distorted features recede. Such patients however are unable to synthesize the good and bad images into a whole person and remain with only the primitive precursors of the superego derived from a period in which loving and hating were still fused rather than synthesized. In treatment we seek to integrate and synthesize the islands of psychic functioning through a kind of psychological grafting, metaphorically analogous to the use of fill to build a causeway between separated islands. If successful, if the degree of compacting is high enough, there will appear little difference in the completed structure from the natural formation. Nevertheless we know all too well that underground movements will always be more dangerous here than where no fill has been necessary.

The specific interpretive interventions that have been utilized to carry out this treatment strategy may be described as attempts to engage the monster in a psychotherapeutic process. By treating him as a common property, a temporary mutual delusion of folie à deux, he may help serve to link together the patient and therapist. Once brought into the analytic hour, the delusional monsters are then available to the same kind of interpretive work as is accorded to the patient. The therapist points out that the monsters seem to serve a positive function despite their cruel sadistic methods. He wonders if they cannot be helped to become more rational so that they can give reasons for what they do. When it is appropriate, the therapist directs his remarks to the monsters. As the process develops, a dialogue ensues between the therapist and the monster who has now become someone with whom the patient and the therapist can negotiate. Through this process, the very nature of the monster is changed in that he becomes more rational and subject to secondary-process reasoning. The patient slowly develops sufficient strength and distance to try, himself, to influence these monsters to help them accomplish their purpose by less punitive, less destructive, and more adaptive means.

Clinical data from the patients referred to above illustrate how such change slowly unfolds in the therapeutic process. The schizophrenic girl describes the present situation vis-à-vis the monster:

I haven't been trying to just get him out of the way or just get him out of my mind or by other means get him out of me . . . remember before how hard I would try? . . . Now I just try to ignore him, that's the best . . . before I would want to get angry at the creature, he's the one who would get me angry, nobody else, he started it and I would want to finish what he started and instead I would wind up doing it to someone else . . . but I found out that's not the best thing to do to tame him . . . the creature bothers me now with a reason.

The schizophrenic boy came into treatment so terrified of his personal devil, Mr. Punishment, that he could not even say the full tabooed word for months but could only refer to Mr. P. The boy has finally come to describe himself as Donald Jones and Donald Punishment, two different parts of one person. After about a year and one-half of treatment, he writes to the therapist:

I have made a big discovery . . . when a person hides himself from other people he builds up in his imagination what he thinks is real. But it is not .. . . because I didn't want to face the real people of my life, I said the inner world for me. Ever since then I have thought Mr. Punishment was important. . . . Then I felt I wasn't doing good at all so I said why not go get someone to teach me how to do things. But this made-up teacher (Mr. Punishment) know only one thing from the first PUNISH PUNISH PUNISH! ! ! So that is why he knows only one way of helping me because I fed into him all I knew then . . . it seems I'm divided into three parts not two. . . . Part one wants to learn, feels he's behind; part two wants to be punished, feels he should suffer; part three thinks he is a genius. So I think I may be more than just Donald Jones and Donald Punishment, I may have a third part, Donald Genius. But the main part is Donald Jones. So it is really good to divide yourself up into three parts.

After writing this letter, this boy brought into treatment a peace treaty, a kind of charter for an intrapsychic United Nations as it were, which read:

DONALD JONES AND DONALD PUNISHMENT PEACE TREATY
January 16, 1965
After many years of torture and punishment, we have come to a decision to become great friends. For a long time we have been enemies and competiters (sic). Now we both realize that we are growing up, And becoming men. IN the past you Donald Punishment, Would always punish Donald Jones. He would think he was doing wrong but, the more you punished him the more wrong he would do. So I ask you, Do you want to continue living in the past or do you want to come up to date? There is much more fun in life than just Punishment. Dr. R.E. will do all he can To Help Us achieve a better life for us in the future.
Just sitting around and dreaming does not get you anywhere at all. . . . Someday we will have to change our ideas for something Else That is more mature and grownup.
Donald Jones & Donald Punishment. do you hereby agree to start working For each other? And form one good person Donald F. Jones?
SIGN HERE I_____
Good luck friends
Signiture of doctor _____
PLEASE SIGN TO MAKE OFFICIAL

We have used as our guiding theme the suggestion that the Lord in Goethe's *Faust* made concerning the use of the devil in order to bring about higher accomplishments. In the beginning it is God who makes the decision that He will like the devil and accept him for what he is, as someone who drives men to accomplishment even though the devil's subjective purpose is to cheat God and fight Him. At the end however the devil literally becomes more human and will start to love God, except that he will project now onto God that God behaves more humanly. Thus Mephisto says about the Lord:

> *I like to see the old man now and then*
> *And try to be not too uncivil.*
> *It's charming in a noble squire when*
> *He speaks humanely with the very devil.*

Our suggestion is that in therapeutic work we must start with the acceptance of the delusional monster and bring about a working alliance with that part of the patient's personality. At a later point of the process we will have helped the patient to accept and to synthesize the monster parts of himself as well as the patient's feelings about the therapist. The interpretive strategy of the taming of the monster, analogous to Freud's dictum that where id was shall ego be, suggests that where unstable introjects ruled, capacity for object relations shall be developed.

REFERENCES

[1] The present authors' Certain phenomenological aspects of the countertransference in the treatment of schizophrenic children, Reiss-Davis Clin. Bull., 2:80, 1964.

[2] Winnicott, D. W. Hate in the countertransference, Int. J. Psychoanal. 30:69, 1949.

[3] Greenson, R. R. The Working Transference and the Therapeutic Alliance, Psychoanal. Quart., 2:155, 1965.

[4] Freud, A. Problems of technique in adult analysis, Bull. Phila. Ass., 4:44, 1954.

[5] Winnicott, D. W. Transitional objects and transitional phenomena, Int. J. Psychoanal., 34:89, 1953.

[6] Knight, R. P. Borderline states, Bull. Menninger Clin., 17:1, 1953.

[7] Lederer, W. Dragons, delinquents and destiny, Psychol. Issues, 3:mono. 15, 1964.

PART SEVEN

TRAINING PROBLEMS

I have, alas, studied philosophy,
jurisprudence and medicine, too.
And, worst of all, theology
with keen endeavor, through and through—
and here I am, for all my lore,
the wretched fool I was before.
Called Master of Arts, and Doctor to boot,
for ten years almost I confute
and up and down, wherever it goes,
I drag my students by the nose—
and see that for all our science and art
we can know nothing. It burns my heart.

JOHANN WOLFGANG VON GOETHE

23

SPECIAL TRAINING PROBLEMS IN PSYCHOTHERAPEUTIC WORK WITH PSYCHOTIC AND BORDERLINE CHILDREN

It almost looks as if analysis were the third of those "impossible" professions in which one can be quite sure in advance of insufficient success. The other two, much longer known, are education and politics.

SIGMUND FREUD

Recently I saw a 15 year old boy. His parents had asked me to determine the type of treatment program which might be suitable for him and to help them find a therapist. This boy suffered from a serious organic deficit, which caused him to drag his feet and to speak haltingly with a severe additional speech defect. His facial expression seemed to give away the organic deficit, and in spite of the courageous struggle which he had put up for years he was hardly likeable. He soon revealed, perhaps as a consequence of his organic deficit and the reaction of the world to it, a functional condition which would put him in a borderline range. At his best, he functioned as a withdrawn, neurotic, anxiety-ridden youngster would; at his worst, he was dominated by fugue states, by blind and uncontrollable rages, which he could hardly remember and which seemed to come over him out of the clear sky. The parents had maintained him at home at times, and sometimes had placed him in private schools for years. Somehow he had maintained a labile, pseudo adjustment which permitted him to continue in school with his own age group. As I became acquainted with him, the thought forced itself upon my mind that it would be practically impossible to find a therapist for him. Anyone I might want to call, in order to refer this child for treatment, might resent the referral and might practically take it as an insult. During these minutes as I was weighing his chances in treatment and trying to think of a person who would have the appropriate technical skill and the patience, I did not see how I might explain to the therapist that a treatment was worthwhile and that this patient was a worthwhile patient. While I thought that way, I recognized quickly that I was actually coping with my own reaction to the child. I started to wonder about a peculiar problem in psychotherapy in which it seems to be necessary that the patient be considered worthwhile. I recalled numerous referrals by telephone call or conference in which colleagues seemed to dwell on the worthwhileness of the case, the social value of the patient, the scientific interest of the case, as if it were necessary to sell the idea of treatment.

I had examined this fact and I had found that this *issue of worthwhileness* was not limited to therapists who had very little time available and therefore could afford to be rather selective. The same issue functioned in private work with less experienced therapists, and it could be found also as part of the referrals that are made to clinics. This "worthwhileness" of the patient as a fantasied or actual condition for treatment is very different from medical referrals in general and deserves our special attention, since it seems characteristic for psychotherapists and for certain aspects of our work. We wonder whether the Hippocratic oath of the physician is to be amended in our field with "provided the patient is worthwhile."

Psychotherapeutic treatment is frequently long and tedious. It requires an involvement on the part of the psychotherapist which is very different from the involvement of the physician who does medical or surgical work only. In treatment processes, the relationship between physician and patient involved in a medical or a surgical program plays an entirely different part from its role in cases of psychotherapy. Psychoanalysis or analytic psychotherapy requires a kind of involvement in which selection of patients and special treatment interests and issues, such as worthwhileness, are dominant considerations. One may very well wonder how psychotherapists in training would react to situations which seem to offer none of the gratifications that are expressed in the word "worthwhileness." I think, of course, of the treatment of psychotic and borderline children who are poor treatment risks, about whose treatment we know very little, and who require many years of involvement, frequently without hope based on reliable treatment techniques.

An ever increasing literature on the treatment of the borderline and psychotic conditions in childhood indicates the rising interest in the treatment of such children. A number of residential centers, hospital clinics, and child guidance clinics, as well as practitioners in private practice are devoted to the treatment of such children. This author, in conjunction with Bryant and Friedman[1] has summed up our current feeling that the treatment of such children is worthwhile in the following statement:

The powerful optimism which pervades the literature concerning the treatment of a number of schizophrenic children is as yet not supported by evidence concerning the prognosis for the whole group. Most reports represent enthusiastic pioneer efforts, and permit the expectation that another survey ten years from now will report consolidated gains. The years from 1936 to 1946 were characterized by an emphasis on diagnosis and therapeutic pessimism. The phase from 1946 to 1956 has been one of therapeutic experimentation and optimism. One may predict, then, or certainly hope, on the basis of accumulated evidence, that the period from 1956 to 1966 will bring further improved treatment techniques which may shift the emphasis from an uncertain prognosis for childhood schizophrenia to one in which there will be increased probability of recovery.

The first enthusiastic case reports have aroused interest, and have caused us to ponder as to how the skill of gifted pioneers can be transmitted to others in the field. This is a prerequisite to bringing about a situation in which the discoveries of these pioneers can be tested and can move from the realm of the miracle cure, by especially intuitive psychotherapists, to one of a transmittible treatment technique, which is based on a clear rationale and verifiable prediction.

I am concerned primarily with methods of supervision for child psychotherapists who engage in the treatment of severely disturbed, frequently psychotic children. The basic philosophy from which I draw and which I wish to apply specifically to the technical problem of training personnel treating severely disturbed children has been summed up by Wallerstein and myself.[2] We have attempted to integrate a variety of different trends in training methods as reflected in the contributions of the basic clinical professions represented in orthopsychiatry: psychoanalysis, psychiatry, social work, and clinical psychology. The techniques developed consist of an attempt to individualize training according to the needs of the individual student. They de-emphasize earlier trends in which rigid attempts were made either to stay completely with didactic issues, or solely with countertransference issues, or to turn the supervisory experience into psychotherapy for the student, or to work solely with the interpersonal relationship between student and teacher. It is suggested that all these elements of teaching may be used according to the pattern of learning in the student and the type of learning problem posed through the patient to be treated. If the student were to need psychotherapy, the supervisor may help him to move toward this resource, but essentially he will not attempt to turn the learning situation into a therapeutic venture.

If for a moment we compare child psychotherapists with therapists who work with adults, we think of two specific issues which separate the two groups, although this separation will not prove a sharp one without transitions.

The first difference concerns the therapist's choice of working with children. It has frequently been suggested, although I know of no formal studies which would offer solid evidence, that child psychotherapists usually have a kind of identification with their patients, the children, which makes them into the natural enemies of the child's parents. It is as if they could only work with the child if they can look at his world with his point of view. The child patient's world, and certainly our case histories of children seem to prove this, is one in which he is constantly traumatized by ignorant or rejecting parents. Accordingly, the child psychotherapist seems constantly troubled by the question whether any cure is possible as long as the child stays with the parent or as long as the parent himself remains essentially unchanged.

It has been suggested that this point of view does not merely stem from etiological considerations but is deeply ingrained in the personality of him who chooses child psychotherapy, intensive work with disturbed children, as a profession. He is in the position of someone who is out to prove that he can do better than his own parents, that he must undo the wrong inflicted upon the child. His basic attitudes towards parents frequently towards all adults, are rebellious ones. The child psychotherapist is thought to be overidentified with the child patient and is frequently hostile towards the parents. The therapist sees many of his difficulties in treating children as difficulties of the parents who are interfering with the treatment, who are sabotaging it, and who must be made to see their responsibility for the child's illness. I am far from believing that this seems to be only the beginning attitude which the unanalyzed student of child psychotherapy brings to professional training. I believe that one can actually find such attitudes in more or less pronounced form in gifted and well-trained people who, even though they have insight into this difficulty, have never quite given up the overidentification with the child and the critical attitude towards the parents. Child analysts have suggested that many women who have been trained in this profession have maintained their active interest as practicing child analysts only as long as they remained unmarried. One might then be tempted to think of psychotherapeutic work with children as a transitional phase in the development of a professional person.

I do not know whether such a concept of the psychology of the child psychotherapist would hold up under more rigorous scientific scrutiny. There are certainly some who fit this category, and there are many, perhaps the majority of our students, who go through such phases in their work with children.

It has occurred to me that the difficulty described should perhaps be considered one which stems from the special technical task rather than one that is inherent in the makeup of the child psychotherapist.

I wish to discuss now the second difference between psychotherapeutic work with children and such work with adult patients. Usually one may work with the adult patient without having to work actively with members of his family. As a matter of fact, we know that usually the psychotherapeutic situation can be maintained only if we avoid getting involved with other members of the family. Classical analytic work is a case in point. This rule certainly does not hold true for children, since we know that it would be impossible to work with children, not only legally but psychologically as well, if we were not to include the parents. He who wishes to work with children and does so because of his special interest in childhood, his overidentification with the plight of the child, and his innate hostility toward authority figures, is certainly in for a strange discovery. He will become a good child psychotherapist only if he is willing to look at his training as a sort of "package deal." Unless he learns also to work successfully with the parent, whom he may have hated, consciously or unconsciously, as he went into training, he cannot truly help the child. The dependency of the child on the parent—psychologically, physically, economically, and legally—creates a psychological situation which is entirely different from the one to which we are accustomed when we work with adult patients.

We do not treat the child alone but we are confronted with the necessity to deal with the child-parent unit. This state of affairs has sometimes been discussed in terms of the transference situation as it applies to adult work and to work with children. In classical analysis, we speak about the analysis of the transference neurosis, that is, the repetition of the infantile neurosis. The child who still lives with his parents and is bound up with them in a special psychological unity, does not repeat past and now-repressed special dependency situations in psychotherapy. At best, he displaces them to the therapist who works with the child while concurrently the educational process is going on. It has been pointed out in recent years that children are sometimes capable of developing transference neuroses in relation to earlier repressed stages of their life, which are then fully reproduced in the psychotherapeutic situation. At the same time, however, they are confronted with transference configurations which are of the displacement type rather than of the repetitive type which is typical for the classical transference neurosis.

This particular child-parent constellation creates a special problem for the psychotherapist. He does not deal with the infantile neurosis as a repetition of the past, but deals with it as a present reality. While the therapist who works with the adult patient may help the patient to reflect on past traumata, the child psychotherapist must frequently help the child with current conflicts which put him into provocative situations. Over-identification with the child frequently must lead to the kinds of reactions which we described earlier in speaking about the child psychotherapist's inclination to be rejecting and hostile to parents. We must not forget that in the countertransference he also may sometimes assume parental educational roles rather than maintain a therapeutic function, thus over-identifying with the parent at the expense of optimum contact with the child.

I have spoken about two differences. The first refers to the inner sources, the motivating forces which the young psychotherapist brings to the profession. The second refers to the specific problem that the child psychotherapist faces as he learns to deal with the child-parent unit.

These two issues are reflected in special training problems which one encounters in supervising child psychotherapists. They are blown up to unusual proportions when the training is concerned with the treatment of that patient group which is diagnosed as borderline or as schizophrenic. The child psychotherapist who works with the more mildly disturbed child may wish to help the child against traumatizing environmental influences. The one who is ready to devote his time to the severely disturbed child, for whom the psychotic threat is a threat to life itself, will identify with the child's inner problem in such a way that he may feel himself as a rescuer of the child. He is dedicated to rescue a child who is otherwise considered as hopeless, whom no one else gives a chance, who is no longer considered worthwhile by the profession at large and is frequently given up as a hopeless case and rejected by his parents because of his lack of response.

Earlier and now untenable notions which try to explain childhood schizophrenia merely in terms of the rejecting mother have been given up. We remain, nevertheless, deeply impressed that in all these situations there exists a hopelessness in the mother-child relationship, a lack of mutual understanding, a lack of capacity for understanding each other's cues. Thus, help for the child is frequently seen in terms of a rescue mission, and frequently as a necessity for deep commitment which will allow the psychotherapist to do the impossible, to become a miracle worker, like Anna Sullivan, who must see in this child the future Helen Keller, who, in spite of all the odds against her, achieves self-realization and has hidden and special worthwhileness.

The psychotic child has not achieved a capacity for object relationship, as is true for the mildly disturbed child. The psychotic mother-child relationship, as compared with the neurotic child's capacity for object relationship, exists in symbiotic rudiments, in fusion states, or is reflected in autistic positions.

Neurotic transference figurations are replaced in the case of the psychotic child by psychotic transference configurations. In these, mother and therapist sometimes are not truly separated in the mind of the child, and in them the mother-child experience, not having yet developed to a state of separation, is reflected in symbiotic fusion experiences.

The child psychotherapist who works with the neurotic child may meet the transference manifestations with his own countertransference potential, but he will have a special problem if the provocations to which he is exposed are psychotic transference manifestations. The issue arises as to what kind of countertransference potential is aroused in order to meet the threat that comes from such children.

When the concept of countertransference is used in work with neurotic or psychotic children, we do not think of this simply as an obstacle to treatment, as was assumed in earlier considerations. Countertransference, if not understood, if not dealt with, if not taken as a cue toward the understanding of the patient, can of course develop into an obstacle to our work. But if it is truly understood and utilized as a clue to the understanding of the patient, it may also be the track upon which treatment may proceed.

One might suggest then that countertransference constitutes a form of regression, a return of the repressed, and in the case of having been provoked through psychotic material, a regression to very early states of one's own relationship with one's own parents. Such *countertransference*, however, if understood and utilized, could be considered, if I may paraphrase Kris, *as regression in the service of the therapeutic ego*. Psychotic children who bring to us the totality of their problem, the terror of their isolation, the plea for rescue, as well as their constant struggle against rescue, can be helped by us only if we somehow respond to them in accepting this challenge. We overidentify with them, and it is as if we can do so only if the hate they experience for the parent and the threat from the parent are experienced by us as a wish to rescue them from those who have traumatized them; to be the good mother for them, as it were.

This ideology protects us from our own difficulties in accepting such children as patients, endorses them to us as worthwhile, and permits us to maintain long and seemingly hopeless treatment relationships. It leads us to the kind of dedication which is necessary in order to commit oneself to treatment programs which until recently were considered hopeless and senseless. It is as if faith has to take over where a perfect rationale for treatment has not yet developed. This conscious or unconscious rescue complex, saviour complex, of which Ernest Jones [3] spoke as the psychotherapist's hidden unconscious notion to be God, seems to be a driving force in many who attempt to treat such children. Frequently, however, the powerful hate directed against the forces which are seen as the causative agent of the child's illness, turns into hate for the child. In the next chapter there is a description of the failure of treatment of a psychotic child, in which countertransference, at first in the service of the therapeutic program, turned into a force which created treatment disruption.

These general observations lead to more complicated problems that must be looked at for the purpose of evaluating specific training difficulties which they create.

The child psychotherapist who wishes to work with severely disturbed children brings to us in an exaggerated way two special problems, which will be reflected in his relationship with the supervisor; in the use that he makes of the supervisor; and in his capacity or lack of capacity for acquiring new techniques in order to cope with the task of treating borderline and psychotic conditions of childhood. He has come to the field, or to this special task, because of his overidentification with the child, his wish to rescue the child from terrible adults, and his belief that he can be the miracle worker who might do it. He also brings into the relationship with his teacher the daily provocations to which he is exposed as he works with the child and the parents. The situation may even be more difficult in that, frequently, he may simply work with the child, while one of the other workers in the institution works with the parent. This complication may exist even when he may not have to work with the parents, since the child is hospitalized in a specific residential center, but he then may have to work with the institutional personnel: cottage parents, nurses, residential staff.

He who had certain expectations of his own parents, he who comes with certain ideas about the parents of the children whom he is to help, will, of course, have similar expectations of other adults, certainly of the administrators and the supervisors in his clinic. The special parent-hating syndrome will frequently be reflected in the use the child psychotherapist makes of his teachers, the administrators, the clinic, or the hospital. It is true, of course, that any student will react towards the supervisor in terms of his specific needs in the face of authority. His learning problems will be influenced by the conscious and unconscious methods which he must use in order to please authority, to rebel against it, to seduce it, to comply with the task, or to arrive at a more mature and collaborative relationship.

In my experience these problems which are experienced throughout the field of therapeutic service, are more pronounced with people who are to be trained in child psychotherapy. I have already given one reason for this in suggesting the motivating forces which bring the child psychotherapist to the field as a cognitive agent for the special nature of his problems with the supervisor; and I believe also that the provocations that the child exposes him to are contributing factors in training complications. I have also noticed that these difficulties are enhanced by the fact that supervisors and administrators in this area, since they, too, are basically identified with child psychotherapeutic work, will bring problems into the situation, problems which are not unlike those that the parent of the sick child brings to the treatment situation. We have then an accumulation of multiple difficulties which must be faced.

The borderline and psychotic child truly depends on the skill and the wisdom, on the deep commitment of the child psychotherapist. The patient confronts the therapist with constant provocations which are frequently enhanced by the reactions of helpless, often very sick parents, who find the task of coping impossible. The child psychotherapist, then, brings to the supervisor the impossible task, the constant emergency, the spilling-over of the therapeutic situation into the social situation, the "interference" of the parents, the lack of wisdom on the part of auxiliary personnel in the residential center. He frequently also brings to the supervisor a kind of involvement with the child, which he frequently cannot communicate either orally or in recorded form. This involvement entails a powerful conviction that he can rescue the child because of his own special understanding and that he does not want his work to be interfered with by either parents or the supervisor. He also brings to the supervisor deep-seated anxieties which psychotic and borderline children provoke and bring to the foreground. When I suggested during a seminar that the psychotherapist will understand such children best if he can find some similar experience in himself, one participant a week later claimed that I had said the child psychotherapist should be potentially psychotic. This was said half in jest perhaps, but gave away the fear that one can help children of this kind only if there is something not quite right with one's self. The supervisor, perhaps, is experienced by the psychotherapist as the person who would drive one, as it were, into dangerous mental states. These children constantly provoke anxiety of a kind which can hardly be contained and which floods the supervisory relationship.

Regardless of how many years of experience any one of us has accumulated in the treatment of psychotic and borderline children and how many contributions he himself may have made in this field, we must all admit, as we try to train psychotherapists for the work with these children, that we are all really hardly more than beginners. We work by trial and error. Each case is for us a new scientific experiment, and each situation is so new to us that very little which we have learned from other cases seems to be transferable. We are teaching when, truly, we ourselves are still searching. We are expected to give prescriptions and to become miracle supervisors for miracle psychotherapists, while at the same time we are also experienced by them as people who intervene, who take away from the worker his independence and free choice. We are seen as immense powers-that-be, and are called upon to interfere with reality situations not conducive to treatment. Sometimes, as the worker wants to share with us some of the problems he has in working with these children, he sees us as the very people who provoke such anxiety-arousing material instead of helping him. In one way or the other we are like the psychotherapist himself, put into a position where we have to learn to maintain seemingly impossible situations against almost unbearable odds. We may feel like the one-eyed man who leads the blind. But in moments of stress when the psychotherapist faces emergencies which he cannot bridge, we are sought out like the Messiah who has the secret cure, the magic words for the recovery of an almost lost situation.

So far I have made a variety of statements which are of a general nature. The specific instances which have given rise to these generalizations strike home for all of us who work with severely disturbed children. I am not singling out any individual by citing behavior or reactions of trainees. But rather than asserting that all the characters described are purely coincidental and are not meant to refer to any living person, I suggest that this material could truly apply to anyone among us, students and teachers. I believe that everyone who has been supervised when working with psychotic and borderline children can easily identify himself with the characters created, and he will thus believe that the generic is a kind of confrontation with his difficulties. Rather than try to prevent such an impression I would consider this as our first attempt to come to grips with the problems of the therapist who wants to learn from others how one can work with such children. One can hardly develop dedicated compassion with skill and scientific insight without going through the storms, the doubts, the wish to escape, and the many other tribulations which are described in this paper. Unfortunately, many of the therapists who try such work will have to go through these storms only in order to find out that they are not suited for this kind of work. We have learned that not even a thorough analysis can guarantee one's capacity for such work. As a matter of fact, a few especially intuitive workers in this field known to me never went through an analytic experience themselves.

As our young child patients struggle for psychic survival, they constantly create emergencies; that is, the chaotic material rises to the surface of consciousness and is translated into external emergency situations which call for rescue or invite despair. Their catastrophic discontinuity must find reverberations in the reactions of the learning psychotherapist. He, even though he has maintained his own continued technical application of his understanding of the case, will show reactions which run parallel to the patient's reactions. These reactions are a weaker edition of the vicissitudes of the patient's inner life, as it becomes translated within the psychotherapeutic context.

The enormity of the patient's problem thus finds its way into the supervisory relationship. The observations dealt with so far would strengthen the belief that powerful countertransference reactions are constantly finding their way into the supervisory relationship. These are sometimes expressed in impossible demands for emergency help; for prescriptive advice from the supervisor; for his being willing to play a reality part in dealing with the parents or the sponsoring institution; or in reactions of anger and hate against him, since the impact of the psychotherapeutic relationship is sometimes felt only in terms of the impact of the learning situation itself. One is impressed with the fact that powerful reactions towards the patient to be treated and towards the supervisor to be learned from, interfere with the more normal kinds of learning problems. As a result, the normal learning problems are beset by crisis, by emergency, by deep-rooted conflict. Such an impression is, to be sure, one-sided, but a first report on problems encountered in supervising students who wish to specialize in work with severely disturbed children will naturally stress what seems emergent and most obvious, what seems to be different from the normal course of supervisory processes. I am reminded of the methods of early historians who stressed the crises of civilizations and nations. Their history was usually a history of wars, of conquests, of the sudden destruction of nations, and the heroic struggles for survival. Wars and revolutions, the sudden disintegration of cultures, and the sudden emergence of new powers are, however, the most vivid points only, and by no means give a decisive picture of the driving forces in history.

The supervisory work that I have started to describe cannot be fully understood if we look only at these "wars," "emergencies," "struggles for survival," or sudden discontinuances of treatment caused by seemingly un-understood and sudden decisions of parents or therapists. We must keep in mind the long haul of the careful gathering of clinical data; the slow, sometimes spontaneous, emergence of insight; the development, after many trials and errors, of stable techniques as applicable in each instance; and the therapist's slowly growing capacity to share with the supervisor all relevant clinical data as well as his own inner reactions about treating and about learning. The sharing of the provocations caused by the treatment process, the sharing of one's thinking, one's doubts, one's hesitancies, and one's affects, creates a tremendous burden for psychotherapist and supervisor alike. The degree of professional intimacy which is required if earnest psychotherapeutic work, earnest learning, are to be accomplished, is indeed an extraordinary one. Not many people, therapists or teachers, are willing to assume such burdens. It is for this reason that the rate of training failure, the giving-up of training, the angry or unhappy desertion of patients, the disappointment with supervisor-therapist or parent is much higher than is the case in training for work with more mildly disturbed patients.

But if the process succeeds, and often indeed it does, the gratification is enormous. The trainee makes rapid progress, becomes more and more intrigued with the task ahead, and frequently will develop his skill, his understanding, his curiosity to such a degree that both his dedication and his relationship with the supervisor will soon lead toward collaboration on a scientific level. This outcome is almost unavoidable. It seems to me that psychotherapeutic work with severely disturbed children can only be learned and taught against the background of honest experimentation, of scientific curiosity, and of earnest dedication. It is interesting that the supervision of psychotherapists in this particular field is characterized at one end of its range by powerful, hostile, and negative reactions, while at the other end of its range it will slowly turn into scientific collaboration. This latter factor is perhaps the best counterweight against the earlier aspects which we consider unavoidable, but which we feel can be overcome if they can lead to the self-discipline of scientific experimentation and therapeutic devotion.

I have suggested earlier that these powerful reactions toward the supervisor are frequently reflections of the countertransference. They are the responses to the parent-child situation in the case of childhood psychosis, which are frequently expressed as a problem about learning rather than a learning problem, a problem about and with the supervisor rather than, as yet, a technical problem. I believe our insight will be more complete if we see another facet of the problem in the person of the supervisor. We are, of course, referring primarily to supervisors who themselves have thorough experience in the treatment of psychotic and borderline children, and who are devoted to the problems of such children. They will then be psychotherapists who have been willing to work with them and who have succeeded with some of them. They will have succeeded in treating such children and in training psychotherapists in their treatment of them, if they combine a deep understanding of the psychotic process in childhood with a therapeutic dedication, a therapeutic commitment which is willing to face whatever emergencies might have to be encountered. When one admires such supervisors, one may speak of them as dedicated teachers who make strict but justified demands and who are willing to give fully of all their knowledge. When angry with them one may like to think of them as driven, overdemanding personalities; their dedication is seen as unreasonable, megalomanic persistence. Such teachers, who study constantly, work hard, and are never satisfied with either their own answers or those of their students, are not apt to bring out mild responses in those with whom they work. Their students will be deeply committed to them, heavily involved with them, and may sometimes violently turn away from them. They may not be able to turn away from the work in the self-recognition that this is not the kind of work they should do. But they can do so in being disappointed with the teacher and bringing about an angry break of the learning relationship.

Once I heard August Aichhorn speak about certain successful psychotherapists. He ascribed their success not so much to their skill and training but more to their charismatic properties. Patients take to such psychotherapists instantly. These psychotherapists seem to bring out in the patient a transference readiness simply because of the kind of inner qualities they convey. Of teachers in the field of childhood psychosis it may also be true that they can convey without words their dedication, devotion, curiosity, and deep commitment to the student. But they will bring out not only strong positive reactions in the service of the development of the psychotherapist, but equally strong negative reactions. It is as though one can avoid being caught in their enthusiasm, their commitment, their scientific curiosity, their willingness to work only if one stays away from them or escapes them. One might say that they are favored by positive, charismatic qualities and that they are also disfavored by negative, charismatic properties.

Inner commitment may become the shining example for some, may invite "collaboration on the highest level," and may be experienced by others as driven overcommitment. I have found this to be of significance in the development of training processes, even though the training techniques used included, of course, a deep commitment on the part of the supervisor to offer the student a genuine choice toward or away from this work. Some of the experiences I have had in the training of people who were not involved with processes with such children, but were trained to work with the more normal patient load, are entirely different from experiences encountered with children who suffer from severe disturbances.

A word must also be said about the administrative function as we face training issues. In some administrative settings, administrative function is separated from the supervisory function. This is not always true for organizations dedicated to the treatment of children. These clinics or hospitals or residential centers are usually small units, and therefore we frequently find that the chief of the clinic may also be the main teacher. Furthermore I believe that *the desire to combine supervisory and administrative function often has something to do with the nature of work with children.* We have described earlier the peculiar nature of child psychotherapists, so frequently still in rebellion with parents, and at the same time so much, of course, in need of a parent within the clinical setting. For them the meaning of the administrator seems to be quite different from that of other categories of workers. It is equally true that he who chooses administrative work in a clinic for children may have a stronger need for a paternalistic role, a need which is met by the type of personnel that work in such clinics. If this were the case, we would find it more difficult to develop a supervisory system in which the administrative function and the supervisory function are separated. I think of children's clinics and residential centers where the director in charge was the main teacher, the one who set, as it were, the theoretical and clinical convictions, and who operated as the father-surrogate for the staff.

If such a director is capable of developing an administrative conviction in which the separation of functions is stressed, he will encounter a variety of problems, the backwash as it were, of those processes which have been discussed earlier. He will be involved more frequently in emergency types of situations. He will find more frequently that psychotherapists within his setting, unable to tolerate the learning process smoothly, will resort to him in order to attempt to solve problems which they could not allow themselves to resolve with the supervisor. The supervisor himself will have more need for the help of the administrator. The next chapter examines in detail such a teaching situation in which there developed the involvement of total staff and administration.

I would like to extend Freud's aphorism about the three "impossible" professions of educating, healing, and governing. I suggest that the training of psychotherapists who are to work with borderline and psychotic children combines four "impossible" professions. The processes of healing, of supervising, of administering such programs are combined with the research process. In this particular field, many may say that the expectation of a yield of scientific results for technical intervention is an impossible one. The difficulties of this fourfold impossibility are undeniable. They include the disturbed mother-child unit; the symbiotic and autistic struggles for survival; the ups and downs in the struggle for contact; the withdrawals; the ego deficiencies; the fusion states and the lack of stable objects; the wildly fluctuating psychotic transference in these children—all make special problems for the psychotherapist. He himself may be one who is dedicated to the idea of rescuing the child from the traumatizing source; who himself is in direct or indirect rebellion with parent figures and authority; who struggles for independence but is in need of help and consequently has special problems with his teacher. The character of his work will often increase his problems. The training will suffer from the fact that people who work with psychotic and borderline children will possess not only special talents and gifts but also idiosyncrasies, which does not make it easy for them to fall into the conventional pattern. The same, of course, might be said of administrators of such programs, as well as of teachers who are ready to teach in a field in which there is not as yet a stable body of knowledge or theory, and in which available research does not keep up with the need or the demand. It is as if we ask our students to do research while they learn, that we ask them to be learners as well as discoverers, recipients of available skill as well as explorers of unknown regions of the mind. Students and teachers in this strange field will have to have a great deal of tolerance for each other and they will have to be committed to their mutual task in the same dedicated way as they are dedicated to their patients.

The German poet Schiller is said to have done his writing while he had rotten apples in the drawers of his desk. The smell inspired his poetry, and it is alleged that he was not able to do without these apples. I believe I have discussed some of the rotten apples which seem to accompany our work. The impatient person may feel that we could do just as well if we were to clean out the drawers and throw away the rotten apples. I suspect it will be more helpful to each of us if we tolerate each other's rotten apples. It is perhaps the task of the teacher in this field to discover what his student's rotten apples might be and to learn to tolerate them although they may not fit into the conventional scheme of teaching. Perhaps the student who wishes to enter the field of psychotherapeutic treatment of psychotic children will also have to learn some tolerance toward the rotten apples of his teacher. One of our rotten apples is that we like to communicate our findings. I don't think that we want the smell—or is it fragrance? —to spread, but somehow we hope that it will inspire communication which will lead toward the improvement of our training methods.

REFERENCES

[1] Ekstein, R., Bryant, K., and S. W. Friedman. Childhood Schizophrenia, in L. Bellak, ed., Schizophrenia—a Review of the Syndrome, New York, Logos Press, 1958.

[2] —— and Wallerstein, R. The Teaching and Learning of Psychotherapy, New York, Basic Books, 1958.

[3] Jones, E. The God Complex, in Essays in Applied Psycho-Analysis, London, Hogarth Press, 1951, II.

24

COUNTERTRANSFERENCE IN THE RESIDENTIAL TREATMENT OF CHILDREN*

The scientific results of psychoanalysis are at present only a by-product of its therapeutic aims, and for that reason it is often just in those cases where treatment fails that most discoveries are made.

SIGMUND FREUD

In order to understand the complexities of countertransference in residential treatment, one must be willing to study treatment failure. That this represents an unwelcome undertaking is not primarily because our vanity does not allow failure, or because it is painful to be reminded of suffering which has gone unrelieved, but in large measure because residuals of the experience persist long after the patient's discharge. The would-be observer, still feeling somewhat involved, is reluctant to look back. In this way, countertransference raises a barrier to its own examination.

It is well known that treatability is a function of the conjoined answer to two questions: What influence can we expect to exert on the patient? And, what influence may we expect him to exert upon us? Yet, within the residential treatment center for children, the complex interrelationship of these issues needs further study. In particular, the growing proportion of borderline and psychotic children among the patients has added many new and relatively obscure factors to the delicately balanced, intense, and oftentimes disequilibrious interaction between the treatment staff and the child.

The essence of the residential treatment process is that as each child projects his inner world against the macrocosm of the residence, by and

* Judith Wallerstein and Arthur Mandelbaum are coauthors of this chapter.

428

large the staff will find within itself the strength to resist stepping into the projected transference roles. For clearly, to the extent that the child succeeds in evoking from the residence or hospital staff the response which he evoked within his own family, the treatment will founder. Generally we know that the greater the child's disturbance, the more difficult it becomes to restrain the push of counterfantasies and counterbehavior and to resist entanglements.

Our interest here is to examine some of the elusive psychological processes characterizing these entanglements which appear to be inherent in prolonged exposure to very disturbed children. Specifically, we are concerned with understanding reactions evoked within a residential setting by a child with a symbiotic psychosis. We propose to follow the pre-admission history and residential experience of an eight year old boy who was discharged after seven months because, despite his encouraging response to intensive psychotherapy, he was found to be untreatable within the structure of a residential setting.* Unquestionably, many weighty factors dictated this particular child's discharge and he was, in fact, maintained as long as seven months in the face of formidable difficulties. Our interest is not with the rightness or wrongness of the decision but rather with the psychological underpinnings which were revealed with unusual clarity. Our experience emphasizes that while countertransference responses may, at times, be contained or counterbalanced by factors making for more stability and a different outcome, in one or another guise such responses are always present and, inevitably, threaten the continuity of all residential treatment of children in these clinical groups.

Within the established confines of the standard psychoanalytic situation, transference and countertransference in the treatment of children are distinguishable from their counterparts in the treatment of adults. It has been understood for some time that children's transference manifestations include not only the projection of early repressed relationships but also displacements of the crucial relationships with the living contemporary parents. We suggest that, corollary to this, the countertransference potential in work with children embraces the parent-child unit as well, and includes the therapist's responses to the parents as well as to the child's transferences and displacements. The child therapist, in relation to the parents, faces countertransferences which are every bit as complex as those which involve the child and which can best be understood when considered as part of a unit response to the child and his parents. Thus, the reality recognition that work with children necessarily includes the parents,

* During this patient's experience at the Southard School, the functions of the authors were: Dr. Rudolf Ekstein, training consultant; Judith Wallerstein child psychotherapist; Arthur Mandelbaum, chief residential worker.

is the clinical reflection of the psychological reality of the parent-child unit within the transference and countertransference. This position is supported by the observation regarding the extent to which beginning workers with children commonly invoke fantasies of magically rescuing the child from the wickedness of his parents. Such fantasies can be said to reflect the strong defense against archaic guilt and anxiety generated in reaction to the fantasied replacement of the child's parents, and "parents" more generically.

The potential intensity of reactions to the parent-child unit is magnified many times within the residential setting because the residence actually assumes the parental function in taking over care of the child. It follows that whatever unconscious guilt would attach to fantasies elaborated around the replacement of the child's parents would be correspondingly magnified. Out of this unconscious guilt comes support for the counterfantasy that the staff represent the "good" parents who replace the child's "bad" parents. Categorizations of good and bad, loving and rejecting, eager-to-help and uncooperative, which are used subtly to differentiate treatment staff and parents, are current in some measure in all settings where children are treated. These displacements have been given theoretical underpinnings by the orientation which views the sick child as the helpless victim of psychological traumata inflicted by the parents. Fully extended, this is the concept of the "schizophrenogenic mother." And while these concepts may theoretically be outmoded, their emotional roots remain and continue to find expression within the countertransference. Some of the many seemingly insuperable difficulties which frequently beset the relationship between the real parents and the residential center can be linked to these feelings. Generally, children who have endured a particularly unhappy life experience or whose conditions call forth immediate pity are more likely to evoke rescue fantasies and concomitant rage against the parents. Sometimes, as in the case we describe, the impact of a particular child can evoke these fantasies and feelings in a total staff with extraordinary swiftness and intensity.

This kind of identification with the loving mother and the living-out of the magical helping fantasy may represent in residential treatment a useful and even necessary point of departure. Surely, it makes for therapeutic optimism and a willingness to undertake treatment situations under very difficult conditions. When, however, the expected change in the child does not appear, bewilderment and anxiety may ensue and the helplessness which every magical rescue fantasy obscures will show through. The anger and disappointment caused by the child can only with difficulty be displaced onto the parents who are not within the treatment residence situation. Therefore, new displacement objects may be sought. This, we suggest, is one of the continuing problems of residential treatment of very disturbed children because of the inevitable disappointments encountered during the course of their treatment.

It may be observed generally that the close relationship between psychotherapist and child represents a specific emotional constellation within the residential setting. We have already suggested that in the familiar outpatient treatment of children, the parent-child unit often becomes the object of countertransference projections of the psychotherapist. Within the residential treatment center and in the continued absence of the real parent, the particular constellation of therapist and child can be said to fulfill a similar psychological function for the remainder of the treatment staff. Corollary to this, the psychotherapist, also in the absence of the real parent, tends to project countertransference feelings upon that unit consisting of child-care staff and child. Clearly, psychological phenomena such as transference and countertransference within this multigroup setting are more complex and varied than those described within the one-to-one relationship of psychoanalyst and patient. Many aspects of the responses to children which occur within the shifting tensions and harmonies of the residential setting require the refinement of present concepts and the development of new ones. At this point in our knowledge we may say, however, that the relationship between the residential staff and the psychotherapist, by virtue of crisscrossing countertransference responses, represents one of the major seams of the treatment community, a seam which is never completely invisible since it quickly tends to show the effects of the conflicting tugs and strains upon it.

The kind of unity which exists between psychotherapist and psychotic child, a child with a symbiotic psychosis, imposes a special strain. Frequently with such children, the treatment strategy, as in the case described below, renders the therapist a magical extension of the child in accord with the dominant transference. In their psychological roles vis-à-vis the child, the psychotherapist and those directly occupied with the psychotherapy almost inevitably share in the intense love and hate feelings aroused by the child.

In general, countertransference gains immeasurably in force and complexity as it is linked to psychotic transference manifestations. Winnicott [1] described some of the fears and angers attached to therapeutic work with psychotic patients which have, in his view, no counterpart in the treatment of the neurotic. He distinguished between the reawakening of infantile anxiety in the therapist and the objective hate which must necessarily arise in the therapist because of the patient's demands on him. He stressed his conviction that unless the therapist can appreciate both the depth of the response stirred up within him and the objective basis of a considerable part of his anger, these feelings will insidiously immobilize his capacity both to understand the patient and to help him disentangle his feelings and relationships. Thus, borderline and psychotic children invite a countertransference potential, both in relation to themselves and to the child-parent unit, of an entirely different kind and magnitude from that which obtains in work with neurotic children.

These children, besides the anxiety and hate which they stimulate, call forth an extraordinary investment of love, infinite patience, tenderness, skill, and devotion. Since both love and hate are present, any treatment disruption that occurs always reflects feelings of sadness and personal failure, even if these are covered by anger which finds forceful expression at these times.

In dealing with psychotic children, whatever his treatment framework or function, the worker necessarily finds that his understanding fails many times. Unlike the parent who, as Money-Kryle [2] suggests, has a variety of ways which he can employ to reach and comfort the child, each worker is bound by his single avenue of approach and clinical understanding, by his particular set of skills, and by the limits imposed by the nature of his helping effort. When these seem inadequate to their task, he will feel distressed and anxious. Although individual supervision, group meetings, and other familiar devices are unquestionably useful at such times, the residential staff generally does not have the safeguards provided by either personal analysis or extensive training. Consequently, the residential worker becomes more susceptible to the push of a child's projections. And while the group offers help to its members in providing the camaraderie and relief of shared feelings, it also supplies the conditions for a contagion of countertransference responses which can rapidly become an epidemic that is difficult, if not impossible, to check. Moreover, the group itself often tends to act rather than to reflect. As a result of all these factors, one of the distinguishing attributes of countertransference in residential treatment may well be its capacity to erupt precipitously into what Gitelson has called "acting out in the countertransference." [3]

In the case which we have selected, a schizophrenic child cast his psychological shadow against the background of the treatment center. The psychotic transference consisted of a continual re-enactment of his attempted murder by the mother which had in reality occurred several years prior to his admission. In this enactment, the child, alternately, simultaneously, and symbolically assumed the fragmented roles of murderer and victim, assigning complementary roles to the psychotherapist, the residential setting, and its various representatives.

For a period of time, the staff was able to maintain its helping role and separateness in the face of the child's onslaught and to support the psychotherapeutic relationship and the residential experience with extraordinary persistence. Eventually, however, the child succeeded in evoking a response from the staff parallel to that which he had evoked within his own family. At this time the treatment came to an end.

Ken was brought to Southard School at the age of eight. He was a skinny, undersized, little boy whose face most frequently appeared drawn, tense but impassive, and in marked contrast to his hands and, especially, his feet. These were engaged in rapid unremitting activity, usually of a destructive nature and, in this endeavor, seemed to operate with a strength and vitality all their own. This contrast, coupled with a heightened alertness to distant auditory stimuli, lent an odd, almost simian, quality to the child's appearance, which became especially striking when he was engaged in climbing trees and buildings, an activity which he undertook frequently with extraordinary daring, grace, and agility. When in repose, his taut body stance expressed a constant expectation of attack from every quarter. He seemed poised for rapid flight or, if this were impossible, for counterattack by means of savage, random, and essentially uncontrollable destructiveness. Sometimes, the rigidity of the child's facial mask would give way to what appeared to be wild glee in anticipation of mischief or in satisfaction of having bested the adult. At other times, the child curled upon the floor, sucking and smelling, hands and toes together, eyes glazed, rhythmically rocking and inaccessible to immediate stimuli; yet still acutely attuned to faraway sounds and especially to distant music. On rare occasions he would approach the adult with a pitiable expression of whimpering, panting, and smelling of the person approached. These positions defined the range of relationships available to him at the time of the initial examination.

The parents complained of obstreperousness, wanton destructiveness and obscene language, of open masturbation, sucking and rocking, nonconformity to the simplest family routines except in the face of severe punishment (among which the most effective was ignoring the child). They also reported the need for constant attendance, attention, and entertainment, and many other irksome demands, of the kind described by Kanner,[4] which seemed aimed at preventing change of any kind in the environment.

The disturbance was described as extending back to infancy and pervading all aspects of the personality. Retardation and disturbance were evident in thought, language, all modes of behavior, habit training, and all relationships. More recently the child had shown some signs of capacity for more integrative behavior and curiosity for knowledge of mechanical objects. He had acquired for himself some of the rudiments of written language and numbers and had made some tentative moves towards imitative play with other children.

The parents had apparently been able to manage and control the boy during the past two-and-a-half years which he had spent at home by a combination of extraordinarily large doses of sedatives and tranquillizing drugs, various punishments, and by submitting to his tyranny over the family life. They were desperate for a solution short of life-long hospitalization in a mental hospital.

Ken was an unplanned and unwanted child. The family was already sore beset with a chronic and severe addictive illness of the mother, the self-absorption and cold detachment of the father, and three older children who were showing sufficient neurotic difficulties to occupy fully whatever emotional reserves the parents had available. The mother's addiction began shortly before this, her second marriage. The marriage itself had been replete with stress and misery from the start, interspersed with many moves, opposition from both families, repeated psychotic episodes and hospitalizations for the mother, and increasingly constricted life for the father who more and more substituted his business for other aspects of his life.

The mother was sick and unhappy and using sedatives heavily during her pregnancy with the patient, yet steadfastly refused a therapeutic abortion although this was strongly recommended by the physician who attended her. The child was delivered healthy and was described as healthy and happy for the first few months of his life. Very early, however, within a few months, he began to look "ugly" to the parents who, when they returned from a vacation of a few weeks, felt there was something "missing" from his face. By two years and ten months he was brought for psychiatric examination and diagnosed as an autistic child. At that time he was without speech, without interest in his surroundings, without smiling, without willingness to look up, and refusing to eat unless his mouth was pried open by the mother and the food poured into it. Furthermore, destructiveness ensued when he was taken from the crib. The psychiatric recommendation was for immediate long-term placement which could offer "love therapy." These recommendations were followed despite the mother's enormous hurt and rage which were probably not fully expressed at the time.

During the two and a half years that followed, the child lived with a foster mother. With infinite patience, tenderness, and sensitivity, and with some psychiatric direction, she gradually nursed the child to the point that he fed himself, slept well, mastered language, gave up tantrums, accepted toilet training, began to imitate the play of other children, and seemed happy and demonstrably affectionate. Yet each time the child was returned home for a visit a severe setback was precipitated, wiping out entirely the new-found gains. For instance, during his third year the child was left for a few days with the mother. When found, both mother and child required emergency hospitalization with the child described as emaciated, dehydrated, suffering severe cold, and behaving like a wild animal. The mother was stuporous.

At the age of five and a half, Ken was returned to his home by the foster mother who could no longer keep him. A few weeks following his arrival, the mother, again stuporous, attacked the child in his bed at night, attempting to kill him. She was intercepted, whereupon she retreated to her room and tried to commit suicide. She stated of this episode, "I thought if I did away with the two sickest members of the family the rest would be better off." She was admitted to a hospital, with a diagnosis of acute depressive psychosis, and remained there for several months.*

There was general concurrence at the child's final evaluation conference in a diagnosis of "schizophrenia of childhood in a child of at least average and probably superior intelligence." The recommendation was for long-term residential treatment together with individual intensive psychotherapy for the child and casework or psychotherapy for the parents. The suggestion was that outpatient psychotherapy be instituted immediately on a once-a-week basis during the few weeks' waiting period although this was not a common practice of the treatment center. The hope was that the child could begin to establish a relationship with the psychotherapist which would facilitate his separation from the mother and his transition into the school. Similarly, it was thought that the mother might make use of the casework during this period in order to help separate from the child. Considerable note was taken of the relationship between mother and child and of the mother's attempt to destroy herself and the child together. It was feared that although the child himself might be treatable, the mother-child unity, i.e., the hostile symbiosis which characterized the relationship between Ken and his mother, might prevent treatment in that the mother would probably repeatedly attempt to disrupt the treatment experience.

* The psychological report on the mother during her hospitalization was made by a psychologist who was not informed of the mother-child relationship or of the episode preceding hospitalization. It read in part: "The test material indicates great stress and involvement in her relationship to her son (or sons) and what the son (sons) means to her unconsciously. The content of the Rorschach response which is most revealing of her break with reality and her delusional thinking is tied up with concern about proper conduct and with a son. One wonders if her son represents to her the worst part in her personality and thus is mixed up with her superego conflict." These observations are of especial interest in view of the clinical finding of a symbiotic psychosis in the child.

By and large, doubts regarding the child's treatability were omitted. No extended consideration was given to his impact upon the residential setting nor his needs within the setting, although his extraordinary destructiveness and need for constant surveillance had been abundantly clear during the two-week examination period.

From a close examination of the records of this intake conference, one may discern those conflicts which were to grow to major proportions. For instance, it appears that two contradictory frames of reference were simultaneously in operation: namely, that which viewed the child and his mother as caught within a mesh of mutually interacting psychoses; and that which viewed the child as capable of forming a relationship with the psychotherapist which, on a once-a-week basis, would be sufficient to alleviate significantly his anxiety regarding separation from the mother.

If we take such confusion in an experienced staff as symptomatic of conflict, then we may add as further symptoms the significant omissions from consideration: the additional staff time which the child would require; the physical and psychological toll upon staff and children which his presence could be expected to exact; and, centrally for our thesis, doubts or misgivings about the child's treatability, considering the degree of emotional crippling and the long-standing nature of his illness. Corollary to these omissions was the considerable concern with the mother's role in threatening the treatment continuity; whatever recognition there was of threat to treatment could be experienced only as coming from the outside, i.e., from the mother-child unit.

When the figure of the child is placed between the figure of the mother, of whom it was feared that she might disrupt the treatment, and the figure of the psychotherapist, of whom it was thought that in a short time she would establish a meaningful and comforting relationship with the child, the emotional response becomes clear. In accord with the view which we have stated, the three figures together reflect the countertransference response. We surmise that what happened was a very quick identification with the child, perhaps because of the extent of his disturbance and some pathetic appealing quality in his chronic terror, or perhaps because of his extraordinary history of an attempted murder by the mother. Hand in hand with this identification went the taking over of the positive aspects of the healing mother who will save the child. And, inseparable from this fantasy of the "good" mother, we find the projection upon the "bad" mother of the cause for illness and possibilities for treatment rupture. The taking over of the role of the "good" mother found expression in the magical overevaluation of the psychotherapist as the representative of the rescue fantasy; in the magical overestimation of the influence and power of the residential experience; and in the failure to estimate correctly the serious degree of the child's psychopathology.

This kind of identification with the child with its concomitant fantasies is by no means unusual in work with severely disturbed children (Chapter 23). In fact, it can be argued that the capacity for quick identification with the child is of pivotal importance in therapeutic work with children. Particularly, in work with schizophrenic children it may be that one must believe in one's own omnipotence and find therapeutic failure unacceptable as Eissler[5] has suggested. The attitude of identifying with the "good" parent and projecting the blame upon the "bad" parent who "abandoned" the child to residential treatment is the beginning bias of the residential worker. Such a bias may be necessary for work with a disturbed child where the child care worker sees himself as the "good" parent who has been given the responsibility for therapeutic care of the child after the real parent has found it necessary to give him to others. This attitude surely assists the worker in becoming that "good" parent but it may cause considerable irritation when he discovers that being a "good" parent is not the only requirement for therapeutic care and can lead to serious frustrations when the satisfactions reasonably expected by all "good" parents are not forthcoming.*

At about the time that Ken began treatment, a research project was initiated at the treatment center in which an effort was to be made to envision expected developments within the psychotherapy. Specifically, the project was designed to make use of the evaluation material, therapy hours, and control hours in order to make explicit the treatment strategy and to extrapolate expected transference developments and expected changes in behavior within the residence. In this way, we hoped to consider more systematically some of the theoretical formulations which had evolved in recent years in our work with borderline and psychotic children. We present here the second and third psychotherapy hours with Ken which, together with several others and the evaluation material, led us to guarded encouragement regarding the child's accessability to intensive psychotherapy and enabled us to arrive at some formulations regarding expectable developments within the psychotherapeutic process.

My second hour with Ken began by his recognizing me immediately and coming with a marked lack of hesitancy. He grinned mischievously

---

* It may be argued that the essential mistake made was to accept the child for treatment. The validity of this argument is in itself an indication of strong countertransference responses at the time of the initial evaluation. For in view of the knowledge of the child, his history, and his behavior, which was entirely available to the staff at the time of the evaluation, a mistake can only be understood as reflecting countertransference response.

with a little of a private grin and mumbled he was going to crash things around today as we went upstairs together. He ran into the playroom, threw his shoes and socks toward the ceiling with a vigorous gesture, scrambled into the sandpile and started to throw great quantities of sand around with wild gestures, accompanying this throwing with an entirely mask-like face and a set grin. I said that I was beginning to understand why he crashed things around. In response to this, Ken threw more wildly. I said we would have "holding time" and as I held him I said very slowly and softly that I thought he was afraid to stop throwing and that he throws because he is really too afraid to stop. He answered by sitting quietly for a while and for the first time he did not become limp with terror as I held him. He then asked me whether I had gotten him some toys. I said that I had and showed him some little trucks in his cupboard. He explored these with what looked like a brief moment of genuine pleasure but this could not last and he returned to throwing sand and toys. Again I restrained him by holding him. I repeated what I had said, adding that I doubted if he could stop throwing things alone even if he should want to and that he needed help in this.

At this point Ken saw a baby bottle and ran excitedly to fill it with water. He started to spill water all around the room and said something about being naughty rather gleefully. I agreed he was having an awfully hard time being naughty and he couldn't play with any of the toys or have any fun. He then took one of the puppets and started to fill it with water with savagery from below the puppet's skirt. I asked whether he was Mama Ken and he said vigorously and laughingly that he was. (This play was interspersed with considerable throwing of the dolls, the bottles, the sand, and every toy within reach and was by no means really continuous although it makes up some kind of a complete unit.) I asked whether he was Mama Ken feeding the baby and he agreed and said that it was a hungry baby. I asked whether it would get enough to eat and surely hoped it would. "The water is poison," he yelled at me, "and I am killing the baby." I asked why, and he said because the baby is naughty and mean. I said that I understand that because I knew a little boy who was very frightened. He thought his mother had tried to hurt him very much and would try to hurt him very much and he was so terribly frightened that he threw things all the time. As if in direct confirmation of this, Ken started to throw but this time there was some real feeling and excitement that came through in the throwing in that his hands were no longer divorced from the child. I held him again for "holding time" and he sat quietly but not limply. As I held him I said over and over again that I would never hurt him, that I knew it frightened him when I held him and I knew it frightened him when he threw things, and sometimes it frightened him more when I held him than when he threw things but I would never hurt him and I wanted him to know that. He mounted then with lightning rapidity to the window and attempted to pry it open. I pulled him back and repeated that I would not hurt him nor would I let him hurt himself.

Ken ran wildly in and out of the room several times and finally said he wanted to play with the phonograph. I offered him the pretend phonograph of the crate with building blocks in it and he asked me quietly whether I would help him remove the blocks. I said that what I wanted to do most was to help him. Together we removed the blocks and this time he did so without throwing the blocks, but when he came across pieces of chalk in the box he picked them up and ground them under his feet as if just seeing something that could be ground stimulated the activity which seemed isolated from the rest of his attention and behavior. He finally got into the box telling me he was a long-playing record. I said I wanted so much to hear a long-playing record. He directed me to the imaginary controls of the phonograph and told me to shut and open the top of the box like in a real phonograph while he got inside, and that I should turn the record on. I did as he directed and he started to kick wildly inside of the box. I asked him what that was and he said, "That's the record." I agreed that it was and stated that it sounded like an angry and frightened little record kicking around in the box and trying to get out. He continued to kick for some time, opening the box and shutting it down on himself and almost catching his fingers dangerously under the very heavy lid, with complete lack of concern about this. I said that I very much liked long-playing records and I was pretty sure there were many tunes this particular record could play and I would like to hear them when the time came. On this note the hour ended and I took him back to his mother. As he saw her, he dismissed me from the landscape.

In the third interview which was the last interview before he came into the school, Ken was very agitated, ran wildly and terror-stricken around the room, round and round like a hunted animal, throwing everything he could get hold of. He urinated all over the room and seemed most of the time oblivious to my presence. Twice he approached me crying pitifully and wringing his hands saying he would never see me again because he was going to be coming to Southard School. It was quite clear he had fused me with the mother and felt himself in great danger, but my attempts to get through to him in anything I did or said went unheard and unnoticed.

The original evaluation material and the early interviews as noted provided the basis for a long and detailed analysis of the case from which we have taken the following excerpts. It is relevant that all of this thinking was discussed in detail with the entire staff at the time the child entered the residence and was shared with the team members throughout the child's stay.

Ken's basic relationship position is that of a hostile symbiosis with the mother and his core conflict is his struggle towards and away from this position. The symbiotic arrangement with the mother is experienced as hostile and destructive, threatening to engulf him and bringing with it the loss of even the precursors of self. He attempts to escape from the symbiotic position by returning to an autistic world which shuts out the mother figure, expressing itself in total self-preoccupation and/or loss of contact. Alternately he attempts to find another more advanced independent solution which consists for him of blind impulsivity, wild destructiveness, seeming lack of control eventuating in ego fragmentation, and the return to the autistic position.

The "Jack-in-the-box" fantasy which dominated the first hours of psychotherapy reflects the core conflict. Hiding in different boxes, Ken stated that he was a long-playing record and requested the psychotherapist to manipulate the knobs which control the record machine. As the long-playing record, the child kicked violently against the walls of the box while remaining within the box. As the child emerged from box, he threw different objects violently and wildly and seemingly without control.

His dilemma as expressed in this fantasy is his wish for and dread of being contained in the "mother box." For this problem he envisages two possible solutions, both of which end disastrously. One solution is that of a violent kicking struggle for independence which eventuates in castration, ego fragmentation, destruction, and self-destruction. The other solution is that of autistic isolation and death. In reality, for this patient, kicking within the confines of the symbiotic relationship (kicking inside the mother box) signifies to be alive.

Ken has no integrated self-image and no clearly cathected ego boundaries; his perception of himself is fragmented and fluid. At times he thinks of himself as an armless and lifeless "big turnip." At other times, various objects such as spinning toys are grafted onto his body image. Feet particularly are experienced alternately as enemies and love objects, alternately included and ejected from his ego boundaries. Thus the outside world shifts its boundaries and consists, at times, of those parts of his body which are used for motoric activity. At such times, his self-concept is characterized by an effort to conquer feet and arms which are experienced as external enemies that do not wish to become part of the self-organization.

Transference paradigm: It is expected that during the many months of initial treatment the transference will primarily reflect the dominant symbiotic relationship, showing both its hostile and positive components, and accompanied by escape into the autistic position, as his symbiosis becomes too threatening, and by thrusts toward independent separate activity, as the symbiosis offers assurance. Specifically the patient will utilize the therapist as an extension of himself and as a means toward achieving various primitive gratifications. When the hostile aspects of the symbiosis become dominant, the patient will, in identification with the fantasied aggressor, play act murder of the therapist and self-destruction in various ways. He will also escape into autism via hiding, primitive self-preoccupations, and periodic loss of contact.

The loving aspect of the symbiosis may give rise to erotic feelings which will, in becoming too threatening, also lead to withdrawal, hostile acting out, primitive erotic rituals (of a masturbatory nature), and contact loss. At the same time, the patient may attempt to utilize the grafted strength of this symbiotic relationship to live out magical fantasies of omnipotence and phallic concepts of masculine strength, which will probably lead him to act out what will seem like delinquent manifestations.

If the child is enabled to stabilize his symbiotic relationship and to find it not as fearful as expected, then we may expect a cumbersome attempt to introject certain aspects of the therapist via imitation and cue-taking. We may begin to see some beginning emergence of the precursors of neurotic mechanisms, particularly the precursors of obsessive-compulsive mechanisms.

The therapeutic strategy is to facilitate the development of a positive symbiotic transference since we are of the opinion that only out of the consolidation of a positive symbiotic relationship with the mother substitute can the precursors of identification, i.e., imitation and introjection, emerge. And the first goal is, therefore, to help the child establish this kind of positive symbiosis by diminishing his fear of annihilation at the hands of the symbiotic mother-equal-therapist. This may perhaps be achieved by accepting the magical role of an all-powerful extension of the child, by repeated assurances of protection, by imitation of the child in offering oneself as a partner in his endeavors, and by interpretation of his fears of being destroyed.

Among the many foreseeable technical problems are those which relate to setting limits on the behavior as it swings from anti-social to very regressed behavior, the extent to which such limits are necessary, therapeutic, etc., and of course, the primary problem of doing therapy with a child unable to reflect upon his own behavior.

One of the interesting aspects of this report is that, despite the fact that there was considerable coincidence between developments in the therapy and in the residence and those predicted in this case analysis, it contains too little recognition of the countertransference problem. Thus, while the analyzed data all pointed to the deep well of primitive responses which could reasonably be expected to be stirred up by the entrance of the child upon the scene of the residence, yet this detailed spelling-out of the child's psychosis remained separate from a recognition of the countertransference potential. And it may be that this omission prevented these formulations from being as useful as they might have been in helping to maintain the continuity of the child's treatment.

In the residence Ken's behavior made it possible to begin to make

plans for the treatment in the living situation. When Ken entered the
school, his behavior was that of a child in mortal danger and a desperate
struggle for survival, and that of one who had lost all of his physical
strength as a result of separation from his parents. He insisted upon being
fed, complaining of the lack of strength in his arms, and confined his
eating to dry cereal and milk. Initially at mealtime, while being fed, his
entire body expressed a complete total passivity except for masturbatory
activity. His mouth was kept wide open to receive the food as if he were
an automaton. Within a few days, Ken began to attack the walls of his
room, systematically breaking off large pieces of plaster with great strength.
He repeated over and over again the play of enclosing himself in a box,
closet, or any dark place, only to burst out again using his feet vigorously.
On occasion he would crawl out of his window onto the roof of the house
into a precarious position. When the windows were closed, he broke
through and smashed the outer screen as if he always needed an escape
route. His toilet habits were regressed. He made no use of bathroom
facilities. He defecated and urinated in his room, in drawers, in closets.
Sometimes he would consent to go outside, but generally he expressed
fear of using the bathroom. His most integrated behavior in these early
weeks was a game of tying a weight to a piece of string and, while seated
on top of the stairs, lowering the string up and down in seemingly endless
repetition. (This, of course, calls immediately to mind the play of the 18
month old child as classically described by Freud.[6])

The therapeutic care Ken required in the residence had to provide
safety against his own swift destructive attacks against himself, against
other children, adults, and property, as well as to meet Ken's most regressed
infantile needs, such as requiring to be fed and clothed. Three workers
were assigned to his individual care, and because of Ken's difficulty in
maintaining a constant image and memory of persons coming and going,
each worker kept the same shift so as to provide the most constancy and
stability.

As in the psychotherapy, the aim of the child-care worker relationship
with Ken was to assist in the development of a relationship designed to
diminish his fear of annihilation by protecting him from attacks by the
other children and from his attacking them when they came too close.
His relationships with the adults in the residence also offered him nurturing care; feeding him as he wished to be fed, bathing him so he did not
experience terror and panic, allowing him to urinate and defecate in places
of safety until he might gradually learn to use the bathroom.

The child-care staff became familiar with Ken's interests, especially
with his intense love of music, his preoccupations with radios, phono-
graphs, batteries, odd bits of machinery. They structured for him activities

which had play and educational value and which gave him the feeling that he was doing as the other children were when they attended their school. There is no doubt that Ken was one of the sickest children ever accepted by the residence in the sense that his needs were expressed in most infantile and primitive ways. Any excellent care which met his most basic needs also tended to get too close to the child and resulted in fusion fantasies followed by panic and swift physical attack. At the same time, too much distance from Ken also brought panic and fears of being abandoned, neglected, and left to be destroyed; this, too, was followed instantaneously by swift rage attacks. The child-care workers assigned to Ken needed to learn and test constantly that optimum distance, neither too close nor too far, which gave the child his greatest feeling of comfort and security. The three workers assigned directly to him required more frequent supervision than other child-care staff, for a great deal needed to be understood quickly about Ken's behavior, i.e., his fascination with entering closets and boxes, enclosing himself and then bursting out furiously, his curiosity with electrical motors and wiring of the residence, his intense desire for a radio and then his wild attacks on it. The child-care staff, together with their supervisor and the psychotherapist, constantly explored ways in which protection and care could be afforded Ken. They met his savage attacks with firm nonretaliatory limits and encouraged him from autistic withdrawal by their availability and by providing him, in a most imaginative way, with objects he greatly desired and which had great emotional significance to him, and they helped him to play with them. This was the philosophy underlying the residential treatment of the child.

In response to Ken's behavior, the entire staff at first was able to take an attitude of extraordinary patience and interest. Their observations were acute and perceptive, as evidenced in the detailed notes on the child's frequently incoherent rambling which the child-care staff kept in the hope that the psychotherapist might be able to use this material in the therapy. The sensitivity and interest of the entire staff are perhaps epitomized in the remark of one of the cooks who said that Ken wanted to be fed and not use his hands because otherwise he might throw food.

Gradually, the tolerance gave way. By the time several weeks had gone by, feelings of anger and retaliation were aroused. This the staff experienced and expressed by seeing the child's aggression as deliberately designed to control and provoke them. They began to make use of the concept of "testing" as applied to Ken's destructive activity, implying willful and conscious behavior, particularly in regard to his toilet habits. The fact that at times when limits were placed on his behavior, the child seemed able to make a real effort to conform emphasized and reinforced this opinion. Also, there was considerable jealousy, disturbance, and regressive behavior among the other children which undoubtedly contributed greatly to the child-care staff's discomfort. Nevertheless, in this initial period the dominant attitude was a sober recognition of the serious nature of the child's disturbance coupled with many feelings of sympathy and a wish to protect him from the other children. And in general, the first few weeks of the child's stay reflect the intent of the total staff to master feelings of repugnance, anxiety, anger, and frustration and, with great devotion, to make the child's treatment possible by providing a total change in his milieu and by facilitating his individual psychotherapy.

The first indication of the emergence of the kind of countertransference which threatens treatment continuity occurred vis-à-vis the psychotherapy in a particular incident. In the seventh week of Ken's stay in the residence, he and the psychotherapist were playing with mud on a little wooden porch in back of the office building. Ken was engaged in making mud pies with considerable pleasure, and his usual primitiveness and untidiness soon made for a mud-smeared porch. An experienced staff member, who assumed no direct psychotherapeutic responsibility but had considerable understanding of the privacy of psychotherapy by virtue of his semiprofessional and administrative position, passed by. Apparently unable to restrain himself, he said directly to the child, "Do you know what happens to little boys who make a mess of the director's nice clean porch?" After a slight pause, he continued, "They have to clean it up." After making several similar remarks, and continuing to ignore the therapist who was standing by the child, he quickly left the scene. There followed a precipitous regression in the child from the advance of the mud playing to wild defecating coupled with psychotic incoherences while, wide-eyed with terror, running in circles around the yard.

It is of central importance in understanding this episode that the staff member was evidently in intense conflict regarding this intervention. Since he acted in the face of his unquestioned knowledge that such intervention was not acceptable, we infer the extraordinary push of anxiety which could not be contained. Furthermore, it is relevant that this particular staff member had the confidence of the custodial and kitchen staff and expressed in his behavior a groundswell of opinion which had not yet reached the ears of the professional staff.

We present this incident in detail for several reasons. At the beginning of the child's admission into the school, we described a magical overevaluation of psychotherapy. It had been fully expected that the therapist would, in a few weeks, establish a relationship with Ken which would have considerable influence in alleviating his anxiety. Here one can see the opposite: an intervention into the therapy hour with a disregard of its privacy; a shunting aside of therapy and therapist; in effect, a devaluation of psychotherapy. Parenthetically, we note that we do not consider this incident either unique or extraordinary, but rather that such incidents are more numerous than many have been willing to believe.

This particular incident heralded the gradual emergence of a counter-transference pattern. The therapist, the therapist's supervisor, and the special child-care workers who were assigned to work with Ken were pushed, as it were, into being viewed as the partners of the child's illness, as party to his destructiveness; in effect, as symbiotic partners of the child. It was as if the projection of wickedness onto the departed mother had been moved and was now reprojected onto the psychotherapist and the other workers engaged in direct work with the child. Especially the psychotherapist, in her inability to fulfill the magical expectations that she would contain the child and curb his impulses, became a partner, a stimulus, and in its final extension, a "schizophrenogenic" mother. This was borne out in various ways. When Ken attacked one of the children who had been brought to the school for evaluation and the therapist was standing nearby, the therapist was blamed for "permitting" Ken to attack the other child. When property was damaged, similar statements were made. Gradually, incidents such as these began to multiply, and their emotional charge became increasingly intense.

The mud incident is important also because of its impact upon the therapist. It led to her abrupt and uncomfortable recognition that in achieving her goal of being included within the child's psychological orbit, she had come as well to share responsibility for his misbehavior and destructiveness. Beyond this, the incident, in precipitating a psychotic regression and undermining the child's concept of the psychotherapist as a magical protector, had particular repercussions which undoubtedly magnified its immediate importance; it collided directly with the therapeutic strategy. It was at this time that the seam between therapist and the remainder of the staff, which we have mentioned before, began to show the strain of conflicting tugs and to require reinforcement.

Within both a practical and a psychological framework, psychotherapy with Ken depended in considerable measure upon the active support of those administratively and directly responsible for the child. In practical terms, during many weeks of therapy, Ken was unable to remain in the playroom without panics. These occurred without discernible warning and were marked by destructiveness which was heedless of the value of the object attacked. For many successive hours in the initial phase of treatment, Ken and the therapist crawled together in the subbasement of the residence looking for underground hiding places and subterranean passages where they could remain for a brief respite away from the rest of the world. Several weeks were spent in therapy in water play with a hose in which the attempt was to channel the "nasty nasty" (the child's term for water) in order to avoid the "flood" which threatened to break through the dikes which he and the therapist built and rebuilt. Sometimes the "flood" occurred despite the dikes and the efforts to contain it. At times Ken climbed ten to fifteen trees in rapid, breathless succession in order to distinguish "loving" trees from "angry" trees and needed to be forcibly restrained from going up telegraph poles. He discovered a stagnant pool on a neighboring property and would return to it at intervals to ask plaintively and despairingly of the therapist whether it could ever be cleared, how it got that way, and whether he could be protected from rats and mosquitoes. Sometimes he demanded to be carried to therapy and he rarely arrived except accompanied by his radio, from which he was inseparable, and sometimes he requested that big motors and other equipment which he had salvaged from the junkyard be carried to therapy along with him. All of this behavior placed heavy demands upon the staff and represented, at the very least, a chronic nuisance about which the therapist could not help but feel concerned.

The therapeutic decision to attempt to join the child to the extent possible at the level of his regression, within this nightmare in which every reality stimulus was either potentially or actually dangerous, in which the child's hope was to stay ahead of the terror but never to escape it completely, depended on the actual help or, at the very least, upon the tacit support of the environment. Practically speaking, the attitudes of the surrounding staff, whether expressed or inexpressed, have particular relevance to this kind of therapeutic effort. These attitudes combine to create a psychological climate which ultimately determines whether this kind of therapy can or cannot develop. For, regardless of the extent to which the child therapist is able to identify with the primary-process world of the psychotic child, as an adult she faces within herself the demands of adult society. This double foothold in the psychotic world of the patient and in the reality world of everyday living must be maintained at an even balance which permits free motion and spontaneity. In order to deal with the kind and degree of anxiety and physical exhaustion induced by this kind of patient, the therapist needs to rely upon the structure of the setting and its essential friendliness towards what she is attempting to accomplish. Necessarily she is made anxious and angry by the patient and by her own reawakened opposition to parental images. The approval or disapproval of the surrounding staff represents in this a reinforcement of either permissions or prohibitions within the therapist herself. It becomes difficult to maintain the necessary psychological balance in the face of a living-out of inner prohibitions by the surrounding environment. Moreover, the attitude of the staff, which came to view the psychotherapist as responsible for the destructive and deviate behavior of the child, converged with the child's psychotic transferences. These also held the mother-therapist responsible for the illness. Both together placed a heavy burden upon the maintenance of spontaneity in the therapeutic process.

It is interesting that together with the staff's view of the psychotherapist as a partner of the child's in his illness was the constancy of their surprise when the child repeatedly made clear the significance of his relationship to the therapist. Over and over again the daily notes reflected the amazement of the child-care staff when Ken mentioned his "therapy" in many contexts throughout the day. Much of his behavior during the entire day represented seemingly endless repetitions of activities begun in his therapy hours. It was as if in some very primitive way he was trying to remember, to retain, or to continue the experience, much as sucking continues the nursing experience. Frequently he addressed himself to his radio, promising that he would take his radio to see his "therapy." He called his turtle a "therapy turtle," and he tenderly clipped pictures of hoses from magazines and pinned them to the wall of his room during the period of water play in therapy. It is interesting that the other children in the residence learned quickly that they could reduce Ken to terror by taunting him with the threat that they were going to take away his psychotherapist. Yet, it is almost as if the psychological need to make a symbiotic unit out of therapist-child generated so much anxiety that at one and the same time the intimacy and significance of the therapeutic relationship needed to be denied by a large part of the staff.

In actuality, the child could play out little else but variations of the central conflict, whether in his psychotherapy hours or in the residence. We infer that the fact of the continued amazement of the staff about the significance of the therapeutic relationship to Ken was their need to displace their own anger and anxiety from the child onto the therapist. In defense against their own unacceptable anger against the child, they could see her as the hostile symbiotic parent and themselves remain as the loving parents.

It soon became apparent that Ken evoked a wide and varied spectrum of fearful and angry feelings. In part, resentment derived from the continual rebuffs which the adults received from this child in response to good intentions, kindness, and love generously proffered. These rebuffs, coupled with physical and verbal abuse, gradually generated latent disappointment and anger which could not find an acceptable place within the training and orientation of the total staff. These feelings, always at the verge of breaking through, exacerbated anxiety and unconscious guilt and required the stiffening of characteristic defenses. One worker referred to Ken as being like an old model car, an antique for which no parts could be obtained, or a unique prototype of car which no one could know how to fix or care for. In its uppermost meaning, the worker's statement conveys his feeling that Ken was beyond repair, with no spare parts available to make him function well, and ready, therefore, only for the junk heap. Of considerable interest, however, is the distance of the example (removed in space and time from current car models and almost beyond recognition) and the gross denial of the child's impact which was surely as high-powered as the most up-to-date car.

Beyond this, however, one approached what Winnicott [7] referred to as "the anxiety of psychotic quality and . . . hate produced in those who work with severely ill psychiatric patients." The strange and intense pre-occupations which characterized Ken's behavior, the fading in and out of people and objects, the fluidity of ego boundaries, the primitive animism alongside of the devitalization and fragmentation of living things combined to create great stress. For, inevitably, they called forth counterfantasies against which normal defensive operations in the external devices of individual supervision and group meetings seemed to be of little avail. Thus, in order to defend against the fusion impact of the child, the ego boundaries of those who worked with him were necessarily overcathected.

Much of Ken's behavior appeared like action in a dream accompanied by the kind of reality testing which the sleepwalker retains. He utilized himself and his many extensions, namely, his turtle, his motors, his radios, to represent at different times the all-powerful destructive mother and the impotent anxiety-ridden mother; the all-powerful pseudo-phallic boy and the helpless whimpering infant. In each of these rapidly shifting identities his capacity to mobilize anxiety in the people around him was tremendous, since each identity seemed total, all-engulfing, and unmodified by other identities. On one occasion he savagely stomped a dead turtle to pieces with his bare feet, and while the onlookers were still recovering from the shock, he calmly and efficiently picked up the remains and flushed them away. At such times we were tempted to hazard that the fluctuation itself, namely the fact that each identity did not endure indefinitely, made it possible to withstand anxieties which he called forth.

An additional problem in work with Ken was the seeming separation between impulsive behavior and feeling. It was shocking to observe that the link between impulsive behavior and affect did not obtain and that destruction could occur without anger or panic. Gradually one realized that the surrealistic movies which make use of dream symbols—the man being pursued by the hostile eyes, and the upraised fist—were all reasonably close to portraying the inner life of this child in its lack of full-dimensioned introjects and inability to make connections. A child who behaves in this way evokes stark fear comparable to the panic experience in a nightmare.

One of the most interesting aspects of the total experience was what we have called its peripheral spread. It was striking that people not directly involved with the patient, with the psychotherapy, or with the management of the child became emotionally involved and contributed their own anxieties to the countertransference problem. Somehow, gradually and insidiously, the child began to dominate the entire structure of the residence. His ubiquitousness was extraordinary, and he seemed to be everywhere at the same time, disturbing each function of the setting. Those most concerned with administrative responsibility became increasingly troubled about the safety and physical well-being of the child as well as for the high cost of his care and his destructiveness. The kitchen staff felt aggrieved and put out because he refused to eat the food that they had prepared and confined his eating to dry cereal and milk. The custodial staff was greatly troubled by the wanton destruction of property which recurred. The child-care staff resented the special rest periods and the special privileges accorded those staff members who were employed to take care of Ken and for whom such arrangements were necessary. In short, the disturbance reverberated through every aspect of the residence.

In the face of all of these difficulties the treatment was sustained. Few would question that cogent reality reasons for discharge could surely be derived from the occurrences up to this point. Yet, it is germane to our thesis that only as the child finally entered upon an activity which evoked intense rage and despair, coupled with feelings of utter helplessness, was the treatment abruptly brought to a close. Thus the treatment end can be linked to a particular psychological constellation vis-à-vis the child.

It is not within the scope or purpose of this presentation to delineate all of the complex factors which led to the administrative decision to discharge the child. Our purpose is to describe the psychological impact Ken had on the residence and the ways in which countertransference powerfully influenced the decision to accept the child for in-patient treatment and then how the countertransference also dictated his discharge. Ken had within him the capacity to arouse the generosity of people to rescue him, and also the opposing capacity to activate great amounts of hostility. These fed each other back and forth, with wider and more intense fluctuations to the negative side. It may be said that the sympathy created by the child and his tragic life made it possible for him to be accepted for treatment, and the rising negative feelings he could arouse caused him to leave it.

When he entered the school Ken had begun to climb out on the roof of the residence and the therapy building. But it was only in the fourth

month of his stay that this gradually became his most frequent symptomatic activity. On snowy days when the roof was icy, on rainy days when
the roof was slippery, he would mount the fire escape and remain up on
the roof, tearing off large pieces of shingle and hurling them down, to the
utter distraction of the workers below. There were several attempts to work
out various plans to prevent this roof-climbing, but these proved abortive,
as if some lack of conviction surrounding each plan rendered it unwork-
able. The fact that he undertook this activity in therapy as well increased
the discouragement. Primarily, there seemed no way to get past the discouragement and feelings of helpless rage caused by the fact that instead
of experiencing limits as protective, he viewed them as forces of destruction which engendered wild panic. Thus, if the child-care worker was
stationed on the fire escape to block the climb, Ken reacted in terror, like
a dreamer who, in his dream, encounters a figure from the outside. It is
relevant to add here that Ken never hurt himself throughout his entire stay
in the residence, although he constantly undertook grave risks which might
well have been fatal to other children his age. As the roof climbing became
his most frequent activity, the decision to discharge was made with the
recommendation to the parents that the child was in need of closed hospital treatment. In the psychological climate surrounding the discharge,
the silences, the sadness, the anger, the blame, the difficulties in discussing
or communicating the decision, the haste that went into the discharge
planning, we may find the counterpart to those feelings which had
welcomed Ken into the residential setting.

Theoretically we may conceptualize treatment disruption as analogous
to play disruption in that it serves the same purpose of keeping the unconscious conflict from coming into conscious awareness. With no attempt
to depreciate the reality considerations, we suggest that the treatment
disruption here served to prevent certain unconscious conflicts in the
treatment staff from coming into consciousness. This disruption served to
keep from consciousness the potential for behaving like the real mother
which the child had so deftly aroused. From the very beginning of Ken's
residential experience, those who worked directly with him and were able
in such an exceptional way to tolerate his behavior reported the presence
of this potential. Over and over in their notes and in their supervisory
conferences they repeated that the most upsetting aspect of his behavior
was his open and desperate pleading to be destroyed, which sometimes
followed his breaking out of bounds. Thus from the outset, the child's
provocation for the adult to step into the role of the murdering mother
was that which needed to be warded off most strongly. And we suggest
that it was this fantasy that was warded off in the striking omission of
misgivings and practical difficulties from the intake process. For in this

way the staff was able to avoid the question, "What is my potential for acting like the mother?" And as the child at long last found a way to reduce the staff to a position of helpless rage without seeming psychological or practical recourse, the accumulated anxieties and angers led to a symbolic re-enactment of the mother's role. In his activity of roof climbing and his consequent discharge, Ken finally succeeded in casting himself again as a helpless victimized child vis-à-vis the anxious destructive mother.

There is a particular aspect to the convergence of psychological events which occurred at the point of discharge which may have implications for the future. It is that the discharge coincided with a change in the clinical picture in the direction which had been predicted, i.e., the beginning emergence of the precursors of compulsive-obsessive defenses. Unfortunately, these changes cannot be evaluated, since they did not sustain the shock of the discharge. The depressed patient is most dangerous to himself as the depression begins to lift. Similarly, it may be that the threat of treatment rupture out of hate, fear, and anxiety in the countertransference is greatest with these clinical groups as the child becomes less sick, begins to give up his autistic preoccupations, and begins increasingly to intrude into relationships around him. What is clear from this material, however, is that there were no indications that the child was less treatable at the time the discharge decision was made, and several indications to the contrary.

An excerpt follows from the child's last hour in therapy before the decision to discharge was made. We suggest that in this we see the beginning emergence of the precursors of obsessive-compulsive defenses in the play around "do not touch."

Ken arrived accompanied by his companion. He bounded into the inner office and asked whether I had gotten the toy which he had requested (a little wind-up washing machine, which I had). He took hold of it excitedly, started to wind it up, and led the way outside. I went to get my coat while he, as usual, waited patiently, and suddenly as I joined him, he noticed John, the child-care worker, who was remaining in order to stay on the fire escape and who was still talking to the receptionist. Ken, realizing John's purpose in being there, pushed his way quickly through the two heavy doors and was off for the roof, getting there, of course, well ahead of John or anyone else. He was, however, sufficiently aware of me to realize that I had not followed him. I returned to the upstairs playroom and after a few minutes I heard Ken calling plaintively, "Where is my therapy, where is my therapy?" He arrived on the second floor, took my hand, and pulled me toward the staircase in a dazed and bewildered way, saying plaintively, "Where did you go?" I answered that I thought that he had run away from me so I was waiting for him in the hope that when he was ready he would come back, since I never, never chased people. Ken listened to me in his characteristic expressionless way, his quivering nostrils providing the only indication of his having heard me. He pulled me out the door and towards the water faucet, where he proceeded to play with the washing machine by sucking water out of the little pipes while keeping the mechanism whirling. His investment in this activity was intense, his eyes were partially closed, and though he was by no means out of contact, the distance between us was very great. I said softly and in a recitative kind of way which I had found helpful before with this child that now Ken can feed himself all by himself. He doesn't have to worry about not getting enough food or the wrong kind of food, he doesn't have to worry about people not being there, and so on. Ken continued this activity for just another minute after I spoke with him and then he put the toy down and started to lead the way to the basement. On the way down the steps he looked up and saw John sitting on the fire escape and he asked blankly, "What's he there for?" I said that John was there so that when Ken got frightened in therapy he wouldn't have to go up on the roof. "I'm going to throw water on him," announced Ken menacingly, getting his hose ready. I said, "John is not going to throw water on you, Ken, or hurt you in any way." Ken then relinquished his awareness of John and proceeded to the basement. He began to inspect the furnace and asked about the various parts with a competence that seemed to reflect some experience and I asked whether he had a furnace like it at home. Yes, he said that he had one in the basement. I asked whether his mother let him look at it there. No, he said, she didn't. I asked why not and Ken said it was because she said he might get hurt. "I see," I stated, "I understand now Ken, that when somebody tells you something is dangerous you think maybe that they are going to hurt you and that's what makes it dangerous. And that's also why you try to do dangerous things to show that you're stronger and that you won't get hurt." As expected, for one long minute there was no direct response to what I said. Then he went directly over and looked at the fire extinguisher. He looked at it long and searchingly. I said nothing but what I did was softly and slowly move closer towards him. He then was able to pass the fire extinguisher without touching it and went outside towards the Sterling Building.

As he led the way into the Sterling Building, he stopped off briefly at Mrs. W.'s office where the door was open and asked her what the different objects in her room were, especially a table tied to the wall. I explained that it was tied there because some children didn't know how to play with it and would destroy it. He listened soberly and led the way into the furnace-room. He pointed gleefully to the fire and identified different parts of the furnace. He then started to open different steel boxes which enclosed equipment and fuse boxes and other boxes whose function I did not know and therefore told him I thought we ought to find out what they were before we played with them; that I did not think he

ought to touch them until we found out whether or not they were dangerous. Ken's activity consisted of his opening the boxes or getting me to
open them, or getting me to hold him so that he could open the boxes.
He would open the door of the box, look at the inside intently and then
say each time, "That's dangerous. You can't touch it." I would respond
that it was a relief to know that some things were dangerous and some
things were not dangerous and what was and what wasn't. This same
activity with the boxes was repeated ten or twelve times in each building
of the school. He would repeat his part and I would repeat mine.

Finally it was the end of the hour and I told this to Ken and he left
with considerable reluctance since we had not finished looking at all the
boxes in the basement. I assured him that we would have lots of time to
do so. He finally agreed to come across the street with me. Once there,
we ran into difficulty since there was nobody to leave him with and the
person who was in charge was not eager to receive him at the moment.
Ken sat down and started to kick a hole in the wall. I restrained him and
told him I would surely not leave him until I found someone who would
take very good care of him. By this time John had arrived. As I said goodbye to Ken I noticed that this was the first time in my entire contact with
the child that he did not need to shut me out as I left him. Instead, to
my considerable surprise, he turned to me and asked me whether I would
bring him another little toy washing machine to our next therapy hour.
I said that I would be happy to and patted his cheek and left him holding
John's hand.

During this same period the child-care staff routed the chief residential
worker out of his bed early one Sunday morning to tell him in great excitement and pleasure that could hardly be contained that Ken was playing
football according to regulations with the other children. This represented
the first time that Ken had been able to engage in any play in its usual
sense or had been able to establish any contact of a nondestructive kind
with the other children. It was also of importance that the other children
were apparently pleased to have him in their game. Also at this time he
remarked to his child care worker that he was a butterfly coming out of
a cocoon; and, in beginning recognition of the world around him, he
painstakingly wrote the names of all the children in the residence on his
arms and legs. This, incidentally, was our first indication that the child
could write since he had no formal schooling at all.

All of these observations, and particularly the football incident, reflect
the love and interest in the child which, despite other feelings, were sustained until the very end. It may well be that as a child begins to improve,
the staff is most vulnerable to the threat of the hate and anxiety countertransference in that their investment in the patient may be at its height.

The résumé of the interview between the chief residential worker and Ken, in which the child was informed of the discharge and the transfer reads:

When I entered Ken's room to tell him the news of his transfer to the X school, he was lying on his bed listening to the radio, his foot up to his nose, sucking his finger. After some interchange, I told him that next week his parents were coming to take him to another school. He began to smile after I reached the words that his parents were coming and then it dawned on him that he was being taken by them to another school rather than home. The smile immediately changed. He came close to me, throwing his arms around my neck. He began to quiver throughout his whole body and to whimper, and I reassuringly patted him as I would an infant in distress and spoke to him about the fact that he would be transferred to this new school. He asked immediately why his parents were taking him to the new school. I told him that after some discussion with his parents it was the decision of the staff here that he would do better in a different kind of school where he would have a chance to be with children like himself and there would be additional protection and care. He gazed several times intensely into my eyes as he asked the questions. As I began answering them, he backed up onto the bed, stating with glee that in the other school he would also climb into the closet, move the bed, and when they attempted to bolt it down, he would make it impossible for them to do so and he would destroy things and he would surely go up on the roof. Several times he lay back on the bed, rolling from side to side, with his foot up to his nose and his fingers in his mouth, making small quaking noises. He asked if the school would have psychotherapy. He also asked if his favorite child-care worker would be able to accompany him. As I was beginning to leave he began to get more restless, hyperactive, and started to run in and out of the hall saying he was going to kill one of the little boys. Later he was reported saying to several people, "But I still have my problems, how can you send me away?"

One cannot help but be struck by the extraordinary coherence of this psychotic child, his recognition of the difficulties in his behavior that were causing his discharge, and his request for therapy and for his favorite child-care worker. To come a full circle again, the child's discharge was followed by a depressive mood which prevented the staff for many months from discussing what had occurred.

It is unfortunately so that children who are constantly threatened by catastrophic discontinuity from within and without, and who therefore need our assurances the most, are those whose treatment is most likely to be disrupted. For they successfully assail in us that which they need most desperately, our sustained capacity for treatment continuity.

It is perhaps inherent in the phenomena which we report that we close ruefully with a lingering doubt as to whether we have in this presentation primarily raised technical questions or whether we have given primary expression to a mood still rooted in the described experience.

REFERENCES

[1] Winnicott, D. W. Hate in the countertransference, Int. J. Psychoanal., 30:69, 1949.

[2] Money-Kryle, R. E. Normal countertransference and some of its deviations, Int. J. Psychoanal., 37:360, 1956.

[3] Gitelson, M. The emotional position of the analyst in the psychoanalytic situation, Int. J. Psychoanal., 33:1, 1952.

[4] Kanner, L. Early infantile autism, Amer. J. Orthopsychiat., 9:416, 1949.

[5] Eissler, K. Remarks on the psychoanalysis of schizophrenia, Int. J. Psychoanal., 32:139, 1951.

[6] Freud, S. Beyond the Pleasure Principle, New York, Liveright, 1950.

[7] Winnicott, D. W. Op. cit., p. 74.

AUTHOR INDEX

(Italics indicate quotations.)

Aichhorn, A., 343, 425

Bak, R., 243
Barrie, James M., 69
Bellak, L., 4
Bernfeld, S., 134, 137
Bibring, E., 142
Bleuler, S., 15, 16, 237, 238
Bornstein, Berta, 336
Brenner, C., 241–242
Bryant, K., 4, 210, 415
Bühler, Charlotte, 285, 296
Bühler, Karl, 231, 232, 233, 234, 235, 293

Carroll, Lewis, 75, 87
Caruth, Elaine, 158n, 298n, 403n
Charcot, M., 138
Coleridge, Samuel Taylor, 114, 120
Collodi, C., 249, 284

Deutsch, Helene, 363
Dorsen, M., 5

Eisenberg, L., 233
Eissler, K., 437
Ekstein, R., 4, 10, 137, 138, 167, 210, 235, 249, 253, 291, 301, 377, 414, 415, 429n
Erikson, E. H., 63, 73, 74, 136, 250, 285, 293, 339
Escalona, S., 4

Federn, P., 207
Fenichel, O., 123, 136, 190
Fliess, R., 98, 99
Frank, J., 313n

Freud, Anna, 15, 136, 233, 250, 334, 363, 406
Freud, S., 1, 7, 13, 70, 75, 87, 91, 94, 125, 126, 127, 128, 129, 130, 131–132, 133, 134, 136, 137, 144, 169, 207, 208, 223, 238, 249, 285, 287, 288, 289, 291, 292, 295, 303, 333–334, 335, 336, 348, 373, 374, 413, 426, 428, 442
Friedman, S. W., 4, 15n, 63n, 167, 169n, 207n, 210, 249, 415
Fuller, Dorothy, 63n

Gitelson, M., 155, 432
Goethe, J. W. von, 143, 403, 411
Goldfarb, W., 5
Greenacre, Phyllis, 172
Greenson, R. R., 246, 406
Gregg, A., 381

Hartmann, H., 89, 140, 171

Isaacs, Susan, 250
Isakower, O., 236

James, William, 365
Jones, Ernest, 133, 420

Kaiser, H., 136
Kanner, L., 233, 237, 433
Kanzer, M., 334, 340
Kekulè, von Stradonitz, Friedrich August, 138
Keller, Helen, 418
Klein, Melanie, 250
Knight, R. P., 381, 382
Kraepelin, E., 16

457

SUBJECT INDEX